Biomedical and Business Applications Using Artificial Neural Networks and Machine Learning

Richard S. Segall
Arkansas State University, USA

Gao Niu
Bryant University, USA

A volume in the Advances in Computational
Intelligence and Robotics (ACIR) Book Series

Published in the United States of America by
    IGI Global
    Engineering Science Reference (an imprint of IGI Global)
    701 E. Chocolate Avenue
    Hershey PA, USA 17033
    Tel: 717-533-8845
    Fax: 717-533-8661
    E-mail: cust@igi-global.com
    Web site: http://www.igi-global.com

Library of Congress Cataloging-in-Publication Data

Names: Segall, Richard, 1949- editor. | Niu, Gao, 1987- editor.
Title: Biomedical and business applications using artificial neural
  networks and machine learning / Richard S. Segall and Gao Niu, editor.
Description: Hershey, PA : Engineering Science Reference, [2022] | Includes
  bibliographical references and index. | Summary: "This book covers
  applications of artificial neural networks (ANN) and machine learning
  (ML) aspects of artificial intelligence to applications to the
  biomedical and business world including their interface to applications
  for screening for diseases to applications to large-scale credit card
  purchasing patterns"-- Provided by publisher.
Identifiers: LCCN 2021035365 (print) | LCCN 2021035366 (ebook) | ISBN
  9781799884552 (hardcover) | ISBN 9781799884569 (paperback) | ISBN
  9781799884576 (ebook)
Subjects: LCSH: Medicine--Research--Data processing. | Neural networks
  (Computer science)
Classification: LCC R853.D37 B56 2022 (print) | LCC R853.D37 (ebook) |
  DDC 610.285--dc23
LC record available at https://lccn.loc.gov/2021035365
LC ebook record available at https://lccn.loc.gov/2021035366

This book is published in the IGI Global book series Advances in Computational Intelligence and Robotics (ACIR) (ISSN: 2327-0411; eISSN: 2327-042X)

British Cataloguing in Publication Data
A Cataloguing in Publication record for this book is available from the British Library.

All work contributed to this book is new, previously-unpublished material. The views expressed in this book are those of the authors, but not necessarily of the publisher.

For electronic access to this publication, please contact: eresources@igi-global.com.

Advances in Computational Intelligence and Robotics (ACIR) Book Series

Ivan Giannoccaro
University of Salento, Italy

ISSN:2327-0411
EISSN:2327-042X

MISSION

While intelligence is traditionally a term applied to humans and human cognition, technology has progressed in such a way to allow for the development of intelligent systems able to simulate many human traits. With this new era of simulated and artificial intelligence, much research is needed in order to continue to advance the field and also to evaluate the ethical and societal concerns of the existence of artificial life and machine learning.

The **Advances in Computational Intelligence and Robotics (ACIR) Book Series** encourages scholarly discourse on all topics pertaining to evolutionary computing, artificial life, computational intelligence, machine learning, and robotics. ACIR presents the latest research being conducted on diverse topics in intelligence technologies with the goal of advancing knowledge and applications in this rapidly evolving field.

COVERAGE

- Computer Vision
- Agent technologies
- Machine Learning
- Fuzzy Systems
- Cognitive Informatics
- Automated Reasoning
- Pattern Recognition
- Artificial Life
- Neural Networks
- Natural Language Processing

IGI Global is currently accepting manuscripts for publication within this series. To submit a proposal for a volume in this series, please contact our Acquisition Editors at Acquisitions@igi-global.com or visit: http://www.igi-global.com/publish/.

Titles in this Series

For a list of additional titles in this series, please visit: http://www.igi-global.com/book-series/advances-computational-intelligence-robotics/73674

Socrates Digital™ for Learning and Problem Solving
Mark Salisbury (University of St. Thomas, USA)
Engineering Science Reference • © 2022 • 383pp • H/C (ISBN: 9781799879558) • US $215.00

Regulatory Aspects of Artificial Intelligence on Blockchain
Pardis Moslemzadeh Tehrani (University of Malaya, Malaysia)
Engineering Science Reference • © 2022 • 273pp • H/C (ISBN: 9781799879275) • US $245.00

Genetic Algorithms and Applications for Stock Trading Optimization
Vivek Kapoor (Devi Ahilya University, Indore, India) and Shubhamoy Dey (Indian Institute of Management, Indore, India)
Engineering Science Reference • © 2021 • 262pp • H/C (ISBN: 9781799841050) • US $225.00

Handbook of Research on Innovations and Applications of AI, IoT, and Cognitive Technologies
Jingyuan Zhao (University of Toronto, Canada) and V. Vinoth Kumar (MVJ College of Engineering, India)
Engineering Science Reference • © 2021 • 570pp • H/C (ISBN: 9781799868705) • US $325.00

Decision Support Systems and Industrial IoT in Smart Grid, Factories, and Cities
Ismail Butun (Chalmers University of Technology, Sweden & Konya Food and Agriculture University, Turkey & Royal University of Technology, Sweden)
Engineering Science Reference • © 2021 • 285pp • H/C (ISBN: 9781799874683) • US $245.00

Deep Natural Language Processing and AI Applications for Industry 5.0
Poonam Tanwar (Manav Rachna International Institute of Research and Studies, India) Arti Saxena (Manav Rachna International Institute of Research and Studies, India) and C. Priya (Vels Institute of Science, Technology, and Advanced Studies, India)
Engineering Science Reference • © 2021 • 240pp • H/C (ISBN: 9781799877288) • US $245.00

AI Tools and Electronic Virtual Assistants for Improved Business Performance
Christian Graham (University of Maine, USA)
Business Science Reference • © 2021 • 300pp • H/C (ISBN: 9781799838418) • US $245.00

701 East Chocolate Avenue, Hershey, PA 17033, USA
Tel: 717-533-8845 x100 • Fax: 717-533-8661
E-Mail: cust@igi-global.com • www.igi-global.com

List of Reviewers

Table of Contents

Martin Chanza, North-West University, South Africa
Gomolemo Motlhwe, North-West University, South Africa

Chapter 13
Jason Michaud, Bryant University, USA

Detailed Table of Contents

Section 1
Introduction

Chapter 1

Richard S. Segall, Arkansas State University, USA

This chapter first provides an overview with examples of what neural networks (NN), machine learning (ML), and artificial intelligence (AI) are and their applications in biomedical and business situations. The characteristics of 29 types of neural networks are provided including their distinctive graphical illustrations. A survey of current open-source software (OSS) for neural networks, neural network software available for free trail download for limited time use, and open-source software (OSS) for machine learning (ML) are provided. Characteristics of artificial intelligence (AI) technologies for machine learning available as open source are discussed. Illustrations of applications of neural networks, machine learning, and artificial intelligence are presented as used in the daily operations of a large internationally-based software company for optimal configuration of their Helix Data Capacity system.

Section 2
Biomedical Applications

Chapter 2

Richard S. Segall, Arkansas State University, USA

The purpose of this chapter is to illustrate how artificial intelligence (AI) technologies have been used for COVID-19 detection and analysis. Specifically, the use of neural networks (NN) and machine learning (ML) are described along with which countries are creating these techniques and how these are being used for COVID-19 diagnosis and detection. Illustrations of multi-layer convolutional neural networks (CNN), recurrent neural networks (RNN), and deep neural networks (DNN) are provided to show how these are used for COVID-19 detection and prediction. A summary of big data analytics for COVID-19 and some available COVID-19 open-source data sets and repositories and their characteristics for research and analysis are also provided. An example is also shown for artificial intelligence (AI) and neural network (NN) applications using real-time COVID-19 data.

Son Nguyen, Bryant University, USA
Matthew Quinn, Harvard University, USA
Alan Olinsky, Bryant University, USA
John Quinn, Bryant University, USA

In recent years, with the development of computational power and the explosion of data available for analysis, deep neural networks, particularly convolutional neural networks, have emerged as one of the default models for image classification, outperforming most of the classical machine learning models in this task. On the other hand, gradient boosting, a classical model, has been widely used for tabular structure data and leading data competitions, such as those from Kaggle. In this study, the authors compare the performance of deep neural networks with gradient boosting models for detecting pneumonia using chest x-rays. The authors implement several popular architectures of deep neural networks, such as Resnet50, InceptionV3, Xception, and MobileNetV3, and variants of a gradient boosting model. The authors then evaluate these two classes of models in terms of prediction accuracy. The computation in this study is done using cloud computing services offered by Google Colab Pro.

Viswanathan Rajagopalan, New York Institute of Technology College of Osteopathic
    Medicine at Arkansas State University, USA & Arkansas State University, USA & Center
    for No-Boundary Thinking at Arkansas State University, USA
Houwei Cao, New York Institute of Technology, USA

Despite significant advancements in diagnosis and disease management, cardiovascular (CV) disorders remain the No. 1 killer both in the United States and across the world, and innovative and transformative technologies such as artificial intelligence (AI) are increasingly employed in CV medicine. In this chapter, the authors introduce different AI and machine learning (ML) tools including support vector machine (SVM), gradient boosting machine (GBM), and deep learning models (DL), and their applicability to advance CV diagnosis and disease classification, and risk prediction and patient management. The applications include, but are not limited to, electrocardiogram, imaging, genomics, and drug research in different CV pathologies such as myocardial infarction (heart attack), heart failure, congenital heart disease, arrhythmias, valvular abnormalities, etc.

Fan Wu, Purdue University, USA
Juan Shu, Purdue University, USA

COVID-19, one of the most contagious diseases and urgent threats in recent times, attracts attention across the globe to study the trend of infections and help predict when the pandemic will end. A reliable prediction will make states and citizens acknowledge possible consequences and benefits for the policymaker among the delicate balance of reopening and public safety. This chapter introduces a deep learning technique and long short-term memory (LSTM) to forecast the trend of COVID-19 in the United States. The dataset from the New York Times (NYT) of confirmed and deaths cases is utilized in the research. The results include discussion of the potential outcomes if extreme circumstances happen and the profound effect beyond the forecasting number.

Chapter 6
Zizhe Gao, Columbia University, USA
Hao Lin, Northeastern University, USA

Entering the 21st century, computer science and biological research have entered a stage of rapid development. With the rapid inflow of capital into the field of significant health research, a large number of scholars and investors have begun to focus on the impact of neural network science on biometrics, especially the study of biological interactions. With the rapid development of computer technology, scientists improve or perfect traditional experimental methods. This chapter aims to prove the reliability of the methodology and computing algorithms developed by Satyajit Mahapatra and Ivek Raj Gupta's project team. In this chapter, three datasets take the responsibility to testify the computing algorithms, and they are S. cerevisiae, H. pylori, and Human-B. Anthracis. Among these three sets of data, the S. cerevisiae is the core subset. The result shows 87%, 87.5%, and 89% accuracy and 87%, 86%, and 87% precision for these three data sets, respectively.

Chapter 7
Fangjun Li, University of Connecticut, USA
Gao Niu, Bryant University, USA

For the purpose of control health expenditures, there are some papers investigating the characteristics of patients who may incur high expenditures. However fewer papers are found which are based on the overall medical conditions, so this chapter was to find a relationship among the prevalence of medical conditions, utilization of healthcare services, and average expenses per person. The authors used bootstrapping simulation for data preprocessing and then used linear regression and random forest methods to train several models. The metrics root mean square error (RMSE), mean absolute percent error (MAPE), mean absolute error (MAE) all showed that the selected linear regression model performs slightly better than the selected random forest regression model, and the linear model used medical conditions, type of services, and their interaction terms as predictors.

Section 3
Business Applications

Chapter 8

Xiang Li, Cornell University, USA
Jingxi Liao, University of Central Florida, USA
Tianchuan Gao, Columbia University, USA

Machine learning is a broad field that contains multiple fields of discipline including mathematics, computer science, and data science. Some of the concepts, like deep neural networks, can be complicated and difficult to explain in several words. This chapter focuses on essential methods like classification from supervised learning, clustering, and dimensionality reduction that can be easily interpreted and explained in an acceptable way for beginners. In this chapter, data for Airbnb (Air Bed and Breakfast) listings in London are used as the source data to study the effect of each machine learning technique. By using the K-means clustering, principal component analysis (PCA), random forest, and other methods to help build classification models from the features, it is able to predict the classification results and provide some performance measurements to test the model.

Chapter 9

Xiangming Liu, University of Connecticut, USA
Gao Niu, Bryant University, USA

This chapter presents a thorough descriptive analysis of automobile fatal accident and insurance claims data. Major components of the artificial neural network (ANN) are discussed, and parameters are investigated and carefully selected to ensure an efficient model construction. A prediction model is constructed through ANN as well as generalized linear model (GLM) for model comparison purposes. The authors conclude that ANN performs better than GLM in predicting data for automobile fatalities data but does not outperform for the insurance claims data because automobile fatalities data has a more complex data structure than the insurance claims data.

Chapter 10

Zichen Zhao, Yale University, USA
Guanzhou Hou, Johns Hopkins University, USA

Artificial neural network (ANN) has been showing its superior capability of modeling and prediction. Neural network model is capable of incorporating high dimensional data, and the model is significantly complex statistically. Sometimes, the complexity is treated as a Blackbox. However, due to the model complexity, the model is capable of capture and modeling an extensive number of patterns, and the prediction power is much stronger than traditional statistical models. Random forest algorithm is a combination of classification and regression trees, using bootstrap to randomly train the model from a set of data (called training set) and test the prediction by a testing set. Random forest has high prediction speed, moderate variance, and does not require any rescaling or transformation of the dataset. This study validates the relationship between the U.S. unemployment rate and economic indices during the COVID-19 pandemic and constructs three different predictive modeling for unemployment rate by economic indices through neural network, random forest, and generalized linear regression model.

The credit card has been one of the most successful and prevalent financial services being widely used across the globe. However, with the upsurge in credit card holders, banks are facing a challenge from equally increasing payment default cases causing substantial financial damage. This necessitates the importance of sound and effective credit risk management in the banking and financial services industry. Machine learning models are being employed by the industry at a large scale to effectively manage this credit risk. This chapter presents the application of the various machine learning methods like time series models and deep learning models experimented in predicting the credit card payment defaults along with identification of the significant features and the most effective evaluation criteria. This chapter also discusses the challenges and future considerations in predicting credit card payment defaults. The importance of factoring in a cost function to associate with misclassification by the models is also given.

Chapter 12

This study examines the performance of seasonal autoregressive integrated moving average (SARIMA), multilayer perceptron neural networks (MLPNN), and hybrid SARIMA-MLPNN model(s) in modelling and forecasting inflation rate using the monthly consumer price index (CPI) data from 2010 to 2019 obtained from the South African Reserve Bank (SARB). The forecast errors in inflation rate forecasting are analyzed and compared. The study employed root mean squared error (RMSE) and mean absolute error (MAE) as performance measures. The results indicate that significant improvements in forecasting accuracy are obtained with the hybrid model (SARIMA-MLPNN) compared to the SARIMA and MLPNN. The MLPNN model outperformed the SARIMA model. However, the hybrid SARIMA-MLPNN model outperformed both the SARIMA and MLPNN in terms of forecasting accuracy/accuracy performance.

Chapter 13

For popular sports brands such as Nike, Adidas, and Puma, value often depends upon the performance of star athletes and the success of professional leagues. These leagues and players are watched closely by many around the world, and exposure to a brand may ultimately cause someone to buy a product. This can be explored statistically, and the interconnectedness of brands, athletes, and the sport of basketball are covered in this chapter. Specifically, data about the NBA and Google Ngrams data are explored in relation to the stock price of these various sports brands. This is done through both statistical analysis and machine learning models. Ultimately, it was concluded that these factors do influence the stock price of Nike, Adidas, and Puma. This conclusion is supported by the machine learning models where this diverse dataset was utilized to accurately predict the stock price of sports brands.

Foreword

Rapid technological advances have generated a large exploding volume of data, leading to dramatic growth in the need for big data analytics and automated machine learning. This has brought much scientific and technological research into an unprecedented data-driven era, whereas intelligent computational methods are essential for big data analytics.

The book *Biomedical and Business Applications Using Artificial Neural Networks and Machine Learning* edited by Dr. Richard S. Segall and Dr. Gao Niu meets the challenges in the era of big data, and is timely for utilizing Artificial Intelligence (AI) and machine learning techniques to advance biomedical and business data analytics.

Machine learning leverages algorithms to sift through large-scale and heterogeneous datasets to capture intrinsic data patterns which may be undetectable even by well-trained professionals. These data patterns are valuable for modeling complex relationships among data, predicting future events and making data-driven decisions.

Recent innovations in machine learning and AI techniques open inimitable opportunities for its applications in various fields. In the last few years, breakthroughs and fast developments in deep learning have established a new paradigm in machine learning and AI.

This book keeps pace with the rapid advancements in machine learning, business analytics, data tools and infrastructure, and practices that can help solve real-world problems. It is perceivably beneficial for data scientists, biomedical researchers and industry users to understand the latest state-of-art algorithms and apply these techniques to facilitate business management and operation, and biomedical research and clinical applications.

The book covers a wide spectrum of machine learning and AI algorithms and open source software in chapter 1, biomedical applications in chapters 2-7, and business applications in chapters 8-13. In particular, chapter 2 and chapter 6 present AI and deep-learning models for COVID-19 prediction and diagnosis, which is just-in-time to tackle the critical challenges posed by COVID-19 pandemic that currently have created profound impacts on human health and economic growth worldwide.

I believe a broad range of researchers, professionals and students will find this book useful. I highly recommend this book to the communities of machine learning, biomedical research, data analytics and business intelligence.

Mary Yang
University of Arkansas at Little Rock, USA

Mary Yang, *PhD, is a Professor of Engineering and Information Science and Director of MidSouth Bioinformatics Center and Joint Bioinformatics Graduate Programs of University of Arkansas at Little Rock (UALR) and University of Arkansas for Medical Sciences (UAMS). Her Systems Genomics Laboratory has been funded by NIH (National Institutes of Health), FDA (Food and Drug Administration) and NSF (National Science Foundation) for data analytics, deep learning and genomics research investigations. Dr. Yang received the MS, MSECE and Ph.D. degrees from Purdue University, West Lafayette. She joined the National Human Genome Research Institute (NHGRI) in 2005, where she worked on various large-scale projects related to genomics and systems biology. She has been Founding Editor-in-Chief of International Journal of Computational Biology and Drug Design (IJCBDD), and is on the Editorial boards of The Journal of Supercomputing and International Journal of Pattern Recognition and Artificial Intelligence (IJPRAI). Dr. Yang had been a Visiting Associate Professor of Genetics at Yale University, conducting single-cell genomics investigations. She is the recipient of the Bilsland Dissertation Fellowship, the Purdue Research Foundation Fellowship, IEEE Bioinformatics and Bioengineering Outstanding Achievement Award, the NIH Fellows Award for Research Excellence and NIH Academic Research Enhancement Awards. Dr. Yang has published over a hundred research articles and her research focus on computational intelligence and big-data analytics with applications in biomedical sciences.*

Preface

During these uncertain and turbulent times, intelligent technologies including artificial neural networks (ANN) and machine learning (ML) have played an incredible role in being able to predict, analyze, and navigate unprecedented circumstances across a number of industries, ranging from healthcare to hospitality.

Multi-factor prediction in particular has been especially helpful in dealing with the most current pressing issues such as COVID-19 prediction, pneumonia detection, cardiovascular diagnosis and disease management, automobile accident prediction, and vacation rental listing analysis. To date, there has not been much research content readily available in these areas, especially content written extensively from a user perspective.

This book is designed to cover a brief and focused range of essential topics in the field with perspectives, models, and first-hand experiences shared by prominent researchers, discussing applications of artificial neural networks (ANN) and machine learning (ML) for biomedical and business applications and provides listings of current open-source software for neural networks, machine learning, and artificial intelligence. It also presents summaries of currently available open-source software that utilize neural networks and machine learning.

The book is ideal for professionals, researchers, students, and practitioners who want to more fully understand in a brief and concise format the realm and technologies of artificial neural networks (ANN) and machine learning (ML) and how they have been used for prediction of multi-disciplinary research problems in a multitude of disciplines.

Figure 1 shows an Overview of the layout and contents of the entire book that consists of Section 1, Section 2, and Section 3. Section 1 consists of only one chapter as an "Overview of Multi-Factor Prediction using Deep Neural Networks, Machine Learning and their Open-Source Software" that serves as an introduction to the entire book of edited chapters.

The subsequent chapters of Section 2 as shown in Figure 1 pertain to biomedical applications of related techniques of artificial intelligence and machine learning to COVID-10 prediction and diagnosis, Pneumonia, cardiovascular disorders, and Protein-Protein interactions (PPI), and medical expense analysis in the United States.

The subsequent chapters of Section 3 as also shown in Figure 1 pertain to business applications of neural networks, artificial intelligence and machine learning to Bed-and-Breakfast accommodation listings, analysis of automobile fatal accident and insurance claims, unemployment rate prediction by economic indices in COVID-19 pandemic, prediction of default of credit card payments, inflation rate modeling, and value analysis and prediction of popular basketball brands.

Figure 1. Layout of sections of this book and chapters contained within

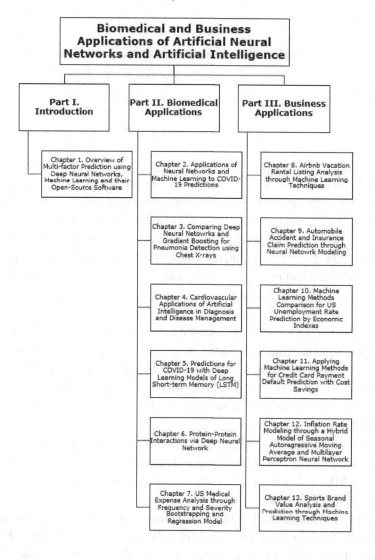

This book is focused on many academic areas that include but not limited to the following: Applications of Machine Learning Methods, Applications of Neural Networks and Machine Learning to COVID-19 Predictions, Artificial Neural Networks, Cardiovascular Applications of Artificial Intelligence, Deep Learning Models, Deep Neural Networks, Image Identification and Damage Estimation Through Convolutional Neural Network, Machine Learning Methods Comparison for Unemployment Rate Prediction, Machine Learning Techniques, Multilayer Perceptron Neural Network, Neural Networks, Open Source Software, and Protein-Protein Interactions via Deep Neural Network. Table 1 of this Preface shows which of the 13 chapters of this book pertains to these specific applications of these academic areas.

Table 1. Directory of chapter number for academic topics discussed within

TOPIC	CHAPTER NUMBER												
	1	2	3	4	5	6	7	8	9	10	11	12	13
Applications of Machine Learning Methods	x	x						x					x
Applications of Neural Networks and Machine Learning to COVID-19 Predictions		x								x			
Artificial Neural Networks	x	x							x				
Cardiovascular Applications of Artificial Intelligence				x									
Deep Learning Models	x	x	x		x	x							
Image Identification and Damage Estimation Through Convolutional Neural Network									x				
Machine Learning Methods Comparison for Unemployment Rate Prediction										x			
Machine Learning Techniques	x							x			x		x
Multilayer Perception Neural Network			x		x								
Neural Networks		x								x	x	x	
Open-Source Software	x												
Protein-Protein Interaction via Deep Neural Networks						x							

Section 1: Introduction

Section 1 consist of one chapter for introduction.

Chapter 1, "Overview of Multi-Factor Prediction Using Deep Neural Networks, Machine Learning, and Their Open-Source Software," by Richard S. Segall includes a highlight Figure 2 which borrowed with permission from the Asimov Institute of The Neural Network Zoo that provides illustrations of 29 types of Neural Networks, and Table 1 that provides characteristics for each of these Neural Network categories. Other highlights of this Chapter 1 are individual tables of open-source software for neural networks, open-source software for machine learning, and open-source artificial intelligence technologies for machine learning and neural networks.

Specific real-world applications of neural networks are shown in Chapter 1 as used in 1.) BMC a large international software company who provided us with permission illustrations of cognitive routing by neural network suing chatbot and example of neural network of "intelligence swarming" with ticket routing. 2.) the use of Visual Analytics with neural networks and machine learning to predict: (i.) spending of mall customers by characteristics of age, gender and estimated salary, (ii.) churn model for bank customers, (iii.) Uber traffic delays in India based on time periods, and (iv.) cancer prediction.

Section 2: Biomedical Applications

Section 2 consist of six chapters on "Biomedical Applications."

Chapter 2, "Survey of Applications of Neural Networks and Machine Learning to COVID-19 Predictions," by Richard S. Segall presents illustrations of Multi-layer Convolutional Neural Networks (CNN), Recurrent Neural Networks (RNN), and Deep Neural Networks (DNN) to show how these are used for COVID-19 detection and prediction with figures for the flow charts of step sequences.

Highlights of this Chapter 2 include several tables listing dates and authors of recent publications in: (i.) Big Data Analytics for COVID-19, (ii.) Artificial Intelligence techniques used for COVID-19 detection and analysis, (iii.) Neural Network used for COVID-19 detection and analysis, (iv.) Applications of Machine Learning to COVID-19, and (v.) COVID-19 open-source repositories of data. Other highlights of this Chapter 2 are figures for data visualization that were created using Rapid Miner, Tensor Flow and Deep Learning Toolbox of MATLAB such as death rate and recovery rate from the active and confirmed cases of COVID-19 in geographic regions.

Chapter 3, "Comparing Deep Neural Networks and Gradient Boosting for Pneumonia Detection Using X-Rays," by Son Nguyen, Mathew Quinn, Alan Olinsky, and John Quinn presents an overview of deep neural networks, gradient boosting, and the problem of detecting pneumonia from chest x-rays. The main difference between the deep neural network models and the gradient boosting models is that deep neural networks are designed to handle image data while gradient boosting models often excel at tasks utilizing regular tabular data. The study confirms the superiority of deep neural network models. While under certain conditions, gradient boosting could compete with deep neural networks, it does not have the flexibility to benefit from the information gained by increasing image resolution.

Chapter 4, "Cardiovascular Applications of Artificial Intelligence in Research, Diagnosis, and Disease Management," by Viswanathan Rajagopala and Houwei Cao presents state-of-the-art artificial intelligence (AI) and machine learning (ML) tools that includes support vector machine (SVM), gradient boosting machine, and deep learning models, and their applicability to advance cardiovascular (CV) diagnosis and disease classification, and risk prediction and patient management. The applications include, but not limited to, electrocardiogram, imaging, genomics and drug research in different CV pathologies such as myocardial infarction (heart attack), heart failure, congenital heart disease, arrhythmias, valvular abnormalities, etc.

This Chapter 4 also presents a tabular Appendix listing a "Summary of Neural Network or Machine Learning Features of References."

Chapter 5, "Predictions for COVID-19 With Deep Learning Models of Long Short-Term Memory (LSTM)," by Fan Wu and Juan Shu uses the modern deep learning method Long Short-Term Memory (LSTM) to forecast the new cases and deaths and discusses the potential influence of the new Delta variants. The year 2020 was defined by the coronavirus pandemic and undoubtedly the worst pandemic since 1900. As of June 2020, COVID-19 has caused more than 181 million cases and 3.19 million deaths worldwide. The illness has affected nearly every aspect of life, from work and school, mental health and everyday life. Governments and international organizations are facing rigorous challenges as the pandemic is still rampaging the countries around the globe. Measurements of human interaction within the virus are challenging tasks. The forecasting results could benefit the governments to determine proper operations.

Chapter 6, "Protein-Protein Interactions (PPI) via Deep Neural Networks," by Hao Lin and Zizhe Gao presents their only goal to verify the experimental conclusion proposed by Satyajit Mahapatra and Ivek Raj Gupta's project team (Mahapatra et al., 2021) that Deep Neuron Network (DNN) can use the

Deep Neural Network to extract advanced discrimination features from common protein descriptions. As the analysis of the Deep Neuron Network (DNN) method described in this chapter, it can be concluded that the Deep Neuron Network (DNN) method can indeed improve the identification and research on Protein-to-Protein Interactions (PPI).

Chapter 7, "US Medical Expense Analysis through Frequency and Severity Bootstrapping and Regression Model" by Fangjun Li and Gao Niu analyzes US medical expenses by medical conditions and type of services through frequency and severity bootstrapping and regression model. This chapter starts with data preprocessing where bootstrapping method is used to construct simulation datasets. Then predictive models, such as linear regression models and random forest method are trained. Several metrics to measure goodness-of-fit of regression models are employed to select the best performed model. Under this scenario, linear regression model and random forest model shows equivalent prediction accuracy, and linear regression model shows a slightly better results for Root Mean Square Error (RMSE), Mean Absolute Percent Error (MAPE) and Mean Absolute Error (MAE). The results can be applied to insurance industry and health service management.

Section 3: Business Applications

Section 3 consists of six chapters on "Business Applications."

Chapter 8, "Airbnb (Air Bed and Breakfast) Listing Analysis Through Machine Learning Techniques," by Xiang Li, Jingxi Liao and Tianchuan Gao focuses on machine learning using the data of Airbnb (Air Bed & Breakfast) listings in London, UK. To make it concise and easy to understand, the authors concentrate on classification from supervised learning, clustering, and dimensionality reduction. The process consists of three steps. The first step is data classification that utilizes K-means clustering, hierarchical clustering and Principal Component Analysis (PCA) that were constructed using classification models based on different features in the Airbnb. The second step is data prediction that utilizes decision tree and random forest processes. Finally, the authors evaluate the model efficiency and accuracy.

Chapter 9, "Automobile Accident and Insurance Claim Prediction Through Neural Network Modeling," by Xiangming Liu and Gao Niu analyzed automobile fatal accident data and automobile insurance claims data through Artificial Neural Network (ANN). The authors also tested the data by Generalized Linear Model (GLM) for comparison purpose. This chapter first presents the two datasets with their key descriptive analysis. Then ANN and GLM models were constructed with detailed parameter testing, such as activation functions, validation dataset, hidden layers, and batch size. GLM variables were selected based on correlation analysis, a basic model is constructed for comparison purposes.

Chapter 10, "U.S. Unemployment Rate Prediction by Economic Indices in COVID-19 Pandemic Using Neural Network, Random Forest, and Generalized Linear Regression," by Zichen Zhao and Guanzhou Hou presents the idea of using machine learning models of neural network and random forest to predict the U.S. unemployment rate during the COVID-19 pandemic based on economic performance of mainly stock market indexes. The model provides insights of drivers for unemployment that policy makers could take advantage of.

Chapter 11, "Applying Machine Learning Methods for Credit Card Payment Default Prediction With Cost Savings," by Siddharth Vinoh Jain and Manoj Jayabalan present the application of the various machine learning methods such as time series models and deep learning models experimented in predicting the credit card payment defaults along with identification of the significant features and the most effective evaluation criteria. This being an anomaly detection study, the datasets available are generally imbalanced, and hence employing balancing techniques improve model performance considerably. Hyperparameter tuning using a ten-fold cross-validation process further boosts the prediction power of the models.

Chapter 12, "Inflation Rate Modelling Through a Hybrid Model of Seasonal Autoregressive Moving Average and Multilayer Perceptron Neural Network," by Gomolemo Motlhwe, Martin Chanza, and Mogari I. Rapoo, examines the performance of Seasonal Autoregressive Integrated Moving Average (SARIMA), Multilayer Perceptron Neural Networks (MLPNN), and hybrid SARIMA-MLPNN model(s) in modelling and forecasting inflation rate using the monthly Consumer Price Index (CPI) data from 2010 to 2019 obtained from the South African Reserve Bank (SARB). The forecast errors in inflation rate forecasting are analyzed and compared. The study employed Root Mean Squared Error (RMSE) and Mean Absolute Error (MAE) as performance measures. The results indicate that significant improvements in forecasting accuracy are obtained with the hybrid model (SARIMA-MLPNN) compared to the SARIMA and MLPNN. The MLPNN model outperformed the SARIMA model. However, the hybrid SARIMA-MLPNN model outperformed both the SARIMA and MLPNN in terms of forecasting accuracy/accuracy performance.

Chapter 13, "Value Analysis and Prediction Through Machine Learning Techniques for Popular Basketball Brands," by Jason Michaud Chapter 13 "Value Analysis and Prediction through Machine Learning Techniques for Popular Basketball Brands" by Jason Michaud discusses how for popular sports brands such as Nike, Adidas, and Puma, value often depends upon the performance of star athletes and the success of professional leagues. These leagues and players of NBA are watched closely by many around the world, and exposure to a brand may ultimately cause someone to buy a product.

The data collected includes both data on the National Basketball Association (NBA) itself, and frequency data from Google Ngrams that are explored in relation to the stock price of these various sports brands.

This can be explored statistically, and the interconnectedness of brands, athletes, and the sport of basketball are covered in this chapter and done through both statistical analysis and machine learning models.

After statistical analysis of the dataset, machine learning models are then built with the goal of accurately predicting the stock price for Nike, Adidas, and Puma. Ultimately, it was concluded that these factors do influence the stock price of Nike, Adidas, and Puma. This conclusion is supported by the machine learning models where this diverse dataset was utilized to accurately predict the stock price of sports brands. Another goal of this chapter is to explore the differences between simple machine learning models and complex machine learning models.

All chapters went through several internal revisions between the Editors and the chapters' authors before being sent for external blind refereeing process by at least three reviewers before final acceptance.

Richard S. Segall
Arkansas State University, USA

Gao Niu
Bryant University, USA

REFERENCE

Mahapatra, S., Gupta, V. R., Sahu, S. S., & Panda, G. (2021). Deep Neural Network and Extreme Gradient Boosting Based Hybrid Classifier for Improved Prediction of Protein-Protein Interaction. *IEEE/ACM Transactions on Computational Biology and Bioinformatics*, 1. doi:10.1109/tcbb.2021.3061300

Acknowledgement

The following individuals need to be acknowledged as external reviewers of contributing chapters who were not authors of any contributing chapters:

Hyacinthe Aboudja, Oklahoma City University; Daniel Berleant, University of Arkansas at Little Rock; Wenjing Fang, Prudential Financial; Michael Howell, University of Arkansas at Little Rock; Aifang Li, University of Connecticut; Phanuel Mariano, Union College; Jake Qualls, Arkansas State University; Xin Qi, American International Group, Inc.; Deepak Rapaka, Deloitte US; Vidhya Sankarasubbu, Arkansas State University; Jonathan Stubblefield, Arkansas State University; Tianyi Song, Liberty Mutual Insurance Company; Junsen Tang, University of St. Thomas; Yucheng Tian, Tencent; Pei Wang, Willis Towers Watson; Peng Zhao, Indiana State University; Yoahua Zhang, Vertex Pharmaceuticals; Jinggong Zhang, Nanyang Technological University; and Rong Zheng, Western Illinois University.

The following authors of contributing chapters need to be recognized for their additional work as serving as reviewers of contributing chapters:

Zizhe Gao, Columbia University; Hao Lin, Northeastern University; Sun Nguyen and Alan Olinsky, Bryant University; Viswanathan Rajagopalan, New York Institute of Technology School of Osteopathic Medicine, and Fan Wu, Purdue University.

Acknowledgement needs to be made for funding to support this book project provided from the Arkansas Biosciences Institute (ABI) located on the campus of Arkansas State University by the 2021 Summer Research Program for Undergraduates for Proposal written with undergraduate student Vidhya Sankarasubbu titled "COVID-19: Survey of Applications of Neural Network, Machine Learning and other Artificial Intelligence (AI) Techniques for this World-Wide Pandemic".

Recognition needs to be made to both the Neil Griffin College of Business at Arkansas State University and Bryant University for purposes of providing the facilities and computer support for completion of this project.

Finally, last but not least, Gianna Walker and Angelina Olivas, the Managing Editors assigned to this project, and entire Editorial staff at IGI Global need to be acknowledged for the continued support and communication throughout the writing process; without their help this project would not have not been possible.

Richard S. Segall
Arkansas State University, USA

Gao Niu
Bryant University, USA

Section 1
Introduction

Chapter 1
Overview of Multi–Factor Prediction Using Deep Neural Networks, Machine Learning, and Their Open–Source Software

Richard S. Segall
Arkansas State University, USA

ABSTRACT

This chapter first provides an overview with examples of what neural networks (NN), machine learning (ML), and artificial intelligence (AI) are and their applications in biomedical and business situations. The characteristics of 29 types of neural networks are provided including their distinctive graphical illustrations. A survey of current open-source software (OSS) for neural networks, neural network software available for free trail download for limited time use, and open-source software (OSS) for machine learning (ML) are provided. Characteristics of artificial intelligence (AI) technologies for machine learning available as open source are discussed. Illustrations of applications of neural networks, machine learning, and artificial intelligence are presented as used in the daily operations of a large internationally-based software company for optimal configuration of their Helix Data Capacity system.

1. INTRODUCTION

1.1. Neural Networks (NN)

A Neural Network (NN) is a network consisting or arcs and nodes or circuit of neurons. An Artificial Neural Network (ANN) is composed of artificial neurons or nodes. (Wikipedia, 2021). A Neural Network (NN) can be either a biological neural network, made up of real biological neurons, or an Artificial Neural Network, for solving Artificial Intelligence (AI) problems. (Wikipedia, 2021a).

DOI: 10.4018/978-1-7998-8455-2.ch001

Figure 1 shows a basic Neural Network with an input layer, processing layer, and output layer of nodes. The connections of the biological neuron are modeled as weights. A positive weight reflects an excitatory connection, while negative values mean inhibitory connections. All inputs are modified by a weight and summed. This activity is referred to as a linear combination. An activation function controls the amplitude of the output. For example, an acceptable range of output is usually between 0 and 1, or it could be −1 and 1. (Wikipedia, 2021a)

Figure 1. Feed Forward Neural Network used for Image Classification Task with Machine Learning

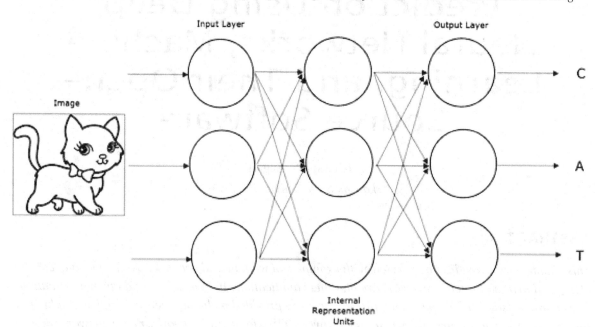

The reader is referred to previous work on computer modeling of neural networks that includes comparing learning rules using computer graphics in Segall (2004, 2003, 2001, 1996, 1995), in Segall & Zhang (2006) for applications of neural networks and genetic algorithm data mining techniques in bioinformatics discovery, Fish & Segall (2002) for a visual analysis of learning rule effects and variable importance for neural networks employed in data mining operations, and Biedenbender et al. (2011) for text mining using rule based and neural network based approaches. A basic overview of neural networks for beginners is presented by Russo (2019), SAS (2020b), Taylor (2017), and Haykin (2020).

1.2. Machine Learning (ML)

Machine learning (ML) is the study of computer algorithms that improve automatically through experience, and is a subset of artificial intelligence. Machine learning algorithms build a model based on sample data, known as "training data". (Wikipedia, 2021b)

Machine learning approaches are traditionally divided into three broad categories of (1.) supervised learning, (2.) unsupervised learning, and (3.) reinforcement learning. Supervised learning is when the computer is presented with example inputs and desired outputs. Unsupervised learning is when learning is on its own to find structure in its input such as discover hidden patterns in data, Reinforcement learning is when a computer program interacts with a dynamic environment in which it must perform a pre-specified goal. (Wikipedia, 2021b)

A basic overview of machine learning is presented in Henderson (2019). Other related research on machine learning were presented by Chouldechove and Roth (2020), David (2020), Geron (2020), G2 (2020), Hasan (2020), Haykin (2020), Jensen (2018), Jones (2018), Kelleher et al. (2015), McForckman (2020), Meng et al. (2015), Ramezani (2020), Rhys (2020), SAS (2020c), and TrustRadius (2020). One hundred and one (101) machine learning algorithms for data science with 'cheat sheets' was presented by Piccini (2019). Open-Source machine learning tools are discussed by Algorithmia (2019) and Springboard India (2019), Yegulalp (2020) and well as others as discussed in Table 3 of this chapter.

1.3. Artificial Intelligence (AI)

Artificial intelligence (AI), is intelligence demonstrated by machines, unlike the natural intelligence displayed by humans and animals. (Wikipedia, 2021c).

Current work in Artificial Intelligence (AI) is presented by Campesato (2020) for a book on AI, ML and deep learning, Hasan (2020) on best AI and machine learning software and framework, McFrockman (2020) with AI mastery with "4 Books in 1", SAS (2020a) of what AI is and why it matters, and Stone (2019) on mathematics of deep learning.

An article by Daley (2021) presented details of studies on "twenty-three examples of artificial intelligence shaking up business as usual" that included examples in manufacturing robots, self-driving cars, disease mapping, automated financial investing, virtual travel booking agent, social media monitoring, inter-team chat tool, conversational marketing bot, and natural language processing (NLP) tools.

1.4 Applications of Neural Networks to Biomedical and Business Applications

Ruano and Ruano (2013) authored an article on the use of artificial neural networks (ANN) as a classifier, dynamic model, and diagnosis tool for biomedical applications that included: blood flow emboli classification, tissue temperature modeling, and identification of ischemic cerebral vascular accident areas based on computer tomography images.

Lisboa et al. (2000) authored an entire book on the real-world business applications of neural networks that includes the use of neural networks for analysis of travel preference data, developments in accurate consumer risk assessment technology, novel techniques for profiling and fraud detection in mobile communications, and detecting payment card fraud with neural networks.

Vieira and Ribeiro (2018) authored a book with technical examples as an introduction to deep learning (DL) business applications for developers' potential applications, challenges, and opportunities of deep learning from a business perspective. These applications include image recognition, segmentation and annotation, video processing and annotation, voice recognition, intelligent personal assistants, automated translation, and autonomous vehicles.

1.5 Applications of Machine Learning to Biomedical and Business Applications

Faggella (2020) presented seven applications of machine learning in pharma and medicine that includes: (1.) disease identification/diagnosis, (2.) personalized treatment/behavioral modification, (3.) drug discovery/manufacturing. (4.) clinical trial research, (5.) radiology and radiotherapy, (6.) smart electronic health records, and (7.) epidemic outbreak prediction.

Thomas (2020) presented fifteen examples of machine learning in healthcare that are revolutionizing medicine in the categories of: (1.) Smart records, (2.) medical imaging and diagnostics, (3.) drug discovery and development, (4.) medical data, and (5.) treatment and diagnosis of disease. An example of drug discovery and development is that Pfizer uses machine learning for immune-oncology research about how the body's immune system can fight cancer.

Pratt (2020) presented ten common uses for machine learning applications in business that includes: (1.) real-time chatbot agents. (2.) decision support systems (DSS), (3.) customer recommendation engines, (4.) customer churn modeling, (5.) dynamic pricing tactics, (6.) market research and customer segmentation, (7.) fraud detection, (8.) image classification and image recognition, (9.) operational efficiencies, and (10.) information extraction.

A "chatbot" as listed above in Pratt (2020) as first common use is as described as Brush (2019) is sometime referred to as a chatterbot is programming that simulates the conversation or "chatter" of a human through text or voice interactions. There are several types of "chatbots" as described by Pratt (2020) as: (1.) scripted or quick reply chatbots, (2.) keyword recognition-based chatbots, (3.) hybrid chatbots, (4.) contextual chatbots, and (5.) voice-enabled chatbots.

The use of "chatbots" is presented in the next section for a real large international software company.

Castle (2017) presented six common machine learning applications for business that includes: (1.) customer lifetime value modeling, (2.) churn modeling, (3.) dynamic pricing, (4.) customer segmentation, (5.) image classification, and (6.) recommendation engines. In this list is customer churn modeling that can identify which customers are likely to stop engaging with your business and why. Also in this list is image classification that according to Castle (2017) has a wide range of business applications including 3D construction plans based on 2D designs, social media photo tagging, and informing medical diagnoses.

2. NEURAL NETWORK (NN) MODELING

2.1 Twenty-Nine Types of Neural Networks

There are many types of Neural Networks and the below Figure 2 of Asimov Institute by Van Veen and Leijnen (2019) shows twenty-nine different variants from which Table 1 was constructed that provides characteristics of each of these. The Key in Figure 2 define the fourteen types of cells utilized that includes: Input cell, Backfed Input Cell, Noisy Input Cell, Hidden Cell, Probabilistic Hidden Cell, Spiking Hidden Cell, Capsule Cell, Output Cell, Match Input Output Cell, Recurrent Cell, Memory Cell, Gated Memory Cell, Kernel and Convolution or Pool.

This chapter also presents Table 2 of Open-Source Software (OSS) for Neural Networks (NN), and Table 3 of Neural Network Software available for free trail download.

This chapter then presents how Neural Network algorithms are used by a large software company BMC that is a privately held multinational firm operating in North America, South America, Australia, Europe, and Asia and has multiple offices located around the world with its international headquarters located in Houston, Texas, United States.

Figure 2. Chart of 29 Types of Neural Networks

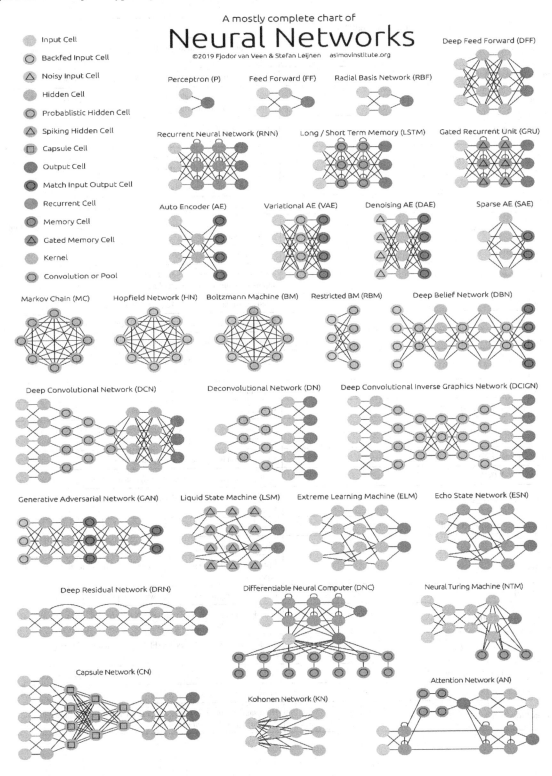

Table 1. Characteristics of 29 Types of Neural Networks (Derived from Van Veen, F. & Leijnen, S. (2019))

Neural Network Category from Figure 2	Characteristics
Auto Encoder (AE)	Encode information automatically with network that always resemble an hourglass shape.
Attention Network (AN)	Use an attention mechanism to combat information decay.
Boltzmann Machine (BM)	Starts with random weights and learns through back-propagation with neurons mostly having binary activation patterns.
Capsule Network (CapsNet)	Neurons are connected with multiple weights (vector) instead of just one weight (scalar).
Deconvolutional Network (DN)	Also called Inverse Graphical Networks (IGNs) and are reversed convolutional neural networks.
Deep Belief Network (DBN)	Effectively trainable stack-by-stack.
Deep Convolutional Inverse Graphics Network (DCIGN)	Can learn to model complex transformations on images.
Deep Convolutional Network (DCN)	Primarily used for image processing but can be used for other types of input such as audio.
Deep Feed Forward (DFF)	Multi-layers of inner processing nodes.
Deep Residual Network (DRN)	Very deep Feed-Forward Neural Networks with extra connections passing inputs from one layer to a later layer as well as next layer.
Denoising AE (DAE)	Feeds input data with noise (e.g., grainy images)
Differential Neural Computers (DNC)	Enhanced Neural Turing Machines with scalable memory.
Echo State Network (ESN)	Random connections between neurons causing unorganized sets of layers.
Extreme Learning Machine (ELM)	Start with random weights and train the weights un a single step according to least-squares fit.
Feed Forward (FF)	Feed information from the input to output layers.
Gated Recurrent Unit (GRU)	Contain an update gate.
Generative Adversarial Network (GAN)	Consists of any 2 networks: one to gnat content and the other to judge content.
Hopfield Network (HN)	Every neuron is connected t every other neuron.
Kohonen Network (KN)	Utilize competitive learning to classify data without supervision.
Liquid State Machine (LSM)	Uses threshold functions and each neuron is also an accumulating memory cell.
Long/Short Term Memory (LSTM)	Contain forget gate.
Markov Chain (MC)	Every state you end up in depends completely on the previous state.
Neural Turing Machine (NTM)	Instead of coding a memory cell directly into a neuron, the memory is separated.
Perceptron (P)	Consists of only one output node with its input nodes.
Radial Basis Network (RBF)	Feed-Forward Neural Networks (FFNNs) with radial basis functions as activation functions.
Recurrent Neural Network (RNN)	Feed-Forward Neural Networks (FFNNs) that have connections between passes.
Restricted Boltzmann Machine (RBM)	Only connect every different group of neurons to every other group.
Sparse Autoencoders (SAE)	Encodes information in more space.
Variational Autoencoders (VAE)	Have same architecture as AE but have an approximated probability distribution of the input samples.

2.2 Neural Networks as Used In Large International Software Company

A large international software company BMC uses neural network algorithms for what we call "cognitive routing." Most chatbots only transfer to the next available agent. The company uses NLP to find the best agent to resolve the problem the employee/customer is having. Example: If requesting a visa application, the request will be routed to HR.

2.2.1 Text Summarization – Understand Content

Chatbot – employee is talking to chatbot. After conversation. Chatbot not able to answer user question. We ask if they want a live agent. Once transfer happens, the live agent is provided a conversation summary (that occurred with chatbot) before engaging with employee. This is shown in Figure 3 below.

Figure 3. Illustration of Cognitive Routing by Neural Network using Chatbot by Large Software Company (Figure provided upon written permissions from BMC Software (2020)).

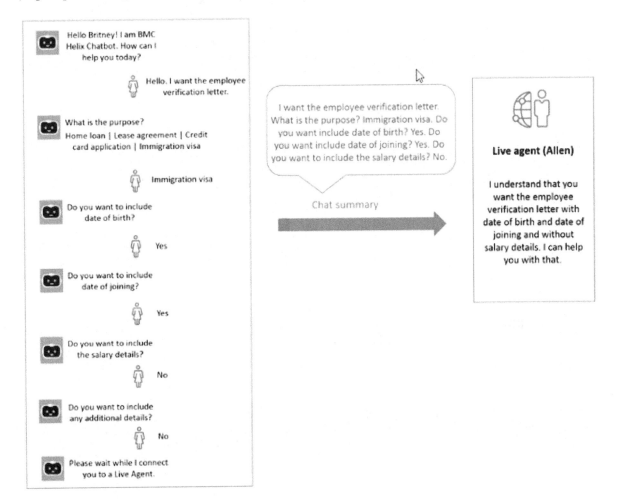

2.2.2 Ticket Summarization

Another example is "intelligent swarming." BMC uses AI to route a ticket to a group of people. As the group works on the incident, the AI/neural network algorithm is used to then decide who is the best person to work on the incident.

Whenever an employee/customer raises a ticket, a machine answers back. If the machine is unable to resolve the issue, the ticket is then assigned to an agent. If agent is unable to resolve, the ticket may get transferred to a second agent. The ticket history is summarized and prepared for this new agent. This is done through the use of NLP and neural networks, and is illustrated in Figure 4 below. (BMC (2020))

Figure 4. Example of Neural Network of "Intelligent Swarming" with Ticket Routing
(Figure provided upon written permissions from BMC Software (2020)).

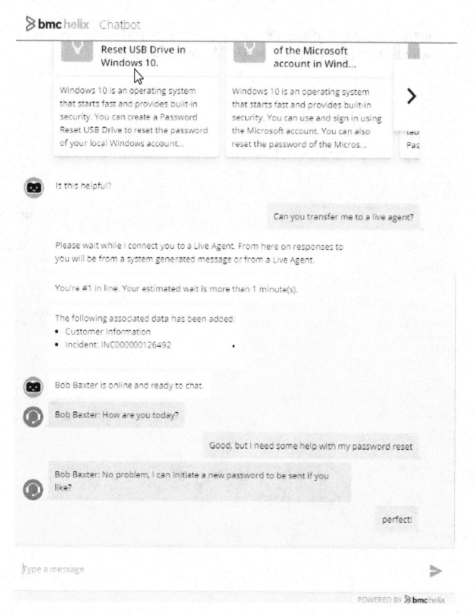

2.3 Open-Source Software for Neural Networks

Table 2. Open-Source Software for Neural Networks

Software	Overview	Important Features	URL
Darknet	Written in C and CUDA, fast and easy to install and supports CPU and GPU computation.	YOLO (You Look Only Once): Real-Time Object Detection, ImageNet Classification, RNN (Recurrent Neural Networks) to represent data that changes over time.	https://pjreddie.com/darknet/
DNNGraph	Deep Neural Network Model Generation.	Visualization of network structure.	https://github.com/ajtulloch/dnngraph
JustNN	Trains, validates and queries neural networks.	Can import data files of text, CSV, binary, XLS.	http://www.justnn.com/
MemBrain	Widely used in industrial manufacturing and technical control applications.	Can set neuron properties such as normalization settings, activation function, output recovery time, etc.	https://membrain-nn.de/english/download_en.htm
Neocognitron	Specially designed to simulate hierarchical, multilayered artificial neural networks.	Preloaded project samples, lets user set input panel size as per the number of layers, can view output routings as well as optimal winner value and pattern.	https://www.softpedia.com/get/Network-Tools/Misc-Networking-Tools/Neocognitron.shtml
Neural Designer	Cross-platform neural network software with pre-loaded examples of projects in multi-disciplines.	Intuitive interface with Task Manager, Neural Editor/Viewer; can export data as TXT, CSV, XLX files, export R scripts, and Python files.	https://www.neuraldesigner.com/download
Sharky Neural Network	Displays points graph and real-time error graph	Can select network architecture from pre-defined ones, and shape to display learning points on graph.	https://download.cnet.com/Sharky-Neural-Network/3000-2054_4-10967073.html
Simbrain	Inputs many network types (Back-prop, Competitive network, Echo State Network, Feed Forward, etc.)	Provides many simulation types (Actor-Critic, Agent Trails, and Cortical Circuit). Can visualize network simulation with bar charts, tine series, projection plot, raster plot, etc.	http://simbrain.net/Downloads/downloads_main.html
Spice-Neuro	Provides multi-layer neural network (MLP) application	Can select training parameters of activation functions for hidden and output layer, splitting data, and stop conditions; can view learning rate in Training and Testing.	https://spiceneuro.wordpress.com/english/

Table 3. Neural Network Software available for Free Trail Download

Software	Overview	Important Features	URL
AForge.Neuro	Provides Neural Network library containing sets of classes for creating different types of neural networks.	Calculating XOR functions, Multilayer Feed Forward, Kohonen Self Organizing Map.	http://www.aforgenet.com/framework/features/neural_networks.html http://www.aforgenet.com/framework/downloads.html
ConNetJS	JavaScript library for training Deep Neural Networks	Ability to specify and train Convolutional Networks that processes images, and contains an experimental reinforcement learning module based on Deep Q Learning.	https://cs.stanford.edu/people/karpathy/convnetjs/
Cuda-convnet2	New Python backend called cudanet for integration into Nervana's neon framework.	Support for non-texture kernels and multi-way costs, Python interface to GPU memory.	https://github.com/NervanaSystems/cuda-convnet2
DN2A	Set of highly decoupled JavaScript modules for Neural Network and AI Development.	Performs training by Step-By-Step, Step-By-Goal, Continuous.	https://github.com/antoniodeluca/dn2a
goBrain	Includes just basic functions such as Feed Forward and Recurrent Neural Network	Feed Forward, Elman Recurrent Neural Network.	https://github.com/goml/gobrain
HNN (Haskell Neural Network)	Powerful library for Feed Forward Neural Networks written in Haskell.	Haskell is general-purpose, statically typed, purely functional programming language.	https://github.com/alpmestan/hnn
Keras	High-level neural networks library written in Python.	Capable of running on top of either TensorFlow or Theano.	https://github.com/keras-team/keras
LambdaNet	Library written in Haskell that abstracts network creation, training, and use as higher order functions.	Quadratic error cost function.	https://github.com/MrVPlusOne/LambdaNet
Neon	Python-based deep learning library.	Swappable hardware backends, provides support for convnets, RNNs, LSTMs, and autoencoders.	https://www.predictiveanalyticstoday.com/neon/
NeuralN	C++ Neural Network Library for Node.js.	Works with large datasets and multi-threaded training available.	https://github.com/totemstech/neuraln
Neuroph	Lightweight Java neural network framework.	Data normalization, image recognition support, and stock market prediction sample.	http://neuroph.sourceforge.net/

Continued on following page

Table 3. Continued

Software	Overview	Important Features	URL
NeuroSolutions	For both novice and advanced developers.	Cluster Analysis, Sales Forecasting, Sports Predictions, Medical Classification	www.neurosolutions.com
RustNN	Feedforward neural network library.	Networks trained via backpropagation using incremental training mode.	https://github.com/jackm321/RustNN
Stuttgart Neural Network Simulator (SNNS)	Library containing many standard implementations of neural networks.	Accessibility of all of the SNNS algorithmic functionality from R.	https://cran.r-project.org/web/packages/RSNNS/
Tflearn	Deep learning library built on top of TensorFlow.	Easy graph visualization with details about weights, gradients, activations and more.	Tflearn.org

3. EXAMPLES OF MACHINE LEARNING (ML) IN ARTIFICAL INTELLIGENCE (AI) SYSTEMS

The following four examples were provided to the author by BMC Corporation as illustrations of their applications of machine learning for obtaining their optimal configuration of their Helix Data Capacity system.

Example 1: Performance of Information Technology (IT) Infrastructure Resource for Business Applications and Services

Use AI/machine learning to understand how IT infrastructure resources are used (compute, storage, and network). In the Figure 5 screen shot below, a summary view of resource use is provided. Through regular analysis, the performance of the infrastructure resources support business applications and business services is reflected. The red means there that an IT resource is about to be saturated and will soon impact the performance of the application. Yellow means you headed towards saturation that could affect performance and green means resources are in good state. The grid provides this view by individual applications or business service (group of applications that deliver a service.

For example, an online buying experience typically includes several applications. And the bottom right shows the state of all IT resources. Companies need to understand the health/usage status of the IT resources that run their applications to prevent application failures (like an online shopping service failing because it cannot support the number of transactions that are occurring. This is a common situation for special events like Black Friday, Superbowl Sunday, Insurance open enrollment, University enrollment, etc.) (BMC (2020))

Figure 5. Capacity Optimization Dashboard (Figure provided upon written permissions from BMC Software (2020)).

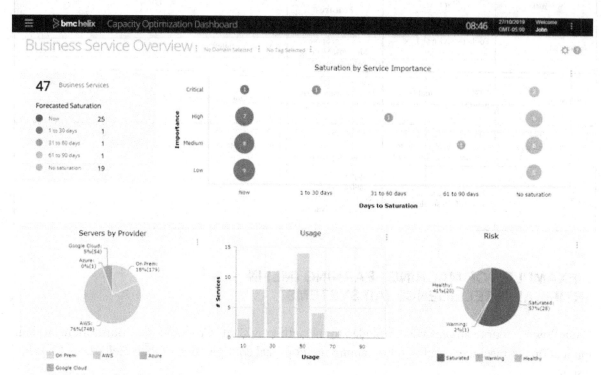

Example 2. Detecting Idle Virtual Machines (VMs) in Public Cloud Services

AI/ML used to identify virtual machines in the public cloud that you have purchased, but are not using. These are detected using ML (Machine Learning) as shown in Figure 6. Algorithms look for usage of these virtual machines (VMs) over a period of time, such as 3 or 6 months, depending on what the business wants to define. Any VMs identified as idle can be automatically shut down so the company does not waste money on paying for cloud resources they are not using. (BMC (2020))

Example 3: Probably Cause Analysis

Using AI/ML algorithms, data is gathered and analyzed to determine where the most like cause of a problem is that is causing an application to fail or run poorly. This is done by analyzing the data to identify changes is events that are collected. By analyzing event data and understand what is normal and not normal, the algorithm can determine the most likely cause of the problem as shown in Figure 7. (BMC (2020))

Figure 6. Cloud Cost Dashboard in BMC Helix (Figure provided upon written permissions from BMC Software (2020)).

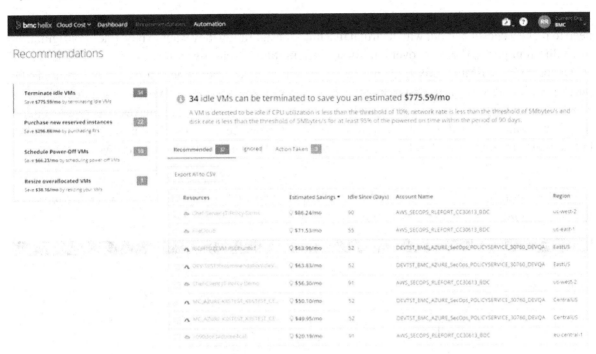

Figure 7. Probability Cause Analysis in BMC Helix (Figure provided upon written permissions from BMC Software (2020)).

Example 4: Migrating Data Center Workloads to Public Cloud

Companies are moving applications and workloads from their data center to the public cloud. They need to make a decision about which virtual machine configuration they want to buy. Each configuration has a different price. There are over a million configurations to choose from.

Using AI/ML, BMC Helix Capacity Optimization makes a recommendation for what should be purchased. It does this by understanding the historical usage patterns of the virtual machine in the data center. Using this information, it then analyzes the cloud configurations and makes a recommendation based on capacity needed (CPU, memory, storage), performance, and cost. In the Figure 8 screen shot below, there is comparative data for the data center VM and the recommended Cloud VM. (BMC (2020))

Figure 8. Migration Simulation using AI/ML for New Web Portal Service of BMC Helix (Figure provided upon written permissions from BMC Software (2020)).

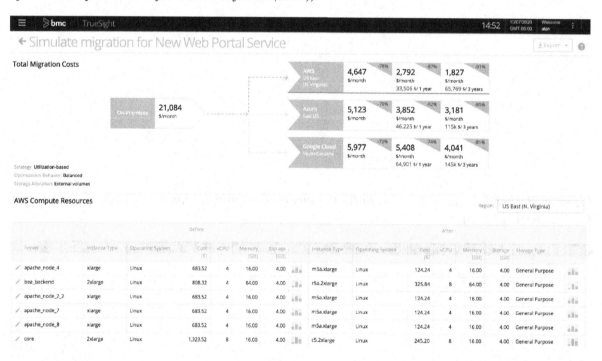

Example 5: Machine Learning and Neural Network Applications Using Business Model and Medical Datasets

Using business and medical model datasets from Kaggle, the following images/visualizations were created. Tensor Flow, Machine learning and Deep learning Toolbox of MATLAB were used to construct Figures.

Figures 9 to 11 below were created by student Vidhya Sankarasubbu under the supervision of author of this chapter as faculty mentor, and who was awarded a 2021 Summer Internship Research Award for a research proposal for support in writing this book as funded by Arkansas Biosciences Institute (ABI)

located on the campus of Arkansas State University (A-STATE) in Jonesboro. Figures 9 to 11 are shown upon written permission of student Vidha Sankarasubbu.

Figure 9. Clustered Chart to predict the spending of Mall Customers using age, customer id, gender and estimated salary using Machine Learning Toolbox (MATLAB). [Created by student Vidha Sankarasubbu and used with written permission.]

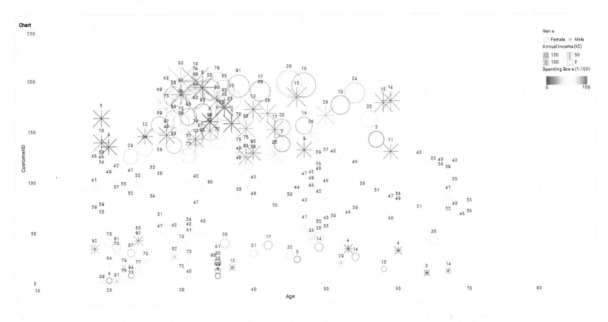

Using Kaggle datasets of customer ranges who spend more at the mall, the following clustered chart is predicted. This graph indicates that people with low salaries and those who are older spend less and save more. Despite their modest salaries, people in their younger years spend more. There are individuals that have a high income and a high spending score, indicating that they are frequent consumers of the mall. People with high incomes have a low spending score in one category. According to the predictions used to anticipate this data, mall authorities should target those with high income and low expenditure scores.

The Kaggle dataset of restaurants was utilized for a project in which the goal was to construct a top-n list of restaurants based on consumer preferences and significant attributes based on restaurant evaluations. The bar graphs of this Figure 10 depict the growth in sales of a restaurant based on regardless or not it was a franchise.

Figure 10. Bar Graph showing the restaurant sales based on their franchises. [Created by student Vidha Sankarasubbu and used with written permission.]

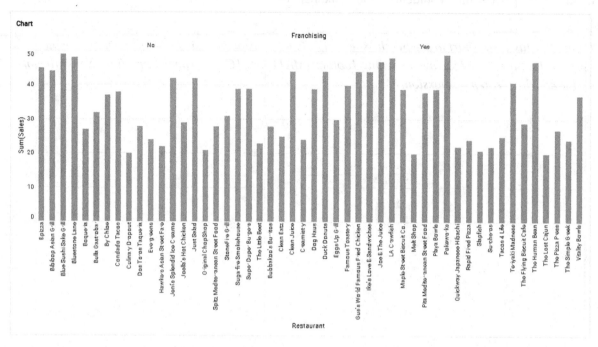

Figure 11. Prediction of Target Customers for the bank based on their age, job description and the campaign method using TensorFlow. [Created by student Vidha Sankarasubbu and used with written permission.]

Based on their age, campaign mode (contacted by telephone/cellular and number of times contacted), and job roles the Kaggle dataset was utilized to estimate the intended customer reaction from campaigns. The retirees between the ages of 60 and 80 who had only been approached once were the most successful. Students who were approached several times had the highest failure rate.

Figure 12. Facet Boxplot prediction of Churn Model – Customers leaving the Bank. [Created by student Vidha Sankarasubbu and used with written permission.]

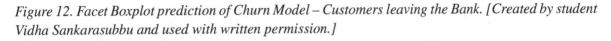
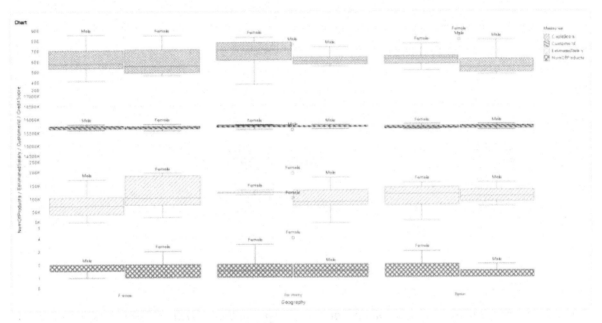

Figure 12 is based on the geographic location, age, credit score, estimated salary, the unique ID given to each customer, and the number of products they are assigned with such as loans, deposits, mortgages, and so on, the data was collected from Kaggle to predict the customers and the reason for leaving the bank using Machine Learning Toolbox (MATLAB). Some consumers are portrayed to have left the bank based on the prediction, yet they have just left a product in the bank and continue to maintain an account. Some people are unpredictable, such as those who have money in their accounts but are no longer customers.

The data for Figure 13 was collected from Kaggle and is based on Indian traffic and the reasons for Uber travel delays based on time periods. The clusters are color and pattern coded to show the differences and the travel time in seconds based on what time a customer is travelling and the reviews given by the driver after each ride. The Uber is delayed more mostly in the early mornings and is more on time in the evenings.

Figure 13. Cluster analysis prediction for Uber traffic and the reason for delays. [Created by student Vidha Sankarasubbu and used with written permission.]

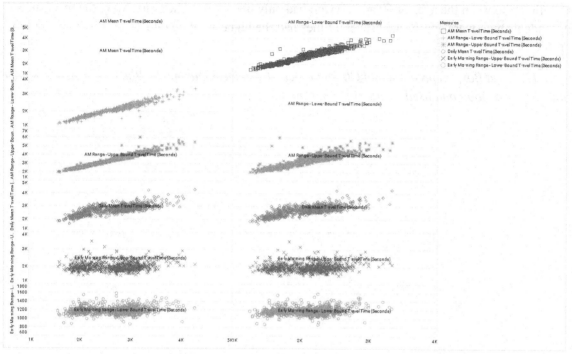

Figure 14. Cancer predictions using neural networks and machine learning algorithms based on the fractal dimension and concavity compared with the compactness. [Created by student Vidha Sankarasubbu and used with written permission.]

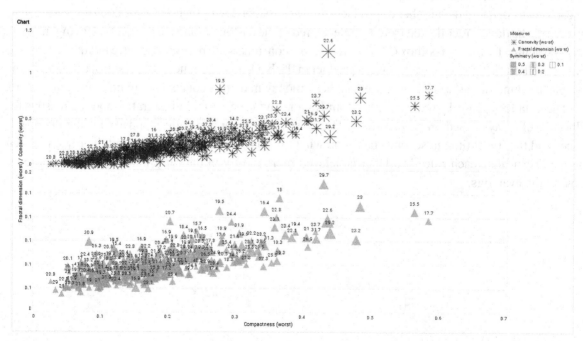

The predictions in Figure 14 show the impact of cancer in human body and the stages of cancer based on the intensity of the concavity and fractal dimension, and if the person is diagnosed for cancer before or if the symptom is new.

OPEN-SOURCE SOFTWARE FOR MACHINE LEARNING

Table 4. Open-Source Software for Machine Learning

Software	Important Features	Language	Algorithms
Accord.Net	Cross-platform that provides machine learning libraries for image and audio-processing.	C#	Classification Regression Clustering
Apache Mahout	Extension of Apache Hadoop Platform and use of the MapReduce paradigms.	Java, Scala	Regression Clustering
Apache Spark MLlib	Apache Spark's scalable machine learning library that allows users to implement machine learning in real time.	APIs in Java, Scala, Python, and R.	Classification Regression Gradient Boosting Decision Trees
Keras	Cross-platform, high-level Deep Learning API that makes it very simple to train and run neural networks	Python	Neural Networks (Convolutional and recurrent)
KNIME (Konstanz Information Miner)	Can work with large data volume.	Java	Supports text mining and image mining through plug-ins
PyTorch	Uses Tensors and can develop dynamic graphs to accelerate your machine learning processes.	Python, C++, CUDA	Deep Neural Networks
Scikit Learn	Built on NumPy, SciPy and matplotlib, and provides a library for Python programming language.	Python, Cython, C, C++	Classification Regression Clustering Dimensionality reduction Preprocessing Model Section
Shogun	You can use it with all sorts of languages including Java, Python, C#, R and Matlab.	C++	Regression Classification Distribution
TensorFlow	For numerical computation using data flow graphs. It was originally developed by Google.	Python, C++, CUDA	The most basics type of TensorFlow is a tensor that is a multi-dimensional array.
Weka	These machine learning algorithms help in data mining.	Java	Data preparation Classification Regression Clustering Visualization Association rules mining

OPEN-SOURCE ARTIFICIAL INTELLIGENGE TECHNOLOGIES FOR MACHINE LEARNING AND NEURAL NETWORKS

Table 5. AI Technologies for Machine Learning available as Open Source (Derived using David (2020).)

AI Technology	Features	Language	URL
AdaNet	TensorFlow-based framework	Python	https://github.com/tensorflow/adanet
Analytics Zoo	Able to scale data from laptop size files to large clusters to big data.	Python	https://github.com/intel-analytics/analytics-zoo
Blocks	Constructs parametrized Theano operations called "bricks" to optimize neural network models.	Python	https://github.com/mila-iqia/blocks
ConvNetJS	Trains Convolutional Networks for images	JavaScript	https://github.com/karpathy/convnetjs
Datum Box	Provides pre-trained models for different tasks	Java	https://github.com/datumbox/datumbox-framework
DeepDetect	Machine Learning API	C++	https://github.com/jolibrain/deepdetect
Dopamine	Allows fast prototyping of reinforcement learning algorithms	Python	https://github.com/google/dopamine
Flair	Applies state-of-art Natural Language Processing (NLP) to Named Entity Recognition (NER) and part-of-speech tagging (PoS)	Python	https://github.com/flairNLP/flair
Mljar	Can train ML models for binary classification, multi-class classification, and regression.	Python	https://github.com/mljar/mljar-supervised
NNI (Neural Network Intelligence)	Manages Automated Machine Learning (AutoML) experiments.	Python	https://github.com/Microsoft/nni
Plato	Supports interactions through text, speech, and dialogue acts.	Python	https://github.com/uber-research/plato-research-dialogue-system
Streamlit	Tool to build interactive web applications	JavaScript & Python	https://github.com/streamlit/streamlit
TuriCreate	ML tasks of image, sound, activity and text classification	Python	https://github.com/apple/turicreate

Table 6. Open-Source Tools for Artificial Intelligence

Software Name	Features	URL
CNTK (Computational Network Toolkit)	Computational Network Toolkit of Microsoft primarily used for research in speech recognition.	https://www.cntk.ai
NUPIC	Based om Hierarchical Temporal Memory (HTM)	https://numenta.com
OpenCog	Diverse assemblage of cognitive algorithms	https://opencog.org
Opencyc	Useful for rich domain modeling and game AIs	https://www.cyc.com/opencyc

CONCLUSION

Multi-Factor Prediction is used for evaluation or estimates of factors of complex systems. It is also used in Multifactor Dimensionality Reduction (MDR) that is a statistical approach, also used in Machine Learning (ML) automatic approaches, for detecting and characterizing combinations of attributes or independent variables that interact to influence a dependent or class variable. (Wikipedia (2021e))

This chapter presents 29 types of neural networks and their characteristics and images of each of these. A summary of available open-source software (OSS) for neural networks is presented that includes that for Deep Neural Networks (DNN) for solving multi-layer networks for complex systems that is the foundation of many modern artificial intelligence applications. Deep learning is subset of neural networks that in turn is a subset of machine learning and artificial intelligence that in turn can be used with Big Data Analytics.

This chapter presented examples that were provided to the author by BMC Corporation as illustrations of their applications of machine learning for obtaining their optimal configuration of their Helix Data Capacity system. Several examples were also presented of applications of Machine Learning and Neural Network using business models and medical datasets.

There are limitless applications of multi-factor predictions with Big Data Analytics using machine learning and the many types of neural networks, and this chapter also presents some of the available open-source software for the reader and all others to utilize from the public domain.

ACKNOWLEDGMENT

The author needs to gratefully acknowledge the permission of using Figures 5 to 8 that were created by BMC Software, as well as the time the members of BMC Software spent with me to describe and understand the corresponding Examples 1, 2, 3 and 4 as shown in this chapter.

The author also needs to acknowledge the assistance of student Vidhya Sankarasubbu who was awarded a 2021 Summer Internship Research Award for a research proposal for support in writing this book that was funded by Arkansas Biosciences Institute (ABI) located on the campus of Arkansas State University (A-STATE) in Jonesboro. For this chapter, Vidhya Sankarasubbu created Figures 9 to 14 and their corresponding verbal descriptions.

REFERENCES

G2. (2020). *Best machine learning software.* Retrieved May 31, 2020 from https://www.g2.com/catego-ries/machine-lcarning#grid

Algorithmia. (2019). *Six Open-Source Machine Learning Tools you should know.* Retrieved November 24, 2020 from https://algorithmia.com/blog/six-open-source-machine-learning-tools-you-should-know

Allen, R. (2017). *Cheat Sheet of Machine Learning and Python (and Math) Cheat Sheets.* Retrieved December 30, 2020 from https://medium.com/machine-learning-in-practice/cheat-sheet-of-machine-learning-and-python-and-math-cheat-sheets-a4afe4e791b6

Biedenbender, C., Berleant, D., Eversole, K., E. Hood, E., Leach, L., Mustell, R., R. Segall, R., & Vicuna, D. (2011). Text Mining: Using Rule Based and Neural Network Based Approaches. *2011 University of Arkansas at Little Rock (UALR) Student Research Expo.*

BMC. (2021). *BMC Helix Capacity Optimization.* BMC Datasheet. Retrieved February 18, 2021 from https://www.bmc.com/it-solutions/bmc-helix-capacity-optimization.html

Bogacz, M. (2021, January 30). *Restaurant business RANKINGS 2020.* Kaggle. https://www.kaggle.com/michau96/restaurant-business-rankings-2020

Brush, K. (2019). *Chatbot.* Retrieved May 9, 2021 from https://searchcustomerexperience.techtarget.com/definition/chatbot?vgnextfmt=print

Cai, F. (2020). DarwinAI open-source COVID-Net as medical image in COVID-19 diagnosis debate continues. *Synced: AI Technology & Industry Review.* Retrieved May 17, 2020 from https://syncedreview.com/2020/04/02/darwinai-open-sources-covid-net-as-medical-imaging-in-covid-19-diagnosis-debate-continues/

Campesato, O. (2020). *Artificial Intelligence, Machine Learning, and Deep Learning.* Mercury Learning & Information.

Castle, N. (2017). *6 Common Machine Learning Applications for Business.* Retrieved May 9, 2021 from https://blogs.oracle.com/ai-and-datascience/post/6-common-machine-learning-applications-for-business

Chouldechova, A., & Roth, A. (2020, May). A snapshot of the frontiers of fairness in machine learning. *Communications of the ACM, 63*(5), 82–89. doi:10.1145/3376898

Cook, A. (2019, March 18). *Interesting data to visualize.* Kaggle. https://www.kaggle.com/alexisbcook/data-for-datavis

Daley, S. (2021). *23 Examples of Artificial Intelligence Shaking up Business as Usual.* Retrieved May 9, 2021 from https://builtin.com/artificial-intelligence/examples-ai-in-industry

David, D. (2020). *15 Undiscovered & Open Source Machine Learning Frameworks You Need to Know in 2020.* #Machine Learning. Retrieved November 24, 2020 from https://www.freecodecamp.org/news/15-undiscovered-open-source-machine-learning-frameworks-you-need-to-know-in-2020/

Faggella, D. (2020). *7 Applications of Machine Learning in Pharma and Medicine*. Emerj AI Research and Advisory Company. Retrieved May 9, 2021 from https://emerj.com/ai-sector-overviews/machine-learning-in-pharma-medicine/

Fish, K. E., & Segall, R. S. (2002). *A Visual Analysis of Learning Rule Effects and Variable Importance for Neural Networks Employed in Data Mining Operations*. Acxiom Data Engineering Laboratory Working Paper Series, ADEL-WP-02-03, Publication in Collaboration with University of Arkansas at Little Rock (UALR) Donaghey Cyber College.

Gallagher, M. B. (2020). Model quantifies the impact of quarantine measures of COVID-19's spread. *MIT News*. Retrieved May 17, 2020 from https://news.mit.edu/2020/new-model-quantifies-impact-quarantine-measures-covid-19-spread-0416

Geron, A. (2020). *Hands-On Machine Learning with Scikit-Learn, Keras, and TensorFlow: Concepts, Tools, and Techniques to Build Intelligent Systems* (2nd ed.). O'Reilly Media.

Hasan, M. (2020). *Top 20 best AI and machine learning software and framework in 2020*. Retrieved May 31, 2020 from https://www.ubuntupit.com/best-ai-and-machine-learning-software-and-frameworks/

Haykin, S. (2020). Neural Networks and Learning Machines (3rd ed.). Pearson India Education Services.

Henderson, M. (2019). Machine learning for beginners 2019. Independently Published.

Jansen, S. (2018). *Hands-On Machine Learning for Algorithmic Trading*. Packt Publishing, Ltd.

Jones, H. (2018). *Machine Learning: The Ultimate Guide to machine learning, neural networks and deep learning for beginners who want to understand applications, artificial intelligence, data mining, big data and more*. CreateSpace Independent Publishing Platform.

Kahn, A. I., Shah, A. I., & Bhat, M. (2020). *CoroNet: A Deep Neural Network for Detection and Diagnosis of COVID-19 from Chest X-ray Images*. Retrieved May 16, 2020 from https://www.researchgate.net/publication/340598559_CoroNet_A_Deep_Neural_Network_for_Detection_and_Diagnosis_of_Covid-19_from_Chest_X-ray_Images

Kelleher, J. D., Mac Namee, B., & D'Arcy, A. (2015). *Fundamentals of Machine Learning for Predictive Data Analytics: Algorithms, Worked Examples, and Case Studies*. The MIT Press.

Learning, U. C. I. M. (2017, September 27). *Restaurant data with consumer ratings*. Kaggle. https://www.kaggle.com/uciml/restaurant-data-with-consumer-ratings

Leong, B., & Jordon, S. (2020). *Artificial Intelligence and the COVID-19 Pandemic*. Retrieved May 16, 2020 from https://fpf.org/2020/05/07/artificial-intelligence-and-the-covid-19-pandemic/

Lisboa, P. J. G., Vellido, A., & Edisbury, B. (2000). *Business Applications of Neural Networks: The state-of-the-art of real-world applications*. World Scientific Press. doi:10.1142/4238

Lu, S., Sears, A., Radish, J., Segall, R. S., & Hahn, T. F. (2014). Discovery of Strong Association Rules for Attributes from Data for Program of All-Inclusive Care for the Elderly. *Journal of Systemics, Cybernetics and Informatics, 12*(1), 21–26.

Lu, S., & Segall, R. S. (2013). Linkage in Medical Records and Bioinformatics Data. *International Journal of Information and Decision Sciences, 5*(2), 169–187. doi:10.1504/IJIDS.2013.053803

McFrockman, J. (2020). Artificial Intelligence Mastery: 4 Books in 1: Machine Learning and Artificial Intelligence for beginners+AI for Business+AI Superpowers and Data Analytics+IOT, Data Science and DL, Updated Edition. Independently Published.

Meng, X., Bradley, J., Yavuz, B., Sparks, E., Venkataraman, S., Liu, D., Freeman, J., Tsai, D. B., & Zadeh, R. (2015). *MLlib: Machine Learning in Apache Spark.* arXiv:1505.06807.

Ozlurk, T., Talo, M., Yildirim, E. A., Baloglu, U. B. Y., & Rajendra-Acharya, U. (2020). Automated detection of COVID-19 cases using deep neural networks with X-ray images. *Computers in Biology and Medicine.* Retrieved May 16, 2020 from https://www.ncbi.nlm.nih.gov/pmc/articles/PMC7187882/ doi:10.1016/j.compbiomed.2020.103792

Pal, R., Sekh, A. A., Kar, S., & Prasad, D. K. (2020). *Neural Network Based Country Wise Risk Prediction of COVID-19.* doi:10.20944/preprints202004.0421.v1

Piccini, N. (2019). *101 Machine Learning Algorithms for Data Science with Cheat Sheets.* R-bloggers. Retrieved January 17, 2021 from https://blog.datasciencedojo.com/machine-learning-algorithms/

Pratt, M. K. (2020). 10 Common Uses for Machine Learning Applications in Business. *Tech Target.* Retrieved May 9, 2021 from https://searchenterpriseai.techtarget.com/feature/10-common-uses-for-machine-learning-applications-in-business

Ramezani, N. (2020). Modern Statistical Modeling in Machine Learning and Big Data Analytics: Statistical models for continuous and categorical variables. Handbook of Research on Big Data Clustering and Machine Learning, 135-151.

Rhys, H. I. (2020). *Machine Learning with R, the Tidyverse, and Mlr* (1st ed.). Manning Publications.

Rosebrock, A. (2020). *Detecting COVID-19 in x-ray images with Keras, TensorFlow, and Deep Learning.* Retrieved May 17, 2020 from https://www.pyimagesearch.com/2020/03/16/detecting-covid-19-in-x-ray-images-with-keras-tensorflow-and-deep-learning/

Ruano, M. G., & Ruano, A. E. (2013). On the Use of Artificial Neural Networks for Biomedical Applications. In Soft Computing, AISC 195, 433-451. doi:10.1007/978-3-642-33941-7_40

Russo, R. R. (2019). Neural Networks for Beginners: An Easy Textbook for Machine Learning Fundamentals to Guide You Implementing Neural Networks with Python and Deep Learning. Independently Published.

SAS. (2020a). *Artificial intelligence: What is it and why it matters.* Retrieved May 31, 2020 from https://www.sas.com/en_us/insights/analytics/what-is-artificial-intelligence.html

SAS. (2020b). *Neural Networks: What they are and why they matter.* Retrieved May 31, 2020 from https://www.sas.com/en_us/insights/analytics/neural-networks.html

SAS. (2020c). *SAS Visual Data Mining and Machine Learning.* Retrieved May 31, 2020 from https://www.sas.com/en_us/software/visual-data-mining-machine-learning.htm

Segall, R. S. (1995, July). Some Mathematical and Computer Modelling of Neural Networks. *Applied Mathematical Modelling, 19*(7), 386–399. doi:10.1016/0307-904X(95)00021-B

Segall, R. S. (1996). Comparing Learning Rules of Neural Networks Using Computer Graphics; *Proceedings of the Twenty-seventh Annual Conference of the Southwest Decision Sciences Institute.*

Segall, R. S. (2001). Final Report for U. S. Air Force Summer Faculty Fellowship (AF/SFFP): Applications of Neural Networks, Data Mining and Warehousing to Artificial Intelligence and Sensor Array Pattern Recognition. National Research Council (NRC).

Segall, R. S. (2003). *Incorporating Data Mining and Computer Graphics for Modeling of Neural Networks.* Acxiom Data Engineering Laboratory Working Paper Series, ADEL-WP-03-02, Publication in Collaboration with University of Arkansas at Little Rock (UALR) Donaghey Cyber College.

Segall, R. S. (2004). Incorporating Data Mining and Computer Graphics for Modeling of Neural Networks. *Kybernetes: The International Journal of Systems & Cybernetics, 33*(8), 1258–1276. doi:10.1108/03684920410545252

Segall, R. S., & Lu, S. (2014). *Linkage Discovery with Glossaries. In Encyclopedia of Business Analytics & Optimization* (pp. 1411–1421). IGI Global. doi:10.4018/978-1-4666-5202-6.ch128

Segall, R. S., & Lu, S. (2015). Information Retrieval by Linkage Discovery. In Encyclopedia of Information Science & Technology (pp. 3932–3939). IGI Global.

Segall, R. S., & Lu, S. (2018). Data Linkage Discovery Applications. In Encyclopedia of Information Science and Technology (IST), 4th edition. IGI Global.

Segall, R. S., & Zhang, Q. (2006). Applications of Neural Network and Genetic Algorithm Data Mining Techniques in Bioinformatics Knowledge Discovery – A Preliminary Study. *Proceedings of the Thirty-seventh Annual Conference of the Southwest Decision Sciences Institute, 37*(1).

Segall, R. S., & Zhang, Q. (2009). Comparing Four Data Mining Software. In Encyclopedia of Data Warehousing and Mining (2nd ed., pp. 269-277). IGI Global Publishing Inc.

Singh, D., Kumar, V., & Kaur, M. (2020). Classification of COVID-19 patients from chest CT images using multi-objective differential evolution-based convolutional neural networks. *European Journal of Clinical Microbiology & Infectious Diseases*. Retrieved May 16, 2020 from https://link.springer.com/content/pdf/10.1007/s10096-020-03901-z.pdf

So, D. (2020). *Alibaba News Roundup: Tech Takes on the Outbreak.* Retrieved May 17, 2020 from https://www.alizila.com/alibaba-news-roundup-tech-takes-on-the-outbreak/

Srivastava, S. (2019, February 27). *Uber traffic data visualization.* Kaggle. https://www.kaggle.com/shobhit18th/uber-traffic-data-visualization

Stone, J. V. (2019). *Artificial Intelligence engines: A tutorial introduction to the mathematics of deep learning.* Sebtel Press.

Talylor, M. (2017). *Neural Networks: A visual introduction for beginners.* Blue Windmill Media.

Theobald, O. (2017). Machine Learning for Absolute Beginners (2nd ed.). Independently Published.

Thomas, M. (2020). *15 Examples of Machine Learning in Healthcare that are Revolutionizing Medicine.* Built in. Retrieved May 9, 2021 from https://builtin.com/artificial-intelligence/machine-learning-healthcare

TrustRadius. (2020). *Machine Learning Tools.* Retrieved May 31, 2020 from https://www.trustradius.com/machine-learning

Van Veen, F., & Leijnen, S. (2019). *A mostly complete chart of Neural Networks.* The Neural Network Zoo. Retrieved December 28, 2020 from https://www.asimovinstitute.org/neural-network-zoo

Vieira, A., & Ribeiro, B. (2018). Introduction to Deep Learning Business Applications for Developers: From Conversational Bots in Customer Service to Medical Image Processing. Apress.

Wang, L. (2020). Convolutional Neural Network detects COVID-19 from Chest Radiography Images. *Vision Systems Design.* Retrieved May 16, 2020 from https://www.vision-systems.com/non-factory/life-sciences/article/14173262/covid-19-chest-radiography-deep-learning-virus-detection

Wang, L., & Wong, A. (2020). *COVID-Net: A Tailored Deep Convolutional Neural Network Design for Detection of COVID-19 Cases from Chest X-Ray Images.* Retrieved May 16, 2020 from https://arxiv.org/abs/2003.09871

Wikipedia. (2021a). *Neural Networks.* Retrieved January 2, 2021 from https://en.wikipedia.org/wiki/Neural_network

Wikipedia. (2021b). *Machine Learning.* Retrieved January 2, 2021 from https://en.wikipedia.org/wiki/Machine_learning

Wikipedia. (2021c). *Artificial Intelligence.* Retrieved January 2, 2021 from https://en.wikipedia.org/wiki/Artificial_intelligence

Wikipedia. (2021d). *Open Source Software.* Retrieved February 18, 2021 from https://en.wikipedia.org/wiki/Open-source_software

Wikipedia. (2021e). *Multifactor Dimensionality Reduction (MDR).* Retrieved February 18, 2021 from https://en.wikipedia.org/wiki/Multifactor_dimensionality_reduction

Zhao, H. (2020). AI CT Scan Analysis for CONVID-19 Detection and Patient Monitoring. *Synced: AI Technology & Industry Review.* Retrieved May 17, 2020 from https://syncedreview.com/2020/03/18/ai-ct-scan-analysis-for-covid-19-detection-and-patient-monitoring/

Zhao, J., Zhang, Y., He, X., & Xie, P. (2020). *COVID-CT-Dataset: A CT scan dataset about COVID-19.* Retrieved May 17, 2020 from https://arxiv.org/pdf/2003.13865.pdf

Zunicd. (n.d.). *Zunicd/Bank-Churn-Prediction: Bank customers churn dashboard with predictions from several machine learning models.* GitHub. https://github.com/zunicd/Bank-Churn-Prediction

ADDITONAL READING

Drone (2021). 10 Open Source Tools Frameworks for Artificial Intelligence. Retrieved January 24, 2021 from https://dzone.com/articles/10-opensource-toolsframeworks-for-artificial-intel

Garbade, M. J. (2018). Top 8 Open Source AI Technologies In Machine Learning.Opensource.com Retrieved November 24, 2020 from https://opensource.com/article/18/5/top-8-open-source-ai-technologies-machine-learning

Grigorev, A. (2021). Machine Learning Bootcamp, Manning Publications Co., Shelter Island, NY.

Hudgeon, D., & Nichol, R. (2020). *Machine Learning for Business: Using Amazon SageMaker and Jupyter*. Manning Publications Co.

Mattman, C. A. (2021). Machine Learning with TensorFlow, Second Edition, Manning Publications Co., Shelter Island, NY.

Nanalyze (2021). Free Artificial Intelligence (AI) Software. Retrieved January 24, 2021 from https://www.nanalyze.com/2017/03/free-artificial-intelligence-ai-software/

Negro, A. (2021). Graph-Powered Machine Learning, Manning Publications Co., Shelter Island, NY, ISBN 9-781-61729-564-5

Rich, C., Prasad, R., & Ganguli, S. (2019). Market Guide for AI Ops Platforms, ID G00378587. Retrieved November 29, 2020 from https://www.gartner.com/doc/reprints?id=1-1XRR9HDN&ct=191115&st=sb

SAS. (2020). Machine learning: What it is and why it matters https://www.sas.com/en_us/insights/analytics/machine-learning.html

Sourceforge (2021). Free Open Source Windows Machine Learning Software. A List of 15 Free AI Software Programs to Download. https://sourceforge.net/directory/science-engineering/ai/machinelearning/os:windows/

Springboard India. (2019). Top 15 Open-Source Machine Learning Tools to Learn in 2020. December 5. Retrieved November 24, 2020 from https://in.springboard.com/blog/machine-learning-tools/

Wikipedia. (2020). List of datasets for machine-learning research. Retrieved November 29, 2020 from https://en.wikipedia.org/wiki/List_of_datasets_for_machine-learning_research

Yegulalp, S. (2020). 14 Open Source Tools to Make the Most of Machine Learning, *InfoWorld*. IDG Communications, Inc. Retrieved November 24, 2020 from https://www.infoworld.com/article/3575420/14-open-source-tools-to-make-the-most-of-machine-learning.html

KEY TERMS AND DEFINITIONS

Artificial Intelligence (AI): Intelligence demonstrated by machines, unlike the natural intelligence displayed by humans and animals, which involves consciousness and emotionality (Wikipedia, 2021c).

Deep Neural Networks (DNN): Also referred to as "deep learning" are capable of learning high-level features with more complexity and abstraction than shallower neural networks (Sse et al., 2020, pp. 3, 7).

Helix Capacity Optimization: BMC Helix Capacity Optimization is a capacity optimization solution that aligns Information Technology (IT) resources with business service demands, optimizing resource usage and reducing costs (BMC, 2021).

Machine Learning (ML): A part of artificial intelligence that is the study of computer algorithms that improve automatically through experience. Machine learning algorithms build a model based on sample data, known as "training data," in order to make predictions or decisions without being explicitly programmed to do so (Wikipedia, 2021b).

Multi-Factor Prediction: Used for evaluation or estimates of factors of complex systems.

Neural Networks (NN): A network or circuit of neurons, or in a modern sense, an artificial neural network, composed of artificial neurons or nodes (Wikipedia, 2021a).

Open-Source Software (OSS): A type of computer software in which source code is released under a license in which the copyright holder grants users the rights to use, study, change, and distribute the software to anyone and for any purpose (Wikipedia, 2021d).

Section 2
Biomedical Applications

Chapter 2
Survey of Applications of Neural Networks and Machine Learning to COVID–19 Predictions

Richard S. Segall
Arkansas State University, USA

ABSTRACT

The purpose of this chapter is to illustrate how artificial intelligence (AI) technologies have been used for COVID-19 detection and analysis. Specifically, the use of neural networks (NN) and machine learning (ML) are described along with which countries are creating these techniques and how these are being used for COVID-19 diagnosis and detection. Illustrations of multi-layer convolutional neural networks (CNN), recurrent neural networks (RNN), and deep neural networks (DNN) are provided to show how these are used for COVID-19 detection and prediction. A summary of big data analytics for COVID-19 and some available COVID-19 open-source data sets and repositories and their characteristics for research and analysis are also provided. An example is also shown for artificial intelligence (AI) and neural network (NN) applications using real-time COVID-19 data.

BACKGROUND OF COVID-19

Corona Virus Disease 2019 (COVID-19) is a contagious disease caused by severe acute respiratory syndrome coronavirus 2 (SARS-CoV-2). The first case was identified in Wuhan, China, in December 2019. It has since spread worldwide, leading to an ongoing pandemic. (Wikipedia, 2021)

European Centre for Disease Prevention and Control (ECDC) (2021) has been posting weekly open-source COVID-19 related datasets for free download that includes data on hospital and ICI admission rates and current occupancy for COVID-19, and data on testing for COVID-19 by week and country.

The Office of Data Science Strategy (ODSS) of National Institute of Health (NIH) (2020) has made available open-access data and computational resources to address COVID-19 that includes CAS CO-VID-19 antiviral candidate compounds dataset of nearly 50,000 chemical substances for use in applications including research, data mining, machine learning, and analytics.

DOI: 10.4018/978-1-7998-8455-2.ch002

Artificial Intelligence (AI) techniques used for diagnosis of COVID-19 include AI-empowered medical image acquisition, segmentation, diagnosis and follow-up. Many investigators have used different image segmentation methods in COVID-19 applications (Shi et al. (2020)).

Recent extensive studies have been presented in several books with detailed COVID-19 related studies of applications of artificial intelligence used for creating predictive models for decision making in this pandemic and include those of Abdelrahman (2020), Bandyopadhyay and Dutta (2020), Hassaniem et al. (2020), Santosh and Joshi (2021), Zhang (2020), Al-Turjan et al. (2021), Marques et al. (2021), and Raza (2021). Further discussions of these extensive studies are presented in this chapter.

MACHINE LEARNING AND COVID-19

Machine learning (ML) is based on the premise that an intelligent machine should be able to learn and adapt from its environment based on its experiences without being explicitly programmed. The availability of open-source data sets with COVID-19 data allows the experimentation of using machine learning techniques and deep neural networks for the prediction and diagnosis of COVID-19 using Computed Tomography (CT) scans and x-rays. CT scans show detailed images of any part of the body, including the bones, muscles, fat, organs and blood vessels.

Shuja et al. (2020) provided a comprehensive survey of open-source data sets that included categories of biomedical images, textual, and speech data. As COVID-19 test kits are in short supply, medical image-based diagnosis provides an alternative method of COVID-19 diagnosis. According to Shuja et al. (2020), the combination of artificial intelligence (AI) and open-source data sets practical solution for COVID-19 diagnosis that can be implemented in hospitals worldwide.

According to the World Health Organization (WHO) (2020) some of the leading hospitals across the world are utilizing artificial intelligence and machine learning algorithms to diagnose COVID-19 cases using Computed Tomography (CT) scans and X-ray images.

Rao and Vazuez (2020) showed that identification of COVID-19 can be quicker through artificial intelligence framework with use of machine learning algorithm when used with a mobile phone-based survey when cities and towns are under quarantine.

Bandyopadhyay and Dutta (2020) provided a validation of COVID-19 by Machine Learning approach using performance metrics of accuracy and Root-Mean Square-Error (RMSE) using a Recurrent Neural Network method.

Zoabi et al. (2021) created a model that predicted COVID-19 test results with high accuracy using only eight binary features: sex, age '60 years, known contact with an infected individual, and the appearance of five initial clinical symptoms. Zoabi et al. (2021) indicate that their framework of can be used, among other considerations, to prioritize testing for COVID-19 when testing resources are limited.

NEURAL NETWORKS AND COVID-19

Pham (2020) presented a comprehensive study on classification of COVID-19 on computed tomography with pretrained convolutional neural networks (CNN). Pham (2020) found that using certain parameter specification and training strategy for the networks, this study found very high performance of several of the 16 pretrained CNNs for COVID-19 diagnosis using CT scans.

Wang et al. (2020) used five pretrained convolutional neural networks (CNN) for COVID-19 diagnosis in chest x-ray images that achieved an overall accuracy of 95%.

Bassi and Attux (2020) showed that chest x-rays used together with Deep Neural Networks (DNN) and Layer-wise Relevance Propagation (LRP) to generate heatmaps can become a cheap and accurate method for COVID-19 diagnosis. Hanfi (2020) also discussed a neural network approach to, detect CO-VID-19 through chest x-ray. The below Figure 1 was created based upon reading these and other related works to show a representative Deep Neural Network approach to detect COVID-19 with chest x-rays.

Figure 1. Sample Deep Neural Network (DNN) framework to detect COVID-19 using chest x-rays [CO-VID+ (presence), COVID- (absence)]

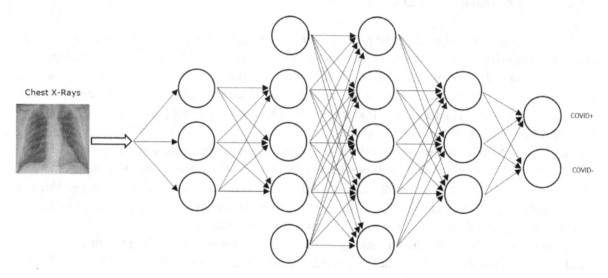

Wieczorek at al. (2020) created a neural network powered COVID-19 spread forecasting model with results in some cases reaches above 99% accuracy.

Abdulaal et al. (2020) made prognostic modeling as a point-of-admission mortality risk scoring system for COVID-19 using an adaptive Artificial Neural Network (ANN) for patient data in the United Kingdom (UK) that was predicted with 86.25% accuracy.

Irmak (2020) presented implementations of two powerful and robust convolutional neural networks (CNN) approaches for COVID-19 disease detection. The first is architecture is able to determine a given chest x-ray image of a patient contains COVID-19 with 98.92 average accuracy. The second architecture presented by Irmak (2020) is able to divide a given chest x-ray image of patient into three classes: COVID-19, normal, and pneumonia with 98.27% accuracy and used databases of over 1,500 images for each of these three categories.

The below Figure 2 presents an example of a Convolutional Neural Network (CNN) that consists of 12 layers for COVID-19 detected and was created after reading Irmak (2020).

Figure 2. Example of Multi-layer Convolutional Neural Network (CNN) for COVID-19 detection

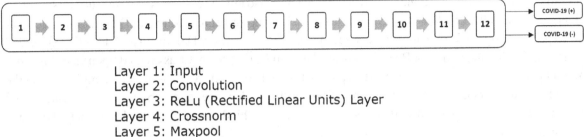

Layer 1: Input
Layer 2: Convolution
Layer 3: ReLu (Rectified Linear Units) Layer
Layer 4: Crossnorm
Layer 5: Maxpool
Layer 6: Convolution
Layer 7: ReLu (Rectified Linear Units) Layer
Layer 8: Maxpool
Layer 9: Dropout
Layer 10: Fully Connected
Layer 11: Soft max
Layer 12: Classification

Nicholson (2020) presented a beginner's guide to Long-Short Term Memory Units (LSTMs) and Recurrent Neural Networks (RNN). Nicholson (2020) explains that Recurrent Neural Networks (RNN) are a type of Artificial Neural Network (ANN) designed to recognize patterns in sequences of data, such as numerical times series data emanating from sensors, stock markets, and government data.

Figure 3. Illustration of Recurrent Neural Network (RNN)

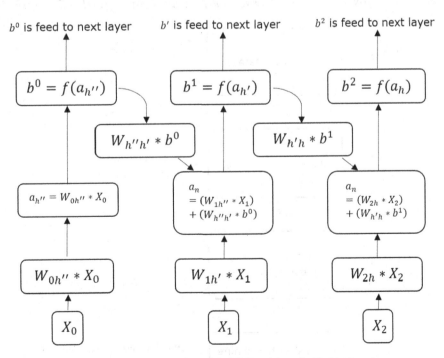

Drawn using A.I. wiki: "A Beginner's Guide to
LSTMs and Recurrent Neural Networks" (2020)
[https://wiki.pathmind.com/lstm]

According to Wikipedia (2021b), Long Short-Term Memory (LSTM) has feedback connections and can not only process single data points (such as images), but also entire sequences of data (such as speech or video). For example, LSTM is applicable to tasks such as unsegmented, connected handwriting recognition, speech recognition, and anomaly detection in network traffic or IDSs (intrusion detection systems).

Figure 3 is an illustration of Recurrent Neural Networks (RNN) that was created upon studying work of Nicholson (2020). Figure 3 shows the span of time where each "x" is an input example, "w" is the "weight" that filters inputs, "a" is the "activation" of the hidden layer (a combination of weighted input and the previous hidden state), and "b" is the "output of the hidden layer" after it has been transformed by the function "f".

MACHINE LEARNING AND NEURAL NETWORKS USED TOGETHER FOR COVID-19

Wang et al. (2020) presented an efficient mixture of deep and machine learning models for COVID-19 diagnosis in chest X-ray images using Deep Neural Networks (DNN) and Machine Learning (ML). The following Figure 4 was constructed upon reading work of Wang et al. (2020) that includes a Step 3 for Pre-trained Deep Learning Models using Deep Neural Networks (DNN) and a Step 4 that classifies the results of Step 3 using Machine Learning (ML) classification methods such as decision trees, random forest, AdaBoost, Bagging and SVM (Support Vector Method) Networks. Figure 4 below presents a flowchart of Deep Neural Networks (DNN) and Machine Learning (ML) for COVID-19 diagnosis.

Figure 4. Flowchart of Deep Neural Networks (DNN) and Machine Learning (ML) for COVID-19 diagnosis.

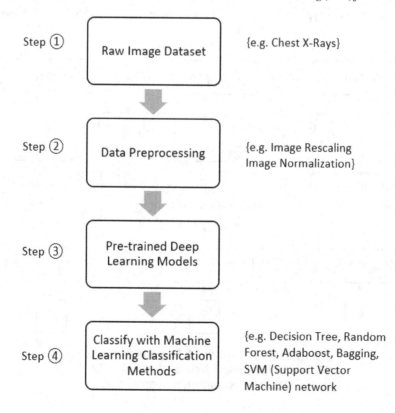

METHODOLOGY FOR SELECTING THE BEST MODEL FOR COVID-19 PREDICTION

Researchers are confronted with multi-criteria decision-making to select the best model or models for predictions of COVID-19. Figure 5 below created by author RS Segall shows a flowchart of steps for selecting the best candidate model for COVID-19 prediction results using multiple metrics based on accuracy, specificity, sensitivity and precision based on numerical values of True Positive (TP), True Negative (TN), False Positive (FP), and False Negative (FN), and Room Mean Square Error (RMSE). The investigator needs to determine which of these Potential Metrics or other Metric is the most useful or suitable criteria for determining the best model for COVID-19 prediction.

Long Short-Term Memory (LSTM) used as Model 1 in Figure 5 is a type of Recurrent Neural Network (RNN) capable of learning order dependence in sequence prediction problems as a behavior required in complex problem domains like machine translation, speech recognition, and more. (Brownlee (2017))

Gated Recurrent Unit (GRU) used as Model 2 in Figure 5 is a gating mechanism in Recurrent Neural Networks, introduced in 2014 by Kyunghyun Cho et al. (2014). The GRU is like a long short-term memory with a forget gate, but has fewer parameters than LSTM, as it lacks an output gate. (Wikipedia, 2021a).

Figure 5. Flowchart of steps for selecting best candidate model for COVID-19 prediction results.

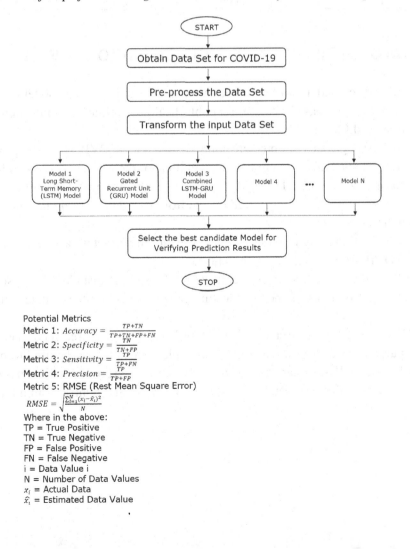

Potential Metrics

Metric 1: $Accuracy = \frac{TP+TN}{TP+TN+FP+FN}$

Metric 2: $Specificity = \frac{TN}{TN+FP}$

Metric 3: $Sensitivity = \frac{TP}{TP+FN}$

Metric 4: $Precision = \frac{TP}{TP+FP}$

Metric 5: RMSE (Rest Mean Square Error)

$$RMSE = \sqrt{\frac{\sum_{i=1}^{N}(x_i - \hat{x}_i)^2}{N}}$$

Where in the above:

TP = True Positive
TN = True Negative
FP = False Positive
FN = False Negative
i = Data Value i
N = Number of Data Values
x_i = Actual Data
$\hat{x}_i$ = Estimated Data Value

BIG DATA ANALYTICS AND EMERGING ARTIFICIAL INTELLIGENCE TECHNOLOGIES FOR BATTLING COVID-19

Table 1 below shows some illustrations of Big Data Analytics for battling COVID-19. The work of Elghamrawy (2020) uses a Deep Learning model H2O based on Deep Learning Big Data analytics (DLBD-COV) for early diagnosis of COVID019 using Computer Tomography (CT) or X-ray images.

Table 1. Big Data Analytics for COVID-19

DATE	AUTHOR(S)	Big Data Contribution	COUNTRY
July 24, 2020	Agbehali et al. (2020)	Review of Big Data Analytics and AI Computing Models	South Africa
March 30, 2020	Kent, J. (2020b)	Google makes COVID-19 Datasets freely available to Researchers	United States
September 21, 2020	Kent, J. (2020c)	Big Data Analytics shows COVID-19 spread by Region.	United States
December 24, 2020	Kent, J. (2020d)	Intersection of Big Data Analytics, COVID-19 Top Focus of 2020.	United States
2020	Elghamrawy (2020)	H20 Deep Learning-Inspired Model on Big Data Analytics	Egypt

APPLICATIONS OF ARTIFICIAL INTELLIGENCE (AI) TO COVID-19

Unnithan et al. (2021) discussed use of both forecasting models and dynamic models in modeling CO-VID-19 data in Canada, and AI-based solutions for public health surveillance for informing public health strategies in Australia and Canada.

Arora and Soni (2021) presented a pre-screening approach for COVID-19 testing based on Belief Rule-Based Expert System (BRBES)to predict the likelihood of the person to be tested for COVID-19.

Srikusan and Karunamoorthy (2021) used Anomaly Detection (AD) to detect COVID-19 like disease outbreaks by comparing expected or forecasted results from past data that mimics the region-specific seasonal infection disease patterns.

Bhapkar et al. (2021) used Rough Set theory that is used for imperfect information in the AI province in the context of COVID-19 to predict symptomatic cases.

Kaiser et al. (2021) discussed the use of healthcare robotics to combat COVID-19 such as supporting patient care at the hospital and home, disinfecting places, collecting the sample from a patient for screening.

Chawki (2021) discussed Smart Screening for High Body Temperature, Surveillance, monitoring treatment, multi-purpose AI or IoT (Internet of Things) platforms that can be used to monitor people that are in compulsory COVID-19 quarantine. Chawki also discussed cross-population train/test models so that the model can be utilized to detect COVID-19 in a different country from a model trained in Wuhan, China.

Arya and Devi (2021) discussed the known AI-models that were earlier trained for different systems as being re-trained using COVID-19 data to assist in predicting and identifying those potentially infected with COVID-19.

Table 2 below shows some applications of Artificial Intelligence (AI) for COVID-19 detection and analysis for year 2020 and Table 3 for year 2021.

Table 2. Year 2020: Artificial Intelligence techniques used for COVID-19 detection and analysis

DATE	AUHTOR(S)	ARTIFICAL INTELLIGENCE (AI) TECHNIQUES	COUNTRY
February 21, 2020	So, D.	New AI algorithm that can diagnose suspected cases in 20 seconds with 96 percent accuracy.	China
March 18, 2020	Zhao, H.	AI-based deep learning image analysis system based on CT chest scans	Israel and United States
April 2, 2020	Cai, F.	GSInquire, a generative synthesis based explain-ability method for critical factors of DarwinAI	Canada
April 28, 2020	Ozturk, T. et al.	DarkNet model used as a classifier if the You Only Look Once (YOLO) real time object detection system.	Turkey, UK, Singapore, Taiwan.
May 7, 2020	Leong, B. & Jordan, S.	Focus on apps directed to health care professionals that leverage audio-visual data, text analysis, chatbots, and sensors.	United States
June 2020	Lalmuanawma, S. et al.	Digital contact tracing process using Bluetooth, Global Positioning System (GPS), Social graph, network-based API, & mobile tracking data.	India United Kingdom (UK)
August 25, 2020	Abdulaah et al.	Artificial Neural Networks (ANN)	United Kingdom
November 10, 2020	Chen, Y. et al.	AI-based imaging analysis methods including chest-imaging techniques.	China
November 2020	Bullock, J. et al.	Molecular, clinical and societal applications at different scales: including medical imaging and risk assessment	United States, United Kingdom, Switzerland
2020	Dalip, D.	AI merged with Global Positioning System (GPS)to prevent spread of COVID-19	India
2020	Jat, D.S. & Singh, C.	Robotic drone applications	Namibia and USA
2020	Gupta, D., Mahajan, A. & Gupta, S.	AI aid in facilitating social distancing	India

Table 3. Year 2021: Artificial Intelligence techniques used for COVID-19 detection and analysis

DATE	AUHTOR(S)	ARTIFICAL INTELLIGENCE (AI) TECHNIQUES	COUNTRY
January 2021	Unnithan, C. et al.	Blue tooth technology used in contact tracing apps, AI methods in predictive modeling.	Australia, Canada
January 2021	Arora, T. & Soni, R.	Belief Rule-Based Expert System (BRBES)	India
January 2021	Srikusan, R. & Karaunamoorthy, M.	Anomaly Detection (AD)	India
January 2021	Bhapkar, H.R. et al.	Rough set theory in COVID-19 to predict symptomatic cases.	India, Denmark, United Kingdom (UK)
January 2021	Kaiser, M.S. et al.	Heathcare Robots	Bangladesh, United Kingdom (UK)
January 2021	Chawki, M.	Smart Screening, Surveillance, Cross-Population Train/Test AI-Driven models	France
January 2021	Arya, M.S. & Devi, S.P.	Retraining of AI models for COVID data	India
January 2021	Agarwal, M. et al.	9 AI Models on cognitive systems in Next Generation Network (NGN).	India Italy
February 2021	Al-Turjman, F.	Cognitive Systems in Next Generation Networks (NGN)	Spain
February 2021	Nawaz, M.S. et al.	Sequential pattern mining (SPM), sequence prediction models, genome analysis.	China United States Japan
March 2021	Lv, D. et al.	Cascade Squeeze-Excitation and Moment Exchange (Cascade-SEME) framework	China United States United Kingdom
April 2021	Verde, L. & et.	Speech and Voice Analysis	Italy Saudi Arabia Egypt
April 2021	Huang, S., Yang, J., Fong, S. & Zhao, Q.	Literature review of challenges & perspectives of AI diagnosis of COVID-19	China
May 2021	Tali, S.H.S. et al.	Sensor and biosensor devices, including diagnostic imaging devices	Canada
May 2021	Ahmed, S. et al.	High-Resolution Network (HRNet) for feature extraction embedding with the UNet for segmentation purposes	Japan Bangladesh

APPLICATIONS OF NEURAL NETWORKS (NN) TO COVID-19

Table 4 shows some applications in year 2020 of neural networks for COVID-19 detection and analysis, and Table 5 for year 2021.

Table 4. Year 2020: Neural Networks used for COVID-19 detection and analysis

DATE	AUTHOR(S)	NEURAL NETWORK TECHNIQUES	COUNTRY
March 16, 2020	Rosebrock, A.	X-ray images wih Keras, TensorFlow, and Deep Learning	Canada
March 22, 2020	Wang, L & Wong, A.	Introduced COVID-Net, a deep convolutional neural network design tailored for the detection of COVID-19 cases from chest X-ray (CXR) images that is open-source and available to the general public.	Canada
March 30, 2020	Zhao,J. et al.	COVIDE-CT-Dataset used with deep learning methods which predicts COVID-19 by analyzing CT scans.	United States
April 2020	Khan, A.I., Shah, J.L. & Bhar, M.	CoroNet: A deep neural network for detection and diagnosis of COVID-19 from chest x-ray images	India
April 24, 2020	Pal, R. et al.	Long Short-Term Memory (LSTM) based neural network to predict the risk category of a country.	Norway and India
April 27, 2020	Singh, D. et al.	Chest CT images using multi-objective differential evolution (MODE) based convolutional neural networks.	India
June 12, 2020	Mollalo, et al.	Multilayer perceptron (MLP) Neural Network	United States
August 15, 2020	Wieczorek et al.	Recurrent Neural Network (RNN)	Poland
October 9, 2020	Pham, T.D.	Pretrained Convolutional Neural Networks (CNN)	Saudi Arabia
October 22, 2020	Irmak, E.	Convolutional Neural Networks (CNN)	Turkey
December 11, 2020	Bassi & Attux	Deep Convolutional Neural Networks (CNN) with Layer-wise Relevance Propagation (LPR)	Brazil
December 13, 2020	Hanfi, S.A.	6-Layer Convolutional Neural Network (CNN)	

Table 5. Year 2021: Neural Networks used for COVID-19 detection and analysis

DATE	AUTHOR(S)	NEURAL NETWORK TECHNIQUES	COUNTRY
2021	Marques et al.	Long Short-Term Memory (LSTM) Networks	Brazil and Macao
2021	Hamadneh et al.	Multi-Layer Perception Neural Network (MLPNN)	Saudi Arabia, Vietnam, Jordan
2021	Bahrami & Sadeddin	Convolutional Neural Network (CNN) identifying COVID-19 coughs and the MIT AI model detecting asymptomatic COVID-19 infections using cough recordings	United States
2021	Colak	Prediction of Infection and Death Ratio of COVID-19 Virus in Turkey by Using Artificial Neural Network (ANN)	Turkey
2021	Kaliyar et al.	MCNNet: Generalizing Fake News Detection with a Multichannel Convolutional Neural Network using a Novel COVID-19 Dataset	India
March 2021	Alsaade, F.W., Al-Adhaileh, T.H. & Al-Adhaileh, M.H.	Developing a Recognition System for Classifying COVID-19 Using a Convolutional Neural Network Algorithm	Saudi Arabia
March 2021	Rahimzadeh, M., Attar, A., & Sakhaei, S.M.	A fully automated deep learning-based network for detecting COVID-19 from a new and large lung CT scan dataset	Iran
April 2021	Taresh, M.M., Zhu, N., Ali, T.A., Hameed, A.S. & Mutar, M.L.	Transfer Learning to Detect COVID-19 Automatically from X-Ray Images Using Convolutional Neural Networks (CNN)	China Iraq Malaysia
May 2021	DeGrave, A.J., Janizek, J.D., & Lee, S-I.	Convolutional Neural Network (CNN) for radiographic COVID-19 detection.	United States
May 2021	Eron, G., Janizek, J.D., Sturmfels, P. et al.	Improving performance of deep learning models with axiomatic attribution priors and expected gradients.	United States
May 2021	Mukherjee, H., Ghosh, S., Dhar, A. et al.	Deep neural network to detect COVID-19: one architecture for both CT scans and Chest X-rays.	India United States
May 2021	Narin, A., Kaya, C. & Pamuk, Z.	Automatic detection of coronavirus disease (COVID-19) using X-ray images and deep Convolutional Neural Networks (CNN)	Turkey
June 2021	Fouladi, S., Ebadi, M. J., Safaei, A. A., Bajuri, M. Y., & Ahmadian, A.	Convolutional Neural Network (CNN), Convolutional Auto-Encoder Neural Network (CAENN), and machine learning (ML) methods are proposed for classifying Chest CT Images of COVID-19.	Iran Malaysia
July 2021	N. N. Hamadneh, W. A. Khan, W. Ashraf, S. H. Atawneh, I. Khan et al.,	Multilayer perceptron neural network (MLPNN) is used in this study together with prey-predator algorithm (PPA). The proposed model is called the MLPNN–PPA.	Saudi Arabia

APPLICATIONS OF MACHINE LEARNING (ML) TO COVID-19

Table 6 presents some applications of machine learning to COVID-19 detection and analysis for year 2020 and Table 7 for year 2021.

Table 6. Year 2020: Machine Learning (ML) techniques used for COVID-19 detection and analysis

DATE	AUTHOR(S)	MACHINE LEARNING (ML) TECHNIQUES	COUNTRY
April 16, 2020	Gallagher, M.B.	Machine learning algorithm combines data on the disease's spread with a neural network, to help predict when infections will slow down on each country.	United States
June 25, 2020	Lalmuanawma et al.	Survey Paper of many methods	India and United Kingdom
September 29, 2020	Li et al.	eXtreme Gradient Boosting algorithm (XGBoost)	United States
October 30, 2020	An et al.	Least Absolute Shrinkage and Selection Operator (LASSO), Random Forest learning method	Korea
November 17, 2020	Wang et al.	Machine Learning Classification methods combined with Pre-trained deep learning models	China
2021	Marques et al.	H_2O AutoML	Brazil and Macao

Table 7. Year 2021: Machine Learning (ML) techniques used for COVID-19 detection and analysis

DATE	AUTHOR(S)	MACHINE LEARNING (ML) TECHNIQUES	COUNTRY
2021	Fernandes, F.T., et al.	Trained five machine learning algorithms: (artificial neural networks, extra trees, random forests, catboost, and extreme gradient boosting).	Brazil
2021	Miliard, M.	Gradient boosted decision trees, or XGBoost	United States
January 4, 2021	Zoabi et al.	Gradient-Boosting machine model with decision-tree base-learners.	Israel
February 15, 2021	Ackerman, D. MIT News Release	Used algorithms that infer causality in interacting systems to turn their undirected network into a causal network.	United States
March 2021	Roberts, D. et al.	Review of machine learning-based models for 2020 using standard-of-care chest x-rays (CXR) or chest computed tomography (CT) images.	United Kingdom
May 2021	Halasz, G. et al.	Developed a machine learning–based score—the Piacenza score—for 30-day mortality prediction in patients with COVID-19 pneumonia.	Italy Switzerland
June 2021	Argyris, Y.A. et al.	Multi-method approach that includes supervised classification algorithm for categorizing tweets.	Canada United States
June 2021	Peng, Y. et al.	Real-time Prediction of the Daily Incidence of COVID-19 in 215 Countries and Territories Using Machine Learning; Model Development & Validation	China

COVID-19 OPEN-SOURCE DATA REPOSITORIES

The below Table 8 provides COVID-19 Open-Source Data Sets for Research & Analysis that includes authors, characteristics and country.

The COVID-19 data repository by Johns Hopkins University Center for Systems Science and Engineering (JHU CSSE) is provided to the public by GitHub and cloud service BigQuery and includes 1TB of free Big Query processing each month that can be used to run queries on this public dataset.

Other COVID-19 open-source data sets provided in Table 8 include that of Machine Learning Repository of University of California at Irvine (UCI), Open Data for Deep Learning of Pathmind, Inc., Allen Institute of Artificial Intelligence, Coronavirus World Data, The Office of Data Science Strategy (ODSS) of National Institutes of Health (NIH), The National Center for Advancing Translational Science (NCATS) of National Institutes of Health (NIH), and Big Queries Public Datasets Program.

Reactome is fast-tracking the annotation of Human Coronavirus infection pathways in collaboration with the COVID-19 Disease Map group. Reactome release 74 features the SARS-CoV-2 (COVID-19) infection pathway. (Reactome (2020)).

Below is Table 8 of Open-Source data sets that is available in the public domain for no charge to users for research and analysis.

Table 8. COVID-19 Open-Source Data Sets for Research & Analysis

DATE/NAME & URL	AUTHOR(S)	CHARACTERISTICS	COUNTRY
March 30, 2020	Jennings & Glass	COVID-19 Public Dataset Program on Google Cloud	United States
March 30, 2020	Health IT Analytics (owned by Google)	Google makes COVID-19 datasets freely available to researchers	United States
September 21, 2020	Shuja et al.	A Comprehensive Survey of COVID-19 Open Source Data Sets	Pakistan and Saudi Arabia
Machine Learning Repository https://archive.ics.uci.edu/ml/index.php	UCI (University of California at Irvine)	Widely used by students, educators, and researchers all over the world as primary source of machine learning data sets.	United States
Open Data for Deep Learning https://wiki.pathmind.com/	Pathmind, Inc.	Maintained by a model deployment platform called Skymind	United States (San Francisco, CA)
COVID-19 Open Research Dataset (CORD-19) https://www.semanticscholar.org/cord19	Allen Institute for AI https://allenai.org/	Contains over 44,000 scholarly articles about COVID-10	United States (Seattle, WA)
Johns Hopkins University COVID-19 data https://github.com/CSSEGISandData/COVID-19	JHU CSSE (Johns Hopkins University Center for Systems Science and Engineering)	Data repository for the COVID-19 Dashboard aggregated from many sources including WHO, CDC, WorldoMeters, etc.	United States
Coronavirus World Data https://worlddata.ai/coronavirus	World Data AI (https://worlddata.ai)	World's Largest Data Platform (3.3 Billion Datasets)	United States (Houston, TX)
National Institutes of Health (NIH) https://datascience.nih.gov/covid-19-open-access-resources	The Office of Data Science Strategy (ODSS)	Open-Access Data & Computational Resources to Address COVID-19	United States
National Institutes of Health (NIH) https://opendata.ncats.nih.gov/covid19/index.html	National Center for Advancing Translational Science (NCATS)	Open Data for COVID-19	United States
https://console.cloud.google.com/marketplace/product/bigquery-public-datasets/covid19-open-data	Big Query Public Datasets Program	Daily time-series data related to COVID-19 globally	United States & European Union (EU)

Example AI and NN Applications Using Real-Time COVID -19 Data

Using COVID-19 datasets from GitHub, the following images/visualizations were created. Rapid Miner, Tensor Flow, and the Deep Learning Toolbox of MATLAB were used to construct the following Figures: Figure 6 to Figure 11. The images show some of the AI and NN applications that can be used with real-time COVID-19 data. The data was aggregated and automated into figures that provide a full explanation of the death rate, recovery rate, active cases, case fatality ratio, confirmed cases, state where it is less and more, and time range where the cases are still much lower. The figures have been color-coded to make it easy to see when the cases were high and to see if there was a pattern. The figure 6 shows the sample of the data that was used.

Figure 6. Sample of Covid-19 Datasets used to create the visualizations shown in Figure 7 to Figure 11 (Github)
[Created by student Vidha Sankarasubbu and used with written permission.]

.Country_Re...	Last_Update	Lat	Long_	Confirmed	Deaths	Recovered	Active	Combined_...	Incident_R...	Case_Fatali...
Categorical ▼	Datetime ▼	Number ▼	Number ▼	Number ▼	Number ▼	Number ▼	Number ▼	Text ▼	Number ▼	Number ▼
Country_Re...	Last_Update	Lat	Long_	Confirmed	Deaths	Recovered	Active	Combined_...	Incident_Ra...	Case_Fatalit...
Afghanistan	2/15/2021 ...	33.93911	67.709953	55492	2427	48395	4670	Afghanistan	142.5491007	4.373603402
Albania	2/15/2021 ...	41.1533	20.1683	93075	1555	56764	34756	Albania	3234.241434	1.670695676
Algeria	2/15/2021 ...	28.0339	1.6596	110711	2939	75999	31773	Algeria	252.4706197	2.654659429
Andorra	2/15/2021 ...	42.5063	1.5218	10503	107	9911	485	Andorra	13593.47699	1.018756546
Angola	2/15/2021 ...	-11.2027	17.8739	20366	492	18795	1079	Angola	61.96626888	2.415791024
Antigua an...	2/15/2021 ...	17.0608	-61.7964	427	9	199	219	Antigua an...	436.0346377	2.107728337

Figure 7. Centroid Chart Clustered Data using Rapid Miner Studio with COVID-19 Dataset
[Created by student Vidha Sankarasubbu and used with written permission.]

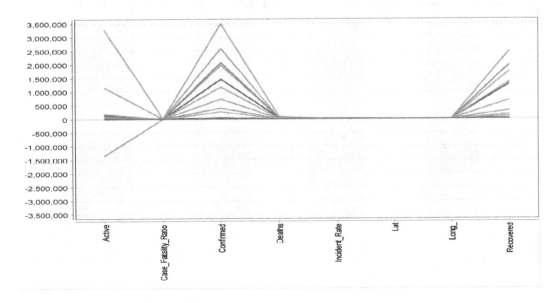

Figures 6 to 11 below were created by student Vidhya Sankarasubbu under the supervision of author of this chapter as faculty mentor, and who was awarded a 2021 Summer Internship Research Award for a research proposal for support in writing this book as funded by Arkansas Biosciences Institute (ABI) located on the campus of Arkansas State University (A-STATE) in Jonesboro. Figures 6 to 11 are shown upon written permission of student Vidha Sankarasubbu.

The clustered chart for COVID datasets is shown in Figure 7. Based on the population rate, latitude, and longitude, the graph depicts the number of active cases as well as the number of deaths. The graph also shows the number of recovered cases, as well as the case fatality ratio and incident rate.

Figure 8. Sample Bubble Graph showing death rate and recovered rate from the active and confirmed cases of COVID-19 in each country region created using Rapid Miner
[Created by student Vidha Sankarasubbu and used with written permission.]

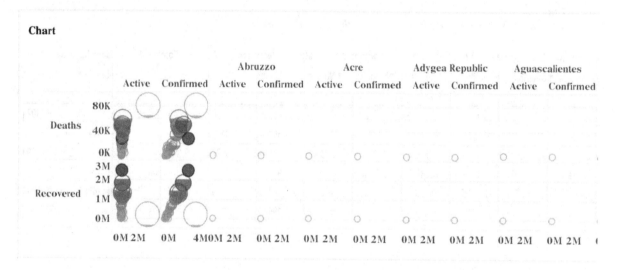

Figure 8 depicts a portion of the whole bubble graph that explains the death rate and current cases by geographic region. Because the data is multivariable, a bubble graph is employed. It is used to compare the number of deaths and the rate of survival in active cases based on geography.

Figure 9. The normalized magnitude and frequency graph and the time domain and amplitude for CO-VID-19 cases in 2021 using Deeplearning Toolbox of MATLAB.
[Created by student Vidha Sankarasubbu and used with written permission.]

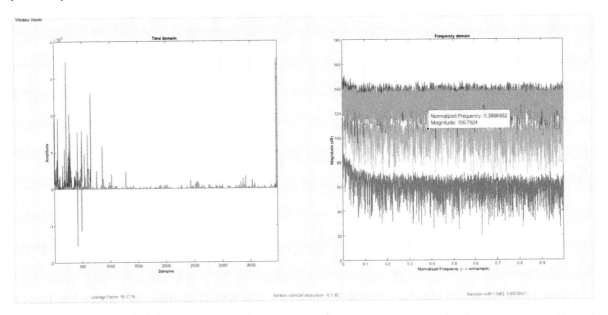

A Bode plot, or graph of magnitude (in dB) vs frequency, is shown in Figure 9. This is used to determine the frequency of death and the rate of recovery in COVID-19 patients. This method has the advantage of demonstrating how circuit parts influence frequency response. In the design of frequency-selective circuits, this is very significant.

Figure 10. Bubble Graph showing maximum of active cases of COVID-19 in each country and their death rate in 2020 using Deeplearning Toolbox of MATLAB
[Created by student Vidha Sankarasubbu and used with written permission.]

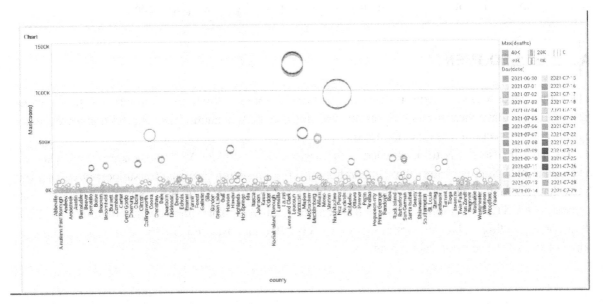

Figure 11. Line Graph of Reorder Attributes using Rapid Miner to show the number of deaths in a particular population rate and time range of recovery.
[Created by student Vidha Sankarasubbu and used with written permission.]

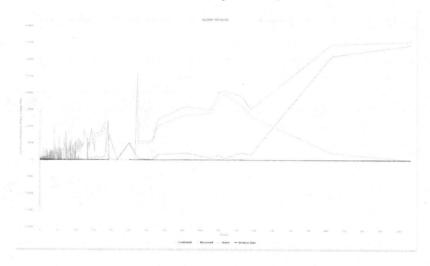

Figure 11 shows how to use chart sorting to reorder the data set's properties and create a line graph. The population and time range are arranged in this graph, which illustrates the pattern of the cases

CONCLUSION

This chapter has presented a survey of many current applications of artificial intelligence, neural networks and machine learning to the pandemic COVID-19 as attempts to search for solutions to this world-wide pandemic. It appears that the continuation of applications of these techniques will be used as valuable insights to COVID-19 and other diseases. Machine learning, neural networks and other artificial intelligence techniques can be combined together to obtain even more powerful insights into this COVID-19 pandemic and the international community is actively pursuing these applications.

ACKNOWLEDGMENT

The author needs to acknowledge the assistance of Co-Editor Gao Niu for his computer software generation of images that appear in this chapter that transformed the five hand-drawn figures that were created by this chapter's author and Lead Co-Editor.

The author also needs to acknowledge the assistance of student Vidhya Sankarasubbu who was awarded a 2021 Summer Internship Research Award for a research proposal for support in writing this book that was funded by Arkansas Biosciences Institute (ABI) located on the campus of Arkansas State University (A-STATE) in Jonesboro. For this chapter, Vidhya Sankarasubbu created Figures 6 to 11 and their corresponding verbal descriptions using COVID-19 data posted on GitHub as well as research for some of the 2021 events of Tables 5 and 7.

REFERENCES

Abdelrahman, A.A. (2020). *Artificial Intelligence and COVID-19: Identify COVID-19 from chest X ray Images by Artificial Intelligence.* LAP LAMBERT Academic Publishing.

Abdulaal, A., Patel, A., Charani, E., Denny, S., Mughal, N., & Moore, L. (2020, August 25). Prognostic Modeling of COVID-19 Using Artificial Intelligence in the United Kingdom: Model Development and Validation. *Journal of Medical Internet Research, 22*(8), e20259. doi:10.2196/20259 PMID:32735549

Ackerman, D. (2021). *A machine-learning approach to finding treatment options for Covid-19.* MIT News Release. Retrieved February 16, 2021 from https://www.eurekalert.org/pub_releases/2021-02/miot-ama021221.php

Agarwal, M., Saba, L., Gupta, S. K., Carriero, A., Falaschi, Z., Paschè, A., Danna, P., El-Baz, A., Naidu, S., & Suri, J. S. (2021, January 26). A Novel Block Imaging Technique Using Nine Artificial Intelligence Models for COVID-19 Disease Classification, Characterization and Severity Measurement in Lung Computed Tomography Scans on an Italian Cohort. *Journal of Medical Systems, 45*(3), 28. doi:10.100710916-021-01707-w PMID:33496876

Agbehadji, I. E., Awuzie, B. O., Ngowi, A. B., & Millham, R. C. (2020, August). Review of Big Data Analytics, Artificial Intelligence and Nature-Inspired Computing Models towards Accurate Detection of COVID-19 Pandemic Cases and Contact Tracing. *International Journal of Environmental Research and Public Health, 17*(15), 5330. doi:10.3390/ijerph17155330 PMID:32722154

Ahmed, S., Hossain, T., Hoque, O. B., Sarker, S., Rahman, S., & Shah, F. M. (2021). Automated COVID-19 Detection from Chest X-Ray Images: A High-Resolution Network (HRNet) Approach. *Sn Comput. Sci, 2*(4), 294. doi:10.100742979-021-00690-w PMID:34056622

Al-Turjman, F. (2021). *Artificial Intelligence and Machine Learning for COVID-19.* Springer. doi:10.1007/978-3-030-60188-1

Allen Institute for AI. (2021, July 13). *COVID-19 open Research Dataset Challenge (CORD-19).* Kaggle. https://www.kaggle.com/allen-institute-for-ai/CORD-19-research-challenge?select=metadata.csv

Alsaade & Al-Adhaileh. (2021). Developing a recognition system for classifying covid-19 using a convolutional neural network algorithm. *Computers, Materials & Continua, 68*(1), 805–819. doi:10.32604/cmc.2021.016264

Arga, K.Y. (2020). COVID-19 and the future of machine learning. *OMICS: A Journal of Integrative Biology,* 512-514. doi:10.1089/omi.2020.0093

Argyris, Y., Monu, K., Tan, P., Aarts, C., Jiang, F., & Wiseley, K. (2021). Using machine learning to compare provaccine and antivaccine discourse among the public on social media: Algorithm Development Study. *JMIR Public Health and Surveillance, 7*(6), e23105. doi:10.2196/23105 PMID:34185004

Arora, T., & Soni, R. (2021). A pre-screening approach for COVID-19 testing based on Belief Rule-Based Expert System. In COVID-19: Prediction, Decision-Making, and its Impacts. Springer Singapore. doi:10.1007/978-981-15-9682-7_3

Arya, S., & Devi, S. P. (2021). Prediction to Service Delivery: AI in Action. In COVID-19: Prediction, Decision-Making, and its Impacts. Springer Singapore. doi:10.1007/978-981-15-9682-7_12

Bahrami, M., & Sadeddin, S. (2021). *Classifying Cough Sounds to Predict COVID-19 Diagnosis.* Retrieved February 15, 2021 from https://blog.wolfram.com/2021/02/10/classifying-cough-sounds-to-predict-covid-19-diagnosis/

Bassi, P. R. A. S., & Attux, R. (2020). *A Deep Convolutional Neural Network Model for COVID-19 Detection using Chest X-rays.* Retrieved January 17, 2020 from https://arxiv.org/abs/2005.01578

Bhapkar, H. R., Mahalle, P. N., Shinde, G. R., & Mahmud, M. (2021). Rough Sets in COVID-19 to Predict Symptomatic Cases. In COVID-19: Prediction, Decision-Making, and its Impacts. doi:10.1007/978-981-15-9682-7_7

Brownlee, J. (2017). *A Gentle Introduction to Long Short-Term Memory Networks by the Experts.* Retrieved December 26, 2020 from https://machinelearningmastery.com/gentle-introduction-long-short-term-memory-networks-experts/

Bullock, J., Luccioni, A., Pham, K. H., & Luengo-Oroz, M. (2020). Mapping the Landscape of Artificial Intelligence Applications against COVID-19. *Journal of Artificial Intelligence Research*, 69, 807–845. doi:10.1613/jair.1.12162

Cai, F. (2020). DarwinAI open-source COVID-Net as medical image in COVID-19 diagnosis debate continues. *Synced: AI Technology & Industry Review.* Retrieved May 17, 2020 from https://syncedreview.com/2020/04/02/darwinai-open-sources-covid-net-as-medical-imaging-in-covid-19-diagnosis-debate-continues/

Chawki, M. (2021). Artificial Intelligence (AI) joins the Fight against COVID-19. In COVID-19: Prediction, Decision-Making, and its Impacts. Springer Singapore. doi:10.1007/978-981-15-9682-7_1

Chen, Y., Jiang, G., Li, Y., Tang, Y., Xu, Y., Ding, S., Xin, Y., & Lu, Y. (2020). A Survey on Artificial Intelligence in Chest Imaging of COVID-19. *BIO Integration*, 1(3), 137–146. doi:10.15212/bioi-2020-0015

Cho, K., van Merrienboer, B., Gulcehre, C., Bahdanau, D., Bougares, F., Schwenk, H., & Bengio, Y. (2014). *Learning Phrase Representations using RNN Encoder-Decoder for Statistical Machine Translation.* doi:10.3115/v1/D14-1179

Colak, A. B. (2021). COVID-19 Projections Using Machine Learning. *Coronaviruses: The World's First International Journal Dedicated to Coronaviruses.* Retrieved August 9, 2020 from https://www.eurekaselect.com/node/185917/article/prediction-of-infection-and-death-ratio-of-covid-19-virus-in-turkey-by-using-artificial-neural-network-ann

Dalip, D. (2020). AI-Enabled Framework to Prevent COVID-19 from Further Spreading. In *Intelligence Systems and Methods to Combat Covid-19* (pp. 29–33). Springer Press. doi:10.1007/978-981-15-6572-4_4

DeGrave, A. J., Janizek, J. D., & Lee, S. I. (2021). AI for radiographic COVID-19 detection selects shortcuts over signal. *Nature Machine Intelligence*, 3(7), 610–619. Advance online publication. doi:10.103842256-021-00338-7

Elghamrawy, S. (2020) An H2O's Deep Learning-Inspired Model Based on Big Data Analytics for Coronavirus Disease (COVID-19) Diagnosis. In Big Data Analytics and Artificial Intelligence Against COVID-19: Innovation Vision and Approach. Springer. doi:10.1007/978-3-030-55258-9_16

Erion, G., Janizek, J. D., Sturmfels, P., Lundberg, S. M., & Lee, S.-I. (2021). Improving performance of deep learning models with axiomatic attribution priors and expected gradients. *Nature Machine Intelligence*, *3*(7), 620–631. Advance online publication. doi:10.103842256-021-00343-w

European Centre for Disease Prevention and Control (ECDC). (2021). *Download COVID-19 datasets.* Retrieved January 17, 2021 from https://www.ecdc.europa.eu/en/covid-19/data

Fernandes, F. T., de Oliveira, T. A., Teixeira, C. E., Batista, A. F. M., Dalla Costa, G., & Chiavegatto Filho, A. D. P. (2021). A multipurpose machine learning approach to predict COVID-19 negative prognosis in São Paulo, Brazil. *Scientific Reports*, *11*(1), 3343. doi:10.103841598-021-82885-y PMID:33558602

Fouladi, S., Ebadi, M. J., Safaei, A. A., Bajuri, M. Y., & Ahmadian, A. (2021). Efficient deep neural networks for classification of COVID-19 based on CT images: Virtualization via software defined radio. *Computer Communications*, *176*, 234–248. doi:10.1016/j.comcom.2021.06.011 PMID:34149118

Gallagher, M. B. (2020). Model quantifies the impact of quarantine measures of COVID-19's spread. *MIT News*. Retrieved May 17, 2020 from https://news.mit.edu/2020/new-model-quantifies-impact-quarantine-measures-covid-19-spread-0416

Goswami, P. N. (2021). MCNNet: Generalizing Fake News Detection with a Multichannel Convolutional Neural Network using a Novel COVID-19 Dataset. *CODS COMAD 2021: 8th ACM IKDD CODS and 26th COMAD*. Retrieved February 15, 2021 from https://dl.acm.org/doi/10.1145/3430984.3431064

Gupta, D., Mahajan, A., & Gupta, S. (2020). Social Distancing and Artificial Intelligence-Understanding the Duality in the Times of COVID-19. In *Intelligence Systems and Methods to Combat Covid-19* (pp. 75–81). Springer Press. doi:10.1007/978-981-15-6572-4_9

Halasz, G., Sperti, M., Villani, M., Michelucci, U., Agostoni, P., Biagi, A., Rossi, L., Botti, A., Mari, C., Maccarini, M., Pura, F., Roveda, L., Nardecchia, A., Mottola, E., Nolli, M., Salvioni, E., Mapelli, M., Deriu, M., Piga, D., & Piepoli, M. (2021). A Machine Learning Approach for Mortality Prediction in COVID-19 Pneumonia: Development and Evaluation of the Piacenza Score. *Journal of Medical Internet Research*, *23*(5), e29058. doi:10.2196/29058 PMID:33999838

Hamadneh, N. N., Khan, W. A., Ashraf, W., Atawneh, S. H., Khan, I., & Hamadneh, B. N. (2021). *Artificial Neural Networks for Prediction of COVID-19 in Saudi Arabia.* Computers, Materials & Continua. doi:10.32604/cmc.2021.013228

Hanfi, S. A. (2020). *A Neural Networks based approach to detect Covid-19 through Chest X-Ray.* Retrieved December 24, 2020 from https://sohailahmedhanfi.medium.com/a-neural-networks-based-approach-to-detect-covid-19-through-chest-x-ray-c11c2b44824d

Huang, S., Yang, J., Fong, S., & Zhao, Q. (2021). Artificial intelligence in the diagnosis of COVID-19: Challenges and perspectives. *International Journal of Biological Sciences*, *17*(6), 1581–1587. doi:10.7150/ijbs.58855 PMID:33907522

Inside Big Data Editorial Team. (2021, February 5). *AI Solving Real-world Problems and AI Ethics Among Top Trends for 2021, According to Oxylabs' AI and ML Advisory Board*. Retrieved February 15, 2021 from https://insidebigdata.com/2021/02/05/ai-solving-real-world-problems-and-ai-ethics-among-top-trends-for-2021-according-to-oxylabs-ai-and-ml-advisory-board/

Irmak, E. (2020). Implementation of convolutional neural network approach for COVID019 disease detection. *Physiological Genomics*, *52*(12), 590–601. doi:10.1152/physiolgenomics.00084.2020 PMID:33094700

Jat, D. S., & Singh, C. (2020). Artificial Intelligence-Enabled Robotic Drones for COVID-19 Outbreak. In *Intelligence Systems and Methods to Combat Covid-19* (pp. 37–46). Springer Press. doi:10.1007/978-981-15-6572-4_5

Jennings, C. W., & Glass, S. (2020). *COVID-19 public dataset program: Making data freely accessible for better public outcomes*. Retrieved December 25, 2020 from https://cloud.google.com/blog/products/data-analytics/free-public-datasets-for-covid19

Joshi, A., Dey, N., & Santosh, K. C. (2020). *Intelligence Systems and Methods to Combat Covid-19*. Springer Press. doi:10.1007/978-981-15-6572-4

Kahn, A. I., Shah, A. I., & Bhat, M. (2020). *CoroNet: A Deep Neural Network for Detection and Diagnosis of COVID-19 from Chest X-ray Images*. Retrieved May 16, 2020 from https://www.researchgate.net/publication/340598559_CoroNet_A_Deep_Neural_Network_for_Detection_and_Diagnosis_of_Covid-19_from_Chest_X-ray_Images

Kaiser, M. S., AlMamun, A., Mahmud, M., & Tania, M. H. (2021). COVID-19: Prediction, Decision-Making, and its Impacts. Springer Singapore. doi:10.1007/978-981-15-9682-7_10

Kaliyar, R. K., Goswami, A., & Narang, P. (2021). *MCNNet: Generalizing Fake News Detection with a Multichannel Convolutional Neural Network using a Novel COVID-19 Dataset*. Retrieved February 15, 2021 from https://dl.acm.org/doi/10.1145/3430984.3431064

Kent, J. (2020a). *Machine Learning Models Forecast Likelihood of COVID-19 Mortality*. Retrieved November 26, 2020 from https://healthitanalytics.com/news/machine-learning-models-forecast-likelihood-of-covid-19-mortality

Kent, J. (2020b). Google Makes COVID-19 Datasets Freely Available to Researchers. *Health IT Analytics*. Retrieved December 24, 2020 from https://healthitanalytics.com/news/google-makes-covid-19-datasets-freely-available-to-researchers

Kent, J. (2020c). Big Data Analytics Show COVID-19 Spread, Outcomes by Region. *HealthITAnalytics*. Retrieved February 15, 2021 from https://healthitanalytics.com/news/big-data-analytics-show-covid-19-spread-outcomes-by-region

Kent, J. (2020d). Intersection of Big Data Analytics, COVID-19 Top Focus of 2020. *HealthITAnalytics*. Retrieved February 15, 2021 https://healthitanalytics.com/news/intersection-of-big-data-analytics-covid-19-top-focus-of-2020

Khosla, P. H., Mittal, M., Sharma, D. & Goyal, L. M. (2021). *Predictive and Preventive Measures for Covid-19 Pandemic.* Springer.

Lalmuanawma, S., Hussain, J., & Chhakchhuak, L. (2020, October). Applications of machine learning and artificial intelligence for Covid-19 (SARS-CoV-2) pandemic: A review. *Chaos, Solitons, and Fractals, 139,* 110059. doi:10.1016/j.chaos.2020.110059 PMID:32834612

Leong, B., & Jordon, S. (2020). *Artificial Intelligence and the COVID-19 Pandemic.* Retrieved May 16, 2020 from https://fpf.org/2020/05/07/artificial-intelligence-and-the-covid-19-pandemic/

Li, W., Ma, J., Shende, N., Castaneda, G., Chakladar, J., Tsai, J. C., Apostol, L., Honda, C. O., Xu, J., Wong, L. M., Zhang, T., Lee, A., Gnanasekar, A., Honda, T. K., Kuo, S. Z., Yu, M. A., Chang, E. Y., Rajasekaran, M. R., & Ongkeko, W. M. (2020). Using machine learning of clinical data to diagnose COVID-19: A systematic review and meta-analysis. *BMC Medical Informatics and Decision Making, 20*(1), 247. Retrieved December 24, 2020, from. doi:10.118612911-020-01266-z PMID:32993652

Lv, D., Wang, Y., Wang, S., Zhang, Q., Qi, W., Li, Y., & Sun, L. (2021, May). A Cascade-SEME network for COVID-19 detection in chest x-ray images. *Medical Physics, 48*(5), 2337–2353. doi:10.1002/mp.14711 PMID:33778966

Majhi, R., Thangeda, R., Sugasi, R. P., & Kumar, N. (2020). Analysis and prediction of COVID-19 trajectory: A machine learning approach. *Journal of Public Affairs, e2537.* doi:10.1002/pa.2537 PMID:33349741

Marques, J. A. L., Gois, F. N. B., Xavier-Neto, J., & Fong, S. J. (2021). *Predictive Models for Decision Support in the COVID-19 Crisis.* Springer. doi:10.1007/978-3-030-61913-8

Miliard, M. (2021). Northwell machine learning model can predict COVID-19 respiratory failure. *Heath Care IT News.* Retrieved February 16, 2021 from https://www.healthcareitnews.com/news/northwell-machine-learning-model-can-predict-covid-19-respiratory-failure

Mohanty, S. N., Saxena, S. K., Chatterjee, J. M., & Satpathy, S. (2021). *Application of Artificial Intelligence in COVID-19.* Springer.

Mollalo, A., Rivera, K. M., & Vahedi, B. (2020). Artificial Neural Network Modeling of Novel Coronavirus (COVID-19) Incidence Rates across the Continental United States. *International Journal of Environmental Research and Public Health, 17*(12), 4204. doi:10.3390/ijerph17124204 PMID:32545581

Mukherjee, H., Ghosh, S., Dhar, A., Obaidullah, S. M., Santosh, K. C., & Roy, K. (2021). Shallow Convolutional Neural Network for COVID-19 Outbreak Screening Using Chest X-rays. *Cognitive Computation.* Advance online publication. doi:10.100712559-020-09775-9 PMID:33564340

Narin, A., Kaya, C., & Pamuk, Z. (2021). *Automatic detection of coronavirus disease (COVID-19) using X-ray images and deep convolutional neural networks.* Pattern Anal Applic. doi:10.100710044-021-00984-y

National Institutes of Health. (2020). *Open-Access Data and Computational Resources to Address COVID-19.* Office of Data Science Strategy. Retrieved December 24, 2020 from https://datascience.nih.gov/covid-19-open-access-resources

Nawaz, M. S., Fournier-Viger, P., Shojaee, A., & Fujita, H. (2021). Using artificial intelligence techniques for COVID-19 genome analysis. *Applied Intelligence, 51*(5), 3086–3103. doi:10.100710489-021-02193-w PMID:34764587

Niazkar, H. R., & Niazkar, M. (2020). Application of artificial neural networks to predict the COVID-19 outbreak. *Global Health Research and Policy, 5*(1), 50. doi:10.118641256-020-00175-y PMID:33292780

Nicholson, C. (2020). *A Beginner's Guide to LSTMs and Recurrent Neural Networks.* Retrieved December 26, 2020 from https://wiki.pathmind.com/lstm

NYTimes. (n.d.). *Nytimes/Covid-19-Data.* GitHub. https://github.com/nytimes/covid-19-data/tree/30c c9e39b9695393f91c0a61a50c659195cbfb49

Ozlurk, T., Talo, M., Yildirim, E. A., & Baloglu, U. B. (2020). Automated detection of COVID-19 cases using deep neural networks with X-ray images. *Computers in Biology and Medicine.* Retrieved May 16, 2020 from https://www.ncbi.nlm.nih.gov/pmc/articles/PMC7187882/ doi:10.1016/j.comp-biomed.2020.103792

Pal, R., Sekh, A. A., Kar, S., & Prasad, D. K. (2020). *Neural Network Based Country Wise Risk Prediction of COVID-19.* doi:10.20944/preprints202004.0421.v1

Peng, Y., Chen, X., Rong, Y., Pang, C., Chen, X., & Chen, H. (2021). Real-time prediction of the daily incidence of COVID-19 in 215 countries and territories using machine learning: Model Development and Validation. *J Med Internet, 23*(6), e24285. doi:10.2196/24285 PMID:34081607

Pham, T. D. (2020). A comprehensive study on classification of COVID-19 on computed tomography with pretrained convolutional neural networks. *Scientific Reports, 10*(1), 16942. doi:10.103841598-020-74164-z PMID:33037291

Poulopoulos, D. (2020). 5 Datasets About COVID-19 you can Use Right Now. *Towards Data Science.* Retrieved December 25, 2020 from https://towardsdatascience.com/5-datasets-about-covid-19-you-can-use-right-now-46307b1406a

Rahimzadeh, M., Attar, A., & Sakhaei, S. M. (2021). A fully automated deep learning-based network for detecting COVID-19 from a new and large lung CT scan dataset. *Biomedical Signal Processing and Control, 68*(July), 102588. Advance online publication. doi:10.1016/j.bspc.2021.102588 PMID:33821166

Ramchandani, A., Fan, C., & Mostafavi, A. (2020). DeepCOVIDNet: An Interpretable Deep Learning Model for Predictive Surveillance of COVID-19 Using Heterogeneous Features and Their Interactions. *IEEE Access: Practical Innovations, Open Solutions, 8*, 159915–159930. doi:10.1109/ACCESS.2020.3019989 PMID:34786287

Rao, A. S. R. S., & Vazquez, J. A. (2020, July). Identification of COVID-19 can be quicker through artificial intelligence framework using a mobile phone-based survey when cities and towns are under quarantine. *Infection Control and Hospital Epidemiology, 41*(7), 826–830. doi:10.1017/ice.2020.61 PMID:32122430

Reactome. (2020). *COVID-19: SARS-CoV-2 infection pathway released.* Retrieved February 16, 2021 from https://reactome.org/about/news/161-version-74-released

Roberts, M., Driggs, D., Thorpe, M., Gilbey, J., Yeung, M., Ursprung, S., Aviles-Rivero, A. I., Etmann, C., McCague, C., Beer, L., Weir-McCall, J. R., Teng, Z., Gkrania-Klotsas, E., Rudd, J. H. F., Sala, E., & Schönlieb, C.-B. (2021). Common pitfalls and recommendations for using machine learning to detect and prognosticate for COVID-19 using chest radiographs and CT scans. *Nature Machine Intelligence*, *3*(3), 199–217. doi:10.103842256-021-00307-0

Rosebrock, A. (2020). *Detecting COVID-19 in x-ray images with Keras, TensorFlow, and Deep Learning*. Retrieved May 17, 2020 from https://www.pyimagesearch.com/2020/03/16/detecting-covid-19-in-x-ray-images-with-keras-tensorflow-and-deep-learning/

Santosh, K. C., & Joshi, A. (2021). COVID-19: Prediction, Decision-Making, and its Impacts. Springer Nature Singapore Pte Ltd.

Sarki, R., Ahmed, K., Wang, H., Zhang, Y., & Wang, K. (2021). *Automated Detection of COVID-19 through Convolutional Neural Network using Chest x-ray images*. Retrieved February 15, 2021 from https://www.medrxiv.org/content/10.1101/2021.02.06.21251271v1

Segall, R. S. (2020). *Applications of Artificial Intelligence to COVID-19*. Invited Virtual Plenary Address at 24th Multi-conference on Systemics, Cybernetics, and Informatics (WMSCI 2020), September 13-16, 2020.

Segall, R. S. (2021). *Applications of Machine Learning and Neural Networks for COVID-19*. 2021 Virtual Conference of MidSouth Computational and Bioinformatics Society (MCBIOS 2021), April 26-30, 2021.

Shi, F., Wang, J., Shi, J., Wu, Z., Wang, Q., Tang, Z., He, K., Shi, Y., & Shen, D. (2020). *Review of Artificial Intelligence Techniques in Imaging Data Acquisition, Segmentation and Diagnosis for COVID-19*. IEEE Rev Biomed Eng.

Shuja, J., Alanazi, E., Alasmary, W., & Alashaikh, A. (2020). COVID-19 open source data sets: A comprehensive survey. *Applied Intelligence*, 1–30. Advance online publication. doi:10.100710489-020-01862-6 PMID:34764552

Singh, D., Kumar, V., & Kaur, M. (2020). Classification of COVID-19 patients from chest CT images using multi-objective differential evolution-based convolutional neural networks. *European Journal of Clinical Microbiology & Infectious Diseases*. Retrieved May 16, 2020 from https://link.springer.com/content/pdf/10.1007/s10096-020-03901-z.pdf

So, D. (2020). *Alibaba News Roundup: Tech Takes on the Outbreak*. Retrieved May 17, 2020 from https://www.alizila.com/alibaba-news-roundup-tech-takes-on-the-outbreak/

Srikusan, R., & Karunamoorthy, M. (2021). Implementing Early Detection System for COVID-19 using Anomaly Detection. In COVID-19: Prediction, Decision-Making, and its Impacts. Springer Singapore. doi:10.1007/978-981-15-9682-7_5

Subramanian, B. (2021, January 31). *Deep Learning: Fighting Covid-19 with Neural Networks*. Data Science Foundation, U.K. Retrieved February 15, 2021 from https://datascience.foundation/science-whitepaper/deep-learning-fighting-covid-19-with-neural-networks

Tali, S. H. S., LeBlanc, J. J., Sadiq, Z., Oyewunmi, O. D., Camargo, C., Nikpour, B., Armanfard, N., Sagan, S. M., & Jahanshahi-Anbuhi, S. (2021, May 12). Tools and Techniques for Severe Acute Respiratory Syndrome Coronavirus 2 (SARS-CoV-2)/COVID-19 Detection. *Clinical Microbiology Reviews*, *34*(3), e00228–e20. doi:10.1128/CMR.00228-20 PMID:33980687

Taresh, M.M., Zhu, N., Ali, T.A.A., Hameed, A.S., & Mutar, M.L. (2021). Transfer Learning to Detect COVID-19 Automatically from X-Ray Images Using Convolutional Neural Networks. *International Journal of Biomedical Imaging*. doi:10.1155/2021/8828404

Umer, M., Ashraf, I., & Ullah, S. (2021). *COVINet: A convolutional neural network approach for predicting COVID-19 from chest X-ray images. J Ambient Intell Human Comput*. doi:10.100712652-021-02917-3

Unnithan, C., Hardy, J., & Lilley, N. (2021). AI for Covid-19: Conduits for Public Heath Surveillance. In COVID-19: Prediction, Decision-Making, and its Impacts. Springer Singapore. doi:10.1007/978-981-15-9682-7_2

Vaid, A., Somani, S., Russak, A. J., De Freitas, J. K., Chaudhry, F. F., Paranjpe, I., Johnson, K. W., Lee, S. J., Miotto, R., Richter, F., Zhao, S., Beckmann, N. D., Naik, N., Kia, A., Timsina, P., Lala, A., Paranjpe, M., Golden, E., Danieletto, M., ... Glicksberg, B. S. (2020). Machine Learning to Predict Mortality and Critical Events in a Cohort of Patients With COVID-19 in New York City: Model Development and Validation. *Journal of Medical Internet Research*, *22*(11), e24018. doi:10.2196/24018 PMID:33027032

Verde, L., De Pietro, G., Ghoneim, A., Alrashoud, M., Al-Mutib, K. N., & Sannino, G. (2021). Exploring the Use of Artificial Intelligence Techniques to Detect the Presence of Coronavirus Covid-19 Through Speech and Voice Analysis. *IEEE Access: Practical Innovations, Open Solutions*, *9*, 65750–65757. doi:10.1109/ACCESS.2021.3075571

Wang, D., Mo, J., Zhou, G., Xu, L., & Liu, Y. (2020) An efficient mixture of deep and machine learning models for COVID-19 diagnosis in chest X-ray images. *PLoS ONE, 15*(11). Retrieved December 25, 2020 from https://journals.plos.org/plosone/article?id=10.1371/journal.pone.0242535 doi:10.1371/journal.pone.0242535

Wang, L. (2020). Convolutional neural network detects COVID-19 from chest radiography images. *Vision Systems Design*. Retrieved May 16, 2020 from https://www.vision-systems.com/non-factory/life-sciences/article/14173262/covid-19-chest-radiography-deep-learning-virus-detection

Wang, L., & Wong, A. (2020). *COVID-Net: A Tailored Deep Convolutional Neural Network Design for Detection of COVID-19 Cases from Chest X-Ray Images*. Retrieved May 16, 2020 from https://arxiv.org/abs/2003.09871

Wieczorek, M., Siłka, J., & Woźniak, M. (2020). Neural network powered COVID-19 spread forecasting model. *Chaos, Solitons, and Fractals*, *140*, 110203. doi:10.1016/j.chaos.2020.110203 PMID:32834663

Wikipedia. (2020). *Comparison of Deep Learning Software*. https://en.wikipedia.org/wiki/Comparison_of_deep-learning_software

Wikipedia. (2021a). *Gated Recurrent Unit (GRU)*. Author.

Wikipedia. (2021b). *Long Short-Term Memory*. Retrieved January 24, 2021 from https://en.wikipedia.org/wiki/Long_short-term_memory

Wikipedia. (2021c). *Tensor Flow*. Retrieved February 16, 2021 from https://en.wikipedia.org/wiki/TensorFlow

World Health Organization (WHO). (2020). *Coronavirus disease 2019 (COVID-19), Situation Report 162*. WHO.

Yates, E. J., Yates, L. C., & Harvey, H. (2018, September). Machine learning "red dot": Open-source, cloud, deep convolutional neural networks in chest radiograph binary normality classification. *Clinical Radiology*, *73*(9), 827–831. doi:10.1016/j.crad.2018.05.015 PMID:29898829

Zhang, C. (2020). A Survey of China's Artificial Intelligence Solutions in Response to the COVID-19 Pandemic: 87 Case Studies from 700+ AI Vendors in China. *Synced Review*.

Zhao, H. (2020). AI CT scan analysis for CONVID-19 detection and patient monitoring. *Synced: AI Technology & Industry Review*. Retrieved May 17, 2020 from https://syncedreview.com/2020/03/18/ai-ct-scan-analysis-for-covid-19-detection-and-patient-monitoring/

Zhao, J., Zhang, Y., He, X., & Xie, P. (2020). *COVID-CT-Dataset: A CT scan dataset about COVID-19*. Retrieved May 17, 2020 from https://arxiv.org/pdf/2003.13865.pdf

Zoabi, Y., Deri-Rozov, S., & Shomron, N. (2021, January 4). Machine learning-based prediction of COVID-19 diagnosis based on symptoms. *NPJ Digital Medicine*, *4*(1), 3. doi:10.103841746-020-00372-6 PMID:33398013

ADDITIONAL READING

Arga, K.Y. (2020). COVID-19 and the future of machine learning, OMICS: A Journal of Integrative Biology, pp.512-514.http://doi.org/ doi:10.1089/omi.2020.0093

Deb, T., Roy, A., Genc, S., Slater, N., Mallya, S., Kass-Hout, T. A., & Hanumaiah, V. (2020). Introducing the COVID-19 Simulator and Machine Learning Toolkit for Predicting COVID-19 Spread. *Artificial Intelligence*. Retrieved November 26, 2020 from https://aws.amazon.com/blogs/machine-learning/introducing-the-covid-19-simulator-and-machine-learning-toolkit-for-predicting-covid-19-spread/

Gu, Y. (2020). COVID-19 Projections Using Machine Learning, retrieved January 24, 2021 from https://covid19-projections.com/

Kahn, A. H., Cao, X., & Li, S. (Eds.). (2021). *Management and Intelligent Decision-Making in Complex Systems: An Optimization-Driven Approach*. Springer Singapore. doi:10.1007/978-981-15-9392-5

Kent, J. (2020). Machine Learning Models Forecast Likelihood of COVID-19 Mortality, Retrieved November 26, 2020 from https://healthitanalytics.com/news/machine-learning-models-forecast-likelihood-of-covid-19-mortality

Khosla, P. K., Mittal, M., Sharma, D., & Goyal, L. M. (Eds.). (2021). *Predictive and Preventive Measures for COVID-19 Pandemic*. Springer Singapore. doi:10.1007/978-981-33-4236-1

Majhi, R., Thangeda, R., Sugasi, R. P., & Kumar, N. (2020). Analysis and prediction of COVID-19 trajectory: A machine learning approach. *Journal of Public Affairs, e2537*. Retrieved January 25, 2021, from. doi:10.1002/pa.2537

Marques, J. A. L., Gois, F. N. B., Xavier-Neto, J., & Fong, S. J. (2021). *Predictive Methods for Decision Support in the COVID-19 Crisis*. Springer International Publishing. doi:10.1007/978-3-030-61913-8

Ramchandani, A., Fan, C., & Mostafavi, A. (2020). DeepCOVIDNet: An Interpretable Deep Learning Model for Predictive Surveillance of COVID-19 Using Heterogeneous Features and Their Interactions. *IEEE Access: Practical Innovations, Open Solutions, 8*, 159915–159930. doi:10.1109/ACCESS.2020.3019989 PMID:34786287

Raza, K. (Ed.). (2021). *Computational Intelligence Methods in COVID-19: Surveillance, Prevention, Prediction and Diagnosis*. Springer Singapore. doi:10.1007/978-981-15-8534-0

Santosh, K. C., & Joshi, A. (Eds.). (2021). *COVID-19: Prediction, Decision-Making, and its Impacts*. Springer Singapore. doi:10.1007/978-981-15-9682-7

Taulli, T. (2019). Artificial Intelligence Basics: A Non-Technical Introduction. Springer Science+ Business Media, New York. https://doi.org/ doi:10.1007/978-1-4842-5028-0

The Mount Sinai Hospital / Mount Sinai School of Medicine. (2021, January 18). Researchers build models using machine learning technique to enhance predictions of COVID-19 outcomes. ScienceDaily. Retrieved February 14, 2021 from www.sciencedaily.com/releases/2021/01/210118113109.htm

Udgata, S. K., & Suryadevara, N. K. (Eds.). (2019). *Internet of Things and Sensor Network for COVID-19*. Springer Singapore.

Vaid, A., Somani, S., Russak, A. J., De Freitas, J. K., Chaudhry, F. F., Paranjpe, I., Johnson, K. W., Lee, S. J., Miotto, R., Richter, F., Zhao, S., Beckmann, N. D., Naik, N., Kia, A., Timsina, P., Lala, A., Paranjpe, M., Golden, E., Danieletto, M., ... Glicksberg, B. S. (2020). Machine Learning to Predict Mortality and Critical Events in a Cohort of Patients With COVID-19 in New York City: Model Development and Validation. *Journal of Medical Internet Research, 22*(11), e24018. doi:10.2196/24018 PMID:33027032

KEY TERMS AND DEFINITIONS

Convolutional Neural Networks (CNN): In deep learning, a convolutional neural network (CNN, or ConvNet) is a class of deep neural networks, most commonly applied to analyzing visual imagery.

COVID-19: Coronavirus disease 2019 (COVID-19) is a contagious disease caused by severe acute respiratory syndrome coronavirus 2 (SARS-CoV-2). The first case was identified in Wuhan, China, in December 2019.

Deep Neural Networks: Deep learning is a class of machine learning algorithms that uses multiple layers to progressively extract higher-level features from the raw input.

H$_2$O AutoML: Learning algorithm within H$_2$O open-source distributed machine learning platform that overlooks the process of finding candidate models using large datasets (Marques et al., 2021).

Keras: Keras is an open-source software library that provides a Python interface for artificial neural networks. It is a High-level Python neural network library that runs on the top layer of TensorFlow (Hanfi, 2020).

Long Short-Term Memory (LSTM): A type of Recurrent Neural Network (RNN) capable of learning order dependence in sequence prediction problems as a behavior required in complex problem domains like machine translation, speech recognition, and more (Brownlee, 2017).

Recurrent Neural Networks (RNN): Class of Artificial Neural Networks (ANN) also called Feedback Neural Networks (FNN) where connections between nodes form a directed graph along a temporal sequence (Wikipedia, 2020).

TensorFlow: Open-source software library originally developed by Google Brian Team for numerical computation using data flow graphs. TensorFlow is a free and open-source software library for machine learning. It can be used across a range of tasks but has a particular focus on training and inference of deep neural networks (Wikipedia, 2021c).

Chapter 3
Comparing Deep Neural Networks and Gradient Boosting for Pneumonia Detection Using Chest X–Rays

Son Nguyen
Bryant University, USA

Matthew Quinn
Harvard University, USA

Alan Olinsky
Bryant University, USA

John Quinn
Bryant University, USA

ABSTRACT

In recent years, with the development of computational power and the explosion of data available for analysis, deep neural networks, particularly convolutional neural networks, have emerged as one of the default models for image classification, outperforming most of the classical machine learning models in this task. On the other hand, gradient boosting, a classical model, has been widely used for tabular structure data and leading data competitions, such as those from Kaggle. In this study, the authors compare the performance of deep neural networks with gradient boosting models for detecting pneumonia using chest x-rays. The authors implement several popular architectures of deep neural networks, such as Resnet50, InceptionV3, Xception, and MobileNetV3, and variants of a gradient boosting model. The authors then evaluate these two classes of models in terms of prediction accuracy. The computation in this study is done using cloud computing services offered by Google Colab Pro.

DOI: 10.4018/978-1-7998-8455-2.ch003

INTRODUCTION

In this chapter, the authors give an overview of deep neural networks, gradient boosting, and the problem of detecting pneumonia from chest x-rays. The main difference between the deep neural network models and the gradient boosting models is that deep neural networks are designed to handle image data while gradient boosting models often excel at tasks utilizing regular tabular data. Detailed structures of these models are provided below.

Neural Networks and Deep Learning

In parametric supervised learning, one wants to establish the relation between the input values and the output value by a specific function. To find this specific function (the solution), one searches in the class of functions identified by parameters (hence the term "parametric") to find values for the parameters that minimize a predetermined objective function or loss function. For example, in linear regression, the least squares regression line is the solution found from a class of linear functions identified by the slope and intercept parameters. These values of the slope and intercept of the least squares regression line are those that minimize the squared loss.

A neural network represents a class of functions. The structure, or architecture, of a neural network, is the combination of several nodes and edges. The edges, or weights, are parameters of the functions. In neural networks, a linear combination of the nodes in one layer is input to a function, called an activation function, of a node in the next layer. The values in the first layer, or the input values, will go through this calculation process, followed by all the hidden layers to ultimately produce the output value in the output layer. Training a neural network entails finding the set of parameters or weights that minimizes a predetermined loss function.

It is easy to see that the linear model is also a neural network with no hidden layers. That is, a linear model effectively takes a linear combination of the input variables to directly produce an output value in a single step. However, including hidden layers increases the flexibility of the neural network, which can help it model more complex scenarios. In fact, it has been shown that any given continuous function can be approximated to any desired precision by a neural network with only a single hidden layer (Nielsen, 2016).

Deep learning models, or deep neural networks, are neural network models with multiple hidden layers (Schmidhuber, 2015). The word "deep" indicates there are many hidden layers. In the past decades, with the explosion in the amount of data available and the rapid development in computing hardware, deep neural networks have been very successful and are usually the default models for tasks in computer vision, such as image recognition and object detection. The initial success of deep neural networks dates back to 2012 when the AlexNet model (Krizhevsky et al., 2012) won the ImageNet Large Scale Visual Recognition Challenge (ILSVRC) with a top-5 error of 15.3%, which was 10.8 percentage points lower than the runner up. Since then, deep neural networks have shown state-of-the-art accuracy on the ImageNet competition (He et al., 2016).

Figure 1. Architecture of a neural network. [The circles are neurons. The connections between two neurons are the edges, or weights, which are parameters of the neural network. The first layer is the input layer, the last layer is the output layer, and the layers between the input layer and output layer are hidden layers.]

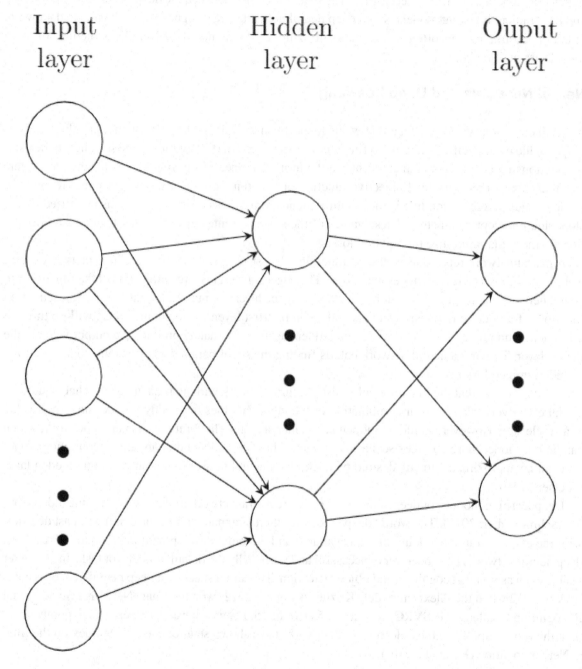

Input
layer

Hidden
layer

Ouput
layer

Figure 2. Values flow from one layer to a neuron of the next layer (say, layer 2). å represents the linear combination of x_1, x_2, x_3 with the corresponding coefficients or weights w_1, w_2, w_3. f is the activation function used at the neuron.

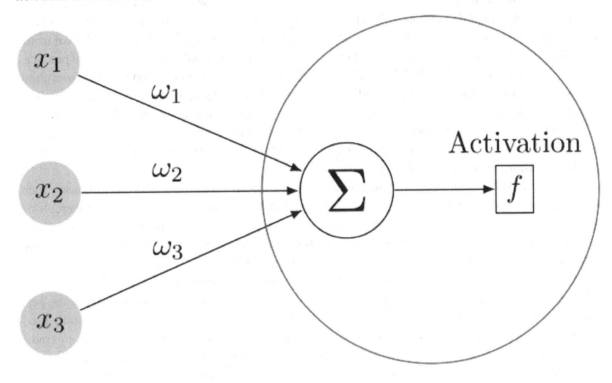

Gradient Boosting Models

Gradient boosting models are boosting models, which are the combinations of multiple weak models trained on different versions of the original data (Friedman, 2001). Weak models are very simple models that have a low accuracy. Examples of weak models include predicting by using the average of the target or using a decision tree with only one split (usually called a "stump"). The idea behind boosting models is to train a weak model into a strong model by having the weak learner learn from their "mistakes". In gradient boosting, this idea is implemented by continuously changing the target variable in one round of training by the error of the previous round. The final prediction is the vote among the weak models from all the rounds where higher voting powers are given to those weak models that perform better.

The authors chose gradient boosting to challenge deep learning models because gradient boosting has been well-known as one of the best models for structured data (data that can be presented in a table). Gradient boosting has won multiple data competitions and is usually the top choice for machine learning practitioners when building predictive models. Among the data competitions that gradient boosting has won include the Twitter RecSys Challenge 2020 (Schifferer, 2020), the KDD Cup 2016 competition (Sandulescu and Chiru, 2016), the 2017 ACM RecSys challenge (Volkovs et al., 2017), and many other Kaggle competitions.

Pneumonia Detection From Chest X-Rays

Pneumonia is an infection of the lungs that can cause mild to severe illness in people of all ages (Centers for Disease Control and Prevention, 2020). Each year, there are about 200 million cases of viral community-acquired pneumonia, half of them being in children (Ruuskanen et al., 2011). The problem of using chest x-rays to study and identify pneumonia patients has been long studied in the literature and practice. In 2017, Rajpurkar et al. built CheXNet, a deep learning model that can identify pneumonia from chest x-rays at a level that exceeds practicing radiologists. Ayan et al. (2019) demonstrated the effectiveness of deep learning models Vgg16 and Xception in detecting pneumonia patients from their chest x-rays. Other work on detecting pneumonia using deep learning includes Hammoud et al. (2021), Rahman et al. (2020), Jaiswal et al. (2019), Stephen et al. (2019), Zech et al. (2018), Asnaoui et al. (2020), Hurt et al (2020), Rahimzadeh and Attar (2020), Ni et al. (2020)

In addition to pneumonia, deep learning models have also been utilized to detect other diseases, such as tuberculosis. For example, Stirenko et al. (2018) used deep learning models to analyze tuberculosis patients and Becker et al. (2018) used deep learning models to detect tuberculosis patterns in photographs of chest x-ray images. Other research using deep learning to analyze chest x-ray or medical image include Zhang et al. (2020), Litjens et al. (2017), and Mahapatra et al. (2018).

In this work, the authors do not strive to develop a competitive deep learning model to the models existing in the literature for detecting diseases from chest x-rays. Instead, the authors compare the performances of deep learning models with gradient boosting, which is a method that is not generally used for this specific type of prediction. In the study, the authors implement several configurations of gradient boosting models and architectures of deep neural networks to detect pneumonia patients. These two classes of models are trained on a dataset that includes x-rays of pneumonia patients and healthy people. The authors use multiple popular architectures of neural networks, including MobileNetV3, Resnet50, and InceptionV3. For gradient boosting models, the authors form different variants by changing its main parameter, the number of iterations. All these models are run on the cloud computing service offered by Google Colab.

DEEP NEURAL NETWORK TECHNIQUES

In this section, two commonly used types of deep neural network layers and three techniques often used when training deep neural networks, which are data augmentation, optimizers, and transfer learning, are described. These techniques are also implemented in the authors' experiment.

Convolutional layers

Convolutional layers are the building blocks of deep neural networks. The main idea behind using convolutional layers is to share a set of the same weights to connect nodes between two layers instead of using different weights, as in the case of traditional neural networks. This same set of weights is referred to as a "filter" or "kernel". Convolutional layers reduce the number of parameters of the neural network, which helps avoid overfitting and also helps detect important visual features of the previous layer.

Pooling layers

In pooling layers, neighboring values coming out of one layer will be grouped together into multiple sets and each set will be presented by a number. The presented number could be the maximum value (feature) of the set, as with max pooling layers, or the average. Pooling layers help reduce the dimensions of the data and do not add more parameters to the model. Since features are presented by aggregating information, the pooling layers help the model recognize the overall global representation of the images.

Data augmentation

Data augmentation refers to a set of techniques that increases the size or improves the quality of the training data or images (Shorten, 2019). Data augmentation could include multiple transformations of each input image to the training data. These transformations could be reflections, different rotations, or cropping of the original images. Data augmentation could also include artificial images that are generated from the input data (Sandfort, 2019).

Data augmentation techniques help reduce overfitting, which is an issue where the model learns the training data well (i.e., the training accuracy is relatively high) but fails to generalize that knowledge to perform well on the test data (i.e., the testing accuracy is relatively low). Overfitting often occurs when the training dataset is not big enough to train the large number of parameters in a deep neural network (the number of parameters in a neural network generally increases with how "deep" the network is). In the experiment, the authors use the following data augmentation or transformation techniques.

- Randomly flip each image horizontally.
- Randomly rotate each image in the angle range of $(-0.4\pi, 0.4\pi)$ radians.
- Randomly zoom out of each image by 20%.

Examples of the data augmentation that the authors used are illustrated in Figure 3.

Optimizers

To train the neural networks, one needs to find the set of weights that minimizes the preselected loss function. In contrast to the case of linear regression, the loss function (function of the weights) in a deep neural network is not a quadratic function and there exists no closed form solution for the optimization problem.

Gradient descent (or batch gradient descent) and its variants have been some of the most popular workhorse algorithms to solve for the approximated solution of minimizing the loss function in deep neural networks (Ruder, 2016). In gradient descent, one first initializes a set of weights for the network then iteratively updates the weights toward the direction of the gradient vector of the loss function. Variants of gradient descent that are mentioned frequently in the literature of deep neural networks are mini batch gradient descent and stochastic gradient descent. These algorithms can be considered as stochastic approximations of gradient descent used to quicken the convergence of gradient descent.

In mini batch gradient descent, instead of using all of the data points, or images, to construct the loss function and its gradient, only a batch of data points, or images, are used at one iteration to update the weights. The entire dataset is divided into multiple batches and these batches are iteratively used to update the weights. In stochastic gradient descent, only one single data point, or image, is used to update the weights in an iteration. Stochastic gradient descent can be considered as a special case of mini batch gradient descent where the size of the batch is 1.

Gradient descent and its variants do not use the full amount of the gradient to update the weights, but only a fraction of it. This fraction is referred as the learning rate and it takes a value between 0 and 1, but usually less than 0.01. Traditionally, this learning rate is pre-determined and is a constant during the training process. However, this is where the traditional gradient descent algorithm presents challenges. Since the learning rate does not change during the entire training process and since it applies to all parameters, it does not adapt to the characteristic of the data. Also, choosing the optimal learning rate is a challenging task and could severely affect the training time. Too small of a learning rate leads to slow convergence, while a too large learning rate may lead to divergence.

Optimizers refer to the set of techniques or algorithms that are extensions of stochastic algorithms that offer more effective ways to update the weights in training deep neural networks. Momentum (Qian, 1999) is an algorithm allowing the weights to move faster in the relevant direction, which helps accelerate the speed of convergence. Adagrad (Duchi et al., 2011) adjusts the learning rate based on parameters where parameters associated with frequent variables (features) will receive a larger learning rate. Some other popular optimizers in the literature include Adadelta (Zeiler, 2012), Adam, or Adaptive Moment Estimation, (Kingma and Ba, 2014), Nadam (Nesterov-accelerated Adaptive Moment Estimation) (Dozat, 2016), AMSGrad (Reddi, 2019)

In the study, the authors implement the Adam optimizer (Kingma and Ba, 2014) for all the deep neural networks. Adam is considered very robust with different architectures of deep neural networks (Goodfellow, 2016).

Transfer learning

To train a neural network, one needs to first initialize the weights on the connections of neurons and then iteratively change the weights to minimize a selected loss function. Since deep neural network models have been famous for being data hungry (Marcus, 2018), it requires a large dataset to train one. This makes deep neural network models impractical when the available data are not large enough. Transfer learning is the bridge between "small" data and deep learning. Transfer learning refers to a set of techniques that can store the knowledge acquired from learning one problem (dataset) to another problem (West et al., 2007). For instance, a model that can recognize different types of housecats may be useful to train a model to recognize different types of lions. Transfer learning can also be useful in cases where outdated data need to be updated (Pan and Yang, 2009).

The knowledge of a deep neural network model can be interpreted as its weights. Using transfer learning to train a neural network A, one can use the weights found in a trained neural network B without retraining A to learn these weights. Here A and B are similar networks and the data used to train A are also similar to the data used to train B. Thus, A is just needed to be trained to find the "remainder" weights, which are usually far fewer in quantity compared to those weights borrowed from B. These "remainder" weights would often account for any layers in network A which are not present in network B. For instance, networks A and B may be nearly identical in their architectures, except that network A has a couple of extra hidden layers immediately before the output layer. In this case, most weights in network A can be transferred from network B, but the "remainder" weights that need to be trained in network A would include those for the extra hidden layers towards the end of the network.

In this study, when transfer learning is used, the weights are "transferred" from the corresponding baseline network trained on the ImageNet dataset. Since all the deep neural network models that the authors implemented are designed to classify more than two categories of images, the authors added on top of these models' extra layers so that they can be used to recognize two classes of images as in this study.

DEEP NEURAL NETWORK ARCHITECTURES

A neural network is defined by its architecture, which specifies the number of layers, the types of layers, and the activation functions used at each neuron. The authors include in this study both the authors' own architectures and those developed by well-recognized corporations, such as Microsoft and Google. Here the authors briefly introduce the architectures of the neural network models that the authors use for the comparison with gradient boosting models.

BasicNet

Since all the deep neural networks the authors implemented in this study were designed for and tested on certain large and well-known datasets, such as ImageNet and CIFAR-100, the authors also include in this study a shallower network that may be appropriate for this smaller chest x-ray dataset. For reference, the authors called this neural network "BasicNet", as it follows the very basic principles of a convolutional neural network. For all convolutional layers, BasicNet uses the "same" padding (i.e., the layers do not change the sizes of their corresponding input images). All activation functions used are Rectified Linear Unit (ReLU) activation functions (Nair and Hilton, 2010). The probability of dropping out at the dropout layer is 20%. The architecture of the authors' network is as follows.

Inception

Inception, or Google's Inception Convolutional Neural Network, was introduced during the ImageNet Recognition Challenge and was developed by researchers at Google, the University of North Carolina, Chapel Hill, and the University of Michigan (Szegedy et al., 2015). The name "Inception" was motivated from the quote "'we need to go deeper" from Christopher Nolan's film, Inception, implying that deeper neural networks have the potential to achieve better accuracy. To go "deeper," the authors make extensive use of a kernel of the size 1x1 to reduce the computational expenses which deeper neural networks tend to require when being trained. The first version of Inception, which has 22 layers, has won the ILSVRC (ImageNet Large Scale Visual Recognition Competition) 2014. (Szegedy et al., 2015).

Table 1. Architecture of BasicNet. For all convolutional layers, the "same" padding is used so that the layers do not change the sizes of their corresponding input images. All activation functions used are ReLU activation functions. The probability of dropping out at the dropout layer is 20%.

Layer	Filters/Kernels	Number of Parameters
Input Layer (Sequential)		
Rescaling		
Convolutional Layer	16 filters of size 3x3	448
Max Pooling Layer		
Convolutional Layer	32 filters of size 3x3	4940
Max Pooling Layer		
Convolutional Layer	64 filters of size 3x3	18496
Max Pooling Layer		
Dropout		
Flatten		
Dense		663680
Dense		258

Resnet

Resnet, or Residual Network, is a deep neural network developed by researchers at Microsoft (He et al., 2016). Resnet introduced the concept of residual block to resolve the problem of gradient vanishing, which often happens when training very deep neural networks. Gradient vanishing occurs when the approximated gradient of the loss function in training becomes infinitesimally small, resulting in no improvement in minimizing the loss function of the network. By using residual block, Resnet can have a very deep structure up to 152 layers (Resnet152). Resnet is widely considered the second breakthrough in deep learning after AlexNet and has won first place in ILSVRC and COCO 2015 competitions in ImageNet Detection, ImageNet localization, Coco detection, and Coco segmentation (He et al., 2016).

MobileNet

MobileNets are small and efficient deep neural networks developed by researchers at Google (Howard et al., 2017) to be used in mobile and embedded applications. In order to reduce the computation to make an efficient model, MobileNets invented depthwise separable convolutions as a replacement to the standard convolutional operation. A depthwise separable convolution is a composition of a depthwise convolution and pointwise convolution. Counting both of these convolutional layers, MobileNets have 28 layers. Since it was introduced, MobileNet has been updated to version 3 (MobileNetV3).

EfficientNet

Since the success of AlexNet, there have been efforts to scale up the model to achieve better performance. Scaling up a deep neural network could be done in three ways: adding more neurons to layers (width scaling), adding more layers to the network (depth scaling), or increasing the resolution of input images (resolution scaling). Tan and Le (2019) have shown that scaling a network individually along only one of these three dimensions could achieve higher accuracy, but the improvement will stagnate at a certain stage. The authors proposed a systematic way of scaling the network by scaling all three dimensions at the same time, called Compound Model Scaling. The authors' proposed model, EfficientNet-B7, has achieved the state-of-the-art performance on multiple datasets, such as ImageNet (Deng et al., 2009) and CIFAR-100 (Krizhevsky and Hinton, 2009), while having a smaller structure and faster running time compared to the best existing neural network.

Xception

Xception, or an extreme version of Inception (Chollet, 2017), modified the Depthwise Separable Convolution module in the Inception model to design a deep neural network that performed better than InceptionV3 on the ImageNet dataset and JFT dataset (Hinton et al., 2015). In addition, Xception still has the same number of parameters as InceptionV3.

To implement these models, the authors use TensorFlow 2.5, which is a free open-source library developed by Google for machine learning and, in particular, deep learning. The authors also implemented the data preprocessing techniques that are specifically designed for each model before fitting the data to that model. For each model, the authors set the batch size to be 32 and the number of epochs to be 50. The readers can refer to the section "KEY TERMS AND DEFINITIONS" at the end of this chapter for brief definitions of epoch and batch size.

GRADIENT BOOSTING MODELS

To implement gradient boosting models, the authors use CatBoost, which is a free open-source library developed by Yandex (Prokhorenkova et al., 2017 and Dorogush et al., 2018). The implemented gradient boosting models are specified in Table 2. To transform the images into the tabular data for training gradient boosting models, the authors used the Python Imaging Library to convert images to matrices as follows. Each image of resolution D x W will be extracted to three matrices of size D x W where each matrix presents the color density of the images for the three colors: red, green, and blue. All the three matrices then be concatenated into a single row, presenting the information of the image in the table data. In the experiment, the authors tested two different resolution 96x96 and 160x160.

Figure 3. Different transformations of the same chest x-ray. Data augmentation adds these transformed images to the training data to help reduce overfitting. The images in the figure are either rotations or zoomed out version of the original image.

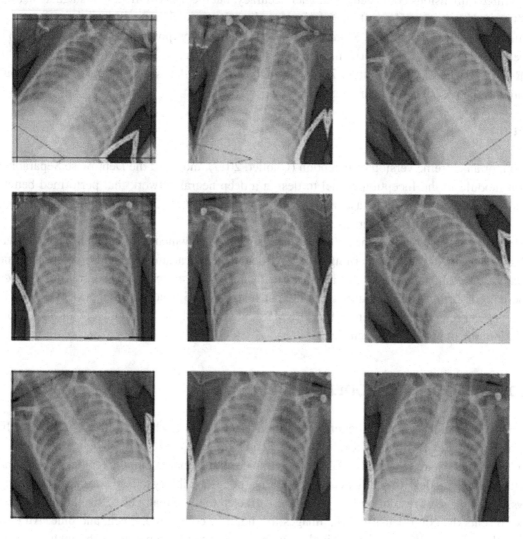

Table 2. Variants of gradient boosting used in the study. For gradient boosting with 1000 trees (GB1000), the authors also implement different variants with different tree depths (Figure 7).

Model	Iterations
GB100	100
GB500	500
GB1000	1000
GB2000	2000
GB5000	5000
GB10000	10000

DATA

The authors use the Labeled Optical Coherence Tomography (OCT) and Chest X-Ray Images (Kermany et al., 2018). In the original data, the distribution of "Pneumonia" images and "Normal" images is unbalanced (about 85% for Pneumonia images and 15% for Normal images). This represents a case of an imbalanced dataset where there is a very large percentage of the majority class with a corresponding small percentage of the minority class. This imbalance could lead to issues with imbalanced classification for the model (Chawla, 2002). For instance, if the imbalance is extremely severe (e.g., 99% majority vs. 1% minority) then all observations could be predicted to be the majority class with an accuracy of 99%. Thus, no predictions would be made for the minority class even though the overall accuracy is nearly perfect.

Two of the original principal approaches for handling imbalanced data are Random Undersampling (RUS) and Random Oversampling (ROS). The goal for both of these methods is to ensure that there is an equal balance between both types of observations. In RUS, randomly selected majority observations are deleted so that there are equal numbers of each class. In ROS, randomly selected minority observations are duplicated and included in the dataset so that the number of these observations matches the number of majority cases. Bonas et al. (2020) discuss these two methods on pages 123 and 124:

"RUS is one of the simpler methods under the larger umbrella that is undersampling. Essentially, random undersampling is accomplished by randomly selecting majority class observations and removing them from the dataset. This then will create a smaller, balanced subset of the original dataset which has the benefit of a faster run-time relative to the original data, oversampling techniques, and even some other undersampling techniques. One major drawback of this technique is that by removing majority observations entirely from the dataset some valuable information could be lost which would then negatively affect the predictive power of the model overall (Shelke et al., 2017). Similar to random undersampling, random oversampling is one of the simpler models under its respective resampling category. It is virtually the exact opposite of RUS where it is accomplished by randomly selecting minority class observations and duplicating them until there are enough observations to make the dataset balanced. This will then create a larger dataset than the original dataset where now the original dataset is a subset of this resampled set. The major benefit of ROS is that none of the original information in the dataset is lost and that there is minimal bias injected into the dataset because existing observations are only being duplicated versus new observations being synthetically created. The downside of ROS is that it takes a longer time to run the model due to the larger size of the resampled dataset." (Shelke et al., 2017).

Bonas et al. (2020, page 134) concluded: "when the datasets were resampled, that the majority of them had their highest balanced accuracy scores around the area of random undersampling… that random undersampling performed as well as, if not better than, random oversampling in all cases. From the results it could be argued that one should almost always choose to use RUS over ROS because of how well it performs, in terms of balanced accuracy. Additionally, one could argue to choose RUS because of how quickly it completes its runs, relative to the speed of ROS."

In the experiment, the authors rebalanced the original data using RUS by eliminating randomly selected observations of the pneumonia cases. The distribution of the two categories in the revised training dataset is 50:50 (1,000 images for each image class). The authors also keep this same 50:50 distribution in the test dataset so that the accuracy metric is relevant to compare the overall performance of the models. A sample of these images is shown in Figure 4.

Figure 4. Sample chest x-ray images from the dataset. All the images are grouped into two classes: Pneumonia and Normal.

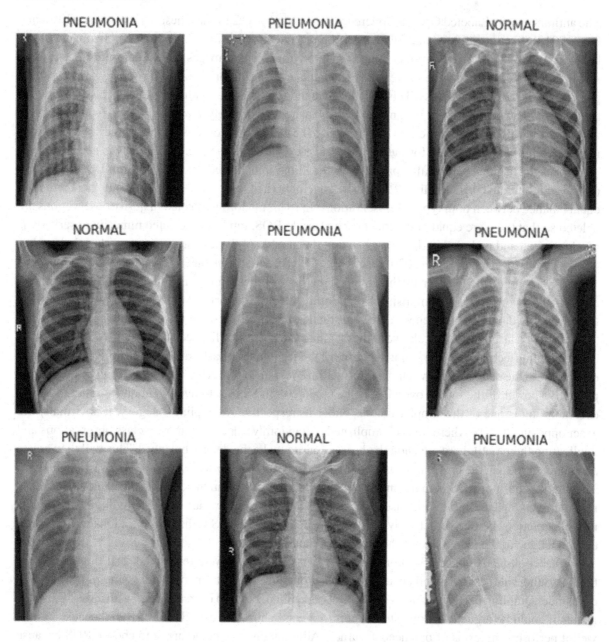

RESULTS

The authors compare the two classes of models, deep neural networks, and gradient boosting, on four different settings based on the resolutions of 96x96 and 160x160, and whether data augmentation and transfer learning techniques are applied when training the neural networks. For deep neural network models, the authors use the Tensorflow platform and for gradient boosting models, the authors use the

Catboost platform. The results for the test accuracy can be seen in Table 3, Table 4, Table 5, Figure 5, Figure 6, and Figure 7.

The authors find that deep learning models significantly outperform gradient boosting models in term of accuracy overall. One of the cases when gradient boosting models score higher in accuracy is when BasicNet, the "shallower" convolutional neural network, is used with no data augmentation or transfer learning. However, when data augmentation and transfer learning are applied, BasicNet improves substantially and becomes better than all of the gradient boosting models. Similarly, MobileNetV3 scores lower (0.77) than the gradient boosting models at 96x96 resolution with data augmentation and transfer learning applied, but at 160x160 resolution, the MobileNetV3 is able to improve its accuracy (0.829) to outperform the gradient boosting models.

The authors also observe that almost all of the deep learning models benefit from the resolution increase from 96x96 to 160x160, but that this is not the case for the gradient boosting models. Gradient boosting largely could not improve its accuracy when training on higher resolution images. Suspecting that the gradient boosting models might be too simple, such that they may underfit the data, the authors increased the depth of the trees in the gradient boosting models to investigate their performance. However, the authors find that even with more complex gradient boosting models, their accuracy does not improve (Figure 7).

The results are not surprising. One of the reasons for the relatively low performance of gradient boosting models could be that when converting the data from the 3D structure of images to tabular data to train the gradient boosting models, the information indicating the positions of the variables (which are the pixels' coordinates in the images) is lost. The authors know that the positions of the columns/variables in the table do not affect the performance of the gradient boosting models. However, this is not true for deep neural networks, as they can natively handle the original 3D structure of the data.

Table 3. The accuracy of the models when data augmentation and transfer learning techniques are applied when training the deep learning models. The dimensions of 96 and 160 correspond to the image resolutions of 96x96 and 160x160, respectively.

Model	Dimension=96	Dimension=160
BasicNet	0.8903	0.8397
InceptionV3	0.7827	0.8418
MobileNetV3	0.77	0.8291
Resnet50	0.8059	0.8734
EfficientNetB7	0.8629	0.8713
Xception	0.7975	0.8354
GB100	0.789	0.7764
GB500	0.7911	0.7932
GB1000	0.7975	0.7869
GB2000	0.801	0.7869
GB5000	0.7996	0.7869
GB10000	0.7932	0.7869

In the experiment, the authors also find that transfer learning does not help to improve accuracy. The reason for this could be that the "knowledge" that the baseline deep learning model learned from the previously used data is not applicable for the task at hand. That is, the previously used data, namely the ImageNet dataset, is too "different" from the chest x-ray data for transferred weights to be helpful.

The model that gives the best performance in the experiment is the Xception model trained on 160x160 resolution images with 0.922 accuracy, when not using data augmentation or transfer learning.

Table 4. The accuracy of the models when data augmentation and transfer learning techniques are applied when training the deep learning models. The dimensions of 96 and 160 correspond to the image resolutions of 96x96 and 160x160, respectively.

Model	Dimension=96	Dimension=160
BasicNet	0.7616	0.7089
InceptionV3	0.8861	0.8987
MobileNetV3	0.8734	0.9072
Resnet50	0.8502	0.903
EfficientNetB7	0.9093	0.8713
Xception	0.8861	0.9219
GB100	0.789	0.7764
GB500	0.7911	0.7932
GB1000	0.7975	0.7869
GB2000	0.801	0.7869
GB5000	0.7996	0.7869
GB10000	0.7932	0.7869

Table 5. The accuracy of gradient boosting with 1000 trees (GB1000) when using different tree depths. The image resolution used is 160x160.

Tree Depth	Accuracy
Depth = 6	0.7869
Depth = 8	0.789
Depth = 10	0.7848
Depth = 12	0.7806
Depth = 14	0.7764
Depth = 16	0.7764

Figure 5. The accuracy of the models when data augmentation and transfer learning techniques are applied when training the deep learning models. The dimensions of 96 and 160 correspond to the image resolutions of 96x96 and 160x160, respectively.

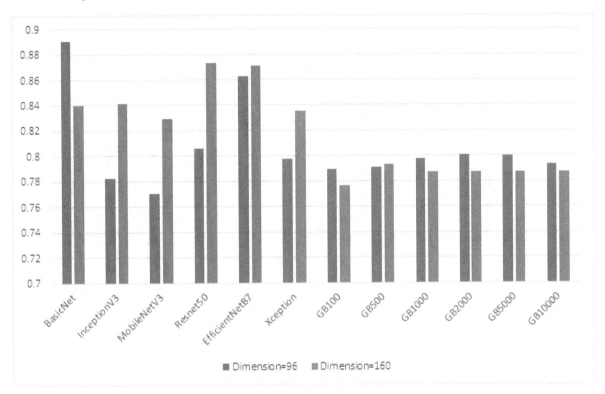

CONCLUSION

In this study, the authors compare the performance of deep neural network models, the default models for computer vision in the past ten years, to gradient boosting, one of the top performing models for structured/tabular data, in the task of detecting pneumonia from chest x-rays. The study confirms the superiority of deep neural network models. While under certain conditions, gradient boosting could compete with deep neural networks, it does not have the flexibility to benefit from the information gained by increasing image resolution. In addition, deep learning models also offer a variety of techniques and an abundance of hyperparameters that can be configured to work well with the available data to improve model performance.

Figure 6. The accuracy of the models when data augmentation and transfer learning techniques are not applied when training the deep learning models. The dimensions of 96 and 160 correspond to the image resolutions of 96x96 and 160x160, respectively.

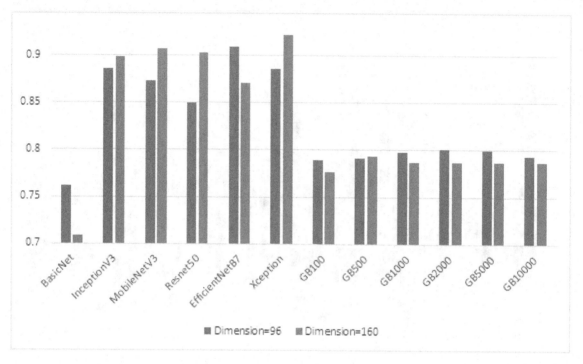

Figure 7. The accuracy of gradient boosting with 1000 trees (GB1000) when using different tree depths. The image resolution used is 160x160.

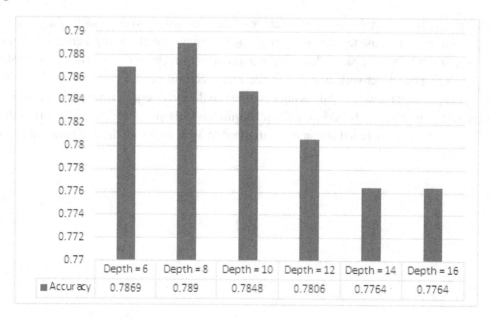

REFERENCES

Asnaoui, K. E., Chawki, Y., & Idri, A. (2020). *Automated methods for detection and classification pneumonia based on x-ray images using deep learning.* arXiv preprint arXiv:2003.14363.

Ayan, E., & Ünver, H. M. (2019, April). Diagnosis of pneumonia from chest x-ray images using deep learning. In *2019 Scientific Meeting on Electrical-Electronics & Biomedical Engineering and Computer Science (EBBT)* (pp. 1-5). IEEE.

Becker, A. S., Blüthgen, C., Sekaggya-Wiltshire, C., Castelnuovo, B., Kambugu, A., Fehr, J., & Frauenfelder, T. (2018). Detection of tuberculosis patterns in digital photographs of chest X-ray images using Deep Learning: Feasibility study. *The International Journal of Tuberculosis and Lung Disease*, *22*(3), 328–335.

Bonas, M., Nguyen, S., Olinsky, A., Quinn, J., & Schumacher, P. (2020). A Method to Determine the Size of the Resampled Data in Imbalanced Classification. *Contemporary Perspectives in Data Mining*, *4*, 119.

Centers for Disease Control and Prevention. (2020, March 9). *Pneumonia.* Centers for Disease Control and Prevention. https://www.cdc.gov/pneumonia/index.html

Chawla, N. V., Bowyer, K. W., Hall, L. O., & Kegelmeyer, W. P. (2002). SMOTE: Synthetic minority over-sampling technique. *Journal of Artificial Intelligence Research*, *16*, 321–357.

Chollet, F. (2017). Xception: Deep learning with depthwise separable convolutions. In *Proceedings of The IEEE Conference on Computer Vision And Pattern Recognition* (pp. 1251-1258). IEEE.

Deng, J., Dong, W., Socher, R., Li, L.-J., Li, K., & Fei-Fei, L. (2009). Imagenet: A large-scale hierarchical image database. In *2009 IEEE Conference on Computer Vision and Pattern Recognition* (pp. 248–255). IEEE.

Dorogush, A. V., Ershov, V., & Gulin, A. (2018). *CatBoost: gradient boosting with categorical features support.* arXiv preprint arXiv:1810.11363.

Dozat, T. (2016). Incorporating Nesterov momentum into Adam. *Workshop Track of ICLR 2016.* Retrieved July 10, 2021 from https://openreview.net/pdf/OM0jvwB8jIp57ZJjtNEZ.pdf

Duchi, J., Hazan, E., & Singer, Y. (2011). Adaptive subgradient methods for online learning and stochastic optimization. *Journal of Machine Learning Research*, *12*(7).

Friedman, J., Hastie, T., & Tibshirani, R. (2009). The Elements of Statistical Learning: Data Mining, Inference, and Prediction. New York: Springer. https://doi.org/ doi:10.1007/978-0-387-84858-7

Goodfellow, I., Bengio, Y., & Courville, A. (2016). *Deep learning.* MIT Press.

Hammoudi, K., Benhabiles, H., Melkemi, M., Dornaika, F., Arganda-Carreras, I., Collard, D., & Scherpereel, A. (2021). Deep learning on chest x-ray images to detect and evaluate pneumonia cases at the era of covid-19. *Journal of Medical Systems*, *45*(7), 1–10.

He, K., Zhang, X., Ren, S., & Sun, J. (2016). Deep residual learning for image recognition. In *Proceedings of The IEEE Conference on Computer Vision and Pattern Recognition* (pp. 770-778). IEEE.

Hinton, G.E., Vinyals, O. & Dean, J. (2015). *Distilling the knowledge in a neural network.* ArXiv, abs/1503.02531.

Howard, A. G., Zhu, M., Chen, B., Kalenichenko, D., Wang, W., Weyand, T., . . . Adam, H. (2017). *Mobilenets: Efficient convolutional neural networks for mobile vision applications.* arXiv preprint arXiv:1704.04861.

Hurt, B., Kligerman, S., & Hsiao, A. (2020). Deep learning localization of pneumonia: 2019 coronavirus (COVID-19) outbreak. *Journal of Thoracic Imaging, 35*(3), W87-W89. doi:10.1097/RTI.0000000000000512

Jaiswal, A. K., Tiwari, P., Kumar, S., Gupta, D., Khanna, A., & Rodrigues, J. J. (2019). Identifying pneumonia in chest X-rays: A deep learning approach. *Measurement, 145,* 511–518.

Kermany, D., Zhang, K., & Goldbaum, M. (2018). Labeled optical coherence tomography (OCT) and Chest X-Ray images for classification. *Mendeley Data, 2.* Advance online publication. doi:10.17632/rscbjbr9sj.2

Kingma, D. P., & Ba, J. (2014). *Adam: A method for stochastic optimization.* arXiv preprint arXiv:1412.6980.

Krizhevsky, A. (2009). *Learning Multiple Layers of Features from Tiny Images.* Technical Report TR-2009, University of Toronto.

Krizhevsky, A., Sutskever, I., & Hinton, G. E. (2012). Imagenet classification with deep convolutional neural networks. *Advances in Neural Information Processing Systems, 25,* 1097–1105.

Litjens, G., Kooi, T., Bejnordi, B. E., Setio, A. A. A., Ciompi, F., Ghafoorian, M., ... Sánchez, C. I. (2017). A survey on deep learning in medical image analysis. *Medical Image Analysis, 42,* 60–88.

Mahapatra, D., Ge, Z., Sedai, S., & Chakravorty, R. (2018, September). Joint registration and segmentation of xray images using generative adversarial networks. In *International Workshop on Machine Learning in Medical Imaging* (pp. 73-80). Springer.

Marcus, G. (2018). *Deep learning: A critical appraisal.* arXiv preprint arXiv:1801.00631.

Nair, V., & Hinton, G. E. (2010). Rectified linear units improve restricted boltzmann machines. *Proceedings of the 27th International Conference on Machine Learning (ICML-10),* 807-814.

Ni, Q., Sun, Z. Y., Qi, L., Chen, W., Yang, Y., Wang, L., ... Zhang, L. J. (2020). A deep learning approach to characterize 2019 coronavirus disease (COVID-19) pneumonia in chest CT images. *European Radiology, 30*(12), 6517–6527.

Nielsen, M. (2016). A visual proof that neural nets can compute any function. In *Artificial Neural Networks and Deep Learning.* Determination Press. http://neuralnetworksanddeeplearning.com/chap4.html

Pan, S. J., & Yang, Q. (2009). A survey on transfer learning. *IEEE Transactions on Knowledge and Data Engineering, 22*(10), 1345–1359.

Prokhorenkova, L., Gusev, G., Vorobev, A., Dorogush, A. V., & Gulin, A. (2017). *CatBoost: unbiased boosting with categorical features.* arXiv preprint arXiv:1706.09516.

Qian, N. (1999). On the momentum term in gradient descent learning algorithms. *Neural Networks, 12*(1), 145–151.

Rahimzadeh, M., & Attar, A. (2020). A modified deep convolutional neural network for detecting CO-VID-19 and pneumonia from chest X-ray images based on the concatenation of Xception and ResNet50V2. *Informatics in Medicine Unlocked, 19*, 100360.

Rahman, T., Chowdhury, M. E., Khandakar, A., Islam, K. R., Islam, K. F., Mahbub, Z. B., ... Kashem, S. (2020). Transfer learning with deep convolutional neural network (CNN) for pneumonia detection using chest X-ray. *Applied Sciences (Basel, Switzerland), 10*(9), 3233.

Rajpurkar, P., Irvin, J., Zhu, K., Yang, B., Mehta, H., Duan, T., . . . Ng, A. Y. (2017). *Chexnet: Radiologist-level pneumonia detection on chest x-rays with deep learning.* arXiv preprint arXiv:1711.05225.

Reddi, S. J., Kale, S., & Kumar, S. (2019). *On the convergence of adam and beyond.* arXiv preprint arXiv:1904.09237.

Ruder, S. (2016). *An overview of gradient descent optimization algorithms.* arXiv preprint arXiv:1609.04747.

Ruuskanen, O., Lahti, E., Jennings, L. C., & Murdoch, D. R. (2011). Viral pneumonia. *Lancet, 377*(9773), 1264–1275.

Sandfort, V., Yan, K., Pickhardt, P. J., & Summers, R. M. (2019). Data augmentation using generative adversarial networks (CycleGAN) to improve generalizability in CT segmentation tasks. *Scientific Reports, 9*(1), 1–9.

Sandulescu, V., & Chiru, M. (2016). *Predicting the future relevance of research institutions-The winning solution of the KDD Cup 2016.* arXiv preprint arXiv:1609.02728.

Schifferer, B. (2020, September 23). *Winning Solution of RecSys2020 Challenge.* Medium. https://medium.com/rapids-ai/winning-solution-of-recsys2020-challenge-gpu-accelerated-feature-engineering-and-training-for-cd67c5a87b1f

Schmidhuber, J. (2015). Deep learning in neural networks: An overview. *Neural Networks, 61*, 85–117.

Shelke, M. M. S., Deshmukh, P. R., & Shandilya, V. K. (2017, April). A Review on imbalanced data handling using undersampling and oversampling technique. *International Journal of Recent Trends in Engineering & Research, 3*(4). Advance online publication. 1 doi:0.23883/IJRTER.2017. 3168.0UWXM

Shorten, C., & Khoshgoftaar, T. M. (2019). A survey on image data augmentation for deep learning. *Journal of Big Data, 6*(1), 1–48.

Stephen, O., Sain, M., Maduh, U. J., & Jeong, D. U. (2019). An efficient deep learning approach to pneumonia classification in healthcare. *Journal of Healthcare Engineering.*

Stirenko, S., Kochura, Y., Alienin, O., Rokovyi, O., Gordienko, Y., Gang, P., & Zeng, W. (2018, April). Chest X-ray analysis of tuberculosis by deep learning with segmentation and augmentation. In *2018 IEEE 38th International Conference on Electronics and Nanotechnology (ELNANO)* (pp. 422-428). IEEE.

Szegedy, C., Liu, W., Jia, Y., Sermanet, P., Reed, S., Anguelov, D., . . . Rabinovich, A. (2015). Going deeper with convolutions. In *Proceedings of The IEEE Conference On Computer Vision and Pattern Recognition* (pp. 1-9). IEEE.

Tan, M., & Le, Q. (2019, May). Efficientnet: Rethinking model scaling for convolutional neural networks. In *International Conference on Machine Learning* (pp. 6105-6114). PMLR.

Volkovs, M., Yu, G. W., & Poutanen, T. (2017). Content-based neighbor models for cold start in recommender systems. In *Proceedings of the Recommender Systems Challenge 2017* (pp. 1-6). Academic Press.

West, J., Ventura, D., & Warnick, S. (2007). *Spring research presentation: A theoretical foundation for inductive transfer.* Brigham Young University, College of Physical and Mathematical Sciences. https://web.archive.org/web/20070801120743/http://cpms.byu.edu/springresearch/abstract-entry?id=861

Zech, J. R., Badgeley, M. A., Liu, M., Costa, A. B., Titano, J. J., & Oermann, E. K. (2018). Variable generalization performance of a deep learning model to detect pneumonia in chest radiographs: A cross-sectional study. *PLoS Medicine, 15*(11), e1002683.

Zeiler, M. D. (2012). *Adadelta: An adaptive learning rate method.* arXiv preprint arXiv:1212.5701.

Zhang, J., Xie, Y., Li, Y., Shen, C., & Xia, Y. (2020). *Covid-19 screening on chest x-ray images using deep learning based anomaly detection.* arXiv preprint arXiv:2003.12338

ADDITIONAL READING

Al Mamlook, R. E., Chen, S., & Bzizi, H. F. (2020, July). Investigation of the performance of Machine Learning Classifiers for Pneumonia Detection in Chest X-ray Images. *In 2020 IEEE International Conference on Electro Information Technology (EIT)* (pp. 098-104). IEEE.

Brunese, L., Mercaldo, F., Reginelli, A., & Santone, A. (2020). Explainable deep learning for pulmonary disease and coronavirus COVID-19 detection from X-rays. *Computer Methods and Programs in Biomedicine, 196,* 105608.

Karthik, R., Menaka, R., & Hariharan, M. (2021). Learning distinctive filters for COVID-19 detection from chest X-ray using shuffled residual CNN. *Applied Soft Computing, 99,* 106744.

Mahmud, T., Rahman, M. A., & Fattah, S. A. (2020). CovXNet: A multi-dilation convolutional neural network for automatic COVID-19 and other pneumonia detection from chest X-ray images with transferable multi-receptive feature optimization. *Computers in Biology and Medicine, 122,* 103869.

Meng, Z., Meng, L., & Tomiyama, H. (2021). Pneumonia Diagnosis on Chest X-Rays with Machine Learning. *Procedia Computer Science, 187,* 42–51.

Pham, H. H., Le, T. T., Tran, D. Q., Ngo, D. T., & Nguyen, H. Q. (2021). Interpreting chest X-rays via CNNs that exploit hierarchical disease dependencies and uncertainty labels. *Neurocomputing, 437,* 186–194.

Rajaraman, S., Siegelman, J., Alderson, P. O., Folio, L. S., Folio, L. R., & Antani, S. K. (2020). Iteratively pruned deep learning ensembles for COVID-19 detection in chest X-rays. *IEEE Access : Practical Innovations, Open Solutions, 8,* 115041–115050.

Shams, M. Y., Elzeki, O. M., Abd Elfattah, M., Medhat, T., & Hassanien, A. E. (2020). Why are generative adversarial networks vital for deep neural networks? A case study on COVID-19 chest X-ray images. In *Big Data Analytics and Artificial Intelligence against COVID-19: Innovation Vision and Approach* (pp. 147–162). Springer.

KEY TERMS AND DEFINITIONS

Activation Functions: In neural network architecture, these are the pre-determined functions at each node or neuron, determining the output value of the node or neuron. These inputs to these functions are the linear combinations of the values at each node in the previous layer. Activation functions are often continuous functions. However, some activation functions are not differentiable everywhere, such as the Rectified Linear Units (ReLU) function, which is not differentiable at 0.

Backpropagation: Widely used in training neural networks, backpropagation is an algorithm to compute the gradient of the loss function of a neural network. Backpropagation computes the gradient of the loss function by using the chain rule. The gradient is computed one layer at a time and is iterated backward from the last layer.

Batch: A batch is a subset of the data. When training a neural network, the entire dataset is divided into batches. Batch size refers to the number of data points (or images) in a batch.

Convolutional Neural Network: A neural network where the hidden layers include layers that perform convolutional operations. The convolutional layers are usually followed by pooling layers and dense layers. At the convolutional layers, a filter (a vector or a multi-dimension tensor) will slide through the neurons to take the inner product with these neurons to provide values for the next layer.

Data Augmentation: Data augmentation refers to a set of techniques that increases the size or improves the quality of the training data or images. Data augmentation could include multiple transformations of each input image in the training data. These transformations could be reflections, different rotations, or cropping of the original images. Data augmentation could also include artificially produced images that are generated from the input data.

Epoch: When training a neural network, a set of data points or images are passed forward and backward sequentially. One epoch is completed when all the data points are passed forward and backward through the neural network.

Gradient Descent: Gradient descent is an algorithm to find a local minimum of a differentiable function. The algorithm starts by initiating a guess and then iteratively improves that guess by moving in the opposite direction of the gradient of the function. The algorithm stops when the gradient is zero, which means the current position is at a local minimum.

Learning Rate: This concept appears in several machine learning models. In neural network models, the learning rate is the fraction of the gradient vector that the weight vectors descend. The learning rate affects the speed and convergence of the training process. In gradient boosting, the learning rate decides how quickly or slowly the next tree corrects the error of the current tree. A learning rate that is too small might lead to a long training time, while a learning rate that is too large might not lead to convergence.

Stump: A decision tree with only one split or two leaves. This is the simplest decision tree that can be used as a weak learner in boosting algorithms.

Transfer Learning: Transfer learning refers to a set of techniques that can store the knowledge acquired from learning one problem (dataset) to another problem. For instance, a model that can recognize different types of housecats may be useful to train a model to recognize different types of lions. Transfer learning can also be useful in the case where outdated data needs to be updated (Pan, 2009).

Chapter 4
Cardiovascular Applications of Artificial Intelligence in Research, Diagnosis, and Disease Management

Viswanathan Rajagopalan

New York Institute of Technology College of Osteopathic Medicine at Arkansas State University, USA & Arkansas State University, USA & Center for No-Boundary Thinking at Arkansas State University, USA

Houwei Cao

New York Institute of Technology, USA

ABSTRACT

Despite significant advancements in diagnosis and disease management, cardiovascular (CV) disorders remain the No. 1 killer both in the United States and across the world, and innovative and transformative technologies such as artificial intelligence (AI) are increasingly employed in CV medicine. In this chapter, the authors introduce different AI and machine learning (ML) tools including support vector machine (SVM), gradient boosting machine (GBM), and deep learning (DL) models, and their applicability to advance CV diagnosis and disease classification, and risk prediction and patient management. The applications include, but are not limited to, electrocardiogram, imaging, genomics, and drug research in different CV pathologies such as myocardial infarction (heart attack), heart failure, congenital heart disease, arrhythmias, valvular abnormalities, etc.

INTRODUCTION

Cardiovascular (CV) diseases claim the greatest number of deaths both worldwide and across the United States (Virani et al., 2021). The CV healthcare costs are enormous despite several advancements in diagnostic and therapeutic products. The CV system can be negatively impacted at various clinical levels. These broadly include heart valve abnormalities such as stenosis (narrowing) or regurgitation (backflow),

DOI: 10.4018/978-1-7998-8455-2.ch004

myocardial infarction (heart attack), heart failure, congenital heart disease (birth defects) and arrhythmias (electrical defects). Thus, novel technologies such as those offered by artificial intelligence (AI) has potential to enhance further progress in the field and may offer significant improvements in health outcomes along with reductions in costs.

As one of the fastest emerging technologies, AI plays major roles in practically every sector of our daily lives. For example, virtual assistants such as Alexa, Siri or Google Assistant can help customers perform searches, order products online, answer questions, set reminders, adjust local environment, etc. Many e-commerce websites improve customers' online shopping experience with personalized recommendations and more streamlined buying processes. Voice verification, facial recognition, and biometric systems have been widely used to enhance security and surveillance.

AI also plays an increasingly important role in healthcare. AI and Machine Learning (ML) techniques have been widely used to improve both patient care and administrative processing. ML and Deep Learning (DL) techniques have been successfully applied to diagnose, analyze, and predict the course of various types of diseases, and in monitoring patient health conditions as well. Natural Language Processing (NLP) techniques can be used to understand and classify unstructured clinical documentations and assist in structuring patient and medication information. AI systems and robotics are also helping with day-to-day administrative and routine functions of health facilities, thus reducing physical workload of medical personnel, minimizing human errors and maximizing efficiency.

AI and ML techniques have been applied to improve CV research and health (Figure 1). This chapter is aimed to provide an overview of AI advancements in diverse areas within the CV field, however, it is not meant be a complete resource of all developments. For a comprehensive collection, the readers are suggested to explore several published review articles (Antoniades, Asselbergs, & Vardas, 2021; Benjamins, Hendriks, Knuuti, Juarez-Orozco, & van der Harst, 2019; C. Krittanawong et al., 2019; Mathur, Srivastava, Xu, & Mehta, 2020; Quer, Arnaout, Henne, & Arnaout, 2021). AI will also be discussed in the context of aforesaid disorders along with imaging, basic and biomedical sciences, precision medicine, drug discovery and development and robotics. The Coronavirus Disease 2019 (COVID-19) pandemic has significantly affected the CV health as well, (Abu Mouch et al., 2021; Chung et al., 2021; Farshidfar, Koleini, & Ardehali, 2021; Gedefaw et al., 2021; Nishiga, Wang, Han, Lewis, & Wu, 2020; Patil, Singh, Henderson, & Krishnamurthy, 2021; Rosner et al., 2021; Wenger & Lewis, 2021; Yiangou, Davis, & Mummery, 2021), however, this chapter will not delve into the topic, as a separate chapter is dedicated for COVID-19 in this volume. Before we dive into the clinical and biomedical aspects, we shall first introduce state-of-the-art AI and ML techniques, and subsequently discuss how those techniques are applied and are beneficial in diverse CV applications.

Figure 1. Schematic of areas where Artificial Intelligence and Machine Learning impact Cardiovascular sciences and medicine.

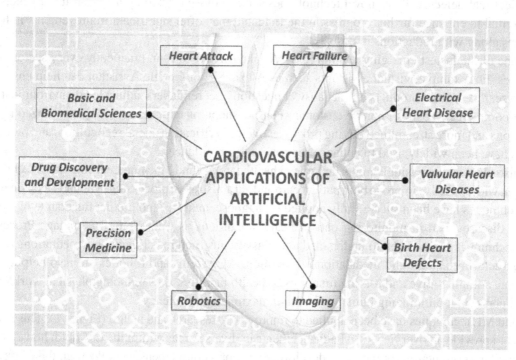

STATE-OF-THE-ART AI AND ML TOOLS

As a part of AI, ML refers to the study of computer algorithms that improve automatically through experience and by the use of data (Mitchell, 1997). Based on the nature of the signal and feedback available to the learning system, ML can be divided into different categories including supervised leaning, unsupervised learning, semi-supervised learning, reinforcement learning, etc.

Supervised Learning

Supervised learning is one of the most common methods of ML. It builds a mathematical model, i.e., a mapping function, that maps inputs to the desired outputs based on a set of training examples of input-output pairs. Here, the inputs X can be considered as features and the outputs Y can be considered as labels. Figure 2 shows a classic example of supervised learning. *Classification* and *regression* are the two major tasks in supervised learning. Classification is the process of finding the mapping function to map the input X to the categorical output Y. A model is trained on the training dataset aiming to categorize the data into different classes. For example, in a study by Sengupta et al. (P. Sengupta et al., 2016), clinical data and the imaging data have been combined together to train classifiers to discriminate cardiac abnormalities. On the other hand, regression is the process of finding the correlations between dependent and independent variables, and the task of the regression is to find the mapping function to map the input X to the continuous output Y. For example, in a study by Lee et al. (J. Lee et al., 2016), regression models have been trained to predict fractional flow reserve from coronary computed tomography (CT) angiography images.

Figure 2. Classic example of Supervised Learning. The labeled data and labels pass on to the model generating prediction of test data.

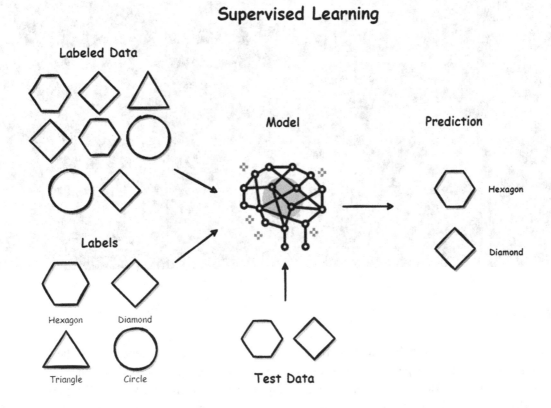

Common supervised learning algorithms include logistic regression (Gortmaker, Hosmer, & Lemeshow, 2013), linear regression (Seber & Lee, 2012), naive Bayes (Zhang, 2004), decision tree (Quinlan, 2004), random forest (Cutler, Cutler, & Stevens, 2011), support vector machine (SVM) (Boser, Guyon, & Vapnik, 1996), k-nearest neighbors (KNN) (Altman, 1992), artificial neural network (ANN) (Daniel, 2013), and ensemble learning methods (Rokach, 2010).

Logistic Regression

Logistic regression, also known as maximum-entropy classification, is a linear model for classification. It is a statistical model that uses a logistic function to model probability of a certain class or event such as healthy/sick. It has been successfully applied in disease prediction including prediction of CV diseases for decades.

Linear Regression

Linear regression is a linear approach to model relationship between the input variables and target variable by fitting a linear equation to observed data. It is a regression model commonly used to predict continuous values. For example, it can be used to predict the CV risk assessment score (Ismail & Anil, 2014). Figure 3 shows graphical representations of linear and logistic regression.

Figure 3. Graphical representation of Linear and logistic Regression

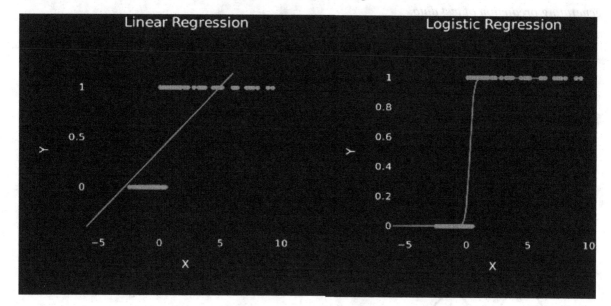

Naive Bayes

Naive Bayes are simple probabilistic classifiers based on applying Bayes' theorem with the "naive" assumption of conditional independence between every pair of features given the value of the class variable. Despite the over-simplified assumption, the naive Bayes classifiers have worked well in many complex real-world situations. They only require a small number of training data to estimate the parameters for classification, and can be trained extremely fast compared to other sophisticated learning methods. In a study by Miranda et al. (Miranda, Irwansyah, Amelga, Maribondang, & Salim, 2016), naive Bayes classifiers had shown very promising results in detection of CV disease risk's level for adults.

Decision Tree

Decision tree (DT) is one of the most popular supervised learning methods which can be used to solve both classification and regression problems. It has been widely applied in various CV applications. It is a non-parametric method that aims to create a model that predicts the value of a target variable by learning simple decision rules inferred from the data features. DT models are easily interpreted that have high accuracy and stability. DTs are also non-linear models which make them great for predicting and solving more complex problems. As shown in Figure 4, each node in the DT represents a decision binary on a feature, the branches from the nodes represent the outcome of the decision, and the last nodes of the tree (the leaves) represent the final classification/estimation of the data.

Figure 4. Architecture of a decision tree. The root and intermediate nodes test on features and the leaves predict the data.

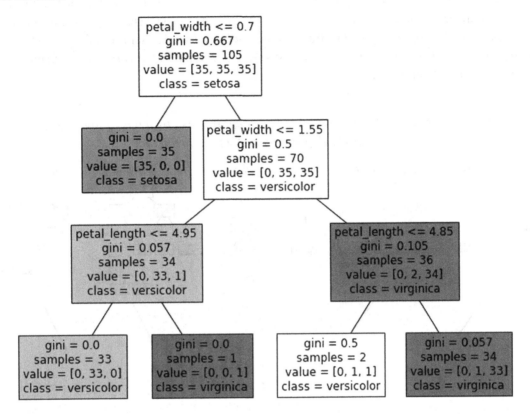

Random Forest

Random forests are an ensemble learning method by constructing a multitude of decision trees at training time. Figure 5 shows an example of random forest ensemble learning. Similar to DT, they can be used to solve both classification and regression problems. For the classification tasks, the output of the random forest is the class selected by most trees. For regression tasks, the output is the mean or average prediction of the individual trees. Random forests generally outperform decision trees as they can help to correct the overfitting from single decision tree. They have been proven successful in many studies on CV disease classification and risk prediction (Xu et al., 2017) (Caballé, Castillo-Sequera, Gomez-Pulido, Gómez, & Polo-Luque, 2020).

Support Vector Machine

Support Vector Machines or SVMs are one of the most robust prediction methods for classification and regression based on statistical learning frameworks. Generally speaking, the objective of SVMs is to find a hyperplane in an *N*-dimensional space that has the maximum margin, i.e. the maximum distance between data points of both classes to distinctly classify the data points. Samples on the margin are called the support vectors. Maximizing the margin distance provides some safety margin such that a slight error in measurement will not cause a misclassification, and future data points can be classified with more confidence. SVMs can be used to solve both linear and non-linear problems and work well on many practical problems including the CV applications. Through non-linear transformation, SVMs can project nonlinear separable samples onto another higher dimensional space by using different types of kernel functions. Common kernel functions include linear kernel, Radial Basis Function kernel, and polynomial kernel. For example, Figure 6 shows decision boundary for a binary classification problem, with three types of kernel functions.

Figure 5. Example of Random Forest Ensemble Learning. It works by aggregating output of different decision trees via majority vote or averaging to generate a final prediction.

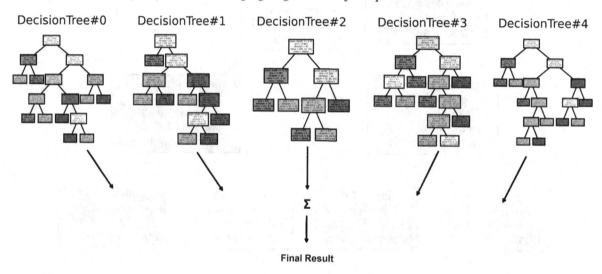

Figure 6. SVM example - Decision boundary for Different Kernels. Dash lines plot support vectors of the models and the solid lines plot decision boundaries of different models.

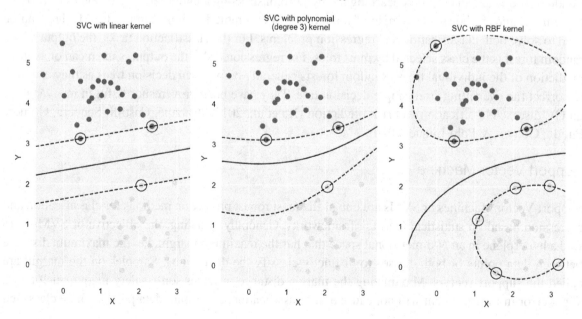

K-Nearest Neighbors

K-nearest neighbors (k-NN) is a non-parametric classification method which can be used to solve both classification and regression problems. In classification, the input consists of the k closest training examples in data set and the output is classified by a plurality vote of its k neighbors. While in regression, the output is the average values of the k nearest neighbors. The selection of the right k is crucial for the success of the algorithm. For example, a small value of k indicates that noise will have a significant impact on the result, while a large value makes it computationally expensive. One common application of k-NN on CV domain is heart disease prediction (Enriko, Suryanegara, & Gunawan, 2016). Although k-NN is a simple and easy-to-implement non-parametric algorithm, it should be noted that it gets significantly slower as the number of examples or predictors increase. In addition, it is also very sensitive to the local structure of the data.

Artificial Neural Network

Artificial neural networks (ANNs) are computing systems in accordance with biological neural networks from animal brains. They can be used to model different kinds of complex, nonlinear or discontinuous relationships. As shown in Figure 7, ANN models consist of input layer, one or more hidden layers and output layer. In each of the layers in ANN, there are nodes called neurons. These nodes are connected to each other with associated weights and thresholds and processes the data in the network through a sum and transfer function. Based on the depth of layers in neural network, ANN models can be further divided into basic neural network and DL models. Basic neural network models usually contain less than or equal to three hidden layers while DL models normally consist of deeper networks with more than three hidden layers. We will discuss various DL algorithms in detail in later sections.

Ensemble Learning

Ensemble learning methods are techniques that combine multiple learning models together to improve predictive performance, which usually produce more accurate solutions than any of the constituent learning algorithm alone. Figure 8 shows an example of the ensemble learning system. Ensemble models tend to produce better results when there is a significant diversity among the models. As a result, many ensemble methods tend to promote diversity among the models they combine (Kuncheva & Whitaker, 2003). Bagging method involves having each model in the ensemble vote with equal weight and is a common ensemble algorithm designed to improve stability and accuracy of model performance. The random forest algorithm that we introduced earlier is a bagging method. Boosting is another type of ensemble method which involves incrementally building an ensemble by training each new model instance to emphasize the training instances that previous models misclassified. Adaptive Boosting (AdaBoost) (Freund, Iyer, Schapire, & Singer, 2003), is one of the most popular boosting method. It helps to combine multiple "weak classifiers" into a single "strong classifier" by putting more weight on difficult to classify instances and less on those already handled well. Ensemble classifiers have been successfully applied in neuroscience, proteomics and medical diagnosis including clinical decision support system for CV disease (Eom, Kim, & Zhang, 2008).

Figure 7. A basic ANN example with a 5-perceptron input layer, a 10-perceptron hidden layer and a 4-perceptron output layer.

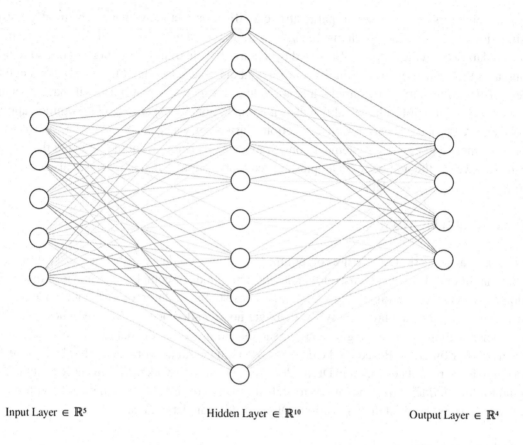

Input Layer $\in \mathbb{R}^5$ Hidden Layer $\in \mathbb{R}^{10}$ Output Layer $\in \mathbb{R}^4$

Figure 8. Example of ensemble learning output and prediction by providing same data to 3 different models and aggregating the output to final prediction.

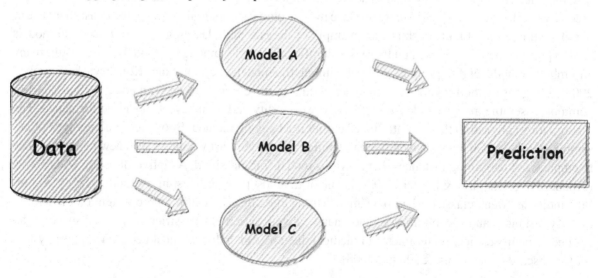

Unsupervised Learning

Unlike supervised learning that tries to fit input data with output labels, unsupervised learning works on its own to discover inherent structure within an input dataset without target labels. The three main tasks of unsupervised learning are clustering, association and dimensionality reduction (Hinton & Sejnowski, 1999).

Clustering

Clustering analysis is a task for grouping unlabeled data based on their similarities or differences such that within a group the observations must be as similar as possible, while observations belonging to different groups must be as different as possible. Figure 9 summarizes different types of cluster algorithms. Among them, hierarchical clustering and k-means clustering are the two main algorithms in clustering analysis. The k-means clustering algorithm assigns similar data points into k groups. The number k needs to be fixed in advance and it represents the size of the grouping and granularity. While hierarchical clustering is generally used for an unknown number of classes and helps to determine the optimal number. Clustering analysis has been used in many fields, including pattern recognition, image analysis, bioinformatics, etc. One common application of cluster analysis in CV research is to identify underlying risk factors for coronary artery disease (Guo et al., 2017). Unpublished data from Rajagopalan group using unsupervised hierarchical clustering showed significant alterations in expression of noncoding RNAs from left ventricles in a model of heart failure (HF) with preserved contractile function (expanded later) as seen in human disease. These findings offer enormous opportunities with potential diagnostic and therapeutic solutions in this type of HF for which there is no clear treatment available.

Figure 9. Types of Cluster Algorithms

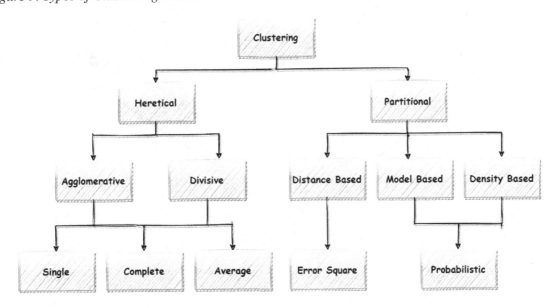

Association

Association is another type of unsupervised learning method that uses different rules to find relationships between variables in a given dataset. It is frequently used to identify items that have an affinity or often appear together. Figure 10 shows downward-closure property of the association method. It can also be used for identifying dependent or associated events as seen in a study (Nahar, Imam, Tickle, & Chen, 2013) in which association rules have been used to detect factors which contribute to heart disease in males and females respectively.

Figure 10. The downward-closure property

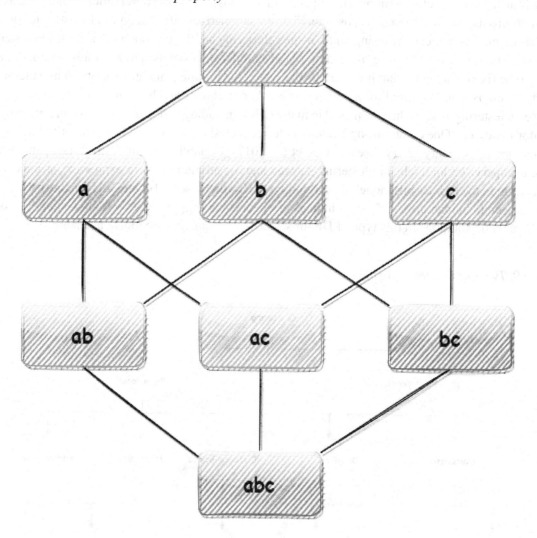

Dimensionality Reduction

Dimensionality reduction is a learning technique used when the number of features in a given dataset is too high. It is the transformation of data from a high-dimensional space into a low-dimensional space while still preserving data integrity. It can be divided into linear and non-linear approaches (van der Maaten, Postma, & Herik, 2007). Principal Component Analysis (PCA) is one of the most common linear techniques for dimensionality reduction. It is an orthogonal linear transformation that transforms the data to a lower-dimensional space such that the variance of the data in the low-dimensional representation is maximized. PCA has been widely used in signal processing, neuro-informatics, and bioinformatics. On the other hand, auto-encoder is a type of neural network used to learn non-linear dimension reduction functions and efficient codings together with an inverse function. It has been used in biomedical image processing, e.g., to remove noise from visual data to improve picture quality and also in drug discovery (Zagribelnyy et al., 2019).

Figure 11. Dimensionality Reduction via PCA, t-SNE, UMAP, LDA (reduced original data from 784 dimensions to 3 dimensions)

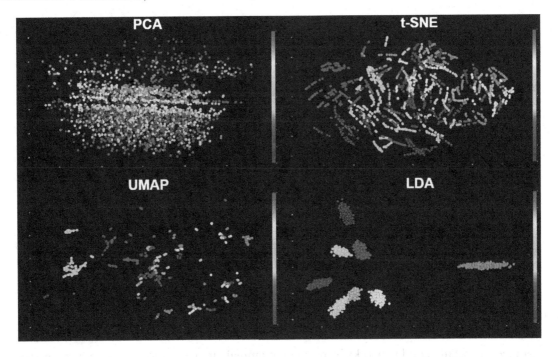

Deep Learning

Deep Learning, DL, based on ANN with representation learning, has emerged as a new area of AI over the past decade (Yoshua Bengio, Courville, & Vincent, 2013; LeCun, Bengio, & Hinton, 2015). DL techniques can be used to extract complex and concealed information from large number of raw data using multiple hidden layers, i.e., tens or hundreds, where each layer is a representation that is a high-level abstraction of the representation from the previous layer of the neural networks. The word "deep" refers to the number of layers through which the data is transformed. The greater the number of hidden layers is, the deeper the network is. For example, when we build DL models for face recognition, the input may be a matrix of pixels from raw images, the first layer may abstract the pixels and encode edges from the image, the second layer may compose and encode arrangements of edges, the third layer may encode nose and eyes, and the fourth layer may recognize that the image contains a face and match the face with registered users.

Common DL models include convolutional neural networks (CNNs), recurrent neural networks (RNNs), deep belief networks (DBNs), deep auto-encoder, etc. They have been widely used in speech recognition, computer vision, natural language processing, bioinformatics, robotics, drug design, medical image analysis and more. (Deng, 2014; Schmidhuber, 2015).

Figure 12. Classic Example of Deep Learning Neural Networks with a 5-perceptron input layer, 4 hidden layers with 8-perceptron, and a 4-perceptron output layer.

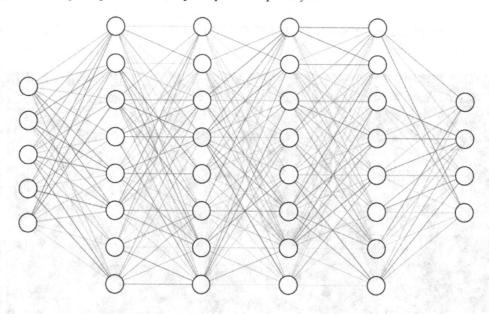

Input Layer $\in \mathbb{R}^5$ Hidden Layer $\in \mathbb{R}^8$ Hidden Layer $\in \mathbb{R}^8$ Hidden Layer $\in \mathbb{R}^8$ Hidden Layer $\in \mathbb{R}^8$ Output Layer $\in \mathbb{R}^4$

Convolutional Neural Networks (CNN)

CNNs are feed-forward neural networks inspired by mammalian visual cortex that contains very small neuronal cells sensitive to specific areas of the visual field, i.e., some neurons respond when exposed to vertical edges and some when exposed to horizontal edges (Hubel & Wiesel, 1962). All these neurons which appear to be spatially arranged in columnar structures are able to produce visual perception. Accordingly, CNNs are proposed with succession layers of convolution, activation, pooling, and fully-connected layers to obtain the final outputs. The convolution layers are the most important part of a CNN, which are composed of a set of filters to extract different features from input data. For instance, the first convolution layer extracts low-level features such as lines, edges, and corners, and higher-level layers extract higher-level features. CNNs are now the dominant approach for various computer vision tasks including medical image analysis.

Figure 13. A Comprehensive Guide to Convolutional Neural Networks. Eight convolution filters with 128×128 input, 8 convolution filters with 64×64 input, 16 convolution filters with 48×48 input, 16 convolution filters with 16×16 input followed by 2 fully connected layers with 256 and 128 units respectively.

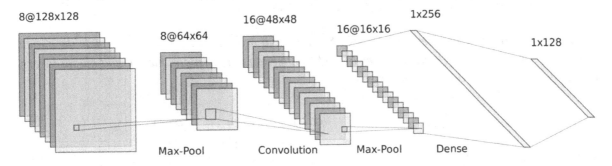

Recurrent Neural Networks (RNN)

Distinct from CNNs with feed-forward networks, RNNs include feedback components that permit signals from one layer to be fed back to the previous layer (Olurotimi, 1994). Moreover, RNN is a type of deep neural network with an internal state (memory) which can be used to store long-term information and process variable length sequences of inputs (Y. Bengio, Simard, & Frasconi, 1994). In addition, RNNs can not only process single data points (such as images), but also entire sequences of data (such as speech and video). It should be noted that basic RNNs may fail to model long-term dependences of data and suffers from gradient vanishing. To overcome these drawbacks, Long-Short-Term Memories (Hochreiter & Schmidhuber, 1997) and Gated Recurrent Units (Cho et al., 2014) have been proposed. Both these models add gates and memory cells in the hidden layer to control the amount of information entering the unit, the amount that will be stored and the information that will be passed to the next units. RNNs have been introduced to various types of CV applications in the last few years. For example, in a study by Choi et al. (Choi, Schuetz, Stewart, & Sun, 2016), the RNN models were applied for early detection of HF onset.

BRIEF, SIMPLIFIED HEART ANATOMY AND PHYSIOLOGY

Human heart begins to form and function quite early in gestational period. The heart comprises 4 chambers, 2 atria (upper) and 2 ventricles (lower). The right atrium receives deoxygenated blood from all parts of the body and pumps out to the lungs for purification via right ventricle and pulmonary artery. The left atrium receives oxygenated purified blood from the lungs and delivers to left ventricle. The left ventricle pumps the blood out with greater force and pressure to all parts of the body via the Aorta. The pumping activities are the result of specialized sarcomeric protein molecules within the major heart cells called cardiomyocytes. The repetitive mechanical activities of alternating contractions and relaxations are the result of immediately preceding electrical activities elicited by specialized cells residing at different regions of heart tissues.

Before entering and leaving each heart chamber, the blood passes through specific valves. The valves are specialized tissue flaps (leaflets) that act as one-way outflow orifices and prevent backward flow of blood. While the bicuspid (mitral) valve is located between left atrium and left ventricle, the tricuspid valve is located between right atrium and right ventricle. Correspondingly, the aortic valve is located between left ventricle and aorta, and the pulmonary valve is located between right ventricle and pulmonary artery.

Figure 14. Recurrent Neural Networks (RNN). X is the input layer, h is the hidden layer, o is the output layer. W, U, and V are weighting matrices of each connection among input, hidden and output layers. The (t-1), (t), and (t+1) are the time steps.

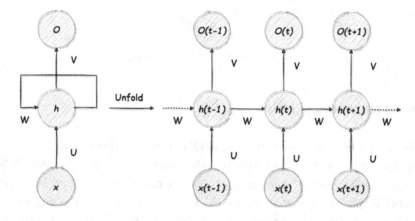

APPLICATIONS OF AI IN CV SPACE

AI in Electrical Heart Disease

Fetal primitive human heart begins to beat towards later part of the first month of gestational period. In order for the heart to pump effectively for rest of the life, it is crucial that the beats are rhythmic and of optimal frequency. Abnormalities in electrical activities including conduction and rhythm (arrhythmias), inherited or acquired, may result in life-threatening CV anomalies such as ventricular tachycardia (VT) or ventricular fibrillation (VF).

Rogers et al. (Rogers et al., 2021) recorded 5706 ventricular monophasic action potentials during steady-state pacing in 42 patients with coronary artery disease and left ventricular (LV) ejection fraction (contractile function) £40%. Using SVMs and CNNs, they showed c-statistics of 0.90 for sustained VT/VF and 0.91 for mortality. In silico modeling also revealed higher L-type calcium current or sodium-calcium exchanger as predominant phenotypes for VT/VF. Future studies in relation to magnetic resonance (MR) imaging-determined scar or *in vivo* optical imaging would be valuable.

Atrial fibrillation (AF) is considered to be the most common rhythm disorder sometimes presenting with serious complications such as stroke. The UK DISCOVER registry comprising primary care population of greater than 600,000 individuals was studied using an ML prediction algorithm to detect AF (Sekelj et al., 2021). Results of this retrospective cohort study showed negative predictive value of

96.7% and sensitivity of 91.8% among patients aged [3]65 years ($n = 117,965$). Attia et al. (Attia, Nose-worthy, et al., 2019) employed CNN using Keras Framework with Tensorflow backend and Python to detect electrocardiogram (ECG) signature of AF present during normal sinus rhythm using standard 10-second, 12-lead ECGs. They employed a total of more than 454,000 ECGs from almost 181,000 patients and achieved 0.9 area under the curve (AUC). These strategies can help in the development of rapid, inexpensive, point-of-care approaches to detect AF.

The widely marketed Apple Watch with proprietary AI features in conjunction with Apple iPhone was tested for its ability to detect AF. In a population of almost 420,000 participants over a median of 117 days of monitoring, the Turakhia group (Perez et al., 2019) aimed at estimating the proportion of notified participants with atrial fibrillation shown on ECG patch. Results showed that 84% of notifications were concordant with AF. To enhance the power of smartwatch towards multiple-lead ECGs, Spacca-rotella et al. (C. A. M. Spaccarotella et al., 2020) placed the Watch in different body locations to obtain 9 bipolar ECG tracings that correspond to Einthoven leads I, II, III and precordial leads, V1-V6 that were compared with simultaneous standard 12-lead ECGs. In a small population set of 100 participants, the findings offer promise by demonstrating that the device was able to record multichannel ECGs in agreement with standard ECGs with comparable ST-segment changes. Taken together, such approaches may help in timely detection and potential prevention of deadly complications including those resulting from myocardial infarction (expanded later), particularly, in asymptomatic individuals. In a case report, they were also able to show ST-segment changes reflective of the rare condition, Brugada syndrome similar to that documented in standard ECG following Ajmaline infusion in an adult male patient (C. Spaccarotella, Santarpia, Curcio, & Indolfi, 2021).

AI in CV Imaging

Imaging technologies play vital role in diagnosis and prognosis of CV diseases. With the development of ML and DL, AI has made remarkable achievements in cardiac imaging (Leiner et al., 2019). This includes improvements in imaging efficiency and quality along with automation in image analyses and interpretations to further assist in the detection and management of CV disorders.

Image Acquisition and Reconstruction

Various AI techniques including compressed sensing and real-time image processing have been applied to enhance cardiac imaging methodologies such as Cardiac CT and MR imaging in the past decade (Graff & Sidky, 2015; Kido et al., 2016; Vasanawala et al., 2010). Recently, DL models have been in-troduced to further improve medical image acquisition and reconstruction. One study (Yang, Sun, Li, & Xu, 2016) proposed a novel deep architecture, dubbed ADMM-Net, which is defined over a data flow graph from iterative procedures in Alternating Direction Method of Multipliers algorithm for optimiz-ing compressed sensing-based MRI models. Their proposed models can reconstruct MR images from a small number of under-sampled data in k-space, and thus accelerate data acquisition in MRI. Another study (Qin et al., 2019) proposed an advanced convolutional recurrent neural network model which can reconstruct high quality cardiac MR images from highly under-sampled k-space data by jointly exploiting dependencies of temporal sequences as well as iterative nature of traditional optimization algorithms. DL techniques have also shown high potential to reduce reconstruction time and improve visual image quality for highly accelerated 3D or 4D data. For example, Kustner et al. proposed a novel 4D (3D+time)

DL-based reconstruction network, termed 4D CINENet, for prospectively under-sampled 3D Cartesian CINE imaging (Küstner et al., 2020). The proposed model outperforms iterative reconstructions related to visual image quality, contrast, and reconstruction time.

Image Registration

ML and DL techniques have been applied to improve accuracy and speed for image registration as well (X. Chen, Diaz-Pinto, Ravikumar, & Frangi, 2020). DL models have been used to generate learnable, data-driven interpretations of similarity metrics, which outperform conventional similarity metrics in robustness and flexibility (Fan, Cao, Xue, & Yap, 2018; Haskins et al., 2018). Moreover, they have been widely used in estimating the parameters of spatial transformation for registration. In a study by Rohe et al., a novel fully convolutional network was proposed (Rohe, Datar, Heimann, Sermesant, & Pennec, 2017). It consists of contracting layers to detect relevant features and a symmetric expanding path that matches them together to output the transformation parametrization. The proposed model was used for inter-patient heart registration and has shown significant improvement over the state-of-the-art optimization-based algorithms. Another study (Sang & Ruan, 2020) proposed a convolutional auto-encoder network with a novel deformation representation model to achieve spatially variant conditioning on deformation vector field (DVF) for 3D cardiac MRIs, which can accomplish registration with physically and physiologically more feasible deformation vector fields, and improve the registration network performance significantly.

Image Segmentation

Image segmentation has a long history and various ML and DL approaches have been explored (Peng et al., 2016; Petitjean & Dacher, 2010). DL-based models such as CNNs, are currently the new state-of-the-art in the field (Ronneberger, Fischer, & Brox, 2015). Such DL frameworks have been successfully applied on segmentation of MR images involving cardiac chambers by using pixel-based classification. For example, a standard CNN model was used to segment short-axis cardiac MR images (Romaguera, Perdigón Romero, Costa Filho, & Costa, 2017). Another approach is to perform regression to produce smooth epicardial and endocardial contours rather than pixel classification. In a study by Du et al., a deep belief network based regression segmentation framework was proposed to delineate boundaries of bi-ventricle from cardiac MR images (Du et al., 2018).

Diagnosis and Prediction

AI has been widely used in image-based cardiac diagnosis and prediction as well (Martin-Isla et al., 2020). ML and DL models have been trained with conventional imaging indices, radiomics features, or raw imaging data for diagnosis of various types of CV diseases. In a study by Larroza et al., SVM models were used to predict myocardial infarction based on radiomics features extracted from MRI (Larroza et al., 2018). Wolterink et al. used random forest models for diagnosis of various cardiomyopathies by using conventional MRI imaging indices (Wolterink, Leiner, Viergever, & Išgum, 2018). Another study (Snaauw et al., 2019) proposed end-to-end DL models based on raw MR images for cardiac diagnoses.

AI in Heart Attack

AI and ML techniques have been successfully applied to predict risk of heart attack, also referred as myocardial infarction. Numerous studies have applied ML models to predict cardiac events primarily in patients presenting with acute coronary syndrome (ACS). For example, both basic ML models such as random forests and DL models have shown high accuracy in prediction of 1-year mortality after hospital discharge in patients with ACS (Barrett, Payrovnaziri, Bian, & He, 2019; Sherazi, Jeong, Jae, Bae, & Lee, 2019).

AI and ML techniques have also contributed to heart attack risk management. In a study by Mandair et al., a deep neural network model was trained to predict 6-month incident myocardial infarction based on harmonized electronic health record (EHR) data from more than 2 million individuals (Mandair, Tiwari, Simon, Colborn, & Rosenberg, 2020). Another study (Knott et al., 2020) applied AI techniques to predict heart attacks and strokes by using perfusion mapping to provide instantaneous quantification of myocardial perfusion based on magnetic resonance. Recently, researchers at the University of Oxford (Oikonomou et al., 2018), developed a new "CaRi-Heart technology", which can identify people at high risk of a fatal heart attack at least 5 years before it strikes. It applies a deeper observation into coronary CT angiogram scans based on DL models, and identifies a new biomarker, called Fat Radiomic Profile. This fingerprint detects biological red flags in perivascular space lining blood vessels which supply blood to the heart. It can more accurately identify inflammation, scarring and changes to these blood vessels, which are all pointers to future heart attack. This new AI tool measuring Fat Attenuation Index Score, FAI-Score is now reported to have received approval from the European Union, which can be used by physicians across the UK and Europe.

In another study (Poplin et al., 2018), scientists from Google Research discovered a new approach to assess risk of CV disease. They applied DL models to extract data using retinal fundus images from the back of patient's eyes, and predict their risk of suffering a major cardiac event, i.e., heart attack, with comparable accuracy as current leading methods based on blood test.

Another interesting multi-center cross-sectional study tried to associate facial features with increased risk of coronary artery disease (CAD) (Lin, li, Fu, & etc, 2020). A deep convolutional neural network model was successfully applied to detect CAD (at least one coronary lesion stenosis >/= 50% based on coronary angiography or coronary CT angiography) using facial images in diverse Chinese populations (5796 patients). Although specificity was not high, the algorithm yielded a sensitivity of 0.8 and an AUC of 0.73. It also outperformed scores typically used in assessing CAD pre-test probability, interestingly, the part of the face that contributed the most to the algorithm's predictions appeared to be the cheek. The proposed model can be used for pre-test CAD probability assessment in outpatient clinics or CAD screening in community.

AI in Heart Failure

Heart Failure (HF) is the decreased ability of the heart to provide sufficient blood to all parts of the body. In patients with HF, the incidence of all-cause hospitalizations is 63% (Tuppin et al., 2014) and can account for more than a third of CV deaths. HF is responsible for 30% of avoidable hospitalizations (Mercier, Georgescu, & Bousquet, 2015), and remains the leading cause of hospitalization for people over 65 years of age (Duflos et al., 2020). The prevalence of HF continues to rise over time, with aging of the population and is expected to increase by 46% by 2030 (Braunwald, 2013; Virani et al., 2021). The overall lifetime risks for HF range from 20% to 45% in those from 45 through 95 years of age. HF is the most frequent complication of MI associated with coronary artery diseases (the most common pathology behind adult CV disease) and also a critical prognostic factor. The chronic incidence of HF following MI is significantly high (Velagaleti et al., 2008). There are two broad types of HF—the well-studied HF with reduced ejection fraction (HFrEF) and the less well-understood HF with preserved ejection fraction (HFPEF). The former results in impaired ventricular systolic (contractile) function, while the latter is more prominently associated with impaired ventricular diastolic (relaxational) properties with systolic function not significantly impaired. HFpEF may be observed in about 55% of patients diagnosed with HF making it a major unmet need necessitating attention (Bursi et al., 2006).

Although the recent Sacubitril/Valsartan is considered as the first drug approved for HFPEF, the combination did not achieve primary endpoint of significantly lowering rate of total hospitalizations for heart failure and death from CV causes among patients with HF and an EF of 45% or higher based on PARAGON trial (Solomon et al., 2019). However, the current indication also serves patients who are sometimes referred as those with mid-range EF (Branca, Sbolli, Metra, & Fudim, 2020), but in the range adjacent to reduced EF. Such issues expose the complexity and the need to understand pathophysiology and biology of the umbrella of HFPEF, and AI offers the potential to study the patient population in a large-scale manner and may identify subgroups that are more suitable for available treatment options (Kitzman et al., 2010; Luo, Ahmad, & Shah, 2017; Pitt et al., 2014).

One study (Cole et al., 2015) concluded that reproducibility of visual grading of LV function and LVEF estimation of echocardiographic cine loops is dependent on image quality, however, individual operators could not themselves identify when poor image quality disrupts their LV function estimate. Nonetheless, coupled with the revolutionary point-of-care ultrasound and handheld imaging devices, AI may play important role in improving consistency, reproducibility, accuracy, accessibility and affordability. Using a CNN trained with Keras with a Tensorflow backend, a study from Mayo clinic was able to detect patients with suspected EF less than or equal to 35% with ECG alone (in the absence of prior transthoracic echocardiogram) (Attia, Kapa, et al., 2019). The study also suggested that false positives may be reduced by assessing NT-pro-BNP (an important biomarker for HF) after the initial "positive screen." Porumb et al. (Porumb, Iadanza, Massaro, & Pecchia, 2020) showed that their CNN model accurately (100%) identified congestive HF on the basis of single raw ECG heartbeat. The study trained and tested using publicly available ECG datasets with a total of over 490,000 heartbeats. In a small patient population, Nirschl et al. (Nirschl et al., 2018) tested a CNN classifier to detect clinical HF from Hematoxylin & Eosin stained whole-slide images. The algorithm was able to show 99% sensitivity and 94% specificity in detection of HF or severe pathology. The CNN was also reported to have outperformed two expert pathologists by nearly 20%.

Recently, Cerna et al. (Ulloa Cerna et al., 2021) showed that their CNN trained on raw pixel data in 812,278 echocardiographic videos from more than 34,000 individuals provided superior predictions of one-year all-cause mortality. The predictions outperformed the widely used pooled cohort equations, the Seattle Heart Failure score, and a ML model involving 58 human-derived variables from echocardiograms and EHR-derived 100 clinical variables. They also showed that cardiologists assisted by the model, while maintaining prediction specificity, substantially improved sensitivity of one-year all-cause mortality predictions by 13%.

AI in Valvular Heart Diseases

Another chronic and progressive condition in patients with CV diseases is valvular heart disease which presents with increasing prevalence especially in growing aging populations including in the Western world (J. Chen, Li, & Xiang, 2020). They may also be detected at later stages of disease development and needs novel approaches for earlier diagnosis and therapy.

Stenosis (narrowing or constriction) of heart valves is a relatively common and potentially fatal condition (Pawade, Newby, & Dweck, 2015). It is characterized by progressive fibro-calcific remodeling and thickening of the valve leaflets that evolve over years to can cause severe obstruction to cardiac blood flow. Aortic valves are crucial for directing blood flow from LV to aorta, and calcific aortic valve disease is considered to be the third most common form of heart disease. Diagnosis and staging of aortic stenosis are based on assessment of severity of obstruction and LV systolic function by doppler echocardiography and presence of symptoms (Lindman et al., 2016). Chang et al. (Chang et al., 2021) aimed to develop a DL-based algorithm for automated quantification of aortic valve calcium from non-enhanced electrocardiogram-gated cardiac CT scans. Their accuracy of DL-measured valve calcium volume for grading was 97.0% with AUC of 0.964 in the test set. In addition, accuracy of DL-measured Agatston score for grading was 92.9% with AUC of 0.933 in the test set thus outperforming radiologist reader group. In ML, weak supervision relies on noisy heuristics to programmatically generate large-scale, imperfect training labels. In order to overcome barriers to use of unlabeled biomedical repositories (e.g., UK Biobank) for supervised ML, Ashley, Ré and Priest groups (Fries et al., 2019) developed a weakly supervised DL model for classification of aortic valve malformations using up to 4,000 unlabeled cardiac MR sequences. In the orthogonal validation study using health outcomes data, their model identified individuals with a 1.8-fold increase in risk of a major adverse cardiac event.

Similar to the aortic valve, AI application has also been explored for disease of mitral valve (crucial for directing blood flow from left atrium to LV). One study aimed to generate an ML-based algorithm to predict in-hospital mortality after Transcatheter Mitral Valve Repair in a total of 849 patients (Hernandez-Suarez et al., 2021). Using random forest and SVM approaches, the authors showed that history of coronary artery disease, chronic kidney disease and smoking were the three most significant predictors of in-hospital mortality. Nonetheless, the study warrants additional studies with contemporary and more granular data to improve the model's discriminatory performance and applicability. Another study presented preliminary experience of an AI-based semiautomated software for analysis of tricuspid valve (crucial for directing blood flow from right atrium to right ventricle) (Fatima et al., 2020). The authors concluded that the software offered high correlation to surgical inspection throughout the cardiac cycle with higher reproducibility of data analysis, and reduces interobserver variability with minimal need for manual intervention.

In another study of 13,639 eligible patients extracted from the Chinese Low Intensity Anticoagulant Therapy after Heart Valve Replacement database (all 3 valves above) from 15 centers across China, the authors reported that Back Propagation Neural Network model showed promise for predicting warfarin maintenance dose after heart valve replacement compared with multiple linear regression model (Li et al., 2020). The former presented a higher ideal prediction percentage in external validation group, best prediction accuracy in intermediate-dose subgroup, high predicted percentage in high-dose subgroup and poor performance in the low-dose subgroup.

Furthermore, mobile AI-enabled stethoscopes and FDA-approved softwares used with digital stethoscopes in smartphones or computers are useful for automated detection of cardiac murmurs (unusual sounds across heart valves) including automated heart rate detection. Although they may not offer complete explanation for the decision provided and are more expensive than conventional stethoscopes (Thoenes et al., 2021), they can serve as cost-effective screening tools and reduce over-referrals to echocardiography, and can be more user- and telemedicine-friendly.

AI in Birth Heart Defects

Congenital Heart Diseases (CHD) are defects in one or more structures of the heart and associated anatomy and are generally present from birth. These can be life-threatening with significant negative impact on function of the heart, especially directionality of blood flow and oxygen saturation, and are mainly seen in pediatric population with significant hereditary component. Diagnostic and therapeutic advancements have enabled newborns with CHD to survive through childhood and well into adulthood. In addition, some disease conditions may not manifest until later in adult life. AI tools can be used for diagnostic imaging (classification and segmentation), clinical outcomes prediction and also disease prevention (Orwat, Arvanitaki, & Diller, 2021).

Diller et al. (Diller et al., 2019) studied over 10,000 patients with adult CHD from a single institution with neural network architecture designed in R using Keras and Tensorflow. Algorithms based on over 44,000 medical records categorized diagnosis, disease complexity and NYHA class with all their accuracies above 90% in the test sample. Cardiac MR offers reliable analysis of cardiac function and anatomy in CHD; however, analysis can be time-consuming. To circumvent this issue, Karimi-Bidhendi et al. (Karimi-Bidhendi et al., 2020) developed an automated deep fully convolutional network-based model showing strong agreement with manual segmentation, and no significant statistical difference was found by two independent statistical analyses.

Chest radiography with X-rays is one of the most widely used diagnostic tools across the world for CV and related disorders including CHDs. However, their predictive value can be limited by subjective and/or qualitative nature of interpretation. In a study using deep CNN approach developed by Google already trained with everyday color images from ImageNet, the diagnostic concordance rate of the DL model was significantly high (Toba et al., 2020). Although the model was not highly sensitive for detecting a high pulmonary to systemic flow ratio, the specificity was 0.95, and the AUC was 0.88.

While several genes associated with CHD have been identified and characterized so far, many more are yet to be discovered (Pierpont et al., 2018; Sifrim et al., 2016). Bicuspid aortic valve (aortic valve with only two cusps/flaps instead of three) is the most common congenital valvular heart disease (0.6%–1.0% of adult population), and is attributed to be the primary cause of about half of isolated severe aortic stenosis discussed earlier requiring aortic valve replacement. It is also frequently associated with aortic aneurysm and aortic dissection (LeMaire et al., 2011; Yutzey et al., 2014). The Srivastava group (Theodoris et al., 2021) developed a K-nearest neighbors ML algorithm approach to identify small molecules that broadly correct gene networks dysregulated in N1 haploinsufficiency in isogenic human induced pluripotent stem cell-derived endothelial cells from patients with aortic valvular stenosis and calcific aortic valve disease relevant to bicuspid valves. Gene network correction by the most efficacious therapeutic candidate (XCT790) generalized to patient-derived primary aortic valve cells and was sufficient to prevent and treat N1-dependent aortic valve disease *in vivo* in a mouse model.

AI in Basic and Biomedical CV Sciences

AI technologies have been successfully employed in the understanding of biological, developmental and preclinical aspects of CV sciences. Ahmad et al. (Ahmad et al., 2014) combined ML sequence features with chromatin immunoprecipitation data for key cardiac regulators to computationally classify cell type-specific cardiac enhancers of *Drosophila melanogaster* (fruit flies). Using these strategies, the authors identified heart regulatory elements on a genome-wide scale, their shared and unique sequence motifs, and novel cardiogenic transcription factors. They also validated computational predictions using *in vivo* experiments. In addition, they identified novel cardiac and cell type-specific regulatory motifs by clustering top-scoring classifier sequence features.

Stem cells have had a resurgence in CV research over the past two decades and development of pluripotent stem cell-derived cardiomyocytes and engineered cardiac tissues have made significant progress. The potential for applications in cardiac regeneration and drug screening is enormous. In a recent study, Lee et al. (E. K. Lee et al., 2017) described use of supervised ML to comprehensively analyze several functional parameters from force readouts of human pluripotent stem cell-derived ventricular cardiac tissue strips electrically paced at a range of frequencies and exposed to a library of drug compounds. Each contraction of the myocytes was considered as an individual data point for the ML analysis. They developed a classification model that can not only automatically determine if a compound is cardioactive, but can also predict mechanistic action of unknown cardioactive drugs.

Imaging at histological, cellular and molecular levels are becoming inevitable aspects of fundamental research in CV biology. Improvements in automating detection, localization and analyses of cellular organelles and molecules are crucial for better efficiency and quality of research. In a study by Orita et al., (Orita, Sawada, Matsumoto, & Ikegaya, 2020) the authors optically detected contractility of confluent cultured human-induced pluripotent stem-cell-derived cardiomyocytes using bright-field microscopy. They reported discrimination between functionally normal and abnormal contractions of the stem cell-derived cardiomyocytes using data preprocessing, data augmentation, dimensionality reduction and SL.

Ali et al. (Ali, Nguyen, Wang, Jiang, & Sadek, 2020) developed a proof-of-principle methodology to detect cardiomyocyte nuclei and distinguish from nonmyocyte nuclei using a global nuclear stain (DAPI) along with cardiomyocyte structural protein (troponin T) immunostained images from 8 μm-thick, frozen sections. Ground truth nuclei labeling was accomplished by immunostaining young adult alpha myosin heavy chain promoter-driven transgenic mouse cardiac tissues for Cre recombinase. Using an image-to-image DL U-net style architecture model with TensorFlow, the authors showed that the prediction closely matched expectations with an AUC of about 0.94. Further development of such models will also help in the assessment of pathological clinical samples routinely used for CV patients.

AI in CV Drug Discovery and Development

AI plays crucial roles in current drug discovery and development strategies. Many biopharmaceutical companies, including Bayer, Roche, and Pfizer have worked very closely with information technology companies from drug discovery to pharmaceutical product management (Mak & Pichika, 2018). ML algorithms such as random forest, naive Bayes, SVM as well as DL models including CNN, RNN, and autoencoder have been included in diverse sectors in CV drug discovery including drug design, chemical synthesis, polypharmacology, drug repurposing, and drug screening (Jing, Bian, Hu, Wang, & Xie,

2018; Patel, Shukla, Huang, Ussery, & Wang, 2020; Paul et al., 2020; Vamathevan et al., 2019; Yeung, Benjamins, van der Harst, & Juárez-Orozco, 2021).

In drug design, AI techniques and ML models can be used to determine drug activity, predict 3D structure of target protein and drug-protein interactions and improve the molecular de novo design. For example, studies using deep generative adversarial autoencoder or generative adversarial network with transcriptomic data have shown their potential to generate new or hit-like molecules (Kadurin, Nikolenko, Khrabrov, Aliper, & Zhavoronkov, 2017; Mendez-Lucio, Baillif, Clevert, Rouquie, & Wichard, 2020). In polypharmacology, DL models have been successfully applied to help the design of bio-specific and multi-target drug molecules. ML and DL models have been widely used in chemical synthesis studies as well such as predicting retrosynthesis pathways and designing synthetic routes. In drug screening, AI has shown advantages in prediction of toxicity, identification and classification of target cells, etc. (Lavecchia, 2019).

In late 2020, the Google AI offshoot, DeepMind presented a revolutionary breakthrough in the world of fundamental biology by developing DL algorithm to accurately predict three-dimensional structure of protein using physical and geometric constraints that determine how a protein folds (Callaway, 2020). Instead of predicting relationships between amino acids, the network predicts a target protein sequence's final structure. This, AlphaFold, has huge implications and offers optimism in the ability to develop drugs to combat numerous pathologies including CV diseases. The methodology has recently been published (Jumper et al., 2021; Tunyasuvunakool, et al., 2021) as open source code, and this could open enormous opportunities both for industry and academia to advance various fields forward.

AI in Precision CV Medicine

Precision medicine is a relatively new approach to disease prevention and treatment, which try to optimize medical care provided to individual patients by considering factors such as their genetics, environment, and lifestyle. AI and ML play especially important roles in advancing precision medicine (Ho et al., 2020; Subramanian et al., 2020). By integrating existing medical variables, multi-omics, lifestyle, and environmental data together, AI techniques have great potential to digitize future clinical trials, and discover novel therapies (Chayakrit Krittanawong, Johnson, Hershman, & Tang, 2018). They have been applied in CV medicine to explore novel genotypes and phenotypes in existing diseases, enable cost-effectiveness, improve the quality of patient care, and reduce readmission and mortality rates (Chayakrit Krittanawong, Zhang, Wang, Aydar, & Kitai, 2017).

In a study by Choi et al., RNNs with gated recurrent units were used to model temporal relations among events in EHRs, which can improve model performance in predicting initial diagnosis of HF (Choi et al., 2016). Another study (Juhola, Joutsijoki, Penttinen, & Aalto-Setälä, 2018) showed that it was possible to separate different genetic cardiac diseases on the basis of Ca^{2+} transients by using basic ML methods including KNN, Random Forest and SVM models. AI and ML techniques are commonly used in high throughput differential gene expression analyses as well, which can be used to identify genes that are altered in patients but not in controls. For example, PCA and logistic regression models were used to investigate relationship between familial hypercholesterolemia mutations and high polygenic score, to early-onset myocardial infarction (Khera et al., 2018).

In addition, ML and DL techniques have been used to advance risk prediction and patient management. For example, in a study by Zhao et al., different types of ML models including logistic regression, random forest, gradient-boosted trees, CNN, and Long-Short-Term Memories, have been applied to predict 10-year CV events, by using the features extracted from longitudinal EHRs (Zhao et al., 2019). The prediction results show that all ML models perform significantly better than the American College of Cardiology and the American Heart Association pooled cohort risk equation. Another study (Bellot & Schaar, 2018) investigated the problem of personalizing survival estimates of patients in heterogeneous populations for clinical decision support. A novel probabilistic survival model which can flexibly capture individual traits through a hierarchical latent variable formulation was proposed to enable survival prognosis in heterogeneous populations.

AI in CV Robotics

Robotic surgeries have attracted a lot of attention recently. Many systems including the laparoscopy-based Da Vinci robot, the endovascular catheter platforms such as the Corpath system, and the more electro-mechanically advanced Magellan robot, have been developed for CV surgery in the past decade. AI techniques can be used to enhance productivity and minimize scope of errors in robotic surgeries (Daglius Dias, Shah, & Zenati, 2020; Feizi, Tavakoli, Patel, & Atashzar, 2021; Jones, Reed, & Hayanga, 2020).

AI techniques can be used to improve surgical decision making by combining diverse sources of information including patient risk factors, anatomy and disease natural history. Rapid developments of computer vision, automatic control, and reinforcement learning make usage of autonomous and semi-autonomous robotic systems more realistic, which may have great potential to reduce trauma to patients, improve surgical safety and shorten hospital stays (Moustris, Hirides, Deliparaschos, & Konstantinidis, 2011). For instance, autonomous and semi-autonomous robots can provide faster and higher-accuracy procedures than surgeons, particularly for simple surgeries involving standard and repetitive operations (Shademan et al., 2016; Sousa et al., 2020). A retrospective analysis of 300 surgeries showed that integration of robotic-assisted minimally invasive direct coronary artery bypass procedures in the surgical landscape can be safely achieved and complication rates can quickly be reduced below those expected in traditional coronary artery bypass grafting (Van den Eynde et al., 2021)

Social robotics and our understanding of human-robot interactions are improving (Darling K, 2021). A recent study (Céspedes et al., 2021) investigating benefits of using socially assistive robots for long-term cardiac rehabilitation suggested that robots increase adherence and faster completion of rehabilitation program. The patients had more rapid improvement in their recovery heart rate, better physical activity performance and higher improvement in cardiovascular functioning.

Moreover, use of autonomous robots can reduce radiation exposure for clinicians performing remote procedures associated with use of digital subtraction angiography or for infectious exposures during crisis such as the COVID-19 viral pandemic.

FUTURE DIRECTIONS AND CONCLUSION

The potential of AI towards progress in CV sciences and health can be best realized by comprehensive integration of big data from various sources and aspects of both individual subjects and the environment. This could span across genomics, epigenomics, transcriptomics, proteomics, metabolomics, microbiomics, physiomics, radiomics, foodomics, etc. Realistically, even algorithms well-designed for clinical applications may face executional challenges associated with availability of high-quality, annotated and structured data for algorithm training and validation, and of data that are representative of real-world conditions.

In addition, some countries may have regulatory barriers in data sharing, privacy restrictions, intellectual property considerations or incomplete reporting. To overcome some of these challenges including improving reproducibility and credibility of ML studies, standards have been developed by different groups ("Machine learning in translation," 2021; Topol, 2020). These include Standard Protocol Items: Recommendations for Interventional Trials (SPIRIT), Consolidated Standards of Reporting Trials (CONSORT), Standards for Reporting of Diagnostic Accuracy Studies (STARD) guidelines, Checklist for Artificial Intelligence in Medical Imaging (CLAIM) best-practice guide and Proposed Requirements for CV Imaging-Related Machine Learning Evaluation (PRIME) (Cruz Rivera et al., 2020; Liu et al., 2020; Mongan, Moy, & Kahn, 2020; P. P. Sengupta et al., 2020; Sounderajah et al., 2020). The Butte group (Norgeot et al., 2020) also developed Minimum Information about Clinical Artificial Intelligence Modeling (MI-CLAIM).

The future is bright for incorporation of AI in day-to-day aspects of the CV space both in healthcare practice and continuing research. Simplification and automation using AI protocols can allow CV experts to focus their energies on more pressing questions towards the universal goal of reducing mortality and morbidity and accelerate novel biological, diagnostic and therapeutic advancements.

ACKNOWLEDGMENT

The authors need to acknowledge the work of student Vidhya Sankarasubbu at Arkansas State University who was the recipient of a 2021 Arkansas Biosciences Institute (ABI) Summer Internship Award for a funded grant proposal to work on this project.

REFERENCES

Abu Mouch, S., Roguin, A., Hellou, E., Ishai, A., Shoshan, U., Mahamid, L., Zoabi, M., Aisman, M., Goldschmid, N., & Berar Yanay, N. (2021). Myocarditis following COVID-19 mRNA vaccination. *Vaccine*, *39*(29), 3790–3793. doi:10.1016/j.vaccine.2021.05.087 PMID:34092429

Ahmad, S. M., Busser, B. W., Huang, D., Cozart, E. J., Michaud, S., Zhu, X., Jeffries, N., Aboukhalil, A., Bulyk, M. L., Ovcharenko, I., & Michelson, A. M. (2014). Machine learning classification of cell-specific cardiac enhancers uncovers developmental subnetworks regulating progenitor cell division and cell fate specification. *Development*, *141*(4), 878–888. doi:10.1242/dev.101709 PMID:24496624

Ali, S. R., Nguyen, D., Wang, B., Jiang, S., & Sadek, H. A. (2020). Deep learning identifies cardiomyocyte nuclei with high precision. *Circulation Research*, *127*(5), 696–698. doi:10.1161/CIRCRESAHA.120.316672 PMID:32486999

Altman, N. (1992). An introduction to kernel and nearest-neighbor nonparametric regression. *The American Statistician*, *46*, 175–185.

Antoniades, C., Asselbergs, F. W., & Vardas, P. (2021). The year in cardiovascular medicine 2020: Digital health and innovation. *European Heart Journal*, *42*(7), 732–739. doi:10.1093/eurheartj/ehaa1065 PMID:33388767

Attia, Z. I., Kapa, S., Yao, X., Lopez-Jimenez, F., Mohan, T. L., Pellikka, P. A., Carter, R. E., Shah, N. D., Friedman, P. A., & Noseworthy, P. A. (2019). Prospective validation of a deep learning electrocardiogram algorithm for the detection of left ventricular systolic dysfunction. *Journal of Cardiovascular Electrophysiology*, *30*(5), 668–674. doi:10.1111/jce.13889 PMID:30821035

Attia, Z. I., Noseworthy, P. A., Lopez-Jimenez, F., Asirvatham, S. J., Deshmukh, A. J., Gersh, B. J., Carter, R. E., Yao, X., Rabinstein, A. A., Erickson, B. J., Kapa, S., & Friedman, P. A. (2019). An artificial intelligence-enabled ECG algorithm for the identification of patients with atrial fibrillation during sinus rhythm: A retrospective analysis of outcome prediction. *Lancet*, *394*(10201), 861–867. doi:10.1016/S0140-6736(19)31721-0 PMID:31378392

Barrett, L., Payrovnaziri, S. N., Bian, J., & He, Z. (2019). Building computational models to predict one-year mortality in ICU patients with acute myocardial infarction and post myocardial infarction syndrome. *AMIA Joint Summits on Translational Science Proceedings. AMIA Joint Summits on Translational Science*, *2019*, 407–416. PMID:31258994

Bellot, A., & Schaar, M. (2019). A hierarchical Bayesian model for personalized survival predictions. *IEEE Journal of Biomedical and Health Informatics*, *23*(1), 72–80. doi:10.1109/JBHI.2018.2832599 PMID:29994056

Bengio, Y., Courville, A. C., & Vincent, P. (2013). Representation learning: A review and new perspectives. *IEEE Transactions on Pattern Analysis and Machine Intelligence*, *35*(8), 1798–1828. doi:10.1109/TPAMI.2013.50 PMID:23787338

Bengio, Y., Simard, P., & Frasconi, P. (1994). Learning long-term dependencies with gradient descent is difficult. *IEEE Transactions on Neural Networks*, *5*(2), 157–166. doi:10.1109/72.279181 PMID:18267787

Benjamins, J. W., Hendriks, T., Knuuti, J., Juarez-Orozco, L. E., & van der Harst, P. (2019). A primer in artificial intelligence in cardiovascular medicine. *Netherlands Heart Journal; Monthly Journal of the Netherlands Society of Cardiology and the Netherlands Heart Foundation*, *27*(9), 392–402. doi:10.100712471-019-1286-6 PMID:31111458

Boser, B. E., Guyon, I. M., & Vapnik, V. N. (1992). A training algorithm for optimal margin classifiers. *Proceedings of the Fifth Annual ACM Workshop on Computational Learning Theory*, 144-152. 10.1145/130385.130401

Branca, L., Sbolli, M., Metra, M., & Fudim, M. (2020). Heart failure with mid-range ejection fraction: Pro and cons of the new classification of heart failure by European Society of Cardiology guidelines. *ESC Heart Failure*, *7*(2), 381–399. doi:10.1002/ehf2.12586 PMID:32239646

Braunwald, E. (2013). Heart failure. *JACC. Heart Failure*, *1*(1), 1–20. doi:10.1016/j.jchf.2012.10.002 PMID:24621794

Bursi, F., Weston, S. A., Redfield, M. M., Jacobsen, S. J., Pakhomov, S., Nkomo, V. T., Meverden, R. A., & Roger, V. L. (2006). Systolic and diastolic heart failure in the community. *Journal of the American Medical Association*, *296*(18), 2209–2216. doi:10.1001/jama.296.18.2209 PMID:17090767

Caballé, N., Castillo-Sequera, J., Gomez-Pulido, J. A., Gómez, J., & Polo-Luque, M. (2020). Machine learning applied to diagnosis of human diseases: A systematic review. *Applied Sciences (Basel, Switzerland), 10*(15), 5135. Advance online publication. doi:10.3390/app10155135

Callaway, E. (2020). 'It will change everything': DeepMind's AI makes gigantic leap in solving protein structures. *Nature, 588*(7837), 203–204. doi:10.1038/d41586-020-03348-4 PMID:33257889

Céspedes, N., Irfan, B., Senft, E., Cifuentes, C. A., Gutierrez, L. F., Rincon-Roncancio, M., Belpaeme, T., & Múnera, M. (2021). A socially assistive robot for long-term cardiac rehabilitation in the real world. *Frontiers in Neurobototics, 15*, 1–19. doi:10.3389/fnbot.2021.633248 PMID:33828473

Chang, S., Kim, H., Suh, Y. J., Choi, D. M., Kim, H., Kim, D. K., Kim, J. Y., Yoo, J. Y., & Choi, B. W. (2021). Development of a deep learning-based algorithm for the automatic detection and quantification of aortic valve calcium. *European Journal of Radiology, 137*, 109582. Advance online publication. doi:10.1016/j.ejrad.2021.109582 PMID:33578089

Chen, J., Li, W., & Xiang, M. (2020). Burden of valvular heart disease, 1990-2017: Results from the Global Burden of Disease Study 2017. *Journal of Global Health, 10*(2), 020404. Advance online publication. doi:10.7189/jogh.10.020404 PMID:33110570

Chen, X., Diaz-Pinto, A., Ravikumar, N., & Frangi, A. F. (2020). Deep learning in medical image registration. *Progress in Biomedical Engineering, 3*(1). Advance online publication. doi:10.1088/2516-1091/abd37c

Cho, K., van Merrienboer, B., Gulcehre, C., Bahdanau, D., Bougares, F., Schwenk, H., & Bengio, Y. (2014). Learning phrase representations using RNN Encoder-Decoder for statistical machine translation. *arXivLabs*. https://arxiv.org/abs/1406.1078v3

Choi, E., Schuetz, A., Stewart, W., & Sun, J. (2016). Using recurrent neural network models for early detection of heart failure onset. *Journal of the American Medical Informatics Association: JAMIA, 24*(2), 361–370. doi:10.1093/jamia/ocw112 PMID:27521897

Chung, M. K., Zidar, D. A., Bristow, M. R., Cameron, S. J., Chan, T., Harding, C. V. III, Kwon, D. H., Singh, T., Tilton, J. C., Tsai, E. J., Tucker, N. R., Bernard, J., & Loscalzo, J. (2021). COVID-19 and cardiovascular disease: From bench to bedside. *Circulation Research, 128*(8), 1214–1236. doi:10.1161/CIRCRESAHA.121.317997 PMID:33856918

Cole, G. D., Dhutia, N. M., Shun-Shin, M. J., Willson, K., Harrison, J., Raphael, C. E., Zolgharni, M., Mayet, J., & Francis, D. P. (2015). Defining the real-world reproducibility of visual grading of left ventricular function and visual estimation of left ventricular ejection fraction: Impact of image quality, experience and accreditation. *The International Journal of Cardiovascular Imaging, 31*(7), 1303–1314. doi:10.100710554-015-0659-1 PMID:26141526

Cruz Rivera, S., Liu, X., Chan, A.-W., Denniston, A. K., Calvert, M. J., Darzi, A., Holmes, C., Yau, C., Moher, D., Ashrafian, H., Deeks, J. J., Ferrante di Ruffano, L., Faes, L., Keane, P. A., Vollmer, S. J., Lee, A. Y., Jonas, A., Esteva, A., Beam, A. L., ... Rowley, S. (2020). Guidelines for clinical trial protocols for interventions involving artificial intelligence: The SPIRIT-AI extension. *Nature Medicine, 26*(9), 1351–1363. doi:10.103841591-020-1037-7 PMID:32908284

Cutler, A., Cutler, D. R., & Stevens, J. R. (2012) Random forests. In C. Zhang & Y. Ma (Eds.), Ensemble Machine Learning (pp. 157-175). Springer. doi:10.1007/978-1-4419-9326-7_5

Daniel, G. G. (2013). Artificial Neural Network. In A. L. C. Runehov & L. Oviedo (Eds.), *Encyclopedia of Sciences and Religions*. Springer. doi:10.1007/978-1-4020-8265-8_200980

Darling, K. (2021). *The new breed: What our history with animals reveals about our future with robots.* Henry Holt and Company.

Deng, L. (2014). A tutorial survey of architectures, algorithms, and applications for deep learning. *APSIPA Transactions on Signal and Information Processing*, *3*(E2), e2. Advance online publication. doi:10.1017/atsip.2013.9

Dias, R. D., Shah, J., & Zenati, M. A. (2020). Artificial intelligence in cardiothoracic surgery. *Minerva Cardioangiologica*, *68*(5), 532–538. doi:10.23736/S0026-4725.20.05235-4 PMID:32989966

Diller, G.-P., Kempny, A., Babu-Narayan, S. V., Henrichs, M., Brida, M., Uebing, A., Lammers, A. E., Baumgartner, H., Li, W., Wort, S. J., Dimopoulos, K., & Gatzoulis, M. A. (2019). Machine learning algorithms estimating prognosis and guiding therapy in adult congenital heart disease: Data from a single tertiary centre including 10 019 patients. *European Heart Journal*, *40*(13), 1069–1077. doi:10.1093/eurheartj/ehy915 PMID:30689812

Du, X., Zhang, W., Zhang, H., Chen, J., Zhang, Y., Warrington, J. C., Brahm, G., & Li, S. (2018). Deep regression segmentation for cardiac bi-ventricle MR images. *IEEE Access: Practical Innovations, Open Solutions*, *6*, 3828–3838. doi:10.1109/ACCESS.2017.2789179

Duflos, C., Troude, P., Strainchamps, D., Segouin, C., Logeart, D., & Mercier, G. (2020). Hospitalization for acute heart failure: The in-hospital care pathway predicts one-year readmission. *Scientific Reports*, *10*(1), 10644. Advance online publication. doi:10.103841598-020-66788-y PMID:32606326

Enriko, I. K. A., Suryanegara, M., & Gunawan, D. (2016). Heart disease prediction system using k-nearest neighbor algorithm with simplified patient's health parameters. *Journal of Telecommunication. Electronic and Computer Engineering*, *8*(12), 59–65.

Eom, J.-H., Kim, S.-C., & Zhang, B.-T. (2008). AptaCDSS-E: A classifier ensemble-based clinical decision support system for cardiovascular disease level prediction. *Expert Systems with Applications*, *34*(4), 2465–2479. doi:10.1016/j.eswa.2007.04.015

Fan, J., Cao, X., Xue, Z., Yap, P. T., & Shen, D. (2018). Adversarial similarity network for evaluating image alignment in deep learning based registration. In A. Frangi, J. Schnabel, C. Davatzikos, C. Alberola-López, & G. Fichtinger (Eds.), *MICCAI 2018. Lecture notes in computer science, 11070.* Medical image computing and computer assisted intervention. Springer. doi:10.1007/978-3-030-00928-1_83

Farshidfar, F., Koleini, N., & Ardehali, H. (2021). Cardiovascular complications of COVID-19. *JCI Insight*, *6*(13), e148980. Advance online publication. doi:10.1172/jci.insight.148980 PMID:34061779

Fatima, H., Mahmood, F., Sehgal, S., Belani, K., Sharkey, A., Chaudhary, O., Baribeau, Y., Matyal, R., & Khabbaz, K. R. (2020). Artificial intelligence for dynamic echocardiographic tricuspid valve analysis: A new tool in echocardiography. *Journal of Cardiothoracic and Vascular Anesthesia, 34*(10), 2703–2706. doi:10.1053/j.jvca.2020.04.056 PMID:32540242

Feizi, N., Tavakoli, M., Patel, R., & Atashzar, S. (2021). Robotics and AI for teleoperation, tele-assessment, and tele-training for surgery in the era of COVID-19: Existing challenges and future vision. *Frontiers in Robotics and AI, 8*, 610677. Advance online publication. doi:10.3389/frobt.2021.610677 PMID:33937347

Freund, Y., Iyer, R., Schapire, R. E., & Singer, Y. (2003). An efficient boosting algorithm for combining preferences. *Journal of Machine Learning Research, 4*, 933–969.

Fries, J. A., Varma, P., Chen, V. S., Xiao, K., Tejeda, H., Saha, P., Dunnmon, J., Chubb, H., Maskatia, S., Fiterau, M., Delp, S., Ashley, E., Ré, C., & Priest, J. R. (2019). Weakly supervised classification of aortic valve malformations using unlabeled cardiac MRI sequences. *Nature Communications, 10*(1), 3111. Advance online publication. doi:10.103841467-019-11012-3 PMID:31308376

Gedefaw, L., Ullah, S., Leung, P. H. M., Cai, Y., Yip, S. P., & Huang, C. L. (2021). Inflammasome activation-induced hypercoagulopathy: Impact on cardiovascular dysfunction triggered in COVID-19 patients. *Cells, 10*(4), 916. doi:10.3390/cells10040916 PMID:33923537

Gortmaker, S. L., Hosmer, D. W., & Lemeshow, S. (2013). Applied Logistic Regression. *Contemporary Sociology, 23*, 89–151. Advance online publication. doi:10.1002/9781118548387.ch4

Graff, C. G., & Sidky, E. Y. (2015). Compressive sensing in medical imaging. *Applied Optics, 54*(8), C23–C44. doi:10.1364/AO.54.000C23 PMID:25968400

Guo, Q., Lu, X., Gao, Y., Zhang, J., Yan, B., Su, D., Song, A., Zhao, X., & Wang, G. (2017). Cluster analysis: A new approach for identification of underlying risk factors for coronary artery disease in essential hypertensive patients. *Scientific Reports, 7*(1), 43965. Advance online publication. doi:10.1038rep43965 PMID:28266630

Haskins, G., Kruecker, J., Kruger, U., Xu, S., Pinto, P. A., Wood, B. J., & Yan, P. (2018). Learning deep similarity metric for 3D MR–TRUS image registration. *International Journal of Computer Assisted Radiology and Surgery, 14*(3), 417–425. doi:10.100711548-018-1875-7 PMID:30382457

Hernandez-Suarez, D. F., Ranka, S., Kim, Y., Latib, A., Wiley, J., Lopez-Candales, A., Pinto, D. S., Gonzalez, M. D., Ramakrishna, H., Sanina, C., Nieves-Rodriguez, B. G., Rodriguez-Maldonado, J., Maldonado, R. F., Rodriguez-Ruiz, I. J., da Luz Sant'Ana, I., Wiley, K. A., Cox-Alomar, P., Villablanca, P. A., & Roche-Lima, A. (2021). Machine-learning-based in-hospital mortality prediction for transcatheter mitral valve repair in the United States. *Cardiovascular Revascularization Medicine, 22*, 22–28. doi:10.1016/j.carrev.2020.06.017 PMID:32591310

Hinton, G., & Sejnowski, T. J. (1999). *Unsupervised learning: Foundations of neural computation.* Bradford Books. doi:10.7551/mitpress/7011.001.0001

Ho, D., Quake, S. R., McCabe, E. R. B., Chng, W. J., Chow, E. K., Ding, X., Gelb, B. D., Ginsburg, G. S., Hassenstab, J., Ho, C.-M., Mobley, W. C., Nolan, G. P., Rosen, S. T., Tan, P., Yen, Y., & Zarrinpar, A. (2020). Enabling technologies for personalized and precision medicine. *Trends in Biotechnology*, *38*(5), 497–518. doi:10.1016/j.tibtech.2019.12.021 PMID:31980301

Hochreiter, S., & Schmidhuber, J. (1997). Long short-term memory. *Neural Computation*, *9*(8), 1735–1780. doi:10.1162/neco.1997.9.8.1735 PMID:9377276

Hubel, D. H., & Wiesel, T. N. (1962). Receptive fields, binocular interaction and functional architecture in the cat's visual cortex. *The Journal of Physiology*, *160*(1), 106–154. doi:10.1113/jphysiol.1962.sp006837 PMID:14449617

Ismail, B., & Anil, M. (2014). Regression methods for analyzing the risk factors for a life style disease among the young population of India. *Indian Heart Journal*, *66*(6), 587–592. doi:10.1016/j.ihj.2014.05.027 PMID:25634389

Jing, Y., Bian, Y., Hu, Z., Wang, L., & Xie, X.-Q. (2018). Deep learning for drug design: An artificial intelligence paradigm for drug discovery in the big data era. *The AAPS Journal*, *20*(3), 58–58. doi:10.120812248-018-0210-0 PMID:29603063

Jones, B., Reed, B., & Hayanga, J. W. A. (2020). Autonomously driven: Artificial intelligence in cardiothoracic surgery. *The Annals of Thoracic Surgery*, *110*(2), 373. doi:10.1016/j.athoracsur.2020.02.074 PMID:32277880

Juhola, M., Joutsijoki, H., Penttinen, K., & Aalto-Setälä, K. (2018). Detection of genetic cardiac diseases by Ca^{2+} transient profiles using machine learning methods. *Scientific Reports*, *8*(1), 9355. Advance online publication. doi:10.103841598-018-27695-5 PMID:29921843

Jumper, J., Evans, R., Pritzel, A., Green, T., Figurnov, M., Ronneberger, O., Tunyasuvunakool, K., Bates, R., Žídek, A., Potapenko, A., Bridgland, A., Meyer, C., Kohl, S. A. A., Ballard, A. J., Cowie, A., Romera-Paredes, B., Nikolov, S., Jain, R., Adler, J., ... Hassabis, D. (2021). Highly accurate protein structure prediction with AlphaFold. *Nature*, *596*(7873), 583–589. doi:10.103841586-021-03819-2 PMID:34265844

Kadurin, A., Nikolenko, S., Khrabrov, K., Aliper, A., & Zhavoronkov, A. (2017). druGAN: An advanced generative adversarial autoencoder model for de novo generation of new molecules with desired molecular properties in Silico. *Molecular Pharmaceutics*, *14*(9), 3098–3104. doi:10.1021/acs.molpharmaceut.7b00346 PMID:28703000

Karimi-Bidhendi, S., Arafati, A., Cheng, A. L., Wu, Y., Kheradvar, A., & Jafarkhani, H. (2020). Fully-automated deep-learning segmentation of pediatric cardiovascular magnetic resonance of patients with complex congenital heart diseases. *Journal of Cardiovascular Magnetic Resonance*, *22*(1), 80. Advance online publication. doi:10.118612968-020-00678-0 PMID:33256762

Khera, A. V., Chaffin, M., Zekavat, S. M., Collins, R. L., Roselli, C., Natarajan, P., Lichtman, J. H., D'Onofrio, G., Mattera, J., Dreyer, R., Spertus, J. A., Taylor, K. D., Psaty, B. M., Rich, S. S., Post, W., Gupta, N., Gabriel, S., Lander, E., Chen, Y.-D. I., ... Kathiresan, S. (2018). Whole-genome sequencing to characterize monogenic and polygenic contributions in patients hospitalized with early-onset myocardial infarction. *Circulation*, *139*(13), 1593–1602. doi:10.1161/CIRCULATIONAHA.118.035658 PMID:30586733

Kido, T., Kido, T., Nakamura, M., Kouki, W., Schmidt, M., Forman, C., & Mochizuki, T. (2016). Compressed sensing real-time cine cardiovascular magnetic resonance: Accurate assessment of left ventricular function in a single-breath-hold. *Journal of Cardiovascular Magnetic Resonance*, *18*(1), 50. Advance online publication. doi:10.118612968-016-0271-0 PMID:27553656

Kitzman, D. W., Hundley, W. G., Brubaker, P. H., Morgan, T. M., Moore, J. B., Stewart, K. P., & Little, W. C. (2010). A randomized double-blind trial of enalapril in older patients with heart failure and preserved ejection fraction: Effects on exercise tolerance and arterial distensibility. *Circulation: Heart Failure*, *3*(4), 477–485. doi:10.1161/CIRCHEARTFAILURE.109.898916 PMID:20516425

Knott, K., Seraphim, A., Augusto, J., Xue, H., Chacko, L., Aung, N., Petersen, S. E., Cooper, J. A., Manisty, C., Bhuva, A. N., Kotecha, T., Bourantas, C. V., Davies, R. H., Brown, L. A. E., Plein, S., Fontana, M., Kellman, P., & Moon, J. (2020). The prognostic significance of quantitative myocardial perfusion: An artificial intelligence-based approach using perfusion mapping. *Circulation*, *141*(16), 1282–1291. doi:10.1161/CIRCULATIONAHA.119.044666 PMID:32078380

Krittanawong, C., Johnson, K. W., Hershman, S. G., & Tang, W. H. W. (2018). Big data, artificial intelligence and cardiovascular precision medicine. *Expert Review of Precision Medicine and Drug Development*, *3*(5), 305–317. doi:10.1080/23808993.2018.1528871

Krittanawong, C., Johnson, K. W., Rosenson, R. S., Wang, Z., Aydar, M., Baber, U., Min, J. K., Tang, W. H. W., Halperin, J. L., & Narayan, S. M. (2019). Deep learning for cardiovascular medicine: A practical primer. *European Heart Journal*, *40*(25), 2058–2073. doi:10.1093/eurheartj/ehz056 PMID:30815669

Krittanawong, C., Zhang, H., Wang, Z., Aydar, M., & Kitai, T. (2017). Artificial intelligence in precision cardiovascular medicine. *Journal of the American College of Cardiology*, *69*(21), 2657–2664. doi:10.1016/j.jacc.2017.03.571 PMID:28545640

Kuncheva, L. I., & Whitaker, C. J. (2003). Measures of diversity in classifier ensembles and their relationship with the ensemble accuracy. *Machine Learning*, *51*(2), 181–207. doi:10.1023/A:1022859003006

Küstner, T., Fuin, N., Hammernik, K., Bustin, A., Qi, H., Hajhosseiny, R., Masci, P. G., Neji, R., Rueckert, D., Botnar, R. M., & Prieto, C. (2020). CINENet: Deep learning-based 3D cardiac CINE MRI reconstruction with multi-coil complex-valued 4D spatio-temporal convolutions. *Scientific Reports*, *10*(1), 13710. Advance online publication. doi:10.103841598-020-70551-8 PMID:32792507

Larroza, A., López-Lereu, M. P., Monmeneu, J. G., Gavara, J., Chorro, F. J., Bodí, V., & Moratal, D. (2018). Texture analysis of cardiac cine magnetic resonance imaging to detect non-viable segments in patients with chronic myocardial infarction. *Medical Physics*, *45*(4), 1471–1480. doi:10.1002/mp.12783 PMID:29389013

Lavecchia, A. (2019). Deep learning in drug discovery: Opportunities, challenges and future prospects. *Drug Discovery Today, 24*(10), 2017–2032. doi:10.1016/j.drudis.2019.07.006 PMID:31377227

LeCun, Y., Bengio, Y., & Hinton, G. (2015). Deep learning. *Nature, 521*(7553), 436–444. doi:10.1038/nature14539 PMID:26017442

Lee, E. K., Tran, D. D., Keung, W., Chan, P., Wong, G., Chan, C. W., Costa, K. D., Li, R. A., & Khine, M. (2017). Machine learning of human pluripotent stem cell-derived engineered cardiac tissue contractility for automated drug classification. *Stem Cell Reports, 9*(5), 1560–1572. doi:10.1016/j.stemcr.2017.09.008 PMID:29033305

Lee, J. H., Ó Hartaigh, B., Han, D., Rizvi, A., Lin, F. Y., & Min, J. K. (2016). Fractional flow reserve measurement by computed tomography: An alternative to the stress test. *Interventional Cardiology (London, England), 11*(2), 105–109. doi:10.15420/icr.2016:1:2 PMID:29588715

Leiner, T., Rueckert, D., Suinesiaputra, A., Baeßler, B., Nezafat, R., Išgum, I., & Young, A. A. (2019). Machine learning in cardiovascular magnetic resonance: Basic concepts and applications. *Journal of Cardiovascular Magnetic Resonance, 21*(1), 61. Advance online publication. doi:10.118612968-019-0575-y PMID:31590664

LeMaire, S. A., McDonald, M.-L. N., Guo, D. C., Russell, L., Miller, C. C. III, Johnson, R. J., Bekheirnia, M. R., Franco, L. M., Nguyen, M., Pyeritz, R. E., Baravia, J. E., Devereux, R., & Maslen, C. (2011). Genome-wide association study identifies a susceptibility locus for thoracic aortic aneurysms and aortic dissections spanning FBN1 at 15q21.1. *Nature Genetics, 43*(10), 996–1000. doi:10.1038/ng.934 PMID:21909107

Li, Q., Wang, J., Tao, H., Zhou, Q., Chen, J., Fu, B., Qin, W. Z., Li, D., Hou, J. L., & Zhang, W. H. (2020). The prediction model of warfarin individual maintenance dose for patients undergoing heart valve replacement, based on the Back Propagation Neural Network. *Clinical Drug Investigation, 40*(1), 41–53. doi:10.100740261-019-00850-0 PMID:31586305

Lin, S., Li, Z., Fu, B., Chen, S., Li, X., Wang, Y., Wang, X., Lv, B., Xu, B., Song, X., Zhang, Y.-J., Cheng, X., Huang, W., Pu, J., Zhang, Q., Xia, Y., Du, B., Ji, X., & Zheng, Z. (2020). Feasibility of using deep learning to detect coronary artery disease based on facial photo. *European Heart Journal, 41*(46), 4400–4411. doi:10.1093/eurheartj/ehaa640 PMID:32818267

Lindman, B. R., Clavel, M.-A., Mathieu, P., Iung, B., Lancellotti, P., Otto, C. M., & Pibarot, P. (2016). Calcific aortic stenosis. *Nature Reviews Disease Primers, 2. Artricle, 16006*(1). Advance online publication. doi:10.1038/nrdp.2016.6 PMID:27188578

Liu, X., Cruz Rivera, S., Moher, D., Calvert, M. J., Denniston, A. K., Ashrafian, H., Beam, A. L., Chan, A.-W., Collins, G. S., Deeks, A. D. J. J., ElZarrad, M. K., Espinoza, C., Esteva, A., Faes, L., Ferrante di Ruffano, L., Fletcher, J., Golub, R., Harvey, H., Haug, C., ... Yau, C. (2020). Reporting guidelines for clinical trial reports for interventions involving artificial intelligence: The CONSORT-AI extension. *The Lancet. Digital Health, 2*(10), e537–e548. doi:10.1016/S2589-7500(20)30218-1 PMID:33328048

Luo, Y., Ahmad, F. S., & Shah, S. J. (2017). Tensor factorization for precision medicine in heart failure with preserved ejection fraction. *Journal of Cardiovascular Translational Research, 10*(3), 305–312. doi:10.100712265-016-9727-8 PMID:28116551

Machine learning in translation [Editorial]. (2021). *Nature Biomedical Engineering, 5*, 485–486. doi:10.1038/s41551-021-00758-1

Mak, K.-K., & Pichika, M. R. (2018). Artificial intelligence in drug development: Present status and future prospects. *Drug Discovery Today, 24*(3), 773–780. doi:10.1016/j.drudis.2018.11.014 PMID:30472429

Mandair, D., Tiwari, P., Simon, S., Colborn, K. L., & Rosenberg, M. A. (2020). Prediction of incident myocardial infarction using machine learning applied to harmonized electronic health record data. *BMC Medical Informatics and Decision Making, 20*(1), 252. Advance online publication. doi:10.118612911-020-01268-x PMID:33008368

Martin-Isla, C., Campello, V. M., Izquierdo, C., Raisi-Estabragh, Z., Baeßler, B., Petersen, S. E., & Lekadir, K. (2020). Image-based cardiac diagnosis with machine learning: A review. *Frontiers in Cardiovascular Medicine, 7*(1), 1. Advance online publication. doi:10.3389/fcvm.2020.00001 PMID:32039241

Mathur, P., Srivastava, S., Xu, X., & Mehta, J. L. (2020). Artificial intelligence, machine learning, and cardiovascular disease. *Clinical Medicine Insights. Cardiology, 14*. Advance online publication. doi:10.1177/1179546820927404 PMID:32952403

Méndez-Lucio, O., Baillif, B., Clevert, D.-A., Rouquie, D., & Wichard, J. (2020). De novo generation of hit-like molecules from gene expression signatures using artificial intelligence. *Nature Communications, 11*(1), 10. Advance online publication. doi:10.103841467-019-13807-w PMID:31900408

Mercier, G., Georgescu, V., & Bousquet, J. (2015). Geographic variation in potentially avoidable hospitalizations in France. *Health Affairs, 34*(5), 836–843. doi:10.1377/hlthaff.2014.1065 PMID:25941286

Miranda, E., Irwansyah, E., Amelga, A. Y., Maribondang, M. M., & Salim, M. (2016). Detection of cardiovascular disease risk's level for adults using naive Bayes classifier. *Healthcare Informatics Research, 22*(3), 196–205. doi:10.4258/hir.2016.22.3.196 PMID:27525161

Mitchell, T. M. (1997). *Machine learning.* McGraw-Hill.

Mongan, J., Moy, L., & Kahn, C. E. Jr. (2020). Checklist for Artificial Intelligence in Medical Imaging (CLAIM): A guide for authors and reviewers. *Radiology. Artificial Intelligence, 2*(2), e200029. doi:10.1148/ryai.2020200029 PMID:33937821

Moustris, G. P., Hirides, S. C., Deliparaschos, K. M., & Konstantinidis, K. M. (2011). Evolution of autonomous and semi-autonomous robotic surgical systems: A review of the literature. *International Journal of Medical Robotics and Computer Assisted Surgery, 7*(4), 375–392. doi:10.1002/rcs.408 PMID:21815238

Nahar, J., Imam, T., Tickle, K. S., & Chen, Y.-P. P. (2013). Association rule mining to detect factors which contribute to heart disease in males and females. *Expert Systems with Applications, 40*(4), 1086–1093. doi:10.1016/j.eswa.2012.08.028

Nirschl, J. J., Janowczyk, A., Peyster, E. G., Frank, R., Margulies, K. B., Feldman, M. D., & Madabhushi, A. (2018). A deep-learning classifier identifies patients with clinical heart failure using whole-slide images of H&E tissue. *PLoS One*, *13*(4), e0192726. doi:10.1371/journal.pone.0192726 PMID:29614076

Nishiga, M., Wang, D. W., Han, Y., Lewis, D. B., & Wu, J. C. (2020). COVID-19 and cardiovascular disease: From basic mechanisms to clinical perspectives. *Nature Reviews. Cardiology*, *17*(9), 543–558. doi:10.103841569-020-0413-9 PMID:32690910

Norgeot, B., Quer, G., Beaulieu-Jones, B. K., Torkamani, A., Dias, R., Gianfrancesco, M., Arnaout, R., Kohane, I. S., Saria, S., Topol, E., Obermeyer, Z., Yu, B., & Butte, A. J. (2020). Minimum information about clinical artificial intelligence modeling: The MI-CLAIM checklist. *Nature Medicine*, *26*(9), 1320–1324. doi:10.103841591-020-1041-y PMID:32908275

Oikonomou, E. K., Mohamed, M. M., Desai, M. Y., Mancio, J., Alashi, A., Hutt, E., Centeno, E. H., Thomas, S., Herdman, L., Kotanidis, C. P., Thomas, K. E., Griffin, B. P., Flamm, S. D., Antonopoulos, A. S., Shirodaria, C., Sabharwal, N., Deanfield, J., Neubauer, S., Hopewell, J. C., ... Antoniades, C. (2018). Non-invasive detection of coronary inflammation using computed tomography and prediction of residual cardiovascular risk (the CRISP CT study): A post-hoc analysis of prospective outcome data. *Lancet*, *392*(10151), 929–939. doi:10.1016/S0140-6736(18)31114-0 PMID:30170852

Olurotimi, O. (1994). Recurrent neural network training with feedforward complexity. *IEEE Transactions on Neural Networks*, *5*(2), 185–197. doi:10.1109/72.279184 PMID:18267790

Orita, K., Sawada, K., Matsumoto, N., & Ikegaya, Y. (2020). Machine-learning-based quality control of contractility of cultured human-induced pluripotent stem-cell-derived cardiomyocytes. *Biochemical and Biophysical Research Communications*, *526*(3), 751–755. doi:10.1016/j.bbrc.2020.03.141 PMID:32265031

Orwat, S., Arvanitaki, A., & Diller, G. P. (2021). A new approach to modelling in adult congenital heart disease: Artificial intelligence. *Revista Espanola de Cardiologia*, *74*(7), 573–575. doi:10.1016/j.recesp.2020.12.009 PMID:33478913

Patel, L., Shukla, T., Huang, X., Ussery, D. W., & Wang, S. (2020). Machine learning methods in drug discovery. *Molecules (Basel, Switzerland)*, *25*(22), 5277. doi:10.3390/molecules25225277 PMID:33198233

Patil, M., Singh, S., Henderson, J., & Krishnamurthy, P. (2021). Mechanisms of COVID-19-induced cardiovascular disease: Is sepsis or exosome the missing link? *Journal of Cellular Physiology*, *236*(5), 3366–3382. doi:10.1002/jcp.30109 PMID:33078408

Paul, D., Sanap, G., Shenoy, S., Kalyane, D., Kalia, K., & Tekade, R. K. (2020). Artificial intelligence in drug discovery and development. *Drug Discovery Today*, *26*(1), 80–93. doi:10.1016/j.drudis.2020.10.010 PMID:33099022

Pawade, T. A., Newby, D. E., & Dweck, M. R. (2015). Calcification in aortic stenosis: The skeleton key. *Journal of the American College of Cardiology*, *66*(5), 561–577. doi:10.1016/j.jacc.2015.05.066 PMID:26227196

Peng, P., Lekadir, K., Gooya, A., Shao, L., Petersen, S. E., & Frangi, A. F. (2016). A review of heart chamber segmentation for structural and functional analysis using cardiac magnetic resonance imaging. *Magnetic Resonance Materials in Physics. Biology and Medicine (Aligarh)*, *29*(2), 155–195. doi:10.100710334-015-0521-4 PMID:26811173

Perez, M. V., Mahaffey, K. W., Hedlin, H., Rumsfeld, J. S., Garcia, A., Ferris, T., Balasubramanian, V., Russo, A. M., Rajmane, A., Cheung, L., Hung, G., Lee, J., Kowey, P., Talati, N., Nag, D., Gummidipundi, S. E., Beatty, A., Hills, M. T., Desai, S., ... Turakhia, M. P. (2019). Large-scale assessment of a smartwatch to identify atrial fibrillation. *The New England Journal of Medicine*, *381*(20), 1909–1917. doi:10.1056/NEJMoa1901183 PMID:31722151

Petitjean, C., & Dacher, J.-N. (2010). A review of segmentation methods in short axis cardiac MR images. *Medical Image Analysis*, *15*(2), 169–184. doi:10.1016/j.media.2010.12.004 PMID:21216179

Pierpont, M. E., Brueckner, M., Chung, W. K., Garg, V., Lacro, R. V., McGuire, A. L., Mital, S., Priest, J. R., Pu, W. T., Roberts, A., Ware, S. M., Gelb, B. D., & Russell, M. W. (2018). Genetic basis for congenital heart disease: Revisited: A scientific statement from the American Heart Association. *Circulation*, *138*(21), e653–e711. doi:10.1161/CIR.0000000000000606 PMID:30571578

Pitt, B., Pfeffer, M. A., Assmann, S. F., Boineau, R., Anand, I. S., Claggett, B., Clausell, N., Desai, A. S., Diaz, R., Fleg, J. L., Gordeev, I., Harty, B., Heitner, J. F., Kenwood, C. T., Lewis, E. F., O'Meara, E., Probstfield, J. L., Shaburishvili, T., Shah, S. J., ... McKinlay, S. M. (2014). Spironolactone for heart failure with preserved ejection fraction. *The New England Journal of Medicine*, *370*(15), 1383–1392. doi:10.1056/NEJMoa1313731 PMID:24716680

Poplin, R., Varadarajan, A. V., Blumer, K., Liu, Y., McConnell, M. V., Corrado, G. S., Peng, L., & Webster, D. R. (2018). Predicting cardiovascular risk factors from retinal fundus photographs using deep learning. *Nature Biomedical Engineering*, *2*(3), 158–164. doi:10.103841551-018-0195-0 PMID:31015713

Porumb, M., Iadanza, E., Massaro, S., & Pecchia, L. (2020). A convolutional neural network approach to detect congestive heart failure. *Biomedical Signal Processing and Control*, *55*, 101597. Advance online publication. doi:10.1016/j.bspc.2019.101597

Qin, C., Schlemper, J., Caballero, J., Price, A. N., Hajnal, J. V., & Rueckert, D. (2019). Convolutional recurrent neural networks for dynamic MR image reconstruction. *IEEE Transactions on Medical Imaging*, *38*(1), 280–290. doi:10.1109/TMI.2018.2863670 PMID:30080145

Quer, G., Arnaout, R., Henne, M., & Arnaout, R. (2021). Machine learning and the future of cardiovascular care: *JACC* state-of-the-art review. *Journal of the American College of Cardiology*, *77*(3), 300–313. doi:10.1016/j.jacc.2020.11.030 PMID:33478654

Quinlan, J. R. (1986). Induction of decision trees. *Machine Learning*, *1*(1), 81–106. doi:10.1007/BF00116251

Rogers, A. J., Selvalingam, A., Alhusseini, M. I., Krummen, D. E., Corrado, C., Abuzaid, F., Baykaner, T., Meyer, C., Clopton, P., Giles, W., Bailis, P., Niederer, S., Wang, P. J., Rappel, W.-J., Zaharia, M., & Narayan, S. M. (2021). Machine learned cellular phenotypes in cardiomyopathy predict sudden death. *Circulation Research*, *128*(2), 172–184. doi:10.1161/CIRCRESAHA.120.317345 PMID:33167779

Rohé, M.-M., Datar, M., Heimann, T., Sermesant, M., & Pennec, X. (2017). SVF-Net: Learning deformable image registration using shape matching. In M. Descoteaux, L. Maier-Hein, A. Franz, P. Jannin, D. Collins, & S. Duchesne (Eds.), Medical image computing and computer assisted intervention: Vol. 10433. *MICCAI 2017. Lecture notes in computer science.* Springer. doi:10.1007/978-3-319-66182-7_31

Rokach, L. (2010). Ensemble-based classifiers. *Artificial Intelligence Review*, *33*(1-2), 1–39. doi:10.100710462-009-9124-7

Romaguera, L. V., Romero, F. P., Filho, C. F. F. C., & Costa, M. G. F. (2017). Myocardial segmentation in cardiac magnetic resonance images using fully convolutional neural networks. *Biomedical Signal Processing and Control*, *44*, 48–57. doi:10.1016/j.bspc.2018.04.008

Ronneberger, O., Fischer, P., & Brox, T. (2015). U-Net: convolutional networks for biomedical image segmentation. In N. Navab, J. Hornegger, W. Wells, & A. Frangi (Eds.), Medical image computing and computer-Assisted intervention: Vol. 9351. *MICCAI 2015. Lecture notes in computer science.* Springer. doi:10.1007/978-3-319-24574-4_28

Rosner, C. M., Genovese, L., Tehrani, B. N., Atkins, M., Bakhshi, H., Chaudhri, S., Damluji, A. A., de Lemos, J. A., Desai, S. S., Emaminia, A., Flanagan, M. C., Khera, A., Maghsoudi, A., Mekonnen, G., Muthukumar, A., Saeed, I. M., Sherwood, M. W., Sinha, S. S., O'Connor, C. M., & deFilippi, C. R. (2021). Myocarditis temporally associated with COVID-19 vaccination. *Circulation*, *144*(6), 502–505. doi:10.1161/CIRCULATIONAHA.121.055891 PMID:34133885

Sang, Y., & Ruan, D. (2020). Enhanced image registration with a network paradigm and incorporation of a deformation representation model. *2020 IEEE 17ᵗʰ International Symposium on Biomedical Imaging (ISBI)*, 91-92. 10.1109/ISBI45749.2020.9098395

Schmidhuber, J. (2015). Deep learning in neural networks: An overview. *Neural Networks*, *61*, 85–117. doi:10.1016/j.neunet.2014.09.003 PMID:25462637

Seber, G. A. F., & Lee, A. J. (2012). *Linear regression analysis* (2nd ed.). John Wiley & Sons.

Sekelj, S., Sandler, B., Johnston, E., Pollock, K. G., Hill, N. R., Gordon, J., Tsang, C., Khan, S., Ng, F. S., & Farooqui, U. (2021). Detecting undiagnosed atrial fibrillation in UK primary care: Validation of a machine learning prediction algorithm in a retrospective cohort study. *European Journal of Preventive Cardiology*, *28*(6), 598–605. doi:10.1177/2047487320942338 PMID:34021576

Sengupta, P. P., Huang, Y.-M., Bansal, M., Ashrafi, A., Fisher, M., Shameer, K., Gall, W., & Dudley, J. T. (2016). Cognitive machine-learning algorithm for cardiac imaging: A pilot study for differentiating constrictive pericarditis from restrictive cardiomyopathy. *Circulation: Cardiovascular Imaging*, *9*(6), e004330. doi:10.1161/CIRCIMAGING.115.004330 PMID:27266599

Sengupta, P. P., Shrestha, S., Berthon, B., Messas, E., Donal, E., Tison, G. H., Min, J. K., D'hooge, J., Voigt, J.-U., Dudley, J., Verjans, J. W., Shameer, K., Johnson, K., Lovstakken, L., Tabassian, M., Piccirilli, M., Pernot, M., Yanamala, N., Duchateau, N., ... Arnaout, R. (2020). Proposed requirements for cardiovascular imaging-related machine learning evaluation (PRIME): A checklist: Reviewed by the American College of Cardiology Healthcare Innovation Council. *JACC: Cardiovascular Imaging*, *13*(9), 2017–2035. doi:10.1016/j.jcmg.2020.07.015 PMID:32912474

Shademan, A., Decker, R. S., Opfermann, J. D., Leonard, S., Krieger, A., & Kim, P. C. W. (2016). Supervised autonomous robotic soft tissue surgery. *Science Translational Medicine, 8*(337), 337ra64. Advance online publication. doi:10.1126citranslmed.aad9398 PMID:27147588

Sherazi, S. W. A., Jeong, Y. J., Jae, M. H., Bae, J.-W., & Lee, J. Y. (2019). A machine learning-based 1-year mortality prediction model after hospital discharge for clinical patients with acute coronary syndrome. *Health Informatics Journal, 26*(2), 1289–1304. doi:10.1177/1460458219871780 PMID:31566458

Sifrim, A., Hitz, M. P., Wilsdon, A., Breckpot, J., Turki, S. H., Thienpont, B., McRae, J., Fitzgerald, T. W., Singh, T., Swaminathan, G. J., Prigmore, E., Rajan, D., Abdul-Khaliq, H., Banka, S., Bauer, U. M. M., Bentham, J., Berger, F., Bhattacharya, S., Bu'Lock, F., ... Hurles, M. E. (2016). Distinct genetic architectures for syndromic and nonsyndromic congenital heart defects identified by exome sequencing. *Nature Genetics, 48*(9), 1060–1065. doi:10.1038/ng.3627 PMID:27479907

Snaauw, G., Gong, D., Maicas, G., van den Hengel, A., Niessen, W. J., Verjans, J., & Carneiro, G. (2019, 04). End-to-end diagnosis and segmentation learning from cardiac magnetic resonancei Imaging. *2019 IEEE 16th International Symposium on Biomedical Imaging (ISBI 2019),* 802-805. 10.1109/ISBI.2019.8759276

Solomon, S. D., McMurray, J. J. V., Anand, I. S., Ge, J., Lam, C. S. P., Maggioni, A. P., Martinez, F., Packer, M., Pfeffer, M. A., Pieske, B., Redfield, M. M., Rouleau, J. L., van Veldhuisen, D. J., Zannad, F., Zile, M. R., Desai, A. S., Claggett, B., Jhund, P. S., Boytsov, S. A., ... Lefkowitz, M. P. (2019). Angiotensin-neprilysin inhibition in heart failure with preserved ejection fraction. *The New England Journal of Medicine, 381*(17), 1609–1620. doi:10.1056/NEJMoa1908655 PMID:31475794

Sounderajah, V., Ashrafian, H., Aggarwal, R., De Fauw, J., Denniston, A. K., Greaves, F., Karthikesalingam, A., King, D., Liu, X., Markar, S. R., McInnes, M. D. F., Panch, T., Pearson-Stuttard, J., Ting, D. S. W., Golub, R. M., Moher, D., Bossuyt, P. M., & Darzi, A. (2020). Developing specific reporting guidelines for diagnostic accuracy studies assessing AI interventions: The STARD-AI Steering Group. *Nature Medicine, 26*(6), 807–808. doi:10.103841591-020-0941-1 PMID:32514173

Sousa, P. L., Sculco, P. K., Mayman, D. J., Jerabek, S. A., Ast, M. P., & Chalmers, B. P. (2020). Robots in the operating room during hip and knee arthroplasty. *Current Reviews in Musculoskeletal Medicine, 13*(3), 309–317. doi:10.100712178-020-09625-z PMID:32367430

Spaccarotella, C., Santarpia, G., Curcio, A., & Indolfi, C. (2021). The smartwatch detects ECG abnormalities typical of Brugada syndrome. *The Journal of Cardiovascular Medicine.* Advance online publication. doi:10.2459/JCM.0000000000001216 PMID:34054105

Spaccarotella, C. A. M., Polimeni, A., Migliarino, S., Principe, E., Curcio, A., Mongiardo, A., Sorrentino, S., De Rosa, S., & Indolfi, C. (2020). Multichannel electrocardiograms obtained by a smartwatch for the diagnosis of ST-segment changes. *JAMA Cardiology, 5*(10), 1176–1180. doi:10.1001/jamacardio.2020.3994 PMID:32865545

Subramanian, M., Wojtusciszyn, A., Favre, L., Boughorbel, S., Shan, J., Letaief, K. B., Pitteloud, N., & Chouchane, L. (2020). Precision medicine in the era of artificial intelligence: Implications in chronic disease management. *Journal of Translational Medicine, 18*(1), 472. Advance online publication. doi:10.118612967-020-02658-5 PMID:33298113

Theodoris, C. V., Zhou, P., Liu, L., Zhang, Y., Nishino, T., Huang, Y., Kostina, A., Ranade, S. S., Gifford, C. A., Uspenskiy, V., Malashicheva, A., Ding, S., & Srivastava, D. (2021). Network-based screen in iPSC-derived cells reveals therapeutic candidate for heart valve disease. *Science, 371*(6530), eabd0724. Advance online publication. doi:10.1126cience.abd0724 PMID:33303684

Thoenes, M., Agarwal, A., Grundmann, D., Ferrero, C., McDonald, A., Bramlage, P., & Steeds, R. P. (2021). Narrative review of the role of artificial intelligence to improve aortic valve disease management. *Journal of Thoracic Disease, 13*(1), 396–404. doi:10.21037/jtd-20-1837 PMID:33569220

Toba, S., Mitani, Y., Yodoya, N., Ohashi, H., Sawada, H., Hayakawa, H., Mirayama, M., Futsuki, A., Yamamoto, N., Ito, H., Konuma, T., Shimpo, H., & Takao, M. (2020). Prediction of pulmonary to systemic flow ratio in patients with congenital heart disease using deep learning-based analysis of chest radiographs. *JAMA Cardiology, 5*(4), 449–457. doi:10.1001/jamacardio.2019.5620 PMID:31968049

Topol, E. J. (2020). Welcoming new guidelines for AI clinical research. *Nature Medicine, 26*(9), 1318–1320. doi:10.103841591-020-1042-x PMID:32908274

Tunyasuvunakool, K., Adler, J., Wu, Z., Green, T., Zielinski, M., Žídek, A., Bridgland, A., Cowie, A., Meyer, C., Laydon, A., Velankar, S., Kleywegt, G. J., Bateman, A., Evans, R., Pritzel, A., Figurnov, M., Ronneberger, O., Bates, R., Kohl, S. A. A., ... Hassabis, D. (2021). Highly accurate protein structure prediction for the human proteome. *Nature, 596*(7873), 590–596. doi:10.103841586-021-03828-1 PMID:34293799

Tuppin, P., Cuerq, A., de Peretti, C., Fagot-Campagna, A., Danchin, N., Juillière, Y., Alta, F., Allemand, H., Bauters, C., Drici, M.-D., Hagège, A., Jondeau, G., Jourdain, P., Leizorovica, A., & Paccaud, F. (2014). Two-year outcome of patients after a first hospitalization for heart failure: A national observational study. *Archives of Cardiovascular Diseases, 107*(3), 158–168. doi:10.1016/j.acvd.2014.01.012 PMID:24662470

Ulloa Cerna, A. E., Jing, L., Good, C. W., vanMaanen, D. P., Raghunath, S., Suever, J. D., Nevius, C. D., Wehner, G. J., Hartzel, D. N., Leader, J. B., Alsaid, A., Patel, A. A., Kirchner, H. L., Pfeifer, J. M., Carry, B. J., Pattichis, M. S., Haggerty, C. M., & Fornwalt, B. K. (2021). Deep-learning-assisted analysis of echocardiographic videos improves predictions of all-cause mortality. *Nature Biomedical Engineering, 5*(6), 546–554. doi:10.103841551-020-00667-9 PMID:33558735

Vamathevan, J., Clark, D., Czodrowski, P., Dunham, I., Ferran, E., Lee, G., Li, B., Madabhushi, A., Shah, P., Spitzer, M., & Zhao, S. (2019). Applications of machine learning in drug discovery and development. *Nature Reviews. Drug Discovery, 18*(6), 463–477. doi:10.103841573-019-0024-5 PMID:30976107

Van den Eynde, J., Vaesen Bentein, H., Decaluwé, T., De Praetere, H., Wertan, M. C., Sutter, F. P., Balkhy, H. H., & Oosterlinck, W. (2021). Safe implementation of robotic-assisted minimally invasive direct coronary artery bypass: Application of learning curves and cumulative sum analysis. *Journal of Thoracic Disease, 13*(7), 4260–4270. doi:10.21037/jtd-21-775 PMID:34422354

Van der Maaten, L., Postma, E., & van den Herik, J. (2009). *Dimensionality reduction: A comparative review.* https://members.loria.fr/moberger/Enseignement/AVR/Exposes/TR_Dimensiereductie.pdf

Vasanawala, S. S., Alley, M. T., Hargreaves, B. A., Barth, R. A., Pauly, J. M., & Lustig, M. (2010). Improved pediatric MR imaging with compressed sensing. *Radiology*, 256(2), 607–616. doi:10.1148/radiol.10091218 PMID:20529991

Velagaleti, R. S., Pencina, M. J., Murabito, J. M., Wang, T. J., Parikh, N. I., D'Agostino, R. B., Levy, D., Kannel, W. B., & Vasan, R. S. (2008). Long-term trends in the incidence of heart failure after myocardial infarction. *Circulation*, 118(20), 2057–2062. doi:10.1161/CIRCULATIONAHA.108.784215 PMID:18955667

Virani, S. S., Alonso, A., Aparicio, H. J., Benjamin, E. J., Bittencourt, M. S., Callaway, C. W., Carson, A. P., Chamberlain, A. M., Cheng, S., Delling, F. N., Elkind, M. S. V., Evenson, K. R., Ferguson, J. F., Gupta, D. K., Khan, S. S., Kissela, B. M., Knutson, K. L., Lee, C. D., Lewis, T. T., ... Tsao, C. W. (2021). Heart disease and stroke statistics—2021 update: A report from the American Heart Association. *Circulation*, 143(8), e254–e743. doi:10.1161/CIR.0000000000000950 PMID:33501848

Wenger, N. K., & Lewis, S. J. (2021). Incremental change versus disruptive transformation: COVID-19 and the cardiovascular community. *Circulation*, 143(19), 1835–1837. doi:10.1161/CIRCULATIONAHA.121.053860 PMID:33820438

Wolterink, J., Leiner, T., Viergever, M. A., & Išgum, I. (2018). Automatic segmentation and disease classification using cardiac cine MR images. In M. Pop, M. Sermesant, J. Zhao, S. Li, K. McLeod, A. Young, K. Rhode, & T. Mansi (Eds.), Statistical atlases and computational models of the heart. Atrial segmentation and LV quantification challenges (pp. 101-110). Springer. doi:10.1007/978-3-319-75541-0_11

Xu, S., Zhang, Z., Wang, D., Hu, J., Duan, X., & Zhu, T. (2017, March 10–12). *Cardiovascular risk prediction method based on CFS subset evaluation and random forest classification framework* [Paper presentation]. 2017 IEEE 2nd International Conference on Big Data Analysis (ICBDA), Beijing, China. 10.1109/ICBDA.2017.8078813

Yang, Y., Sun, J., Li, H., & Xu, Z. (2016, December 5-12). *Deep ADMM-Net for compressive sensing MRI* [Paper presentation]. *Annual Conference on Neural Information Processing Systems*, Barcelona, Spain.

Yeung, M. W., Benjamins, J. W., van der Harst, P., & Juárez-Orozco, L. (2021). Machine learning in cardiovascular genomics, proteomics, and drug discovery. In S. J. Al'Aref, G. Singh, L. Baskaran, & D. Metaxas (Eds.), *Machine learning in cardiovascular medicine* (pp. 325–352). Academic Press. doi:10.1016/B978-0-12-820273-9.00014-2

Yiangou, L., Davis, R. P., & Mummery, C. L. (2021). Using cardiovascular cells from human pluripotent stem cells for COVID-19 research: Why the heart fails. *Stem Cell Reports*, 16(3), 385–397. doi:10.1016/j.stemcr.2020.11.003 PMID:33306986

Yutzey, K. E., Demer, L. L., Body, S. C., Huggins, G. S., Towler, D. A., Giachelli, C. M., Hofmann-Bowman, M. A., Mortlock, D. P., Rogers, M. B., Sadeghi, M. M., & Aikawa, E. (2014). Calcific aortic valve disease: A consensus summary from the Alliance of Investigators on Calcific Aortic Valve Disease. *Arteriosclerosis, Thrombosis, and Vascular Biology*, 34(11), 2387–2393. doi:10.1161/ATVBAHA.114.302523 PMID:25189570

Zhang, H. (2004). The optimality of naive Bayes. *Proceedings of Florida Artificial Intelligence Research Society (FLAIRS)*. https://www.aaai.org/Papers/FLAIRS/2004/Flairs04-097.pdf

Zhao, J., Feng, Q., Wu, P., Lupu, R. A., Wilke, R. A., Wells, Q. S., Denny, J. C., & Wei, W.-Q. (2019). Learning from longitudinal data in electronic health record and genetic data to improve cardiovascular event prediction. *Scientific Reports*, 9(1), 717. doi:10.103841598-018-36745-x PMID:30679510

Zhavoronkov, A., Ivanenkov, Y. A., Aliper, A., Veselov, M. S., Aladinskiy, V. A., Aladinskaya, A. V., Terentiev, V. A., Polykovskiy, D. A., Kuznetsov, M. D., Asadulaev, A., Volkov, Y., Zholus, A., Shayakhmetov, R. R., Zhebrak, A., Minaeva, L. I., Zagribenlnyy, B. A., Lee, L. H., Soll, R., Madge, D., ... Aspuru-Guzik, A. (2019). Deep learning enables rapid identification of potent DDR1 kinase inhibitors. *Nature Biotechnology*, 37(9), 1038–1040. doi:10.103841587-019-0224-x PMID:31477924

ADDITIONAL READING

Frohlich, E. D., & Quinlan, P. J. (2014). Coronary heart disease risk factors: Public impact of initial and later-announced risks. *The Ochsner Journal*, 14(4), 532–537. https://www.ncbi.nlm.nih.gov/pmc/articles/PMC4295729/ PMID:25598717

Kent, J. (2020, February 18). AHA awards $2M to artificial intelligence, precision medicine studies. *HealthITAnalytics*. https://healthitanalytics.com/news/aha-awards-2m-to-artificial-intelligence-precision-medicine-studies

Kent, J. (2020, August 5). Artificial intelligence may accelerate heart failure diagnosis. *Health IT Analytics*. https://healthitanalytics.com/news/artificial-intelligence-may-accelerate-heart-failure-diagnosis

Lopez-Jimenez, F., Attia, Z., Arruda-Olson, A. M., Carter, R., Chareonthaitawee, P., Jouni, H., Kapa, S., Lerman, A., Luong, C., Medina-Inojosa, J. R., Noseworthy, P. A., Pellikka, P. A., Redfield, M. M., Roger, V. L., Sandhu, G. S., Senecal, C., & Friedman, P. A. (2020). Artificial intelligence in cardiology: Present and future. *Mayo Clinic Proceedings*, 95(5), 1015–1039. https://www.mayoclinicproceedings.org/article/S0025-6196(20)30138-5/fulltext. doi:10.1016/j.mayocp.2020.01.038 PMID:32370835

Pai, A. (2020, February 17). CNN vs. RNN vs. ANN—Analyzing 3 types of neural networks in deep learning. *Analytics Vidhya*. https://www.analyticsvidhya.com/blog/2020/02/cnn-vs-rnn-vs-mlp-analyzing-3-types-of-neural-networks-in-deep-learning/

Roy, S. S., Mallik, A., Gulati, R., Obaidat, M. S., & Krishna, P. V. (2017). A deep learning based artificial neural network approach for intrusion detection. In D. Giri, R. Mohapatra, H. Begehr, & M. Obaidat (Eds.), *Mathematics and Computing. ICMC 2017. Communications in Computer and Information Science* (Vol. 655). Springer., doi:10.1007/978-981-10-4642-1_5

Tatan, V. (2019, December 23). Understanding CNN (Convolutional Neural Network. *Towards Data Science*. https://towardsdatascience.com/understanding-cnn-convolutional-neural-network-69fd626ee7d4

Walter, M. (2021, March 16). AI model predicts death from cardiovascular disease, coronary artery disease better than other advanced techniques. *Cardiovascular Business*. https://www.cardiovascularbusiness.com/topics/imaging-physiology/ai-model-cardiovascular-disease-coronary-artery-disease

KEY TERMS AND DEFINITIONS

Arrhythmia: Arrhythmias are heart rhythm abnormalities that occur when electrical impulses that coordinate heartbeats are anomalous and can lead to impaired heart contraction or relaxation or both.

Artificial Intelligence: Artificial intelligence is the ability of computer systems to perform tasks that normally require human intelligence.

Deep Learning: A class of machine learning based on artificial neural networks that include multiple hidden layers to progressively extract higher level features from the raw data.

Genome: Complete set of genetic instructions needed to build and sustain an organism. This may include interactions of genes with one another and the environment (epigenome).

Heart Failure: Heart failure occurs when heart muscle does not pump sufficient blood to meet the demands of the body secondary to several conditions including heart attack, hypertension, heart valve disease, congenital (birth) heart defects, etc.

Machine Learning: A study of computer algorithms that can access data and use the data to learn by themselves.

Myocardial infarction: Sometimes referred as heart attack, myocardial infarction occurs when blood flow to the heart tissues is interrupted secondary to obstruction from buildup of fat and other substances within blood vessels called coronary arteries.

APPENDIX

Table 1. Summary of Neural Network or Machine Learning Features of References

AUTHORS	FEATURE
Abu Mouch S, Roguin A, Hellou E, Ishai A, Shoshan U, Mahamid L, Zoabi M, Aisman M, Goldschmid N, Berar Yanay N.	Myocarditis following COVID-19 mRNA vaccination
Shaad M. Ahmad, Brian W. Busser, Di Huang, Elizabeth J. Cozart, Sébastien Michaud, Xianmin Zhu, Neal Jeffries, Anton Aboukhalil, Martha L. Bulyk, Ivan Ovcharenko, Alan M. Michelson	Machine learning classification of cell-specific cardiac enhancers uncovers developmental subnetworks regulating progenitor cell division and cell fate specification
Ali SR, Nguyen D, Wang B, Jiang S, Sadek HA.	Deep Learning Identifies Cardiomyocyte Nuclei with High Precision.
Altman, N.	An Introduction to Kernel and Nearest-Neighbor Nonparametric Regression.
Antoniades C, Asselbergs FW, Vardas P.	The year in cardiovascular medicine 2020: digital health and innovation.
Attia ZI, Kapa S, Yao X, Lopez-Jimenez F, Mohan TL, Pellikka PA, Carter RE, Shah ND, Friedman PA, Noseworthy PA.	Prospective validation of a deep learning electrocardiogram algorithm for the detection of left ventricular systolic dysfunction.
Attia ZI, Noseworthy PA, Lopez-Jimenez F, Asirvatham SJ, Deshmukh AJ, Gersh BJ, Carter RE, Yao X, Rabinstein AA, Erickson BJ, Kapa S, Friedman PA.	An artificial intelligence-enabled ECG algorithm for the identification of patients with atrial fibrillation during sinus rhythm: a retrospective analysis of outcome prediction.
Barrett LA, Payrovnaziri SN, Bian J, He Z.	Building Computational Models to Predict One-Year Mortality in ICU Patients with Acute Myocardial Infarction and Post Myocardial Infarction Syndrome.
A. Bellot and M. van der Schaar	A Hierarchical Bayesian Model for Personalized Survival Predictions
Bengio Y, Courville A, Vincent P.	Representation learning: a review and new perspectives.
Y. Bengio, P. Simard and P. Frasconi	Learning long-term dependencies with gradient descent is difficult
Benjamins JW, Hendriks T, Knuuti J, Juarez-Orozco LE, van der Harst P.	A primer in artificial intelligence in cardiovascular medicine.
Boser, B., Guyon, I., & Vapnik, V.	A Training Algorithm for Optimal Margin Classifier.
Branca, L., Sbolli, M., Metra, M., & Fudim, M	Heart failure with mid-range ejection fraction: pro and cons of the new classification of Heart Failure by European Society of Cardiology guidelines.
Braunwald, E.	Heart failure.
Bursi F, Weston SA, Redfield MM, Jacobsen SJ, Pakhomov S, Nkomo VT, Meverden RA, Roger VL.	Systolic and diastolic heart failure in the community.
Caballé, N., Castillo-Sequera, J., Gomez-Pulido, J. A., Gómez, J., & Polo-Luque, M.	Machine Learning Applied to Diagnosis of Human Diseases: A Systematic Review.
Callaway, E.	'It will change everything': DeepMind's AI makes gigantic leap in solving protein structures.
Chang, S., Kim, H., Suh, Y. J., Choi, D. M., Kim, H., Kim, D. K., Choi, B. W.	Development of a deep learning-based algorithm for the automatic detection and quantification of aortic valve calcium.
Chen, J., Li, W., & Xiang, M.	Burden of valvular heart disease, 1990-2017: Results from the Global Burden of Disease Study 2017.
Chen, X., Diaz-Pinto, A., Ravikumar, N., & Frangi, A.	Deep learning in medical image registration.
Cho, K., van Merriënboer, B., Gulcehre, C., Bougares, F., Schwenk, H., & Bengio, Y.	Learning Phrase Representations using RNN Encoder-Decoder for Statistical Machine Translation.

continued on following page

Table 1. Continued

AUTHORS	FEATURE
Choi, E., Schuetz, A., Stewart, W., & Sun, J.	Using recurrent neural network models for early detection of heart failure onset.
Chung, M. K., Zidar, D. A., Bristow, M. R., Cameron, S. J., Chan, T., Harding, C. V., Loscalzo, J.	COVID-19 and Cardiovascular Disease: From Bench to Bedside.
Cole, G. D., Dhutia, N. M., Shun-Shin, M. J., Willson, K., Harrison, J., Raphael, C. E., Francis, D. P.	Defining the real-world reproducibility of visual grading of left ventricular function and visual estimation of left ventricular ejection fraction: impact of image quality, experience and accreditation.
Cruz Rivera, S., Liu, X., Chan, A. W., Denniston, A. K., Calvert, M. J.	Guidelines for clinical trial protocols for interventions involving artificial intelligence: the SPIRIT-AI extension.
Cutler, A., Cutler, D., & Stevens, J., Daglius Dias, R., Shah, J., & Zenati, M.	Artificial intelligence in cardiothoracic surgery.
Daniel, G. o., mez Gonz\'a,lez.	Artificial Neural Network.
Deng, L.	A tutorial survey of architectures, algorithms, and applications for deep learning
Diller, G. P., Kempny, A., Babu-Narayan, S. V., Henrichs, M., Brida, M., Uebing, A., Gatzoulis, M. A.	Machine learning algorithms estimating prognosis and guiding therapy in adult congenital heart disease: data from a single tertiary centre including 10,019 patients.
Du, X., Zhang, W., Zhang, H., Chen, J., Zhang, Y., Warrington, J., Li, S.	Deep Regression Segmentation for Cardiac Bi-Ventricle MR Images.
Duflos, C., Troude, P., Strainchamps, D., Segouin, C., Logeart, D., & Mercier, G.	Hospitalization for acute heart failure: the in-hospital care pathway predicts one-year readmission.
Enriko, I. K., Suryanegara, M., & Gunawan, D.	Heart disease prediction system using k-Nearest neighbor algorithm with simplified patient's health parameters.
Eom, J.-H., Kim, S.-C., & Zhang, B.-T.	A classifier ensemble-based clinical decision support system for cardiovascular disease level prediction.
Fan, J., Cao, X., Xue, J., & Yap, P.-T.	Adversarial Similarity Network for Evaluating Image Alignment in Deep Learning Based Registration.
Farshidfar, F., Koleini, N., & Ardehali, H.	Cardiovascular complications of COVID-19.
Fatima, H., Mahmood, F., Sehgal, S., Belani, K., Sharkey, A., Chaudhary, O., Khabbaz, K. R.	Artificial Intelligence for Dynamic Echocardiographic Tricuspid Valve Analysis: A New Tool in Echocardiography.
Feizi, N., Tavakoli, M., Patel, R., & Atashzar, S.	Robotics and AI for Teleoperation, Tele-Assessment, and Tele-Training for Surgery in the Era of COVID-19: Existing Challenges, and Future Vision.
Freund, Y., Iyer, R. D., Schapire, R. E., & Singer, Y.	An Efficient Boosting Algorithm for Combining Preferences.
Fries, J. A., Varma, P., Chen, V. S., Xiao, K., Tejeda, H., Saha, P., Priest, J. R.	Weakly supervised classification of aortic valve malformations using unlabeled cardiac MRI sequences.
Gedefaw, L., Ullah, S., Leung, P. H. M., Cai, Y., Yip, S. P., & Huang, C. L.	Inflammasome Activation-Induced Hypercoagulopathy: Impact on Cardiovascular Dysfunction Triggered in COVID-19 Patients.
Gortmaker, S. L., Hosmer, D., & Lemeshow, S.	Applied Logistic Regression.
Graff, C., & Sidky, E.	Compressive sensing in medical imaging
Guo, Q., Lu, X., Gao, Y., Zhang, J., Yan, B., Su, D., Wang, G.	Cluster analysis: A new approach for identification of underlying risk factors for coronary artery disease in essential hypertensive patients.
Haskins, G., Kruecker, J., Kruger, U., Xu, S., Pinto, P., Wood, B., & Yan, P.	Learning deep similarity metric for 3D MR–TRUS image registration.
Hernandez-Suarez, D. F., Ranka, S., Kim, Y., Latib, A., Wiley, J., Lopez-Candales, A., Roche-Lima, A.	Machine-Learning-Based In-Hospital Mortality Prediction for Transcatheter Mitral Valve Repair in the United States.

continued on following page

Table 1. Continued

AUTHORS	FEATURE
Hinton, G., & Sejnowski, T.	Unsupervised learning foundations of neural computation
Ho, D., Quake, S., McCabe, E., Chng, W., Chow, E., Ding, X., Zarrinpar, A.	Enabling Technologies for Personalized and Precision Medicine.
Hochreiter, S., & Schmidhuber, J.	Long Short-term Memory.
Hubel, D. H., & Wiesel, T. N.	Receptive fields, binocular interaction and functional architecture in the cat's visual cortex.
Ismail, B., & Anil, M.	Regression methods for analyzing the risk factors for a life style disease among the young population of India.
Jing, Y., Bian, Y., Hu, Z., Wang, L., & Xie, X.-Q.	Deep Learning for Drug Design: An Artificial Intelligence Paradigm for Drug Discovery in the Big Data Era.
Jones, B., Reed, B., & Hayanga, J.	Autonomously Driven: Artificial Intelligence in Cardiothoracic Surgery.
Juhola, M., Joutsijoki, H., Penttinen, K., & Aalto-Setälä, K.	Detection of genetic cardiac diseases by Ca^{2+} transient profiles using machine learning methods.
Kadurin, A., Nikolenko, S., Khrabrov, K., Aliper, A., & Zhavoronkov, A.	An Advanced Generative Adversarial Autoencoder Model for de Novo Generation of New Molecules with Desired Molecular Properties in Silico.
Karimi-Bidhendi, S., Arafati, A., Cheng, A. L., Wu, Y., Kheradvar, A., & Jafarkhani, H.	Fully automated deep learning segmentation of pediatric cardiovascular magnetic resonance of patients with complex congenital heart diseases.
Khera, A., Chaffin, M., Zekavat, S., Collins, R., Roselli, C., Natarajan, P., Kathiresan, S.	Whole-Genome Sequencing to Characterize Monogenic and Polygenic Contributions in Patients Hospitalized with Early-Onset Myocardial Infarction.
Kido, T., Kido, T., Nakamura, M., Kouki, W., Schmidt, M., Forman, C., & Mochizuki, T.	Compressed sensing real-time cine cardiovascular magnetic resonance: accurate assessment of left ventricular function in a single-breath-hold.
Kitzman, D. W., Hundley, W. G., Brubaker, P. H., Morgan, T. M., Moore, J. B., Stewart, K. P., & Little, W. C.	A randomized double-blind trial of enalapril in older patients with heart failure and preserved ejection fraction: effects on exercise tolerance and arterial distensibility.
Knott, K., Seraphim, A., Augusto, J., Xue, H., Chacko, L., Aung, N., Moon, J.	The Prognostic Significance of Quantitative Myocardial Perfusion: An Artificial Intelligence Based Approach Using Perfusion Mapping.
Krittanawong, C., Johnson, K., Hershman, S., & Tang, W. H.	Big data, artificial intelligence, and cardiovascular precision medicine.
Krittanawong, C., Johnson, K. W., Rosenson, R. S., Wang, Z., Aydar, M., Baber, U., Narayan, S.	Deep learning for cardiovascular medicine: a practical primer.
Krittanawong, C., Zhang, H., Wang, Z., Aydar, M., & Kitai, T.	Artificial Intelligence in Precision Cardiovascular Medicine.
Kuncheva, L. I., & Whitaker, C. J.	Measures of Diversity in Classifier Ensembles and Their Relationship with the Ensemble Accuracy.
Küstner, T., Fuin, N., Hammernik, K., Bustin, A., Qi, H., Hajhosseiny, R., . . . Prieto, C.	CINENet: deep learning-based 3D cardiac CINE MRI reconstruction with multi-coil complex-valued 4D spatio-temporal convolutions.
Larroza, A., López-Lereu, M., Monmeneu, J., Gavara, J., Chorro, F., Bodí, V., & Moratal, D.	Texture analysis of cardiac cine magnetic resonance imaging to detect non-viable segments in patients with chronic myocardial infarction.
Lavecchia, A.	Deep learning in drug discovery: opportunities, challenges and future prospects.
LeCun, Y., Bengio, Y., & Hinton, G.	Deep Learning.
Lee, E. K., Tran, D. D., Keung, W., Chan, P., Wong, G., Chan, C. W., Khine, M.	Machine Learning of Human Pluripotent Stem Cell-Derived Engineered Cardiac Tissue Contractility for Automated Drug Classification.
Lee, J., Ó Hartaigh, B., Han, D., Rizvi, A., Lin, F., & Min, J.	Fractional Flow Reserve Measurement by Computed Tomography: An Alternative to the Stress Test.

continued on following page

Table 1. Continued

AUTHORS	FEATURE
Leiner, T., Rueckert, D., Suinesiaputra, A., Baeßler, B., Nezafat, R., Išgum, I., & Young, A.	Machine learning in cardiovascular magnetic resonance: Basic concepts and applications.
LeMaire, S. A., McDonald, M. L., Guo, D. C., Russell, L., Miller, C. C., 3rd, Johnson, R. J., Milewicz, D.	Genome-wide association study identifies a susceptibility locus for thoracic aortic aneurysms and aortic dissections spanning
Li, Q., Wang, J., Tao, H., Zhou, Q., Chen, J., Fu, B., Zhang, W. H.	The Prediction Model of Warfarin Individual Maintenance Dose for Patients Undergoing Heart Valve Replacement, Based on the Back Propagation Neural Network.
Lin, S., li, Z., Fu, B.,	Feasibility of using deep learning to detect coronary artery disease based on facial photo.
Lindman, B. R., Clavel, M. A., Mathieu, P., Iung, B., Lancellotti, P., Otto, C. M., & Pibarot, P.	Calcific aortic stenosis.
Liu, X., Cruz Rivera, S., Moher, D., Calvert, M. J., Denniston, A. K., Spirit, A. I., & Group, C.-A. W.	Reporting guidelines for clinical trial reports for interventions involving artificial intelligence: the CONSORT-AI extension.
Luo, Y., Ahmad, F. S., & Shah, S. J.	Tensor Factorization for Precision Medicine in Heart Failure with Preserved Ejection Fraction.
Mak, K.-K., & Pichika, M.	Artificial intelligence in drug development: present status and future prospects.
Mandair, D., Tiwari, P., Simon, S., Colborn, K., & Rosenberg, M.	Prediction of incident myocardial infarction using machine learning applied to harmonized electronic health record data.
Martin-Isla, C., Campello, V., Izquierdo, C., Raisi, Z., Baeßler, B., Petersen, S., & Lekadir, K.	Image-Based Cardiac Diagnosis with Machine Learning: A Review.
Mathur, P., Srivastava, S., Xu, X., & Mehta, J. L.	Artificial Intelligence, Machine Learning, and cardiovascular disease.
Mendez-Lucio, O., Baillif, B., Clevert, D. A., Rouquie, D., & Wichard, J.	De novo generation of hit-like molecules from gene expression signatures using artificial intelligence.
Mercier, G., Georgescu, V., & Bousquet, J. (2015).	Geographic variation in potentially avoidable hospitalizations in France.
Miranda, E., Irwansyah, E., Amelga, A. Y., Maribondang, M. M., & Salim, M.	Detection of Cardiovascular Disease Risk's Level for Adults Using Naive Bayes Classifier.
Mitchell, T. M.	Machine Learning (1 ed.): McGraw-Hill, Inc.
Mongan, J., Moy, L., & Kahn, C. E., Jr.	Checklist for Artificial Intelligence in Medical Imaging (CLAIM): A Guide for Authors and Reviewers.
Moustris, G., Hirides, S., Deliparaschos, K., & Konstantinidis, K.	Evolution of autonomous and semi-autonomous robotic surgical systems: A review of the literature.
Nahar, J., Imam, T., Tickle, K., & Chen, Y.-P. P.	Association rule mining to detect factors which contribute to heart disease in males and females.
Nirschl, J. J., Janowczyk, A., Peyster, E. G., Frank, R., Margulies, K. B., Feldman, M. D., & Madabhushi, A.	A deep-learning classifier identifies patients with clinical heart failure using whole-slide images of H&E tissue.
Nishiga, M., Wang, D. W., Han, Y., Lewis, D. B., & Wu, J. C.	COVID-19 and cardiovascular disease: from basic mechanisms to clinical perspectives.
Norgeot, B., Quer, G., Beaulieu-Jones, B. K., Torkamani, A., Dias, R., Gianfrancesco, M., Butte, A. J.	Minimum information about clinical artificial intelligence modeling: the MI-CLAIM checklist.
Oikonomou, E., Mohamed, M., Desai, M., Mancio, J., Alashi, A., Hutt, E., Antoniades, C.	Non-invasive detection of coronary inflammation using computed tomography and prediction of residual cardiovascular risk (the CRISP CT study): a post-hoc analysis of prospective outcome data.
Olurotimi, O.	Recurrent Neural Network Training with Feedforward Complexity.
Orita, K., Sawada, K., Matsumoto, N., & Ikegaya, Y.	Machine-learning-based quality control of contractility of cultured human-induced pluripotent stem-cell-derived cardiomyocytes.

continued on following page

Table 1. Continued

AUTHORS	FEATURE
Orwat, S., Arvanitaki, A., & Diller, G. P.	A new approach to modelling in adult congenital heart disease: artificial intelligence.
Patel, L., Shukla, T., Huang, X., Ussery, D. W., & Wang, S.	Machine Learning Methods in Drug Discovery.
Patil, M., Singh, S., Henderson, J., & Krishnamurthy, P.	Mechanisms of COVID-19-induced cardiovascular disease: Is sepsis or exosome the missing link?
Paul, D., Sanap, G., Shenoy, S., Kalyane, D., Kalia, K., & Tekade, R.	Artificial intelligence in drug discovery and development.
Pawade, T. A., Newby, D. E., & Dweck, M. R.	Calcification in Aortic Stenosis: The Skeleton Key.
Peng, P., Lekadir, K., Gooya, A., Shao, L., Petersen, S., & Frangi, A.	A review of heart chamber segmentation for structural and functional analysis using cardiac magnetic resonance imaging.
Perez, M. V., Mahaffey, K. W., Hedlin, H., Rumsfeld, J. S., Garcia, A., Ferris, T.	Large-Scale Assessment of a Smartwatch to Identify Atrial Fibrillation.
Petitjean, C., & Dacher, J.-N.	A review of segmentation methods in short axis cardiac MR images.
Pierpont, M. E., Brueckner, M., Chung, W. K., Garg, V., Lacro, R. V., McGuire, A. L.	Precision, M. (2018). Genetic Basis for Congenital Heart Disease: Revisited: A Scientific Statement from the American Heart Association.
Pitt, B., Pfeffer, M. A., Assmann, S. F., Boineau, R., Anand, I. S., Claggett, B.,	Spironolactone for heart failure with preserved ejection fraction.
Poplin, R., Varadarajan, A., Blumer, K., Liu, Y., McConnell, M., Corrado, G., Webster, D	Predicting Cardiovascular Risk Factors from Retinal Fundus Photographs using Deep Learning.
Porumb, M., Iadanza, E., Massaro, S., & Pecchia, L.	A convolutional neural network approach to detect congestive heart failure.
Qin, C., Schlemper, J., Caballero, J., Price, A. N., Hajnal, J. V., & Rueckert, D.	Convolutional Recurrent Neural Networks for Dynamic MR Image Reconstruction.
Quer, G., Arnaout, R., Henne, M., & Arnaout, R.	Machine Learning and the Future of Cardiovascular Care: JACC State-of-the-Art Review.
Quinlan, J. R.	Induction of Decision Trees.
Rogers, A. J., Selvalingam, A., Alhusseini, M. I., Krummen, D. E., Corrado, C., Abuzaid, F., Narayan, S. M.	Machine Learned Cellular Phenotypes in Cardiomyopathy Predict Sudden Death.
Rohe, M.-M., Datar, M., Heimann, T., Sermesant, M., & Pennec, X.	SVF-Net: Learning Deformable Image Registration Using Shape Matching.
Rokach, L.	Ensemble-based classifiers.
Romaguera, L., Perdigón Romero, F., Costa Filho, C., & Costa, M.	Myocardial segmentation in cardiac magnetic resonance images using fully convolutional neural networks.
Ronneberger, O., Fischer, P., & Brox, T.	U-Net: Convolutional Networks for Biomedical Image Segmentation.
Rosner, C. M., Genovese, L., Tehrani, B. N., Atkins, M., Bakhshi, H., Chaudhri, S., deFilippi, C. R.	Myocarditis Temporally Associated with COVID-19 Vaccination.
Sang, Y., & Ruan, D.	Enhanced Image Registration with a Network Paradigm and Incorporation of a Deformation Representation Model.
Schmidhuber, J.	Deep learning in neural networks: An overview.
Seber, G., & Lee, A.	Linear Regression Analysis
Sekelj, S., Sandler, B., Johnston, E., Pollock, K. G., Hill, N. R., Gordon, J., Farooqui, U.	Detecting undiagnosed atrial fibrillation in UK primary care: Validation of a machine learning prediction algorithm in a retrospective cohort study.
Sengupta, P., Huang, Y.-M., Bansal, M., Ashrafi, A., Fisher, M., Khader, S., & Gall, W.	Cognitive Machine-Learning Algorithm for Cardiac Imaging: A Pilot Study for Differentiating Constrictive Pericarditis from Restrictive Cardiomyopathy.

continued on following page

Table 1. Continued

AUTHORS	FEATURE
Sengupta, P. P., Shrestha, S., Berthon, B., Messas, E., Donal, E., Tison, G. H., Arnaout, R.	Proposed Requirements for Cardiovascular Imaging-Related Machine Learning Evaluation (PRIME): A Checklist: Reviewed by the American College of Cardiology Healthcare Innovation Council.
Shademan, A., Decker, R., Opfermann, J., Leonard, S., Krieger, A., & Kim, P.	Supervised autonomous robotic soft tissue surgery.
Sherazi, S. W. A., Jeong, Y., Jae, M., Bae, J.-W., & Lee, J.	A machine learning–based 1-year mortality prediction model after hospital discharge for clinical patients with acute coronary syndrome.
Sifrim, A., Hitz, M. P., Wilsdon, A., Breckpot, J., Turki, S. H., Thienpont, B., Hurles, M. E.	Distinct genetic architectures for syndromic and non- syndromic congenital heart defects identified by exome sequencing.
Snaauw, G., Gong, D., Maicas, G., Hengel, A., Niessen, W. J., Verjans, J., & Carneiro, G.	End-To-End Diagnosis and Segmentation Learning from Cardiac Magnetic Resonance Imaging.
Solomon, S. D., McMurray, J. J. V., Anand, I. S., Ge, J., Lam, C. S. P., Maggioni	Angiotensin-Neprilysin Inhibition in Heart Failure with Preserved Ejection Fraction.
Sounderajah, V., Ashrafian, H., Aggarwal, R., De Fauw, J., Denniston, A. K., Greaves, F., Darzi, A.	Developing specific reporting guidelines for diagnostic accuracy studies assessing AI interventions: The STARD-AI Steering Group.
Sousa, P., Sculco, P., Mayman, D., Jerabek, S., Ast, M., & Chalmers, B.	Robots in the Operating Room During Hip and Knee Arthroplasty.
Spaccarotella, C., Santarpia, G., Curcio, A., & Indolfi, C.	The smartwatch detects ECG abnormalities typical of Brugada syndrome.
Spaccarotella, C. A. M., Polimeni, A., Migliarino, S., Principe, E., Curcio, A., Mongiardo, A., Indolfi, C.	Multichannel Electrocardiograms Obtained by a Smartwatch for the Diagnosis of ST-Segment Changes.
Subramanian, M., Wojtusciszyn, A., Favre, L., Boughorbel, S., Shan, J., Letaief, K., Chouchane, L.	Precision medicine in the era of artificial intelligence: implications in chronic disease management.
Theodoris, C. V., Zhou, P., Liu, L., Zhang, Y., Nishino, T., Huang, Y., Srivastava, D.	Network-based screen in iPSC-derived cells reveals therapeutic candidate for heart valve disease.
Thoenes, M., Agarwal, A., Grundmann, D., Ferrero, C., McDonald, A., Bramlage, P., & Steeds, R. P.	Narrative review of the role of artificial intelligence to improve aortic valve disease management.
Toba, S., Mitani, Y., Yodoya, N., Ohashi, H., Sawada, H., Hayakawa, H., Takao, M.	Prediction of Pulmonary to Systemic Flow Ratio in Patients with Congenital Heart Disease Using Deep Learning-Based Analysis of Chest Radiographs.
Topol, E. J.	Welcoming new guidelines for AI clinical research.
Tuppin, P., Cuerq, A., de Peretti, C., Fagot-Campagna, A., Danchin, N., Juilliere, Y., Paccaud, F.	Two-year outcome of patients after a first hospitalization for heart failure: A national observational study.
Ulloa Cerna, A. E., Jing, L., Good, C. W., van Maanen, D. P., Raghunath, S., Suever, J. D., Fornwalt, B. K.	Deep-learning-assisted analysis of echocardiographic videos improves predictions of all-cause mortality.
Vamathevan, J., Clark, D., Czodrowski, P., Dunham, I., Ferran, E., Lee, G., Zhao, S.	Applications of machine learning in drug discovery and development.
van der Maaten, L., Postma, E., & Herik, H.	Dimensionality Reduction: A Comparative Review.
Vasanawala, S., Alley, M., Hargreaves, B., Barth, R., Pauly, J., & Lustig, M.	Improved Pediatric MR Imaging with Compressed Sensing1.
Velagaleti, R. S., Pencina, M. J., Murabito, J. M., Wang, T. J., Parikh, N. I., D'Agostino, R. B., Vasan, R. S.	Long-term trends in the incidence of heart failure after myocardial infarction.
Virani, S. S., Alonso, A., Aparicio, H. J., Benjamin, E. J., Bittencourt, M. S., Callaway, C. W., Stroke Statistics, S.	Heart Disease and Stroke Statistics-2021 Update: A Report from the American Heart Association.
Wenger, N. K., & Lewis, S. J.	Incremental Change Versus Disruptive Transformation: COVID-19 and the Cardiovascular Community.

continued on following page

Table 1. Continued

AUTHORS	FEATURE
Wolterink, J., Leiner, T., Viergever, M., & Išgum, I.	Automatic Segmentation and Disease Classification Using Cardiac Cine MR Images.
Xu, S., Zhang, Z., Wang, D., Hu, J., Duan, X., & Zhu, T.	Cardiovascular risk prediction method based on CFS subset evaluation and random forest classification framework.
Yang, Y., Sun, J., Li, H., & Xu, Z.	Deep ADMM-Net for Compressive Sensing MRI.
Yeung, M. W., Benjamins, J. W., van der Harst, P., & Juárez-Orozco, L.	Machine learning in cardiovascular genomics, proteomics, and drug discovery.
Yiangou, L., Davis, R. P., & Mummery, C. L.	Using Cardiovascular Cells from Human Pluripotent Stem Cells for COVID-19 Research: Why the Heart Fails.
Yutzey, K. E., Demer, L. L., Body, S. C., Huggins, G. S., Towler, D. A., Giachelli, C. M., Aikawa, E.	Calcific aortic valve disease: a consensus summary from the Alliance of Investigators on Calcific Aortic Valve Disease.
Zagribelnyy, B., Zhavoronkov, A., Aliper, A., Polykovskiy, D., Terentiev, V., Aladinskiy, V., .Shayakhmetov, R.	Deep learning enables rapid identification of potent DDR1 kinase inhibitors.
Zhang, H.	The Optimality of Naive Bayes. Paper presented at the FLAIRS Conference.
Zhao, J., Feng, Q., Wu, P., Lupu, R., Wilke, R., Wells, Q., Wei, W.-Q.	Learning from Longitudinal Data in Electronic Health Record and Genetic Data to Improve Cardiovascular Event Prediction.

Chapter 5
Predictions For COVID-19 With Deep Learning Models of Long Short-Term Memory (LSTM)

Fan Wu
Purdue University, USA

Juan Shu
Purdue University, USA

ABSTRACT

COVID-19, one of the most contagious diseases and urgent threats in recent times, attracts attention across the globe to study the trend of infections and help predict when the pandemic will end. A reliable prediction will make states and citizens acknowledge possible consequences and benefits for the policymaker among the delicate balance of reopening and public safety. This chapter introduces a deep learning technique and long short-term memory (LSTM) to forecast the trend of COVID-19 in the United States. The dataset from the New York Times (NYT) of confirmed and deaths cases is utilized in the research. The results include discussion of the potential outcomes if extreme circumstances happen and the profound effect beyond the forecasting number.

INTRODUCTION

Coronavirus disease (COVID-19) is a dangerous and infectious disease caused by Severe Acute Respiratory Syndrome Coronavirus-2 (SARS-CoV2) has become a pandemic that has shaken the whole world. Currently, in June 2020, according to the data posted by Johns Hopkins University of Baltimore, Maryland USA and New York Times (NYT), more than 181 million cases have been reported across the world, while deaths tragically climbed to 3.93 million. The United States leads the world in total cases at 33.6 million, and the deaths toll around 604,000. Fortunately, based on the latest data from the Centers of Disease Control and Prevention (CDC), nearly 131 million people are fully vaccinated, and 66% of the total population have received at least one dose. Daily new cases plummed to a relatively low

DOI: 10.4018/978-1-7998-8455-2.ch005

number by the protection of the vaccine. However, the delta variant, also known as B.1.617.2, is still one of the concern viruses as it seems to be around 60% more transmissible and may cause more severe symptoms. Due to the delta variant, despite being fully vaccinated, breakthrough infections could occur and rapidly increase new cases reported in Israel and India.

The World Health Organization (WHO) warns that COVID-19 could be spread starting with one person, then exaggerated through contact and respiratory spay. Pandemic has always been individually but shared worldwide. According to the character of this virus, many countries have to close their borders and enforce a partial or complete lock-down which had a devastating impact on tons of industry workers. The sudden lock-down often creates a large wave of problems in terms of agriculture, transportation, especially for third-world countries and low-income communities. Overwhelmed hospitals and lack of oxygen made the patient unable to have enough treatment and finally lost their lives. As the pandemic destroyed standard lifestyle, governments urgently know whether the peak of this pandemic is passed away? When is the proper time to reopen? Under this circumstance, prediction of the COVID-19 new cases and deaths becomes crucial to help the governments and healthcare systems prepare in advance about what kind of policy is more appropriate for their situation and check whether the policy undertaken is effective or not.

Prominent computational and statistical models have been unrealistic as the dynamic transmission of the epidemic, highly nonlinear, long interval (several days and months), and high variance, is hard to describe by traditional methods. Thanks to enough good data and computational resources, machine learning and deep learning techniques have recently gained lots of progress, known as solving more complex models and acquiring relationships without providing too much prior information. Recurrent Neural Networks (RNN) is a powerful tool to model sequence data by its unique connection structure and has been widely used in recognition tasks (Robinson et al., 2002; Graves et al., 2013; Sak et al., 2014). Based on the Recurrent Neural Network, Long Short-Term Memory (LSTM) (Sepp et al., 1997) adds a feedback connection to its structure. It makes it possible to process data sequentially while keeping robustness against the long-term dependency issue. LSTM is also well-known for its outstanding performance among handwriting recognition, speech recognition, and making predictions based on time series data.

Benefit from the high accuracy prediction behavior of deep learning. Several studies were published about modeling the diagnosing and spreading procedure. COVID-19 infection forecasting of all states in India has been investigated through the Long Short-Term Memory (LSTM) and predicted the new cases of the next few days (Arora et al., 2020; Chandra et al., 2020; Shahid et al., 2020; Shastri et al., 2020). The mutation rate of COVID-19 has been modeled and forecasted using the Recurrent Neural Networks (RNN) based technique (Pathan et al., 2020). As the current data of confirmed cases and death is available to the public, we consider using the relative model on this up-to-date data and conducting our prediction and discussion after the fitting procedure.

This chapter will first discuss the foundational background information about Long Short-Term Memory (LSTM), COVID-19 data set, dropout procedure, and performance indices. Then, how to build a Long Short-Term Memory (LSTM) based network to predict COVID-19 new cases in Python 3.9 is explored and illustrated step by step. Next, how to build up a similar deep learning model to predict the deaths toll is showed but skips too many details. Their fitting and predicting performances are compared, and their advantages and limitations when working with this form of data are discussed.

BACKGROUND

In this work, one of the deep learning techniques is well established for COVID-19 predictions. In the first part, the structure of Long Short-Term Memory (LSTM) is discussed, whereas, in the next phase, the introduction of the dropout technique is presented. The data set information and performance measures are also mentioned in this part. An overview will be provided to deliver the work scheme, where data is collected, processed, then transferred to two models and evaluated by error measures.

Long Short-Term Memory (LSTM) Network Models

Recurrent Neural Networks (RNN) are beneficial for processing sequential data by their loop structure. The output connects with the current input and the hidden states, and the previous information. Therefore, Recurrent Neural Networks (RNN) could incorporate the current state and inputs to transmit a vital message into future states and then to the final output. However, RNN has the hurdle to train the long-term dependencies data.

Long Short-Term Memory (LSTM), anticipated by Hochreiter and Schmidhuber, is an extension of Recurrent Neural Networks (RNN) that implements a forgetting mechanism to handle long-sequence inputs, as it could add or removes information on the state of the cell. Long Short-Term Memory (LSTM) also has a chain structure as Recurrent Neural Networks (RNN), but the repeating module has a unique design. Instead of having a single neural network layer, more complex structures are used in Long Short-Term Memory (LSTM). In each vanilla Long Short-Term Memory (LSTM) unit, an input gate, external-input gate, forget gate, and output gate can be found. The work of the input gate and output gate is used to qualify the flow of input and outputs into the rest of the network. The memory mechanism is complied by two parts, memory cell C_t And working cell h_t. Memory cells are responsible for the retention of the sequence controlled with forgetting gate f_t, which is a crucial technique in Long Short-Term Memory (LSTM). The working memory h_t is recorded as the output of each memory cell, and output gate o_t determine which part of the former state and the current input to be remembered in the memory cell. The former state and current input jointly process to the nonlinear activation function. The Long Short-Term Memory (LSTM) network computes the mapping between the input sequence and output sequence. Updating by the following equations:

Forgot gate: $f_t = \sigma\left(W_f \cdot [h_{t-1}, x_t] + b_f\right)$ (1)

Input gate: $i_t = \sigma(W_i \cdot [h_{t-1}, x_t] + b_i)$ (2)

Update gate: $C_t = \tanh(W_c \cdot [h_{t-1}, x_t] + b_c)$ (3)

$c_t = f_t \cdot c_{t-1} + i_t \cdot C_t$ (4)

Output fate: $o_t = \sigma \left(W_o \cdot [h_{t-1}, x_t] + b_o \right)$ (5)

$h_t = o_t \bullet \tan h(c_t)$ (6)

Dropout

Neural Nets need a large number of parameters to get a fantastic performance on fitting specific datasets. Deep neural networks compromise multiple nonlinear hidden layers and much more cells so that they can learn very complicated relationships between inputs and outputs. However, relatively small datasets can cause a severe problem—overfitting. This could impact the model to focus more on statistical noise in the training data, leading to a poor prediction result on the testing dataset. Generalization error increases due to overfitting.

To reduce this problem, one of the commonly used methods is the dropout, which Nitish Srivastava proposed in 2014.

Dropout is a regularization method that approximates training a large number of neural networks with different architectures in parallel. Better than the ensemble method, dropout is no need for multiple models to be fit and stored, which can be a big challenge when models turn to be complex, requiring days even weeks to train. For the dropout method, some layer outputs are randomly eliminated from the network during the training process. Dropout has a side effect: it will encourage the network to learn a sparse representation, and hidden units turn sparsed. It also reduces the model capacity and thins the network, whereas a broader network is required when using this method. For a single-layer model, the dropout step is more likely to filter the nodes. However, we will keep the dropout at our model for further studies on more layers and more complicated models.

COVID-19 Dataset

The New York Times (NYT) tracked the first coronavirus case in the United States in Washington State on January 21, 2020. Since then, The New York Times (NYT) has kept following all the new claims based on the reports from state and local health agencies. In this research, we only focus on the national level.

Therefore, we utilize the .csv file of confirmed cased, death cases of the United States. On their website (https://www.nytimes.com/interactive/2021/us/covid-cases.html.), the visualization of newly reported cases is provided, and it's convenient for us to have the latest update of COVID-19. The data is preprocessed before treating them as input for our Long Short-Term Memory (LSTM) model.

Figure 1. Coronavirus in the U.S.: Latest Map and Case Count. Picture from https://www.nytimes.com/interactive/2021/us/covid-cases.html.

New reported cases

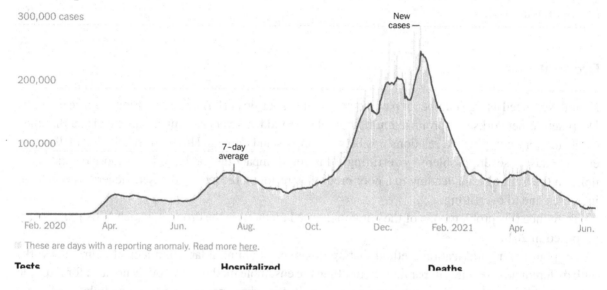

These are days with a reporting anomaly. Read more here.

Tests　　　　　　　　　**Hospitalized**　　　　　　　　　**Deaths**

Prediction Accuracy Measurement

Initially, the Long Short-Term Memory (LSTM) models planned to be trained on the training data set, and the model's prediction was validated among the testing data. To better measure the loss function and prediction performance of the trained model. The Mean Squared Error (MSE), Root Mean Square Error (RMSE) and Mean Absolute Error (MAE) are all considered in our matric. Three measurements are calculated as the following equation:

$$MAE = \frac{1}{N}\sum_{i=1}^{N}|y_i - y| \tag{7}$$

$$MSE = \frac{1}{N}\sum_{i=1}^{N}(y_i - y)^2 \tag{8}$$

$$RMSE = \sqrt{\frac{1}{N}\sum_{i=1}^{N}(y_i - y)^2} \tag{9}$$

Where, y is model predicted value, y_i is the actual value.

To evaluate the model performance on the testing data, we will calculate the accuracy, precision, recall, and the F1-score, which are very commonly used indicators of measuring measure of the degree of closeness of a measured or calculated value to actual value. We will provide this information in the fitting section.

Methodology Framework

The experiments are conducted using python 3.9 with commonly used open-source libraries such as keras (Chollet et al., 2020), Numpy (Oliphant et al., 2015), Pandas (Mckinney et al., 2010), Tensorflow (Abadi et al., 2016). The experimental setup is based on a local computational environment having Intel® Core i7@ 3.1GHz with 16 GB RAM under MacOS Big Sur Version 11.4.

Once we have the raw COVID-19 datasets, normalizing data is required before training Long Short-Term Memory (LSTM) models. After normalizing, historical datasets of confirmed and death cases are given to the Long Short-Term Memory (LSTM) model for model training. The number of hidden layers, return sequences, epoch size, dense layers, kernel size, and optimizer are preset. All the parameters will modify to a proper number based on the model evaluation. Model testing is followed after training, and all three prediction accuracy measurements are used to select the best parameters for Long Short-Term Memory (LSTM). The optimizing process will stop when the MAE, MSE, and RMSE are not significantly improved from the previous setting. The output picture will illustrate the best model prediction.

BUILDING UP LSTM PREDICTION MODEL WITH COVID-19 CONFIRMED DATA

Data Processing

First, required libraries are needed to import before importing raw COVID-19 data. In this section, we only focus on the prediction of the new confirmed cases in the United States, so that we will only use "new" color and transfer "data" to a readable formula. Then we separate the whole data set into training and testing tests. We use 0.85 as the split percent, which means that 85% of the whole data is used to train our Long Short-Term Memory (LSTM) model, while 15% of the data is used to evaluate our model performance. Since the data set covers from January 23, 2020, to June 8, 2021. We need to balance the train and test cases ratio to get a more realistic forecasting performance. Careful with df['new'].values, as we have to make it become Numpy array instead of the single vector nor a data frame. Python 3.9 code is showed as follow:

```
import numpy as np
import keras
import tensorflow as tf
from keras.preprocessing.sequence import TimeseriesGenerator
import pandas as pd
np.random.seed(36)
import plotly.graph_objects as go
df = pd.read_csv\
('/Users/Desktop/Predictions For COVID-19 With Long Short-Term Memory/Covid-19/USA/usdata.csv')
df['date'] = pd.to_datetime(df['date'])
df.set_axis(df['date'], inplace=True)
```

```
#df.drop(columns=['deaths'], inplace=True
Inew_data = df['new'].values
new_data = new_data.reshape((-1,1))
Isplit_percent = 0.85
split = int(split_percent*len(new_data))
Inew_train = new_data[:split]
new_test = new_data[split:]
Idate_train = df['date'][:split]
date_test = df['date'][split:]
Iprint(len(new_train))
print(len(new_test))
print(date_train)
print(date_test)
```

Next, Long Short-Term Memory (LSTM) is very sensitive to the sequential data fluctuations and capturing the pattern in the time series data. We have to normalize the data set before feeding it to our Long Short-Term Memory (LSTM) model. We transform data into the same scale and avoid unnecessary bias during the training and validation process. The mathematical representation of MinMaxScaler is defined as:

$$x_i = \frac{x - x_{min}}{x_{max} - x_{min}} \tag{10}$$

Where x is, the input training data set and x_i is the output of the normalized training dataset. Python code as showed as following:

```
from sklearn.preprocessing import MinMaxScaler
scaler=MinMaxScaler()
new_train=scaler.fit_transform(new_train)
new_test=scaler.transform(new_testtest)
```

Data Structure Creation

A unique data structure is needed to handle a specific time window, based on which Long Short-Term Memory (LSTM) will predict the next value. After training the data and compare different model performances, we put 12 as a lookback window. TimeseriesGenerator is used here to provide us the data in the specific format that is critical for our model. Batch size is also an important factor that may influence model performance. Therefore, we need to put a resealable number based on experimentation.

```
look_back = 12
from keras.preprocessing.sequence import TimeseriesGenerator
train_generator = TimeseriesGenerator(new_train, new_train, length=look_back, batch_size=20)
test_generator = TimeseriesGenerator(new_test, new_test, length=look_back, batch_size=1)
```

Model Building

Fundamentally, we have come to create the Long Short-Term Memory (LSTM) model. First, we need to initialize the model. Then, add the 1ˢᵗ Long Short-Term Memory (LSTM) layer with the Dropout layer followed.

from keras.models import Sequential
from keras.layers import Dense
from keras.layers import LSTM
from keras.layers import Dropout
Imodel = Sequential()
I# Adding the first LSTM layer and some Dropout regularization
model.add(LSTM(unites = 52, activation='relu', input_shape=(look_back, 1)))
model.add(Dropout(0.20))

Note for the Long Short-Term Memory (LSTM) layer, the number of units representing the total number of neurons in the layer is the most critical parameter. Fifty-two neurons would allow the model to handle high dimensional data and be large enough to capture the different directions trends. Return_sequence needs to be set as True if more layer is needed. In this study, we find one layer is large enough to handle this data set. Dropout, a valuable tool for avoiding overfitting, results in 20% of 52 neurons being eliminated randomly during each iteration.

Following provide the sample code as if more layer of Long Short-Term Memory (LSTM) is needed.

 # Adding a second LSTM layer and some Dropout regularization
#model.add(LSTM(units=45, return_sequences=True))
I
 # Adding a third LSTM layer and some Dropout regularization
#model.add(LSTM(10, return_sequences=True))
#model.add(Dropout(0.1))
I# Adding a fourth LSTM layer and some Dropout regularization
#model.add(LSTM(units=45))
#model.add(Dropout(0.2))

Finally, add the output layer. Under this circumstance, we have created a Long Short-Term Memory (LSTM) model.

model.add(Dense(units=1))

Model Compiling

After successfully creating the model, we compile our model by choosing an SGD (Stochastic Gradient Descent) algorithm and an appropriate loss function. For the optimizer, Adam, a safe choice, is used in the first case. For the loss function, we deter using MAE as the mean of the absolute value of errors between actual values and predictions. We will also check the MSE (Mean Square Error) and RMSE (Root Mean Square Error) to ensure our model is suitable for predicting the future trend.

model.compile(optimizer='adam', loss='mae')

Model Fitting

Fitting our Long Short-Term Memory (LSTM) model is the next step.

num_epochs = 2000
model.fit(train_generator, epochs=num_epochs, batch_size=12)
fitted = model.predict_generator(train_generator)

Long Short-Term Memory (LSTM) weights are updated every 12 days' data of COVID-19 with the batch size set to 12. Make sure the epochs are large enough to get a relatively small loss. Different batches and epochs are no harm to try if the loss of the model is not converging to a fair number. The model generates the fitted value by predict_generator.

model.fit(train_generator, epochs=num_epochs, batch_size=12)
fitted = model.predict_generator(train_generator)

Since we have already processed the testing data, we use the same function on test_generator as we want to get the prediction values on the testing data set. We also need to reshape the data and visualize the output to review the model fitting and evaluation step.

```
#print(predict)
prediction = model.predict_generator(test_generator)
new_train = new_train.reshape((-1))
new_test = new_test.reshape((-1))
prediction = prediction.reshape((-1)
fitted = fitted.reshape((-1))
#forecast = forecast.reshape((-1))
import plotly.graph_objects as go
import numpy as np
trace1 = go.Scatter(
    x = date_train,
    y = new_train,
    mode = 'lines',
    name = 'Data'
)
trace2 = go.Scatter(
    x = date_train,
    y = fitted,
    mode = 'lines',
```

```
        name = 'Fitted'
)
trace3 = go.Scatter(
    x = date_test,
    y = prediction,
    mode = 'lines',
    name = 'Prediction'
)
trace4 = go.Scatter(
    x = date_test,
    y = new_test,
    mode='lines',
    name = 'Ground Truth'
)
layout = go.Layout(
    title = "New Cases",
    xaxis = {'title': "Date"},
    yaxis = {'title': "Cases"}
)

fig = go.Figure(data=[trace1, trace2, trace3, trace4], layout=layout)
fig.show()
```

After the iteration, we get the loss function to decrease to 12489 and keep stable on the training data. For the testing part, we get 0.860 of accuracy, 0.924 of precision, 0.926 of recall, and the F1-score of 0.925.

Figure 2. Fitting and evaluating results for the confirmed new cases. Blueline is the train data, while the red line shows the fitting value on the train data set. For the evaluation part. The purple line illustrates the ground truth of the actual number as the green line represents the prediction of our LSTM model.

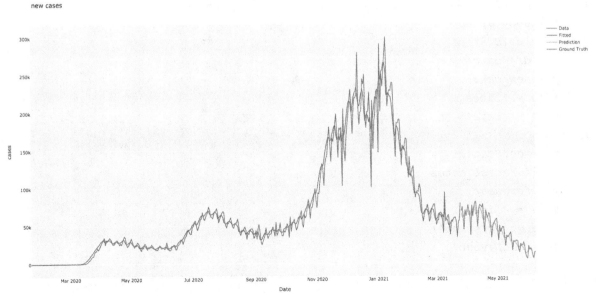

Data Forecasting

One of the differences between regular regression models and time series models is how we run predictions. According to linear regression or generalized linear models, we could simply take the last 12 months as the train data and conduct the forecast step. How do we predict in Long Short-Term Memory (LSTM)? The magic part is that the "first prediction" needs to be added to the last 11 training data. In this way, a new set of 12 data points has been created, and the model could use the 12 data points to predict the next one. Then we try to forecast the next 60 day's situation and visualize it as a plot. Python code is provided as follow:

```python
new_data = new_data.reshape((-1))
def predict(num_prediction, model):
    prediction_list = new_data[-look_back:]
    for _ in range(num_prediction):
        x = prediction_list[-look_back:]
        x = x.reshape((1, look_back, 1))
        out = model.predict(x)[0][0]
        prediction_list = np.append(prediction_list, out)
    prediction_list = prediction_list[look_back - 1:]
    return prediction_list

def predict_dates(num_prediction):
    last_date = df['date'].values[-1]
    prediction_dates = pd.date_range(last_date, periods=num_prediction +
1).tolist()
    return prediction_dates

num_prediction = 60
forecast = predict(num_prediction, model)
forecast_dates = predict_dates(num_prediction)
import plotly.graph_objects as go
import numpy as np
trace1 = go.Scatter(
    x = df['date'],
    y = new_data,
    mode = 'lines',
    name = 'Data'
)
trace2 = go.Scatter(
    x = forecast_dates,
    y = forecast,
    mode = 'lines',
    name = 'Forecast')
layout = go.Layout(
```

```
    title = "Future",
    xaxis = {'title': "Date"},
    yaxis = {'title': "Cases"}
)



fig = go.Figure(data=[trace1, trace2], layout=layout)
fig.show()
```

Figure 3. Forecasting result for the confirmed new cases of the next 60 days. Fluctuate, and the decreasing trend is shown in our forecasting result.

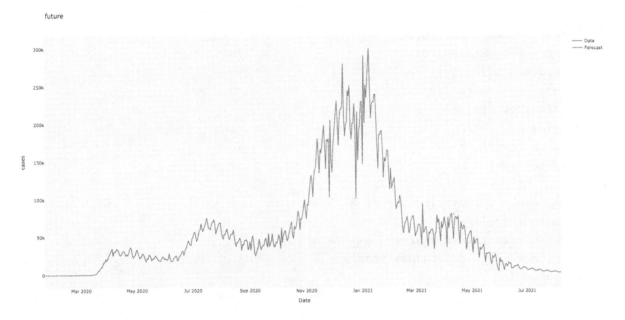

BUILDING UP LONG SHORT-TERM MEMORY (LSTM) PREDICTION MODEL WITH COVID-19 DEATHS TOLL

In this section, we use the death toll in the original COVID-19 data set. We follow a similar scheme: Data processing, Model building, model compiling, Model fitting, and Data forecasting. We modify the look back number to 7 and Long Short-Term Memory (LSTM) units to 40, which shows the number of deaths is highly dependent on the last seven days as the confirmed cases have a long-term dependency.

```
import pandas as pd
import numpy as np
import keras
import tensorflow as tf
from keras.preprocessing.sequence import TimeseriesGenerator
import pandas as pd
```

```
np.random.seed(24)

import plotly.graph_objects as go
df = pd.read_csv\
    ('/Users/Predictions For COVID-19 With Long Short-Term Memory /Covid-19/
USA/usdatad.csv')
df['date'] = pd.to_datetime(df['date'])
df.set_axis(df['date'], inplace=True)
#df.drop(columns=['deaths'], inplace=True)
Inew_data = df['deaths'].values
new_data = new_data.reshape((-1,1))
Isplit_percent = 0.85
split = int(split_percent*len(new_data))
Inew_train = new_data[:split]
new_test = new_data[split:]
Idate_train = df['date'][:split]
date_test = df['date'][split:]
Iprint(len(new_train))
print(len(new_test))
print(date_train)
print(date_test)


from sklearn.preprocessing import MinMaxScaler
scaler=MinMaxScaler()
new_train=scaler.fit_transform(new_train)
new_test=scaler.transform(new_test)
look_back = 7
Itrain_generator = TimeseriesGenerator(new_train, new_train, length=look_back,
batch_size=20)


test_generator = TimeseriesGenerator(new_test, new_test, length=look_back,
batch_size=1)
Ifrom keras.models import Sequential
from keras.layers import Dense
from keras.layers import LSTM
from keras.layers import Dropout
Imodel = Sequential()
I# Adding the first LSTM layer and some Dropout regularization
model.add(LSTM(40, activation='relu', input_shape=(look_back, 1)))
model.add(Dropout(0.20))



# Adding a second LSTM layer and some Dropout regularisation
```

```
#model.add(LSTM(units=45, return_sequences=True))
I# Adding a third LSTM layer and some Dropout regularization
#model.add(LSTM(10, activation='relu'))
#model.add(Dropout(0.1))
# Adding a fourth LSTM layer and some Dropout regularization
#model.add(LSTM(units=45))
#model.add(Dropout(0.2))
# Adding the output layer

model.add(Dense(units=1))
Imodel.compile(optimizer='adam', loss='mae')
Inum_epochs = 20000 model.fit(train_generator, epochs=num_epochs, batch_
size=24) fitted = model.predict_generator(train_generator) #print(predict)
prediction = model.predict_generator(test_generator) new_train = new_train.
reshape((-1)) new_test = new_test.reshape((-1)) prediction = prediction.re-
shape((-1)) fitted = fitted.reshape((-1)) #forecast = forecast.reshape((-1))
import plotly.graph_objects as go import numpy as np trace1 = go.Scatter( x =
date_train, y = new_train, mode = 'lines', name = 'Data' )
trace2 = go.Scatter(
 x = date_train,
 y = fitted,
 mode = 'lines',
 name = 'Fitted'
) trace3 = go.Scatter( x = date_test, y = prediction, mode = 'lines', name =
'Prediction' ) trace4 = go.Scatter( x = date_test, y = new_test, mode='lines',
name = 'Ground Truth' ) layout = go.Layout( title = "New Deaths", xaxis =
{'title': "Date"}, yaxis = {'title': "Deaths"} ) fig = go.Figure(data=[trace1,
trace2, trace3, trace4], layout=layout)
fig.show()
Inew_data = new_data.reshape((-1))
def predict(num_prediction, model):
    prediction_list = new_data[-look_back:]
I    for _ in range(num_prediction):
        x = prediction_list[-look_back:]
        x = x.reshape((1, look_back, 1))
        out = model.predict(x)[0][0]
        prediction_list = np.append(prediction_list, out)
    prediction_list = prediction_list[look_back - 1:]
    return prediction_list
Idef predict_dates(num_prediction):

    last_date = df['date'].values[-1]
    prediction_dates = pd.date_range(last_date, periods=num_prediction +
1).tolist()
```

```
    return prediction_dates
num_prediction = 60
forecast = predict(num_prediction, model)
forecast_dates = predict_dates(num_prediction)
Iimport plotly.graph_objects as go
import numpy as np

trace1 = go.Scatter(
    x = df['date'],
    y = new_data,
    mode = 'lines',
    name = 'Data'
)
trace2 = go.Scatter(
    x = forecast_dates,
    y = forecast,
    mode = 'lines',
    name = 'Forecast'
)
layout = go.Layout(
    title = "Future",
    xaxis = {'title': "Date"},
    yaxis = {'title': "Deaths"}
)

fig = go.Figure(data=[trace1, trace2], layout=layout)
fig.show()
```

On the training data, as the death toll is much smaller than the confirmed cases, we get the loss function decrease to 235.431 and get slightly fluctuate among the iterations. For the testing part, we get 0.876 for accuracy, 0.959 for precision, 0.910 for recall, and the F1-score of 0.934.

Figure 4. Fitting and evaluation result for the new deaths toll. Blueline is the train data, while the red line shows the fitting value on the train data set. For the evaluation part, the purple line illustrates the ground truth of the actual number as the green line represents the prediction of our LSTM model.

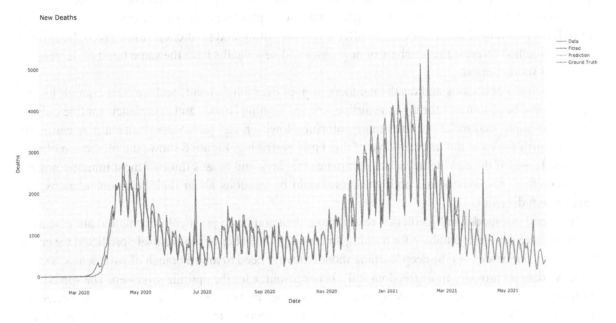

Figure 5. Forecasting result for the number of new deaths of the next 60 days.

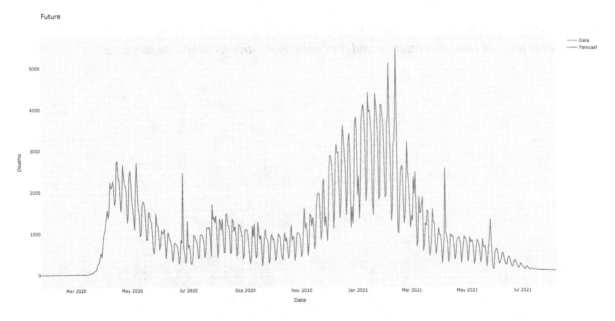

DISCUSSION

The numerical statistic analysis among the test data shows that we get high precision and recall scores on both confirmed and death cases. The fitting and testing plots send the same message that the Long Short-Term Memory (LSTM) model can offer a reliable fitting and prediction result given the limited data. Our method forecast the numbers of new cases and new deaths have the same trend of decreasing in the next future period.

The declined new cases and deaths numbers prompt everyone's heart, and we bear enough for the pandemic and hope to travel through the airline, cruise. Visiting friends and experiencing a fine cuisine refresh our minds and make our lives more colorful. However, any premature decision may cause the third or fourth waves as the transmissible of this virus is striking. Figure 6 shows the prediction of new confirmed cases if the new delta variant dominates this area and breaks through most immune protection. Therefore, researchers and policymakers should be cautious about their recommendations and management decision.

To amend our model and prediction result, more data and more practical information are essential. When we have a broader database for training and testing, the better or more closely predicted we could expect from our model. As the deep learning models always need to tune a branch of parameters, a more extensive data set provides more freedom and a better resource for the optimization step. The spread and multiple variants of Covid-19, the delay of confirmed cases and death toll data collection, the effect of vaccines, and executive order of lock-down add a lot of uncertainties and challenges in predicting the next trend. The population of the county, local economic situation, and local specific culture will also influence the spread of the virus, thus make it so difficult to seek a reliable forecasting result. Therefore, we should daily update our database and include more factors as best we can.

Figure 6. Forecasting results for the number of new confirmed cases with extreme conditions if the vaccines cannot provide enough protection and the contiguous variants dominate this area.

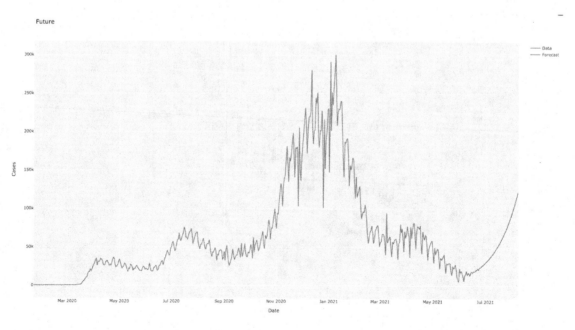

On the other hand, nurses and doctors can nap from the overwhelmed condition as hospitalized numbers decrease. However, many people may face Mental health issues on or after this pandemic.

The World Health Organization (WHO) mentioned that mental health conditions contribute to poor health outcomes, premature death, human rights violations, and global and national economic loss. Unfortunately, nationally, about one in five adults suffers from a mental illness. People may have more chance of suffering from a mental illness increases when experiencing economic troublesome; the lower a person's socioeconomic status, the higher their risk is for suffering from some sort of mental illness or even hospitalization (Hudson, et al., 2005).

Due to a lack of access to health care, individuals and families of lower-income status are less likely to seek out health care unless in an emergency; if they do, the care they receive is usually poor (Becker et al ., 2003). Kilbourne proposed that only a third of those in need receive adequate mental health care. Though the economy, tax return, and new infrastructure plan have raised more media and public attention. No significant improvement for mental health in the United States. Some people feel that physical fitness is more important than mental health, and therefore seek out care when the situation is too late to have a professional doctor intervene. However, according to WHO's research, the only way to achieve the highest standard of health is to ensure a person's mental health and well-being. What's worse, many mental care facilities were forced to temporarily or permanently closed as the pandemic swept the whole world.

Mental health is essential for human beings, and it is a disaster when mental care is limited. The importance of treating mental health conditions should be widely spread, and more people need to recognize that it's essential to have a healthy mental illness. Depression, which may lead to tragic suicide, has also been associated with an increased risk of coronary heart disease. Those who experienced very high levels of distress were 32% more likely to die of cancer (Mental Health Foundation, 2016). Even though the pandemic has changed everyone's life, the federal and local governments also need to take responsibility for those eager for a mental health service.

CONCLUSION

Long Short-Term Memory (LSTM) is a deep learning method that could capture the relationship among the time-series dynamics. This chapter verifies the ability of Long Short-Term Memory (LSTM) to fit and predict the COVID-19 growth curve feeding enough training data. The results show that Long Short-Term Memory (LSTM) is a promising tool for predicting potential outbreaks by learning from big data. If no black swan events happen in the next sixty days, the new cases and deaths toll may plummet to a relatively low-level area. The governments should carefully consider their policy to avoid getting subjugated by the COVID-19 pandemic. In future work, it's vital to improve our model and confirm the robustness of the model. Once more data is accessible and more complicated situations among the would, we could compare diverse models like Deep Bidirectional LSTM (Cui et al., 2018), attention mechanism (Vaswani et al., 2017) or consider the Bayesian method to enhance the capacity of capturing different features. We plan to investigate more places and other countries and hope our human beings can rapidly recovery from this pandemic.

FUTURE RESEARCH DIRECTIONS

The biggest problem for training the Long Short-Term Memory (LSTM) is the computational time and resources. Consequently, single-layer Long Short-Term Memory (LSTM)s are often used on local personal computers (P.C.s), while deep Long Short-Term Memory (LSTM) models are always on the cluster with powerful GPUs (Graphical Processing Units) and CPUs (Central Processing Units). Once we could access more computational resources to build a deep and large model, Long Short-Term Memory (LSTM) could be trained and better fitting and forecasting performance. In addition to confirmed cases and death toll prediction, the hospitalization and fully vaccinated data are also worthy of analysis. Furthermore, variants of Long Short-Term Memory models, Stacked Long Short-Term Memory (LSTM), Convolutional Long Short-Term Memory (LSTM), and Bi-directional Long Short-Term Memory (LSTM), have various advantages compared with the original one. It's no harm to reach and attempt to explore the best one. In general, better planning and management are often based on precise forecasting. Further studies and investigations are necessary and crucial for the health departments and governments.

REFERENCES

Abadi, M., Barham, P., Chen, J., Chen, Z., Davis, A., Dean, J., Devin, M., Ghemawat, S., Irving, G., Isard, M., Kudlur, M., Levenberg, J., Monga, R., Moore, S., Murray, D. G., Steiner, B., Tucker, P., Vasudevan, V., Warden, P., . . . Zheng, X. (2016, May 31). *TensorFlow: A system for large-scale machine learning.* https://arxiv.org/abs/1605.08695

Agrebi, S., & Larbi, A. (2020). Use of artificial intelligence in infectious diseases. *Artificial Intelligence in Precision Health*, 415–438. doi:10.1016/B978-0-12-817133-2.00018-5

Alzahrani, S. I., Aljamaan, I. A., & Al-Fakih, E. A. (2020). Forecasting the spread of the COVID-19 pandemic in Saudi Arabia using ARIMA prediction model under current public health interventions. *Journal of Infection and Public Health*, *13*(7), 914–919. doi:10.1016/j.jiph.2020.06.001 PMID:32546438

American Psychological Association. (2017). *Addressing the Mental and Behavioral Health Needs of Underserved Populations.* American Psychological Association. https://www.apa.org/advocacy/workforce-development/gpe/populations

Anand, A., Lamba, Y., & Roy, A. (2020). Forecasting COVID-19 Transmission in India Using Deep Learning Models. *Letters in Applied NanoBioScience*, *10*(2), 2044–2055. doi:10.33263/LIANBS102.20442055

Arias Velásquez, R. M., & Mejía Lara, J. V. (2020). Forecast and evaluation of COVID-19 spreading in USA with reduced-space Gaussian process regression. *Chaos, Solitons, and Fractals*, *136*, 109924. doi:10.1016/j.chaos.2020.109924 PMID:32501372

Arora, P., Kumar, H., & Panigrahi, B. K. (2020). Prediction and analysis of COVID-19 positive cases using Deep Learning Models: A descriptive case study of India. *Chaos, Solitons, and Fractals*, *139*, 110017. doi:10.1016/j.chaos.2020.110017 PMID:32572310

Atkeson, A. (2020). *What Will Be the Economic Impact of COVID-19 in the U.S.?* Rough Estimates of Disease Scenarios. doi:10.3386/w26867

Becker, G., & Newsom, E. (2003, May). Socioeconomic status and dissatisfaction with health care among chronically ill African Americans. *American Journal of Public Health*. https://www.ncbi.nlm.nih.gov/pmc/articles/PMC1447830/

Benvenuto, D., Giovanetti, M., Vassallo, L., Angeletti, S., & Ciccozzi, M. (2020). Application of the ARIMA model on the COVID-2019 epidemic dataset. *Data in Brief*, 29, 105340. doi:10.1016/j.dib.2020.105340 PMID:32181302

Bodapati, S., Bandarupally, H., & Trupthi, M. (2020). COVID-19 Time Series Forecasting of Daily Cases, Deaths Caused and Recovered Cases using Long Short Term Memory Networks. *2020 IEEE 5th International Conference on Computing Communication and Automation (ICCCA)*. 10.1109/ICCCA49541.2020.9250863

Broman, C. L. (2012). Race differences in the receipt of mental health services among young adults. *Psychological Services*, 9(1), 38–48. doi:10.1037/a0027089 PMID:22449086

Centers for Disease Control and Prevention. (2021). *Vaccines for COVID-19*. Centers for Disease Control and Prevention. https://www.cdc.gov/coronavirus/2019-ncov/vaccines/index.html

Chakraborty, T., & Ghosh, I. (2020). Real-time forecasts and risk assessment of novel coronavirus (COVID-19) cases: A data-driven analysis. doi:10.1101/2020.04.09.20059311

Chandra, R., Jain, A., & Chauhan, D. S. (2021, January 28). *Deep learning via LSTM models for COVID-19 infection forecasting in India*. Retrieved September 30, 2021, from https://arxiv.org/abs/2101.11881

Chimmula, V. K., & Zhang, L. (2020). Time series forecasting of COVID-19 transmission in Canada using LSTM networks. *Chaos, Solitons, and Fractals*, 135, 109864. doi:10.1016/j.chaos.2020.109864 PMID:32390691

Chollet, F. (2020). *The Keras Blog*. The Keras Blog ATOM. https://blog.keras.io/author/francois-chollet.html

Chow, J. C.-C., Jaffee, K., & Snowden, L. (2003). Racial/Ethnic Disparities in the Use of Mental Health Services in Poverty Areas. *American Journal of Public Health*, 93(5), 792–797. doi:10.2105/AJPH.93.5.792 PMID:12721146

Connor, J. T., Martin, R. D., & Atlas, L. E. (1994). Recurrent Neural Networks and robust time series prediction. *IEEE Transactions on Neural Networks*, 5(2), 240–254. doi:10.1109/72.279188 PMID:18267794

Counts, P. G. T. N. N. (2016, January 25). Reducing Health Care Costs Through Early Intervention On Mental Illnesses: Health Affairs Blog. *Health Affairs*.

Cruz-Mendoza, I., Quevedo-Pulido, J., & Adanaque-Infante, L. (2020). LSTM perfomance analysis for predictive models based on Covid-19 dataset. *2020 IEEE XXVII International Conference on Electronics, Electrical Engineering and Computing (INTERCON)*. 10.1109/INTERCON50315.2020.9220248

Cui, Z., Ke, R., Pu, Z., & Wang, Y. (2020). Stacked bidirectional and unidirectional LSTM recurrent neural network for forecasting network-wide traffic state with missing values. *Transportation Research Part C, Emerging Technologies*, 118, 102674. doi:10.1016/j.trc.2020.102674

Da Silva, R. G., Ribeiro, M. H., Mariani, V. C., & dos Coelho, L. (2020). Forecasting Brazilian and American COVID-19 cases based on artificial intelligence coupled with climatic exogenous variables. *Chaos, Solitons, and Fractals*, *139*, 110027. doi:10.1016/j.chaos.2020.110027 PMID:32834591

Everitt, B., Landau, S., & Leese, M. (2011). *Cluster analysis* (5th ed.). Wiley Series in Probability and Statistics. doi:10.1002/9780470977811

Fattah, J., Ezzine, L., Aman, Z., El Moussami, H., & Lachhab, A. (2018). Forecasting of demand using ARIMA model. *International Journal of Engineering Business Management*, *10*, 184797901880867. doi:10.1177/1847979018808673

Fernandes, N. (2020). Economic Effects of Coronavirus Outbreak (COVID-19) on the World Economy. SSRN *Electronic Journal*. doi:10.2139/ssrn.3557504

Feroze, N. (2020). Forecasting the patterns of COVID-19 and causal impacts of lock-down in top five affected countries using Bayesian Structural Time Series Models. *Chaos, Solitons, and Fractals*, *140*, 110196. doi:10.1016/j.chaos.2020.110196 PMID:32834662

Fischer, S. H. (2021, January 8). *Use of Telehealth Jumped as Pandemic Shutdown Began; Use Is Highest for Mental Health Services*. RAND Corporation. https://www.rand.org/news/press/2021/01/11/index1.html

Fischer, S. H., Uscher-Pines, L., Roth, E., & Breslau, J. (2021). The Transition to Telehealth during the First Months of the COVID-19 Pandemic: Evidence from a National Sample of Patients. *Journal of General Internal Medicine*, *36*(3), 849–851. doi:10.100711606-020-06358-0 PMID:33409884

Gallagher, W. (2020, July 1). *For People in Underserved Communities, Getting Mental Health Care Is a Struggle*. Black Bear Lodge. https://blackbearrehab.com/blog/for-people-in-underserved-communities-getting-mental-health-care-is-a-struggle/

Gao, J., Zheng, P., Jia, Y., Chen, H., Mao, Y., Chen, S., Wang, Y., Fu, H., & Dai, J. (2020). Mental Health Problems and Social Media Exposure During COVID-19 Outbreak. SSRN *Electronic Journal*. doi:10.2139/ssrn.3541120

Ghany, K. K., Zawbaa, H. M., & Sabri, H. M. (2021). COVID-19 prediction using LSTM algorithm: GCC case study. *Informatics in Medicine Unlocked*, *23*, 100566. doi:10.1016/j.imu.2021.100566 PMID:33842686

Gorbalenya, A. E., Baker, S. C., Baric, R. S., Groot, R. J., Haagmans, B. L., Gulyaeva, A. A., Drosten, C., Ziebuhr, J., Sola, I., Sidorov, I. A., Samborskiy, D. V., Leo, L. M., Poon, L. L. M., Perlman, S., Penzar, D., Neuman, B. W., Leontovich, A. M., & Lauber, C. (2020). The species Severe acute respiratory syndrome-related coronavirus: Classifying 2019-nCoV and naming it SARS-CoV-2. *Nature Microbiology*, *5*(4), 536–544. doi:10.103841564-020-0695-z PMID:32123347

Gower, J. C., & Ross, G. J. (1969). Minimum Spanning Trees and Single Linkage Cluster Analysis. *Applied Statistics*, *18*(1), 54. doi:10.2307/2346439

Graves, A., & Jaitly, N., & Mohamed, A-R. (2013). Hybrid speech recognition with Deep Bidirectional LSTM. *2013 IEEE Workshop on Automatic Speech Recognition and Understanding*. 10.1109/ASRU.2013.6707742

Grawitch, M. (2009). Faulty Assumptions in Creating a Psychologically Healthy Workplace. *PsycEXTRA Dataset*. doi:10.1037/e686382011-001

Henderson, C., Evans-Lacko, S., & Thornicroft, G. (2013). Mental Illness Stigma, Help Seeking, and Public Health Programs. *American Journal of Public Health*, *103*(5), 777–780. doi:10.2105/AJPH.2012.301056 PMID:23488489

Hochreiter, S., & Schmidhuber, J. (1997, November 15). *Long Short-Term Memory*. Neural Computation. https://direct.mit.edu/neco/article/9/8/1735/6109/Long-Short-Term-Memory

Hudson, C. G. (2005). Socioeconomic Status and Mental Illness: Tests of the Social Causation and Selection Hypotheses. *The American Journal of Orthopsychiatry*, *75*(1), 3–18. doi:10.1037/0002-9432.75.1.3 PMID:15709846

Jansson, B. S. (2020). Practicing Policy Advocacy in the Mental Health and Substance Abuse Sector. In Social welfare policy and advocacy: advancing social justice through eight policy sectors (pp. 289–332). Sage.

John Hopkins University (JHU). (2021). *COVID-19 Dashboard by the Center for Systems Science and Engineering (CSSE)*. https://publichealthupdate.com/jhu/

Karra, S. (2020, October 6). *LSTM for Time Series predictions*. Medium. https://sailajakarra.medium.com/lstm-for-time-series-predictions-cc68cc11ce4f

Kaxiras, E., Neofotistos, G., & Angelaki, E. (2020). The first 100 days: Modeling the evolution of the COVID-19 pandemic. *Chaos, Solitons, and Fractals*, *138*, 110114. doi:10.1016/j.chaos.2020.110114 PMID:32834582

Khazan, O. (2016, June 1). It's Hard to Get Therapy Unless You're White. *The Atlantic*. https://www.theatlantic.com/health/archive/2016/06/the-struggle-of-seeking-therapy-while-poor/484970/

Kilbourne, A. M., Beck, K., Spaeth-Rublee, B., Ramanuj, P., O'Brien, R. W., Tomoyasu, N., & Pincus, H. A. (2018). Measuring and improving the quality of mental health care: A global perspective. *World Psychiatry; Official Journal of the World Psychiatric Association (WPA)*, *17*(1), 30–38. doi:10.1002/wps.20482 PMID:29352529

Lalmuanawma, S., Hussain, J., & Chhakchhuak, L. (2020). Applications of machine learning and artificial intelligence for Covid-19 (SARS-CoV-2) pandemic: A review. *Chaos, Solitons, and Fractals*, *139*, 110059. doi:10.1016/j.chaos.2020.110059 PMID:32834612

Li, X., & Wu, X. (2015). Constructing Long Short-Term Memory based deep Recurrent Neural Networks for large vocabulary speech recognition. *2015 IEEE International Conference on Acoustics, Speech and Signal Processing (ICASSP)*. 10.1109/ICASSP.2015.7178826

Maleki, M., Mahmoudi, M. R., Wraith, D., & Pho, K.-H. (2020). Time series modelling to forecast the confirmed and recovered cases of COVID-19. *Travel Medicine and Infectious Disease*, *37*, 101742. doi:10.1016/j.tmaid.2020.101742

Maliszewska, M., Mattoo, A., & van der Mensbrugghe, D. (2020). *The Potential Impact of COVID-19 on GDP and Trade: A Preliminary Assessment*. doi:10.1596/1813-9450-9211

McKinney, W. (2010, January 1). *Pandas: A Foundational Python Library for Data Analysis and Statistics: Semantic Scholar*. Academic Press.

Mental Health Foundation. (2016, July 9). *Physical health and mental health*. https://www.mentalhealth.org.uk/a-to-z/p/physical-health-and-mental-health

Niraula, P., Mateu, J., & Chaudhuri, S. (2021). A Bayesian machine learning approach for spatio-temporal prediction of COVID-19 cases. doi:10.21203/rs.3.rs-636809/v1

Olah, C. (2015). *Understanding LSTM Networks*. Understanding LSTM Networks -- colah's blog. https://colah.github.io/posts/2015-08-Understanding-LSTMs/

Oliphant, T. E. (2015). *Guide to NumPy* (2nd ed.). CreateSpace Independent Publishing Platform.

Owusu-Fordjour, C., Koomson, C. K., & Hanson, D. (2020, January 1). The Impact Of Covid-19 On Learning - The Perspective of the Ghanaian Student. *Semantic Scholar. European Journal of Education Studies*. DOI: doi:10.46827/EJES.V0I0.3000

Pakulis, A. (2020, February 25). *Fact Sheet: Impact of the President's 2021 Budget on Health*. First Focus on Children. https://firstfocus.org/resources/fact-sheet/fact-sheet-impact-of-the-presidents-2021-budget-on-health

Pathan, R. K., Biswas, M., & Khandaker, M. U. (2020). Time series prediction of COVID-19 by mutation rate analysis using recurrent neural network-based LSTM model. *Chaos, Solitons, and Fractals, 138*, 110018. doi:10.1016/j.chaos.2020.110018 PMID:32565626

Pearson, G. S., Hines-Martin, V. P., Evans, L. K., York, J. A., Kane, C. F., & Yearwood, E. L. (2015). Addressing Gaps in Mental Health Needs of Diverse, At-Risk, Underserved, and Disenfranchised Populations: A Call for Nursing Action. *Archives of Psychiatric Nursing, 29*(1), 14–18. doi:10.1016/j.apnu.2014.09.004 PMID:25634869

Ren, H., Zhao, L., Zhang, A., Song, L., Liao, Y., Lu, W., & Cui, C. (2020). Early forecasting of the potential risk zones of COVID-19 in China's megacities. *The Science of the Total Environment, 729*, 138995. doi:10.1016/j.scitotenv.2020.138995 PMID:32353723

Robinson, A. J., Cook, G. D., Ellis, D. P. W., Fosler-Lussier, E., Renals, S. J., & Williams, D. A. G. (2002). Connectionist speech recognition of Broadcast News. *Speech Communication, 37*(1-2), 27–45. doi:10.1016/S0167-6393(01)00058-9

Sak, H., Senior, A., & Beaufays, F. (n.d.). *Long Short-Term Memory Based Recurrent Neural Network Architectures for Large Vocabulary Speech Recognition*. https://www.arxiv-vanity.com/papers/1402.1128/

Schmidhuber, J. (2015). Deep learning in neural networks: An overview. *Neural Networks, 61*, 85–117. doi:10.1016/j.neunet.2014.09.003 PMID:25462637

Shahid, F., Zameer, A., & Muneeb, M. (2020). Predictions for COVID-19 with deep learning models of LSTM, GRU and Bi-LSTM. *Chaos, Solitons, and Fractals, 140*, 110212. doi:10.1016/j.chaos.2020.110212 PMID:32839642

Shastri, S., Singh, K., Kumar, S., Kour, P., & Mansotra, V. (2020). Time series forecasting of Covid-19 using deep learning models: India-USA comparative case study. *Chaos, Solitons, and Fractals, 140*, 110227. doi:10.1016/j.chaos.2020.110227 PMID:32843824

Shi, X., Chen, Z., Wang, H., & Yeung, D.-Y. (1970, January 1). *Convolutional LSTM Network: A Machine Learning Approach for Precipitation Nowcasting*. Advances in Neural Information Processing Systems. https://proceedings.neurips.cc/paper/5955-convolutional-lstm-network-a-machine-learning-approach-for-precipitation-nowcasting

Shim, R., Koplan, C., Langheim, F. J. P., Manseau, M. W., Powers, R. A., & Compton, M. T. (2014). The Social Determinants of Mental Health: An Overview and Call to Action. *Psychiatric Annals*, *44*(1), 22–26. doi:10.3928/00485713-20140108-04

Shirmohammadi-Khorram, N., Tapak, L., Hamidi, O., & Maryanaji, Z. (2019). A comparison of three data mining time series models in prediction of monthly brucellosis surveillance data. *Zoonoses and Public Health*, *66*(7), 759–772. doi:10.1111/zph.12622 PMID:31305019

Shortliffe, E. H. (1976). Copyright. *Computer-Based Medical Consultations: Mycin*. Advance online publication. doi:10.1016/B978-0-444-00179-5.50003-2

Singh, S., Parmar, K. S., Kumar, J., & Makkhan, S. J. (2020). Development of new hybrid model of discrete wavelet decomposition and autoregressive integrated moving average (ARIMA) models in application to one month forecast the casualties cases of COVID-19. *Chaos, Solitons, and Fractals*, *135*, 109866. doi:10.1016/j.chaos.2020.109866 PMID:32395038

Srivastava, N., Hinton, G., Krizhevsky, A., Sutskever, I., & Salakhutdinov, R. (1970, January 1). Dropout: A Simple Way to Prevent Neural Networks from Overfitting. *Journal of Machine Learning Research*. https://jmlr.org/papers/v15/srivastava14a.html

Sun, L. (2021, May 7). *LSTM for Stock Price Prediction*. Medium. https://towardsdatascience.com/lstm-for-google-stock-price-prediction-e35f5cc84165

Tan, P.-N., Steinbach, M., Karpatne, A., & Kumar, V. (2020). *Introduction to Data Mining*. Pearson.

The New York Times. (2021). *Coronavirus (Covid-19) Data in the United States*. GitHub. https://github.com/nytimes/covid-19-data

Thomas, S., Jenkins, R., & Wright, F. (2016). Promoting Mental Health and Preventing Mental Illness in General Practice. *London Journal of Primary Care*. https://pubmed.ncbi.nlm.nih.gov/28250821/

Ting, D. S. W., Carin, L., Dzau, V., & Wong, T. Y. (2020, March 27). Digital technology and COVID-19. *Nature News*. https://www.nature.com/articles/s41591-020-0824-5

U.S. Department of Health and Human Services. (2020). *Mental Illness*. National Institute of Mental Health. https://www.nimh.nih.gov/health/statistics/mental-illness.shtml

Vaswani, A., Shazeer, N., Parmar, N., Uszkoreit, J., Jones, L., Gomez, A. N., Kaiser, L., & Polosukhin, I. (2017, December 6). *Attention is all you need*. Retrieved September 30, 2021, from https://arxiv.org/abs/1706.03762

Wang, H., Li, G., Wang, G., Peng, J., Jiang, H., & Liu, Y. (2016, December 8). Deep learning based ensemble approach for probabilistic wind power forecasting. *Applied Energy*. https://www.sciencedirect.com/science/article/pii/S0306261916317421

Wang, L., & Shen, L. (2020). A CONVLSTM-combined hierarchical attention network for saliency detection. *2020 IEEE International Conference on Image Processing (ICIP)*. 10.1109/ICIP40778.2020.9190788

Wang, P., Zheng, X., Li, J., & Zhu, B. (2020). Prediction of epidemic trends in COVID-19 with logistic model and machine learning technics. *Chaos, Solitons, and Fractals*, *139*, 110058. doi:10.1016/j.chaos.2020.110058 PMID:32834611

Wieczorek, M., Siłka, J., & Woźniak, M. (2020). Neural network powered COVID-19 spread forecasting model. *Chaos, Solitons, and Fractals*, *140*, 110203. doi:10.1016/j.chaos.2020.110203 PMID:32834663

Williams, D., & Williams-Morris, R. (2000). Racism and Mental Health: The African American experience. *Ethnicity & Health*, *5*(3-4), 243–268. doi:10.1080/713667453 PMID:11105267

World Health Organization. (2019). *Special initiative for mental health (2019-2023)*. World Health Organization. https://www.who.int/mental_health/evidence/special_initiative_2019_2023/en/

World Health Organization. (2020). *Coronavirus Disease (COVID-19) Situation Reports*. World Health Organization. https://www.who.int/emergencies/diseases/novel-coronavirus-2019/situation-reports

Yadav, M., Perumal, M., & Srinivas, M. (2020). Analysis on novel coronavirus (COVID-19) using machine learning methods. *Chaos, Solitons, and Fractals*, *139*, 110050. doi:10.1016/j.chaos.2020.110050 PMID:32834604

Yang, J.-H., Cheng, C.-H., & Chan, C.-P. (2017). A Time-Series Water Level Forecasting Model Based on Imputation and Variable Selection Method. *Computational Intelligence and Neuroscience*, *2017*, 1–11. doi:10.1155/2017/9478952 PMID:29250110

Yeşilkanat, C. M. (2020). Spatio-temporal estimation of the daily cases of COVID-19 in worldwide using random forest machine learning algorithm. *Chaos, Solitons, and Fractals*, *140*, 110210. doi:10.1016/j.chaos.2020.110210 PMID:32843823

Zaremba, W., Sutskever, I., & Vinyals, O. (2014, September 11). *Recurrent Neural Network Regularization*. https://arxiv.org/abs/1409.2329v2

ADDITIONAL READING

Boos, D. D., & Stefanski, L. A. (2013). *Essential Statistical Inference: Theory and Methods*. Springer-Verlag. doi:10.1007/978-1-4614-4818-1

Bruhl, R. H. (2018). *Understanding Statistical Analysis and Modeling*. SAGE Publications, Inc.

Chollet, F. (2021). *Deep Learning with Python* (2nd ed.). Manning Publications Co.

Conway, D., & White, J. M. (2012). *Machine Learning for Hackers*. O'Reilly Media.

Goodfellow, I., Bengio, Y., & Courville, A. (2017). *Deep Learning*. The MIT Press.

Harrington, P. (2012). *Machine Learning in Action*. Manning Publications Co.

Hastie, T., Tibshirani, R., & Friedman, J. H. (2017). *The Elements of Statistical Learning: Data Mining, Inference, and Prediction*. Springer-Verlag New York.

James, G., Witten, D., Hastie, T. J., & Tibshirani, R. J. (2017). *An Introduction to Statistical Learning: with applications in R*. Springer.

Kuhn, M., & Johnson, K. (2016). *Applied Predictive Modeling*. Springer-Verlag New York.

Mitchell, T. M. (2017). *Machine Learning*. McGraw Hill.

Mueller, J., & Massaron, L. (2019). *Deep Learning For Dummies*. John Wiley and Sons, Inc.

Müller, A. C., & Guido, S. (2018). *Introduction to Machine Learning With Python: A Guide For Data Scientists*. O'Reilly.

Nocedal, J., & Wright, S. (2006). *Numerical Optimization*. Springer-Verlag New York.

KEY TERMS AND DEFINITIONS

Artificial Intelligence (A.I.): Artificial intelligence is a wide-ranging branch of computer science concerned with building smart machines capable of performing tasks that typically require human intelligence. A.I. is an interdisciplinary science with multiple approaches, but advancements in machine learning and deep learning are creating a paradigm shift in virtually every sector of the tech industry.

Artificial Neural Network (ANN): Artificial neural network referred to as neural network, is a computing system made up of a number of simple, highly interconnected processing elements, which process information by their dynamic state response to the external inputs.

Deep Learning: Deep learning, a subset of machine learning, utilizes a hierarchical level of Artificial Neural Networks to carry out the process of machine learning. It mimics the working of the human brain in processing supervised and unsupervised data in detecting objects, recognizing speech, translating languages, and making decisions.

Dropout: Dropout is a method to capture the information, usually the variability, contained within a dataset at a lower dimension.

Long Short-Term Memory (LSTM): Long short-term memory is an artificial recurrent neural network (RNN) architecture used in deep learning. LSTM has feedback connections so that it's useful for different handle types of time series data. LSTM unit is composed of a cell, an input gate, an output gate, and a forget gate.

Loss Function: Loss function is used to describe the error between the output of our algorithms and the given target value. In layman's terms, the loss function expresses how far off the mark our computed output is (Courville, 2016).

Mental Health: Mental health includes our emotional, psychological, and social well-being. It affects how we think, feel, and act. Mental health is essential at every stage of life, from childhood and adolescence through adulthood.

Prediction Accuracy Measure: Prediction accuracy measure is a numerical measure of the difference between actual and prediction of the trained model. Mean squared error (MSE), root mean squared error (RMSE) and mean absolute error (MAE) are commonly used to evaluate the performance.

Recurrent Neural Network (RNN): Recurrent neural network is a class of artificial neural networks (ANN) where connections between nodes form a directed graph along a temporal sequence.

Chapter 6
Protein–Protein Interactions (PPI) via Deep Neural Network (DNN)

Zizhe Gao
Columbia University, USA

Hao Lin
Northeastern University, USA

ABSTRACT

Entering the 21st century, computer science and biological research have entered a stage of rapid development. With the rapid inflow of capital into the field of significant health research, a large number of scholars and investors have begun to focus on the impact of neural network science on biometrics, especially the study of biological interactions. With the rapid development of computer technology, scientists improve or perfect traditional experimental methods. This chapter aims to prove the reliability of the methodology and computing algorithms developed by Satyajit Mahapatra and Ivek Raj Gupta's project team. In this chapter, three datasets take the responsibility to testify the computing algorithms, and they are S. cerevisiae, H. pylori, and Human-B. Anthracis. Among these three sets of data, the S. cerevisiae is the core subset. The result shows 87%, 87.5%, and 89% accuracy and 87%, 86%, and 87% precision for these three data sets, respectively.

INTRODUCTION

Neural network computing, as the name suggests, is to simulate the operation mode of the computer to achieve the simulation of human brain neural autonomous judgment ability, adaptability, and the ability of multi-project integration and parallel processing. From a biological perspective, the human cerebral cortex contains more than 10 billion neurons connected to form a neural network. Information is collected through the body's sense of touch, taste and other sensory organs. The collected data is transmitted to the central nervous system and the connection points of the neural network. Then the data collected

DOI: 10.4018/978-1-7998-8455-2.ch006

will be screened, sorted out and cleaned by the nerve center system, and then transmitted to the whole body according to different analysis results to coordinate the functions of various organs in the body.

Figure 1. Neural network framework of inputs and functions to produce perceptron.

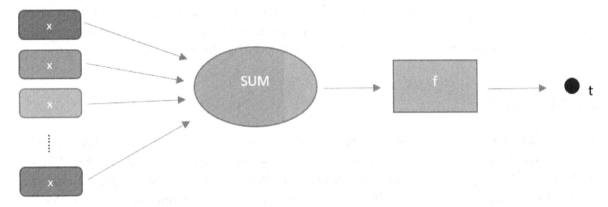

From a historical perspective, in the 1940s, McCulloch and Pitts discovered the work of turning logic devices into neurons (Palm, 1986); In the 1960s, Rosenblatt proposed the Perceptron model (Fig. 1), which utilizes simulated learning and recognition functions. It has several input terminals to represent the reception of signals from input or another perceptron. After summation of these signals, outputs or transmits them to other perceptrons through excitation functions. Nerve cells dendrites and axons, some close connection between neurons, some loose connection, and performance are high on the side of each connection weights on the perception of low, save the weight information is neural network acquisition of "knowledge". However, due to the data dependence, use limitations and forced to end. Until recent years, modern high-tech approaches have provided a solid foundation for research into artificial intelligence, neural networks, deep learning, and other technologies, and the consumer market's expectation of intelligent devices has fueled researchers' enthusiasm for the development of neural networks and other related technologies (Admin, 2021).

Compared with the traditional computing methods, the deep neural network algorithm has the ability to self-adaptation and self-organization (Mahapatra, Gupta, Sahu, & Panda, 2021). The traditional computing methods rely on the knowledge and ability written by the programmers to the systematic program. Hence, it primarily depends on the early programmer to write the code, as well as the maintenance and update of the database. In this traditional model, the computing power and intelligence of the computer will be dramatically limited. They were looking at the new updated deep neuron network. The neural network algorithm provides machines with self-learning, self-identification and this specific ability can develop the computer beyond the capacity of its designer itself. Typically, the program designer sets up a learning method for the neural network algorithm or the content to imitate and periodically provides a sample standard for the computer to replicate. The other way is to let the algorithm learn on its own. In this case, the program designer only needs to build a learning instruction for the algorithm, and the algorithm will learn accordingly to the type and pattern of the imported data sets to achieve the goal of identifying the regularity and characteristics of the environment (Oja, 1994).

From the perspective of actual demand, in the 21st century, with the global outbreak of COVID-19 since late 2020, medical and health care has become the focus of exploring international research institutions. There is also a growing trend in understanding Protein-Protein Interactions (PPIs) around the world, such as the proteins that are the core building blocks of viruses. The PPI can provide series of exchanges of amino acids between protein molecules. After extracting the interactions between the molecules, the deep neuron network algorism can develop an ability to predict the future interactions in any given protein. That is to say, the core of a virus is a protein that interacts with each other to reproduce, which means that understanding these interactions could speed up efforts to defeat the virus.

BACKGROUND

In traditional biological research, biologists have explored a considerable number of experimental methods to explore the relationship between protein interactions. These methods include Tandem Affinity Purification (TAP), affinity chromatography, X-ray crystallography, and Nuclear Magnetic Resonance (NMR) (Du, Zhang, Yao, Hu, & Sun, 2017). The advantage of these experimental methods is that the changes in proteins can be recorded continuously during the testing process. However, their disadvantage is that the seep and accuracy of recording are too much dependent on human capability. The accuracy of recording interactions between proteins can be lower than the speed of protein interaction computed by the deep neuron network algorisms. It can also lead to unreliable conclusions concluded by these experimental methods.

In reality, scientists and researchers developed several usable methodologies based on the deep neuron network algorism to observe PPIs. These include, but are not limited to, DEEPPPI (Du, Zhang, Yao, Hu, & Sun, 2017), Convolutional Neural Network (Baruah, 2017), Domain Frequency & Association Score Base Classification of Protein Pairs (Garima, Navita, & Gulshan, 2012), etc. In order to improve the efficiency of recording protein-protein interaction relationships and improve the reliability of experimental conclusions. The researchers, led by Satyajit Mahapatra as the core member, proposed using Deep Neural Networks (DNN) for Protein-Protein Interactions' prediction.

Traditionally, two models are mainly used to research PPIs, and they are Naive Bayes (NB), K-Nearest Neighbor (KNN).

KNN (K-Nearest Neighbor) is one of the simplest machine learning algorithms and can be used for classification and regression. It is a supervised learning algorithm. The idea is that if most of the K parameters are similar to a dataset in the eigenspace belong to a particular category. That sample also belongs to that category. That is to say, the method only determines the category of the models is divided according to the category of the closest one or several instances.

Although the KNN algorithm is used in a wide range of aspects, as a machine learning algorithm, it still has advantages and disadvantages. From the practical level, the KNN algorithm is simple in logic and mature in theory. It can be used for both classification and regression. When necessary, it can also be used for nonlinear variety. From the technical point of view, the KNN algorithm has no obvious training process. Still, at the beginning of the program, after the data set is loaded into the memory, there is no need for training, direct prediction, so the training time complexity is 0. Secondly, since the KNN method mainly depends on the surrounding limited adjacent samples, rather than the method of discriminating the class domain to determine the category to which it belongs, the KNN method is more suitable than other methods for the sample set to be classified with a lot of crossovers or overlap of the class domain. Any algorithm will have shortcomings. (Zhang, 2016).

Although the KNN algorithm has been very mature, there are still shortcomings. The KNN algorithm needs to calculate the distance between each test point and the training set. When the training set is large, the amount of calculation is quite large, and the time complexity is high, especially when the number of features is relatively large. This means that the KNN algorithm requires a lot of memory and high space complexity. When the sample is unbalanced (that is, some categories have a large sample size and others have a small sample size), the prediction accuracy for rare categories is low. In addition, the KNN algorithm is a lazy learning method, which leads to a slower prediction speed than logistic regression and other algorithms (Zhang, 2016).

Naive Bayes is a straightforward classification algorithm, and it's called Naive Bayes classification because the idea is naive. The ideological basis of Naive Bayes is: for the given category to be classified, solve the probability of each category under the condition of the occurrence of this category. The largest category will be considered the category to which this category belongs (Safri, Arifudin & Muslim, 2018).

As one of the classifications of the Bayesian model, the Naive Bayesian model originated from classical mathematics theory, and its classification efficiency is relatively stable. Especially for small-scale data, performance is outstanding, can be used to process multi-classification tasks, suitable for incremental training, significantly if the amount of data exceeds the memory, can be batch by batch to gradual movement. From the perspective of technical reliability, the algorithm is simple and not sensitive to missing data. Although the Naive Bayes model has high reliability, it still has some shortcomings. The naive Bayes model has the lowest error rate compared with other classification methods. But this is not always the case because the Naive Bayes model assumes that the attributes are independent of each other, and this assumption is often not valid in practice. Although the attribute correlation is small, the Naive Bayes performance is good. However, when the number of attributes is relatively large or the correlation between features is significant, the classification effect is not good (Huang, Lu, & Ling. 2003).

Moreover, when the Naive Bayes model is needed to be used for operation, the model needs to know the prior probability. The prior probability depends on the hypothesis in many cases. The hypothesis model can have a variety of models, which leads to the poor prediction effect due to the assumption of the prior model. From the perspective of the accuracy of the analysis conclusion, the data determine the posterior probability, so there is a specific error rate in the classification decision (Huang, Lu, & Ling. 2003).

Deep Neural Networks (DNN) are used to efficiently and accurately learn protein behavior from common protein descriptions. According to paper by Mahapatra et al. (2021) on DNN, there are several shortcomings in traditional studies on protein interaction relationships. First, traditional research is exceptionally dependent on the professional ability of researchers, and the lack of experience of the researchers on the selection of operational models will lead to significant and fetal experimental errors. On the other hand, the general machine learning method cannot accurately extract the available information for all existing observation sequences, thus reducing the validity of the experimental conclusions. Last but not least, the neural network algorithm can enhance the autonomous screening ability of the selected model so as to realize the power of automatic extraction of advanced discriminant features.

MAIN FOCUS OF THE CHAPTER

In view of these traditional shortcomings, experiment by Mahapatra et al. (2021) shows that the DNN can automatically learn specific sequence motif of RNA-protein; and it can reduce the influence of noise in the original data and learn the fundamental hidden advanced features. In addition, some Deep Neural Network-based methods even artificially introduce noise to reduce overfitting and enhance the generalization and robustness of the model (Mahapatra, Gupta, Sahu, & Panda, 2021).

In order to verify whether the DNN method proposed by Mahapatra et al. (2021) can improve the effectiveness of PPI researches, this paper will test the methodology behind the model and hypothesis proposed by Satyajit Mahapatra from the following aspects.

1. Analyze the Deep Neuron Network (DNN) algorithm and operational logic, verify whether the neural network can automatically extract abstract features from protein sequence features, and verify whether the deep neural network can better promote the recognition of advanced fusion features than K-nearest neighbor and Naive Bayes.
2. Analyze and compare whether the input of each protein as a neural unit can improve the effectiveness of neural network learning

ISSUES AND PROBLEMS

Limitation of Studying PPIs in Vivo and Vitro

Throughout the experiment settings, many problems and issues appear and these issues include not only with technical issues, but also logical issues. The identification of protein-protein interactions in vivo requires validation in vitro (Piehler, 2005). The classic technique for detecting protein-protein interactions in vitro is Tandem Affinity Purification (TAP). TAP, a technique based on affinity purification of a bait protein, is built on immunoprecipitation and pull-down assays. A 'bait' protein tagged with a TAP tag is expressed in a target cell and then analyzed by mass spectrometry and SDS-PAGE (Puig et al., 2001). The main disadvantage of TAP is that an added tag will impact the binding of protein to its interacting partners and protein expression level. Both of them make for errors in results. In addition, TAP requires a well-trained technician to operate in wash step, mass spectrometry and SDS-PAGE (Rigaut et al., 1999).

The Yeast Two-Hybrid (Y2H) system is made to screen Vivo protein-protein interaction (Piehler, 2005). This technique requires a molecular structure of transcription factor that contains DNA-Binding-Domain (DBD) and a Transcription Activation Domain (TAD). A DBD and TAD at non-binding status will inactivate the transcription factor, and its function could be restored by fusing them to two interacting proteins. Therefore, the protein-protein interaction can be detected by combining a 'bait' protein to a DBD and 'prey' proteins (potential interaction partners) to TAD. This technique was used to screen the protein interaction network of S. cerevisiae. (Hendrickson, 1994).

However, the Y2H systems are limited to screen protein-protein interactions in the nucleus, and plasma membrane proteins perform significant physiological functions in cells, which cannot be measured with this technique. In the most available designs, the fluorescence substrates are used to monitor the status of the reaction and identify the protein-protein interactions. A fluorescence substrate work efficiency is affected by several environmental factors, including room temperature, PH value, cellular status and binding, etc. (Hendrickson, 1994). A slight change in experimental and fluorescence substrate storage conditions can result in an experiment fails, including a high false-positive rate by over-activated fluorescence substrates. Thus, a new technique that is relevant independent and excluding the experimental error needs to be developed.

Limitation of Current Algorithms on Interspecies & Intraspecies PPI Prediction

In recent years, people proposed several novel computational techniques that use features extracted from protein sequences to predict intraspecies and interspecies PPI. An auto-covariance method extracts information from protein sequence and predicts PPIs in S. cerevisiae using Support Vector Machines (SVM) (Guo et al., 2008). People use multiscale continuous and discontinuous local feature descriptors using these features for PPI prediction based on the SVM algorithm (You et al., 2013). Zhu-Hongyou and his colleagues utilized the discrete cosine transformation, global encoding and wavelet transformations to distinguish features from substitution matrix representation of protein sequence (You et al., 2019). Moreover, this technique is improved by a fusion of these features is used as input to the weighted sparse classifier for PPI prediction.

A new approach is also created to predict host-pathogen interactions by conducting multiple classifiers, including random forest, Naive Bayes, K-Nearest Neighbor (Kösesoy, Gök, & Öz, 2019). Furthermore, this hybrid classifier yielded the best result in terms of accuracy, F1 score, MCC (Matthews correlation coefficient), AUC (Area Under Curve). A prediction of the host-pathogen interaction is made based on a combination of four features, such as Amino Acid Composition (AAC), Composition-Transition-Distribution (CTD), the relative frequency of amino acid triads, and frequency difference of amino acid triads (Zhou et al., 2018). With this method, the fused feature vectors, a complex high dimensional vector, are used as machine learning input that affects the predictor's accuracy. Lei Wang and his colleague performed a chi-square test to filter low-grade features from the high-dimensional feature set. Subsequently, they employed the rotation forest classifiers for the prediction of PPI (Wang et al., 2017).

Most of the current machine learning techniques used a single type of protein sequence feature or a fusion of multiple components to predict the intraspecies PPI. Still, very little work has been reported for the prediction of interspecies PPI. A prediction of intraspecies PPI helps to understand the process of life, such as hormone regulation, metabolism. In addition, issues such as infective diseases, and host-pathogen interaction, need knowledge of interspecies PPI. However, none of the mentioned predictors predicts both intraspecies and interspecies PPI. And a change of method between data sets can affect the comparison results between results. Thus, the authors aim to create a technique that can handle the prediction of intraspecies and interspecies PPI.

METHODOLOGY

In this section, the authors introduce a blueprint of the DNN (Figure 1). In this experiment, the protein sequences, represented by a letter symbol of 20 types of amino acids, are used as an original input data set. The process starts with feature extraction and follows bypassing feature vectors through the DNN architecture. The DNN architecture helps to find essential protein features that determine the interaction property. Finally, the extracted salient features are passed through the classifier to estimate the PPI class. Moreover, a 5-fold cross-validation method is employed for the assessment of the performance of the classifier.

Figure 2. Blueprint of proposed Deep Neural Network (DNN)

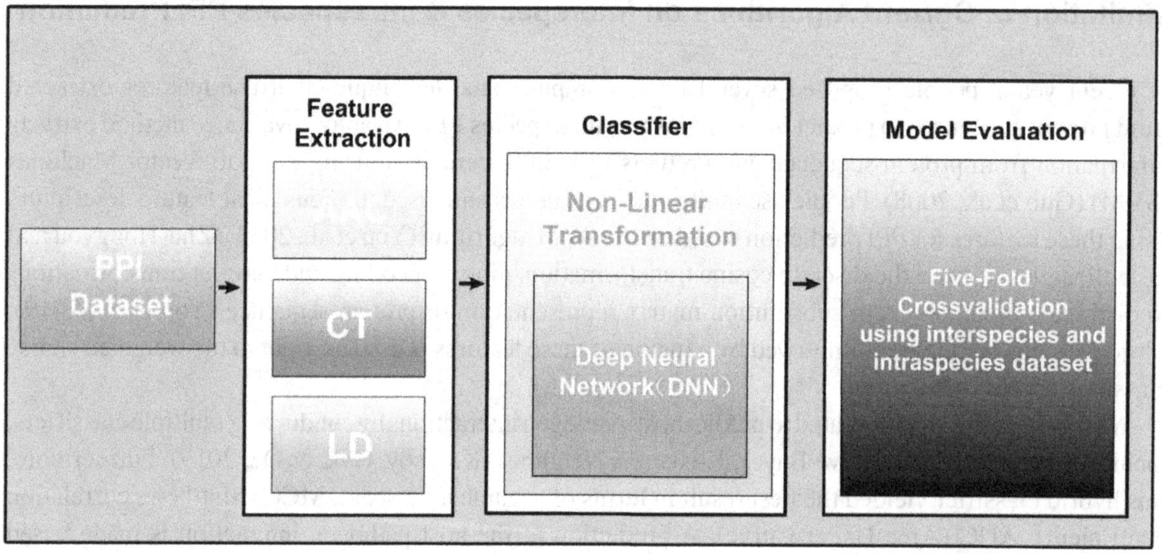

Data Set

A suitable PPI prediction method requires a valid benchmark data set to evaluate the predictor. In this experiment, two intraspecies data sets and one interspecies data set are used.

The intraspecies data set includes Helicobacter pylori data set and Saccharomyces *cerevisiae* data set. Helicobacter *pylori* PPIs data set contains 1458 positive interactions and 1458 negative interactions. Saccharomyces *cescerevisia* data set includes 5594 positive interactions and 5594 negative interactions. These PPI data sets are employed in this experiment to verify the validity of the following method in the intraspecies PPI prediction field.

A human host with Bacillus *anthracis* (B. *Anthracis*) is used as an interspecies data set in this experiment. The Human-B. *anthracis* PPI data set contains 3090 interacting pairs and 9500 non-interacting pairs. Since Human-B. *anthracis* PPI data set has an imbalanced number of samples of positive and negative classes. Therefore, a balanced data set is generated from Human-B. *anthracis* PPI by randomly choosing positive samples equal to the number of negative samples. The proportional data set is obtained and used for testing the feasibility of DNN on the prediction of interspecies PPI.

Feature Extraction

A Deep Neural Network requires a fixed number of inputs for training and testing. Therefore, a piece of global information about protein with variable length is created in the feature extraction step. This information is obtained based on sequence-derived physiochemical and structural features of the protein. The data is highly considered for the prediction of Protein-Protein Interaction.

These three base characteristics classify protein: Amino-Acid Characteristic (AAC), Conjoint Dimer (CD), Composition, Transition, And Distribution (CTD). AAC, CT, and CTD are concatenated to form a high dimensional feature factor for the prediction of PPI.

Amino Acid Composition (AAC)

Note. Formulas from Mahapatra, S., Gupta, V. R., Sahu, S. S., & Panda, G. (2021). Deep Neural Network and Extreme Gradient Boosting Based Hybrid Classifier for Improved Prediction of Protein-Protein Interaction. IEEE/ACM Transactions on Computational Biology and Bioinformatics, 1–1. https://doi. org/10.1109/tcbb.2021.3061300

Amino acid composition gives the fraction of each amino acid type within a protein. An AAC output of protein results in a 1×20-dimensional feature factor is calculated as

$$P_n(a_i) = \frac{f(a_i)}{\sum_{i=1}^{20} f(a_i)}, \quad i=1,2,3,\ldots,20 \tag{1}$$

Where $P_n(a_i)$ is 20 amino acid features, a_i are i[th] amino acid and $f(a_i)$ is the frequency count of ith amino acid.

Conjoint Triad (CT)

Amino acids can be grouped into seven different clusters based on the volume of side chains and dipoles (Shen (2007)). In the conjoint triad test, the amino acids belong to one collection are considered identical.

Thus, the feature obtained is a normalized frequency of occurrence of all 343 triads (7×7×7).

A protein sequence n with L amino acid can be written as:

$$P = a_1, a_2, a_3, \ldots, a_L \tag{2}$$

Make it in triad form:

$$C_n = a_1 a_2 a_3, a_4 a_5 a_6, \ldots, a_{L-2} a_{L-1} a_L \tag{3}$$

If the term is a triad, C_n can be calculated as

$$C_n = T_1, T_2, \ldots, T_I \tag{4}$$

where $T_1 = a_1 a_2 a_3$, $T_2 = a_4 a_5 a_6$, $T_I = a_{L-2} a_{L-1} a_L$ and $I=1,2,\ldots,L-2$.

The conjoint dimer feature is the normalized frequency of occurrence of each triad in C_n is calculated as

$$CT = [f_1, f_2, f_3, \ldots, f_{343}] \tag{5}$$

Where $f_I = \dfrac{T_I}{L-1}$ and T_I is the number of occurrences of each triad.

Concatenating the feature of protein pairs, a CD output of a protein results in a 1×686 (2×343) feature factor.

COMPOSITION, TRANSITION AND DISTRIBUTION (CTD)

In Composition, Transition and Distribution (CTD), a protein with variable length is normalized to vectors based on their physicochemical and structural properties. Amino acids can be divided into three classes to attribute based on properties such as hydrophobicity, van der Waals volume, and polarity. Each amino acid is replaced by one of indices 1,2,3 depends on its class (Dubchak, Muchnik, Holbrook, & Kim, 1995) (Dubchak, Muchnik, Mayor, Dralyuk, & Kim, 1999). The following Table 1 provides amino acid attributes.

Table 1. Amio Acid Classes and Properties [Derived from Journal article by Dubchak et al. (1995).]

ID	Property	Class 1	Class 2	Class 3
[x.1]	Hydrophobicity	RKEDQN	GASTPHY	CLVIMFW
[x.2]	Normalized van der Waals volume	GASTPD	NVEQIL	MHKFRYW
[x.3]	Polarity	LIFWCMVY	PATGS	HQRKNED
[x.4]	Polarizability	GASDT	CPNVEQIL	KMHFRYW
[x.5]	Charge	KR	ANCQGHILMFPSTWYV	DE
[x.6]	Secondary structure	EALMQKRH	VIYCWFT	GNPSD
[x.7]	Solvent accessibility	ALFCGIVW	PKQEND	MPSTHY
[x.8]	Surface tension	GQDNAHR	KTSEC	ILMFPWYV
[x.9]	Protein-Protein Interface hotspot propensity-Bogan	DHIKNPRWY	EQSTGAMF	CLV
[x.10]	Protein-Protein Interface propensity-Ma	CDFMPQRWY	AGHVLNST	EIK
[x.11]	Protein-DNA interface propensity-Schneider	GKNQRSTY	ADEFHILVW	CMP
[x.12]	Protein-DNA interface propensity-Ahmad	GHKNQRSTY	ADEFIPVW	CLM
[x.13]	Protein-RNA interface propensity-Kim	HKMRY	FGILNPQSVW	CDEAT
[x.14]	Protein-RNA interface propensity-Ellis	HGKMRSYW	AFINPQT	CDELV
[x.15]	Protein-RNA interface propensity-Phipps	HKMQRS	ADEFGLNPVY	CITW
[x.16]	Protein-ligand binding site propensity-Khazanov	CFHWY	GILNMSTR	AEDKPQV
[x.17]	Protein-ligand valid, binding site propensity-Khazanov	CFHWYM	DGILNSTV	AEKPQR
[x.18]	Propensity for protein-ligand polar & aromatic non-bonded interactions-Imai	DEHRY	CFKMNQSTW	AGILPV
[x.19]	Molecular Weight	AGS	CDEHIKLMNQPTV	FRWY
[x.20]	cLogP	RKDNEQH	PYSTGACV	WMFLI
[x.21]	No of hydrogen bond donor in side chain	HKNQR	DESTWY	ACGFILMPV
[x.22]	No of hydrogen bond acceptor in side chain	DEHNQR	KSTWY	ACGFILMPV
[x.23]	Solubility in water	ACGKRT	EFHILMNPQSVW	DY
[x.24]	Amino acid flexibility index	EGKNQS	ADHIPRTV	CFLMWY

Note. From Dubchak, I., Muchnik, I., Holbrook, S. R., & Kim, S. H. (1995). Prediction of Protein Folding Class using Global Description of Amino Acid Sequence. *Proceedings of the National Academy of Sciences, 92*(19), 8700–8704. https://doi.org/10.1073/pnas.92.19.8700

The "x" in descriptor ID in the table represents three different feature categories, respectively. Calculation details for each given attribute are as follows:

Composition

It works similar to amino acid composition, but the fraction of each amino acid type is replaced by each encoded class in the sequence. The document gives 72 features that can be defined as

$$C_r = \frac{N_r}{N}, \quad r,s=1,2,3\dots,20 \tag{6}$$

where N_r is the number of r encoded sequence and N is the length of the sequence.

Transition

A transition is used to transform the variable length of protein to a fixed-length vector without losing much information. Transition descriptor gives 72 features, 3×24, that can be defined as

$$T_{yz} = \frac{N_{yz} + N_{zy}}{N}, \quad yz=12,13,23 \tag{7}$$

Where N_{yz}, N_{zy} is the number of dipeptides encodes as yz and zy and N is the length of the sequence

Distribution

The distribution descriptor describes the distribution of each attribute in the sequence. Each attribute has five distribution descriptors, and they are the position per cent in the whole series, in order of the first residue, 25% residues, 50% residues, 75% residues, and the last residue, respectively a specified encoded class. Distribution descriptor gives 360 features that can be defined as

$$D = 10.0 \times \left(\frac{K_0 \times 100}{N} \right), 25.0 \times \left(\frac{K_{25} \times 100}{N} \right), 75.0 \times \left(\frac{K_{50} \times 100}{N} \right), 85.0 \times \left(\frac{K_{75} \times 100}{N} \right), 100.0 \times \left(\frac{K_{100} \times 100}{N} \right) \tag{8}$$

where K_0, K_{25}, K_{50}, K_{75}, K_{100} are the indexes of each residue in such sequences.

Figure 3. Proposed deep neural network for prediction of Protein-Protein Interaction (PPI)

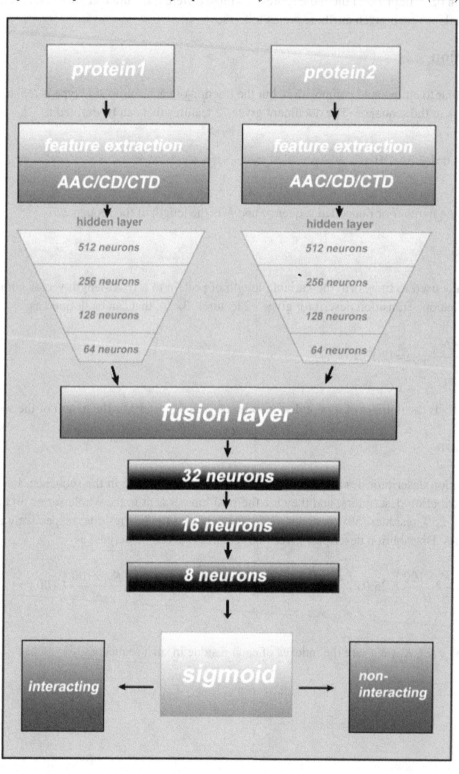

DEEP NEURAL NETWORK (DNN) CONSTRUCTION

A Deep Neural Network (DNN) is an Artificial Neural Network (ANN) built to simulate the neural network found in vivo brain to learn and interpret data. It is an effective tool to combine low-level features with an objective function to discover data rules. A Deep Neural Network consists of layers of interconnected neurons. The number of hidden layers and their maximum width, number of neurons of the hidden layer in a neural network represents its depth.

In this experiment, a Deep Neural Network (DNN) is employed to find the hidden PPI from the raw features of the protein sequence (Figure 3). In general, a DNN is constructed by four or more hidden layers. The input is fed into the first layer, and output is obtained from the last layer. A rectified linear unit function (ReLU) processes the weighted sum generated in the DNN of each hidden layer. ReLU is a simple activation function that reduces the training time by blocking negative values in the weighted sum. In this case, the cross-entropy function is also employed to reduces the training time as a loss function. An error back-propagation with a Stochastic Gradient Descent Algorithm (SGD) is used to train DNN.

The proposed DNN architecture is shown in Figure 3. It has three main components, feature extraction layer, fusion layer and prediction layer. It will output a binary value that represents whether Protein 1 interacts with Protein 2 or not.

A grid search technique is used to obtain optimal hyper-parameters for DNN. The parameters used for the simulation of the deep neuron network is provided in Table 2.

Table 2. Hyperparameters used for the Deep Neural Network. [Derived from Journal article by Mahapatra et al. (2021).]

Hyperparameter Name	Optimal value
Learning rate	0.01
Batch size	64
Momentum rate	0.9
Weight Initialization	glorot_normal
Weight regularization	L2
Per-parameter adaptive learning rate method	SGD
Activation	ReLU
Dropout rate	0.2
Loss Function	binary-crossentropy
Epochs	40

Note. From Mahapatra, S., Gupta, V. R., Sahu, S. S., & Panda, G. (2021). Deep Neural Network and Extreme Gradient Boosting Based Hybrid Classifier for Improved Prediction of Protein-Protein Interaction. IEEE/ACM Transactions on Computational Biology and Bioinformatics, 1–1. https://doi.org/10.1109/tcbb.2021.3061300

Input

The Deep Neural Network takes a pair of protein sequence feature vectors, 1×867 dimensional vectors. The feature vector of protein sequence with n length consists of 20 AAC features, 343 CT features, and 504 CTD features.

Feature Extraction Layer

Two parallel channels consist of the feature extraction layer. Each channel has a structure of four connected layers of 512-256-128-64 computing units. In the feature extraction layer, the raw features of protein sequences are marked by their effective representation of PPI. The output of each layer in this network starts with a dense layer and ends with a dropout layer. The dense layer extracts relevant input from the input and outputs them to the dropout layer as features. Dropout is a technique employed to avoid over-fitting. Some neurons, along with their connections, are assigned zero during training (Figure 3). Here, a rectified linear unit is employed to map all negative values in output to zero.

$$f_{lx} = Dropout\left(ReLU\left(Dense_M\left(P_x\right)\right)\right), \ x=1,2$$

where f_{lx} represents the output vector, x is protein number, M is the number of nodes in layer l.

Figure 4. Hidden layer dropped out neurons architecture

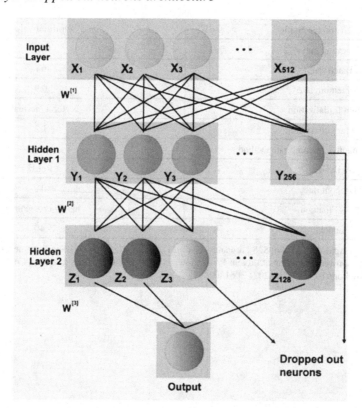

Fusion Layer

The fusion layer concatenates the output from two parallel channels, and its output is given by $F = [f_1 f_2]$.

Prediction Layer

The prediction layer has a structure of three connected dense layers with an activation function ReLU, followed by a neuron with a sigmoid activation function. The sigmoid activation function in the single neuron transforms the input vector J of dimension d from the previous into an output score.

$$O(P_1, P_2) = \sum_{k=1}^{d} J_k W_k + \beta_0 \tag{9}$$

where W_k represents the weights corresponding to the input J_k and $\beta 0$ is the bias vector.

The interaction probability between P_1 and P_2 is computed by the following formula:

$$\tau_{P_1, P_2} = \frac{1}{1 + e^{-O(P_1, P_2)}} \tag{10}$$

And the result is passed through the binary cross-entropy loss function given by:

$$l\big(O(P_1, P_2), \gamma_{P_1 P_2}\big) = -\big(\gamma_{P_1 P_2} \log\big(O(P_1, P_2)\big)\big) + \big(1 - \gamma_{P_1 P_2}\big)\log\big(1 - O(P_1, P_2)\big) \tag{11}$$

where $\gamma_{P_1 P_2} = 1$ and $\gamma_{P_1 P_2}$ are the respective class labels for interacting and non-interacting.

Note. Formulas from Mahapatra, S., Gupta, V. R., Sahu, S. S., & Panda, G. (2021). Deep Neural Network and Extreme Gradient Boosting Based Hybrid Classifier for Improved Prediction of Protein-Protein Interaction. IEEE/ACM Transactions on Computational Biology and Bioinformatics, 1–1. https://doi. org/10.1109/tcbb.2021.3061300

Performance Evaluation

The 5-fold cross-validation method is a standard for the deep neural network, and it is employed to assess the classifier's performance. In the 5-fold cross-validation method, the data set is randomly divided into five subsets. In this experiment, 80% of the data set is used for training, and the remaining 20% is used for testing. The stratified K-fold of the scikit-learn library is used to perform the splitting task. The mean and the standard deviation of these five experiments are final results.

The following assessments compute the accuracy and deviation to evaluate the validity and robustness of a DNN prediction method, and they are defined as follows:

$$Accuracy = \frac{TP + TN}{TP + TN + FP + FN} \tag{12}$$

$$Sensitivity = \frac{TP}{TP+FN} \tag{13}$$

$$Specificity = \frac{TN}{TN+FP} \tag{14}$$

$$Precision = \frac{TP}{TP+FP} \tag{15}$$

$$MCC = \frac{TP \times TN - FP \times FN}{\sqrt{\left(TP+FP\right)\left(TP+FN\right)\left(TN+FP\right)\left(TN+FN\right)}} \tag{16}$$

where TP is the True Positive number, it represents the number of predicted positive PPIs found in positive data set; TN is the True Negative number, it represents the number of predicted negative PPIs found in negative data set; FP is the False Positive, it represents the number of negative PPIs predicted as positive; and FN is the False Negative, it represents the number of positive PPIs predicted as negative.

RESULTS

Performance of PPI Prediction

The proposed predictor is applied to the extracted features of S. *cerevisiae (core subset)*, H. *pylori*, Human-B. A*nthracis* data sets. Table 3 gives the 5-fold cross-validation results of these three data sets.

Table 3. Performance of DNN on S. cerevisiae (core subset), H.pylori, Human-B.Anthracis data sets

Data set	Accuracy (%)	Sensitivity (%)	Specificity (%)	Precision (%)	MCC (%)	AUC (%)
S. *Cerevisiae (core)*	87.01±1.50	86.07±2.86	87.32±1.53	87.26±1.33	74.01±2.86	93.73
H. *pylori*	87.57±0.97	89.71±1.19	85.46±2.05	86.09±1.19	75.27±1.18	92.22
Human-B. *Anthracis*	89.25±0.95	91.34±1.03	87.27±1.49	87.16±1.24	74.92±2.22	94.12

Note. From Mahapatra, S., Gupta, V. R., Sahu, S. S., & Panda, G. (2021). Deep Neural Network and Extreme Gradient Boosting Based Hybrid Classifier for Improved Prediction of Protein-Protein Interaction. IEEE/ACM Transactions on Computational Biology and Bioinformatics, 1–1. https://doi.org/10.1109/tcbb.2021.3061300

The average prediction performance on the proposed method on S. *cerevisiae*(core) data set, such as accuracy, precision, MCC, and AUC, are 87.01%, 87.26%, 74.01%, and 93.73%, respectively. The method also achieved the result on H.pylori data sets, such as accuracy, precision, MCC, and AUC are 87.57%, 86.09%, 75.27%, and 92.22%. On the interspecies data set of Human-B. Anthracis, the proposed method achieved an accuracy of 89.25%, a precision of 87.16%, and MCC of 74.92%, and an AUC of 94.12%, respectively. These results indicate that DNN is indeed a successful method for PPI prediction.

Comparing With K-Nearest Neighbor and Naive Bayes

The comparison of performance between the proposed method and K-Nearest Neighbor (KNN) and Naive Bayes (NB) on the H.pylori data set is given in Figure 5.

Figure 5. Performance comparison of Deep Neural Network (DNN), K-Nearest Neighbor (KNN), and Naïve Bayes (NB) algorithms on H. pylori data set.

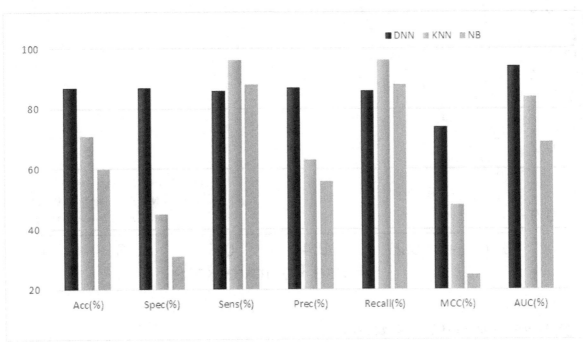

Neither KNN nor NB has a high prediction performance. KNN has average prediction performance, such as accuracy, specificity, precision, MCC, and AUC are 71.00±1.69%, 45.85±2.66%, 63.99±1.30%, 48.61%, and 84.57%, respectively. On the other hand, the accuracy, specificity, precision, MCC, and AUC obtained from NB are 60.11±4.34%, 31.81±4.36%, 88.42±8.68%, 56.95±3.72%, 25.12±6.86%, and 69.85%, respectively. Therefore, the proposed DNN has a better prediction result regarding accuracy, specificity, precision, MCC, and AUC.

The Receiver Operator Characteristic (ROC) curve is a technique used for visualizing the prediction performance. ROC is composed of the actual positive rate and the false positive rate from results, which shows the relative tradeoffs between True Positive and False Positives. In this experiment, the ROC curve is plotted to compare various methods on H. *pylori*. (Figure 6)

Figure 6. Receiver Operator Characteristic (ROC) curve comparison of DNN, NB, and KNN algorithms on H.pylori data set.

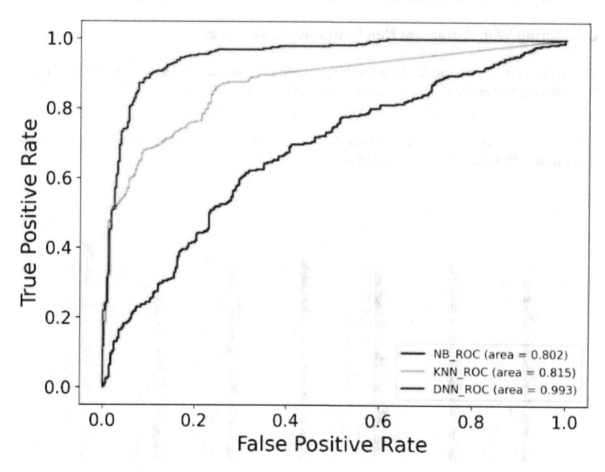

High-Level Featured Visualization

The general idea behind DNN is that it captures more notable features from raw input data through hidden layers, which improve classification performance. A technique, t-SNE, built in python scikit-learn library is used to project high dimensional results into a 2D coordinate graph to visualize this process. (Figure 7).

Figure 7. t-SNE plots of H. pylori data set

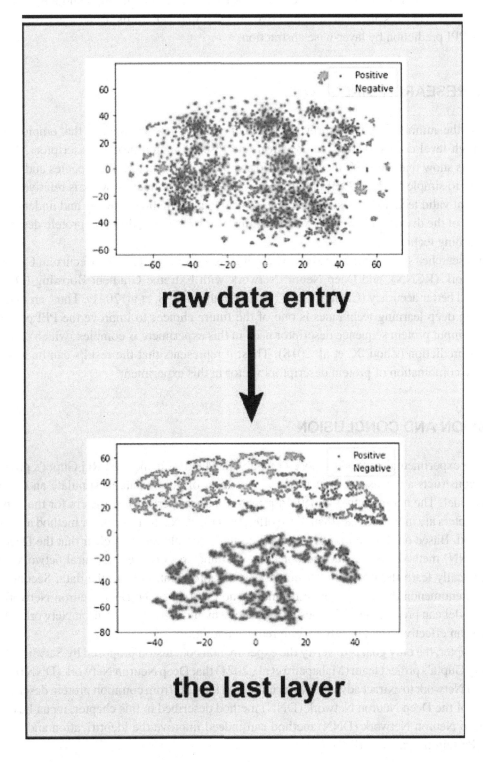

From Figure 7, the negative and positive PPI starts with chaos. After multiple hidden layers involved in training, the two classes are clear split into two clusters. In other words, DNN can extract important features for PPI prediction by layer-wise abstraction.

FUTURE RESEARCH DIRECTIONS

In this work, the authors aimed to improve PPI prediction and propose a method that employs the DNN to extract high-level discriminative features from the fused common protein descriptors. The experimental results show that the DNN classifier performs better on predicting interspecies and intraspecies PPI compare to simple KNN and NB classifiers. However, the accuracy of work is relatively low compare to current valid technique those are capable of analyzing signaling pathway and understanding the pathogenesis of the disease. The accuracy can be improved by utilizing different protein descriptors and machine learning techniques.

Recent researches show some hybrid deep learning algorithm like Residual Recurrent Convolutional Neural Network (RCNN), and Deep Neural Network with Extreme Gradient Boosting (DNN-XGB) have achieved better accuracy (Chen. M. et al. 2019) (Mahapatra. S. et al. 2021). Thus, an investigation of combining deep learning techniques is one of the future choices to improve the PPI prediction. In addition, the input protein sequence descriptor used in this experiment is complex, which can affect the accuracy of prediction (Zhou. X. et al. 2018). Thus, it represents that the results can be improved by changing the combination of protein descriptors vector in this experiment.

DISCUSSION AND CONCLUSION

Based on the experimental method proposed by Satyajit Mahapatra and Ivek Raj Gupta's project team, this paper constructs a consistent framework. It uses a set of public data to simulate and analyze the operation model. The neural network method provides a set of perfect parameters for the experiment. These parameters are more accurate than those offered by the K-Nearest Neighbor method and the Naive Bayes method. Based on the vital information found in the simulation, it is clear that the Deep Neuron Network (DNN) method can provide more accurate parameters because the neural network algorithm can automatically learn the internal distributed feature representation from the data. Second, PPI is a biological phenomenon that can generate infinitely and randomly. The Deep Neuron Network (DNN) operating model can predict these changes in advance, which is why Deep Neuron Network (DNN) has proved to be an effective way to study protein representation.

In this chapter, the only goal is to verify the experimental conclusion proposed by Satyajit Mahapatra and Ivek Raj Gupta's project team (Mahapatra et al., 2021) that Deep Neuron Network (DNN) can use the Deep Neural Network to extract advanced discrimination features from common protein descriptions. As the analysis of the Deep Neuron Network (DNN) method described in this chapter, it can be concluded that the Deep Neuron Network (DNN) method can indeed improve the identification and research on Protein-to-Protein Interactions (PPI). ·

ACKNOWLEDGMENT

As the authors of this article, we know that we could not have finished this work without help from others. First of all, we would like to thank Professor Richard Segall and Professor Niu Gao for giving us this rare opportunity, especially Professor Richard Segall for his continuous support, no matter in terms of professional knowledge, language and literature, or the time of audit, he has given us great tolerance and support. Professor Niu Gao, despite his busy schedule, helped us come up with useful suggestions and gave us a lot to learn from, allowing us to finish such an article in a short time.

In this article, we have borrowed some of the logic from a 2021 IEEE article and we owe our utmost respect to the authors: Satyajit Mahapatra, Vivek Raj Gupta, Sitanshu Sekhar Sahu, and Ganapati Panda. Especially when we met some difficulties, Satyajit Mahapatra responded from India to our emails at the last minute and gave us a very detailed explanation, letting us understand how each step of the experiment was carried out.

REFERENCES

Admin. (2021, January 1). *Perceptron - Deep Learning Basics*. Start-Tech Academy. https://start-techacademy.com/perceptron-deep-learning-basics/#:~:text=In%201958%20Frank%20Rosenblatt%20proposed%20the%20perceptron%2C%20a,was%20refined%20and%20perfected%20by%20Minsky%20and%20Papert

Baruah, L. (2017). Performance Comparison of Binarized Neural Network with Convolutional Neural Network. *Digital Commons @ Michigan Tech*. doi:10.37099/mtu.dc.etdr/487

Chen, M., Ju, C. J. T., Zhou, G., Chen, X., Zhang, T., Chang, K. W., Zaniolo, C., & Wang, W. (2019). Multifaceted protein–protein interaction prediction based on Siamese residual RCNN. *Bioinformatics (Oxford, England)*, *35*(14), i305–i314. doi:10.1093/bioinformatics/btz328 PMID:31510705

Du, X., Zhang, Y., Yao, Y., Hu, C., & Sun, S. (2017). DeepPPI: Boosting Prediction of protein-protein Interactions with Deep Neural Networks. *Journal of Chemical Information and Modeling*, *57*(6), 1499–1510. doi:10.1021/acs.jcim.7b00028 PMID:28514151

Dubchak, I., Muchnik, I., Holbrook, S. R., & Kim, S. H. (1995). Prediction of Protein Folding Class using Global Description of Amino Acid Sequence. *Proceedings of the National Academy of Sciences of the United States of America*, *92*(19), 8700–8704. doi:10.1073/pnas.92.19.8700 PMID:7568000

Dubchak, I., Muchnik, I., Mayor, C., Dralyuk, I., & Kim, S. H. (1999). Recognition of a Protein Fold in the Context of the SCOP Classification. *Proteins*, *35*(4), 401–407. doi:10.1002/(SICI)1097-0134(19990601)35:4<401::AID-PROT3>3.0.CO;2-K PMID:10382667

Garima, S., Navita, S., & Gulshan, W. (2012). Neural Network Model for Prediction of PPI using Domain Frequency & Association Score Base Classification of Protein Pairs. *International Journal of Advanced Research in Computer Science*, *3*(3), 234–238.

Guo, Y., Yu, L., Wen, Z., & Li, M. (2008). Using support vector machine combined with auto covariance to predict protein–protein interactions from protein sequences. *Nucleic Acids Research*, *36*(9), 3025–3030. doi:10.1093/nar/gkn159 PMID:18390576

Hendrickson, H. (1994). Fluorescence-Based Assays of Lipases, Phospholipases, and Other Lipolytic Enzymes. *Analytical Biochemistry*, *219*(1), 1–8. doi:10.1006/abio.1994.1223 PMID:8059934

Huang, J., Lu, J., & Ling, C. X. (2003). Comparing naive Bayes, decision trees, and SVM with AUC and accuracy. *Third IEEE International Conference on Data Mining*, 553-556. 10.1109/ICDM.2003.1250975

Kösesoy, R., Gök, M., & Öz, C. (2019). A New Sequence Based Encoding for Prediction of Host–Pathogen Protein Interactions. *Computational Biology and Chemistry*, *78*, 170–177. doi:10.1016/j.compbiolchem.2018.12.001 PMID:30553999

Mahapatra, S., Gupta, V. R., Sahu, S. S., & Panda, G. (2021). Deep Neural Network and Extreme Gradient Boosting Based Hybrid Classifier for Improved Prediction of Protein-Protein Interaction. *IEEE/ACM Transactions on Computational Biology and Bioinformatics*, 1–1. doi:10.1109/TCBB.2021.3061300 PMID:33621179

Oja, E. (1994). Neural Networks – Advantages and Applications. Machine Intelligence and Pattern Recognition. In E. S. Gelsema & L. S. Kanal (Eds.), *Pattern Recognition in Practice IV: Multiple Paradigms, Comparative Studies and Hybrid Systems* (Vol. 16, pp. 359–365). Elsevier.

Palm, G. (1986). Warren McCulloch and Walter Pitts: A Logical Calculus of the Ideas Immanent in Nervous Activity. *Brain Theory*, 229–230. Advance online publication. doi:10.1007/978-3-642-70911-1_14

Piehler, J. (2005). New Methodologies for Measuring Protein Interactions in Vivo and in Vitro. *Current Opinion in Structural Biology*, *15*(1), 4–14. doi:10.1016/j.sbi.2005.01.008 PMID:15718127

Puig, O., Caspary, F., Rigaut, G., Rutz, B., Bouveret, E., Bragado-Nilsson, E., Wilm, M., & Séraphin, B. (2001). The Tandem Affinity Purification (TAP) Method: A General Procedure of Protein Complex Purification. *Methods (San Diego, Calif.)*, *24*(3), 218–229. doi:10.1006/meth.2001.1183 PMID:11403571

Rigaut, G., Shevchenko, A., Rutz, B., Wilm, M., Mann, M., & Séraphin, B. (1999). A Generic Protein Purification Method for Protein Complex Characterization and Proteome Exploration. *Nature Biotechnology*, *17*(10), 1030–1032. doi:10.1038/13732 PMID:10504710

Safri, Y. F., Arifudin, R., & Muslim, M. A. (2018). K-Nearest Neighbor and Naive Bayes Classifier Algorithm in Determining the Classification of Healthy Card Indonesia Giving to The Poor. *Scientific Journal of Informatics*, *5*(1), 18. doi:10.15294ji.v5i1.12057

Shen, J. (2007). Predicting Protein-Protein Interactions based only on Sequences Information. *Proceedings of the National Academy of Sciences*, *104*(11), 4337–4341. 10.1073/pnas.0607879104

Wang, L., You, Z. H., Xia, S. X., Chen, X., Yan, X., Zhou, Y., & Liu, F. (2017). An Improved Efficient Rotation Forest Algorithm to predict the Interactions among Proteins. *Soft Computing*, *22*(10), 3373–3381. doi:10.100700500-017-2582-y

You, Z. H., Huang, W. Z., Zhang, S., Huang, Y. A., Yu, C. Q., & Li, L. P. (2019). An Efficient Ensemble Learning Approach for Predicting Protein-Protein Interactions by Integrating Protein Primary Sequence and Evolutionary Information. *IEEE/ACM Transactions on Computational Biology and Bioinformatics*, *16*(3), 809–817. doi:10.1109/TCBB.2018.2882423 PMID:30475726

You, Z. H., Lei, Y. K., Zhu, L., Xia, J., & Wang, B. (2013). Prediction of Protein-Protein Interactions from Amino Acid Sequences with Ensemble Extreme Learning Machines and Principal Component Analysis. *BMC Bioinformatics*, *14*(S8), S10. Advance online publication. doi:10.1186/1471-2105-14-S8-S10 PMID:23815620

Zhang, Z. (2016). Introduction to Machine Learning: K-nearest Neighbors. *Annals of Translational Medicine*, *4*(11), 218. doi:10.21037/atm.2016.03.37 PMID:27386492

Zhou, X., Park, B., Choi, D., & Han, K. (2018). A Generalized Approach to Predicting Protein-Protein Interactions between Virus and Host. *BMC Genomics*, *19*(S6), 568. Advance online publication. doi:10.118612864-018-4924-2 PMID:30367586

ADDITIONAL READING

Alipanahi, B., Delong, A., Weirauch, M. T., & Frey, B. J. (2015). Predicting the Sequence Specificities of DNA- and RNA-binding Proteins by Deep Learning. *Nature Biotechnology*, *33*(8), 831–838. doi:10.1038/nbt.3300 PMID:26213851

Baldi, P. (2014). *Proceedings of the 5th ACM Conference on Bioinformatics, Computational Biology, and Health Informatics*. Association for Computing Machinery (ACM). Retrieved October 23, 2021 from https://lib.ugent.be/catalog/ebk01:3780000000084417

Bengio, Y., Courville, A., & Vincent, P. (2013). Representation Learning: A Review and New Perspectives. *IEEE Transactions on Pattern Analysis and Machine Intelligence*, *35*(8), 1798–1828. doi:10.1109/TPAMI.2013.50 PMID:23787338

Huang, Y. A., You, Z. H., Gao, X., Wong, L., & Wang, L. (2015). Using Weighted Sparse Representation Model Combined with Discrete Cosine Transformation to Predict Protein-Protein Interactions from Protein Sequence. *BioMed Research International*, *2015*, 1–10. doi:10.1155/2015/902198 PMID:26634213

Leung, M. K. K., Delong, A., Alipanahi, B., & Frey, B. J. (2016). Machine Learning in Genomic Medicine: A Review of Computational Problems and Data Sets. *Proceedings of the IEEE*, *104*(1), 176–197. doi:10.1109/JPROC.2015.2494198

McCulloch, W. S., & Pitts, W. (1943). A Logical Calculus of the Ideas Immanent in Nervous Activity. *The Bulletin of Mathematical Biophysics*, *5*(4), 115–133. doi:10.1007/BF02478259

Mehla, J., Caufield, J. H., & Uetz, P. (2015). Mapping Protein–Protein Interactions Using Yeast Two-Hybrid Assays. *Cold Spring Harbor Protocols*, *2015*(5). doi:10.1101/pdb.prot086157

Schmidhuber, J. (2015). Deep Learning in Neural Networks: An Overview. *Neural Networks*, *61*, 85–117. doi:10.1016/j.neunet.2014.09.003 PMID:25462637

KEY TERMS AND DEFINITIONS

Amino Acid: An organic acid containing an amino group, and it is the building block of proteins. Mainly from proteolysis, it can also be synthesized chemically or by microbial fermentation.

Amino-Acid Composition (AAC): Amino acid composition gives the fraction of each amino acid type within a protein.

Conjoint Analysis: By assuming that the products have specific attributes, the actual effects are simulated, and then consumers are allowed to evaluate these virtual products according to their preferences. In addition, these characteristics are separated from the utility of attribute level by the mathematical statistics method so that the importance of each attribute and attribute level can be quantitatively evaluated.

Deep Neural Network (DNN): A technology in the field of Machine Learning that can use statistical learning methods to extract high-level features from original sensory data and obtain an adequate representation of input space in a large amount of data.

Grid Search: Grid Search is about traversing every intersection in the grid to find the best combination. The dimension of the grid is the number of over arguments. If we have k super parameters, and each super parameter has m candidates, we have to go through km combinations.

K-Nearest Neighbor (KNN): A more mature method in theory, but also one of the simplest machine learning algorithms. In the feature space, if the majority of the k nearest (i.e., the closest in the feature space) samples in the vicinity of a sample belong to a specific category, then the sample also belongs to this category.

Naive Bayes (NB): NB model is a classification model based on Bayes' theorem and independent assumption of characteristic conditions. It requires few estimated parameters, is not sensitive to missing data, and the algorithm is relatively simple. In theory, the NB model has the smallest error rate compared with other classification methods.

Protein-Protein Interactions (PPI): A reaction in which two or more proteins are joined together by physical contact. Typically, biologists use this method to find new combinations and new.

Receiver Operating Characteristic Curve (ROC): According to a series of different dichotomies (demarcation or determination threshold), the valid positive rate (sensitivity) is plotted on the vertical axis, and the false positive rate (1-specificity) is plotted on the abscissa.

Rectified Linear Unit (ReLU): In the neural network, linear rectification, as the neuron's activation function, defines the nonlinear output of the neuron after the linear transformation. In other words, for the input vectors from the upper layer of the neural network that enters the neuron, the neuron using the linear rectification activation function will be output to the next layer of the neuron or as the output of the entire neural network (depending on the position of the existing neuron in the network structure).

Chapter 7

US Medical Expense Analysis Through Frequency and Severity Bootstrapping and Regression Model

Fangjun Li
University of Connecticut, USA

Gao Niu
Bryant University, USA

ABSTRACT

For the purpose of control health expenditures, there are some papers investigating the characteristics of patients who may incur high expenditures. However fewer papers are found which are based on the overall medical conditions, so this chapter was to find a relationship among the prevalence of medical conditions, utilization of healthcare services, and average expenses per person. The authors used bootstrapping simulation for data preprocessing and then used linear regression and random forest methods to train several models. The metrics root mean square error (RMSE), mean absolute percent error (MAPE), mean absolute error (MAE) all showed that the selected linear regression model performs slightly better than the selected random forest regression model, and the linear model used medical conditions, type of services, and their interaction terms as predictors.

INTRODUCTION

Many studies showed that a few high-cost people account for the majority of health expenditures (Berk & Monheit, 2001-03-01) (Riley, May/Jun2007). Identifying patients who may incur high medical expenditures plays an important role to reduce health expenditures, allocate resources and improve the healthcare system. There are multiple studies comparing the essential attributes of potential high-cost patients. Among the most common attributes include age, self-reported health status, functional limits,

DOI: 10.4018/978-1-7998-8455-2.ch007

etc. (Meehan, Chou, & Khasawneh, 2015). On the other hand, the consistent high-cost users (CHUs), defined as people with high medical costs consistently across multiple consecutive periods, can be a good target. It was observed that CHUs had higher prevalence of chronic and psychosocial conditions than point high-cost users, which may be partially explained by that those conditions need continuous medications (Chang, et al., 2016-09).

There are some studies aim to investigate the economic burden for patients of specific disease (Whitney, Kamdar, Ng, Hurvitz, & Peterson, 2019) (Rodbard, Green, Fox, & Grandy, 2009) (Bhattacharyya, 2011-09), but less are found to be based on overall medical conditions, so the objective of this paper is to find how prevalence of medical conditions and type of health services could affect the average expenses per person with care. We will start with data preprocessing where we will use bootstrapping method to construct simulation datasets. Then for the next section, we can use this dataset to train predictive models, such as linear regression models and random forest method. Several metrics to measure goodness of fit of regression models will be employed to select the best performed model. The result can be applied to insurance industry and health service management.

DATA DESCRIPTION AND PREPROCESSING

The original data was collected by the Medical Expenditure Panel Survey (MEPS). MEPS is a set of large-scale surveys on the health services and the frequency, the cost of using these services, how they are paid, as well as the data about health insurance in the US. Among the two major components of MEPS, the Household Component (HC) provides information on household-reported medical conditions. The sample of families and individuals are from households that participated in the prior year's National Health Interview Survey (conducted by the National Center for Health Statistics) (Agency for Healthcare Research and Quality, 2019).

The data we use come from the HC summary data tables conducted by the American Agency for Healthcare Research and Quality (AHRQ) which provides number of people with care and mean expenditure per person from 2016 to 2018 (Agency for Healthcare Research and Quality, n.d.). The data are grouped by 53 condition categories collapsed from the household-reported conditions coded into ICD-10 and CCSR codes, and six event types (emergency room visits, home health events, inpatient stays, office-based events, outpatient events, prescription medicines).

Number of People with Care

According to the documentation of 2018 Medical Conditions File from MEPS (MEPS HC-207 2018 Medical Conditions, 2020), each year a new panel of sample households of sample size about 15,000 households is selected, and all data for a sampled household are reported by a single household respondent.

To get some idea of how prevalent a condition is and how frequently a type of events is used, we did some summation to plot the following figures. For example, the number of people had condition "hypertension" is the total number of six combinations: hypertension - emergency room visits, hypertension - home health events, hypertension - inpatient stays, hypertension - office-based events, hypertension - outpatient events, hypertension - prescription medicines.

Figure 1. TreeMap for Number of People with care by Condition

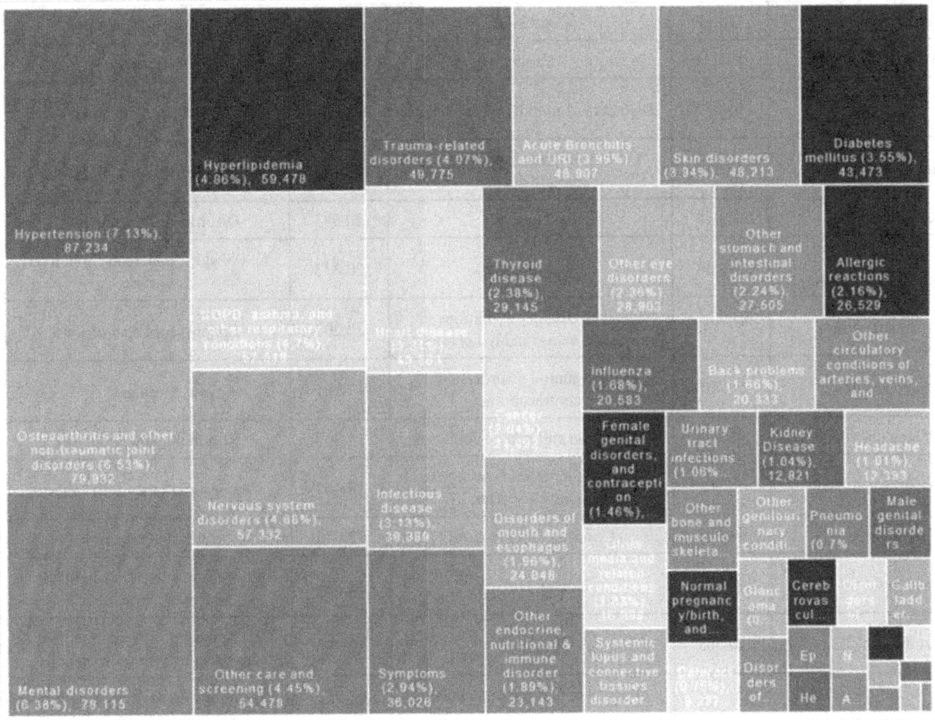

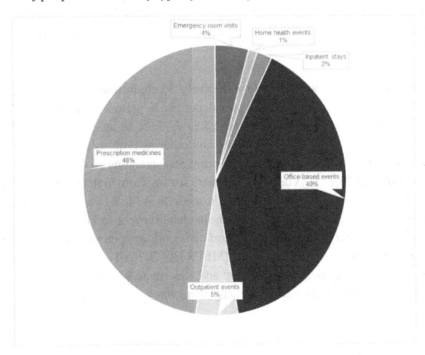

Figure 2. Number of people with care by type of event in year 2018

Table 1. Number of people with care by condition in year 2018

Conditions	Total	Conditions	Total	Conditions	Total
Hypertension	87,234	Cancer	24,992	Glaucoma	7,165
Osteoarthritis and other non-traumatic joint disorders	79,932	Disorders of mouth and esophagus	24,048	Disorders of teeth and jaws	6,880
Mental disorders	78,115	Other endocrine, nutritional & immune disorder	23,143	Cerebrovascular disease	6,576
Hyperlipidemia	59,478	Influenza	20,583	Disorders of the upper GI	6,320
COPD, asthma, and other respiratory conditions	57,518	Back problems	20,333	Gallbladder, pancreatic, and liver disease	5,777
Nervous system disorders	57,332	Other circulatory conditions of arteries, veins, and lymphatics	20,203	Epilepsy and convulsions	3,613
Other care and screening	54,478	Female genital disorders, and contraception	17,961	Hernias	3,548
Trauma-related disorders	49,775	Otitis media and related conditions	16,369	Non-malignant neoplasm	3,126
Acute Bronchitis and URI	48,907	Systemic lupus and connective tissues disorders	13,467	Anemia and other deficiencies	2,807
Skin disorders	48,213	Urinary tract infections	13,073	Intestinal infection	2,379
Diabetes mellitus	43,473	Kidney Disease	12,821	Poisoning by medical and non-medical substances	1,802
Heart disease	40,563	Headache	12,393	Hemorrhagic, coagulation, and disorders of White Blood cells	1,641
Infectious disease	38,389	Other bone and musculoskeletal disease	10,905	Complications of pregnancy/birth, and perinatal conditions	1,490
Symptoms	36,026	Normal pregnancy/birth, and live born	9,890	Non-malignant breast disease	1,312
Thyroid disease	29,145	Cataract	9,232	Congenital anomalies	1,109
Other eye disorders	28,903	Other genitourinary condition	9,060	Tonsillitis	642
Other stomach and intestinal disorders	27,505	Pneumonia	8,592	Complications of surgery or device	0
Allergic reactions	26,529	Male genital disorders	8,164	Overall Total	1,222,931

Figure 1 summarizes the number of people with care of 53 conditions and the corresponding percent in a TreeMap. The top five conditions of high prevalence are hypertension (7.13% or 87,234), osteoarthritis and other non-traumatic joint disorders (6.53% or 79,932), mental disorders (6.38% or 78,115), hyperlipidemia (4.86% or 59,478), COPD, asthma, and other respiratory conditions (4.7% or 57,518), Nervous system disorders (4.68% or 57,332), Other care and screening (4.45% or 54,478) and Trauma-related disorders (4.07% or 49,775). A detailed summary sorting from high to low can be seen in Table 1.

Through Figure 2, it is obvious that prescription medicines (48%) and office-based events (40%) are the most frequently six types of events, while home health events and inpatient stays are the least. Note that because persons can be seen for more than one condition per visit, these frequencies will not match the person or event-level utilization counts (MEPS HC-207 2018 Medical Conditions, 2020). For example, a person had one inpatient hospital stay and was treated for three different conditions, then the total inpatient stay would be three when actually there was only one inpatient stay for this person.

Average and Total Expense

Table 2 summarizes the expenses by conditions. From total cost perspective, Office-based events (28.05%), Prescription medicines (27.54%) and inpatient stays (25.29%) are the main categories of total expenses. Office-based events and prescription medicines have low average cost but their high frequency results high total cost. Inpatient stays has relatively low frequency (1.05% total number of people with care) but high severity ($8,285 average expenses) which end up with high total expenses.

Table 2. Average expense by type of event in year 2018

	Emergency room visits	Home health events	Inpatient stays	Office-based events	Outpatient events	Prescription medicines	Total
Total Number of people with Care (Count)	50,914	12,786	22,733	492,625	63,307	580,566	1,222,931
Total Number of people with Care (%)	4.16%	1.05%	1.86%	40.28%	5.18%	47.47%	100.00%
Average Expense	1,142	8,285	18,878	966	2,533	805	1,388
Total Expense ($)	58,139,817	105,936,880	429,162,594	475,988,228	160,327,119	467,345,319	1,696,899,957
Total Expense (%)	3.43%	6.24%	25.29%	28.05%	9.45%	27.54%	100.00%

Almost all high average expenses per person are from home health events and inpatient stays as shown in Figure 3. Note that the points in this figure are all possible combinations of conditions and type of events. For example, the highest average expense 35,038 is a patient with condition "cancer" and type of event "inpatient stays". Many combinations have average expense equals zero. There are several possible reasons: one is that some combinations do not have occurrence, such as condition "headache" and type of event "inpatient stays"; another is that the data was self-reported, which means it is possible to miss some record. In our following research steps, we will apply bootstrapping method and this method will omit those with no occurrence in the original dataset.

Figure 3. Average expense by type of event with condition distribution in year 2018

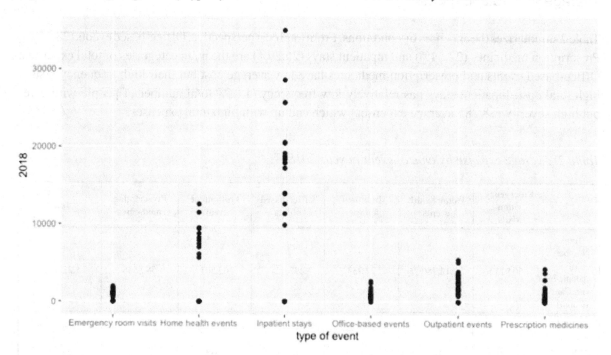

From the perspective of conditions, Table 3 and Figure 4 summarizes the average expenses and total expenses respectively. From Table 3 we can see that the overall average expenses is $1,388. The most expensive conditions are Pneumonia ($5,298), Other care and screening ($5,289), COPD, asthma, and other respiratory conditions ($4,185). From Figure 4, we can see Male genital disorders has the highest total expenses, 7.87% or $133,675,730 of the total expense weas spent on this category. Other categories such as other bone and musculoskeletal disease (7.27%), Disorders of teeth and jaws (7.23%), heart disease (6.82%), Other endocrine, nutritional & immune disorder (6.39%), COPD, asthma, and other respiratory conditions (6.16%), Normal pregnancy/birth, and live born (7.06%), Tonsillitis (5.17%), Diabetes mellitus (4.78%), Hernias (3.6%) and Pneumonia (3.08%) are the main categories where patients spend their money on.

Identifying conditions of high expense is very meaningful for but not limited to insurance policy making. The goal of the model is to investigate the relationship between a medical condition's characteristics, such as prevalence and common treatments received, and its corresponding expenses. However, because the random variables from summary tables are not independent and identically distributed, instead of doing regression directly, we use bootstrapping method to simulate a dataset of 5000 independent patients with specific condition, type of event and expenses, which can provide an estimate for the distribution of the original data.

Table 3. Average expense by conditions in year 2018

Conditions	Average Cost	Conditions	Average Cost	Conditions	Average Cost
Pneumonia	$ 5,298	Diabetes mellitus	$1,412	Congenital anomalies	$ 544
Other care and screening	$ 5,289	Glaucoma	$1,405	Thyroid disease	$ 541
COPD, asthma, and other respiratory conditions	$ 4,185	Hyperlipidemia	$1,399	Infectious disease	$ 493
Allergic reactions	$ 3,872	Nervous system disorders	$1,394	Headache	$ 472
Kidney Disease	$ 2,994	Otitis media and related conditions	$1,321	Female genital disorders, and contraception	$ 444
Other endocrine, nutritional & immune disorder	$ 2,676	Complications of pregnancy/birth, and perinatal conditions	$1,301	Osteoarthritis and other non-traumatic joint disorders	$ 429
Heart disease	$ 2,665	Hemorrhagic, coagulation, and disorders of White Blood cells	$1,113	Other circulatory conditions of arteries, veins, and lymphatics	$ 414
Skin disorders	$ 2,445	Disorders of the upper GI	$1,088	Mental disorders	$ 409
Disorders of teeth and jaws	$ 2,255	Other stomach and intestinal disorders	$ 997	Non-malignant neoplasm	$ 323
Anemia and other deficiencies	$ 2,248	Cataract	$ 976	Non-malignant breast disease	$ 301
Hernias	$ 2,224	Epilepsy and convulsions	$ 960	Systemic lupus and connective tissues disorders	$ 292
Cerebrovascular disease	$ 2,119	Gallbladder, pancreatic, and liver disease	$ 862	Complications of surgery or device	$ 278
Normal pregnancy/birth, and live born	$ 1,797	Poisoning by medical and non-medical substances	$ 751	Hypertension	$ 249
Tonsillitis	$ 1,765	Disorders of mouth and esophagus	$ 744	Symptoms	$ 238
Male genital disorders	$ 1,672	Influenza	$ 729	Urinary tract infections	$ 157
Back problems	$ 1,591	Cancer	$ 698	Intestinal infection	$ 136
Other bone and musculoskeletal disease	$ 1,581	Other genitourinary condition	$ 660	Acute Bronchitis and URI	$ -
Other eye disorders	$ 1,468	Trauma-related disorders	$ 555	Overall Average	$1,388

Figure 4. Total expense by condition in year 2018

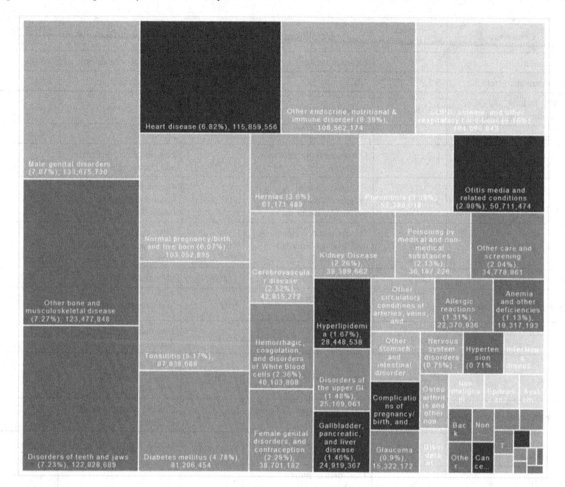

Bootstrapping Sampling on Number of People with Care

Bootstrapping is one of resampling methods that uses random sampling with replacement, and it assigns measures of accuracy (bias, variance, confidence intervals, prediction error, etc.) to sample estimates (Bootstrapping (statistics), 2021). We will use this method to create a set of simulated samples, making conditions and type of event as independent variables, and average expense per person with care as dependent variable.

First, we convert the number of people with care of each condition and event into a probability percent of the total number of people with any condition and any event from year 2016 to year 2018, which is 3,652,509. For example, the number of people with condition "Acute Bronchitis and URI" and received "emergency room" service for year 2018 is 1911, and it is converted to 0.052%. This conversion is repeated for each combination of condition, event and year, and all those probabilities will add up to 1. After that, the cumulative probability is calculated to construct intervals that help determining our bootstrapping sampling. To be more specific, a randomly generated number 0.00085 falls in the interval of [0.00075263, 0.00093415) and thus this number generate a patient with condition "back problems" and "emergency room visit". As a result, generating 5000 random numbers range from 0 to

1 can construct a sample with 5000 patients whose conditions and type of events retain the distribution information of the original data.

Table 4. Examples showing bootstrapping procedures

Condition	Emergency room visits	Probability	Cumulative probability
Acute Bronchitis and URI	1,911	0.0005232	0.0005232
Allergic reactions	838	0.00022943	0.00075263
Anemia and other deficiencies	0	0	0.00075263
Back problems	663	0.00018152	0.00093415
Cancer	0	0	0.00093415
Cataract	0	0	0.00093415
Cerebrovascular disease	797	0.00021821	0.00115236

The original data from year 2016 to 2018 contains 159 rows of data, which are 53 conditions times 3 years. By bootstrapping, we obtained a simulated sample with 5000 independent patients. And we constructed two tables to test whether the simulated sample correctly captures the frequencies of the original data. Table 5 is the list of five highest occurrence and five least occurrence conditions from the 5000 simulated patients, and Table 6 is the list from the original data that averages over three years. The percent column is calculated as the occurrence of a specific condition divided by the total number of people with care. For example, 380 patients of hypertension were simulated in this dataset and as mentioned earlier the dataset's sample size is 5000, then the percent of "hypertension" is 380/5000 = 7.6%. By comparing these two tables, we can see that the top five conditions of high prevalence are the same for simulated dataset and original data. And though the least five conditions have slight differences, the differences of percent between simulated and original data are relatively small and can even be smaller if the simulated dataset has larger sample size.

Table 5. The highest 5 and least 5 occurred conditions and their respective percent from the simulated dataset

Sort by percent	Conditions	Percent
1	Hypertension	7.60%
2	Osteoarthritis and other non-traumatic joint disorders	6.62%
3	Mental disorders	5.42%
4	Nervous system disorders	4.96%
5	Hyperlipidemia	4.80%
49	Complications of pregnancy/birth, and perinatal conditions	0.12%
50	Non-malignant breast disease	0.10%
51	Congenital anomalies	0.10%
52	Tonsillitis	0.08%
53	Complications of surgery or device	0.08%

Table 6. The highest 5 and least 5 occurred conditions and their respective percent from the original data

Sort by percent	Conditions	Percent
1	Hypertension	7.28%
2	Osteoarthritis and other non-traumatic joint disorders	6.38%
3	Mental disorders	6.06%
4	Hyperlipidemia	4.99%
5	Nervous system disorders	4.64%
49	Poisoning by medical and non-medical substances	0.11%
50	Complications of surgery or device	0.10%
51	Congenital anomalies	0.10%
52	Tonsillitis	0.08%
53	Hemorrhagic, coagulation, and disorders of White Blood cells	0.07%

The more detailed tables showing distribution probabilities of each condition, each type of events, and cross categories can be seen in appendix. Because the simulated sample size is relatively small compared with the original total number of people of any category, some combinations of condition and event type that have low frequency are also drawn less and even never drawn in the bootstrapping procedure. Some combinations like "hypertension" and "office-based events", "Osteoarthritis and other non-traumatic joint disorders" and "office-based events", which have very high frequency in the original data, also have high percent in the simulated sampling. Comparing the grand total probabilities of each condition or event type also shows that the bootstrapping sample captures the original distribution and thus is appropriate to replace it to be the predictors in a regression model.

Bootstrapping Average Expense Per Person

After a sample of patients with various conditions and events that are generated by bootstrapping, each patient's expense is generated from three years' average expense data assuming lognormal distribution. Table 7 shows three sample combinations' original average expense data from year 2016 to 2018 and the simulated expenses. For example, condition "hypertension" and event "home health events" have 7879, 7487, 7100 dollars of average expense per person in year 2018, 2017, 2016 respectively. The mean and variance of these three years' data are 7488.67 and 101141.56. Based on the relation between lognormal and normal distribution, we back up the μ and σ which are the parameters for lognormal distribution, and for this case μ equals 8.92 and σ equals 0.042. Then a random number range from 0 to 1 is treated as a probability to generate a standard score z, and the simulated average expense is calculated as $e^{\mu + z * \sigma}$. In our simulated sample there are four patients with "hypertension" and "home health events", and their simulated expenses are 7446, 7550, 7109, 7101, which are reasonable compared with the past three years' data.

Table 7. Examples of original record and simulated average expenses

Condition	Type of event	2018	2017	2016	Simulated expenses rounded
hypertension	home health events	7879	7487	7100	7446, 7550, 7109, 7101
Infectious disease	Inpatient stays	25659	16817	20049	20394, 21982
Thyroid disease	Office-based events	506	469	469	496, 508, 506, 494, 459, 473, 511, 497, 499, etc.

Figure 5 and Figure 6 demonstrate the distribution of simulated average expenses grouped by medical conditions and type of services respectively. Some relationships are obvious, for example, most of patients have low expenses and few patients incurred high expenses. The conditions with top average expenses are "cancer", "other care and screening", "heart disease" and "cerebrovascular disease". And the type of service "inpatient stays" has significantly higher expenses that even its lower quartile is higher than the others, while "home health" is the second.

Figure 5. Simulated average expense grouped by medical conditions

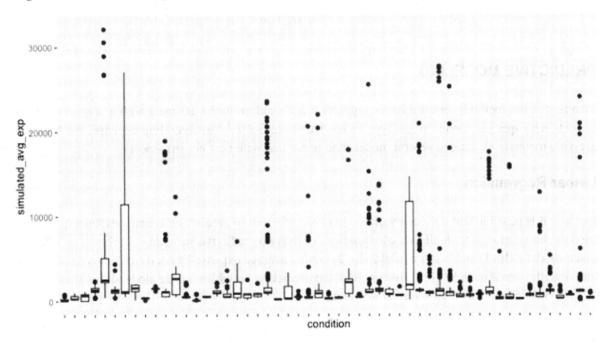

Figure 6. Simulated average expense grouped by type of services

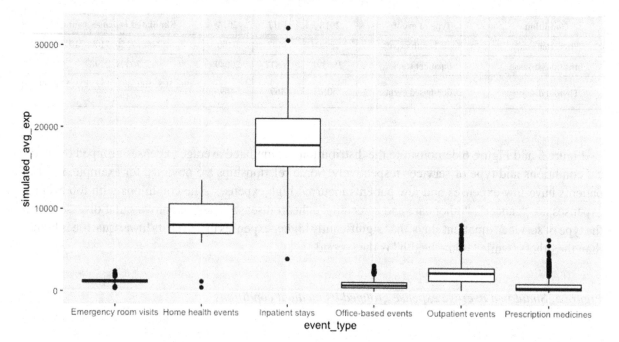

PREDICTIVE MODELING

Two regression methods, general linear regression and random forest are used with a dataset of 5000 patients with specific condition and type of service to predict the corresponding expense. For both regression methods we trained several models and select one with best performance.

Linear Regression

Because it is possible that only one variable may be sufficient to predict the average expenses, we first tried the linear models with all four combinations of the two predictive variables. As shown in Table 8, linear model 1 (lm 1) and linear model 2 (lm 2) predict average expense by conditions or type of events individually; linear model 3 (lm 3) uses both of the predicting variables; linear model 4 (lm 4) uses both and also take account of their interaction effect.

Table 8. Description of four linear models

Models	Descriptions
lm1	Average expense ~ conditions
lm2	Average expense ~ type of events
lm3	Average expense ~ conditions + type of events
lm4	Average expense ~ conditions + type of events + conditions * type of events

The simulated sample was divided into train set and test set with ratio 8:2. The models are trained with the train set and then applied to both train set and test set. The prediction values are then compared with the true values which are the simulated average expenses, as shown in Figure 7 that the matrix of comparison visualizes their prediction accuracy. If the model is a good fit, the points should be close to the straight line which means the predicted value equals the true value. Through the figures of each row, we can see that lm4 is the best fit, while lm1 and lm2 are the worst. Further observation can lead to the speculation that (lm1) only using conditions to predict may tend to underestimate the average expenses, and (lm2) only using type of events make the model insufficient of variable levels and thus can't make accurate predictions.

Figure 7. Predicted value versus simulated value for train set and test set of linear models 1 to 4, respectively

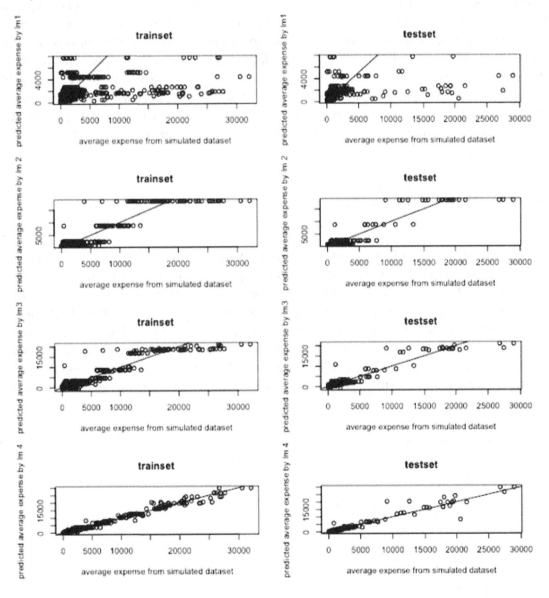

To select a model among the four, we used three metrics: multiple R-squared, adjusted R-squared and Akaike's Information Criteria (AIC). The R-squared, also known as coefficient of determination, is the proportion of the variation in dependent variable that can be explained by the independent variables. It is measured with two sums of squares equations, $SS_{residual}$ the sum of squared residuals between observed values y_i and fitted data f_i, and SS_{total} the sum of squared residuals between observed values y_i and mean of the observed data $\bar{y}$. If a model perfectly fits the data, which means $y_i = f_i$, then $SS_{residual}$ equals zero and R^2 equals 1, so a model with R^2 close to 1 is usually more preferable.

$$R^2 = 1 - \frac{SS_{residual}}{SS_{total}} = 1 - \frac{\sum(y_i - f_i)^2}{\sum(y_i - \bar{y})^2} \tag{1}$$

However, increasing the number of predictive variables can always increase R^2 so it is inappropriate to compare models with different number of predictive variables by R^2. Adjusted R^2 is more appropriate because it takes into account the number of variables. In RStudio the adjusted R^2 is calculated as below, where n is the sample size and p is the number of independent variables. For example, in lm2 there are 4000 observations in the train set (n = 4000) and 5 variables (p=5). Note that though the independent variable "type of events" has 6 levels, RStudio treats "emergency room visits" as a base level so the model has five variables (see details in appendix). If the newly added variables are not useful to predict, the resulted adjusted R^2 becomes smaller as the number of predictors gets larger while R^2 only increases by a small extent.

$$adjusted\ R^2 = 1 - (1 - R^2) * \frac{n - 1}{n - p - 1} \tag{2}$$

Similar to adjusted R^2, AIC measures model goodness while balancing the tradeoffs between the model goodness and the model complexity by adding a penalty term (Rachel T. Silvestrini, 2018). In RStudio AIC is calculated as the function below, where $\mathcal{L}$ is the maximum likelihood of the model, k equals 2 for AIC, and *NPAR* is the number of parameters in the model (AIC, n.d.). The penalty term 2*npar will become larger as the model become more complex, so a model with lower AIC is preferred. However, the AIC value only tells the quality of a model relative to the other candidates, rather than its absolute quality (Akaike information criterion, n.d.), and this is the reason why we also incorporated metrics R^2 and adjusted R^2 which can provide information of how well observed outcomes are predicted by the model.

$$AIC = -2 * \log \mathcal{L} + k * npar \tag{3}$$

Table 9. Comparison of four linear models based on metrics

Models	Multiple R-squared	Adjusted R-squared	AIC
lm1	0.1417	0.1304	73,964
lm2	0.8544	0.8542	66,773
lm3	0.9011	0.8997	65,330
lm4	0.9856	0.9849	57,886

Table 9 summarizes the metrics of four linear models. By multiple R^2 we can see lm3 and lm4 have good fit that more than 90% of the variation can be explained by the predictive variables. After taking into account the complexity of models, lm4 still performs well with the highest adjusted R^2 and the lowest AIC values, even though the number of estimated parameters for lm4 is much larger than the other three. And thus, we can choose lm4 as a representative of linear models.

Random Forest

Random Forest is an ensemble learning method that construct many independent trees using different bootstrap subset samples of data, and the prediction is based on a simple majority vote (Breiman, Random Forests, 2001). That is to say, random forest incorporates the ideas of decision trees and bagging method. Bagging is abbreviation of bootstrap aggregating, a method designed to improve accuracy by training several models on randomly generated train sets with replacement and then predicting by plurality votes (for classification) or averages over the versions (for regression) (Breiman, Bagging Predictors, 1994). In terms of random forest, bagging is applied to trees with randomly selected samples of train set and also a randomly selected subset of features at each candidate split.

Table 10. Illustrative example of random forest procedures

patient	condition	Event type	age	gender	expense
1	Other eye disorders	Prescription medicines	57	M	558
2	Hyperlipidemia	Prescription medicines	35	M	445
3	Hyperlipidemia	Prescription medicines	52	F	388
4	Mental disorders	Prescription medicines	58	F	926
5	Symptoms	Home health events	49	F	8605
6	Heart disease	Emergency room visits	68	M	1623
7	Infectious disease	Office-based events	41	F	342
8	Heart disease	Office-based events	64	M	811
9	Cataract	Office-based events	78	M	1001
10	Female genital disorders…	Prescription medicines	38	F	450

Assume the above ten samples are the entire dataset, the first step is to create a bootstrapped dataset. For example, train set 1 is consisted by patients 1, 3, 4, 9, 2, 1, 5, 8, and note that a sample can be selected more than once because of replacement, while patients 6, 7, 10 who are not selected can be the test set. The second step is to develop tree 1 by using train set 1 and at each node only a random subset of predictive variables is considered as candidates. For example, at root node event type and age are randomly selected, and if event type did a better job it is chose to split the node; then for the next node condition and age are considered and condition is choosing to split the node; and tree 1 is developed by building more branches. Then by repeating these steps hundreds of times we can get a random forest. Compared with standard trees which tend to select important variables repeatedly, the trees in random forest are less correlated because each tree is forced to consider different subsets of variables. And random forest at most times outperforms decision trees with higher accuracy.

Two parameters of random forest algorithm in RStudio, mtry and ntree, can be adjusted to improve its performance. Different from standard decision trees in which each node is split by the best among all variables, in random forest each node is split by the best among the subset of predictors randomly chosen at that node (Liaw & Wiener, 2002). And mtry is the number of variables randomly sampled as candidates at each split, and its default is set as $\sqrt{p}$ for classification or $\dfrac{p}{3}$ for regression, where p is number of variables. But because our data only have two predictive variables, we tried both when mtry equals 1 (rf1) and when mtry equals 2 (rf2) and by comparing the two models we can choose a more appropriate mtry with smaller error. In other words, each node of trees in rf1 only considers one of the predictive variables, "conditions" or "type of events", while rf2 considers both at each node. As shown in Table 11, rf2 has lower mean of squared residuals and higher percent of variability explained than rf1, so we chose to set mtry equal to 2.

Table 11. Comparison of random forest models

Random forest models	Mean of squared residuals	% Var explained
rf1	392084.1	94.64
rf2	267838.6	96.34
rf3	306740.1	95.69

On the other hand, ntree means the number of trees to grow and its default is 500. Note that ntree should not be too low so that every input row is able to get predicted least a few times, and it should not be too high because it may cause overfitting problem. After setting mtry equals 2, ntree can be specified depending on Figure 8 which plots the error of random forest regression when ntree range from 0 to 500. The plot shows that the error stabilizes after ntree reaches about 150, we choose to construct rf3 with mtry = 2 and ntree =400 to be conservative. As Table 11 shows rf3 has slightly higher mean of squared residuals and slightly lower percent of variability explained than rf2, so we chose rf2 as a representative model for random forest regression algorithm.

Figure 8. Error of rf2 when ntree is set from 0 to 500

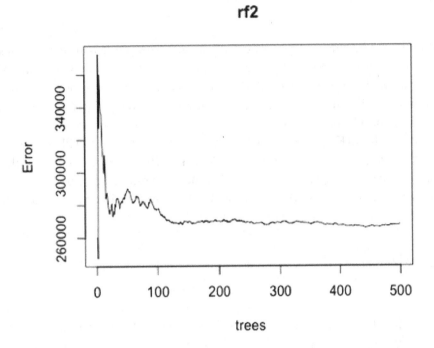

MODEL COMPARISON AND SELECTION

To compare the selected linear regression model lm4 and the selected random forest rf2, three measures of prediction accuracy are used, root-mean-square error (RMSE), mean absolute percentage error (MAPE) and mean absolute error (MAE). We used more than one measure of accuracy because any of them has pros and cons.

RMSE, or the root-mean-square deviation (RMSD), is a frequently used measure of the difference between predicted values f_i and observed values y_i, with function as below where n is the number of observations. Compared with MSE, RMSE takes the root of MSE and brings the unit back to the same as dependent variable, thus it has the advantage to be interpreted directly. In general, a lower RMSE is better and RMSE = 0 means perfect fit of data. RMSE's drawback is that it is sensitive to outliers that few large errors in the sum may produce a significant increase, and the test does not differentiate between underestimation and overestimation (Kambezidis, 2012). As discussed earlier in data description part, the dataset we use has several extreme values of high expenses so using RMSE as the only measure would cause some concerns.

$$RMSE = \sqrt{\frac{\sum(y_i - f_i)^2}{n}}$$

(4)

MAE uses the absolute value so it won't be affected by outliers as much as RMSE but if the outliers contain important information MAE cannot capture it.

$$MAE = \frac{1}{n} * \sum |y_i - f_i| \tag{5}$$

MAPE measures the accuracy of prediction as a percentage and it is usually defined as follows. The advantage is that it is very intuitive to interpret relative error and lower MAPE means lower error. MAPE is similar to MAE but normalizes MAE by true observations, so it resolved one problem that MAE provides little insight into the error when comparing across data of different scales (Bahl, 2019). But it also brings the disadvantage of MAPE that it produces infinite or undefined values for zero or close-to-zero actual values (Kim & Kim, 2016). Another drawback of MAPE is that it puts heavier penalty on negative errors than positive errors (Makridakis, 1993). For example, for the actual value 100 and estimated value of 90, the MAPE is 0.10. For the same estimated value and actual value of 80, the MAPE is 0.125. As a result, if MAPE is used as an objective function, the estimator prefers smaller values and can be biased towards negative errors (Bahl, 2019).

$$MAPE = \frac{100}{n} * \sum \left| \frac{y_i - f_i}{y_i} \right| \tag{6}$$

The response variable average expenses per person have a wide range from 15.257 to 32108.9, so we employed different metrics to avoid limitations. Here the metrics are applied to the whole dataset instead of test set. As shown in Table 12, the two models have similar performance and lm4 is lightly better with lower RMSE, lower MAPE, and lower MAE, which means lm4 has slightly better prediction accuracy than rf2.

Table 12. Comparison of lm4 and rf2

	RMSE	MAPE	MAE
Linear Regression lm4	422.0867	0.1107812	125.8517
Random Forest rf2	429.6108	0.1186094	131.8507

Furthermore from Figure 9 we can observe that these two models have very similar prediction results. Compared with the figure of lm4 against observations and the figure of rf2 against observations, the points of lm4 against rf2 are closer to form a line. And because of the categorical property of predictive variables, both regression models have the problem that a group of resulted predictions is equal to one value even the true observation varies by large amount.

Figure 9. Comparison of rf2 and lm4 predicted values against the true (simulated) value

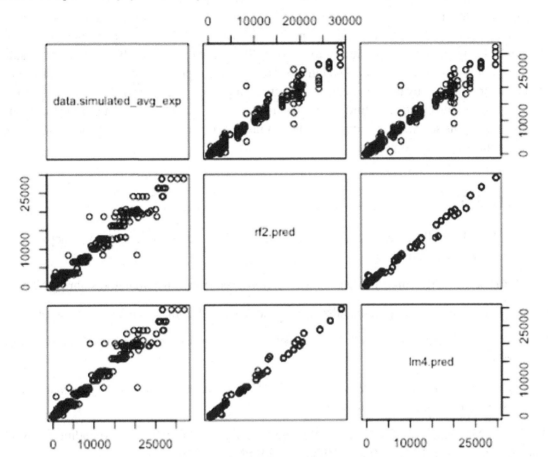

CONCLUSION AND FUTURE RESEARCH

The goal of this paper is to predict the average expenses by medical conditions and type of services. To do this, we mainly did two phases of work – simulating samples and predictive modeling. The reason that we need to do sample simulation in data preprocessing is that the original summary tables retrieved from AHRQ cannot be directly applied to regression models. The method we used is bootstrapping because it makes the simulated samples retain the statistics of the original data, such as frequency, variance, etc. The simulated dataset contains 5000 independent patients of various conditions, type of services and corresponding expense and it was applied to linear regression and random forest models. The best performed linear regression model uses medical conditions, type of services and their interaction terms as predictive variables. And the best performed random forest is when the number of variables at each split equals 2 and the forest has 400 trees. These two models have similar prediction accuracy and three commonly used metrics RMSE, MAPE and MAE shows the linear model lm4 is slightly better than random forest rf2.

Limitation of our study is that both table of the number of people with care and table of average expense per person retrieved from AHRQ have been categorized into medical conditions and type of events, which may miss information about those couldn't be categorized into the table. And this causes another concern that some estimates in the summary tables are suppressed due to inadequate precision, and some estimates' relative standard error is greater than 30% (Agency for Healthcare Research and Quality, n.d.). Another limitation is that because MEPS-HC conditions are coded into ICD-10 cods starting in 2016, we didn't include data from 1996 to 2015 which was using ICD-9 and as a result the data we used only covers three years. Though we can use bootstrapping method to construct simulated sample with larger size, only using larger original data could provide new information about distribution or other statistic characteristics. Future studies can use a more comprehensive dataset to train models.

The results of this study may be applied to health insurance planning, health service resource management, insurance policy strategy, etc.

REFERENCES

Agency for Healthcare Research and Quality. (2019, June 25). Retrieved from https://meps.ahrq.gov/mepsweb/survey_comp/household.jsp

Agency for Healthcare Research and Quality. (n.d.). Retrieved from https://datatools.ahrq.gov/meps-hc

AIC. (n.d.). Retrieved from https://stat.ethz.ch/R-manual/R-devel/library/stats/html/AIC.html

Akaike information criterion. (n.d.). In *Wikipedia*. https://en.wikipedia.org/wiki/Akaike_information_criterion

Bahl, A. (2019, November 22). *MAPE v/s MAE% v/s RMSE*. Retrieved from https://agrimabahl.medium.com/mape-v-s-mae-v-s-rmse-3e358fd58f65

Berk, M. L., & Monheit, A. C. (2001, March 01). The concentration of health care expenditures, revisited. *Health Affairs*, 20(2), 9–18. doi:10.1377/hlthaff.20.2.9 PMID:11260963

Bhattacharyya, N. (2011). Incremental Healthcare Utilization and Expenditures for Allergic Rhinitis in the United States. *The Laryngoscope*, 121(9), 1830-1833.

Bootstrapping (statistics). (2021, July 15). Retrieved from https://en.wikipedia.org/wiki/Bootstrapping_(statistics)#Advantages

Breiman, L. (1994). *Bagging Predictors*. Technical Report.

Breiman, L. (2001). Random Forests. *Machine Learning*, 45(1), 5–32. doi:10.1023/A:1010933404324

Chang, H.-Y., Boyd, C. M., Leff, B., Lemke, K. W., Bodycombe, D. P., & Weiner, J. P. (2016, September). (2016-09). Identifying Consistent High-cost Users in a Health Plan: Comparison of Alternative Prediction Models. *Medical Care*, 54(9), 852–859. doi:10.1097/MLR.0000000000000566 PMID:27326548

Kambezidis, H. (2012). *Comprehensive Renewable Energy*. Elsevier.

Kim, S., & Kim, H. (2016). A new metric of absolute percentage error for intermittent demand forecasts. *International Journal of Forecasting*, 32(3), 669–679. doi:10.1016/j.ijforecast.2015.12.003

Liaw, A., & Wiener, M. (2002). Classification and Regression by Random Forest. *R News*, 2/3. doi:10.1057/9780230509993

Makridakis, S. (1993). Accuracy measures: Theoretical and practical concerns. *International Journal of Forecasting*, *9*(4), 527–529. doi:10.1016/0169-2070(93)90079-3

Meehan, J., Chou, C.-A., & Khasawneh, M. T. (2015). Predictive modeling and analysis of high-cost patients. *IIE Annual Conference. Proceedings*, 2566-2575.

MEPS. (2020). *HC-207 2018 Medical Conditions*. Retrieved from https://meps.ahrq.gov/data_stats/download_data/pufs/h207/h207doc.pdf

Riley, G. (2007). Long-Term Trends in the Concentration of Medicare Spending. *Health Affairs*, *26*(3), 808-816.

Rodbard, H. W., Green, A. J., Fox, K. M., & Grandy, S. (2009). Impact of type 2 diabetes mellitus on prescription medication burden and out-of-pocket healthcare expenses. *Diabetes Research and Clinical Practice*, *87*(3), 360–365. doi:10.1016/j.diabres.2009.11.021 PMID:20047768

Silvestrini, R. T., & Burke, S. E. (2018). *Linear Regression Analysis with JMP and R*. ASQ Quality Press.

Whitney, D. G., Kamdar, N. S., Ng, S., Hurvitz, E. A., & Peterson, M. D. (2019). Prevalence of high-burden medical conditions and health care resource utilization and costs among adults with cerebral palsy. *Clinical Epidemiology*, *11*, 469–481. doi:10.2147/CLEP.S205839 PMID:31417318

ADDITIONAL READING

Mooney, C. Z., & Duval, R. D. (1993). *Bootstrapping: A Nonparametric Approach to Statistical Inference*. Sage Publications. doi:10.4135/9781412983532

Niu, G., & Olinsky, A. (2020). Generalized Linear Model for Automobile Fatality Rate Prediction in R. In R. S. Segall, & G. Niu, Open Source Software for Statistical Analysis of Big Data: Emerging Research and Opportunities (pp. 137-161). Hershey: IGI Global.

Niu, G., Segall, R. S., Zhao, Z., & Wu, Z. (2021). A Survey of Open Source Statistical Software (OSSS) and Their Data Processing Functionalities. *International Journal of Open Source Software and Processes*, *12*(1), 1–20. doi:10.4018/IJOSSP.2021010101

Segall, R. S., Cook, J. S., & Niu, G. (2019). Overview of Big Data - Intensive Storage and its Technologies for Cloud and Fog Computing. *International Journal of Fog Computing*, *2*(1), 74–113. doi:10.4018/IJFC.2019010104

Segall, R. S., & Niu, G. (2018). Overview of Big Data and Its Visualization. In R. S. Segall, & J. S. Cook, Handbook of Research on Big Data Storage and Visualization Techniques (pp. 1-32). Hershey: IGI Global.

Segall, R. S., & Niu, G. (2018). Big Data and Its Visualization with Fog Computing. *International Journal of Fog Computing*, *1*(2), 51–82. doi:10.4018/IJFC.2018070102

Smith, C. (2017). *Decision Trees and Random Forests: A Visual Introduction for Beginners*. Blue Windmill Media.

Wu, Z., Zhao, Z., & Niu, G. (2020). Introduction to the Popular Open Source Statistical Software (OSSS). In R. S. Segall, & G. Niu, Open Source Software for Statistical Analysis of Big Data: Emerging Research and Opportunities (pp. 73-110). Hershey: IGI Global

KEY TERMS AND DEFINITIONS

Adjusted R-Squared: It indicates how well terms fit a curve or line but adjusts for the number of terms in a model.

Akaike's Information Criteria (AIC): It is a standard to measure the goodness of statistical model fitting. Based on the concept of entropy, the criterion can weigh the complexity of the estimated model and the goodness of the model fitting data.

Bagging: Bagging is an acronym for Bootstrap Aggregating. It is an ensemble meta-algorithm that is commonly used to reduce variance within a noisy dataset. Several data samples are generated by random selection with replacement, and then weak models are then trained independently to yield a more accurate estimate.

Bootstrapping: A resampling method used to estimate statistics on a population by sampling a dataset with replacement. The process resamples a single dataset to create many simulated samples.

Data Preprocessing: One important step in machine learning. Manipulating data before it is used to build a model for example, in order to enhance performance and more applicable to algorithms or models. It usually involves steps such as data cleaning, data integration, data reduction, and data transformation.

Goodness of Fit: The goodness of fit of a statistical model describes how well it fits a set of observations. Some commonly used metrics include R squared, chi-squared test, etc.

Linear Regression: Linear approach for modelling the relationship between a scalar response and one or more explanatory variables. The case of one explanatory variable is called simple linear regression; for more than one, the process is called multiple linear regression.

Mean Absolute Error (MAE): MAE measures the average magnitude of the errors in a set of predictions, without considering their direction.

Mean Absolute Percentage Error (MAPE): A measure of how accurate a forecast system is and measures this accuracy as a percentage.

Medical Conditions: The data we used are after 2016, when the household-reported conditions are coded into ICD-10 codes and then collapsed into the Condition categories in the tables.

MTRY: A parameter in Random Forest modeling that represents the number of variables sampled at each split.

Multiple R-Squared: Also known as coefficient of determination, multiple R-squared is the proportion of the variation in dependent variable that can be explained by the independent variables. It provides a measure of how well observed outcomes are replicated by the model.

Node: A node of a decision tree represents a "test" on an attribute. A root node is at the beginning of a tree where the entire population are analyzed. And each leaf node represents a class label.

NTREE: A parameter in Random Forest modeling that represents the number of trees to grow.

Predictive Modeling: A commonly used statistical technique to predict future behavior. Predictive modeling solutions are a form of data-mining technology that works by analyzing historical and current data and generating a model to help predict future outcomes.

Random Forest: An ensemble learning method for classification, regression and other tasks that operates by constructing a multitude of decision trees at training time. It has a wide range of application prospects, from marketing to healthcare insurance. It can not only be used to model marketing simulation, to count customer origin, retention, and churn, but also to predict the risk of disease and the susceptibility of patients.

Root-Mean-Square Error (RMSE): A frequently used measure of the differences between values predicted by a model or an estimator and the values observed, and it is sensitive to outliers.

Simulated Dataset: New datasets that resemble but are not identical to the existing dataset by methods such as bootstrapping.

Split: One node can split into several branches and each branch represents the outcome of the test.

Type of Events: A home health event is defined as one month during which home health service was received. For prescription medicines, an event is defined as a purchase or refill.

APPENDIX

Figure 10. Number of people with care by conditions from original data

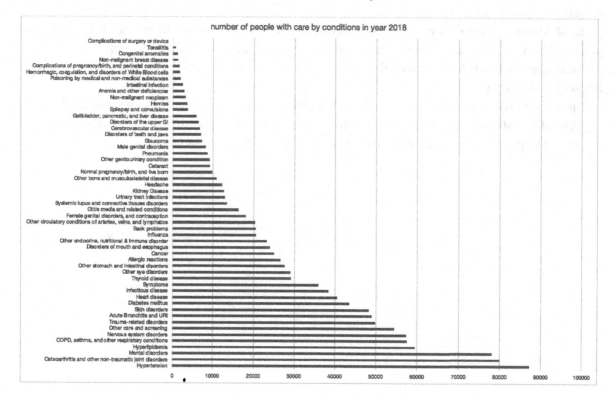

Figure 11. Simulated dataset distribution summary

Count of simulated_avg_exp	Emergency room visits	Home health events	Inpatient stays	Office-based events	Outpatient events	Prescription medicines	Grand Total
Acute Bronchitis and URI	0.04%	0.00%	0.00%	1.60%	0.10%	2.02%	3.76%
Allergic reactions	0.06%	0.00%	0.00%	0.88%	0.00%	1.38%	2.32%
Anemia and other deficiencies	0.00%	0.00%	0.00%	0.14%	0.00%	0.10%	0.24%
Back problems	0.06%	0.00%	0.00%	1.24%	0.10%	0.44%	1.84%
Cancer	0.00%	0.04%	0.10%	0.94%	0.36%	0.42%	1.86%
Cataract	0.00%	0.00%	0.00%	0.50%	0.04%	0.08%	0.62%
Cerebrovascular disease	0.06%	0.08%	0.12%	0.22%	0.00%	0.14%	0.62%
Complications of pregnancy/birth, and perinatal conditions	0.00%	0.00%	0.00%	0.10%	0.00%	0.02%	0.12%
Complications of surgery or device	0.00%	0.00%	0.00%	0.06%	0.00%	0.02%	0.08%
Congenital anomalies	0.00%	0.00%	0.00%	0.10%	0.00%	0.00%	0.10%
COPD, asthma, and other respiratory conditions	0.26%	0.08%	0.16%	1.56%	0.16%	2.26%	4.46%
Diabetes mellitus	0.04%	0.04%	0.00%	1.44%	0.16%	1.98%	3.66%
Disorders of mouth and esophagus	0.00%	0.00%	0.00%	0.32%	0.14%	1.64%	2.10%
Disorders of teeth and jaws	0.00%	0.00%	0.00%	0.04%	0.00%	0.56%	0.60%
Disorders of the upper GI	0.00%	0.00%	0.00%	0.12%	0.00%	0.56%	0.68%
Epilepsy and convulsions	0.00%	0.00%	0.00%	0.24%	0.00%	0.06%	0.30%
Female genital disorders, and contraception	0.00%	0.00%	0.00%	0.54%	0.04%	1.28%	1.86%
Gallbladder, pancreatic, and liver disease	0.02%	0.00%	0.02%	0.34%	0.08%	0.12%	0.56%
Glaucoma	0.00%	0.00%	0.00%	0.26%	0.00%	0.26%	0.52%
Headache	0.02%	0.00%	0.00%	0.40%	0.00%	0.28%	0.70%
Heart disease	0.34%	0.10%	0.32%	1.44%	0.20%	1.36%	3.76%
Hernias	0.00%	0.00%	0.00%	0.04%	0.04%	0.10%	0.18%
Hyperlipidemia	0.00%	0.00%	0.00%	1.42%	0.12%	3.26%	4.80%
Hypertension	0.10%	0.08%	0.06%	2.48%	0.20%	4.88%	7.80%
Infectious disease	0.16%	0.00%	0.04%	1.44%	0.18%	1.48%	3.30%
Influenza	0.06%	0.00%	0.00%	0.88%	0.00%	0.56%	1.50%
Intestinal infection	0.04%	0.00%	0.00%	0.10%	0.00%	0.12%	0.26%
Kidney Disease	0.10%	0.00%	0.06%	0.28%	0.12%	0.32%	0.88%
Male genital disorders	0.00%	0.00%	0.00%	0.18%	0.00%	0.58%	0.76%
Mental disorders	0.14%	0.20%	0.08%	1.72%	0.16%	3.12%	5.42%
Nervous system disorders	0.14%	0.10%	0.04%	2.06%	0.26%	2.36%	4.96%
Non-malignant breast disease	0.00%	0.00%	0.00%	0.10%	0.00%	0.00%	0.10%
Non-malignant neoplasm	0.00%	0.00%	0.00%	0.32%	0.02%	0.00%	0.34%
Normal pregnancy/birth, and live born	0.04%	0.00%	0.26%	0.32%	0.06%	0.14%	0.82%
Osteoarthritis and other non-traumatic joint disorders	0.14%	0.18%	0.10%	3.24%	0.52%	2.44%	6.62%
Other bone and musculoskeletal disease	0.00%	0.00%	0.00%	0.34%	0.12%	0.36%	0.82%
Other care and screening	0.12%	0.02%	0.12%	2.00%	0.22%	1.66%	4.14%
Other circulatory conditions of arteries, veins, and lymphatics	0.12%	0.00%	0.06%	0.88%	0.18%	0.46%	1.70%
Other endocrine, nutritional & immune disorder	0.20%	0.00%	0.00%	0.54%	0.10%	1.38%	2.22%
Other eye disorders	0.00%	0.00%	0.00%	1.60%	0.08%	0.70%	2.36%
Other genitourinary condition	0.00%	0.00%	0.00%	0.24%	0.04%	0.34%	0.62%
Other stomach and intestinal disorders	0.18%	0.00%	0.16%	0.72%	0.22%	0.82%	2.10%
Otitis media and related conditions	0.04%	0.00%	0.00%	0.70%	0.04%	0.74%	1.52%
Pneumonia	0.08%	0.00%	0.04%	0.18%	0.00%	0.24%	0.54%
Poisoning by medical and non-medical substances	0.00%	0.00%	0.00%	0.06%	0.00%	0.08%	0.14%
Skin disorders	0.14%	0.00%	0.00%	1.78%	0.16%	1.72%	3.80%
Symptoms	0.16%	0.08%	0.02%	1.12%	0.20%	1.18%	2.76%
Systemic lupus and connective tissue disorders	0.00%	0.00%	0.00%	0.52%	0.14%	0.34%	1.00%
Thyroid disease	0.00%	0.00%	0.00%	0.80%	0.14%	1.52%	2.46%
Tonsillitis	0.00%	0.00%	0.00%	0.06%	0.00%	0.00%	0.06%
Trauma-related disorders	0.92%	0.02%	0.10%	1.70%	0.28%	1.00%	4.02%
Urinary tract infections	0.06%	0.00%	0.00%	0.38%	0.00%	0.92%	1.36%
Grand Total	3.84%	1.00%	1.86%	40.71%	4.98%	47.61%	100.00%

Figure 12. Original dataset distribution summary

Condition	Emergency room visits	Home health events	Inpatient stays	Office-based events	Outpatient events	Prescription medicines	Grand Total
Acute Bronchitis and URI	0.16%	0.00%	0.00%	2.08%	0.12%	1.97%	4.33%
Allergic reactions	0.07%	0.00%	0.00%	0.82%	0.00%	1.45%	2.34%
Anemia and other deficiencies	0.00%	0.00%	0.00%	0.13%	0.00%	0.12%	0.25%
Back problems	0.06%	0.00%	0.00%	1.04%	0.16%	0.53%	1.79%
Cancer	0.00%	0.04%	0.08%	1.17%	0.30%	0.44%	2.02%
Cataract	0.00%	0.00%	0.00%	0.47%	0.07%	0.17%	0.70%
Cerebrovascular disease	0.07%	0.06%	0.07%	0.16%	0.00%	0.18%	0.53%
Complications of pregnancy/birth, and perinatal conditions	0.00%	0.00%	0.00%	0.07%	0.00%	0.06%	0.13%
Complications of surgery or device	0.00%	0.00%	0.00%	0.05%	0.00%	0.05%	0.10%
Congenital anomalies	0.00%	0.00%	0.00%	0.10%	0.00%	0.00%	0.10%
COPD, asthma, and other respiratory conditions	0.27%	0.06%	0.11%	1.58%	0.19%	2.40%	4.60%
Diabetes mellitus	0.05%	0.06%	0.00%	1.39%	0.15%	1.98%	3.63%
Disorders of mouth and esophagus	0.00%	0.00%	0.00%	0.43%	0.07%	1.48%	1.99%
Disorders of teeth and jaws	0.00%	0.00%	0.00%	0.11%	0.00%	0.63%	0.74%
Disorders of the upper GI	0.00%	0.00%	0.00%	0.18%	0.00%	0.37%	0.55%
Epilepsy and convulsions	0.02%	0.00%	0.00%	0.12%	0.00%	0.20%	0.34%
Female genital disorders, and contraception	0.02%	0.00%	0.00%	0.47%	0.09%	0.95%	1.53%
Gallbladder, pancreatic, and liver disease	0.06%	0.00%	0.04%	0.17%	0.07%	0.12%	0.47%
Glaucoma	0.00%	0.00%	0.00%	0.30%	0.00%	0.29%	0.59%
Headache	0.08%	0.00%	0.00%	0.40%	0.00%	0.53%	1.01%
Heart disease	0.26%	0.10%	0.22%	1.18%	0.27%	1.27%	3.31%
Hemorrhagic, coagulation, and disorders of White Blood cells	0.00%	0.00%	0.00%	0.04%	0.00%	0.02%	0.07%
Hernias	0.00%	0.00%	0.00%	0.13%	0.07%	0.07%	0.28%
Hyperlipidemia	0.00%	0.00%	0.00%	1.49%	0.12%	3.38%	4.99%
Hypertension	0.12%	0.07%	0.03%	2.08%	0.13%	4.84%	7.28%
Infectious disease	0.18%	0.00%	0.06%	1.37%	0.10%	1.45%	3.16%
Influenza	0.11%	0.00%	0.00%	0.65%	0.00%	0.57%	1.32%
Intestinal infection	0.03%	0.00%	0.00%	0.14%	0.00%	0.11%	0.28%
Kidney Disease	0.11%	0.00%	0.05%	0.40%	0.11%	0.28%	0.96%
Male genital disorders	0.00%	0.00%	0.00%	0.21%	0.00%	0.44%	0.65%
Mental disorders	0.14%	0.14%	0.08%	2.18%	0.15%	3.38%	6.06%
Nervous system disorders	0.16%	0.12%	0.06%	1.89%	0.28%	2.12%	4.64%
Non-malignant breast disease	0.00%	0.00%	0.00%	0.11%	0.00%	0.00%	0.11%
Non-malignant neoplasm	0.00%	0.00%	0.00%	0.25%	0.02%	0.00%	0.27%
Normal pregnancy/birth, and live born	0.04%	0.00%	0.23%	0.37%	0.07%	0.13%	0.84%
Osteoarthritis and other non-traumatic joint disorders	0.17%	0.14%	0.08%	3.27%	0.47%	2.24%	6.38%
Other bone and musculoskeletal disease	0.00%	0.00%	0.00%	0.42%	0.08%	0.37%	0.87%
Other care and screening	0.09%	0.12%	0.15%	1.89%	0.33%	1.77%	4.35%
Other circulatory conditions of arteries, veins, and lymphatics	0.11%	0.00%	0.08%	0.64%	0.14%	0.47%	1.45%
Other endocrine, nutritional & immune disorder	0.10%	0.00%	0.05%	0.56%	0.08%	1.06%	1.84%
Other eye disorders	0.00%	0.00%	0.00%	1.51%	0.08%	0.66%	2.25%
Other genitourinary condition	0.00%	0.00%	0.00%	0.25%	0.02%	0.39%	0.66%
Other stomach and intestinal disorders	0.27%	0.00%	0.12%	0.78%	0.16%	0.91%	2.23%
Otitis media and related conditions	0.06%	0.00%	0.00%	0.61%	0.02%	0.64%	1.33%
Pneumonia	0.10%	0.00%	0.08%	0.23%	0.00%	0.26%	0.67%
Poisoning by medical and non-medical substances	0.02%	0.00%	0.00%	0.03%	0.00%	0.06%	0.11%
Skin disorders	0.15%	0.00%	0.02%	1.79%	0.15%	1.71%	3.82%
Symptoms	0.21%	0.08%	0.08%	1.05%	0.16%	1.43%	3.01%
Systemic lupus and connective tissues disorders	0.01%	0.00%	0.00%	0.68%	0.10%	0.49%	1.29%
Thyroid disease	0.00%	0.00%	0.00%	0.70%	0.10%	1.58%	2.38%
Tonsillitis	0.00%	0.00%	0.00%	0.06%	0.00%	0.02%	0.08%
Trauma-related disorders	0.86%	0.07%	0.13%	1.91%	0.34%	0.94%	4.24%
Urinary tract infections	0.09%	0.00%	0.00%	0.46%	0.00%	0.55%	1.10%
Grand Total	**4.26%**	**1.08%**	**1.83%**	**40.63%**	**4.79%**	**47.82%**	**100.00%**

Figure 13. Linear Regression Model 1

Call:
lm(formula = simulated_avg_exp ~ condition, data = trainset)

Residuals:
   Min   1Q Median   3Q   Max
-7207.0 -643.6 -184.3 14.1 27703.8

Coefficients:

	Estimate	Std. Error	t value	Pr(>|t|)	
(Intercept)	173.82	206.02	0.844	0.39889	
conditionAllergic reactions	243.52	335.95	0.725	0.46858	
conditionAnemia and other deficiencies	396.7	778.33	0.51	0.6103	
conditionBack problems	1127.12	356.84	3.159	0.0016	**
conditionCancer	4231.31	353.65	11.965	< 2e-16	***
conditionCataract	1044.45	529.89	1.971	0.04879	*
conditionCerebrovascular disease	7537.67	569.32	13.24	< 2e-16	***
conditionComplications of pregnancy/birth, and perinatal conditions	1127.56	1132.17	0.996	0.31935	
conditionComplications of surgery or device	137.49	1261.61	0.109	0.91322	
conditionCongenital anomalies	1301.22	1132.17	1.149	0.2505	
conditionCOPD, asthma, and other respiratory conditions	1471.6	278.66	5.281	1.35E-07	***
conditionDiabetes mellitus	1961.41	288	6.81	1.12E-11	***
conditionDisorders of mouth and esophagus	413.87	333.61	1.241	0.21485	
conditionDisorders of teeth and jaws	-48.29	569.32	-0.085	0.93241	
conditionDisorders of the upper GI	302.31	506.09	0.597	0.55031	
conditionEpilepsy and convulsions	1042.88	854.98	1.22	0.22262	
conditionFemale genital disorders, and contraception	504.23	343.53	1.468	0.14224	
conditionGallbladder, pancreatic, and liver disease	1380.05	538.81	2.561	0.01047	*
conditionGlaucoma	489.13	569.32	0.859	0.3903	
conditionHeadache	583.43	513.58	1.136	0.25602	
conditionHeart disease	2498.17	288	8.674	< 2e-16	***
conditionHemorrhagic, coagulation, and disorders of White Blood cells	-20.62	2497.86	-0.008	0.99341	
conditionHernias	933.56	854.98	1.092	0.27494	
conditionHyperlipidemia	266.85	273.97	0.974	0.33011	
conditionHypertension	317.03	250.39	1.266	0.20554	
conditionInfectious disease	909.93	298.39	3.049	0.00231	**
conditionInfluenza	76.77	381.74	0.201	0.84062	
conditionIntestinal infection	138.49	813.72	0.17	0.86487	
conditionKidney Disease	2041.38	479.82	4.254	2.14E-05	***
conditionMale genital disorders	281.15	506.09	0.556	0.57857	
conditionMental disorders	1507.82	266.96	5.648	1.74E-08	***
conditionNervous system disorders	1386.44	271.26	5.111	3.36E-07	***
conditionNon-malignant breast disease	812.85	1261.61	0.644	0.51942	
conditionNon-malignant neoplasm	521.18	778.33	0.67	0.50314	
conditionNormal pregnancy/birth, and live born	5007.49	479.82	10.436	< 2e-16	***
conditionOsteoarthritis and other non-traumatic joint disorders	1551.55	256.23	6.055	1.53E-09	***
conditionOther bone and musculoskeletal disease	1096.06	521.5	2.102	0.03564	*
conditionOther care and screening	1697.64	285.34	5.95	2.92E-09	***
conditionOther circulatory conditions of arteries, veins, and lymphatics	1439.03	353.65	4.069	4.81E-05	***
conditionOther endocrine, nutritional & immune disorder	394.63	328.14	1.203	0.22919	
conditionOther eye disorders	472.24	322.18	1.466	0.14279	
conditionOther genitourinary condition	518.05	529.89	0.978	0.32831	
conditionOther stomach and intestinal disorders	1944.76	340.91	5.705	1.25E-08	***
conditionOtitis media and related conditions	133.89	391.28	0.342	0.73224	
conditionPneumonia	986.17	607.12	1.624	0.10438	
conditionPoisoning by medical and non-medical substances	-84.98	1132.17	-0.075	0.94017	
conditionSkin disorders	458.03	292.37	1.567	0.11728	
conditionSymptoms	800.6	315.11	2.541	0.0111	*
conditionSystemic lupus and connective tissues disorders	1115.88	444.26	2.512	0.01205	*
conditionThyroid disease	153.22	325.08	0.471	0.63742	
conditionTonsillitis	448.49	1261.61	0.355	0.72224	
conditionTrauma-related disorders	1291.64	284.91	4.533	5.97E-06	***
conditionUrinary tract infections	53.94	396.49	0.136	0.89179	

Signif. codes: 0 '***' 0.001 '**' 0.01 '*' 0.05 '.' 0.1 ' ' 1

Residual standard error: 2489 on 3947 degrees of freedom
Multiple R-squared: 0.1417,   Adjusted R-squared: 0.1304
F-statistic: 12.53 on 52 and 3947 DF, p-value: < 2.2e-16

Figure 14. Linear Regression Model 2

Call:
lm(formula = simulated_avg_exp ~ event_type, data = trainset)

Residuals:
```
    Min      1Q   Median      3Q      Max
-14518.3   -403.2   -168.6    281.0  13644.2
```

Coefficients:

	Estimate	Std. Error	t value	Pr(>|t|)	
(Intercept)	1224.92	82.94	14.769	< 2e-16	***
event_typeHome health events	7518.48	179.48	41.89	< 2e-16	***
event_typeInpatient stays	17239.73	146.66	117.551	< 2e-16	***
event_typeOffice-based events	-373.51	86.68	-4.309	1.68E-05	***
event_typeOutpatient events	1096.63	110.11	9.959	< 2e-16	***
event_typePrescription medicines	-497.37	86.17	-5.772	8.43E-09	***

Signif. codes: 0 '***' 0.001 '*   *' 0.01 '*   ' 0.05 '.'   0.1 ' '   1

Residual standard error: 1019 on 3994 degrees of freedom
Multiple R-squared: 0.8544,   Adjusted R-squared: 0.8542
F-statistic: 4688 on 5 and 3994 DF, p-value: < 2.2e-16

Figure 15. Linear Regression Model 3

Call:
lm(formula = simulated_avg_exp ~ ., data = trainset)

Residuals:
```
    Min      1Q  Median      3Q     Max
-13935.5  -160.0    -5.4   164.9  11143.3
```

Coefficients:

	Estimate	Std. Error	t value	Pr(>|t|)	
(Intercept)	548.8772	100.8584	5.442	5.59E-08	***
conditionAllergic reactions	264.7936	114.1212	2.32	0.020376	*
conditionAnemia and other deficiencies	423.2785	264.4116	1.601	0.109494	
conditionBack problems	1064.0279	121.6127	8.749	< 2e-16	***
conditionCancer	3227.6298	120.7336	26.733	< 2e-16	***
conditionCataract	1018.1226	180.3606	5.645	1.77E-08	***
conditionCerebrovascular disease	2483.4864	196.1406	12.662	< 2e-16	***
conditionComplications of pregnancy/birth, and perinatal conditions	1151.813	384.6688	2.994	0.002768	**
conditionComplications of surgery or device	162.4568	428.5745	0.379	0.704661	
conditionCongenital anomalies	1322.6423	384.8872	3.436	0.000596	***
conditionCOPD, asthma, and other respiratory conditions	609.8317	94.8241	6.431	1.42E-10	***
conditionDiabetes mellitus	1818.701	97.8505	18.587	< 2e-16	***
conditionDisorders of mouth and esophagus	345.3597	113.5848	3.041	0.002377	**
conditionDisorders of teeth and jaws	-13.9689	193.6082	-0.072	0.942486	
conditionDisorders of the upper GI	335.4755	172.0463	1.95	0.051257	.
conditionEpilepsy and convulsions	1067.452	290.5569	3.674	0.000242	***
conditionFemale genital disorders, and contraception	503.857	116.737	4.316	1.63E-05	***
conditionGallbladder, pancreatic, and liver disease	529.8204	183.3101	2.89	0.00387	**
conditionGlaucoma	518.2929	193.3558	2.681	0.007381	**
conditionHeadache	595.7608	174.5373	3.413	0.000648	***
conditionHeart disease	918.7583	98.4994	9.328	< 2e-16	***
conditionHemorrhagic, coagulation, and disorders of White Blood cells	0.7997	848.4871	0.001	0.999248	
conditionHernias	674.4029	290.6507	2.32	0.020374	*
conditionHyperlipidemia	263.4465	93.09	2.83	0.004678	**
conditionHypertension	143.8202	85.0668	1.691	0.090978	.
conditionInfectious disease	577.1254	101.4558	5.688	1.38E-08	***
conditionInfluenza	90.1766	129.7906	0.695	0.487231	
conditionIntestinal infection	125.9368	276.4609	0.456	0.648752	
conditionKidney Disease	1290.7546	163.4506	7.897	3.68E-15	***
conditionMale genital disorders	313.3294	171.9691	1.822	0.068529	.
conditionMental disorders	985.9724	90.9118	10.845	< 2e-16	***
conditionNervous system disorders	996.0781	92.2413	10.799	< 2e-16	***
conditionNon-malignant breast disease	834.2717	428.8067	1.946	0.051778	.
conditionNon-malignant neoplasm	424.5902	264.8383	1.603	0.108969	
conditionNormal pregnancy/birth, and live born	-921.9155	166.9859	-5.521	3.59E-08	***
conditionOsteoarthritis and other non-traumatic joint disorders	971.6711	87.27	11.134	< 2e-16	***
conditionOther bone and musculoskeletal disease	930.9493	177.31	5.25	1.60E-07	***
conditionOther care and screening	1049.0926	97.065	10.808	< 2e-16	***
conditionOther circulatory conditions of arteries, veins, and lymphatics	830.386	120.5238	6.89	6.48E-12	***
conditionOther endocrine, nutritional & immune disorder	342.1321	111.729	3.062	0.002212	**
conditionOther eye disorders	458.8993	109.7662	4.181	2.97E-05	***
conditionOther genitourinary condition	496.6383	179.9714	2.76	0.005815	**
conditionOther stomach and intestinal disorders	559.1399	116.3087	4.807	1.59E-06	***
conditionOtitis media and related conditions	132.1402	132.8995	0.994	0.320144	
conditionPneumonia	26.147	206.5738	0.127	0.899284	
conditionPoisoning by medical and non-medical substances	-57.8842	384.5422	-0.151	0.880356	
conditionSkin disorders	406.1312	99.376	4.087	4.46E-05	***
conditionSymptoms	311.2435	107.3232	2.9	0.003752	**
conditionSystemic lupus and connective tissues disorders	980.0097	151.0962	6.486	9.91E-11	***
conditionThyroid disease	104.291	110.4712	0.944	0.345199	
conditionTonsillitis	469.9081	428.8067	1.096	0.273211	
conditionTrauma-related disorders	643.9947	98.5608	6.534	7.22E-11	***
conditionUrinary tract infections	77.476	134.6944	0.575	0.56519	
event_typeHome health events	7137.7665	151.2811	47.182	< 2e-16	***
event_typeInpatient stays	17189.1039	125.4801	136.987	< 2e-16	***
event_typeOffice-based events	-396.4774	74.6272	-5.313	1.14E-07	***
event_typeOutpatient events	901.5941	93.5342	9.639	< 2e-16	***
event_typePrescription medicines	-410.6695	74.6974	-5.498	4.09E-08	***

Signif. codes: 0 '***' 0.001 '**' 0.01 '*' 0.05 '.' 0.1 ' ' 1

Residual standard error: 845.4 on 3942 degrees of freedom

Multiple R-squared: 0.9011, Adjusted R-squared: 0.8997

F-statistic: 630.3 on 57 and 3942 DF, p-value: < 2.2e-16

Figure 16. Linear Regression Model 4
(250 rows omitted here)

```
Call:
lm(formula = simulated_avg_exp ~ condition * event_type, data = trainset)

Residuals:
Min    1Q  Median   3Q    Max
-5144.4  -47.6   -1.9   37.5  5144.4

Coefficients: (126 not defined because of singularities)
```

	Estimate	Std. Error	t value	Pr(>|t|)	
(Intercept)	812.638	328.058	2.477	0.013288	*
conditionAllergic reactions	94.557	401.788	0.235	0.813957	
conditionAnemia and other deficiencies	-9.172	167.982	-0.055	0.956458	
conditionBack problems	606.8	378.809	1.602	0.109269	
conditionCancer	3472.04	81.814	42.438	< 2e-16	***
conditionCataract	340.955	167.982	2.03	0.042455	*
conditionCerebrovascular disease	1168.208	378.809	3.084	0.002058	**
conditionComplications of pregnancy/birth, and perinatal conditions	35.149	330.052	0.106	0.915196	
conditionComplications of surgery or device	-2.361	330.052	-0.007	0.994293	
conditionCongenital anomalies	1201.88	152.703	7.871	4.56E-15	***
conditionCOPD, asthma, and other respiratory conditions	334.996	347.958	0.963	0.335735	
conditionDiabetes mellitus	285.923	401.788	0.712	0.476739	
conditionDisorders of mouth and esophagus	351.196	53.385	6.579	5.40E-11	***
conditionDisorders of teeth and jaws	-20.01	81.814	-0.245	0.806799	
conditionDisorders of the upper GI	381.102	76.136	5.006	5.82E-07	***
conditionEpilepsy and convulsions	2008.589	234.784	8.555	< 2e-16	***
conditionFemale genital disorders, and contraception	363.407	56.574	6.424	1.49E-10	***
conditionGallbladder, pancreatic, and liver disease	856.8	463.944	1.847	0.064857	.
conditionGlaucoma	713.327	101.395	7.035	2.35E-12	***
conditionHeadache	1226.627	463.944	2.644	0.008229	**
conditionHeart disease	930.496	339.572	2.74	0.006169	**
conditionHemorrhagic, coagulation, and disorders of White Blood cells	-119.963	330.781	-0.363	0.716874	
conditionHernias	107.819	151.119	0.713	0.475599	
conditionHyperlipidemia	349.58	46.62	7.498	7.99E-14	***
conditionHypertension	228.04	366.78	0.622	0.534153	
conditionInfectious disease	78.584	354.343	0.222	0.824503	
conditionInfluenza	47.227	401.788	0.118	0.906436	
conditionIntestinal infection	-396.799	463.944	-0.855	0.392454	
conditionKidney Disease	918.34	366.78	2.504	0.012329	*
conditionMale genital disorders	317.053	78.768	4.025	5.80E-05	***
conditionMental disorders	364.873	366.78	0.995	0.319896	
conditionNervous system disorders	378.303	354.343	1.068	0.28576	
conditionNon-malignant breast disease	713.509	169.408	4.212	2.59E-05	***
conditionNon-malignant neoplasm	1024.914	378.809	2.706	0.006848	**
conditionNormal pregnancy/birth, and live born	-447.675	463.944	-0.965	0.33464	
conditionOsteoarthritis and other non-traumatic joint disorders	219.736	366.78	0.599	0.549145	
conditionOther bone and musculoskeletal disease	648.246	105.339	6.154	8.34E-10	***
conditionOther care and screening	484.321	366.78	1.32	0.186759	
conditionOther circulatory conditions of arteries, veins, and lymphatics	450.904	359.37	1.255	0.209662	
conditionOther endocrine, nutritional & immune disorder	216.739	344.07	0.63	0.528781	
conditionOther eye disorders	343.209	72.791	4.715	2.50E-06	***
conditionOther genitourinary condition	634.566	97.934	6.48	1.04E-10	***
conditionOther stomach and intestinal disorders	778.576	350.709	2.22	0.026477	*
conditionOtitis media and related conditions	-80.695	463.944	-0.174	0.861928	
conditionPneumonia	116.237	378.809	0.307	0.758976	
conditionPoisoning by medical and non-medical substances	58.646	234.784	0.25	0.802765	
conditionSkin disorders	26.876	354.343	0.076	0.939545	
conditionSymptoms	484.047	347.958	1.391	0.164275	
conditionSystemic lupus and connective tissues disorders	814.585	94.867	8.587	< 2e-16	***
conditionThyroid disease	90.55	54.961	1.648	0.099534	.
conditionTonsillitis	349.145	169.408	2.061	0.039374	*
conditionTrauma-related disorders	338.477	332.237	1.019	0.308371	
conditionUrinary tract infections	152.175	463.944	0.328	0.742928	
event_typeHome health events	4911.793	332.237	14.784	< 2e-16	***
event_typeInpatient stays	19334.527	172.236	112.256	< 2e-16	***
event_typeOffice-based events	-539.475	330.781	-1.631	0.102991	
event_typeOutpatient events	-220.981	378.809	-0.583	0.559687	
event_typePrescription medicines	-734.589	330.052	-2.226	0.026094	*
conditionAllergic reactions:event_typeHome health events	NA	NA	NA	NA	
conditionAnemia and other deficiencies:event_typeHome health events	NA	NA	NA	NA	

Random Forest Models

```
Rf1
Call:
 randomForest(formula = simulated_avg_exp ~ ., data = data, importance = TRUE,
mtry = 1)
               Type of random forest: regression
                     Number of trees: 500
No. of variables tried at each split: 1
         Mean of squared residuals: 392084.1
                   % Var explained: 94.64
Rf2
Call:
 randomForest(formula = simulated_avg_exp ~ ., data = data, importance = TRUE,
mtry = 2)
               Type of random forest: regression
                     Number of trees: 500
No. of variables tried at each split: 2
         Mean of squared residuals: 267838.6
                   % Var explained: 96.34
Rf3
Call:
 randomForest(formula = simulated_avg_exp ~ ., data = trainset,        impor-
tance = TRUE, mtry = 2, ntree = 400)
               Type of random forest: regression
                     Number of trees: 400
No. of variables tried at each split: 2
         Mean of squared residuals: 306740.1
                   % Var explained: 95.69
```

Section 3
Business Applications

Chapter 8
Airbnb (Air Bed and Breakfast) Listing Analysis Through Machine Learning Techniques

Xiang Li
Cornell University, USA

Jingxi Liao
University of Central Florida, USA

Tianchuan Gao
Columbia University, USA

ABSTRACT

Machine learning is a broad field that contains multiple fields of discipline including mathematics, computer science, and data science. Some of the concepts, like deep neural networks, can be complicated and difficult to explain in several words. This chapter focuses on essential methods like classification from supervised learning, clustering, and dimensionality reduction that can be easily interpreted and explained in an acceptable way for beginners. In this chapter, data for Airbnb (Air Bed and Breakfast) listings in London are used as the source data to study the effect of each machine learning technique. By using the K-means clustering, principal component analysis (PCA), random forest, and other methods to help build classification models from the features, it is able to predict the classification results and provide some performance measurements to test the model.

INTRODUCTION

Nowadays, machine learning (ML) is well-known and can be used in solving different types of problems such as probability, convex analysis and approximation theory. It is a type of artificial intelligence (AI) and it mainly focuses on letting the computer learn by itself without the control from humans (Expert.ai Team, 2020). It may look difficult to some beginners, but the method we mentioned here is about classification from supervised learning, clustering, and dimensionality reduction which is easy to explain and

DOI: 10.4018/978-1-7998-8455-2.ch008

understand. Moreover, we want to show not only the effect of machine learning but also how close this technique can be applied to our daily life, so we use the dataset from Airbnb listings to do the analysis.

Airbnb which stands for Air Bed and Breakfast, a famous online marketplace for lodging, is often used by a large number of travelers and landlords. It provides a platform between tenants and renters and helps them match each other easily and conveniently. It was built in 2008 and started in San Francisco, California USA before spreading to all over the world (Bivens, 2019). Based on some statistics, the Airbnb covers 220 countries and regions with active listings, has nearly 500 million guests since its creation and was joined by 14,000 new hosts in each month of 2021 (Deane, 2021). In order to keep our data source comprehensive and multifarious, we select the Airbnb listing from London as a dataset which contains 76,619 numbers of listings information and over 8 features. Then, we use K-means clustering, hierarchical clustering, Principal Component Analysis, random forest to analyze the date we choose and we will use the decision tree to predict the data after the analysis process.

Firstly, We are going to introduce K-means clustering. K-means clustering is one of the unsupervised learning which is easy to explain. Cluster is a common type of data analysis and it is used to separate the original data to different subgroups or clusters, so the data with the same group will be very similar (Dabbura, 2018). Furthermore, K-mean, which is a kind of algorithm of the centroid-based and distance-based, is used to assign different data points to different clusters through the calculation of the distance from the point to the cluster centroid which is randomly selected in the beginning (Sharma, 2019). After that, we will reselect new cluster centroids and redo the assigned process again and again, so our goal in the K-mean cluster is to repeat the select and assign process and find suitable clusters with minimal distance from each data point to the cluster centroid (Sharma, 2019).

The second method we use is hierarchical clustering which is similar to the first method that is a type of unsupervised learning and is to cluster data points but with different standards. In hierarchical clustering, we initially consider each of the data points as different clusters and then find the closest two clusters and merge them together (Patlolla, 2018). Hierarchical clustering is similar to the K-mean cluster in that those processes will run cyclically but it is different that all the data points will be in a single cluster. Compare K-mean clustering with hierarchical clustering, we have the assumption that if the dataset has a large number of variables, it is better to use K-mean clustering and if we want the result explicable and structured, hierarchical clustering is more suitable (Das, 2020).

Moreover, we also mention Principal Component Analysis (PCA) during analyzing the dataset. Principal Component Analysis which is also called PCA is a method to reduce or refine the dimension of a dataset and the smaller dataset which we transferred from the original dataset still contains the important information (Jaadi, 2021). Therefore, our goal in the PCA is to make the dataset concise and effective.

The above method we have introduced is all used in the analysis process. Like we previously said, we will do the data prediction after the analysis process and the method we used is the decision tree. Nowadays, the decision tree usually appears in machine learning and it is a type of supervised machine learning. As its name decision tree, it is used to build a model like a tree and use the tree truck to present all the possible consequences in different kinds of data. Specifically, the tree is made of nodes, leaf and branches with respect to test, class label that is decision and conjunctions that are connected to class labels (Yadav, 2018).

Furthermore, the second method we used in the process of data prediction is random forest which is a type of supervised learning. Just like its named "forest", it is made of many decision trees and these trees will be merged to get an accurate predicted result (Donges, 2019). Compare the decision tree and the random forest, we can get that the decision tree can be explained easily but it is hard for us to pick the optimal ones and the random forest can be used in a large dataset but the training process may take lots of time (Trehan, 2020).

LITERATURE REVIEW

Before starting the research, we have read some literature which is relative to the dataset analysis through machine learning. I find out that Kalehbasti, Nikolenko and Rezaei also did a analysis on Airbnb but they concentrated on price prediction through the Machine Learning and Sentiment Analysis. They select the Airbnb dataset from New York City. The methods they used for price prediction are Ridge Regression, K-means Clustering with Ridge Regression, Support Vector Regression, Neural Network and Gradient Boosting Tree Ensemble. Moreover, they used the Sentiment analysis to evaluate feature from customer review to refine the predictive process. Finally, they conclude that Support Vector Regression is the best among those methods based on the value of R-square and Mean Squared Error. (Kalehbasti, Nikolenko, & Rezaei, 2021)

Moreover, I find another paper which is also about Analysis of Airbnb in machine learning. Dhillon, Eluri, Kaur, Chhipa, Gadupudi, Eravi and Pirouz mainly focus on price prediction of Airbnb. In order to make the predictive process accurately, they initially did the data cleaning and data pre-processing. Then used linear and Logistic regression and Random Forest to predict the price. Finally, they drew a conclusion that the Random Forest Method is the best among those methods base on the least value of RMSE. (Dhillon, et al., 2021)

Furthermore, Kim and Song used the Machine Learning to do a Prediction of Business Status. Different to the paper I previously mention, they used Microsoft Azure Machine Learning Studio program that with many algorithms such as classification and regression to predict the data. Conclusively, they indicated that this program is over 60% accuracy base on the experiment data and the self- employment are recommended to use this model to predict the business status. (Kim & Song, 2018)

DATA DESCRIPTION

The source data we obtain is from inside Airbnb (http://insideairbnb.com/)that Provide data that quantifies the impact of short-term rentals on housing and residential communities. The dataset we choose contains 76,619 numbers of listings information in London that covers a wide range of features like pricing and review score. We select the following features:

Review scores rating: The overall review score for the property in one year.
Price number: The average listing price for this property in one year.
Accommodates: The number of guests this property can accommodate.
Bedrooms: The number of bedrooms this property has.
Maximum nights: The maximum number of nights for stay in this property.
Availability 365: The availability days for this property in one year.
Number of reviews: The number of reviews for this property in one year.
Reviews per month: The average number of reviews for this property in a month.

We also mutate a new column 'min_price' by multiplying the price per night with minimum nights. The reason why we choose these features is that these features can be classified as several types:

1.   price
2.   reviews (score and number of reviews)
3.   features of property,

and all these types can describe most information about a listing so we can consider choosing features as a simple process of reducing dimensions.

Before we apply all the machine learning techniques, we first manipulate the source data and plot the graphs that relate to the features we selected.

Figure 1. The median value of minimum cost of every Airbnb property by neighbourhoods in London

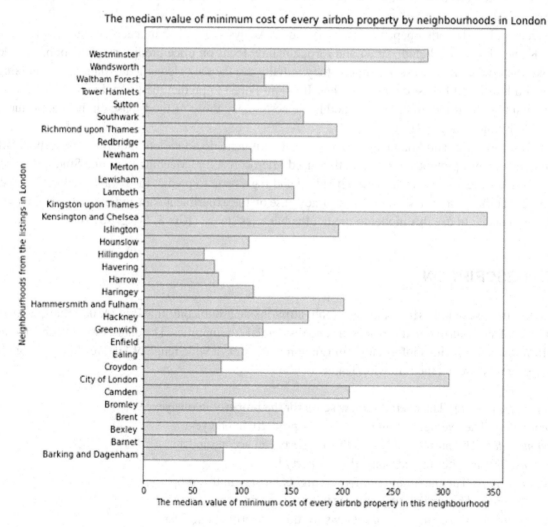

For Figure 1, we first calculate the minimum cost of every property and set it as 'min_price' column Then we plot the bar graph with horizontal direction that shows the median value of minimum cost of every Airbnb property by neighborhoods in London. We can observe that Westminster, Kingston upon Thames and the City of London have the highest median value of minimum cost and this result makes sense because these neighborhoods are filled with famous landmarks so there is a positive association between the minimum cost for staying in an Airbnb property and the prosperity of the neighborhood.

Figure 2. London Airbnb listings location: Price per night and Minimum nights

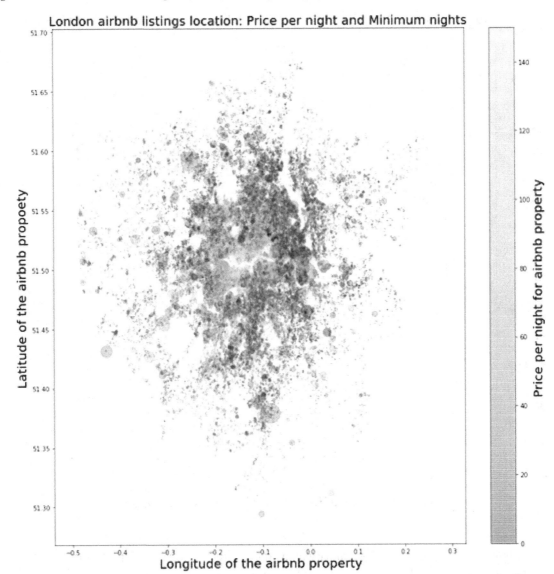

For the Figure 2, we observe that most Airbnb properties locate in the longitude around -0.2 to 0.0, latitude around 51.45 to 51.55. From the size of figure that represent the minimum nights, we also observe that the less price per night, the more minimum nights required by the host because from the plot most purple circles has a relatively large figure. For the color of the plot, we choose 0 to 150 as the range of the color bar because the mean price per night is 114 and 150 is a good measurement to distinguish a high price that is above mean and a lower price under the mean. We observe that most expensive (above mean) listings are located in longitudes of -0.2 to -0.1 and latitude of 51.45 to 51.50 which is in the center of London.

Figure 3. Histogram that shows the distribution of availability days in a year for Airbnb listing

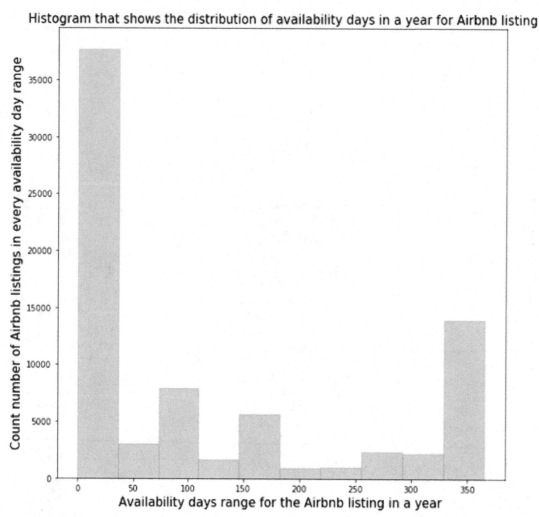

From Figure 3, we observe that the majority of available days in a year for Airbnb listings in London falls in the range of 0 to 45 days and the second largest part is in around 330 to 350 days. We can conclude that there is a polarization for the distribution. Most hosts would choose to list their properties in a short time or fully use Airbnb properties. Not many hosts would choose to list their properties from 200 to 250 days.

As a result, we have an initial view about our feature distribution, and we will then move to apply the machine learning technique to further explore the data.

METHODS

The first kind of machine learning method we use is unsupervised learning. When we observe a data only contains features and there is no associated label (outcome variable) for each observation to be classified. We can introduce unsupervised learning to classify the data by the features to a certain number of clusters. The first clustering method is K-means, K-means clustering aims to partition n observations into k clusters in which each observation belongs to the cluster with the nearest mean, the value of k is set by the tester. The four steps of K-means are as follows:

1. Select initial centroids at random
2. Assign each object to the cluster with the nearest centroid.
3. Compute each centroid as the mean of the objects assigned to it.
4. Repeat previous 2 steps until no change.

Here we use Euclidean distance to measure the distance to centroid, the distance between point p and q in a two- dimensional axis d(p, q) is as follow:

$$d(p,q) = d(q,p) = \sqrt{(p_1-q_1)^2+(p_2-q_2)^2+(p_3-q_3)^2} = \sqrt{\sum_{i=1}^{n}(q_i-p_i)^2} \qquad (1)$$

A good clustering method will produce clusters with high intra-class similarity and low inter-class similarity. Since the number of clusters is chosen by the operator subjectively. Although we can use some performance measurement method like silhouette score to help us decide the cluster number, the clustering quality still can be largely dependent on our choice.

Another clustering method we introduce in this part is hierarchical agglomerative clustering. It uses distance/similarity matrix as clustering criteria. The basic idea can be described as:

1. Starts with each data sample in a separate cluster
2. Repeatedly joins the closest pair of clusters until there is only one cluster.
3. The history of merging forms a binary tree or hierarchy. The specific steps are as follows:

Step 1. Place each point of V in its own cluster (singleton), creating the list of clusters L (initially, the leaves of T): L= V_1, V_2, V_3, ..., V_{n-1}, V_n.

Step 2. Compute a merging cost function between every pair of elements in L to find the two closest clusters {V_i, V_j} which will be the cheapest couple to merge.

Step 3. Remove V_i and V_j from L.

Step 4. Merge V_i and V_j to create a new internal node V_{ij} in T which will be the parent of V_i and V_j in the resulting tree.

Step 5. Go to Step 2 until there is only one set remaining.

The advantages of hierarchical clustering are:

1. Compared to K-means which need to specify the number of clusters in the first and we can only observe the final clustering result based on the k number of clusters we choose; hierarchical clustering instead can easily navigate the result of different number of clusters by dendrogram.
2. The principle of this method is as easy as K-means clustering which make it easy for us to do the clustering.

The disadvantages of hierarchical clustering are:

1. Just like K-means, we need to make some decisions before the analysis that can significantly change the result. First, we need to specify which kind of linkage to calculate the distance between each cluster. (complete linkage, average linkage, single linkage). We also need to specify the condition of ending the clustering process which makes the result depend more on personal decisions.
2. It is also hard to use some data type like categorical data since it is based on calculating distance between each cluster like K-means.
3. It takes more time to finish the hierarchical clustering than K-means based on the complexity of the process of algorithm. As a result, hierarchical clustering can be considered as an alternative clustering method but there is no obvious superiority between K-means and this method so we will stick to K-means in this chapter.

After clustering, we can consider the classification part is completed because we make every observation in the data belong to one of the clusters we obtained from either K-means or hierarchical clustering. We can then consider each cluster as a class and use the class labels as supervised information. We can use a supervised model to perform cluster assignment for new data samples that is to predict the cluster labels of new data. In this particular case, we choose the decision tree algorithm as the major method for supervised training.

Decision tree itself is a decision support tool that uses a tree-like graph or model of decisions and their possible consequences, including chance event outcomes, resource costs, and utility.
There are three major steps in a decision tree:

1. Are all the objects in set D of the same class? If FALSE, proceed to 2.
2. Divided into subsets $D_1, D_2 \ldots D_N$ by some attribute of the data. Proceed to 3.
3. For each subset D_i, return to 1.

As a result, it is a tree structure, in which each internal node represents a judgment on an attribute, each branch represents the output of a judgment result, and finally each leaf node represents a classification result, which is essentially composed of multiple judgment nodes. An important aspect for decision trees is the attribute selection measure. Attribute selection measure is a heuristic for selecting the splitting criterion that partition data into the best possible manner. It is also known as splitting rules because it helps us to determine breakpoints for tuples on a given node. Most popular selection measures are Information Gain, Gain Ratio, and Gini Index Corresponding to ID3 (Iterative Dichotomiser 3) with using information gain and C4.5 (successor of ID3) with using information gain ratio and CART (Classification and Regression Tree) that was termed by Breiman (1984) with using Gini Index.

For ID3 we have information gain, it introduces a concept: Entropy. It measures the impurity of the input set. In physics and mathematics, entropy is referred to as the randomness or the impurity in the system. In information theory, it refers to the impurity in a group of examples. Information gain computes the difference between entropy before split and average entropy after split of the dataset based on given attribute values. We can write Entropy as:

$$H(D) = -\sum_{x \in D} p(x) log(p(x)) \tag{2}$$

Where H(D) is the entropy of the classes in a set of observations D, p(x)log(p(x) represents the probability of class x in the set of observations D. From that, we can then write the formula of information gain:

$$IG(D, A) = H(D) - \sum_{t \in A} p(t) H(t) \tag{3}$$

Where IG (D, A) represents the information gained when splitting a set of observations D by attribute A.

For C4.5 we have a gain ratio, it can be considered as an improvement from ID3 because information gain is biased for the attribute with many outcomes. It means it prefers the attribute with many distinct values. Gain ratio handles the issue of bias by normalizing the information gain using Split Info.

$$splitInfo_A(D) = -\sum_{j=1}^{v} \frac{|D_j|}{|D|} * log_2\left(\frac{|D_j|}{|D|}\right) \tag{4}$$

Where $\frac{|D_j|}{|D|}$ acts as the weight of jth partition and v is the number of discrete values in attribute A. So,

gain ratio can be defined as: $GainRatio(A) = \dfrac{Gain(A)}{splitInfo_A(D)}$.

For CART we have a Gini Index. The Gini Index is calculated by subtracting the sum of the squared probabilities of each class from one. It favors larger partitions. We can write Gini index as:

$$G(D) = \sum_{x \in D} p(x)(1 - p(x)) \tag{5}$$

Where D corresponds to all classes in observation D and p is the probability of class x in observation D. By calculating Gini index for each feature, the winner will be the first feature to split on because its cost is the lowest.

In this study, we select CART which refers to Gini index as the major attribute selection measure, the attribute with minimum Gini index is chosen as the splitting attribute. We then import the data and divide the variables as dependent and independent variables. Dependent variable refers to the label we obtained from K-means, here we use this variable to train the classifier. Independent variable refers to the features we have. Then we split data into Training (90%) and Testing (10%) sets so that we can have enough data to train the classifier and test the performance of the classifier. The base settings of the tree is: class_weight='balanced' this mode uses the values of y to automatically adjust weights inversely proportional to class frequencies in the input data as n_samples / (n_classes * np.bincount(y)) to prevent classification results when we have an unbalanced class distribution from the data.Here max_depth specify the maximum depth of the tree. If it is None, it means that the depth of the tree is not limited until each leaf is pure, that is, all samples in the leaf node belong to the same category. n_samples refers to the number of samples we input in the classifier, n_classes refers to number of classes we want to divide and np.bincount is the Count number of occurrences of y value in array of non-negative integers. We set the max_depth =3 to have classification classes similar to the unsupervised learning. After the tree is trained and test, we also visualize the tree and use classification report and feature importance ranking to check the classification performance.

To optimize our model performance, we also introduce the idea of Grid search, In the machine learning fields, the parameters that need to be manually selected are called hyperparameters. For example, the number of decision trees in the random forest, the number of hidden layers and the number of nodes in each layer in the artificial neural network model, the size of the constant in the regular term etc. They all need to be specified in advance. Inappropriate selection of hyper-parameters will lead to problems of under-fitting or over-fitting. When selecting hyperparameters, there are two ways, one is to fine-tune based on experience, and the other is to select parameters of different sizes, bring them into the model, and select the best-performing parameters.

Grid Search can guarantee that we can find the most accurate parameters within the specified parameter range, but this is also the flaw of grid search. It requires traversing all possible parameter combinations, which is very time-consuming when we have large data sets and multiple parameters. Here we only want grid search to help us find the most appropriate depth and class distribution method. Grid search is a technique for tuning hyperparameter that may facilitate build a model and evaluate a model for every combination of algorithms parameter per grid. Here we also use 10-fold cross-validation to search the best value for that tuning hyperparameter.

In the research and application of many fields, it is usually necessary to have data containing multiple variables because these variables can provide sufficient variation especially in the case of clustering or regression since even adding one variable that is related to the subjects would definitely increase the clustering or regression performance. However, it is not wise to add features blindly, because of the following two major reasons with too many features/variables in the dataset:

1. Some features may have correlation which will increase the complexity of the problem and this kind of problem refers to collinearity in the regression model and we usually need to examine the effect of collinearity separately.
2. This problem refers to the calculation power and time since large number features always involve lots of calculation power and time from the computer and it is not cost-effective when considering the increased model performance compared to the calculation power and time.

On the other hand, if we analyze each feature separately, the analysis will be isolated and cannot fully utilize the information from the data and blindly reducing the features may result in the loss of important information. As a result, we introduce dimensionality reduction technique PCA. PCA is commonly used for dimensionality reduction by projecting each data point onto only the first few principal components to obtain lower-dimensional data while preserving as much of the data's variation as possible, the number of PCs is also decided by the tester. Specifically, it is a statistical procedure that uses an orthogonal transformation to convert a set of observations of possibly correlated variables (entities each of which takes on various numerical values) into a set of values of linearly uncorrelated variables called principal components.

As stated above, the idea of dimensionality reduction is to keep a certain variance of the data along with reduction of variables. In our practice, we always use cumulative explained variance ratio as a function of the number of components to select the ideal number of components corresponding to certain acceptable variance. After that, we can apply classification model like K-means to labels the data and then put into prediction model like random forest or decision tree to be trained and compare the prediction result with the prediction result from the model without PCA so that we can have a direct view about the balance of model performance and model efficacy.

Our final method is the random forest model, this model is derived from the idea of ensemble learning. The idea of ensemble learning is to solve the inherent shortcomings of a single model or a certain set of parameter models, so as to integrate more models, learn from each other, and avoid limitations. Random forest is the product of the idea of ensemble learning, which integrates many decision trees into a forest, and together they are used to predict the final result. There are two major types of ensemble learning: Bootstrap and bagging. The bootstrap method, as the name suggests, is a method that generates many new samples of the same size that are available from the sample itself, and generates from itself similar to itself, so it is called Bootstrap, that is, without using other sample data. The specific meaning of the Bootstrap method is as follows:

If we have a sample of size N, we hope to get m samples of size N for training. Then we can do this: First, randomly select a sample x_1 out of N samples, then write it down, put it back, and then draw a x_2, repeat N times to get a new sample of N, in this new sample There may be duplicates. Repeat m times to get m such samples. In fact, it is a random sampling problem with replacement. Each sample has the same probability (1/N) to be drawn.

This method is useful when the sample is relatively small. For example, our sample is small, but we want to set aside a part for validation. If the traditional method is used for train-validation, the sample will be smaller and the bias will be even greater and this is undesirable. The bootstrap method does not reduce the size of the training sample, but also leaves a validation set (because the training set has repetitions, but this repetition is random), so it has certain advantages. For bagging, this method divides the training set into m new training sets, and then builds a model on each new training set, which is independent of each other. In the final prediction, we integrate the results of the m models. Get the final result. The integration method is: Majority voting is used for classification problems, and the average value is used for regression.

Random forest is actually a special bagging method that uses decision trees as a model in bagging. First, use the bootstrap method to generate m training sets. Then, for each training set, construct a decision tree. When the node finds the features to split, not all the features can be found to maximize the index (such as information gain), But randomly extract a part of the features from the features, find the optimal solution among the extracted features, apply it to the node, and split. The random forest method has bagging, that is, the idea of integration, which is actually equivalent to sampling both samples and features (if the training data is regarded as a matrix, as it is common in practice, then it is a row and all columns are sampled), so overfitting can be avoided.

RESULTS

From the first method we applied, that is the K-means clustering, we want to find the best cluster number by Sum of squared distances of samples to their closest cluster center and Silhouette score. The result is shown in Figure 4. For the sum of squared distances, we use elbow method which Compute K-means clustering algorithm for different values of k and for each k, calculate the total within-cluster sum of square and then plot the curve of sum of squares according to the number of clusters k. Finally, the location of a bend (knee) in the plot is generally considered as an indicator of the appropriate number of clusters from this method, we observe the first elbow when k=3, so we should choose k=3 from this method. For the Average Silhouette Method, the idea is the average silhouette approach measures the quality of a clustering. That is, it determines how well each object lies within its cluster. A high average silhouette width indicates a good clustering. From the result of this method, we observe that both k=3 and k=4 refer to the highest silhouette score. Combining the result from these two methods, we choose k=3 to be the k we use in this case.

Figure 4. Left: Number of Clusters versus Sum of squared distances from samples to closest clusters. Right: Number of Clusters versus Silhouette Score.

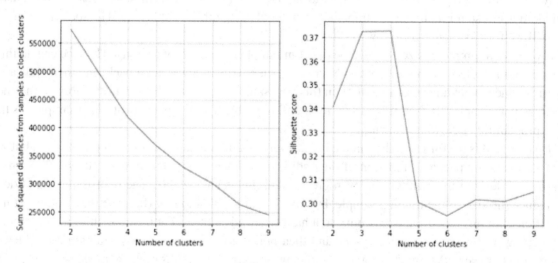

Next, we look at the distribution of each category and observe that there is no extreme large or small number of samples for the three labels. This further proves our decision of the number of k in the previous step. The result is shown in Figure 5:

Figure 5. Cluster Index versus Number of Samples

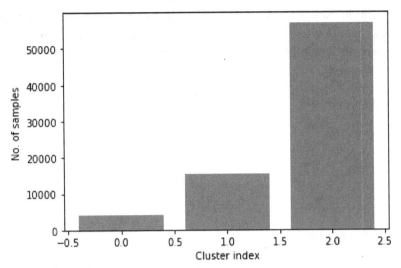

Next, since we are observing a high-dimensional dataset, we need a specific visualization method to give us a clear view of compelling two-dimensional "maps" from data with multiple dimensions. the map is shown in Figure 6:

Figure 6. sSNE_0 Versus tSNE_1

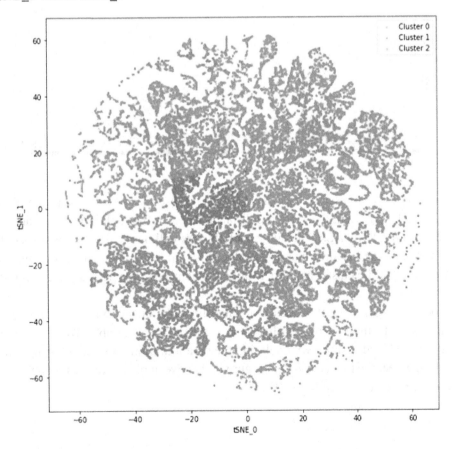

For our second clustering, we use the hierarchical clustering, here we do not know in advance how many clusters we want; in fact, we end up with a tree-like visual representation of the observations, called a dendrogram, that allows us to view at once the clusterings obtained for each possible number of clusters, from 1 to n, the dendrogram is shown in Figure 7:

Figure 7. Dendrogram

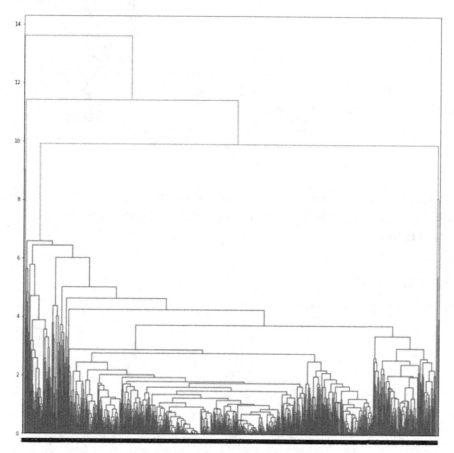

Here the vertical lines represent the distance between these samples and more the distance of the vertical lines in the dendrogram, the more the distance between these clusters. If we add a horizontal line located between 8-10 of y axis. The number of clusters will be the number of vertical lines which are being intersected by the line drawn using the threshold but from this method, we observe that most samples are from the middle cluster and this is quite unbalanced compared to the distribution we have in K-means.

Next, our focus turns to using the labels generated from the unsupervised learning. More specifically, we use the labels from the K-means clustering as the outcome variable. We first use the Decision tree from K-means and grid search. After splitting the data into training set and testing set, we use the training set to fit the tree, the tree is shown in Figure 8, then we apply the trained model into the testing set and observe the prediction accuracy in Table 1.

Figure 8. Decision tree

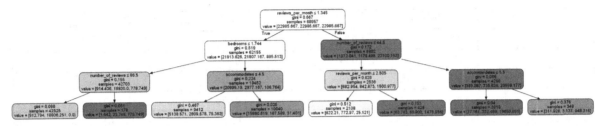

Table 1. Table about prediction accuracy in decision tree

	Precision	Recall	F1-score	Support
0.0	0.99	0.82	0.90	5750
1.0	0.66	0.91	0.76	1549
2.0	0.48	0.96	0.64	363
accuracy			0.85	7662
Macro avg	0.71	0.90	0.77	7662
Weighted avg	0.90	0.85	0.86	7662

From the result, we observe that the precision for each label differs a lot. We have an excellent prediction accuracy from label 0 but a terrible result for label 2 since it is less than 0.48 which means that it is close to random. Here we introduce grid search to improve the model performance and the result from the grid search is in Figure 9, and we find out that the best parameter max depth as 9 and use the parameters from the grid search to refit the decision tree and the result is in Table 2:

Figure 9. Result from the grid search

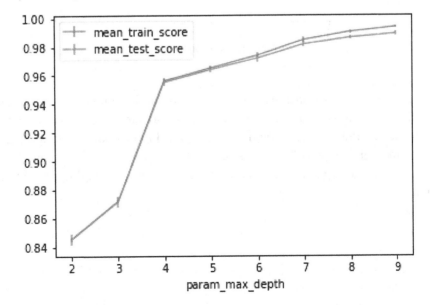

Table 2. Table about prediction accuracy in grid search

	Precision	Recall	F1-score	Support
0.0	0.98	0.99	0.98	1547
1.0	1.00	0.99	0.99	5752
2.0	0.93	0.99	0.96	363
accuracy			0.99	7662
Macro avg	0.97	0.99	0.98	7662
Weighted avg	0.99	0.99	0.99	7662

We can clearly see that the prediction accuracy for all three labels is close and located at a high level which shows a significant improvement from the decision tree without grid search.

At last, we introduce the PCA as our dimensionality reduction technique. Initially, we check the variance explained by the PC (Principal Components), the plot is shown in Figure 10.

Figure 10. The variance explained and the cumulative variance explained by the PCs

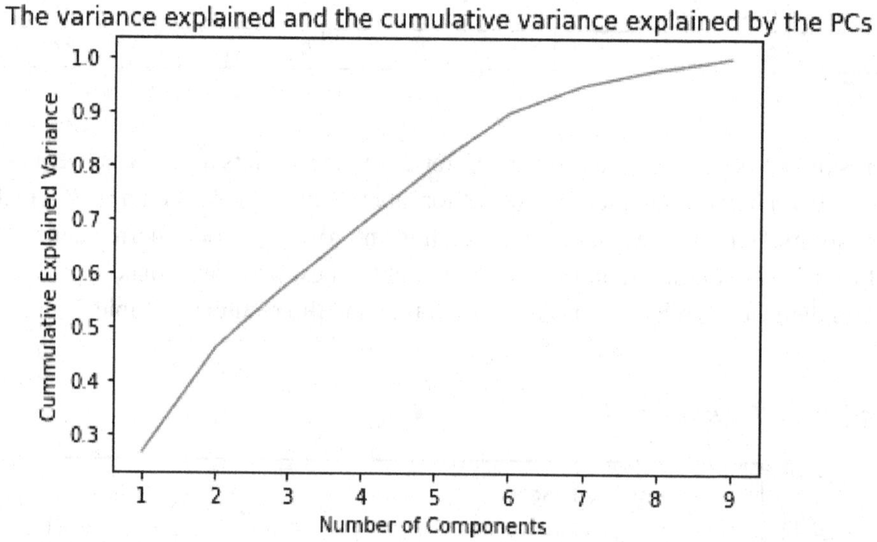

Similarly, we also use the elbow method to choose the appropriate number of components and from this plot and the first elbow is located in 2 which corresponds to almost 50% variance explained, this is not a considerable large number so we should consider to add more component, we then consider the middle of the first elbow and second elbow and select 4 as our number of components. As a result, there are 4 PCs that are required to explain 60% of the variance in the data. After doing the PCA, we observe a biplot shown in Figure 11.

Figure 11. Biplot After doing the PCA (Principal Component Analysis)

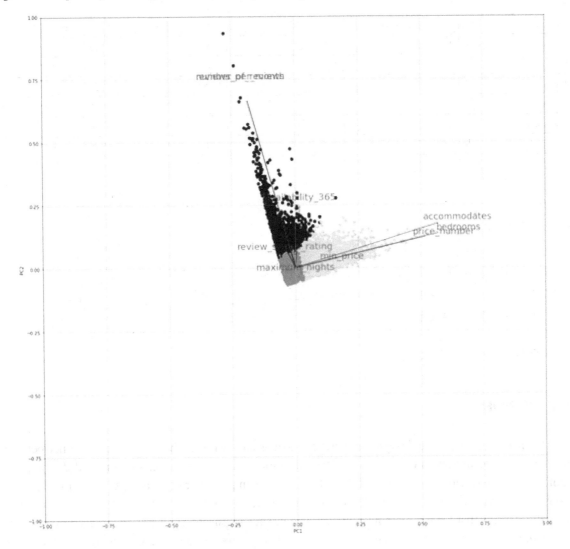

For our final model which is the random forest, we observe a improve performance compared to the decision tree, the result is shown in Table 3 and when we apply the cross validation to consider the test error, the performance of the model still can be considered as solid, the result is shown in Figure 12.

Table 3. Table about prediction accuracy in random forest

	Precision	Recall	F1-score	Support
0.0	1.00	1.00	1.00	5773
1.0	0.99	1.00	0.99	1533
2.0	0.97	0.99	0.98	356
accuracy			1.00	7662
Macro avg	0.99	0.99	0.99	7662
Weighted avg	1.00	1.00	1.00	7662

Figure 12. Code for test error

```
from sklearn.model_selection import cross_val_score
scores1 = cross_val_score(clf, X_train, y_train)
np.mean(scores1)
```

```
0.9944023103604508
```

DISCUSSION

From the K-means clustering, two plots are presented in order to find out the clustering difference between the min-price created by us to measure the true minimum cost to live in this listing and the price per night. The first plot which focuses on the clustering between price per night and number of reviews, we observe a plot with 3 clusters. One with green color centered close to 0 and this cluster can be considered as all the listings that have almost no reviews. The cluster in purple color has relatively low price but a large number of reviews can be considered as the listings that are popular with an acceptable rate of charge. The last cluster represents the listings that cost higher and maybe due to their high price, their number of reviews are relatively low.

The second cluster plot of minimum price versus number of reviews has a similar shape but the number of points in yellow cluster that represent high price, low reviews listings become less and the whole trend become lower than before, this can be explained since many properties may have a high price for every night but lower requirement for minimum stay night, we think use the min-price instead of price per night can be more close to realistic situation since some low-cost properties may have higher minimum stay night. Generally, we can say that price and number of reviews have a negative association. The higher the price becomes, the smaller the number of reviews it will receive.

As we know, K-means clustering requires us to pre-specify the number of clusters K. This can be a disadvantage and Hierarchical clustering is an alternative approach which does not require that we commit to a particular choice of K but we noticed that we have a considerable large data set which involves almost 20 dimension and thousands of observations so in this case the con of this method appears significantly because Hierarchical clustering is computationally demanding, fails on larger sets. In the practice, the hierarchical clustering took almost twice time compared to K-means clustering and from the dendrogram we obtained, the clustering result is not ideal compared to K-means since the majority of samples belongs to one category which is opposite to the result from K-means and since we need the labels from clustering to do our supervised learning task, we finally choose the labels from K-means.

For supervised learning, we have the decision tree as our main method and as we mentioned in the method section that in the ID3 (Iterative Dichotomiser 3) algorithm, we use information gain to select features, and the one with larger information gain is preferred. In the C4.5 (successor of ID3) algorithm, the information gain ratio is used to select features to reduce the problem that the information gain is easy to select features with many feature values. But both ID3 (Iterative Dichotomiser 3) and C4.5 (successor of ID3) are based on the entropy model of information theory, which involves a lot of logarithmic operations. Can the model be simplified without completely losing the advantages of the entropy model? Yes, here we introduce the CART (Classification and Regression Tree) classification tree algorithm which uses the Gini coefficient instead of the information gain ratio. The Gini coefficient represents the impurity of the model. The smaller the Gini coefficient, the lower the impurity and the better the characteristics. This is the opposite of information gain (ratio). After we finish the subset method from the decision tree, we use in this study then there are two ways of model fitting we use, one is to use grid search and cross-validation to find the optimal parameters of the decision tree, and to create a decision tree with optimal parameters, the other is the default decision tree.

In our practice, we began with default decision tree from the result of that tree, we observe that prediction accuracy for label as 2.0 is extremely low and this may due to the overfitting since for label 0, the prediction accuracy is extremely high which is close to 100% so in order to prevent this situation, we should introduce the use of grid search and cross validation. Here for cross-validation we use the k-folding method to divide the training set into equal k parts. Then select one from 1~k each as the test set, and the remaining k-1 as the training set. After training, use a certain scoring rule to score the model, and finally take the highest of the k scores as the model's score. So, from cross-validation, we can easily prevent the problem of overfitting and the problem of randomly dividing training and testing dataset that increase bias or variance. After that, we need to choose a suitable set of parameters for the model. Take a support vector machine as an example. Its parameters are gamma and C, then the two-tuples (1,1), (0.1,1), (1,10) can be regarded as several "grids". Then the grid search is, for the support vector machine model, a cross-validation evaluation is performed for each grid, and finally a set of grids with the highest score is obtained, then finally we have established the optimal model. From our practice of grid search with cross-validation, we observe a significant increase in the model performance since for each label, the prediction accuracy is over 90% which is much better than the default decision tree.

From the PCA, the first thing we did was to decrease the dimension. We checked the variance explained by the Principal Components (PCs) from the plot of the variance explained and the cumulative variance explained by the PCs and we observed an elbow around 2 and 6. Since we have 9 features and we want to maintain the balance between reducing dimensions and a good variance explained by the PCA, we choose 4 PCs since it can explain over 60% variance that means we cut over half dimensions and keep the variance explained to 60%. We observe the result mainly from the biplot. From the plot, the price bedroom and accommodates are fully correlated and min-price is close to them. This can be understood because the features of the property definitely affect the price of the property. Another direction is for the number of reviews and reviews per month. This is because they are all measurements for the reviews. Review ratings and availability in a year is quite close to them because they can be considered as potentially correlated as the reviews. Maximum nights are relatively not so correlated with other features. In conclusion, we can consider this PCA gives me a good result because it reduces significant dimensions without losing relationship between all the features.

From the random forest model, we have observed that it has a stronger prediction performance compared to decision tree and even slightly stronger than the decision tree along with grid search and cross validation, this is mostly due to the idea of ensemble learning behind this algorithm that involves both bootstrap and bagging, so that we can say the following for random forest:

1. *Can be used to solve both classification and regression problems:* Random Forest can handle classification and numerical features at the same time.
2. *Anti-over-fitting ability:* reduce the risk of overfitting by averaging decision trees.
3. *Wrong predictions will only be made when more than half of the base classifiers have errors:* Random Forest is very stable, even if a new data point appears in the data set, the entire algorithm will not be affected too much, it will only affect one decision tree, it is difficult to have an impact on all decision trees.

But if there is no perfect model after all, there are still some deficiencies of this model:

1. If there is noise in the training data for some classification/regression problems, the result from the random forest may contain over-fitting issues.
2. It is more complicated than the decision tree algorithm and has a higher computational cost.
3. Due to their complexity, they require more time to train than other similar algorithms.

From all these methods of unsupervised and supervised learning we apply in this chapter, we realize that for data with multiple dimensions, a simple method of unsupervised and supervised learning is far from enough to give us an exhaustive classification or explanation of the data, instead, we suggest the future direction would be deep learning methods like neural network.

FUTURE RESEARCH DIRECTION

From this chapter, we mainly focus on some categorical or continuous features that are directly obtained from the data but we also notice that there are some variables containing long text like some detailed reviews for the listings. For these variables, we shall consider some techniques to transform these variables to be categorical variables. For example, we can categorize the review from the guest of the listings as "positive", "neutral", "negative". This transformation needs the technique of natural language processing (NLP) that involves using neural networks. Specifically, we can use both Recurrent neural networks (RNN) and convolutional neural networks (CNN). A recurrent neural network (RNN) is a class of artificial neural networks where connections between nodes form a directed graph along a temporal sequence so on the basis of RNN there are a lot of models are built and applied to different input and output architectures (one-to-one, one-to-many, many-to-one and so) and fields that covers both supervised learning and unsupervised learning and it can be directly applied to analyzing sequential data.

Another neural network we can use is the convolutional neural network (CNN) which is mainly used for image recognition and classification. As we know, all these methods are part of deep learning, which is an artificial intelligence (AI) function that imitates the workings of the human brain in processing data and creating patterns for use in decision making.

Deep learning, also known as deep neural learning or deep neural network, is a subset of machine learning in artificial intelligence that has networks capable of learning unsupervised from data that is unstructured or unlabeled. Deep learning uses multiple layers to iteratively extract higher level feature data from raw input. These levels of abstraction generate increasingly more composite representations. Two advantages of deep learning are that it optimizes which features are placed within each of its features and that it has scaled very well with data of higher complexity and dimensionality in terms of performance. As a result, our future direction shall use the deep learning technique to construct a more efficient and sensible model to better explain our classification result that can also help the researchers to have a better idea of the general situation of the Airbnb listing in London.

CONCLUSION

In this chapter, we have applied a few supervised and unsupervised learning algorithms to the clustering, classification and prediction problems exist in our dataset, we can conclude from all these methods that there is no perfect algorithm for every dataset and the best algorithm for each dataset is figured out by our understanding of the problem and also the algorithm.

From the K-means clustering, we can say that price and number of reviews have a negative association. The higher the price becomes, the smaller the number of reviews it will receive. if we use the minimum cost for the property instead of price per night, the result will be more realistic.

From the decision tree method, we can say that grid search with cross-validation is more appropriate in this dataset compared to default decision tree since it not only finds out the best hyperparameters for the tree but also prevent the bias, variance and overfitting problem in the training and testing dataset. We may also consider a random forest method in future study since it also improves the deficiency of the default decision tree.

From the PCA, we think the dimension reduction is successful since we obtain a good correlation between all the features, we got but adding more categorical variables can result in a better explanation for this data.

From the random forest model, we obtain the best classification and prediction result among all models we have and this is due to the characteristics of this algorithm that prevent overfitting.

The limitation of this analysis is mainly from the Not Available (NAs) in the data and for the clustering and PCAs we only must drop the rows that have NAs which can result in incomplete data. Also, we think we should consider some categorical variables since we only use continuous variables in this challenge. Furthermore, the distribution of points in the cluster can be more discrete.

We have already mentioned many methods of machine learning here, but there are still many others which are useful and meaningful to introduce such as the support vector machine and the k nearest neighbor. In the future, we will try our best to do more research in machine learning and an increasing number of methods in this area will be introduced and investigated.

REFERENCES

Bivens, J. (2019, January 30). *The economic costs and benefits of Airbnb*. Retrieved from Economic Policy Institute: https://www.epi.org/publication/the-economic-costs-and-benefits-of-airbnb-no-reason-for-local-policymakers-to-let-airbnb-bypass-tax-or-regulatory-obligations/

Breiman, L., Friedman, J. H., Olshen, R. A., & Stone, C. J. (1984). Classification and regression trees. Wadsworth & Brooks/Cole Advanced Books & Software.

Dabbura, I. (2018, September 17). *K-means Clustering: Algorithm, Applications, Evaluation Methods, and Drawbacks*. Retrieved from towards (data science): https://towardsdatascience.com/K-means-clustering-algorithm-applications-evaluation-methods-and-drawbacks-aa03e644b48a

Das, V. K. (2020, October 11). *K-means clustering vs hierarchical clustering*. Retrieved from Global Tech Council: https://www.globaltechcouncil.org/clustering/K-means-clustering-vs-hierarchical-clustering/

Deane, S. (2021, January 26). *2021 Airbnb Statistics: Usage, demographics, and revenue growth*. Retrieved from STRATOS (Jet Charters, Inc.): https://www.stratosjets.com/blog/airbnb-statistics/

Dhillon, J., Eluri, N. P., Kaur, D., Chhipa, A., Gadupudi, A., Eravi, R. C., & Pirouz, M. (2021). Analysis of Airbnb Prices using Machine Learning Techniques. In *2021 IEEE 11th Annual Computing and Communication Workshop and Conference (CCWC)* (pp. 297-303). IEEE.

Donges, N. (2019, June 16). *A complete guide to the random forest algorithm*. Retrieved from Built In: https://builtin.com/data-science/random-forest-algorithm

Expert.ai Team. (2020, May 06). *What is Machine Learning? A Definition*. Retrieved from expert.ai: https://www.expert.ai/blog/machine-learning-definition/

Jaadi, Z. (2021, April 7). *A step-by-step explanation of Principal Component Analysis (PCA)*. Retrieved from Built In: https://builtin.com/data-science/step-step-explanation-principal-component-analysis

Kalehbasti, P. R., Nikolenko, L., & Rezaei, H. (2021). *Airbnb Price Prediction Using Machine Learning and Sentiment Analysis*. Machine Learning and Knowledge Extraction. doi:10.1007/978-3-030-84060-0_11

Kim, K.-P., & Song, S.-W. (2018). A Study on Prediction of Business Status. *Korea Journal of Artificial Intelligence*, 23–27.

Patlolla, C. R. (2018, December 10). *Understanding the concept of hierarchical clustering technique*. Retrieved from Towards Data Science: https://towardsdatascience.com/understanding-the-concept-of-hierarchical-clustering-technique-c6e8243758ec

Sharma, P. (2019, August 19). *The most comprehensive guide to K-means clustering you'll ever need*. Retrieved from Analytics Vidhya: https://www.analyticsvidhya.com/blog/2019/08/comprehensive-guide-K-means-clustering/

Trehan, D. (2020, July 2). *Why choose random forest and not decision trees*. Retrieved from *Towards AI*: https://towardsai.net/p/machine-learning/why-choose-random-forest-and-not-decision-trees

Yadav, P. (2018, November 13). *Decision tree in machine learning.* Retrieved from *Towards Data Science*: https://towardsdatascience.com/decision-tree-in-machine-learning-e380942a4c96

ADDITIONAL READING

Bansal, A., Sharma, M., & Goel, S. (2017). Improved K-mean clustering algorithm for prediction. *International Journal of Computers and Applications*, *157*(6), 35–40. Advance online publication. doi:10.5120/ijca2017912719

Doddipalli, L., & Usha Rani, K. (2011). Performance evaluation of decision tree classifiers on medical datasets. *International Journal of Computers and Applications*, *26*(4).

Goel, E., & Abhilasha, E. (2017). Random Forest: A Review. *International Journal of Advanced Research*, *7*(1), 251–257. http://ijarcsse.com/Before_August_2017/docs/papers/Volume_7/1_January2017/V7I1-01113.pdf

Karamizadeh, S., Abdullah, S. M., Manaf, A. A., Zamani, M., & Hooman, A. (2013). An Overview of Principal Component Analysis. *Journal of Signal and Information Processing*, *4*(03, no. 3B), 173–175. doi:10.4236/jsip.2013.43B031

Naeem, S., & Wumaier, A. (2018). Study and Implementing K-mean Clustering Algorithm. *International Journal of Computers and Applications*, *182*(31), 7–14. doi:10.5120/ijca2018918234

Priyam, A., Abhijeet, Gupta, R., Rathee, A., & Srivastava, S. (2013). Comparative analysis of decision tree classification algorithms. *International Journal of Current Engineering and Technology*, *3*(2), 334–337.

Sasirekha, K., & Baby, P. (2013). Agglomerative hierarchical clustering algorithm: A review. *International Journal of Scientific and Research Publications*, *3*(3), 1–3.

KEY TERMS AND DEFINITIONS

Classification and Regression Tree (CART): A predictive model, which explains how an outcome variable's values can be predicted based on other values. A CART output is a decision tree where each fork is a split in a predictor variable and each end node contains a prediction for the outcome variable (Breiman, 1984).

Decision Tree: A method that build a tree-like models to present all the possible consequences in different kinds of data is used in the process of data prediction.

Hierarchical Clustering: A method separates different data points to different clusters based on hierarchy and merge different clusters to one.

K-Means Clustering: A kind of algorithm that separates different data points to different clusters based on different values.

Principal Component Analysis (PCA): A method used in data analysis is to refine the size of data and make the dataset effectively.

Random Forest: A method that can be used to do the data prediction is to build many Decision Trees and refine those to get accurate predictive results.

Supervised Learning: A method in machine learning uses the model that has been trained to analyze the data.

Unsupervised Learning: A technique in machine learning that allows users to run the model without supervision.

Chapter 9
Automobile Fatal Accident and Insurance Claim Analysis Through Artificial Neural Network

Xiangming Liu
University of Connecticut, USA

Gao Niu
Bryant University, USA

ABSTRACT

This chapter presents a thorough descriptive analysis of automobile fatal accident and insurance claims data. Major components of the artificial neural network (ANN) are discussed, and parameters are investigated and carefully selected to ensure an efficient model construction. A prediction model is constructed through ANN as well as generalized linear model (GLM) for model comparison purposes. The authors conclude that ANN performs better than GLM in predicting data for automobile fatalities data but does not outperform for the insurance claims data because automobile fatalities data has a more complex data structure than the insurance claims data.

INTRODUCTION

This chapter we analyzed automobile fatal accident data and automobile insurance claims data through Artificial Neural Network (ANN). We also tested the data by Generalized Linear Model (GLM) for comparison purpose. Both ANN and GLM models were constructed in Python, which is one of the most popular and powerful open source statistical software. (Niu, Segall, Zhao, & Wu, 2021) (Wu, Zhao, & Niu, 2020)

The automobile fatal accident data and automobile insurance claims data were used in this study. Analyzing two dataset allows us to have a thorough understanding of how fatal automobile accident

DOI: 10.4018/978-1-7998-8455-2.ch009

happened and how certain key drivers impact insurance claim. The two datasets were not merged. They are analyzed and modeled separately. Results and comparison discussion are included in this chapter. The goal is to measure how efficient ANN and GLM models these two related datasets. Fatal accident data has more variables and observations than the insurance claims dataset. GLM is a widely accepted technique in statistical analysis and predictive modeling. It is picked for comparison purposes.

We first present the two datasets with their key descriptive analysis. Then we constructed ANN and GLM models. ANN models were constructed with detailed parameter testing, such as activation functions, validation dataset, hidden layers and batch size. GLM variables were selected based on correlation analysis, a basic model is constructed for comparison purposes.

GLM for automobile fatality rate predictions in R has been done before. (Niu & Olinsky, Generalized Linear Model for Automobile Fatality Rate Prediction in R, 2020) But this study focuses on comparison between ANN and GLM, also the statistically software used is Python instead R.

DATA DESCRIPTION

There were two groups of data used in this study. The first one is were extracted from the FARS (Fatal Accident Reporting System) collected and organized by the United States Department of Transportation. 2016 to 2019, 4 years of complete data were extracted. One is fatal accident data by person, which includes all relevant information by person who were involved with an accident that had at least one death during the year. We will call this data source 1 in the following content.

The second data used is based on one-year automobile insurance claims data from either 2004 or 2005, downloaded from the following website: http://www.afas.mq.edu.au/research/books/glms_for_insurance_data. The data was used as sample for the book Generalized Linear Models for Insurance Data (Jong & Heller, 2008). In this chapter, the data is analyzed to provide a benchmark comparison between three main statistical models. We will call this data source 2 in the following content.

2016 – 2019 Fatal Accident Data by Person

From 2016 to 2019, there were total of 148,210 people dead due to automobile fatal accidents. Fatal accident is defined as any accident that has at least one automobile involved and at least one people are dead, more than 36,000 people were dead each year. Around 70% are male, 29% are female, and 1% are other. Other includes categories such as not reported, reported as unknown and unknown that recorded in the FARS database. Overalls, total number of deaths is slightly decreasing. The detail number of fatalities are shown in Table 1.

Table 1. 2016-2019 US Auto Accident Fatalities by Gender

	2016	2017	2018	2019	Total
Male	26,773	26,618	26,040	25,634	105,065
Female	10,988	10,806	10,766	10,420	42,980
Other*	45	49	29	42	165
Total	37,806	37,473	36,835	36,096	148,210
* Includes Not Reported, Reported as Unknown, and Unknown					

From location perspective, majority of the accidents happened in the area that has the most population. Texas, California, Florida, Georgia and North Carolina have the top 5 total number of fatalities as shown in Figure 1 and Table 2.

Figure 1. 2016-2019 US Auto Accident Fatalities by Region

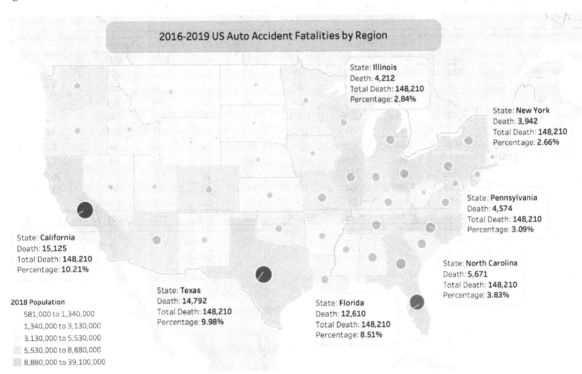

Table 2. 2016-2019 US States with Highest and Lowest Auto Accident Total Fatalities

State	Number of Death				Number of Death Per Million People				2021 Population
	2016	2017	2018	2019	2016	2017	2018	2019	
Texas	3,797	3,732	3,648	3,615	128	126	123	122	29,730,311
California	3,837	3,884	3,798	3,606	97	98	96	91	39,613,493
Florida	3,176	3,116	3,135	3,183	145	142	143	145	21,944,577
Georgia	1,556	1,540	1,505	1,491	144	142	139	138	10,830,007
North Carolina	1,450	1,412	1,436	1,373	136	132	134	128	10,701,022
North Dakota	113	116	105	100	147	151	136	130	770,026
Alaska	84	79	80	67	116	109	110	92	724,357
Rhode Island	51	84	59	57	48	79	56	54	1,061,509
Vermont	62	69	68	47	99	111	109	75	623,251
District of Columbia	27	31	31	23	38	43	43	32	714,153
Total	37,806	37,473	36,835	36,096	114	113	111	109	331,343,567

Overall, 109 people dead per million people in 2019. Table 3 presents the top 5 and bottom 5 number of deaths per million people. Wyoming, Mississippi, New Mexico, South Carolina and Alabama have the highest number of deaths per capita. District of Columbia, New York, Massachusetts, Rhode Island and New Jersey has the least number of fatalities per capita.

Table 3. 2016-2019 US States with Highest and Lowest Auto Accident Fatalities Per Capita

State	Number of Death				Number of Death Per Million People				2021 Population
	2016	2017	2018	2019	2016	2017	2018	2019	
Wyoming	112	123	111	147	193	212	191	253	581,075
Mississippi	687	685	663	643	232	231	224	217	2,966,407
New Mexico	405	380	392	424	192	181	186	201	2,105,005
South Carolina	1,020	989	1,036	1,001	193	187	196	190	5,277,830
Alabama	1,083	948	953	930	219	192	193	188	4,934,193
New Jersey	602	624	563	559	68	70	63	63	8,874,520
Rhode Island	51	84	59	57	48	79	56	54	1,061,509
Massachusetts	387	347	355	334	56	50	51	48	6,912,239
New York	1,041	1,006	964	931	54	52	50	48	19,299,981
District of Columbia	27	31	31	23	38	43	43	32	714,153
Total	37,806	37,473	36,835	36,096	114	113	111	109	331,343,567

Figure 2. 2016-2019 US Auto Accident Fatalities by Month

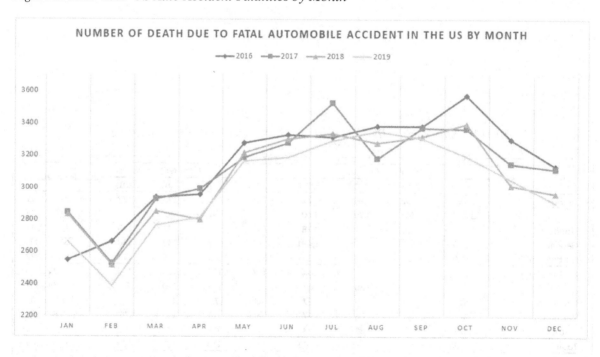

From a season perspective, winter has less fatalities than other seasons in the US as shown in the Figure 2. Start from month November, total fatalities decreases and month February has the lowest number death. One possible contributing factor for this pattern is sleep loss and behavioral changes due to Daylight Saving Time. In the spring, because of the DST change, drivers lose an hour of sleep which causes the significant increase in the number of automobile accidents and fatalities. (Varughese & Allen, 2001) The following figure also shows that 2019 has the lowest number of deaths compared with previous years.

Figure 3 presents the total number of deaths by hour. For the year 2016 to 2019, the pattern has been stable. 4am in the morning and 8am-9am morning rush hour are among the least number of fatalities. From the afternoon until 9pm, number of deaths increases and reaches its peak from 5pm to 9pm.

Figure 3. 2016-2019 US Auto Accident Fatalities by Hour

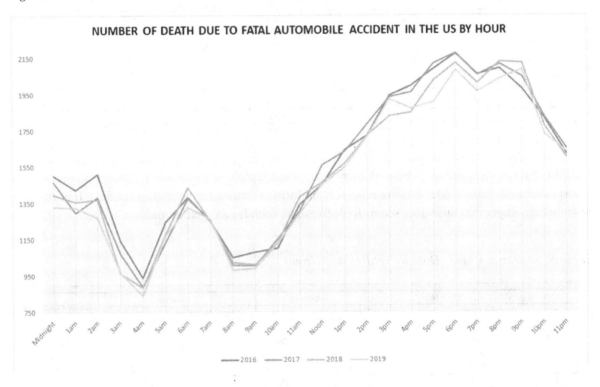

2004 or 2005 Autombile Insurance Claims Data

The insurance claim data used in this chapter is for one policy year. Insurance policies are sold continuously during a year, normally they are annual policies. Policies sold in January 1st 2004, the whole policy is exposed to risk during the year 2004 because by December 31st 2004, the policy would expire. Policies sold in July 1st 2004, half policy is exposed to risk during the year 2004, and half policy is exposed to risk during the year 2005. That's why the data used in this study is labeled 2004 or 2005. All these policies were issued during the year 2004, however it has risk exposure on 2004 or 2005.

10 variables were studied in this chapter within the dataset. They are the following. Vehicle Value ($0 - $350,000), Exposure (0-1), Claim Occurrence (0, 1), Vehicle Age (1 new, 2, 3, 4), Age Band of Policy Holder (1 youngest, 2, 3, 4, 5, 6). Claim Occurrence is the dependent variable we modeled, and rest of the variables were used as independent variables.

Table 4 shows the insurance claims data by car value. We can see that 47.0% of the vehicle insured has a car value between $10,000 to $19,999. This category also has the highest number of exposure (47.1%) as well as number of claims (47.1%). However, vehicle value from $30,000 to $39,000 has the highest claim per exposure of 0.176, which indicates that the it is the riskiest among all car value categories.

Table 4. Insurance Claims Data by Car Value

	Vehicles		Exposure		Claims		Claim Per Exposure
	Total Number	%	Total Number	%	Total Number	%	
<$10,000	16,459	24.3%	7,638	24.0%	960	20.8%	0.126
$10,000 - $19,999	31,911	47.0%	14,990	47.1%	2,179	47.1%	0.145
$20,000 - $29,999	11,097	16.4%	5,255	16.5%	830	17.9%	0.158
$30,000 - $39,999	4,569	6.7%	2,122	6.7%	374	8.1%	0.176
$40,000 - $49,999	2,371	3.5%	1,136	3.6%	182	3.9%	0.160
$50,000 - $59,999	902	1.3%	419	1.3%	68	1.5%	0.162
>=$60,000	547	0.8%	240	0.8%	31	0.7%	0.129
Total	67,856	100.0%	31,801	100.0%	4,624	100.0%	0.145

Table 5 shows the insurance claims data by vehicle age. Except new cars has a relatively lower number of exposure and claims, older cars are relatively uniform in terms of exposure and claims. It is worth to note that claim per exposure does seems to decrease as vehicles are getting older.

Table 5. Insurance Claims Data by Vehicle Age Group

	Vehicles		Exposure		Claims		Claim Per Exposure
	Total Number	%	Total Number	%	Total Number	%	
1 (new)	12,257	18.1%	5,339	16.8%	825	17.8%	0.155
2	16,587	24.4%	7,924	24.9%	1,259	27.2%	0.159
3	20,064	29.6%	9,542	30.0%	1,362	29.5%	0.143
4	18,948	27.9%	8,996	28.3%	1,178	25.5%	0.131
Total	67,856	100.0%	31,801	100.0%	4,624	100.0%	0.145

Table 6 shows the insurance claims data by Age Band of Policy Holder. Both youngest and oldest group has the lowest exposure and claims. However, youngest group has the highest claim per exposure and oldest group has the lowest claim per exposure. The pattern is monotone. The older the policyholder gets, the better the risk is.

Table 6. Insurance Claims Data by Age Band of Policy Holder

	Vehicles		Exposure		Claims		Claim Per Exposure
	Total Number	%	Total Number	%	Total Number	%	
1 (youngest)	5,742	8.5%	2,612	8.2%	496	10.7%	0.190
2	12,875	19.0%	5,892	18.5%	932	20.2%	0.158
3	15,767	23.2%	7,409	23.3%	1,113	24.1%	0.150
4	16,189	23.9%	7,617	24.0%	1,104	23.9%	0.145
5	10,736	15.8%	5,171	16.3%	614	13.3%	0.119
6	6,547	9.6%	3,100	9.7%	365	7.9%	0.118
Total	67,856	100.0%	31,801	100.0%	4,624	100.0%	0.145

ANN MODEL

Introduction of ANN

Artificial neural network (ANN), also known as neural network, is a kind of machine learning that can be used to learn historical patterns and make future predictions. ANN works as a simulation of our brain nervous system, each node in ANN represents a neuron, and one or more nodes in each layer. There isn't a universal rule of how many neurons have the best model performance. However, it is worth to note that too few neurons in the hidden layers could result in large errors or under-fitting, and too many neurons in the hidden layers could result in overfitting (Ahmad, Mourshed, & Rezgui, 2017). Compared to other linear arithmetic models, ANN performs more complex. In an ANN, there are usually three parts, input layer, hidden layer and output layer, infinite possible permutations and combinations make it suitable for big data-based applications. Figure 4 shows a simple artificial neural network framework: there are four parameters in the input layer, one in output later and five nodes in the only hidden layer.

Figure 4. A Simple Artificial Neural Network Framework

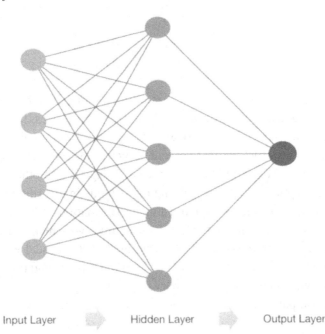

Input Layer → Hidden Layer → Output Layer

Keras is one of the most powerful libraries that often used in building artificial neural network machine learning in Python (Chollet, 2017). It is easy for user to define model type by importing Sequential.

```
from keras.models import Sequential
```

Keras also provide options to improve machine learning performance by tuning such hyperparameters as number of hidden layers, number of nodes for each layer, activation function, early stop, batch size, learning rate, kernel initializer, bias initializer, etc. In this chapter, adding layers and early stop will be used in learning process, thus we import proper packages: Dense and Earlystopping. At the complex network process, the combination of parameters can be tuned to optimize ultimate network. In this chapter, the impact of validating data portion, number of hidden layers and size of batch on machine learning procedure will be detailed discussed in the next subsections.

```
from keras.layers import Dense
from keras.callbacks import EarlyStopping
```

Building an ANN is started by defining its model type as Sequential and input layer dimensions (the number of variables in training data that will be used in learning process). After that, the first hidden layer can be added by indicating its nodes number, activation function, input layer nodes and kernel initializer etc.

Kernel initializer is one of the arguments that helps the model to set up the initial weights on parameters in each layer. There are multiple built-in initializers available. In the following neural network, we initialize the weights as randomly uniform distributed. After setting up the initial weights, neural network will adjust them to optimize loss and accuracy values through activation function.

```
n_cols = x.shape[1]
model = Sequential()
model.add(Dense(15,activation='relu', input_shape=(n_cols,),kernel_
initializer='uniform'))
model.add(Dense(15,activation='relu',kernel_initializer='uniform'))
model.add(Dense(1,activation='sigmoid',kernel_initializer='uniform'))
```

After creating the architecture of the network, compiling the model is the next step. In the compile process, optimizer and loss function can be declared. Optimizer is the process that how the neural network learns from training data and optimize its way to predict. In Keras, there are multiple optimizer options. The classical one is SGD, stochastic gradient descent, which is used by Keras by default, it randomly selects samples from training data set in learning process. Adagrad is another option to be used as an advanced gradient descent optimizing process basing on its adjusting learning rate. In this chapter, we choose the adam optimizer, also called Adaptive Moment Estimation. It has advantages of efficiency with little usage memory, which is suitable for large data sources with many parameters. Loss function is another hyperparameter needs to be defined. After defining it, the model will calculate the loss between the predicted values and actual values during its learning process and try to reduce loss values by adjusting the model's weights on parameters. 'Binary cross-entropy' is a loss function that can be used in predicting categorical outputs. The compile process can be built as bellow.

```
model.compile(optimizer = 'adam', loss = 'binary_crossentropy', metrics =
['accuracy'])
```

The final step in building up the model is to fit the model with the training data and validate it with testing data set. In this process, epochs, batch size and callbacks can be modified to improve neural network performance.

One epoch is defined as a procedure that the neural network learns from the whole training data. after completion of each epoch, model parameters will be updated and optimized. The number of epochs indicates how many times the neural network learns from training data. However, the more epochs do not mean to have better learning capability. Fewer epochs may cause underfitting and too many epochs may lead to overfitting, which might worsen model performance. Early-stop can help the model to stop training if there are no improvements in loss and accuracy and to avoid those problems that may happen. In the example codes, callback is defined as early stopping with patient=10, meaning that the model stops training at next ten epochs with no improvement on loss and accuracy.

```
early_stop = EarlyStopping(patience=10)
model.fit(x_train,y_train, validation_data = (x_test, y_test), epochs=1000,
callbacks = [early_stop])
```

Train on 47499 samples, validate on 20357 samples

Epoch 1/1000
47499/47499 [====] - 2s 44us/step - loss: 0.2567 - accuracy: 0.9340 - val_loss: 0.2567 - val_accuracy: 0.9270
Epoch 2/1000
47499/47499 [====] - 2s 39us/step - loss: 0.2368 - accuracy: 0.9340 - val_loss: 0.2528 - val_accuracy: 0.9270
Epoch 3/1000
47499/47499 [====] - 2s 39us/step - loss: 0.2344 - accuracy: 0.9340 - val_loss: 0.2525 - val_accuracy: 0.9270
Epoch 4/1000
47499/47499 [====] - 2s 38us/step - loss: 0.2344 - accuracy: 0.9340 - val_loss: 0.2523 - val_accuracy: 0.9270
Epoch 5/1000
47499/47499 [====] - 2s 39us/step - loss: 0.2342 - accuracy: 0.9340 - val_loss: 0.2511 - val_accuracy: 0.9270
...

...
Epoch 1000/1000
47499/47499 [====] - 2s 36us/step - loss: 0.2342 - accuracy: 0.9340 - val_loss: 0.2511 - val_accuracy: 0.9270
CPU times: user 2min 42s, sys: 46.4 s, total: 3min 28s
Wall time: 1min 32s

By looking at the loss movement in learning and validating procedures, we will know how the loss function works in neural network and try to minimize loss values based on loss function defined in the model. Let's look at two different loss curves Figure 5 and Figure 6. In Figure 5, the loss curve does not show decreasing trend as epochs increases. After epochs=25, loss on training and testing data sets keeps on a certain value without any improvement. Additionally, the overall loss values on training data are higher than those in testing data. This means that the loss function in this model works better in testing data than in training data. However, we can see a pretty good fit of neural network from the loss curves in Figure 6. Both curves show decreasing tendency along with epochs, without many variations. On the other hand, the figure provides evidence of properly used loss function in this model.

Figure 5. Loss Curves with Inappropriate Loss Function

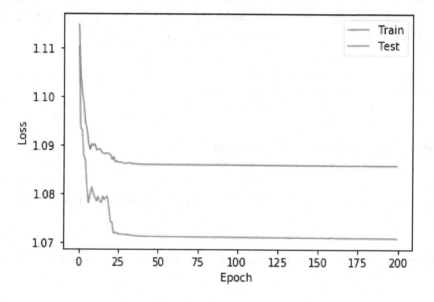

Figure 6. Loss Curve with Appropriate Loss Function

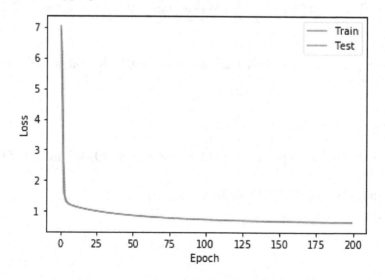

Overall, a sample whole process can be summarized as Figure 7 and Figure 8. Either in workflow table or in network graph, the number of parameters of each layer can easily be recognized. In this example, there are four parameters in the input layer and one outcome in the output layer. And two hidden layers were added into the neural network.

```
from keras.utils.vis_utils import plot_model
plot_model(model, show_shapes = True, show_layer_names = True, rankdir = 'LR')
from ann_visualizer.visualize import ann_viz
from graphviz import Digraph
ann_viz(model, title = "Artificial Neural Network")
```

Figure 7. ANN Model Workflow Table

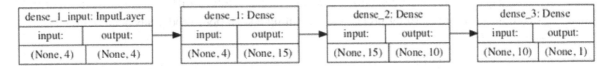

Figure 8. ANN Model Network Graph

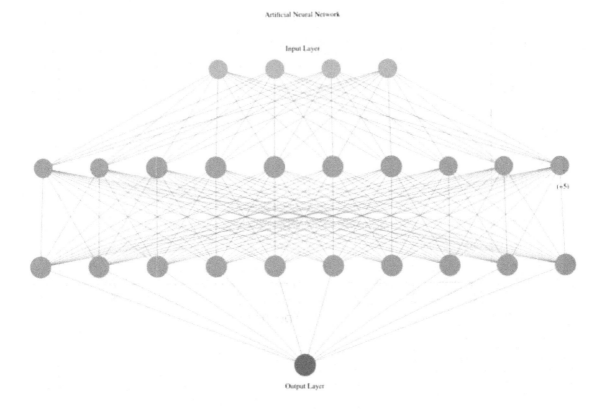

One drawback of the artificial neural network is there is no insights of the model learning process. Thus, the neural network is also called a kind of black-box model. However, we can assess its performance by comparing its loss and accuracy on training and testing data sets. In python, a list of loss and accuracy values can be recapped through evaluation method.

Accuracy curves help us to know the learning and predicting capability of the model. The changes of accuracy on training and testing data sets can be visualized by using codes below.

In Figure 9 and Figure 10, the model performs pretty well in training and predicting process, as the accuracy shows increasing tendency as times of learning procedure increases. Compared with these two figures, the model in Figure 10 performs betters than the one in Figure 9 by looking at the gap between two accuracy curves. In Figure 9, the model seems to be a little underfitting, since the accuracy on testing are generally higher than on training data, which means the model is better in predicting than in training. Its opposite condition is when the testing curve lies under the training one, an indication of possible overfitting. A perfect example can be seen in Figure 10, two accuracy curves show a perfect match, meaning a good model has been built. Now, let's look at a totally different situation in Figure 11. Accuracy decreases as more learning processes, indicating a such poor model has been built.

```
score_train = model.evaluate(x_train,y_train)
score_test = model.evaluate(x_test,y_test)
```

Figure 9. Exemplary Accuracy Graph with Underfitting Issue

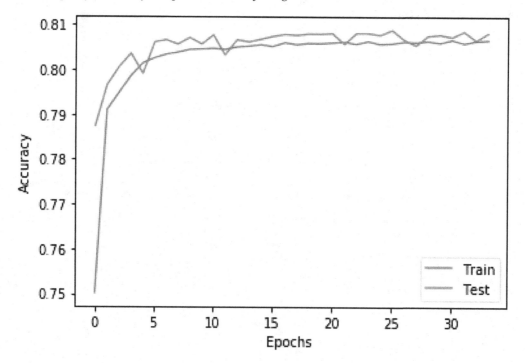

Figure 10. Exemplary Accuracy Graph without Underfitting Issue

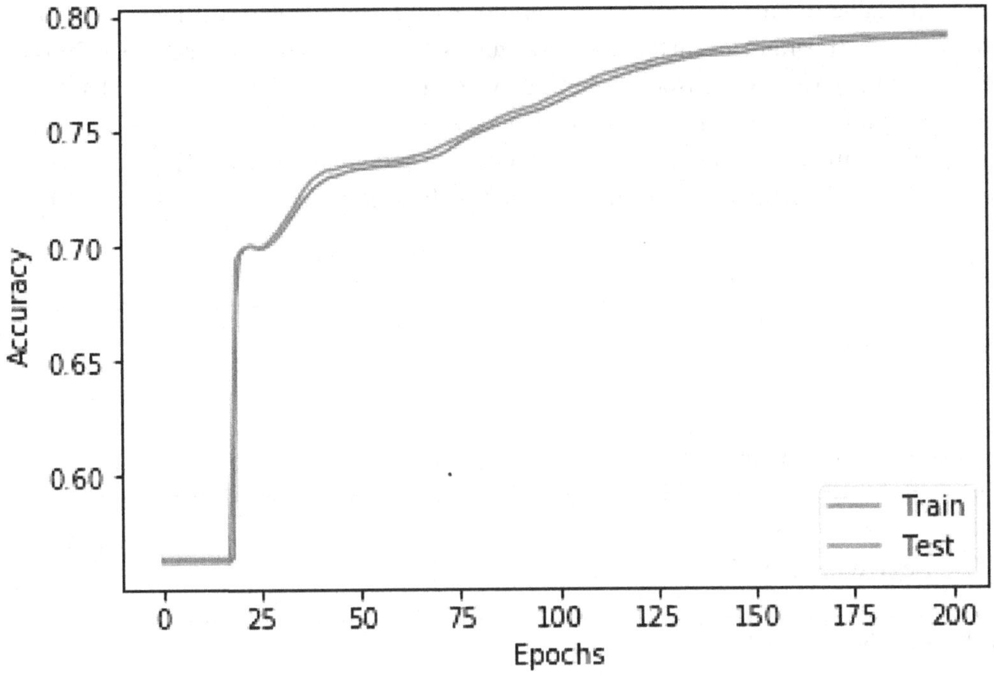

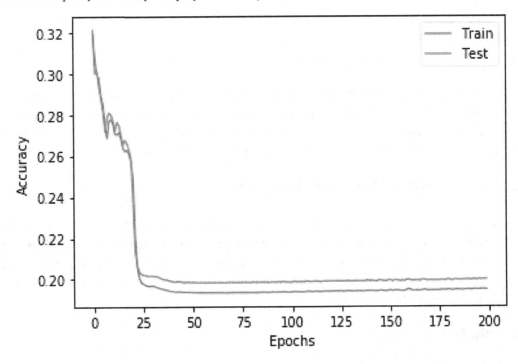

Figure 11. Exemplary Accuracy Graph for a Poorly Constructed Model

Total number of parameters can be obtained by having a look at the model's summary. The following model summary table reveals the total parameters for each layer. Let's have a look at the output layer (dense_6), there are 11 parameters in total, but in Figure 8, there are 10 lines connected to the output node from the last hidden layer. The reason is neural network added bias values in the hidden layer, similar to the way that adding a constant by Linear or Generalized Linear Model. Bias values can be initialized by assigning bias initializer in adding layers procedure. They are adjusted during learning process to optimize model's predictability. However, discussion on bias initializer is not included in this chapter.

```
model.summary()
```

Model: "sequential"

Layer (type) Output Shape Param #
==
======

dense_4 (Dense) (None, 15) 75

---

dense_5 (Dense) (None, 10) 160

---

dense_6 (Dense) (None, 1) 11

==
======

Total params: 246
Trainable params: 246
Non-trainable params: 0

In order to explore impact of hyperparameters on model's accuracy, we keep other factors the same for parallel comparison, such as nodes number, epochs, activation function and Kernel initializer. And the following sections will discuss how percentage of training data set, hidden layers, and batch size affect artificial neural network's learning process and predicting capabilities.

Model Characteristics - Activation Functions

Activation function in layers, is a function that assists neural network to learn from training data. It transforms values from the previous layer into the next layer, with adjusted weights on parameters and adjusted bias values. Activation functions do more complex non-linear work rather than linear function. Proper activation function used in layers will attach power and flexibility to the neural network. There are various types of activation functions.

Linear Activation

Linear activation is defined as the following:

$$g(x) = cx \tag{1}$$

X are inputs or calculated values from previous layer notes. C is a constant that could be positive or negative. Input value range is from negative infinite to positive infinite, the linear features made the activation function very easy to interpret the impact of input locally.

Step Function

Step Function is defined as the following:

$$g(x) = \begin{cases} 1, if x \geq 0 \\ 0, if x < 0 \end{cases} \tag{2}$$

Step function converts calculated value into a binary 0 or 1 data, which captures only the absolute direction of the previous layer output and drops off the magnitude. The benefit of this function is that the model will not be influenced easily by several input outliers. It has a high calculation efficiency.

Rectified Linear Unit (ReLU)

ReLU is short for Rectified Linear Unit, it is defined as the following:

$$g(x) = \max(0, x) \tag{3}$$

It is similar to step function, that drops negative input, but the functions keep the positive portion of the input instead of change them to 1 as what step function does. ReLU is widely chosen in order to produce positive outcomes. In this function, all negative values will be assigned to zero.

Logistics Sigmoid

Logistics Sigmoid often short for Sigmoid, it is defined as the following:

$$g(x) = \frac{e^x}{e^x + 1} \tag{4}$$

Sigmoid function could take in any value from negative infinity to positive infinity, and output a value from 0 to 1. Exponential function has a range of $(0, +\yen)$, and $\frac{e^x}{e^x + 1}$ has a range of $(0, 1)$, where g(x) approaches to 0 when x approaches to $-\yen$, and g(x) approaches to 1 when x approaches to $+\yen$. It is often used for probability modeling.

In the output layer, we assign Sigmoid as its activation function, often used when we expect the probability of results exist between zero and one, with the same logical working on logistic regression.

Model Characteristics - Validation Dataset

The procedure of separating data set into training and testing is helpful in training and estimating model performance, especially when facing a large data source with complex structure. Training data set is used in machine learning procedure and testing data set is for estimating model's predictive capability, thus different portion on these two data sets would differ model's performance. We will discuss two different situations, twenty percent of testing data, which is a widely used choice, and half of testing data.

In Table 7 and Table 8, accuracy values on eighty percent of training and twenty percent of testing are higher than values on half of testing data. Loss values are lower in data source with twenty percent of validation data. Running time spent in learning process on high portion of training data is longer than the other, because higher portion of training data means larger data are used in learning process, model needs more time to learn patterns and make adjustments on parameters. Therefore, from aspects of accuracy and loss, fewer testing data set produces higher accuracy and lower loss than the data set with higher percentage of testing. However, the larger training data set is, the longer running time is required.

Table 7. Model Validation Result on Fatal Accident Data

	80% Training/20% Testing		50% Training/50% Testing	
	Training Data	Testing Data	Training Data	Testing Data
Accuracy	81.1%	81.0%	81.0%	81.1%
Loss	41.7%	42.0%	41.8%	42.0%
Time	239 s		62 s	

Table 8. Model Validation Result on Insurance Claims Data

	80% Training/20% Testing		50% Training/50% Testing	
	Training Data	Testing Data	Training Data	Testing Data
Accuracy	93.2%	93.3%	93.1%	93.3%
Loss	23.9%	23.3%	24.1%	23.6%
Time	258 s		197 s	

Model Characteristics - Hidden Layer

In this section, we'll talk through how the hidden layers will affect neural network's behavior. Hidden layers are somewhat secrets in the 'black-box' of the machine learning. The process of training and adjustments of weights on parameters cannot be seen by us. However, diverse number of hidden layers derive different predicting precisions. Three different conditions on hidden layers will be discussed and compared in the following, model with no hidden layer, 1 hidden layer and two hidden layers.

At the condition of no hidden layers, only input layer and output layer are added. Thus, the procedure of adding layers becomes much simpler.

```
model.add(Dense(1, input_shape = (n_cols,), activation = 'sigmoid', kernel_
initializer ='uniform'))
```

Auto Accident Data (Data Source 1)

Built on Data Source 1, we have 12 input nodes and 1 output node. An extra line that stands for bias is also added by artificial neural network automatically as demonstrated in Figure 12.

Figure 12. Demonstration for Bias

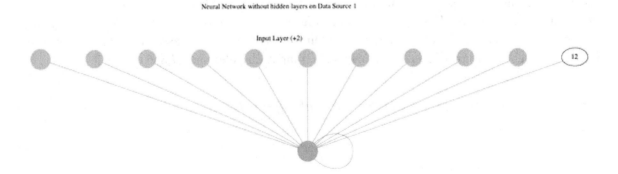

Accuracy values on training and testing data sets are exact the same, thus loss is our only consideration on selecting number of hidden layers. In Figure 13, loss with two hidden layers has the lowest values on training and testing data sets.

Figure 13. Auto Accident Data Accuracy/Loss with different hidden layers

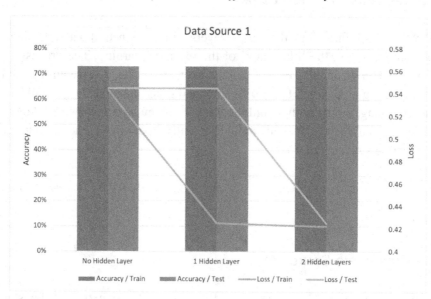

Insurance Claim Data (Data Source 2)

From Figure 14, accuracy on both training data and testing data does not appear any refinements, the same situation as in data source 1. Besides, loss on training and predicting are not consistent in these three conditions. Thus, for Data Source 2, hidden layers are not considered to be a kind of edge that can be added to increase model's accuracy nor diminish loss. One of the reasons may on account of the relative smaller dimension of this data source, only 4 input variables and 67,856 data in it.

Figure 14. Insurance Claim Data Accuracy/Loss with different hidden layers

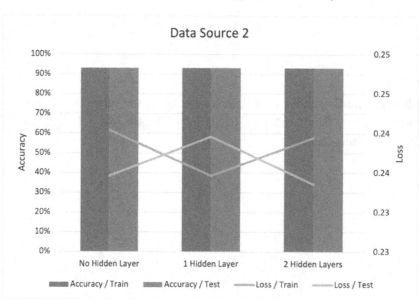

Fanalized Hidden Layer

Comparing with Figure 13 and Figure 14, it is apparent that the more hidden layers, the complex learning process on training data. However, more hidden layers not always generate better neural network. Proper number of hidden layers rely on the dimensions of data set and complexity of data structure. To answer how many hidden layers will produce best model will be complex and not so simple. If variables are linearly correlated, no hidden layers needed in neural network. For data sources, which having complex structure and non-linear relationship between parameters, adding hidden layers are helpful in model learning procedure. However, there is no rule of how many hidden layers should be added, just through trial and error. An important thing that needs to keep in mind is to avoid overfitting or underfitting for better model performance. In most cases, two hidden layers would be more than enough to build a well performed neural network. In some cases, such as the Cascade Correlation Learning Architecture in artificial neural network (Fahlman & Lebiere, 1990) two or more hidden layers will be added. Radial Basis Function (RBF) is an example of neural network with one hidden layer (Orr, 1996).

Model Characteristics - Batch Size

The batch size is the number of samples selected from training dataset. For example, when epoch=5 and batch_size=10 with 100 training data. The whole process of neural network train on 10 batches (100 training data divides batch_size 10) is considered to be one epoch. And this procedure would happen 5 times if no early stop defined ahead. Possible batch size can be any integer ranging from 1 to the total data number in training set, and its default value is 32.

Data Source 1

We experimented on 9 different batch sizes on data source 1, ranging from its default value to its possible maximum value. In order to realize the impacts of batch size on model performance, we compared in three aspects, loss, accuracy and running time. We add running time into consideration and comparison, because the influence is significant under different batch sizes. Additionally, it is an important issue especially when you are dealing with a huge set of data source, longer running time without superior model performance would be inefficient.

From Figure 15 and Figure 16, we notice an overall trend that the large batch size is, the more loss and lower accuracy on both training and testing datasets. However, running time has significant advantage when increasing batch size (Figure 17). From a comprehensive view, choosing a model that runs faster associate with similar loss and accuracy would be smart. In our example, we will assign batch size as 5000.

Figure 15. Auto Accident Data Loss vs Batch Size Analysis

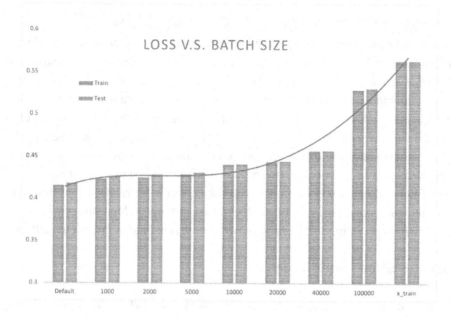

Figure 16. Auto Accident Data Accuracy vs Batch Size Analysis

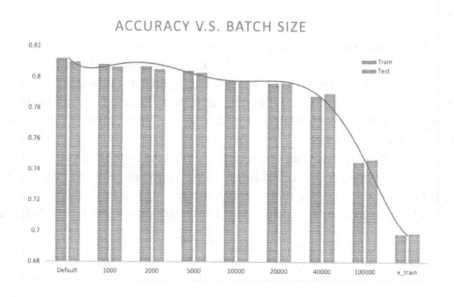

Figure 17. Auto Accident Data Time vs Batch Size Analysis

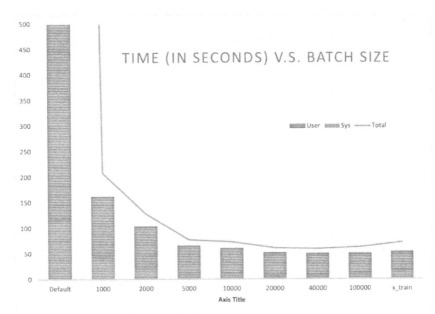

Data Source 2

For data source 2, we trialed on 12 different batch size, also ranging from its default value to its possible maximum value. This time, we compared loss and running time, since accuracy come to exactly same values on all these different conditions. Loss on train and test has tiny difference until batch size equals to 5000, after which shows an increasing trend as batch number increases (Figure 18), the similar situation as data source 1. The trend on running time tells an opposite story, running time decreasing as batch size comes to 5000, almost flat line after that (Figure 19). Thus, batch size equals 5000 would be a sharp choice in this data source.

Figure 18. Insurance Claim Data Loss vs Batch Size Analysis

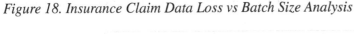

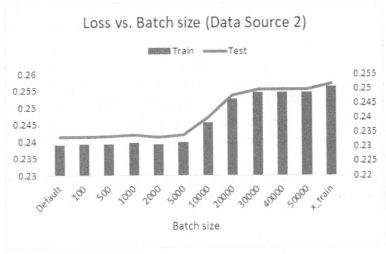

Figure 19. Insurance Claim Data Time vs Batch Size Analysis

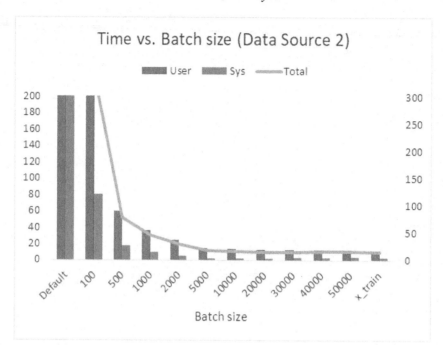

ANN Summary

Artificial neural network is power predictable model, especially for data source with large amount and complex structure. However, building up the learning procedure is more complicated than Generalized Linear Model. Multiple adjustable hyper-parameters lead to innumerable possibilities of combinations.

For train and test split rate, it would depend on the size and complexity of data source. Twenty or thirty percent of testing are often used in most cases, where is a good start of your trial. For a data with simpler structure, the portion of testing data makes little difference, since relationship patterns can easily be captured by model. On the other side, the testing portion will have significant impact on complex structured data. In this kind of condition, propitiate portion will produce a good model in both learning and predicting.

Overfitting or underfitting is one of crucial considerations of how well the model you built in predicting. Overfitting means the model learns pretty well on training data set but works poorly on validation data, it is a commonly problem when building machine learning models. For example, accuracy on training is 0.99, but comes to 0.45 in validation data. When it happens in your model, it seems to be inflexible in predicting other data sets, which means it cannot used to do prediction properly. Underfitting is a opposite issue, that prediction process performs better than training procedure. By having a look at loss and accuracy curves, overfitting or underfitting can be diagnosed. A proper machine learning should has decreasing loss curve and increasing accuracy curve, and the smaller the gap between these two curves is the better.

Neither default value nor possible maximum value of batch size are normally considered to be a good choice. With its default value, time consuming is significant during learning procedure. At its maximum value, loss value comes to high as well. To find out an optimum value in a comprehensive aspect helps the learning process to be well performed and effective.

GENERALIZED LINEAR MODEL (GLM)

GLM is a modeling process that build relationships between variables. It relaxes the restrictive normal assumptions for the traditional linear regression model, which allows GLM capable of analyzing non-normal data. (Jong & Heller, 2008)

In Python, the process of building up a Generalized Linear Model is simpler than the process in ANN. Noting that when your independent variables are in an array, a constant coefficient needs to be added manually, which is the intercept of GLM and not included by default.

There are three main parts in learning process, dependent variable, independent variables and its families. By using summary method, details of GLM results such as model information, estimated values of each dependent variables, along with their statistics. Detailed GLM model results for both automobile fatal accident data and insurance claims data are attached in the appendix II and appendix III.

```
import statsmodels.api as sm
x_train_sm = sm.add_constant(x_train)
model = sm.GLM(y_train, x_train_sm, family = sm.families.Binomial()).fit()
print(model.summary())
```

COMPARISON AND CONCLUSION

In this chapter, artificial neural network (ANN) machine learning technique was built to predict the occurrence of event upon two different sources. Data sources 1 has more complex data relationship structure as well as data size compared with data source 2.

The framework of ANN model has been detailed introduced in section 4, codes to be used in Python have been provided and some of hyper-parameters' effects on model performance are detailed explored as well. From experiments on different data sources and diverse combination of hyper-parameters, we can recognize variations of accuracy in an ANN model's learning and predicting process. In section 4, impacts of three model characteristics were inspected in detail, train and test split rate, number of hidden layers and size of batch. Some possible actions are suggested to make improvements that could boost ANN predictability; 1) use proper portion of data source as validation, twenty or thirty percentage are normally used; 2) two hidden layers are enough in most cases, adding one hidden layer is a good start point of your trial; 3) batch size with default value or its maximum value will not usually bring a good model in consideration of accuracy loss and running time. However, there is no such a rule indicates best parameters, trials and adjustments are required to optimize ultimate model.

In order to investigate the edges of using artificial neural network to make predictions, we created Generalized Linear Model on both of data sources as well. Comparable results are summarized in Table 9. From the point of model accuracy in Data Source 1, ANN performs much better than GLM, with 8.29 percentage greater predicting capability. For data source 2, accuracy values are similar or close between these two models. Therefore, the artificial neural network becomes a standout a model on data sets with larger size and complicated relationship structure. With regards to running time in learning process, GLM performs better because of its simpler algorithm.

Table 9. ANN and GLM Model Comparison

	Data	ANN	GLM
Accuracy	Fatal Accident Data	81.2%	72.9%
	Insurance Claims Data	93.2%	93.1%
Time (in Second)	Fatal Accident Data	175	3.24
	Insurance Claims Data	77	0.532

Thus, ANN could leverage its edge on data sources with complex or non-linear data structures. However, in general, ANN takes longer time in training than traditional techniques like GLM.

In addition, further explorations on ANN model's parameters could be done in many other areas that not included in this chapter. For example, the number of appropriate input variables, learning rate. Research shows that ANN has outstanding performance on larger data sets, data sources provided in this chapter are not large enough in real industry world. In addition, some efforts available that could be made to shorten its running time on CPUs (Vanhoucke, Senior, & Mao, 2011). As a black-box model, the artificial neural network's performance is unpredictable and has possibility of overfitting. However, there are many applications of ANN in various industries. The output quality could be improved by reducing its limitations. Thus, as the increasing demand of ANN applications, further developments on ANN is invaluable.

REFERENCES

Ahmad, M. W., Mourshed, M., & Rezgui, Y. (2017). Trees vs Neurons: Comparison between random forest and ANN for high-resolution prediction of building energy consumption. *Energy and Bulidings*, *147*, 77–89. doi:10.1016/j.enbuild.2017.04.038

Chollet, F. (2017). *Deep Learning with Python*. Manning Publications.

Fahlman, S. E., & Lebiere, C. (1990). The Cascade-Correlation Learning Architecture. In D. S. Touretzky (Ed.), *Advances in Neural Networks in Information Processing Systems 2* (pp. 524–532). Morgan Kaufmann Publishers Inc.

Jong, P. d., & Heller, G. Z. (2008). *Generalized Linear Models for Insurance Data*. Cambridge University Press. doi:10.1017/CBO9780511755408

Niu, G., & Olinsky, A. (2020). Generalized Linear Model for Automobile Fatality Rate Prediction in R. In R. S. Segall & G. Niu (Eds.), *Open Source Software for Statistical Analysis of Big Data: Emerging Research and Opportunities* (pp. 137–161). IGI Global. doi:10.4018/978-1-7998-2768-9.ch005

Niu, G., Segall, R. S., Zhao, Z., & Wu, Z. (2021). A Survey of Open Source Statistical Software (OSSS) and Their Data Processing Functionalities. *International Journal of Open Source Software and Processes, 12*(1), 1–20. doi:10.4018/IJOSSP.2021010101

Orr, M. J. (1996). *Introduction to radial basis function networks.* Centre for Cognitive Science, University of Edinburgh.

Vanhoucke, V., Senior, A., & Mao, M. Z. (2011). Improving the speed of neural networks on CPUs. In *Deep Learning and Unsupervised Feature Learning Workshop*. NIPS.

Varughese, J., & Allen, R. P. (2001). Fatal Accidents Following Changes in Daylight Savings Time: The American Experience. *Sleep Medicine, 2*(1), 31–36. doi:10.1016/S1389-9457(00)00032-0 PMID:11152980

Wu, Z., Zhao, Z., & Niu, G. (2020). Introduction to the Popular Open Source Statistical Software (OSSS). In R. S. Segall & G. Niu (Eds.), *Open Source Software for Statistical Analysis of Big Data: Emerging Research and Opportunities* (pp. 73–110). IGI Global. doi:10.4018/978-1-7998-2768-9.ch003

ADDITIONAL READING

Abiodun, O. I., Jantan, A., Omolara, A. E., Dada, K. V., Mohamed, N. A., & Arshad, H. (2018, November). State-of-the-art in artificial neural network applications: A survey. Retrieved from ScienceDirect: https://www.sciencedirect.com/science/article/pii/S2405844018332067#!

Baareh, A. K. (2017). Solving the Carbon Dioxide Emission Estimation Problem: An Artificial Neural Network Model. Journal of Software Engineering and Applications, 338-342.

Grossi, E., & Buscema, M. (2008, January). Introduction to artificial neural networks. Retrieved from ResearchGate: https://www.researchgate.net/publication/5847739_Introduction_to_artificial_neural_networks

Khalil, B. M., Awadallah, A. G., Karaman, H., & El-Sayed, A. (2012). Application of Artificial Neural Networks for the Prediction of Water Quality Variables in the Nile Delta. *Journal of Water Resource and Protection, 04*(06), 388–394. doi:10.4236/jwarp.2012.46044

Nguyen, S., Niu, G., Quinn, J., Olinsky, A., Ormsbee, J., Smith, R. M., & Bishop, J. (2019). Detecting Non-injured Passengers and Drivers in Car Accidents: A New Under-resampling Method for Imbalanced Classification. In K. D. Lawrence, & R. K. Klimberg, Advances in Business and Management Forecasting (Vol. 13, pp. 93-105). Emerald Publishing Limited. doi:10.1108/S1477-407020190000013011

Offor, U. H., & Alabi, S. B. (2016, July). Artificial Neural Network Model for Friction Factor Prediction. Retrieved from Journal of Materials Science and Chemical Engineering: https://www.scirp.org/journal/paperinformation.aspx?paperid=69055

Otache, M. Y., Musa, J. J., Kuti, I. A., Mohammed, M., & Pam, L. E. (2021). Effects of Model Structural Complexity and Data Pre-Processing on Artificial Neural Network (ANN) Forecast Performance for Hydrological Process Modelling. *Open Journal of Modern Hydrology, 11*(01), 1–18. doi:10.4236/ojmh.2021.111001

Salawu, E. O., Abdulraheem, M., Shoyombo, A., Adepeju, A., Davies, S., Akinsola, O., & Nwagu, B. (2014). Using Artificial Neural Network to Predict Body Weights of Rabbits. *Open Journal of Animal Sciences, 04*(04), 182–186. doi:10.4236/ojas.2014.44023

Sarkar, A., & Kumar, R. (2012). Artificial Neural Networks for Event Based Rainfall-Runoff Modeling. *Journal of Water Resource and Protection, 04*(10), 891–897. doi:10.4236/jwarp.2012.410105

Segall, R. S., Cook, J. S., & Niu, G. (2019). Overview of Big Data - Intensive Storage and its Technologies for Cloud and Fog Computing. *International Journal of Fog Computing, 2*(1), 74–113. doi:10.4018/IJFC.2019010104

Segall, R. S., & Niu, G. (2018). Big Data and Its Visualization with Fog Computing. *International Journal of Fog Computing, 1*(2), 51–82. doi:10.4018/IJFC.2018070102

Segall, R. S., & Niu, G. (2018). Overview of Big Data and Its Visualization. In R. S. Segall & J. S. Cook (Eds.), *Handbook of Research on Big Data Storage and Visualization Techniques* (pp. 1–32). IGI Global. doi:10.4018/978-1-5225-3142-5.ch001

Sharma, V., Rai, S., & Dev, A. (2012). A Comprehensive Study of Artificial Neural Networks. *International Journal of Advanced Research in Computer Science and Software Engineering*, 278–284.

Wibig, T. (2010). Neural Network Performance for Complex Minimization Problem. Communications and Network, 31-37.

KEY TERMS AND DEFINITIONS

Activation Functions: Activation function assists neural network to learn from training data. It transforms values from the previous layer into the next layer, with adjusted weights on parameters and adjusted bias values.

Artificial Neural Network (ANN): A machine learning technique that can be used to learn historical patterns and make future predictions. It works as a simulation of our brain nervous system, each node in ANN represents a neuron, and one or more nodes in each layer.

Automobile Fatal Accident: One of the datasets analyzed in this chapter is from FARS (Fatality Analysis Reporting System), which is recorded for any accident happened in the United States that has at least one person dead accidentally due to automobile accident.

Automobile Insurance Claim: One of the datasets analyzed in this chapter is that captures an automobile insurance company's claims information from 2004 to 2005.

Batch Size: The batch size is the number of samples selected from training dataset. Possible batch size can be any integer ranging from 1 to the total data number in training set.

Generalized Linear Model: A modeling process that build relationships between variables. It relaxes the restrictive normal assumptions for the traditional linear regression model, which allows GLM capable of analyzing non-normal data.

Hidden Layers: Hidden layers are essential components of artificial neural network which significantly enlarges the model's mathematical complexity and improve its capability. It serves as ANN model parameter compared with other traditional statistical modeling.

Linear Activation: Linear activation function has an output range from negative infinity to positivity infinity with a constant coefficient to adjust the weight.

Logistic Sigmoid: Logistic sigmoid is often called sigmoid. It is a type of activation function that converts input value to a non-negative value. It is a commonly used activation function for hidden layers.

Model Validation: A process of model construction that used to validate the model efficiency. Commonly used process for validation include 50%(Training)/50%(Testing), 75%(Training)/25%(Testing), 80%(Training)/20%(Testing), Even-Year(Training)/Odd-Year(Testing), K-Fold Cross Validation, etc.

Neurons: Neurons are key components of ANN, which is responsible processing information by carrying the calculated value forward from input layer to output layer. Too few neurons in each layer could result in large errors or under-fitting, and too many neurons could result in overfitting.

Predictive Modeling: A process that utilize historical and current data to capture patterns, then create models to make future predictions.

ReLU: ReLU is for rectified linear unit. It is a type of activation function that converts input value to a range of (0, 1) exclusively. It is a commonly used activation function for probability model output layer.

Step Function: Step function is a type of activation function that converts input value to a binary 0 or 1 output. It has a high calculation efficiency.

APPENDIX I

Figure 20.

State	Number of Death				Number of Death Per Million People				2021 Population
	2016	2017	2018	2019	2016	2017	2018	2019	
Alabama	1,083	948	953	930	219	192	193	188	4,934,193
Alaska	84	79	80	67	116	109	110	92	724,357
Arizona	952	998	1,011	981	127	133	134	130	7,520,103
Arkansas	561	525	520	505	185	173	171	166	3,033,946
California	3,887	3,884	3,798	3,606	97	98	96	91	39,613,493
Colorado	608	648	632	596	103	110	107	101	5,893,634
Connecticut	304	281	293	249	86	79	82	70	3,552,821
Delaware	119	119	111	132	120	120	112	133	990,334
District of Columbia	27	31	31	23	38	43	43	32	714,153
Florida	3,176	3,116	3,135	3,183	145	142	143	145	21,944,577
Georgia	1,556	1,540	1,505	1,491	144	142	139	138	10,830,007
Hawaii	120	107	117	108	85	76	83	77	1,406,430
Idaho	253	245	234	224	136	132	126	120	1,860,123
Illinois	1,078	1,090	1,035	1,009	86	87	82	80	12,569,321
Indiana	829	916	860	809	122	135	126	119	6,805,663
Iowa	402	330	319	336	127	104	101	106	3,167,974
Kansas	429	461	405	411	147	158	139	141	2,917,224
Kentucky	834	782	724	732	186	175	162	163	4,480,713
Louisiana	757	770	771	727	164	166	167	157	4,627,002
Maine	160	173	136	157	118	128	100	116	1,354,522
Maryland	522	558	512	521	86	92	84	86	6,065,436
Massachusetts	387	347	355	334	56	50	51	48	6,912,239
Michigan	1,065	1,031	977	985	107	103	98	99	9,992,427
Minnesota	392	358	381	364	69	63	67	64	5,706,398
Mississippi	687	685	663	643	232	231	224	217	2,966,407
Missouri	947	932	921	880	154	151	149	143	6,169,038
Montana	190	186	181	184	175	171	167	170	1,085,004
Nebraska	218	228	230	248	112	117	118	127	1,951,996
Nevada	329	311	329	304	103	98	103	95	3,185,786
New Hampshire	136	102	147	101	99	74	107	74	1,372,203
New Jersey	602	624	563	559	68	70	63	63	8,874,520
New Mexico	405	380	392	424	192	181	186	201	2,105,005
New York	1,041	1,006	964	931	54	52	50	48	19,299,981
North Carolina	1,450	1,412	1,436	1,373	136	132	134	128	10,701,022
North Dakota	113	116	105	100	147	151	136	130	770,026
Ohio	1,132	1,179	1,068	1,153	97	101	91	98	11,714,618
Oklahoma	687	657	655	640	172	165	164	160	3,990,443
Oregon	498	439	502	489	116	102	117	114	4,289,439
Pennsylvania	1,188	1,137	1,190	1,059	93	89	93	88	12,804,123
Rhode Island	51	84	59	57	48	79	56	54	1,061,509
South Carolina	1,020	989	1,036	1,001	193	187	196	190	5,277,830
South Dakota	116	129	130	102	129	144	145	114	896,581
Tennessee	1,037	1,024	1,040	1,135	149	147	150	163	6,944,260
Texas	3,797	3,732	3,648	3,615	128	126	123	122	29,730,311
Utah	281	273	260	248	85	82	79	75	3,310,774
Vermont	62	69	68	47	99	111	109	75	623,251
Virginia	760	839	820	831	88	98	95	97	8,603,985
Washington	536	563	539	519	69	72	69	67	7,796,941
West Virginia	269	304	294	260	152	172	166	147	1,767,859
Wisconsin	607	613	589	566	104	105	101	97	5,852,490
Wyoming	112	123	111	147	193	212	191	253	581,075
Total	37,806	37,473	36,885	36,096	114	113	111	109	331,343,567

APPENDIX II

```
              Generalized Linear Model Regression Results (Data Source 1)
================================================================================
Dep. Variable:                  Death   No. Observations:              237214
Model:                            GLM   Df Residuals:                  237201
Model Family:                Binomial   Df Model:                          12
Link Function:                  logit   Scale:                         1.0000
Method:                          IRLS   Log-Likelihood:            -1.2905e+05
Date:                Wed, 26 May 2021   Deviance:                   2.5810e+05
Time:                        13:21:20   Pearson chi2:                 2.83e+05
No. Iterations:                     6
Covariance Type:            nonrobust
================================================================================
                 coef    std err          z      P>|z|      [0.025      0.975]
--------------------------------------------------------------------------------
const          0.4855      0.025     19.756      0.000       0.437       0.534
x1             0.1183      0.016      7.335      0.000       0.087       0.150
x2            -3.9506      0.074    -53.670      0.000      -4.095      -3.806
x3            -1.6579      0.026    -63.576      0.000      -1.709      -1.607
x4             0.6281      0.076      8.266      0.000       0.479       0.777
x5             1.5547      0.029     52.821      0.000       1.497       1.612
x6            -2.1417      0.062    -34.569      0.000      -2.263      -2.020
x7            -0.4621      0.021    -22.485      0.000      -0.502      -0.422
x8            -3.2888      0.066    -49.749      0.000      -3.418      -3.159
x9             0.6552      0.019     33.783      0.000       0.617       0.693
x10           -1.1797      0.027    -44.334      0.000      -1.232      -1.128
x11            4.1378      0.027    151.172      0.000       4.084       4.191
x12            0.2409      0.011     21.571      0.000       0.219       0.263
================================================================================
```

x1	State
x2	Rural Urban Indicator
x3	Automobile Body Type
x4	Model Year
x5	Fire Indicator
x6	Age
x7	Sex
x8	Seat Position
x9	Restraint Type
x10	Air Bag
x11	Ejection
x12	Drinking

APPENDIX III

```
               Generalized Linear Model Regression Results (Data Source 2)
==============================================================================
Dep. Variable:                    clm   No. Observations:                54284
Model:                            GLM   Df Residuals:                    54279
Model Family:                Binomial   Df Model:                            4
Link Function:                  logit   Scale:                          1.0000
Method:                          IRLS   Log-Likelihood:                -13049.
Date:                Sat, 29 May 2021   Deviance:                       26098.
Time:                        15:06:10   Pearson chi2:                 5.35e+04
No. Iterations:                     6
Covariance Type:            nonrobust
==============================================================================
                 coef    std err          z      P>|z|      [0.025      0.975]
------------------------------------------------------------------------------
const          3.2493      0.089     36.468      0.000       3.075       3.424
veh_value     -0.0333      0.016     -2.125      0.034      -0.064      -0.003
exposure      -1.8171      0.061    -29.796      0.000      -1.937      -1.698
veh_age        0.0390      0.019      2.057      0.040       0.002       0.076
agecat         0.0852      0.012      7.007      0.000       0.061       0.109
==============================================================================
```

Chapter 10

U.S. Unemployment Rate Prediction by Economic Indices in the COVID-19 Pandemic Using Neural Network, Random Forest, and Generalized Linear Regression

Zichen Zhao
Yale University, USA

Guanzhou Hou
Johns Hopkins University, USA

ABSTRACT

Artificial neural network (ANN) has been showing its superior capability of modeling and prediction. Neural network model is capable of incorporating high dimensional data, and the model is significantly complex statistically. Sometimes, the complexity is treated as a Blackbox. However, due to the model complexity, the model is capable of capture and modeling an extensive number of patterns, and the prediction power is much stronger than traditional statistical models. Random forest algorithm is a combination of classification and regression trees, using bootstrap to randomly train the model from a set of data (called training set) and test the prediction by a testing set. Random forest has high prediction speed, moderate variance, and does not require any rescaling or transformation of the dataset. This study validates the relationship between the U.S. unemployment rate and economic indices during the COVID-19 pandemic and constructs three different predictive modeling for unemployment rate by economic indices through neural network, random forest, and generalized linear regression model.

DOI: 10.4018/978-1-7998-8455-2.ch010

INTRODUCTION

Literature review

In March of 2020, COVID-19 pandemic started to outbreak in the U.S. All industries have been affected dramatically due to the high transmission rate and population movement in the spring. The downgrade of stock market and upgrade of unemployment rate are two sensible evidence to show the serious impact from COVID-19. The Dow Jones Industrial Average has experienced a sharp decrease from almost 30,000 to a point lower than 20,000 in few days. The majority of secondary industry, for examples airline, food, entertainment, were largely affected by the pandemic. Companies like NPC International Inc, Hertz, CMX Cinemas, J.C. Penney, etc. went bankrupt due to COVID-19. In the fourth quarter of 2020, U.S. GPD had fallen over 2 percent for the year, the unemployment rate averaged 6.7 percent according to U.S. department of treasury.

To explore the relationship between stock market index and the unemployment rate, this paper first reviews and summarizes the past studies and researches.

Unemployment rate and stock market are highly correlated because they are all direct outcomes of the country's economic changes. Also, there should be a lag between the changes of stock market and unemployment rate (stock market changes before the movement of unemployment rate). The phenomena are also studied by Quantifying Macroeconomic Expectations in Stock Markets using Google Trends (Bock, 2018) and The Stock Market's Reaction to Unemployment News: Why Bad News Is Usually Good for Stocks (Boyd et al, 2005). There is a clear positive relationship between capacity scrapping and unemployment rate increasing. (Arestis, Baddeley, & Sawyer, 2007)

There are many different factors that could impact unemployment rate, such as adverse demand shocks, when shocks reserve, unemployment may not fall to previous levels due to insufficient capital. (Arestis & Mariscal, 2000) Other economic data such as lagged values show significant effect on unemployment. (Loungani, Rush, & Tave, 1990) Study shows countries experienced the largest slowdown in capital accumulation per labor hour faced the highest unemployment rate in 1990s. (Gordon, 1997) The focus of this study is to model unemployment rate by economic indexes during COVID-19 pandemic. Thus, other factors such as adverse demand shocks, lagged values and capital accumulation slowdown that cannot be quantified with COVID-19 characteristics were not incorporated in this study.

The reason of such relationship is that, negative impact on stock market could cause lower incentives of firms to invest in hiring. During the periods of high risk, stock market valuations are low and unemployment rises. (Kilic & Wachter, 2018) However, the relationship is not perfectly negatively correlated. The information spillover was found significant between the stock market and labor market, but insignificant in the opposite direction, and significant bi-directionally. (Sibande, Gupta, & Wohar, 2019). Also, there is one-way causal direction from stock prices to the unemployment rate in G7 countries. There is a strong bilateral causal relationship between stock prices and unemployment for other advanced countries. (Pan, 2018)

In summary, unemployment rate and stock market should be highly correlated because they are all direct outcome of the country's economy change. Also, there should be a lag between the changes of stock market and unemployment rate (stock market changes before the movement of unemployment rate). This thought has been confirmed after reviewing Quantifying Macroeconomic Expectations in Stock Markets using Google Trends (Bock, 2018) and The Stock Market's Reaction to Unemployment News: Why Bad News Is Usually Good for Stocks (Boyd et al., 2005). Thus, we decided to test whether

U.S. unemployment rate can be predicted by economic indexes through neural network, random forest and generalized linear regression model. We aimed to compare the prediction power among all three models. Although neural network and random forest are unquestionable machine learning models to use for prediction, the model themselves are usually not interpretable. Thus, we designed to use generalized linear regression model to help us understand the coefficient of each individual variable.

Quantitative methods were used to measure the relationship between unemployment rate and stock prices. Study shows only anticipated unemployment rate has a strong impact on stock prices based on nonparametric granger causality and quantile regression-based tests. (Gonzalo & Taamouti, 2017) Artificial Neural Network (ANN) has been showing its superior capability of modeling and prediction. Neural network model is capable of incorporating a high dimensional data and the model is significantly complex statistically. Sometimes, the complexity is treated as Blackbox. However, due to the model complexity, the model is capable of capture and model an extensive amount pattern and the prediction power is much stronger than traditional statistical modeling. This study validates relationship between U.S. unemployment rate and economic indexes during the COVID-19 pandemic, constructs three different predictive modeling for U.S. unemployment rate by economic indexes through neural network, random forest and generalized linear regression model.

The methodology and the modeling approach adapted in this paper can just be used on the topic of relationship between COVID-19 pandemic and unemployment rate. It could also be used on different scenarios related to social and public health impact on economic, helping policymakers on establishing rules that could impede economic decay.

Random Forest

We had reviewed multiple influential literatures that used random forest model in application. To start our literature review regarding the Random Forests models, our paper first demonstrates the unique characteristics and desirable features of the Random Forests. Many distinguished researches have been conducted over the years and some of those researches are great enlightenment to our paper.

The Random Forests combine the features of independent values of random vector and same distribution for all trees. The errors of the Random Forests model become large as the number of sample increases. The ability of individual predictor places great impact on the overall prediction accuracy (Breiman, 2001) The Random Forests models have many desirable features which can be applied to many research fields. The Random Forests models is efficient in terms of computation, robust to noise, and offer great visualizations for its outputs (Robnik-Šikonja, 2004).

The research of the algorithm foundation of the Random Forests models focuses on the induction of decision trees and the construction of ensembles of randomized trees. The algorithm of the Random Forests models is computational fast, and the ability of interpretation is comprehensive (Louppe, 2014). Boosting and Bagging is viewed as the most accurate method for the Random Forests model, this method requires sample weighting and bootstrapping. Boosting and Bagging provides a computational efficiency way to exercise the Random Forests predication (Gislason, et al., 2006). There have been some extensive researches regarding the accuracy of the Random Forests model, one of the major improvements has been made by analyzing the performance of ensembles of trees. The accuracy of the prediction will receive significant increases under the situation that each tree in the ensemble is grown with parameter (Biau, 2012).

Although the Random Forests models are well researched for many years, the model results are usually uninterpretable in magnitude since the intrinsic calculation behind the model is like a Blackbox. The mathematical properties behind the model receive little attention since it is difficult to analyze the randomization process and the highly data-dependent tree structure at the same time (Scornet et al., 2015). In order to fix this potential limitation, we decided to apply Generalized Linear Model (GLM) to investigate the relationship between unemployment rate and all stock market predictors in certain magnitude.

The research area of improving the prediction accuracy and performance attracts great attention since accuracy remains the crucial concern of any statistic model. Even when the initial prediction is already decent, improvements can still be achieved by some tuning process to enhance the prediction power. Various new approaches have been attempted by researcher to enhance the performance of the Random Forests models.

Adaptive nearest-neighbor methods are an emerging approach to study the Random Forests method. Under this assumption, researchers have been analyzing the effect of terminal node sizes on the prediction accuracy of the Random Forests models (Lin & Jeon, 2006).

The dynamic integration is a distinguish method to improve the prediction performance of Random Forests model. The dynamic integration is based on local performance estimates and replacing the combination function with the dynamic integration will result in better prediction (Tsymbal et al. 2006).

The property and ability of the variables which applied to the Random Forests models have significant impact on the accuracy and comprehensiveness of the prediction outcomes. Thus, the method and principle of variable selection have determining impact on the overall outcomes of the Random Forests models.

Variable selection process remains a crucial part of the Random Forests model as the variables are the determining factors of the prediction. One major variable selection method requires important variables for interpretation, second method demands to rank the importance of explanatory variables (Genuer, 2010).

The Conditional variable importance for the Random Forests models is one of the major research areas. Comparing to the screening method, the Random Forest variable importance measures cover the impact of each variable separately and the interactions with other predictor variables. (Strobl et al., 2008)

The Random Forests models have extensive application possibility in various fields, due to its convenient statistical strength and unique feature, The Random Forests models have advantage in deal with complex modeling problem and simulate real world situations.

One innovative application of the Random Forests models is Intrusion Detection System. The current Intrusion Detection System are rule based and has many limitations on detect novel intrusion. However, the Intrusion Detection System based on the Random Forests models offer better intrusion detection by matching the network activities against the patterns. The Intrusion Detection System based on Random Forests algorithm improve the detection performance by combining the advantages of the misuse and anomaly detection (Zhang, Zulkernine, & Haque, 2008).

Researchers have been using the Random Forests model in the field of ecology and analyzing special cases regarding ecological evolvement. The advantages of using Random Forests model in the field of ecology including high classification accuracy, ability to model complicated situations, flexibility of performing various type of data (Cutler, 2007).

Another crucial aspect of the application regarding the Random Forests model is data mining. Random Forests model remains an efficiency method to obtain useful datasets (Verikas, 2011).

One major application of the Random Forests models is in the field of big data, Random Forests models are powerful nonparametric statistical method which allows to analyze the two-class and multi-class classification problems. Furthermore, scaling Random Forests to big data is one promising research area that we should pay attention to Genuer et al. (2017). Random Forests models are highly data adaptive, and the models are particularly suited for high-dimensional genomic data analysis (Chen & Ishwaran, 2012).

Generalized Random Forests model is one valuable special case among Random Forests models. The Generalized Random Forests model support nonparametric statistical estimation based on Random Forests, this special case allows any quantity of desired variables as the solution of the equations (Athey et al., 2019). As we analysis the Random Forests model, there is a special case which we should pay close attention to: the multivariable Random Forests (Segal & Xiao, 2011).

DATA DESCRIPTION

There are six stock market indexes data and one unemployment data used for this research, and all of them were extracted from Federal Reserve Bank of St. Louis economic data (Federal Reserve Bank of St. Louis, 2020), a free accessed public data. The data included in this study is from 1/1/1986 and 11/1/2020. Figure 1 shows all the economic indexes and US unemployment rate data that are used for this study, and their basic data descriptions are presented.

Figure 1. Economic Indexes and Unemployment Rate Data Description

Data Description					
	Min	**Max**	**Median**	**Mean**	**Standard Deviation**
NASDAQ100	138.63	11893.28	1554.86	2238.93	2316.68
NASDAQCOM	314.54	11794.46	2055.62	2614.75	2304.62
WILL5000PR	2260.46	36521.77	11110.60	12103.29	7996.09
NIKKEI225	7694.78	38115.32	17042.24	17356.79	6093.29
VXOCLS	8.02	65.45	18.11	20.20	8.62
WLEMUINDXD	14.87	1108.58	72.57	96.06	94.32
UNRATE	3.50	14.70	5.60	5.92	1.66

NASDAQ100: NASDAQ 100 Index
NASDAQCOM: NASDAQ Composite Index
WILL5000PR: Wilshire 5000 Price Index
NIKKEI225: Nikkei Stock Average, Nikkei 225
WLEMUINDXD: Equity Market-related Economic Uncertainty Index
VXOCLS: CBOE S&P 100 Volatility Index: VXO
UNRATE: US Unemployment Rate

The NASDAQ 100 Index contains 100 of the largest domestic and international non-financial securities listed on the NASDAQ Stock Market based on market capitalization.

The NASDAQ Composite Index describes market capitalization weighted index with more than 3000 common equities listed on the NASDAQ Stock Market. The types of securities in the index include American depositary receipts (ADRs), common stocks, real estate investment trusts (REITs), and tracking stocks.

The Wilshire 5000 Price Index describes the market-capitalization-weighted index of the market value of all the U.S. trading stocks.

The Nikkei Stock Average (Nikkei 225) is the major stock market index comprising of 225 highly liquid stocks of the Tokyo Stock Exchange. It is expected that US unemployment rate is mainly impacted by the US economy, however, globalization does play a factor in the U.S. employment since international trading movement. The U.S. and Japan have strong and mutually advantageous economic relationship, two countries together account a large portion of world domestic product. NIKKEI225 index is included and tested to reflect the globalization impact.

The Equity Market-related Economic Uncertainty Index is a policy related index to address economic policy uncertainty (Baker, Bloom, & Davis, 2015), which is related to stock price volatility, investment and employment.

The CBOE S&P 100 Volatility Index estimates the expected 30-day volatility of the S&P 100 stock, originally provided by Chicago Board Options Exchange.

The Unemployment Rate represents the number of unemployed as a percentage of the labor force. The labor force is defined as people, living in 1 of the 50 states or the District of Columbia, 16 years of age and older.

The economic indexes data listed above is not an exclusive way to measure all aspect of economic condition. However, it includes major economic indexes from U.S. market and a proxy of globalization. Relationship between the dependent variable and independent variables are the main focus of this study.

DATA CLEANING

Data cleaning requires significant amount of work. Despite the fact that neural network and random forest do not require any specific transformation of the data, it is meaningful and important to construct statistical model effectively. The dataset is extracted from data repository on a daily basis, and then they are combined into monthly basis to avoid observation mismatch. Two possible ways can be utilized when handling missing data. One is to eliminate missing data directly from the data, the other is to use random forest model to impute the missing values by its algorithm. As only little missing values were found in our data and removing them wouldn't make affecting impact to the model results, we decided to remove them from the dataset. There are a limited number of data eliminated so that final data used are a complete matrix without any missing value. Every observation has a dependent variable and valid independent variables.

Economic Indexes Modification

Original economic indexes data are represented in a daily format, yet the unemployment rate is reported monthly. Therefore, we calculated the monthly average of all economic indexes as general performances in that month to make connection with the unemployment rate. Figure 2 displays a linear trend of unemployment rate versus major economic indexes over time.

Figure 2. Unemployment Rate vs Major Economic Indexes

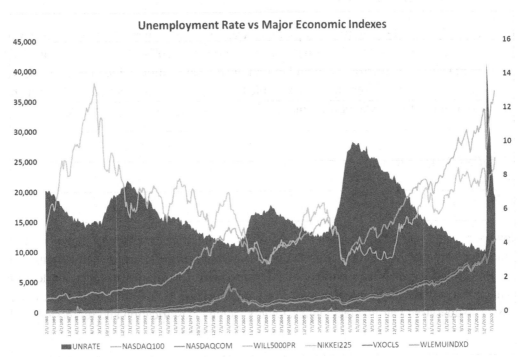

We observe increasing trendlines for the economic indexes overtime as a result of technology development and globalization. However, a decline of economy will generally lead to a consequence of unemployment. Based on our observation, most increases in unemployment rate incurred after a downgrade of economic indexes. For example, unemployment rate had an increasing trend in the middle of 2000 when major indexes started to decline. Also, another decrease of these economic indexes and an increase of unemployment rate occurred in the end of 2008 due to global financial crisis. The same pattern is observed in the beginning of 2020 due to COVID-19. All economic indexes and unemployment rate experienced a terrible decline. With the COVID-19 Economic Relief fact passed by the government, families and small business owners were supported, leading to the start of U.S. economy revival. The observation suggests economic indexes are critical drivers or proxies for unemployment rate prediction.

Unemployment Rate Modification

Unemployment rate was collected numerically and varies by each month, unemployment rate change was used to fit the model. Binary data is modeled as the output layer for the artificial neural network. The number of 0 indicates the unemployment rate of one month has decreased compared to previous month, and the number of 1 indicates the unemployment rate of one month has increased or not changed compared to previous month. The emergence of a sequence of 1 in consecutive months indicate a growing trend of unemployment rate. The emergence of a sequence of 0 in consecutive months indicates a declining trend of unemployment rate.

Testing and Training Separation

The data is randomly separated into two groups, one is training and another is testing for the purposes of validation. Multiple separations thresholds have been tested such as 20%-80%, 30%-70%, 40%-60% and 50%-50%. The model results improve with higher training data allocation, which indicates the model is not completely converged. However, the model is able to reach a more than 90% accuracy which shows statistical relationship between unemployment rate change and major economic indexes.

MODEL DESCRIPTION

Neural Network

The follow graph shows the main categorization of Artificial Intelligence (AI) and computational statistics techniques and their relationships. Search, Optimization, Machine Learning and Language Natural Language Processing are main applications of AI. Supervised Learning, Unsupervised learning and reinforcement learning are popular techniques. The model utilized in this study, neural network, is one of the classical supervised learning techniques. Others include classification and regression.

Figure 3. Artificial Intelligence Categorization

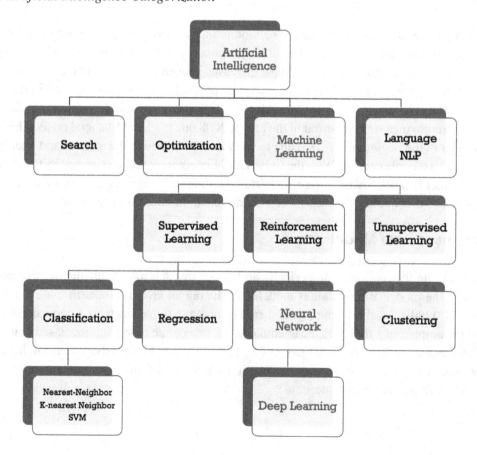

The main topic of this study is to show the economic impact on unemployment rate change. The artificial neural network constructed is a well-defined supervised learning model, because the availability of the target metric (unemployment).

Multiple neural network models were constructed and tested. Figure 4 shows the finalized model and its parameters. There are six neurons each represents an economic index as input. Only one hidden layer was included to enhance model flexibility. Multiple layers' settings were tested, however they showed suboptimal accuracy. Overfitting was the main reason for the inaccurate predictability. There is only one neuron for the output which is a binary data indicating unemployment rate change (1 represents there is an increase between two consecutive months, 0 represents there is a decrease between two consecutive months).

Figure 4. Final Artificial Neural Network Model

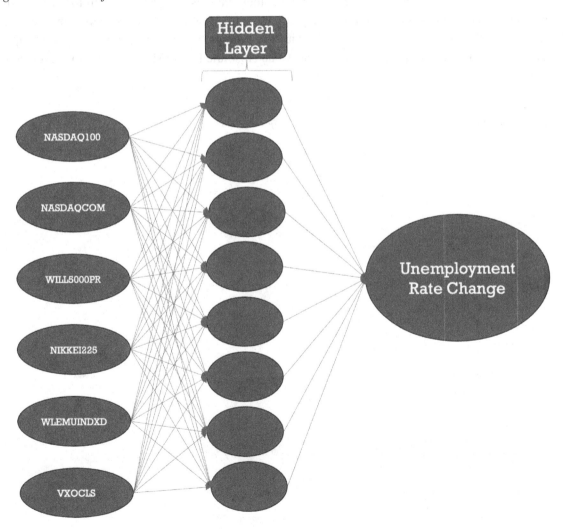

In the hidden layers, rectified linear unit (ReLu) activation function is used. For the final layer (output), sigmoid activation function is selected. Other activation functions such as linear activation function, step function, are also tested. ReLu and Sigmoid are selected because they produce better model accuracy.

Random Forest

Random forest is a learning algorithm that uses decision trees to classify different samples in the dataset. It has high accuracy through cross validation and uses Out-Of-Bag (OOB) error to test the prediction rate. Each decision tree in random forest is trained based on two third of the training set (bootstrap sample), OOB error is computed as a weighted average of the prediction error on the remaining one third of the training set (out of bag sample). It is a common estimate when measuring the prediction error of random forest model or other bootstrap aggregating machine learning models.

In this data, we have six predictors from different stock markets. We used random forest to predict the unemployment rate change based on these predictors and identified the most important variables. This analysis was performed through Rstudio with the following packages: ggplot2, cowplot, dplyr, caret, ranger. The percentage prediction error and Mean Absolute Error (MAE) were also computed for random forest model.

Figure 5. Root Mean Square Deviation for OOB error

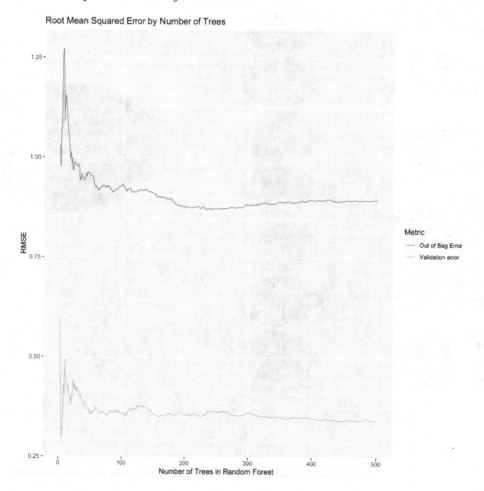

In our models, the data was randomly split into training set and testing set with a ratio of 8:2. Then, we used random forest to build an initial model, and identified the number of trees that are required to stabilize the Root Mean Square Deviation (RMSE) for OOB error and validation error to stabilize the model. As figure 5 shows, the RMSE for OOB error became stable after the number of trees reached 200 and had a lowest RMSE for OOB error when the number of trees is around 250. Since we were aimed to decide an ideal number of trees in random forest before any other tuning process, 250 was set as the number of trees for later models.

In order to find the optimal random forest model that provides the least OOB error, we performed a grid search looping across multiple models with different combinations of hyperparameters through ranger. The major hyperparameters include mtry (the number of variables to randomly sample as candidates at each split), node_size (minimum number of samples within the terminal node), sample_size (the number of samples to train on), OOB RMSE (root mean square deviation of out-of-bag error). The optimal random forest model, as figure 6 shows, has a RMSE of OOB error of 0.9108909 with mtry of 3, node size of 3 and a sample size of 80%.

Figure 6. Random Forest Model Grid Search Results

	Hyperparameters Grid Search			
	mtry	node_size	sample_size	OOB_RMSE
1	3	3	0.800	0.9108909
2	2	3	0.800	0.9117806
3	2	3	0.632	0.9178788
4	3	3	0.700	0.9201665
5	2	3	0.700	0.9238953
6	4	3	0.800	0.9275213
7	2	5	0.800	0.9295682
8	2	3	0.550	0.9307868
9	4	3	0.632	0.9329985
10	3	3	0.550	0.9340923

mtry: the number of variables to randomly sample as candidates at each split
node_size: minimum number of samples within the terminal node
sample_size: the number of samples to train on
OOB RMSE: root mean square deviation of out-of-bag error

After confirming the hyperparameters for the optimal model, we tested the variable importance. Variable importance is an internal calculated value in random forest model measured by recording the decrease in Mean Squared Error (MSE) every time a variable is used as a node split in a tree. After a node split, node impurity is left as a remaining error in predictive accuracy. A variable was considered more important if it reduces this impurity. In our model, the accumulating reduction of MSE was assessed for each variable through all the trees. The variable with the greater accumulation of MSE reduction was more important.

The final step we made for random forest model was to calculate the error rate and MAE by comparing the predicted values and the observed values in testing set, based on previous training process, to systematically check our model accuracy.

Generalized Linear Model (GLM)

Although neural network and random forest all made decent prediction on U.S. unemployment rate, lack of interpretable results is one of the potential limitations for both models. Ordinary Least Squares (OLS) linear regression model is one of the most common linear models used in statistical analysis. In order to investigate the relationship between single response variable and different predictors and interpret our results in certain magnitude, OLS linear regression became an ideal choice to apply to our data. The analysis was performed through Rstudio.

Figure 7. Relationship Between Unemployment Rate and Predictors

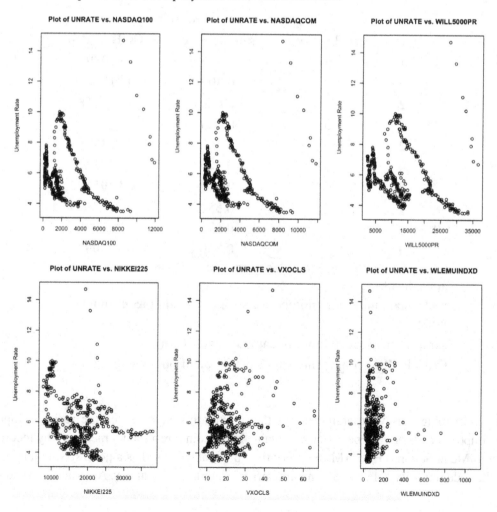

When using OLS regression model, several major assumptions must be tested: 1. Linearity assumption: there are linear relationships between the response variable and the predictors; 2. Independence assumption: the errors are independent; 3. No multicollinearity assumption: there is no correlated relationship among all the predictors; 4. Homoscedasticity assumption: the errors need to have equal variance; 5. Normality assumption: errors are normally distributed.

The assumption of linearity and multicollinearity were firstly tested before we run any model. As figure 7 shows, there were no non-linear relationships found between unemployment rate and all predictors, though the linear relationships were not obviously strong.

The linear relationships were also presented in figure 8, the pairs plot of all variables. In this plot, some collinear relationships were observed between variables NASDAQ100, NSDAQCOM, WILL5000PR. This issued was caused because NASDAQ100 and NSDAQCOM are both indexes from the same stock exchange market, and WILL5000PR is a market capitalization weighted index of market value of all-American stocks traded in the U.S. Therefore, we removed NASDAQ100 and NSDAQCOM to solve multicollinearity issue for our OLS regression model.

Figure 8. Predictors Multicollinearity Testing Result

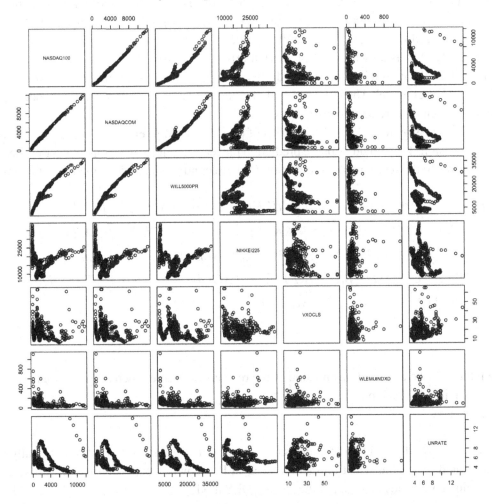

A naïve OLS model was run after validating above two assumptions, the general equation of this model is described as following.

$$UNRATE = \beta_0 + \beta_1 * WILL5000PR + \beta_2 * NIKKEI225 + \beta_3 * VXOCLS + \beta_4 * WLEMUINDXD + \epsilon$$

$\beta0$ is the intercept (the expected mean value of the response variable when all predictors are 0)
βi is the coefficient for each predictor
ϵ is the error term

Model outputs related to adjusted R-squared, p-value of each predictor and Akaike Information Criterion (AIC) were reported. R-squared is a statistical measure which demonstrates the proportion of the variance for the response variable explained by predictors in a regression model. Adjusted R-squared is an adapted version R-squared which adjusted the number of predictors in the model. A higher adjusted R-squared usually indicates better model. P-value is the estimated probability when the alternative hypothesis in our study is true (rejecting the null hypothesis). The null hypothesis for each predictor was assuming the coefficient to be zero (H_0: $\beta i_= 0$ for i =1,2,3,4) at a significance level at α=0.05. A variable was considered significant (rejecting the null hypothesis) if the p-value for that predictor is lower than 0.05 in our study. AIC is a measure of prediction error that is usually used to compare the quality of statistical models. We used it in addition to adjusted R-squared to compare models. A lower AIC generally indicates a better model. Then, the residual plot and Q-Q plot were drawn for this model to test the rest of three assumptions related to error term.

In a linear regression model, quadratic terms of predictors and interaction terms are considered significant on occasion. They could improve prediction power. Therefore, we included all the quadratic and interaction terms to the second model. Equation of the second model is described as following.

$$\begin{aligned}
UNRATE = {} & \beta_0 + \beta_1 * WILL5000PR + \beta_2 * NIKKEI225 + \beta_3 * VXOCLS + \beta_4 * WLEMUINDXD \\
& + \beta_5 * WILL5000PR^2 + \beta_6 * NIKKEI225^2 + \beta_7 * VXOCLS^2 + \beta_8 * WLEMUINDXD^2 \\
& + \beta_9 * WILL5000PR * NIKEEI225 + \beta_{10} * WILL5000PR * VXOCLS + \beta_{11} * WILL5000PR \\
& * WLEMUINDXD + \beta_{12} * NIKKEI225 * VXOCLS + \beta_{13} * NIKKEI225 * WLEMUINDXD \\
& + \beta_{14} * VXOCLS * WLEMUINDXD + \epsilon
\end{aligned}$$

$\beta0$ is the intercept (the expected mean value of the response variable when all predictors are 0)
βi is the coefficient for each predictor
ϵ is the error term

However, simply adding additional terms to a linear regression model is not scientifically rigorous. We implemented a variable selection method used in R, stepwise regression (backward selection), to help us eliminate variables included in the second OLS model for the purpose of achieving the optimal

OLS model. There are three different stepwise regression methods, forward selection, backward selection and bidirectional selection. We chose backward selection since it allowed us to add all possible terms into the model, and then helped us find the ideal model among different combinations of those terms. Finally, the adjusted R-squared, p-value, AIC and coefficient of significant variables were reported for the optimal OLS model.

RESULTS

Neural Network

Multiple testing and training dataset separation scenarios were tested. Smaller testing size which corresponds to larger training size had the best accuracy level of 91.67% as presented in Figure 5. The efficiency of convergence is high as the accuracy improves quite fast.

Table 1. Model Output with Variant Testing/Training Size

Testing/Training Size	Model Output	
	Loss	Accuracy
20%:80%	2.6238	0.9167
50%:50%	70.2971	0.8852
60%:40%	1653.106	0.6853

The accuracy definition is a standard metrics in TensorFlow package, however, there are many other definitions of accuracy measure statistically that could be considered, compared and concluded. This study did not focus on accuracy measurement selection, model structure such as number of layers, number of neurons within each layer and activation function selection were the main focus of the model construction. A consistent accuracy comparison of neural network models is sufficient for model validation.

As the testing size increases, the accuracy levels drop significantly from testing size 50% of 88.52% to testing size 60% of 58.53% as presented in Table 1. The accuracy of the model also depends on the initial random weight selection, however, it does converge to a relatively stable results especially as the training dataset size increases.

Random Forest

The optimal random forest model after our tuning procedures used 250 tress, mtry 3, node size of 3 and a sample size of 80%. It had a root mean square deviation of out of bag error around 0.9108909. The variable importance is reported as following, where Nikkei Stock Average is the most important variable on predicting U.S. unemployment rate, then followed by NASDAQ 100 index, NASDAQ Composite index, Wilshire 5000 Price index, CBOE S&P 100 Volatility index, and Equity Market-related Economic Uncertainty index is the least important variable. Surprisingly, the stock market index for the Tokyo Stock Exchange is even more important than the U.S. domestic stock exchange index on unemployment rate. In our opinion, it can be explained as COVID-19 has largely impeded international trading activities and led to a lack in demand of labor force.

Table 2. Variable Importance from Random Forest

Variable Importance					
NIKKEI225	**NASDAQ100**	**NASDAQCOM**	**WILL5000PR**	**VXOCLS**	**WLEMUINDXD**
257.18440	164.76113	116.66998	88.01111	54.62054	32.06618

In addition to the OOB error, the percent error and the MAE were also calculated for this model. The percent error, computed as the average of the absolute difference of the predicted value and the observed value divided by the observed value for each observation, is 6.73%. The accuracy rate, on the other hand, is 93.27%. The MAE, computed as the sum of the absolute difference of the predicted value and the observed value for all observations divided by the total number of observations, is 0.412. Thus, we can conclude the overall performance of our random forest model is relatively accurate.

Generalized Linear Model (GLM)

The naïve OLS model, simply removing two correlated terms (NASDAQ100 and NASDAQCOM), had a poor performance. The summary table is presented in Table 3. The adjusted R-squared was 0.1578 and only two predictors, WILL5000PR and NIKKEI225, were found significant in this model. Also, the AIC is relatively high, 1543.108. Therefore, the model tuning process was surely needed to improve the model performance.

Table 3. Naïve OLS Model Outputs

	Estimate	Std. Error	t value	p-value
(Intercept)	7.792000	0.364400	21.384000	<2.00e-16
WILL5000PR	-0.000041	0.000010	-4.194000	0.000034
NIKKEI225	-0.000096	0.000013	-7.596000	0.000000
VXOCLS	0.008333	0.008924	0.934000	0.351000
WLEMUINDXD	0.001344	0.000834	1.611000	0.108000
Adjusted R-Squared	0.1578			
AIC	1543.108			

The second OLS model, including all quadratic and interaction terms, was run and we observed some improvements for the model. As Table 4 presented, the adjusted R-squared increased to 0.5146 and AIC slightly decreased to 1322.504. In this revised model, three terms were found significant when predicting U.S. unemployment rate. However, directly adding new terms to the model would improve the model performance but it doesn't lead us to the optimal model, as we mentioned in the method section. Hence, the backward selection was applied to find the best model.

Table 4. Second OLS Model Outputs

	Estimate	Std. Error	t value	p-value
(Intercept)	7.681000	1.523000	5.044000	0.000001
WILL5000PR	-0.000071	0.000060	-1.169000	0.242900
NIKKEI225	0.000139	0.000101	1.382000	0.167700
VXOCLS	-0.054020	0.041740	-1.294000	0.196300
WLEMUINDXD	0.004911	0.005530	0.888000	0.375100
I(WILL5000PR^2)	0.000000	0.000000	13.028000	<2.00e-16
I(NIKKEI225^2)	0.000000	0.000000	-0.320000	0.748900
I(VXOCLS^2)	-0.000188	0.000407	-0.462000	0.644300
I(WLEMUINDXD^2)	-0.000001	0.000003	-0.309000	0.757300
WILL5000PR:NIKKEI225	0.000000	0.000000	-9.858000	<2.00e-16
WILL5000PR:VXOCLS	0.000006	0.000001	6.303000	0.000000
WILL5000PR:WLEMUINDXD	0.000000	0.000000	0.656000	0.512500
NIKKEI225:VXOCLS	-0.000001	0.000001	-0.930000	0.352900
NIKKEI225:WLEMUINDXD	0.000000	0.000000	-2.024000	0.043700
VXOCLS:WLEMUINDXD	0.000115	0.000136	0.850000	0.396000
Adjusted R-Squared	0.5146			
AIC	1322.504			

The optimal model we found through backward selection from stepwise regression slightly improved the performance of the second model, and more terms were reported significant. As Table 5 presented, the optimal OLS model had an adjusted R-squared of 0.5196 and a AIC of 1312.341. More importantly, eight terms were found significant from this model. There were WILL5000PR, NIKKEI225, VXOCLS, WLEMUINDXD, the quadratic term of WILL5000PR, the interaction term of WILL5000PR and NIKKEI225, the interaction term of WILL5000PR and VXOCLS, and the interaction term of NIKKEI225 and WLEMUINDXD.

Table 5. The Optimal OLS Model Outputs

	Estimate	Std. Error	t value	p-value
(Intercept)	7.946000	0.631200	12.588000	<2.00e-16
WILL5000PR	-0.000060	0.000046	-1.289000	0.198136
NIKKEI225	0.000096	0.000025	3.779000	0.000181
VXOCLS	-0.070470	0.012010	-5.870000	0.000000
WLEMUINDXD	0.009822	0.002041	4.812000	0.000002
I(WILL5000PR^2)	0.000000	0.000000	15.304000	<2.00e-16
WILL5000PR:NIKKEI225	0.000000	0.000000	-13.76400	<2.00e-16
WILL5000PR:VXOCLS	0.000005	0.000001	6.482000	0.000000
NIKKEI225:WLEMUINDXD	0.000000	0.000000	-4.662000	0.000004
Adjusted R-Squared	0.5196			
AIC	1312.341			

CONCLUSION

There are multiple potential issues or limitations within the data and models. The neural network model constructed here is extremely simplified and fundamental. However, it still includes 6 (inputs)* 8 (neurons in hidden layer) + 8 (neurons in hidden layer) *1 (output) = 48 + 8 = 56 weights. More sophisticated models, such as more hidden layer and larger number of neurons within each layer were tested. However, they did not show a meaningful improvement and were not selection. When models show equivalent result, the simpler model is preferred according to the rule of "Parsimony". In addition to the rule of "Parsimony", overfitting was another reason that the current model is selected. The random forest model is reliable as it doesn't have many requirements to the dataset. It can reduce overfitting and improve prediction power by its intrinsic mechanism. The result of random forest, however, is not interpretable just like many other machine learning models. Although we applied GLM to find more interpretable results, potential correlation issue still existed since there should be certain relationship among U.S. domestic stock market indexes. Also, all GLM models assume a linear relationship between dependent variable and all independent variables. A nonlinear relationship could reduce the predicting power of GLM models, thus the results from GLM must be proceeded with cautious.

The neural network model does show difference between training/testing data separation variations, which indicates that the model is not completely converged. However, the model is able to reach to more than 90% accuracy which explains the relationship between unemployment rate change and major economic indexes.

The model provides a decent prediction results and accuracy. It is more appropriate to explain the relationship between employment rate change and major economic indexes instead of prediction. The model is still limited because of the small data size. The reason of small size is that unemployment rate is reported in a monthly basis. Even though the starting point of dataset is in the beginning of 1986, the size is still small. The starting weights for the model are randomly chosen, small dataset has a potentially higher risk to achieve converged model result. Also, there exist more economic or stock market related variables, which need to be explored, that could be included in the model. For example, more globalization drivers and more policy related data. However, we must be careful about the correlation issue and linearity assumption in the GLM model.

For future studies, more economical dataset will be investigated. More granular data will be studied and incorporated. The same models could also be tested in another social economy. Furthermore, other techniques within machine learning framework will be researched to see whether it shows a better fit to model such relationship.

All three models deliver different types of messages to the social economy based on the performance of stock market, and they are all helpful reference to the policy maker. We can never predict when the pandemic will come, yet we can predict its impact to the economy. Whenever similar situation happens again, we will be prepared.

REFERENCES

Arestis, P., Baddeley, M., & Sawyer, M. (2007, April). The Relationship Between Capital Stock, Unemployment and Wages in Nine EMU Countries. *Bulletin of Economic Research*, *59*(2), 13–15. doi:10.1111/j.0307-3378.2007.00254.x

Arestis, P., & Mariscal, B.-F. (2000). Capital shortages, unemployment and wages in the UK and Germany. *Scottish Journal of Political Economy*, *47*(5), 487–503. doi:10.1111/1467-9485.00175

Athey, S., Tibshirani, J., & Wager, S. (2019). Generalized random forests. *Annals of Statistics*, *47*(2), 1148–1178. doi:10.1214/18-AOS1709

Baker, R. S., Bloom, N., & Davis, J. S. (2015). *Measuring Economic Policy Uncertainty*. National Bureau of Economic Research. doi:10.3386/w21633

Biau, G. (2012). Analysis of a Random Forests Model. *Journal of Machine Learning Research*, *3*, 1063-1095.

Bock, J. (2018). *Quantifying macroeconomic expectations in stock markets using Google Trends*. Department of Finance, Warwick Business School, University of Warwick. doi:10.2139srn.3218912

Boyd, J. H., Hu, J., & Jagannathan, R. (2005). The Stock Market's Reaction to Unemployment News: Why Bad News Is Usually Good for Stocks. *The Journal of Finance*, *60*(2), 649–672. doi:10.1111/j.1540-6261.2005.00742.x

Breiman, L. (2001). Random Forests. *Machine Learning*, *45*(1), 5–42. doi:10.1023/A:1010933404324

Chen, X., & Ishwaran, H. (2012). Random forests for genomic data analysis. *Genomics*, *99*(6), 323–329. doi:10.1016/j.ygeno.2012.04.003 PMID:22546560

Cutler, D. R. (2007, November 1). Random Forests for Classification in Ecology. *Journal of Ecological Society of America*, *88*(11), 2783–2792. PMID:18051647

Federal Reserve Bank of St. Louis. (2020). *FRED Economic Data*. Retrieved from *Economic Research*: https://fred.stlouisfed.org/

Genuer, R., Poggi, J.-M., & Tuleau-Malot, C. (2010). Variable selection using random forests. *Pattern Recognition Letters*, *31*(14), 2225–2236. doi:10.1016/j.patrec.2010.03.014

Genuer, R., Poggi, J.-M., Tuleau-Malot, C., & Vialaneix, N. (2017). Random Forests for Big Data. Big Data Research, 9, 28-46. doi:10.1016/j.bdr.2017.07.003

Gislason, P.O., Benediktsson, J.A. & Sveinsson, J.R. (2006, March). Random Forests for land cover classification. *Pattern Recognition Letters,* *27*(4), 294-300. doi:10.1016/j.patrec.2005.08.011

Gonzalo, J., & Taamouti, A. (2017, June 23). The reaction of stock market returns to unemployment. *Studies in Nonlinear Dynamics and Econometrics*, *21*(4), 78–80.

Gordon, R. (1997). Is there a trade-off between unemployment and productivity growth? In D. Snower & G. de la Dehesa (Eds.), *Unemployment Policy: Government Options for the Labour Market* (pp. 433–463). Cambridge University Press. doi:10.1017/CBO9780511752025.033

Kilic, M., & Wachter, J. (2018, December). Risk, Unemployment, and the Stock Market: A Rare-Event-Based Explanation of Labor Market Volatility. *Review of Financial Studies*, *31*(12), 4762–4814. doi:10.1093/rfs/hhy008

Lin, Y., & Jeon, Y. (2006). Random Forests and Adaptive Nearest Neighbors. *Journal of the American Statistical Association*, *101*(474), 578–590. doi:10.1198/016214505000001230

Loungani, P., Rush, M., & Tave, W. (1990). Stock market dispersion and unemployment. *Journal of Monetary Economics*, *25*(3), 367–388. doi:10.1016/0304-3932(90)90059-D

Louppe, G. (2014). *Understanding Random Forests: From Theory to Practice* (Ph.D. Dissertation). University of Liège, Faculty of Applied Sciences, Department of Electrical Engineering & Computer Science. Retrieved August 14, 2021 from https://arxiv.org/pdf/1407.7502.pdf

Pan, W.-F. (2018). Does the stock market really cause unemployment? A cross-country analysis. *The North American Journal of Economics and Finance*, *44*(C), 34–43. doi:10.1016/j.najef.2017.11.002

Robnik-Šikonja, M. (2004). Improving Random Forests. *Proceedings of 15th European Conference on Machine Learning (ECML)*, 359-370.

Scornet, E., Biau, G., & Vert, J.-P. (2015, August). Consistency of random forests. *Annals of Statistics*, *43*(4), 1716–1741. doi:10.1214/15-AOS1321

Segal, M., & Xiao, Y. (2011). Multivariate random forests. *WIRES Data Mining and Knowledge Discovery*, *1*(1), 80–87. doi:10.1002/widm.12

Sibande, X., Gupta, R., & Wohar, M. (2019). Time-varying causal relationship between stock market and unemployment in the United Kingdom: Historical evidence from 1855 to 2017. *Journal of Multinational Financial Management*, *49*, 81–88. doi:10.1016/j.mulfin.2019.02.003

Strobl, C., Boulesteix, A.-L., Kneib, T., Augustin, T., & Zeileis, A. (2008). Conditional variable importance for random forests. *BMC Bioinformatics*, *9*(1), 307. Advance online publication. doi:10.1186/1471-2105-9-307 PMID:18620558

Tsymbal, A., Pechenizkiy, M., & Cunningham, P. (2006). Dynamic Integration with Random Forests. *European Conference on Machine Learning*, 801-808. Retrieved August 15,2021 from http://citeseerx. ist.psu.edu/viewdoc/download?doi=10.1.1.391.1720&rep=rep1&type=pdf

Verikas, A., Gelzinis, A., & Bacauskiene, M. (2011, February). Mining data with random forests: A survey and results of new tests. *Pattern Recognition, 44*(2), 330–349. doi:10.1016/j.patcog.2010.08.011

Zhang, J., Zulkernine, M., & Haque, A. (2008, August 19). Random-Forests-Based Network Intrusion Detection Systems. *IEEE Xplore, 38*(5), 649–659.

ADDITIONAL READING

Chua, L. O., & Yang, L. (1988). Cellular neural networks: theory. *IEEE Transactions on Circuits and Systems, 35*(10), 1257-1272. Retrieved August 14, 2021 from https://www.researchgate.net/profile/ Leon-Chua/publication/3183706_Cellular_neural_networks_Theory/links/58c82d5245851591df33faa4/ Cellular-neural-networks-Theory.pdf

Denil, M., Matheson, D., & De Freitas, N. (2014). Narrowing the Gap: Random Forests in Theory and an Practice. In *Proceedings of the 31th International Conference on Machine Learning*, Beijing, China, pp. 665-673.

Latinne, P., Debeir, O., & Decaestecker, C. (2001). Limiting the Number of Trees in Random Forests. In J. Kittler & F. Roli (Eds.), Lecture Notes in Computer Science: Vol. 2096. Multiple Classifier Systems. MCS 2001 (pp. 178–187). Springer., doi:10.1007/3-540-48219-9_18

Matsuki, K., Kuperman, V., & Van Dyke, J. A. (2016). The Random Forests statistical technique: An examination of its value for the study of reading. *Scientific studies of reading: The official journal of the Society for the Scientific Study of Reading, 20*(1), 20–33. https://doi.org/ doi:10.1080/10888438.2 015.1107073

Vellido, A., Lisboa, P. J. G., & Vaughan, J. (1999, July). Neural networks in business: A survey of applications. *Expert Systems with Applications, 17*(1), 51–70. doi:10.1016/S0957-4174(99)00016-0

Wan, L., Zeiler, M., Zhang, S., Cun, Y. L., & Fergus, R. (2013). Regularization of Neural Networks using DropConnect. *Proceedings of the 30th International Conference on Machine Learning*, Atlanta, GA. p.1058-1066.

Wang, X., Girshick, R., Gupta, A., & He, K. (2018). Non-local Neural Networks, *Proceedings of 2018 IEEE/CVPR Conference on Computer Vision and Pattern Recognition*, pp. 7794-7803, doi: 10.1109/ CVPR.2018.00813

Winham, S. J., Winham, R. R., & Biernacka, J. M. (2013). A weighted random forests approach to improve predictive performance. *Statistical Analysis and Data Mining, 6*(6), 496–505. doi:10.1002am.11196 PMID:24501613

Zhang, G., & Lu, Y. (2012). Bias-corrected random forests in regression. *Journal of Applied Statistics, 39*(1), 151–160. doi:10.1080/02664763.2011.578621

Zhou, Z.-H., Wu, J., & Tang, W. (2002). Ensembling neural networks: Many could be better than all. *Artificial Intelligence, 137*(1-2), 239–263. doi:10.1016/S0004-3702(02)00190-X

KEY TERMS AND DEFINITIONS

Artificial Neural Network (ANN): One of the computational models of the machine learning methodology. Artificial Neural Network simulates neurons in human brain, learns from existing patterns and fathom artificial intelligence problems.

Classification Tree: A machine learning algorithm that is similar as random forest. Different from random forest, classification tree usually handles binary decision in each tree node, and it requires less training.

COVID-19 Pandemic: A coronavirus disease caused by SARS-CoV-2 that emerged in December 2019. It is a highly transmissible disease and has caused more than 30 million infections and 400,000 deaths in the U.S. as of July 2021.

Economic Indices: Six stock market-based indexes including NASDAQ 100, NASDAQ Composite, Wilshire 5000 Price, Nikkei Stock Average, Equity Market-related Economic Uncertainty, CBOE S&P 100 Volatility.

Generalized Linear Model (GLM): A widely used statistical modelling technique for data analysis and prediction models. It is a general concept of all linear models including linear regression, logistic regression, and Poisson regression. It assumes a linear relationship between the response variables and all predictors.

Machine Learning: An application of artificial intelligence on the basis of automatically learn and adapt from data. Also known as a data analysis method that utilize intrinsic self-learning system to help on making prediction.

Ordinary Least Squares (OLS) Model: Also known as linear regression model. OLS model is a commonly used statistical model under GLM family. It makes estimation about the relationship between predictors (independent variables) and the response variable (dependent variable), and it is able to report the coefficients of each predictor and overall model fit.

Predictive Modelling: A widely used statistical and mathematical methodology for data analysis. It predicts possible future events based on data mining process of historical data.

Random Forest: One of the computational models of machine learning. Random forest model is a supervised learning algorithm which uses multiple decision trees to make prediction by training a portion of the data. It is a well-known for its highly accurate prediction with less requirements of the dataset.

U.S. Unemployment Rate: A monthly reported rate that demonstrates unemployment change in the U.S. It is calculated by taking the average of daily unemployment rate for each month. Daily unemployment rate is calculated as dividing the total number of unemployed populations by the total number of populations, either employed or unemployed, in the labor market.

Chapter 11
Applying Machine Learning Methods for Credit Card Payment Default Prediction With Cost Savings

Siddharth Vinod Jain
Liverpool John Moores University, UK

Manoj Jayabalan
https://orcid.org/0000-0002-1599-965X
Liverpool John Moores University, UK

ABSTRACT

The credit card has been one of the most successful and prevalent financial services being widely used across the globe. However, with the upsurge in credit card holders, banks are facing a challenge from equally increasing payment default cases causing substantial financial damage. This necessitates the importance of sound and effective credit risk management in the banking and financial services industry. Machine learning models are being employed by the industry at a large scale to effectively manage this credit risk. This chapter presents the application of the various machine learning methods like time series models and deep learning models experimented in predicting the credit card payment defaults along with identification of the significant features and the most effective evaluation criteria. This chapter also discusses the challenges and future considerations in predicting credit card payment defaults. The importance of factoring in a cost function to associate with misclassification by the models is also given.

INTRODUCTION

Credit cards are merely plastics issued by banks and financial institutions. Credit cardholders can use these to make retail purchases physically in stores or digitally from the convenience of their home. Credit card transactions are getting more secured by the day and gradually replacing cash transactions. These credit

DOI: 10.4018/978-1-7998-8455-2.ch011

cards are part of the credit lending business that has been highly profitable for the banking and financial services industry. However, this surge of demand comes with the increased risk of payment defaults.

A payment default is a condition where the credit card holder does not pay back the amount owed to the bank within the payment due date. Payment defaulters impose a significant loss to the lenders globally by not paying back the owed amount and forcing banks to write off these amounts as non-recoverable bad debts in extreme cases. This deep worrying concern necessitated the establishment of a sound risk management system that can predict defaulters in advance and alert banks enabling them to take corrective action thereby mitigating risk. Machine learning models are being employed by the industry at a large scale to effectively manage this credit risk. These machine learning models can identify the significant features and effectively predict the payment defaults in advance.

The existing studies have identified gender, age, marriage, education, payment related variables, repayment related variables, employment status, and limit balance as the most significant features that impact the default prediction (Choubey, 2018; Leong & Jayabalan, 2019; Neema & Soibam, 2017; Sariannidis et al., 2020; Sayjadah et al., 2018; Ullah et al., 2018; Xu et al., 2017; Xu et al., 2018). Leow & Crook (2014) derived features like relationship duration with a bank, transitions between the states of delinquency, average payment amount, and average repayment amount to increase the model performance. Further, few studies have considered macro-economic variables that could potentially impact defaults prediction such as bank interest rate, Consumer Price Index (CPI), Gross Domestic Product (GDP), and unemployment rate (Bellotti & Crook, 2013; Li et al., 2019).

Numerous researchers have shown the application of time series, machine learning, and deep learning models to increase the accuracy of default prediction and minimize loss. The time-series models were implemented on the data spanning across few years to capture the economic conditions. Further, these datasets had several features that could be further classified into static and dynamic features. The factors contributed to the superior performance of time-series models with accuracy close to 95% along with high precision and recall rates (Bellotti & Crook, 2013; Ho Ha & Krishnan, 2012; Leow & Crook, 2014). Machine learning models are typically preferred over time-series models when datasets are not very huge and the period of data does not span over a longer period. Machine learning models like Logistic Regression (LR) have been used for simplicity of implementation and interpretation. Random Forest (RF), eXtreme Gradient Boosting (XGBoost), Artificial Neural Network (ANN), and Recurrent Neural network (RNN) were able to achieve accuracy close to 90% with an equally satisfying precision and recall values (Leong & Jayabalan, 2019; Mazumder, 2020; Neema & Soibam, 2017; Sariannidis et al., 2020; Sayjadah et al., 2018; Ullah et al., 2018; Yontar et al., 2020).

Few studies have experimented with deep learning models as well and achieved high model accuracy (Chishti and Awan, 2019; Ebiaredoh-mienye et al., 2020; Hsu et al., 2019; Sun and Vasarhelyi, 2018). These deep learning models are artificial neural networks that have more than one hidden layer to transform the non-linear relationships effectively. An artificial neural network is an attempt to mimic the functioning of a human brain. Details of these studies are elaborated in a separate subsection.

The purpose of this chapter is to discuss the application of machine learning algorithms to predict credit card payment defaults. As such, it helps the business in making strategic and well-informed decisions thereby minimizing losses substantially. Moreover, the chapter highlights some of the common features, techniques, and evaluation criteria usually considered in the prediction of payment defaults. This chapter is meant to be useful for identifying trends in payment defaults that will allow researchers to focus on areas that need to be improved and new features that could be beneficial to the stakeholders. At the end of this Chapter, you will be able to:

- Understand the functionality of payment default in credit cards and its implications.
- Identify the significant features that contribute to the prediction of credit card payment defaults.
- Review existing studies that employ various data mining techniques to predict payment defaults.
- Understand the latest trends associated with the prediction of credit card payment defaults.
- Appreciate the challenges faced in existing studies and the future recommendations to achieve the state-of-the-art.

DATA ANALYTICS IN PREDICTION OF CREDIT CARD DEFAULTS

This section presents a review of existing studies in the prediction of credit card payment defaults. The significance of data analytics and data mining is discussed in detail along with the contribution of significant features, application of time-series models, machine learning algorithms, and deep learning models in the prediction of credit card payment defaults. A summary of the reviews based on the models, datasets, and evaluation metrics experimented with is depicted in Table 1 in the Appendix section.

Nearly half of the net income from consumer banking of global banks like Citi and Chase is derived from credit cards. Needless to mention that credit card products are drivers of huge profit for most of the major banks and financial institutions across the globe. Banks have to manage the associated risks like frauds and payment defaults that are associated with this product though. These risks can potentially cause huge losses to the banks if not managed effectively. This is where data analytics plays an important role in cardholder lifecycle right from the marketing of cards to origination of new accounts, customer management decisions, fraud management, and collections.

A detailed review of each of these areas mentioned above will help to understand how data analytics contributes significantly to them. For example, data analytics in credit card marketing can help the sales team focus on a segment of customers with a specific type of credit card that is directly linked to credit limits, rewards, privileges, and annual fees. Platinum credit cardholders would typically have a higher credit limit, better rewards program, and privileges as compared to a classic credit cardholder. Data analytics can help identify the right category of people for targeting platinum cards and classic cards with fairly good accuracy based on the available data. Similarly, data analytics can also help in the account origination process by doing the initial screening of applications and only passing the filtered applications for physical verification or review by bank staff to process further. This saves a considerable amount of human effort and hence expense incurred by the bank. Data analytics perform fairly well in rejecting applications that are likely to cause loss to banks in the future, again this is possible because of the history of available data. The probability of human errors is also negated. Fraud management is another area where banks suffer huge losses. Data analytics are largely employed in both real-time (or near real-time) mode as well as offline mode of transactions so that bank staff can alert customers accordingly almost immediately. Thus, banks can mitigate this huge risk that can otherwise cause huge financial damage including brand reputation. Nevertheless, the focus of this chapter is to review the existing studies carried out to predict payment defaults of credit cardholders as elaborated in the next section.

DATA MINING IN PREDICTION OF CREDIT CARD DEFAULTS

Several data mining techniques have been employed over years across industries to extract meaningful data and draw relevant inferences leading to more strategic and well-informed business decisions and higher profitability. These techniques span a wide range starting right from the traditional classical algorithms like Linear and Logistic regression to Decision Trees and then the ensemble algorithms like Random Forest, AdaBoost, XGBoost, and ANN including their respective variations. Apart from these, several techniques have evolved over years to cater to business needs. Several machine learning techniques have been studied to predict credit-card defaults with their performances evaluated using metrics like AUC, Accuracy, Precision, F1-score, and more (Xu et al., 2017; Islam et al., 2018; Leong and Jayabalan, 2019; Sariannidis et al., 2020). Below sections elaborate on the various related studies.

Significant Features Contributing to Prediction of Payment Defaults

Several techniques have been experimented with to identify the significant features that contribute to the prediction of credit card payment defaults. One of the studies used frequency of observations to identify the significant features like gender, education, age, marriage, and limit-balance (amount of credit given) in predicting payment defaults (Ullah et al., 2018). Pearson correlation was used to identify correlations of these significant indicators with the dependent feature payment-default, and it was learned that limit-balance and education were negatively correlated such that the lesser the education and limit-balance, the greater is the probability of payment defaults (Choubey, 2018). Age was found to be positively correlated since the probability of payment defaults increased with an increase in age (Choubey, 2018; Sariannidis et al., 2020).

Another study experimented with the Taiwan credit card default dataset and identified repayment status, credit limit, and payment-related features as the most significant predictors for payment defaults that are based on Correlation Feature Selection (CFS) (Sayjadah et al., 2018). Around 66% of the defaulters delay in making repayment with many of them not making payments for six months consecutively. It was also observed during the study that the approved credit limit of such defaulters was very high which caused huge losses to the banks. A proposal was made to generate alerts to review the credit limit for reduction when repayment is not done for more than five months consecutively. Numerous studies identified limit-balance, age, education, sex, marriage, and repayment status as the most significant predictors (Leong & Jayabalan, 2019; Neema & Soibam, 2017; Xu et al., 2017).

A few studies were carried out using time-series models that experimented with huge datasets spanning across years and containing static variables (demographic data) as well as dynamic variables (transaction-based data). (Leow & Crook, 2014) devised intensity model where Cox's hazard model with time-varying covariates were used. This model was a good example of identifying significant variables by slicing data across time-period that led to the transition into different defined states. It was observed that debtors having a long relationship with the bank had a lesser probability of delinquency and a higher probability of recovering instead, should they go into delinquency. Age and employment status were also significant indicators of delinquency. Applicants aged 21 and above were less likely to move into delinquency states and even recover back from delinquency as compared to the younger applicants. Once in state-2 (two months in arrears), older applicants seemed to be less likely to recover back from delinquency state and instead progress towards default (advance from state-2 which is two months in arrears to state 3 which is three months in arrears and considered as default state) as compared to younger applicants who showed a higher probability of recovering from state-2 (two months in arrears). Applicants with employment status as employed are less likely to default as compared to self-employed or unemployed which can be very well understood even otherwise. Also, a higher proportion of available credit drawn indicates a higher probability of getting into delinquency states. A higher rate of transitions between the states also indicated higher chances of going into delinquency states but not default. Also, they are less likely to make full recoveries.

A discrete-time survival model that included application variables, time-varying behavioral variables, and macro-economic variables was experimented by (Bellotti & Crook, 2013) where they presented a hazard probability graph showing payment defaults peaking at eight months from account opening and then gradually declining over time. Amount-paid-back or payment-status was negatively correlated with defaults as expected since greater ability to pay reduced the probability of defaults. The number of transactions had a positive correlation with defaults indicating that people doing a higher number of transactions showed higher chances of defaulting. From the macro-economic variables, the unemployment rate was observed to be positively correlated with understandable payment default. The bank interest rate was also positively correlated with defaults since increasing interest rates make it even more difficult for customers to pay back thereby increasing chances of defaults. Also, several behavioral variables turned out to be significant explanatory variables of defaults like account balance, repayments, number of transactions within each month, and credit limit.

Cox proportional hazard model was used to study the factors influencing credit card defaults in China. The stability of the customer's work and family was observed to impact the probability of default. Age, sex, and enterprise nature were significant factors in predicting defaults. Especially people aged below 30 show higher chances of defaulting. Males showed a higher probability of defaulting than females, probably because they were willing to take a higher risk of defaults comparatively. Customers employed in state-owned, foreign-funded, private enterprises showed less probability of default as compared to the ones who did not disclose their employer. From the macro-economic factors, defaults had a positive correlation with the consumer price index, GDP, and unemployment rate whereas defaults had a negative correlation with population and investments in fixed assets. Also, economic indicators like bank interest rates, earnings, production index, house price index, unemployment rate, and consumer confidence index were considered for default prediction (Bellotti & Crook, 2013; Li et al., 2019). From the social capital factors, it was observed that customers who lived and worked in registered permanent residences showed a lower probability of default. Also, married people showed higher chances of defaulting as compared to unmarried probably because married people had added responsibilities of mortgages and raising children. Consolidating these together, features like marriage, permanent residence address, and transaction type were also identified as significant.

Similar studies have been done on predicting payment defaults for credits in general and not just specific to credit cards. This credit risk poses a huge potential loss to the banking and financial services industry and hence is generally managed by a separate Risk Management system. Credit scoring forms an integral part of this Risk Management system. Customer's prior payment behavior, limit balance, total authorization amount, individual characteristics like age, education, profession, residence location, the limit of cash withdrawal, grace period, profession, average authorization amount that exceeds the credit limit, and the average number of times the customer has passed due-date along with additional data obtained from commercial credit agencies like unpaid bills, payment request issued by court order, enforcement procedures, and uncovered cheques all were significant features in predicting credit defaults (Mbuvha et al., 2019; Sun & Vasarhelyi, 2018).

Time-Series Models Applied in Prediction of Payment Defaults

Numerous studies were proposed to predict credit card defaults by using time-series models. They were primarily involved in developing a dynamic model (survival analysis) instead of static models (like regression analysis and discriminant analysis). The dynamic models accumulate time-varying variables of the credit cardholders to predict payment defaults. Both timing and occurrence of events can be studied over time. Further, survival analysis was used to identify the relationship of a customer with the bank. This relationship could be any relationship with the bank and not necessarily credit card only.

One study devised a hybrid model that combines a Self-Organizing Map (SOM) which is a form of ANN and Cox's proportional hazard model to improve prediction accuracy (Ho Ha & Krishnan, 2012). The main focus of this study was to predict the probability of recovery from a delinquent state of the debtor which was not done earlier. A SOM was used to cluster the credit card debtors into groups with similar characteristics. It created a topological map from input data through a competitive learning process using the smallest Euclidean distance between the presented pattern and the neighboring neurons. Figure 1 shows the framework devised in this study showing all the discussed functions. As the learning proceeded, each delinquent customer or a debtor within a cluster tended to have similar characteristics as compared to other clustered segments. In this case, five distinct segments were created according to delinquent pattern variables such as delinquency frequency, delinquency period, delinquency amount, the time interval between delinquencies, and delinquency repayment frequency. The resulting segments of credit card delinquents became inputs to Cox's hazard model which belonged to the category of survival analysis and was responsible for analyzing repayment patterns. This Cox's hazard model was chosen because it was useful when an appropriate baseline distribution could not be identified, or a non-parametric method was necessary.

Figure 1. Framework illustrating the prediction model using SOM and Cox's hazard model.

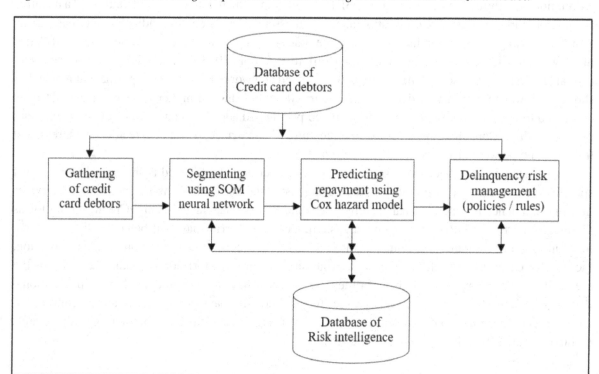

Also, one distinctive characteristic of this model was that it could manipulate imperfect data. A survival analysis used a likelihood function to build the model where survival implies delinquency maintenance. The contributions of this study are significant because: (1) Even though the majority of the studies focused on classifying customers between defaulter and non-defaulter customers, this study made it possible to analyze the delinquent customers who could be recoverable. (2) This study used a Survival analysis to identify influential variables on the rate of credit recovery and to predict the time of credit recovery. (3) This study calculated the expected profit after credit recovery by using a credit prediction model that presented several clues to Management to deal with delinquency risks. However, this study had some limitations for future improvements. (1) It needed a full year of data of all credit debtors, the absence of which causes models not to generalize well, and (2) This study focused on card debtors where all kinds of customers can be encompassed to develop a more complete credit prediction system.

Another study done by (Leow & Crook, 2014) experimented with intensity models and transition probabilities for credit card delinquency prediction. Semi-parametric multiplicative hazard models with time-varying covariates were used here to make delinquency predictions. These intensity estimations allowed for insights into the factors for a transition between the states. The probabilities were estimated for each type of transition and then further used to make delinquency. Such models have several advantages over the regression models or even survival models such as: (1) Users can gain predictions of the probability of moving between the defined states in any future period while incorporating time-varying covariates, (2) additional types of predictions are available like entire transition probability matrix is available for each borrower instead of just the hazard probability of default for a given point of time. For all this to work properly, the input data has monthly observations with continuous-time and hence had to be converted to discrete-time through approximation. These models were not only able to predict the outcome but even able to predict the probability of when it would occur making it a more dynamic framework for predictions.

Some studies considered using application, behavioral, and macro-economic variables to improve the prediction of credit card payment defaults. The behavior data were categorized into online and offline data and the impact of the expansion of internet online transactions on credit card defaults was studied for six months. Macro-economic data was taken from the National Bureau of Statistics (NBS) database. It was observed that the default risk rate grows slowly in the first three years of the opening card account, indicating good repayment habits and trustworthiness during that period. However, this risk grows tremendously in the third year indicating poor card management. This risk again shoots up when card holding lasts for 2000 to 2500 days indicating that after five years of card holding, many cards are canceled or changed.

The inclusion of macro-economic variables enabled them to do a stress test of prediction models since extreme economic conditions could be simulated and included in the model. This is potentially a key tool in helping financial institutions to make successful business strategies, risk management, and capital planning decisions. These studies confirmed that firstly, including behavioral variables improved the model fit in a discreet time hazard model and improved the forecast accuracy. Secondly, not all statistically significant macro-economic variables translate into improved prediction forecasts, and thirdly, including macro-economic variables in the model helped to improve the prediction of default rate. A 3-month lag was considered on macroeconomic variables since the default was defined as a failure to make the minimum payment for three consecutive months or more. For the simulation-based stress test, the Monte Carlo simulation was done. Since macro-economic variables are not normally distributed, Box-Cox transformation was done (Bellotti & Crook, 2013; Li et al., 2019).

Machine Learning Models Applied in Prediction of Payment Defaults

Many of the existing studies have employed popularly used algorithms and successfully experimented with them to predict credit card payment defaults. The algorithms like KNN, SVM, Linear regression, Logistic regression, Naïve Bayes, Decision Trees, and ensemble models like Random Forest, AdaBoost, and XGBoost were applied in these studies. The works of literature generally seem to experiment with the most widely used and popular machine learning algorithms. Ensemble models like decision trees, random forest, and XGBoost perform better than the singular models because ensemble models can collectively make better and more accurate decisions and hence perform better comparatively. Also, ensemble models are more robust because the variance of errors or bias can be reduced as compared to the singular model. The cross-validation process was used for hyperparameter tuning to achieve better prediction accuracy. The performance of models was evaluated primarily using accuracy ranging from 80% to 95% in most of the studies with few of them using AUC ranging from 0.71 to 0.77. Additionally, evaluation metrics like precision, recall, specificity, and F1-score of the models were also measured. (Leong & Jayabalan, 2019; Mazumder, 2020; Sariannidis et al., 2020; Sayjadah et al., 2018; Ullah et al., 2018; Yang and Zhang, 2018; Yontar et al., 2020; Yu, 2020).

A couple of studies included cost function to account for a more specific prediction goal to evaluate the models. The cost function was implemented by applying a higher cost to defaulters that were misclassified as non-defaulters (false negatives, also called type-2 error) and non-defaulters that were classified as defaulters (false positives, also called a type-1 error). Between these two misclassifications, false negatives are much more dangerous since defaulters go unnoticed, and hence appropriate action is not taken on such cases. This cost function helped maintain a healthy balance between Accuracy and Mathew's Correlation Coefficient (MCC) to avoid compromising on losing potential customers (Choubey, 2018; Neema & Soibam, 2017).

Charleonnan (2016) experimented with different machine learning methods RUSMRN and RUSBoost. RUSMRN is a hybrid model ensemble model based on linear and non-linear mapping that combines the RUS balancing technique with an ensemble of three learning models MLP, RBF, and NB classifiers. RUSMRN generated the best results. (Yeh & Lien, 2009) came up with the novel idea of comparing the probability of default prediction based on the understanding that the result of predictive accuracy of the estimated probability of default will be more valuable than the binary result of classification. The sorting smoothing method was presented as a novelty in their study to estimate the real probability of defaults. A simple linear regression result was formulated as $Y = A + BX$ where response feature 'Y' = real probability of defaults and independent feature 'X' = predictive probability of defaults. It turned out that ANN was the only model that could accurately estimate the real probability of defaults as compared to all the six models LR, KNN, DA, NB, Classification Trees (CT), and ANN that were studied. ANN performed best with an AUC of 0.54 and an R2 value of 0.9647 as compared to the other models that were experimented with.

A separate line of the study acknowledged the potential problem of an imbalanced dataset that could impact the performance of machine learning algorithms and hence emphasized correcting the data imbalance using various techniques before implementing the models to predict credit card defaults. One such study done by (Luthra et al., 2019) applied balancing techniques like RUS (Random Under sampling), ROS (Random Over Sampling), SMOTE (Synthetic Minority Oversampling Technique), Tomek, SMOTE-Tomek, ENN, and SMOTE-ENN. The balanced dataset thus created was subsequently used by the models like LR, DT, RF, and NB. WOE and IV were used to identify the most significant features.

They successfully proved that performance of models improved after balancing the dataset. They also mentioned extending their research further in the future by adding models like XGBoost and AdaBoost. Another study was carried out by (Alam et al., 2020) where correcting data imbalance was explored using various balancing techniques encompassing under-sampling methods like RUS, near-miss, cluster centroid, and over-sampling methods like ROS, SMOTE, and Adaptive Synthesis (ADASYN) before implementing machine learning algorithms like Gradient Boosting Decision Trees (GBDT).

A study done by (Xu et al., 2018) proposed an algorithm with hybrid model based on repeated incremental pruning to produce an error reduction called Repeated Incremental Pruning to Produce Error Reduction (RIPPER). A targeted specialized pre-treatment method called RELIEF was used to drop the redundant features and further improve the interpretability of the model. RELIEF is a feature weighted algorithm that assigns weights based on correlations and it drops the features that are below a certain threshold. SMOTE over-sampling balancing technique was also used to balance the input dataset. Finally, the defaults are predicted by taking advantage of the rules generated by the RIPPER algorithm. This SMOTE + RELIEF + RIPPER combined forms the hybrid model called SPR-RIPPER. The evaluation metrics used in this study were F1-score, AUC, Accuracy. SPR-RIPPER showed the best performance with an F1-score of 53.4 and an AUC of 0.70.

A novel idea was presented by (Islam et al., 2018) where a heuristic approach to predict defaults was presented. In this approach, two steps were followed. In the first step, also called as Standard Test, the risk probability was precomputed from all the previous transactional data (offline data) and stored in a database. In the second step, also called the Customer-specific test, risk probability was computed for the current transactions on a real-time basis (online data). Finally, overall risk probability was derived by combining scores from both steps. The rules used for both the steps were different. Besides this heuristic approach, they also proposed a novel machine learning approach called Extremely Randomized Trees (ERT) and these do not resample observations when building a tree which was not applied. This ERT is a tree-based ensemble method used for supervised classification or regression problems where randomness goes beyond that of RF and hence found to perform better than RF also. However, they faced a big challenge here because both offline and online transactional data are not available publicly. To overcome this challenge, they had to decompose the Taiwan dataset into offline and online datasets to proceed with their experiment. The standard machine learning models like KNN, RF, NB, GBM, and ERT. Evaluation metrics like accuracy, precision, recall, and F-score were used to evaluate model performance. ERT showed the best performance with an accuracy of 95.84%, precision of 94.87%, recall of 85.85%, and F-score of 90.14%. As part of decomposition, five batches of online transactions were created in total by creating one batch for every month. They were able to improve the recall rate by almost 10% from the first batch (month 1) to the fifth batch (month 5). Also, computation time was fast which means this model was able to predict near real-time and could predict defaults well in advance making it very cost-efficient. They plan to improve the performance of their heuristic model as compared to standard machine learning models in terms of all the evaluation metrics.

Deep Learning Models Applied in Prediction of Payment Defaults

Several works of literature have considered Artificial Neural Networks (ANN) in addition to the standard Data mining techniques. While the traditional statistical algorithms require a formal relationship between the features, ANNs do not require any such relationship between them and are thus better equipped to learn the patterns in data by capturing non-linear relationships. Hence ANNs generally tend to exhibit superior performance and are capable of learning quickly as well. They are popularly called the Universal approximators. However, at the same time, they run the risk of over-fitting and their predictions are sometimes difficult to explain due to their "black box" nature. A typical structure of ANN has an input layer followed by hidden layers and finally an output layer as depicted in Figure 2. ANNs are broadly categorized into Shallow and Deep networks. A Shallow ANN typically has one hidden layer whereas a Deep ANN has more than one hidden layer where a non-linear transformation of the inputs takes place.

Deep learning models or Deep Neural Networks (DNNs) have evolved from ANNs and have more than one hidden layer enabling them to learn from a massive volume of complex observational data, recognize the underlying pattern and classify data into different categories. DNNs have been successfully applied to a wide range of areas from self-driving cars to playing games, from voice recognition to computer vision, from medical diagnosis to natural language understanding. Studies have proven that DNNs perform better than standard machine learning models. DNNs have much greater representational power than traditional ANNs that have a single hidden layer. DNNs need a sufficiently large amount of data to learn complex underlying patterns. They may not perform better than standard machine learning models or ANNs when the dataset is small or simple, but their performance increases significantly as the scale of data increases and is even more pronounced in the case of unstructured data analysis. Quite a few studies have experimented with deep learning models to predict credit card payment defaults and it was observed that these outperformed the other machine learning models especially when the training dataset is large.

Figure 2. Illustration of a simple artificial neural network structure.

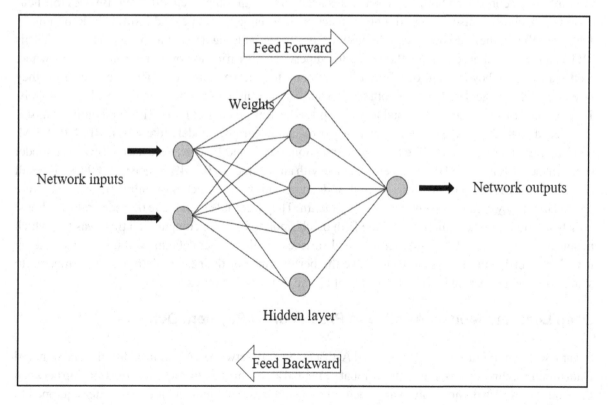

One such study was done by (Sun & Vasarhelyi, 2018) who explored the potential of deep learning in the prediction of the risk of credit card delinquency based on customer characteristics and spending patterns. This study was carried out on Brazil dataset with 6,516,045 records. Optimal hyper-parameters were selected based on grid search where the combination of hyper-parameters with the least validation error was selected. Grid search came up with three hidden layers, 322 neurons in the input layer, the number of neurons in the first, second, and third hidden layers were 175, 350, and 150 respectively. Default Uniform Distribution Initialization (UDI) method was used to randomly initialize the weights. The number of epochs was kept at ten after which the model was overfitting. A learning rate of 0.99 was determined. Epsilon value determined was 1×10^{-8} to ensure that model does not get trapped into local minima. Also, a batch size of 32 was used. Comparing the performance of all models DNN, ANN, LR, NB, and DT, it was observed that DNN performed best with an F1-score of 0.7064, F2 score of 0.6413, F0.5 of 0.7862, overall Accuracy of 99.54%, AUC of 0.955 which was closely followed by ANN and DT. However, the DNN model build time was huge compared to others clocking more than 8 hours. Z-test was additionally performed to confirm that results of DNN are significantly superior to ANN also. Few limitations were presented for future considerations like limited data available including limited time-frame which is indeed a real-life challenge that, when overcome, can significantly improve DNN performance over all other models. Also, DNN could be explored in testing for suspicious cardholders thereby reducing the cost of follow-ups.

One of the studies researched the prediction of credit card defaults using the contemporary approach of ANN which is also known as DNN. They proved that DNN is the only one that can accurately estimate the real probability of defaults. The deep neural network (DNN) was initialized with three hidden layers, each having 28 neurons/nodes. Rectilinear function (RELU) was used as the activation function for the hidden layers and the final output layer's activation function was the Sigmoid function to achieve binary classification into "defaults" and "non-defaults". Stochastic Gradient Descent (SGD) algorithm was used for backpropagation allowing the network to learn through error correction based on the error/loss. The loss function used was 'binary cross-entropy due to binary classification. Also, Accuracy was used as the model's evaluation metric. The model was fit by using different trial values of epochs and batches. Drop-out layers were added after each hidden layer with a drop-out fraction rate of 0.5 which showed satisfactory results. Accuracy of 81.82% was achieved with an F-score of 89.18% (Chishti & Awan, 2019).

RNN has also been used successfully for credit card default prediction especially because these have proven to be useful in time-dependent applications. (Hsu et al., 2019) studied RNN using Gated Recurrent Unit (GRU) as feature extractor on credit card payment history to leverage on time dependencies embedded in these dynamic features. Time dependency is generally ignored in classical classification models. Input sequences are first pre-processed using GRU. These extracted dynamic features along with the static features are used to train an enhanced RNN model combined with Random Forest (RNN-RF) to predict defaults, the architecture of which is shown in Figure 3.

The advantage of RNN-RF model is that static and dynamic features can be combined to provide superior predictive performance. Another variation of RNN, Long Short-Term Memory (LSTM) was not adopted here owing to its complexity. Results of RNN-RF were compared with the classical models like LR, RF, SVM, and KNN. The important point to note here was that GRU and LSTM showed poor lift-index if static features were included which implies that static and dynamic features had to be carefully combined for superior performance. Hence, Classical models were used to extract static features, and GRU was used to extract dynamic features which were later combined and fed to the hybrid RNN-RF model. Additionally, it was noted that the performance of RNN-RF grew steadily with an increase in training data which would happen in real-life industry experience, while classical models did not show considerable improvement.

Figure 3. Illustration of the architecture of the RNN-RF structure

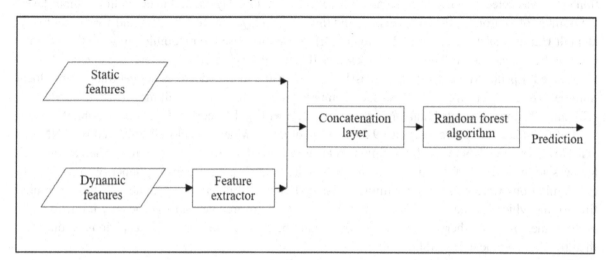

Another different study approach was taken up by (Ebiaredoh-Mienye et al., 2020) where the unsupervised method was used to improve the performance of various classifiers using Stacked Sparse Autoencoder (SSAE). SSAE learns accurate feature representations and the learned features are used to train the classifiers. This study was about comparing the five classifiers with SSAE and the same five classifiers with raw data. The five classifiers experimented with were LR, KNN, CART, SVM, and LDA. Two stacked autoencoders were stacked together to ensure accurate feature representation. The batch normalization technique was applied to prevent overfitting and enhance performance, speed, and stability. It was observed that learned features significantly improve the performance of the classifiers and SSAE-LDA showed the best results with an accuracy of 90% and F1-score of 90% whereas without SSAE, LDA accuracy was 81% and F1-score was 78%.

Evaluation Criteria

The models built on annotated data should generalize well on future unseen data. A decent estimate of the model performance is an important characteristic that is usually computed through measuring accuracy to detect the future predicted behavior. The performance evaluation metrics are broadly classified into the threshold, probability, and ranking metrics. These metrics are scalar group method that presents the classifier performance in a single score value, thus making it easier to compare and contrast the results with other metrics. In most cases, these types of metrics are employed in three different evaluation applications (Hossin & Sulaiman, 2015).

- **Generalization:** In this evaluation, the metrics were used to measure the generalizability and the quality of the summary on the trained classifier. The common metrics utilized for this evaluation consist of accuracy and error.

- **Model Selection:** The best classifier among the different trained classifiers is selected based on the performance of the test set.
- **Discriminator:** The evaluation metrics are employed to discriminate and select the optimum classifier during the validation.

To measure the performance of generalization and model selection, all the three discussed evaluation metrics (threshold, probability, and ranking) can be employed to ensure effectiveness. However, only certain types of metrics from the three categories are utilized for discriminating the classifier such as Receiver Operating Characteristics (ROC) curve and confusion matrix. The commonly used evaluation methods in payment default prediction are listed below.

- **Accuracy:** Measures the correct classification obtained by the classifier in percentage.
- **Precision:** Measures the accuracy of correct predictions out of all the predictions made by the classifier in percentage. It is popularly called a Hit rate.
- **Recall:** Measures the accuracy of correct predictions out of all the actual correct classifications in percentage. It is popularly called a Capture rate.
- **F1-score:** Harmonic mean of precision and recall values of the classifier with a value ranging from 0 to 1 (1 being the best).
- **ROC-AUC:** Measure of the area covered while plotting True Positive Rate (TPR) and False Positive Rate (FPR) together. The value ranges from 0 to 1 with 1 being the best.
- **KS index:** Helps to understand the portion of the population to target to get the highest expected response rate.
- **Gini coefficient:** Indicates a classifier's discriminatory power by showing the effectiveness of discriminating between the class labels.
- **Misclassification cost:** Associated with incorrect classifications by the model. Lower misclassification cost depicts a better-performing model.

DISCUSSIONS AND FUTURE RESEARCH DIRECTIONS

This section presents discussions and future directions of credit card payment defaults. The various significant features that contribute to the prediction of these payment defaults are discussed in detail. Balancing techniques that were experimented with in the existing studies to enhance the prediction power are elaborated in this section. The inclusion of the cost factor into the model performance to give an edge in terms of financial considerations is also presented in this chapter. The section ends with a discussion on the gaps and challenges faced in existing studies and the various ways that can be adopted to achieve the state-of-the-art.

The limit-balance, age, education, times-payment-delayed (derived from repayment-status), and average-payment-amount (derived from payment-amount) seem to be the most significant predictors of credit card payment defaults. Limit-balance is the credit limit of the credit card holder and is negatively correlated with the proportion of defaults. The percentage of defaults seems to decrease substantially with the increase in limit-balance. This makes sense and shows that the banks and financial institutions are doing their part of due diligence in reducing the limit-balance of defaulters thereby minimizing potential loss due to payment defaults. Also, education is observed to be negatively correlated with the proportion of defaults and seems to decrease with an increase in the education level (Choubey, 2018; Sariannidis et al., 2020). Again, this is understandable because higher education level directly relates to a better socio-economic standing and hence lesser defaulters.

The derived variable times-payment-delayed (derived using a count of the number of times payment is delayed for a given customer over 6 months period) is observed as one of the most significant predictors and shows a strong positive correlation with the proportion of defaults (Leong & Jayabalan, 2019). The proportion of defaults increases considerably with the increase in the number of times payment is delayed. Another derived variable average-payment-amount (derived from payment-amount for a given customer over 6 months period) is observed as a significant predictor having a positive correlation with the proportion of defaults. It appears that the defaulters have a lower average-payment-amount as compared to the non-defaulters. This is understandable because defaulters have lower billed-amount (since their limit-balance is lesser compared to non-defaulters) and hence the payment-amount also will be lower as compared to the non-defaulters.

Age is identified as another significant predictor and seems non-linearly related to the proportion of defaults. More specifically, it is observed that the proportion of defaults decrease from the age of the early 20s to the early 30s. Thereafter, a steady increase in the proportion of defaults is observed from the early 30s to the early 60s followed by a sharp decrease in defaults. The proportion of defaults again shows an increase from the early 60s to the 70s, although sample cases reduce substantially. This age is the weakest of the most significant predictors.

The datasets used in anomaly detection (like credit card fraud detection, credit card payment default prediction, and loan default prediction) are generally highly imbalanced with minority class observations being 20% or less of the total observations and majority class observations being 80% or more of the total observations. This class imbalance poses a huge challenge for machine learning models to learn the patterns from the training dataset since data points of the minority class are very few as compared to the majority class. For a dataset with 98% negative events and only 2% positive events, a poorly performing model also could show an accuracy of 98% in predicting negative events and this could be highly misleading since models' accuracy for positive events or anomalies would be minimal which is not desired. Machine learning models are designed assuming a balanced distribution of data points between the class labels for them to learn or train, and hence performance is substantially impacted due to imbalanced datasets. This is where balancing techniques like SMOTE (Synthetic Minority Oversampling Technique) and ADASYN (Adaptive Synthetic) are applied to balance the classes and all models are implemented on balanced and imbalanced datasets for comparing their performance (Alam et al., 2020; Luthra et al., 2019). It is observed that the models implemented on balanced datasets generalize better in testing datasets with better AUC value, F1-score, Gini coefficient and show lesser misclassification cost proving to be more powerful in prediction and cost-effective as compared to the models implemented on the imbalanced dataset. The oversampling balancing techniques balance the classes equally well, helping the classifier models to generalize much better and boost the predictive power in the testing dataset. The overfitting remains a big issue in machine learning algorithms wherein models tend to learn the data points instead of learning the patterns and hence do not generalize well in test datasets.

The misclassification cost is one of the important metrics while determining the most cost-effective prediction classifier models. The misclassification cost is formulated by assigning cost factors to the misclassifications measured through false-positives and false-negatives derived using the confusion matrix. False-Negative refers to misclassification where defaulters are misclassified as non-defaulters. False-Positive refers to misclassification where non-defaulters are misclassified as defaulters. Hence, it makes sense to assign a higher misclassification cost factor to False-Negatives (FN) as compared to False-Positives (FP) because misclassifying defaulters as non-defaulters can potentially cause much higher losses to credit card companies as compared to misclassifying non-defaulters as defaulters.

The concept of drift is another major challenge in credit card defaults since there could be a vast change in the behavior pattern of payment defaulters and non-defaulters over time. For instance, the models that learn these patterns dated fifteen years back may not be able to relevant to predict the recent patterns properly that have changed over time. Hence, the researchers should consider the most recent data so that models remain relevant in predicting defaulters effectively with high precision. Another recommendation is to obtain a larger training database for models to learn more patterns of defaulters so that a better generalization can be achieved thereby improving model performance. Lastly, the default prediction power of machine learning models can be improved further by making more significant variables such as types of other active credits, payment history of other credits, and longer credit history for better learning.

Further works can also include enhanced variants of balancing techniques like SMOTE-ENN, borderline-SMOTE, SVM-SMOTE, and others to better balance the classes and enhance model performance based on experiments done by (Alam et al., 2020; Luthra et al., 2019). Also, tuning the model hyperparameters by first using randomized-search to get a more relevant hyperparameter range and then performing grid-search on the identified hyperparameter range to determine the optimal hyperparameters could also enhance the model performance.

CONCLUSION

Credit card defaults are a huge concern for banking and financial services institutions and several data mining techniques have been experimented with in the existing studies. Data mining techniques comprised machine learning models, deep learning models, and time series models, all being experimented with to predict credit card payment defaults. Including cost-factor in these models enable the business to make better and well-informed strategic decisions. This being an anomaly detection study, the datasets available are generally imbalanced, and hence employing balancing techniques improve model performance considerably. Hyperparameter tuning using a ten-fold cross-validation process further boosts the prediction power of the models. Also, evaluation metrics like AUC, precision, recall, and F1-score tend to be more relevant as compared to accuracy because of the anomalies. This chapter presented the most common issues to be dealt with whilst the organizations adopt effective methods to minimize the losses caused by payment defaults. Moreover, this research highlights some of the research gaps that can be improved upon to achieve the state-of-the-art.

REFERENCES

Alam, T. M., Shaukat, K., Hameed, I. A., Luo, S., Sarwar, M. U., Shabbir, S., Li, J., & Khushi, M. (2020). An Investigation of Credit Card Default Prediction in the Imbalanced Datasets. *IEEE Access: Practical Innovations, Open Solutions*, 8, 201173–201198. doi:10.1109/ACCESS.2020.3033784

Bellotti, T., & Crook, J. (2013). Forecasting and Stress Testing Credit Card Default using Dynamic Models. *International Journal of Forecasting*, *29*(4), 563–574. doi:10.1016/j.ijforecast.2013.04.003

Charleonnan, A. (2016). Credit Card Fraud Detection using RUS and MRN Algorithms. *2016 Management and Innovation Technology International Conference (MITicon)*, MIT-73-MIT-76. 10.1109/MITICON.2016.8025244

Chishti, W. A., & Awan, S. M. (2019). Deep Neural Network a Step-by-Step Approach to Classify Credit Card Default Customer. *2019 International Conference on Innovative Computing (ICIC)*, 1–8. 10.1109/ICIC48496.2019.8966723

Choubey, A. M. (2018). *Predicting Credit Default Risk via Statistical Model and Machine Learning Algorithms* (Masters Thesis in Economics). The University of North Carolina at Charlotte (UNCC).

Datkhile, A., Chandak, K., Bhandari, S., Gajare, H., & Karyakarte, M. (2020). Statistical Modelling on Loan Default Prediction Using Different Models. *IJRESM*, *3*(3), 3–5.

de Castro Vieira, J. R., Barboza, F., Sobreiro, V. A., & Kimura, H. (2019). Machine Learning Models for Credit Analysis Improvements: Predicting low-income families' default. *Applied Soft Computing*, *83*, 105640. doi:10.1016/j.asoc.2019.105640

Ebiaredoh-Mienye, S. A., Esenogho, E., & Swart, T. (2020). *Effective Feature Learning using Stacked Sparse Autoencoder for Improved prediction of Credit Card Default*. Project. https://www.researchgate.net/profile/Ebenezer-Esenogho/publication/341510387_Effective_Feature_Learning_using_Stacked_Sparse_Autoencoder_for_Improved_prediction_of_Credit_Card_Default/links/5ec515a6458515626cb85ac0/Effective-Feature-Learning-using-Stacked-Sparse-Autoencoder-for-Improved-prediction-of-Credit-Card-Default.pdf

Gupta, D. K., & Goyal, S. (2018). Credit Risk Prediction Using Artificial Neural Network Algorithm. *International Journal of Modern Education and Computer Science*, *10*(5), 9–16. doi:10.5815/ijmecs.2018.05.02

Ho Ha, S., & Krishnan, R. (2012). Predicting Repayment of the Credit Card Debt. *Computers & Operations Research*, *39*(4), 765–773. doi:10.1016/j.cor.2010.10.032

Hossin, M., & Sulaiman, M.N. (2015). A Review on Evaluation Metrics for Data Classification Evaluations. *International Journal of Data Mining & Knowledge Management Process*, *52*, 1–11.

Hsu, T. C., Liou, S. T., Wang, Y. P., Huang, Y. S., & Che-Lin. (2019). Enhanced Recurrent Neural Network for Combining Static and Dynamic Features for Credit Card Default Prediction. *ICASSP, IEEE International Conference on Acoustics, Speech and Signal Processing - Proceedings*, 1572–1576. doi:10.1109/ICASSP.2019.8682212

Islam, S. R., Eberle, W., & Ghafoor, S. K. (2018). *Credit Default Mining using Combined Machine Learning and Heuristic Approach*. ArXiv.

Kruppa, J., Schwarz, A., Arminger, G., & Ziegler, A. (2013). Consumer Credit Risk: Individual Probability Estimates using Machine Learning. *Expert Systems with Applications*, *40*(13), 5125–5131. doi:10.1016/j.eswa.2013.03.019

Lai, L. (2020). Loan Default Prediction with Machine Learning Techniques. *2020 International Conference on Computer Communication and Network Security (CCNS)*, 5–9. 10.1109/CCNS50731.2020.00009

Leong, O. J., & Jayabalan, M. (2019). A Comparative Study on Credit Card Default Risk Predictive Model. *Journal of Computational and Theoretical Nanoscience*, *16*(8), 3591–3595. doi:10.1166/jctn.2019.8330

Leow, M., & Crook, J. (2014). Intensity Models and Transition Probabilities for Credit Card Loan Delinquencies. *European Journal of Operational Research*, *236*(2), 685–694. doi:10.1016/j.ejor.2013.12.026

Li, Y., Li, Y., & Li, Y. (2019). What factors are Influencing Credit Card Customer's Default Behavior in China? A study based on survival analysis. *Physica A*, *526*, 120861. doi:10.1016/j.physa.2019.04.097

Luthra, R., Nath, G., & Chellani, R. (2019). *A Review on Class Imbalanced Correction Techniques: A Case of Credit Card Default Prediction on A Highly Imbalanced Dataset*. Praxis Business School.

Mazumder, S. (2020). *Comparative Study of Five Supervised Machine Learning Methods*. doi:10.13140/RG.2.2.16997.14568

Mbuvha, R., Boulkaibet, I., & Marwala, T. (2019). *Automatic Relevance Determination Bayesian Neural Networks for Credit Card Default Modelling*. ArXiv.

Neema, S., & Soibam, B. (2017). The Comparison of Machine Learning Methods to achieve Most Cost-Effective Prediction for Credit Card Default. *Journal of Management Science and Business Intelligence*, *9264*, 36–41. doi:10.5281/zenodo.851527

Sariannidis, N., Papadakis, S., Garefalakis, A., Lemonakis, C., & Kyriaki-Argyro, T. (2020). Default Avoidance on Credit Card Portfolios using Accounting, Demographical and Exploratory Factors: Decision Making based on Machine Learning (ML) Techniques. *Annals of Operations Research*, *294*(1–2), 715–739. doi:10.100710479-019-03188-0

Sayjadah, Y., Hashem, I. A. T., Alotaibi, F., & Kasmiran, K. A. (2018). Credit Card Default Prediction using Machine Learning Techniques. *2018 Fourth International Conference on Advances in Computing, Communication & Automation (ICACCA)*, 1–4. 10.1109/ICACCAF.2018.8776802

Sun, T., & Vasarhelyi, M. A. (2018). Predicting Credit Card Delinquencies: An Application of Deep Neural Networks. *Intelligent Systems in Accounting, Finance & Management*, *25*(4), 174–189. doi:10.1002/isaf.1437

Ullah, M. A., Alam, M. M., Sultana, S., & Toma, R. S. (2018). Predicting Default Payment of Credit Card Users: Applying Data Mining Techniques. *2018 International Conference on Innovations in Science, Engineering and Technology (ICISET), October*, 355–360. 10.1109/ICISET.2018.8745571

Xu, P., Ding, Z., & Pan, M. (2017). An Improved Credit Card Users Default Prediction Model based on RIPPER. *2017 13th International Conference on Natural Computation, Fuzzy Systems and Knowledge Discovery (ICNC-FSKD)*, 1785–1789. 10.1109/FSKD.2017.8393037

Xu, P., Ding, Z., & Pan, M. Q. (2018). A Hybrid Interpretable Credit Card Users Default Prediction Model based on RIPPER. *Concurrency and Computation*, *30*(23), 1–12. doi:10.1002/cpe.4445

Yang, S., & Zhang, H. (2018). Comparison of Several Data Mining Methods in Credit Card Default Prediction. *Intelligent Information Management*, *10*(05), 115–122. doi:10.4236/iim.2018.105010

Yeh, I.-C., & Lien, C. (2009). The Comparisons of Data Mining Techniques for the Predictive Accuracy of Probability of Default of Credit Card Clients. *Expert Systems with Applications*, *36*(2), 2473–2480. doi:10.1016/j.eswa.2007.12.020

Yontar, M., Namli, Ö. H., & Yanik, S. (2020). Using Machine Learning Techniques to develop Prediction Models for Detecting Unpaid Credit Card Customers. *Journal of Intelligent & Fuzzy Systems*, *39*(5), 6073–6087. doi:10.3233/JIFS-189080

Yu, Y. (2020). The Application of Machine Learning Algorithms in Credit Card Default Prediction. *2020 International Conference on Computing and Data Science (CDS)*, 212–218. 10.1109/CDS49703.2020.00050

ADDITIONAL READING

Hu, Y., Ren, Y., & Wang, Q. (2019) A Feature Selection Based on Network Structure for Credit Card Default Prediction. Communications in Computer and Information Science, 1042 CCIS, August, pp.275–286.

Husejinovic, A., Keco, D., & Masetic, Z. (2018). Application of Machine Learning Algorithms in Credit Card Default Payment Prediction. *International Journal of Scientific Research*, *7*(10), 425–426.

Li, W., Ding, S., Chen, Y., Wang, H. and Yang, S., (2019) Transfer learning-based default prediction model for consumer credit in China. *Journal of Supercomputing*, *752*, 862–884. https://doi.org/. doi:10.1007/s11227-018-2619-8

Mei, R., Xu, Y., & Wang, G. (2016). Study on Analysis and Influence Factors of Credit Card Default Prediction Model. *Statistics and Application*, *503*(3), 263–275. doi:10.12677/SA.2016.53026

Ogundimu, E. O. (2019). Prediction of Default Probability by using Statistical Models for Rare Events. *Journal of the Royal Statistical Society. Series A, (Statistics in Society)*, *1824*(4), 1143–1162. doi:10.1111/rssa.12467

Shan, H. (2019). Research on Bank Credit Card Default Prediction Based on Machine Learning. *Hans Journal of Data Mining*, *0904*, 145–152.

Subasi, A., & Cankurt, S. (2019) Prediction of Default Payment of Credit Card Clients using Data Mining Techniques. *Proceedings of the 5th International Engineering Conference, IEC 2019*, pp.115–120. 10.1109/IEC47844.2019.8950597

Wang, Q., Hu, Y., & Li, J. (2018). Community-based Feature Selection for Credit Card Default Prediction. *Studies in Computational Intelligence*, *689*(January), 153–165. doi:10.1007/978-3-319-72150-7_13

KEY TERMS AND DEFINITIONS

ADASYN (Adaptive Synthetic): An algorithm that generates synthetic data, and its greatest advantages are not copying the same minority data, and generating more data for "harder to learn" examples.

Balancing Techniques: These are techniques employed to overcome the class imbalance problem in a given dataset that significantly impacts the performance of the machine learning model. The techniques either employ over-sampling or under-sampling methods to overcome the balancing problem. Some of the popular balancing techniques are ROS, SMOTE, and ADASYN.

Class Imbalance: When the observations or data points associated with an event is rare as compared to the data points or observations associated with the non-event, then the situation is called an imbalanced class. Typically, the data distribution percentage of data points in such cases range from 99:1 to 70:30 between majority and minority class respectively. The data which is available for typical classification problems like fraud detection and default prediction have such severe class imbalance.

Credit Card: Plastic cards issued by Banks or Financial institutions with a pre-assigned credit limit for customers to make purchases at retail stores (also called merchants) or even online.

Cross-Validation: This is a region formed out of the Training dataset with the primary objective of hyperparameter tuning the machine learning models to achieve the best performance. This entire process of hyperparameter tuning using a cross-validation region is called a cross-validation process.

Hyperparameter: These are model parameters that can be manually configured (through expert judgment or empirical results) to achieve optimal performance. Every machine learning model has its own set of hyperparameters.

Hyperparameter Tuning: This is a process of fine-tuning the hyperparameters to achieve optimal model performance. This process typically involves randomized-search or grid-search methods applied in 5-fold or 10-fold cross-validation regions.

Misclassification Cost: Cost associated with the wrong classification of an event. In this chapter, the event is "payment default". Hence, this misclassification cost is assigned to the model that wrongly predicts payment default as a non-default (Type-2 error which is more dangerous) and non-default as a payment default (Type-1 error).

Payment Default: Inability of the customer to make payment of the total due amount owed to the issuer by the specified due date. This applies to credit cards, housing loans, education loans, personal loans, or any similar product offered by banks or financial institutions.

RIPPER (Repeated Incremental Pruning to Produce Error Reduction): Algorithm introduced by W. Cohen in 1995, which improved upon IREP (Incremental Reduced Error Pruning Algorithm) of Furnkranz and Widmer in 1994 by generating rules that match or exceed the performance of decision trees. Having evolved from several iterations of the rule learning algorithm, the RIPPER algorithm can be understood in a three-step process: Grow, Prune, Optimize.

Significant Features: These are the independent or explanatory features or variables that can significantly explain the dependent feature or variable.

SMOTE (The Synthetic Minority Over-Sampling Technique): An oversampling approach that creates synthetic minority class samples.

APPENDIX

Table 1. Summary of reviews based on models, dataset, and primary evaluation metric

Models category	Author(s), Year	Dataset	Number of features	Observations	Data mining technique	Primary evaluation metric and result
Regular machine learning models	(Ullah et al., 2018)	Taiwan	25	30,000	AdaBoost	Accuracy = 88.00%
	(Sariannidis et al., 2020)	Taiwan	25	30,000	SVC	Accuracy = 81.65%
	(Yu, 2020)	Taiwan	25	30,000	Random forest	Accuracy = 82.12%
	(Mazumder, 2020)	Taiwan	25	30,000	Random forest	Accuracy = 90.90%
	(Sayjadah et al., 2018)	Taiwan	25	30,000	Random forest	AUC = 0.77
	(Yontar et al., 2020)	Taiwan bank	24	10,713	CART	Accuracy = 86.00%
	(Yang and Zhang, 2018)	Taiwan	25	30,000	LightGBM	AUC = 0.79
	(Choubey, 2018)	Taiwan	25	30,000	Random forest	AUC = 0.76
	(Neema and Soibam, 2017)	Taiwan	25	30,000	ANN	Accuracy = 82.30%
	(Charleonnan, 2016)	Taiwan	25	30,000	RUSMRN	Accuracy = 79.73%
	(Yeh and Lien, 2009)	Taiwan	25	30,000	ANN	$R^2 = 0.9647$
	(Leong and Jayabalan, 2019)	Taiwan	25	30,000	ANN	AUC = 0.75
	(Xu et al., 2018)	Taiwan	25	30,000	AdaBoost	Accuracy = 88.00%
	(Islam et al., 2018)	Taiwan	25	30,000	ERT	Accuracy = 95.84%
	(Mbuvha et al., 2019)	Taiwan	25	30,000	HMC – ARD	AUC = 0.78
	(Luthra et al., 2019)	Credit defaults	29	Not available	Random forest	AUC = 0.67
	(Alam et al., 2020)	Taiwan	25	30,000	GBDT	Accuracy = 88.70%
Time series models	(Ho Ha and Krishnan, 2012)	Not available	17	Not available	SOM + Cox proportional hazard model	Accuracy = 95.80%
	(Leow and Crook, 2014)	UK bank	Not available	49,000	Intensity model	Accuracy = 83.00%
	(Bellotti and Crook, 2013)	UK bank	23	750,000	Discreet time survival model	MAE = 0.049
	(Li et al., 2019)	China commercial bank	23	60,000	Cox proportional hazard model	Not available

Continued on following page

Table 1. Continued

Models category	Author(s), Year	Dataset	Number of features	Observations	Data mining technique	Primary evaluation metric and result
Deep learning models	(Sun and Vasarhelyi, 2018)	Brazil bank	44	6,516,045	ANN	AUC = 0.95
	(Chishti and Awan, 2019)	Taiwan	25	30,000	RUSMRN	Accuracy = 79.73%
	(Hsu et al., 2019)	Taiwan	25	30,000	RNN – RF	AUC = 0.78
	(Ebiaredoh-mienye et al., 2020)	Taiwan	25	30,000	SSAE – LDA	Accuracy = 90.00%

Chapter 12
Inflation Rate Modelling Through a Hybrid Model of Seasonal Autoregressive Moving Average and Multilayer Perceptron Neural Network

Mogari Ishmael Rapoo
https://orcid.org/0000-0002-3602-7016
North-West University, South Africa

Martin Chanza
North-West University, South Africa

Gomolemo Motlhwe
North-West University, South Africa

ABSTRACT

This study examines the performance of seasonal autoregressive integrated moving average (SARIMA), multilayer perceptron neural networks (MLPNN), and hybrid SARIMA-MLPNN model(s) in modelling and forecasting inflation rate using the monthly consumer price index (CPI) data from 2010 to 2019 obtained from the South African Reserve Bank (SARB). The forecast errors in inflation rate forecasting are analyzed and compared. The study employed root mean squared error (RMSE) and mean absolute error (MAE) as performance measures. The results indicate that significant improvements in forecasting accuracy are obtained with the hybrid model (SARIMA-MLPNN) compared to the SARIMA and MLPNN. The MLPNN model outperformed the SARIMA model. However, the hybrid SARIMA-MLPNN model outperformed both the SARIMA and MLPNN in terms of forecasting accuracy/accuracy performance.

DOI: 10.4018/978-1-7998-8455-2.ch012

INTRODUCTION

Time series predicting is indeed a very powerful and essential area of interest that has grabbed the thinking of academics worldwide. Time series forecasting helps in better preparation for the future. It is widely applied in the field of econometrics, weather forecasting, finance, and engineering. Based on historical values, the ultimate goal is to establish a model where future values can best be predicted (Datta, 2011). Time series forecasting focuses primarily on collecting and analyzing past values to create models that best understands the underlying characteristics of the time series data.

Many time series models have been in use for years to improve the effectiveness and the reliability of predictions. These time series models can either be classified as univariate or multivariate models. Univariate models consist of one variable and observations of that variable are recorded consecutively over the same spaced time intervals, whereas in contrast, multivariate time series models are applicable where there is more than two variables with their respective observations (Chatfield, 2000).

There are a number of commonly applied models to modelling and forecasting time series. Amongst a few, there is Exponential smoothing where the series is decayed into a trend and seasonal element. Other approaches include Multiple Linear Regression (MLR). The disadvantage of using MLR is that it assumes that there is a linear relationship between the predictor and the dependent variables. Both Support Vector Regression (SVR) and MLR are applied in modelling multivariate time series data.

The Autoregressive Integrated Moving Average (ARIMA) model or the Box-Jenkins method is one of the most widely used and acknowledged statistical models of time series forecasting. Furthermore, The Seasonal Autoregressive Integrated Moving Average (SARIMA) model, in particular, includes a seasonal component and is used to capture seasonal trends existing in a time series. Time series modelling and forecasting have often been applied in various fields of econometrics, weather forecasting, finance and engineering (Hyndman & Athanasopoulos, 2018). However, forecasting financial time series is more complex and challenging due to nonlinear trends and random walks, that is where the application of Artificial Neural Networks (ANNs) or simply Neural Networks (NN) came into play.

ANNs are the recent and most widely used methods to forecast and resolve challenges faced by linear models in forecasting more complex and nonlinear time series data. ANNs have the ability to detect any underlying structures in the data, making them appropriate for usage in forecasting. Without human interference, ANNs can automatically learn how to implement predictions on their own (Zhang, Patuwo, & Hu, 1998). There are several kinds of feed-forward artificial neural networks, one type includes a feed-forward Multilayer Perceptron Neural Networks (MLPNNs).

Cang (2011) defines Multilayer Perceptron Neural Networks (MLPNNs) as a type of the Neural Network that is trained to approximate any function, does not make any assumptions regarding the distribution/structure of the data and can model highly nonlinear and irregular data or functions. These types of models are built on the basis of biological neural networks. There has been a lot of development in research in terms of applying hybrid models in forecasting time series data. Most scholars have applied the same logic and argued that this system can improve the forecasting performance of the model.

(Areekul, Senjyu, & Yona, 2010; Ghahnavieh, 2019; Khandelwal, Adhikari, & Verma, 2015; Prayoga, Suhartono, & Rahayu, 2017) suggest that hybrid models can be efficient means of improving the predictive reliability obtained by either of the separately used models. Essentially, the hybrid approach is a mixture of two or several model types. These kinds of models appear to increase the reliability of predictions in forecasting the time series. Motivated by these researches, this study sought to compare the forecasting performance of SARIMA, MLPNN and a hybrid SARIMA-MLPNN in terms of modelling and forecasting inflation rate of South Africa using CPI time series data. The paper is organized as follows. Section 2 will briefly present literature review of the hybrid model, SARIMA and MLPNN models respectively. Section 3 is the presentation of the methodology of the models, whereas in section 4 there is application of the proposed model(s) to Consumer Price Index (CPI) time series data and section 5 will be the last section which will cover concluding remarks of the study.

BACKGROUND

Hybrid Models and Artificial Neural Networks (ANNs)

In the recent past there has been various combinations of models which forms what we call hybrid models or hybrid systems. The sole reason for hybrid models is to use the singular or multiple features that each model has in order to capture all the properties or characteristics presented in a time series data. Hybrid models can either be used as models that are homogenous or heterogeneous. Meaning they can either be used as linear models (homogenous) or being linear and nonlinear models (heterogeneous).

The main aim is to build models that can be able to take care of the properties of the series. This being the case will then tend to improve the forecasting performance of the models because all the aspects of the series would have been taken care of in terms of the modelling part of the series. In terms of neural networks forecasting, both the theoretical and empirical evidence suggests that hybrid models can be effective and efficient way of improving forecasting (Makridakis, 1989; Palm & Zellner, 1992).

Researchers have attempted to create a model that combines two or more models (hybrid models) to account for both linear and nonlinear variation in the data. This sort of model appears to generate better outcomes than individual models in forecasting time series data. Guimaraes Santos and Silva (2014) compared the quality of wavelet–ANN hybrid and ANN models for different average streamflow forecasts. The wavelet-ANN models showed meaningfully improved outcomes for all the cases tested relative to the ANN models. The results they obtained demonstrated and evaluated the advantages of using wavelet transformation in standard streamflow forecasting using ANNs, though perhaps restricted to a single application. This hybrid approach's excellent performance promoted the development of fresh studies on this topic.

Merh, Saxena, and Pardasani (2010) outlined three-layer hybrid models of the ARIMA and ANN to forecast the future index value and trend of the Indian stock market. The ARIMA predicted values in relation to the actual stock value showed to be better than those predicted by the ANNs. The results showed that the BSE 30 (SENSEX), BSE IT and S&P CNX Nifty ANN-ARIMA hybrid model forecast was better than the ARIMA-ANN hybrid, although 100 ARIMA-ANN findings were significantly better than the BSE ANN-ARIMA hybrid model. The hybrid model from ARIMA-ANN revealed a statement of overfitting. The results also showed that BSE Oil & Gas ANN and hybrid ANN-ARIMA were capable of managing input data set and predicting future closing prices, whereas ARIMA and ARIMA-ANN could not predict future values.

Faruk (2010) used ARIMA, ANN and hybrid ARIMA-ANN in his study to model and forecast 108 water quality data for the Buyuk Menderes River. The hybrid model offered much greater precision over ARIMA and neural network models to predict water quality. In particular, the hybrid model results provided a solid modelling framework capable of capturing the non-linear nature of the complex time series and thus producing predictions that were more accurate.

Arunraj and Ahrens (2015) explored the efficiency of sales data modelling and forecasting of SARIMA-MLR and SARIMA-QR models. Their findings showed that the models SARIMAMLR and SARIMA-QR provided improved over-the-counter forecasts compared to seasonal naive forecasts and classical approaches to SARIMA and MLPNN.

Wang, Wang, Zhang, and Guo (2012) developed a hybrid model combining Exponential Smoothing Model (ESM), ARIMA, and Back-Propagation Neural Network (BPNN). The generic algorithm determines the weight of the suggested hybrid model. The actual stock indices dataset was used as illustrative examples to demonstrate the hybrid model's better performance. The Shenzhen Integrated Index (SZII) closure and the Dow Jones Industrial Average Index (DJIAI) opening were used as illustrative examples to evaluate the proposed hybrid model's efficiency. Statistical findings indicated that the suggested model exceeded all traditional models, including BPNN, ESM, EWH, ARIMA, and RWM. A potential future study discussion is the development of a hybrid model for forecasting daily or even hourly information where a more critical problem is how to enhance computation time. For short-term investors, such a model is more essential. A further approach is to investigate the option of mixing other forecasting instruments such as Supporting Vector Regression (SVR) and Multivariate Adaptive Regression Splines (MARS) to further enhance the forecasting of time series.

Ali et al. (2017) applied MLPNN methodology in drought predicting. The study used monthly Standardized Precipitation Evapotranspiration Index (SPEI) time-series data for 17 weather stations in Pakistan and the Northern area. Based on the correlation coefficient, RMSE, and MAE, the MLPNN approach has the potential ability to predict drought. Relevant decision makers can take necessary precautions by utilizing MLPNN as part of their policymaking.

Ali et al. (2017) stated that MLPNN is part of an ANN general class structure called a neural feed-forward network. The neural networks of feed-forward are able to approximate both continuous and integrable processes. The MLPNN's network structure comprises of layered neurons. In the MLPNN model, all input nodes are in one layer and hidden layers are distributed in one or more hidden layers.

Seasonal Autoregressive Integrated Moving Average Model (SARIMA) and Autoregressive Integrated Moving Average (ARIMA) Model

Alnaa and Ahiakpor (2011) used Box Jenkin's methodology to forecast Inflation in Ghana. Ghana Statistical Service was used to obtain monthly data for this variable from June 2000 to December 2010. ARIMA (6, 1, 6) was found to be the most appropriate model to forecast inflation with Root Mean Square Error (RMSE) of 0.115453 which suggests the effectiveness of the model. The forecasts from the model recommended that the ARIMA model may also be competent and capable of predicting Ghana's inflation. The selected model suggested that price increases seem to have a long memory, so precautionary measures to stabilize inflation should be put in place. Whenever the highest peak (spiral) of inflation occurs, bringing it to its steady state can take a period of 12 months.

Chinonso and Justice (2016) used monthly CPI information from January 2001 to December 2015 to model urban and rural inflation in Nigeria. This Consumer Price Index (CPI) is a measure of the average shift in the prices of consumer goods over a period of time, i.e. products and services that individuals purchase for daily living. Box-Jenkins ARIMA Model was used to model 180 monthly CPI figures and was forecast to have 29 monthly CPI figures, which effectively included two quarterly CPI information. The model recognized that both mean and variance were rising over time, the data being dependent and not distributed identically. ARIMA (0, 1, 0), and ARIMA (0, 1, 13) were chosen and showed to be right, the residuals showed small auto-correlated residuals and followed a normal distribution with mean zero and continuous variance.

Nyoni (2018) studied ARIMA and GARCH methods in modelling and forecasting inflation in Kenya. Historical time series data on inflation was collected over the period 1960-2017. After analysis, the resulted models were ARIMA (1, 2, 0), ARIMA (2, 2, 1), GARCH (1, 1) and AR (1) model, as they had the lowest AIC value and Theil's U value. The results of the study indicate that both ARIMA (1, 2, 0) and ARIMA (2, 2, 1) is efficient and adequate to forecast inflation in Kenya. The results further indicated that inflation was expected to remain increasing. The study was intended to assist policy-makers in sustaining and maintaining price levels in Kenya.

Abdulrahman, Ahmed, and Abdellah (2018) applied the Box-Jenkins approach to building an ARIMA model to forecast Sudan's inflation rates. They took the first and second differences to stabilize the series. ARIMA (1, 2, 1) was found to be the most adequate model to forecast Sudan Inflation rates as it had the lowest RMSE. By assessing the performance of the model it was found that there was some overlap between forecasted values and actual values from the year 1970 to 2016. Using forecasted values, inflation appeared to rise in the future.

Nyoni and Nathaniel (2018) studied inflation rates in Nigeria for a period between 1960 and 2016. The study applied the procedures of ARMA, ARIMA, and GARCH models to illustrate and forecast inflation rates in Nigeria. The ADF test suggested that Nigeria's inflation time series data was essentially stationary after the first difference, even though it was in general stationary at a significance level of 10 percent. The analysis identified the ARMA (1, 0, 2) as the best model based on the minimum Theil's U prediction evaluation statistic. Furthermore, standard tests clearly show that the presented models are stable and therefore efficient. Research findings showed that inflation is likely to increase to about 17 percent per year in Nigeria by the end of 2021 and is likely to exceed that level by 2027.

Álvarez-Díaz, González-Gómez, and Otero-Giráldez (2019) compared the performance of ANN (NAR Neural Network), Generic Programming, and SARIMA model. The study utilized monthly international tourism demand in Spain. SARIMA (0, 1, 2) (1, 1, 1) version was selected as the best SARIMA model as it had the lowest BIC and MAPE values in the in-sample period. NAR network outperformed the forecasts of the rest of the models. The non-linear models generate good forecasts in comparison with the SARIMA model. The study recommends that new researches should examine whether combining forecasts can achieve better forecasting results than those given by linear models.

METHODOLOGY

In this section forecasting methods which are SARIMA, MLPNN and hybrid SARIMA-MLPNN are introduced. These models will be subjected to go under appropriate assessments and furthermore model diagnostics will be performed accordingly.

Seasonal Autoregressive Integrated Moving Average (SARIMA) Model

The time series autoregressive integrated moving average (ARIMA) model displaying frequent variations during the same month each year or during the same quarter each year are referred to as seasonal autoregressive integrated moving average (SARIMA) models or SARIMA models for convenience. The SARIMA model is commonly expressed as, where s is the seasonal period. Box-Jenkins now recommends the $ARIMA(p,d,q)(P,D,Q)_s$ model for dealing with time series incorporating seasonal fluctuations which can also be expressed as:

$$\left(1-\varphi_{1B}-\varphi_2 B^2-\ldots-\varphi_p B^p\right)\left(1-\Phi_1 B^s-\ldots-\Phi_p B^{sp}\right)\left(1-B\right)^d\left(1-B\right)^D$$
$$=\left(1-\theta_1 B-\theta_2 B^2-\ldots-\theta_q B^q\right)\left(1-\theta_1 B^s-\ldots-\theta_Q B^{sQ}\right)\varepsilon_t \tag{1}$$

The above formulae (1) can be summarized by the following representation:

$$\varphi B\Phi\left(B^S\right)\nabla^D_S\nabla_d=\theta\left(B\right)\theta\left(B^S\right)\varepsilon_t \tag{2}$$

given that $\tilde{N}_d=(1-B)^d$ are non-seasonal differences, $\tilde{N}^D_S=(1-B^S)^D$ are seasonal differences, $\Phi_1 B^S$ are seasonal autoregressive orders, $\theta 1_B S$ are seasonal moving average orders, $\varphi 1B_a$ re non-seasonal autoregressive orders, $\theta 1$ a$_r$e non-seasonal moving average orders, and εt is the random error, $\varepsilon t\sim WN_{(0},\sigma 2\varepsilon)$ th^a_t is, the error term is white noise (zero mean and constant variance) (Box et al., 2015). This model will be subjected to assessments.

Multilayer Perceptron (MLP) Neural Networks

The principle of artificial neural networks (ANN) has been used for nearly 50 years, it could only be known in the late 1980s that it has achieved substantial use in scientific and technical development. ANN is a mathematical concept with a brain-like structure that is highly connected. A neural network is a device that simulates how the brain performs a particular task. It resembles the brain in two ways: first, through a learning process, the network acquires information from its settings, and second, the strengths of the interneuron relationships are used to store the knowledge acquired, established by synaptic weights (Guresen, Kayakutlu, & Daim, 2011).

A key benefit of ANN models over other nonlinear model categories is that ANNs are generic approximates with a high degree of accuracy that can estimate a large class of functions. Their strength comes from the parallel data processing of information. No previous assumption of the design type is necessary for the model building process. Rather, the network model is strongly influenced by the features of the data. Neural networks can be used to analyze the data and identify trends that can be too difficult and complex for human beings or other analysis techniques to capture through their exceptional ability to infer significance from complicated or unclear data (Guresen et al., 2011).

ANNs are effective computing tools designed to model a number of nonlinear problems. Some benefits include the potential to truly understand how to perform tasks based on the data set as a preparation and initial experience, the ANN can create its own organization or represent the data it collects during the learning process, ANN algorithms can be conducted in parallel, and special hardware devices can be designed and produced using this functionality (Yadav et al., 2014).

An ANN model often involves three layers: the very first layer is the input layer where the data is announced to the network, the network is performed on a digital computer simulation using a software. The second layer is the hidden layer of information processing. This layer is the interface between the layers of input and output. One of the important tasks in this layer is to determine the type of activation function (g) which determines the relationship between the layer of input and output. A widespread activation function(s) is supported by neural networks that are logistic, linear, quadratic and tanh (Khashei & Hajirahimi, 2018). Figure 1 displays the architecture of a Multilayer Perceptron neural network.

Figure 1. MLPNN architecture (Source: Personal Collection)

MLP

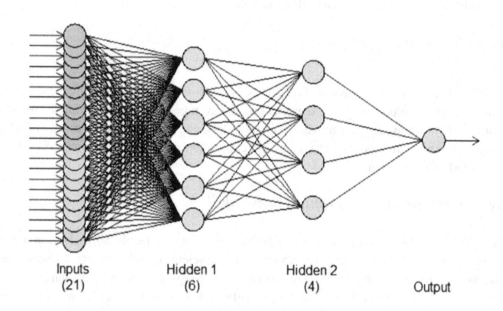

| Inputs (21) | Hidden 1 (6) | Hidden 2 (4) | Output |

The related subject is the choice of a transfer function. The logistic function is often used as the hidden layer transfer function, that is,

$$g(x) = \frac{1}{1+e^{-x}} \tag{3}$$

Khashei and Zahra (2019) further define the tanh function as

$$Tah(x) = \frac{1-e^{-2x}}{1+e^{-2x}} \tag{4}$$

and sigmoid as,

$$sig(x) = \frac{1}{1+e^{-x}} \tag{5}$$

Rezaeian-Zadeh and Tabari (2012) mentioned that the most widely used transfer functions are the logistic sigmoid and tangent functions. They also point out that ANNs with the logistic sigmoid function are more hard to train than ANNs with the tangent function, that training with the tangent function is not only quicker than training with the logistic sigmoid transfer function, but also that the predictions obtained with the tangent networks are slightly higher than those with the logistic sigmoid transfer function and that the current study, therefore, used tangent sigmoid function. The study use the method of min-max method to standardize the values of the series.

The last layer is the output layer which generates the outcomes of the indicated input. Training the model to learn the relationship between input and output parameters is an important step in the neural network. Weights are established by Error Back-Propagation (EBP) algorithms in MLP, which reduce a quadratic cost function by a method of gradient descent. The interconnecting weights between the nodes are changed during the training phase based on the inputs and desired output. The feed-forward multilayer network is the most popular and competitive model (Godarzi et al., 2014).

MLPNN is recognized in predictive analytics functions as a widely used artificial neural network architecture. MLPNN modelling is inspired by the framework of a biological neuron structure capable of parallel processing like a human mind, but these machine learning tools' processing elements have gone far from their biological inspiration. MLPNN has been used successfully by many other sciences, engineering, and forecasting researchers to predict the results of both linear and nonlinear systems without making assumptions implicit in most common statistical techniques. The biggest difficulty with MLPNN, however, is to choose a suitable model as there are different MLPNN model structures, training algorithms, activation functions, learning rate, momentum and number of periods to choose from (Velasco et al., 2019).

The number of input layers, hidden output layers must be specified correctly when constructing ANN design. Mathematical demonstration of the relationship between the inputs:

$y_{t-1}, \ldots, y_{t-p}$, and output y_t is:

$$y_t = \alpha_0 + \sum_{j=1}^{q} \alpha_j g \left(\beta_{0j} + \sum_{i=1}^{p} \beta_{ij} y_{t-i} \right) + \varepsilon_t \tag{6}$$

where $\alpha_j's$ and $\beta_{0j}'s$ are model parameters, q is the number of hidden nodes, p is the number of inputs nodes. For one step forecast, the following formulation is employed:

$$y_t = f\left(y_{t-1}, \ldots, y_{t-p}, w\right) + \varepsilon_t \tag{7}$$

Hence, the MLP model, in fact, performs a nonlinear functional mapping from the past observation $\left(y_{t-1}, y_{t-2} \ldots, y_{t-p},\right)$ to the future value $y_t = f\left(y_{t-1}, \ldots, y_{t-p}, w\right) + \varepsilon_t$ where f is the function determined by the neural network structure and connection weights and w is a vector of all parameters.

It must also be acknowledged that determining the number of nodes in the hidden layer, the number of lagged observations and the input vector dimension in the input layer are essential parts of the artificial neural architecture, however, there is no methodological rule for selecting such parameters and the only way to determine the optimal number is through experimentation method of trial and error (Mehdi Khashei & Hajirahimi, 2019).

The Hybrid Methodology

Artificial neural network (ANN) and autoregressive integrated moving average (ARIMA) (ANN-ARIMA) techniques have been widely used over the past two decades to obtain higher-precision prediction in linear and non-linear data sets; in general, terms, to forecast financial data on various kinds of financial and economic conditions. A hybrid model is a model type in which two or even more models are incorporated Wang et al. (2012) concluded that the hybrid approach incorporating linear and non-linear models can be an effective prediction approach.

Assuming that a time series consists of a linear and nonlinear component can be logical and reasonable. That is,

$$Y_t = L_t + N_t \tag{8}$$

given that L_t represent linear component of the series and N_t represent non-linear component of the series.

From the consumer price index (CPI) results, these components will be expected. Firstly, we require SARIMA to model the static portion of the residuals, followed by the nonlinear component. Residuals are critical for assessing the appropriateness of static models. When linear association frameworks exist in the residuals, the linear model is insufficient. Any noticeable nonlinear behavior in the residuals would reveal the SARIMA's weakness. Let e_t represent the residual of the seasonal ARIMA model at time t, then

$$e_t = y_t - \hat{L}_t \tag{9}$$

given that y_t is the actual series of the SARIMA model at time t, $\hat{L}_t$ is the forecasted value at time t.

Modelling residuals using MLP reveal nonlinear relationships. The MLP model for residuals with input nodes is as follows:

$$e_t = f\left(e_{t-1}, e_{t-2}, \ldots, e_{t-k}\right) + e_t \tag{10}$$

given that $f\left(e_{t-1}, e_{t-2}, \ldots, e_{t-k}\right)$ denotes a nonlinear feature established by the neural networks and e_t is the random error.

The joint forecast will be:

$$\hat{y}_t = \hat{L}_t + \hat{N}_t \tag{11}$$

The study will employ both root mean squared error (RMSE) and mean absolute error (MAE) in comparing the forecasting performance of the models.

$$RMSE = \sqrt{MSE} = \sqrt{\frac{1}{N}\sum_{i=1}^{N}\left(y_t - \hat{y}_t\right)^2} \tag{12}$$

$$MAE = \frac{1}{N}\sum_{i=1}^{N}\left|y_t - \hat{y}_t\right| \tag{13}$$

given that N, y_t and $\hat{y}_t$ is the total number of the series, actual series and the forecasted series of the data respectively.

EMPIRICAL RESULTS

Data Set

The monthly Inflation consumer price index (CPI) data was sourced from South African reserve bank website www.resbank.co.za. The dataset contains price indices from the year 2010/01 to 2019/07 and had a total of 115 observations. According to Mehdi Khashei and Hajirahimi (2019), 75% (86 observations) of the sample was used as a training sample and the remaining 25% (29 observations) as a test sample. Hence, the CPI data was partitioned according to this partition.

Table 1. Period of MLPNN, SARIMA, and SARIMA-MLPNN on training and testing sets

Models	Series	Training	Testing
MLPNN	2010/01 – 2019/07 (115)	2010/01 – 2018/02 (86)	2018/03 – 2019/07 (29)
SARIMA	2010/01 – 2019/07 (115)	2010/01 – 2018/02 (85)	2018/03 – 2019/07 (29)
SARIMA-MLPNN	2010/01 – 2019/07 (115)	2010/01 – 2018/02 (85)	2018/03 – 2019/07 (29)

Note: numbers inside the brackets indicates the total number of observations employed.

The plot has no clear trend. The data is not linear. There is a sudden drop in inflation (CPI) data from the year 2010 to mid-2011. Inflation rate reached a minimum of 3.4 in 2011/02 and 2011/03. There are some prevailing cyclical patterns in the data from mid-2013 to 2017 and some irregularities. There was also a significant decrease from 2017 to 2018.

In the analysis, unit root tests are used as a way of determining more accurately whether differencing is necessary. In our analysis, we use the augmented Dickey-Fuller (ADF) test to check for stationarity. This test may also be used to decide the appropriate order of differences. The result of the test is shown in table 2.

Figure 2. Consumer price index time series plot from 2010/01-2019/07

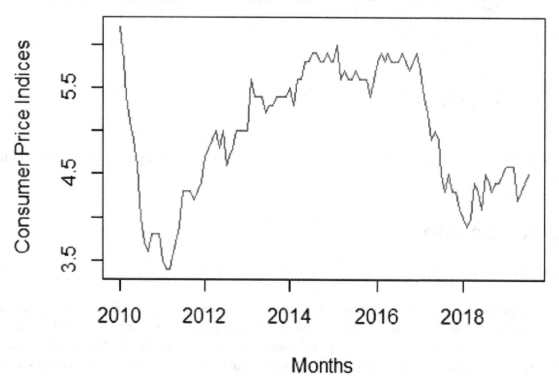

Table 2. ADF test at level(s)

		t-statistic	Prob *
ADF Statistic		-1.0887	0.2786
Test critical values	1% level	-2.58	
	5% level	-4.95	
	10% level	-1.62	

ADF t-statistic value is -1.0887 with the corresponding p-value of 0.2786. Critical values for test statistics are -2.58, -4.95, and -1.62 for 1%. 5% and 10% respectively. The p-value is greater than all the significant levels. We, therefore, accept the null hypothesis and conclude that the series is non-stationary. Thereby showing that the test needs to be conducted at first difference and the results are reported in table 3.

Table 3. ADF test at first difference

		t-statistic	Prob *
ADF Statistic		-9.4731	0.0000054
Test critical values	1% level	-2.58	
	5% level	-4.95	
	10% level	-1.62	

The test statistic is given by -9.4731 and critical values for 1%, 5%, and 10% are -2.58, -1.95 and -1.62 respectively. The probability value is given by 5.439e-16 (approximately 0.0000054). The test statistics are less than the critical value of 1 percent, 5 percent, and 10 percent, indicating acceptance of the null hypothesis. That is, the data is stationary after first difference. The p-value approaches zero.

Results

Five models of SARIMA were estimated in the study. All the models have the same orders of differencing. The ACF has a significant spike at lag 1 and 13, suggesting MA (1) and seasonal MA (1) and the PACF has a significant spike at lag 13, suggesting AR (1) and seasonal AR (1). The competing five models with their corresponding AIC values are:

Table 4. SARIMA model estimation and selection

Models	AIC	BIC
$ARIMA(1,1,1)(1,0,1)_{12}$	-76.67461	-62.99362
$ARIMA(1,1,0)(1,0,1)_{12}$	-71.29686	-60.35206
$ARIMA(1,1,1)(0,0,1)_{12}$	-77.83608	-66.89128
$ARIMA(1,1,0)(0,0,1)_{12}$	-72.84557	-64.63697
$ARIMA(0,1,1)(0,0,1)_{12}$	-72.09076	-63.88216

Note: Model 3 has both the smallest AIC and BIC and hence the study chose it as the best model amongst the five estimated.

Auto ARIMA function suggested model 3 $ARIMA(1,1,1)(0,0,1)_{12}$ to be the best model as compared to the five models estimated. Furthermore, the study did residual analysis as a way of diagnostic checking and normal distribution of the residual was assessed. The results are shown in figure 3.

The residuals (i.e., white noise) are normally distributed. The residual plot revolves around the average of 0 and there is a constant variance. The ACF chart also reveals that the residuals are stationary as the plot does not contain any noticeable spikes. The Normal plot reveals the bell-shaped, indicating the normal distribution of residuals.

The main benefit of ANN methods over other non-linear model types is that ANNs are standard approximators that can estimate a large number of frameworks with a strong level of precision. Their strength comes from the parallel computing of information knowledge. No prior assumption of the design type is required in the model building process. Instead, the network model is strongly influenced by the features of the data.

Figure 3. Residuals Diagnostics

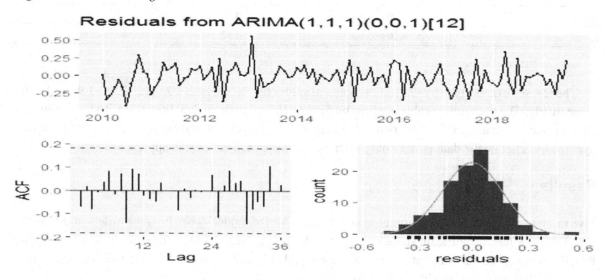

It must be acknowledged that specifying the number of nodes in the hidden layer, the number of lagged measurements and the input vector dimension in the input layer are essential components of the neural network architecture, however there is no methodological rule for selecting such parameters and the only way to pick the appropriate number of p and q is by experimentation or trial and error (Mehdi Khashei & Hajirahimi, 2019).

It should be taken into account that we used the trial and error approach to select the number of hidden layers as well as the number of nodes/neurons. In the analysis, the researcher chose the most appropriate model utilizing 20 different models. The lowest MSE value is the best MLP model. The study estimated 20 multilayer perceptron neural networks model and the best model amongst the twenty estimated was found to be the model with 3 hidden layers (the 1st layer has 5 nodes, the 2nd layer has 1 node and the third layer has 2 nodes) has the lowest MSE value of 0.001. MSE value for this model is closer to zero, hence it is chosen as the best model. The most optimal MLP model has the RMSE value of 0.03144649, MAE is 0.01, and MASE is 0.0177921.

For hybrid SARIMA-MLPNN model this procedure is followed: the residuals obtained from the SARIMA model would be used to fit the MLP model. The training set contains about 86 observations while the testing set contains about 29 observations. The transformed would then be used to fit the MLP models. Since there is no methodical rule for selecting these parameters. In this section, the method of trial and error was also used to find the number of nodes in the hidden layer and the number of hidden layers. Hybrid SARIMA - MLP model (10, 5, 1) hidden nodes and 20 repetitions has the lowest MSE value of 0.0022. Hence, this model is chosen as the most optimal model. Therefore, since all three models are estimated and the optimal models are found, then the three models are compared in terms of forecasting performance of the CPI data series and the results are shown in table 5.

Table 5. Comparing model(s) performance

Models	RMSE	MAE
SARIMA	0.1626621	0.1245401
MLPNN	0.03144649	0.01
Hybrid SARIMA-MLPNN	0.02203298	0.0115682

In view of the outcomes shown in the table above, the traditional linear model of SARIMA is outperformed by the MLPNN model and the hybrid model respectively. The hybrid model has the lowest RMSE value followed by MLPNN. However, MLPNN has the lowest MAE value. This demonstrates the fact that ANNs could be the effective technique for forecasting time series data. Looking at the MAE value for both MLPNN and a hybrid SARIMA-MLPNN, we observe that there is no much difference between them. Hence, we choose a hybrid model as an optimal model.

CONCLUSION

The study fitted SARIMA, MLPNN and a hybrid SARIMA-MLPNN model to the CPI data set using R software. The data showed some seasonal patterns which the Box-Jenkin's seasonal ARIMA (SARIMA) model captures. The chosen SARIMA model was $ARIMA(1,1,1)(0,0,1)_{12}$. The MLP model achieved its definitive model have 5 hidden layers - the 1st layer has 5 nodes, the 2nd layer has 10 nodes and the 3rd layer has 5 nodes, 4th layer has 5 nodes, and the 5th layer has 1 node with a learning rate of 0.05. And the hybrid prototype achieved its definite model to be one with 3 hidden layers with 0.05 learning rate.

Secondly the study compared the three models using RMSE and MAE to measure the overall performance. The results showed SARIMA was outperformed by the MLPNN model and the hybrid model respectively. The hybrid model has the lowest RMSE value followed by MLPNN. However, MLPNN has the lowest MAE value. This demonstrated that ANNs could be the effective technique for forecasting time series data. Looking at the MAE value for both MLPNN and a hybrid SARIMA-MLPNN, we observed that there was no much difference between them. Hence, we chose a hybrid model as the most optimal model. The results have shown that hybrid SARIMA-MLPNN was able to improve forecasting accuracy. The study furthermore recommends that in future research a hybrid model of RBFNN-MLP may also be considered when analyzing time series data and that large data set may also be considered as this may be of the utmost benefit to the researcher.

LIMITATIONS

The study is limited to using monthly historical time series data of consumer price index (CPI) sourced from South African reserve bank and covering the period of January 2010 to July 2019 on the basis of accessibility of data. There are numerous models that are and can be used to model consumer price index (CPI), however for the purpose of the current study, only three models will be used; SARIMA, MLPNN and SARIMA-MLPNN hybrid model. Due to limited sources on machine learning models, the study might use sources older than ten years.

ACKNOWLEDGMENT

The authors of the study would like to offer and express their sincere thanks to the editors and anonymous reviewers for their time and valuable suggestions.

This research received no specific grant from any funding agency in the public, private, commercial, or anywhere else.

REFERENCES

Abdulrahman, B. M. A., Ahmed, A. Y. A., & Abdellah, A. E. Y. (2018). Forecasting of Sudan Inflation Rates using ARIMA Model. *International Journal of Economics Financial Issues*, *8*(3), 17.

Ali, Z., Hussain, I., Faisal, M., Nazir, H. M., Hussain, T., Shad, M. Y., . . . Hussain Gani, S. (2017). Forecasting drought using multilayer perceptron artificial neural network model. Advances in Meteorology.

Alnaa, S. E., & Ahiakpor, F. (2011). ARIMA (autoregressive integrated moving average) approach to predicting inflation in Ghana. *Journal of Economics International Finance*, *3*(5), 328.

Álvarez-Díaz, M., González-Gómez, M., & Otero-Giráldez, M. S. (2019). Forecasting international tourism demand using a non-linear autoregressive neural network and genetic programming. *Forecasting*, *1*(1), 90–106. doi:10.3390/forecast1010007

Areekul, P., Senjyu, T., Toyama, H., & Yona, A. (2010). A Hybrid ARIMA and Neural Network Model for Short-Term Price Forecasting in Deregulated Market. *IEEE Transactions on Power Systems*, *25*(1), 524–530. doi:10.1109/TPWRS.2009.2036488

Arunraj, N. S., & Ahrens, D. (2015). A hybrid seasonal autoregressive integrated moving average and quantile regression for daily food sales forecasting. *International Journal of Production Economics*, *170*, 321–335. doi:10.1016/j.ijpe.2015.09.039

Box, G. E., Jenkins, G. M., Reinsel, G. C., & Ljung, G. M. (2015). *Time series analysis: forecasting and control* (5th ed.). Forecasting and Control.

Cang, S. (2011). A non-linear tourism demand forecast combination model. *Tourism Economics*, *17*(1), 5–20. doi:10.5367/te.2011.0031

Chatfield, C. (2001). *Time-series forecasting*. Chapman & Hall/CRC Press.

Chinonso, U. E., & Justice, O. I. (2016). Modelling Nigeria's urban and rural inflation using Box-Jenkins model. *Scientific Papers. Series Management, Economic Engineering in Agriculture and Rural Development*, *16*(4), 61-68.

Datta, K. (2011). ARIMA forecasting of inflation in the Bangladesh economy. *The IUP Journal of Bank Management*, *10*(4), 7–15.

Faruk, D. Ö. (2010). A hybrid neural network and ARIMA model for water quality time series prediction. *Engineering Applications of Artificial Intelligence*, *23*(4), 586–594. doi:10.1016/j.engappai.2009.09.015

Ghahnavieh, A. E. (2019). Time series forecasting of styrene price using a hybrid ARIMA and neural network model. *Independent Journal of Management & Production*, *10*(3), 915–933. doi:10.14807/ijmp.v10i3.877

Godarzi, A. A., Amiri, R. M., Talaei, A., & Jamasb, T. (2014). Predicting oil price movements: A dynamic Artificial Neural Network approach. *Energy Policy*, *68*, 371–382. doi:10.1016/j.enpol.2013.12.049

Guresen, E., Kayakutlu, G., & Daim, T. U. (2011). Using artificial neural network models in stock market index prediction. *Expert Systems with Applications*, *38*(8), 10389–10397. doi:10.1016/j.eswa.2011.02.068

Hyndman, R.J., & Athanasopoulos, G. (2018). *Forecasting: principles and practice* (2nd ed.). OTexts. OTexts.com/fpp2

Khandelwal, I., Adhikari, R., & Verma, G. J. P. C. S. (2015). Time series forecasting using hybrid ARIMA and ANN models based on DWT decomposition. *Procedia Computer Science*, *48*, 173–179. doi:10.1016/j.procs.2015.04.167

Makridakis, S. (1989). Why combining works? *International Journal of Forecasting*, *5*(4), 601–603. doi:10.1016/0169-2070(89)90017-4

Merh, N., Saxena, V. P., & Pardasani, K. R. (2010). A comparison between hybrid approaches of ANN and ARIMA for Indian stock trend forecasting. *Business Intelligence Journal*, *3*(2), 23–43.

Nyoni, T. (2018). Modeling and Forecasting Inflation in Kenya: Recent Insights from ARIMA and GARCH analysis. *Dimorian Review*, *5*(6), 16–40.

Nyoni, T., & Nathaniel, S. P. (2018). *Modeling rates of inflation in Nigeria: an application of ARMA, ARIMA and GARCH models*. https://mpra.ub.uni-muenchen.de/91351/MPRAPaperNo.91351

Palm, F. C., & Zellner, A. (1992). To combine or not to combine? Issues of combining forecasts. *Journal of Forecasting*, *11*(8), 687–701. doi:10.1002/for.3980110806

Prayoga, Suhartono, & Rahayu. (2017). Forecasting currency circulation data of Bank Indonesia by using hybrid ARIMAX-ANN model. AIP Conference Proceedings, 1842. doi:10.1063/1.4982867

Rezaeian-Zadeh, M., & Tabari, H. (2012). MLP-based drought forecasting in different climatic regions. *Theoretical and Applied Climatology*, *109*(3-4), 407–414. doi:10.100700704-012-0592-3

Santos, C. A. G., & Silva, G. B. L. (2013). Daily streamflow forecasting using a wavelet transform and artificial neural networkhybrid models. *Hydrological Sciences Journal*, *59*(2), 312–324. doi:10.1080/02626667.2013.800944

Velasco, L. C. P., Serquiña, R. P., Zamad, M. S. A. A., & Juanico, B. F. (2019). Performance Analysis of Multilayer Perceptron Neural Network Models in Week-Ahead Rainfall Forecasting. *International Journal of Advanced Computer Science and Applications*, *10*(3). Advance online publication. doi:10.14569/IJACSA.2019.0100374

Wang, J.-J., Wang, J.-Z., Zhang, Z.-G., & Guo, S.-P. (2012). Stock index forecasting based on a hybrid model. *Omega*, *40*(6), 758–766. doi:10.1016/j.omega.2011.07.008

Zhang, G., Patuwo, B. E., & Hu, M. Y. (1998). Forecasting with artificial neural networks: The state of the art. *International Journal of Forecasting*, *14*(1), 35–62. doi:10.1016/S0169-2070(97)00044-7

ADDITIONAL READING

Adebiyi, A. A., Adewumi, A. O., & Ayo, C. K. (2014). Comparison of ARIMA and artificial neural networks models for stock price prediction. *Journal of Applied Mathematics*, *2014*, 2014. doi:10.1155/2014/614342

Babu, C. N., & Reddy, B. E. (2014). A moving-average filter based hybrid ARIMA–ANN model for forecasting time series data. *Applied Soft Computing*, *23*, 27–38. doi:10.1016/j.asoc.2014.05.028

Camara, A., Feixing, W., & Xiuqin, L. (2016). Energy consumption forecasting using seasonal ARIMA with artificial neural networks models. *International Journal of Business and Management*, *11*(5), 231. doi:10.5539/ijbm.v11n5p231

Glišović, N., Milenković, M., & Bojović, N. Comparison of SARIMA-GA-ANN and SARIMA-ANN for prediction of the railway passenger flows. 4th International Symposium & 26th National Conference on Operational Research, Chania, Greece, 4th-6th June, 2015. 181-186.

Kemal, A. (2017). Prediction of Gold Prices Using Artificial Neural Networks. *International Journal of Engineering Research and Development*, *9*, 83–89.

Munandar, D. (2019). Multilayer perceptron (MLP) and autoregressive integrated moving average (ARIMA) models in multivariate input time series data: Solar irradiance forecasting. *International Journal on Advanced Science, Engineering and Information Technology*, *9*(1), 220–228. doi:10.18517/ijaseit.9.1.6426

Nontapa, C., Kesamoon, C., Kaewhawong, N., & Intrapaiboon, P. A Comparative of a New Hybrid Based on Neural Networks and SARIMA Models for Time Series Forecasting. International Conference on Multi-disciplinary Trends in Artificial Intelligence, 2021. Springer, 94-105.

Yarrington, C. S. 2021. Review of Forecasting Univariate Time-series Data with Application to Water-Energy Nexus Studies & Proposal of Parallel Hybrid SARIMA-ANN Model.

KEY TERMS AND DEFINITIONS

Consumer Price Index (CPI): An index of the variation in prices for retail goods and other items.

Data Partitioning: Means the process of physically dividing data into separate data stores.

Hybrid Models: This refers to a situation where two or more models are combined together to solve a certain specific problem presented in a time series data.

Inflation Rate: The rate at which prices increase over time, resulting in a fall in the purchasing value of money.

Mean Absolute Error (MAE): A measure of average magnitude of the errors in predictions without giving preferences to their direction.

Performance Measures or Error Metrics: Is a type of metric used to measure the error of a forecasting model.

Root Mean Square Error (RMSE): Is a frequently used measure of the differences between values predicted by a model or an estimator and the values observed.

Chapter 13
Value Analysis and Prediction Through Machine Learning Techniques for Popular Basketball Brands

Jason Michaud

Bryant University, USA

ABSTRACT

For popular sports brands such as Nike, Adidas, and Puma, value often depends upon the performance of star athletes and the success of professional leagues. These leagues and players are watched closely by many around the world, and exposure to a brand may ultimately cause someone to buy a product. This can be explored statistically, and the interconnectedness of brands, athletes, and the sport of basketball are covered in this chapter. Specifically, data about the NBA and Google Ngrams data are explored in relation to the stock price of these various sports brands. This is done through both statistical analysis and machine learning models. Ultimately, it was concluded that these factors do influence the stock price of Nike, Adidas, and Puma. This conclusion is supported by the machine learning models where this diverse dataset was utilized to accurately predict the stock price of sports brands.

INTRODUCTION

In this chapter, the relationship between popular brands involved in basketball and the sport itself is explored. While the focus here is only on one sport, the principles and techniques shown in this chapter can be applied to others too. For example, if similar data on the National Football league and its players were to be collected, then a prediction of the stock price of connected brands should be achievable. Different varieties of data are utilized in this chapter, and the relationship to brand value is heavily analyzed. The data collected includes both data on the National Basketball Association itself, and frequency data from Google Ngrams. After statistical analysis of the dataset, machine learning models are then built with the goal of accurately predicting the stock price for Nike, Adidas, and Puma. Another goal of this chapter

DOI: 10.4018/978-1-7998-8455-2.ch013

is to explore the differences between simple machine learning models and complex machine learning models. The models of focus are linear regressions and neural networks. The comparison point between these models is the accuracy of the training dataset and the accuracy of the testing dataset.

BACKGROUND

Literature Review

There have been numerous studies that have covered a similar topic area to that of this chapter in the past, whether it be exploring the value of a sports brand or even just the popularity of Michael Jordan. The following studies are not used a basis of this chapter, but rather a springboard for developing the overall topic. Studies are grouped by topic in the below paragraphs.

Effects of Players on Brands

The first study to be examined is a thesis paper written by Paul Andrew Maddock II. This paper covers the economic impact on a brand that an NBA player can have. Regressions were calculated by this author, and both negative and positive impacts on a brand's value could be seen in his results (Maddock II, 2018). Another study focused on a similar topic area as the previous one. It focused on the negative impacts an athlete has on a brand. It even mentioned that this impact can transfer over to other brands too (Shintaro Sato, 2018). Superstar players can also have major effects on the success of their team financially. This study focused on the effects that a superstar player can have on the attendance of games (both home and away), and ultimately concluded that the effect is real (Humphreys, 2019).

Miscellaneous Sports Brand Studies

The next study focused on the impacts of a brand's involvement in grassroots basketball. It further explores why these brands are involved in grassroots sports and even the benefits that they reap from it (Keefe, 2011). Brand loyalty is another factor that ultimately decides the value of a brand. This study explored this through firsthand data collection, and ultimately determined that being loyal to one brand will affect that person's decision to buy a pair of basketball shoes (de Silva, Madhushani, & Jayalath, 2020). Business strategy and models can also affect the value of a brand. This paper explores just that and goes into detail with Nike and Adidas (Ali Mahdi, Abbas, Mazar, & George, 2015).

Michael Jordan and The Effects of Star Athletes

Another paper explores Michael Jordan's decision to return to the NBA from minor league baseball. It explores the effects that decisions like this have on brands that are not directly involved which is significant (Lynette Knowles Mathur, 1997). The final paper to be covered explores what they coin as "The Jordan Effect". This revolves around Michael Jordan's effects on brands just by what he does in life. Any decision he makes can spill over to a brand, and this is something to keep in mind when determining value (Johnson, 1998). Another study focused on the rise and fall of prolific players. They ran various models on this topic and did so for multiple sports as well. While this paper did not cover sports brands directly, the rise and fall of a player can have effects on a brand as evidenced by previous papers referenced in this section (Yupin Yang, 2011).

Data Collection Methods and Principles

For this chapter, statistical analysis was performed on athletic brands that are heavily involved in the sport of basketball. Data utilized includes both frequency data and financial data from a variety of sources. What follows is a background on the methods used to collect the data and a statistical description of what the data itself contains. Table 1 displays a brief summary of this data collection stage.

Year

To allow for predictive models to be ran and basic analysis be performed, a common field was needed. For this time sensitive data, a year field made the most sense. This field is the heart to understanding if certain fields interconnect with one another, whether it be through a correlational matrix or predictive models. It also allows for a sense of organization, as the year value can be associated with the values of every other field in the dataset. This field is basically the first index for the dataset.

Month

On top of a year field, a month field was also added to the dataset. This field was specifically for the stock prices, where the monthly values varied. The other fields stayed the same, as they contained a yearly value and month did not matter. Before adding this field, the dataset had only about 50 rows, which is very small and would not be ideal for running any predictive models. After adding a month field, however, the size of the dataset increased by twelvefold, and the final dataset was then created. Similar to the year field, the month field was treated like a secondary index in order to obtain more rows of data in an organized fashion.

Google Ngrams data

Six of the fields were collected from Google Ngrams. Google Ngrams data is essentially the frequency that a word shows up in literature for each year. The terms that data was collected on are Nike, Adidas, Puma, Reebok, Basketball, and Michael Jordan. Data was collected manually and entered into Excel. It was also collected for the time period of 1970 through 2019 at yearly increments (Google Books Ngram Viewer, n.d.). Figure 1 displays the graph that this data was pulled from.

Stock Price (Nike, Adidas, and Puma)

Stock price was collected for Nike, Adidas, and Puma. Reebok stock price was unavailable, as the company was purchased by Adidas in 2006. The stock symbols used are NKE, ADDYY, and PUM.DE. Monthly price was calculated by using closing price value. This data was collected from Yahoo Finance, and the time periods vary due to companies going public at different times. Data was pulled from the historical data section for each stock symbol. Nike's stock price data is available from 1985 and on, Adidas' data is available from 2006 and on, and Puma's data is available from 1998 and on (Yahoo Finance Historical Data, n.d.). The rows that were left null are for the time periods where no stock price was available.

NBA Finals Average Viewers and Average Ratings

NBA Finals data was collected from a Sports Media Watch article. The data collected is the average rating for each NBA Finals series, and the average viewer count for each series too. The raw data that was collected is just the viewers and ratings per game, so some manual calculation is needed to get an overall average. An NBA Finals series can range from 4 to 7 games depending on how many games it takes for one team to win the series. If they win the first four, they win the series and do not play games 5, 6, and 7 for example. Having a different number of games for each series means that an overall average could not be calculated automatically. An average for each year had to be calculated to obtain an accurate yearly value. This was simply done by entering the raw data in Excel and calculating an average for each year. Another note on the collection of this data involves the year that it is associated with. An NBA season starts in one calendar year and ends in another. Most of the season happens in the second year, so each value is associated with that rather than the first one. For example, the 2001-2002 season data would fall in 2002 in the dataset. (NBA Finals Ratings History (1988-Present), n.d.).

NBA Revenue

NBA Revenue could only be found for the 2001-2002 season through the 2019-2020 season. Like the NBA Finals data, the revenue is associated with the second year of the season too. The data used combines the reported revenue of all 32 teams in the league (National Basketball Association total league revenue from 2001/02 to 2019/20(in billion U.S. dollars), n.d.). This was the largest time frame that could be found for NBA revenue, and no credible sources went back further. This data was only available as yearly, so all of the rows that contain the same year just have the same revenue regardless of month.

Brand shares value

After obtaining the stock price values of each brand, another field was created to capture the total brand shares value for that month. For each brand's stock, the closing price and volume of shares were multiplied. This was then summed to get the final value of all sports brands for that month. As previously mentioned, the data used here was from Yahoo Finance and the new value was calculated in an Excel workbook. The idea behind creating this field is that it gives a field for the total brand value that can be independent of the individual brands, and it is more of an industry wide measure.

Table 1. Summary of Data Collection

Field	Subcategory	Description/Source
Year	Time	Common field that is used as an index for all others.
Month	Time	Secondary index included for the purpose of having more individual rows of stock price data.
Google Ngrams Data	Frequency Data	Term frequency data collected for Nike, Adidas, Puma, Reebok, Basketball, and Michael Jordan (Google Books Ngram Viewer, n.d.).
Stock Price	Financial Data	Monthly closing stock price data collected for Nike (NKE), Adidas (ADDYY), and Puma (PUM.DE) (Yahoo Finance Historical Data, n.d.).
NBA Finals Data	Frequency Data	NBA Finals average viewers and average TV ratings are included here. An average was taken for each individual series, as the number of games differs from season to season (NBA Finals Ratings History (1988-Present), n.d.).
NBA Revenue	Financial Data	Yearly revenue data collected for the NBA. This field is associated with the second calendar year of the season (National Basketball Association total league revenue from 2001/02 to 2019/20(in billion U.S. dollars), n.d.).
Brand Shares Value	Financial Data	To calculate this field, the monthly closing stock price is multiplied by the monthly volume of shares for each brand. This is then summed up to get a total monthly value for all brands. å (Closing Stock Price * Volume of shares).

Interconnectedness of Fields

In Table 1 displayed above, the fields shown are connected in a variety of ways. The stock prices are the target variables, and these are what will be predicted in the machine learning models section of this chapter. The brand shares value is calculated from these stock prices, and this formula can be found in Table 1. Since this chapter is about the value prediction of brands involved in the sport of basketball, the Google Ngrams frequency data is about terms related to both basketball and brands. The remaining data on the NBA is connected to the target variables because this is the premier basketball league for the whole planet.

History of Brands and Statistical Description of Frequency Data

This section covers a brief background description of the major sports brands in this chapter, and some of the other fields that were collected too. The goal here is to generate an understanding of the brand's involvement in the sport of basketball, and why they are so important to this chapter. Table 2 displays a briefer history of these brands in the sport of basketball.

Nike

Starting off with Nike, this brand has a long history with the sport of basketball. The first Nike basketball sneaker models, the "Bruin" and the "Blazer", were released in 1972. It would be numerous years before Nike would gain popularity in the basketball world, and the brand really started to pick up popularity in the early 1980s. It was at this time that the Air Force One was launched and star players were being recruited to promote the brand. The Air Jordan brand was launched in 1985, and Michael Jordan was the headliner of this. Shortly after, Nike entered the college game sponsoring numerous schools who wore the Nike Dunk at the time. Building upon the success of these early sub brands, Nike recruited even more players in the 1990s. This includes Dennis Rodman, Scottie Pippen, Charles Barkley, and Kevin Garnett to name a few players (Nike Basketball History, n.d.).

Having such a rich history in basketball, Nike is an intriguing brand to examine. Referring to Figure 1, Nike has an increase in frequency from the mid-1980s through the late 1990s. This is right around the time that Nike was creating all the previously mentioned basketball sneakers and expanding their roster of sponsored athletes. It is no surprise that the term frequency of Nike was going up during this time window as the brand was gaining traction in the sports world.

Puma

Puma is a brand that has recently been endorsing more and more NBA players. One of Puma's first endorsed NBA players was Isiah Thomas, who wore Puma shoes on the court during his championship winning 1989-1990 season (Dodson). As of 2019, some of Puma's notable endorsed players include: "Skylar Diggins-Smith, Deandre Ayton, Marvin Bagley III, DeMarcus Cousins, Rudy Gay, Danny Green, Kevin Knox, Michael Porter Jr., Terry Rozier and Zhaire Smith." (Dodson, 2019). This list contains many young players who have a chance to become stars on their respective teams, and it shows that Puma is trying to reenter and disrupt the basketball scene where Nike and Adidas have seen so much success.

With this increasing number of sponsorships recently, it will be interesting to examine the data on Puma. Results may not be showing now, but they could be in a few years. Puma had a very gradual increase in frequency from about 1970 to 2010 (Figure 1). They started a slow decline after that though between 2010 and 2018, so these players have not necessarily generated any buzz about the brand yet.

Reebok

Reebok truly entered the basketball scene in 1991. Specifically, Dee Brown of the Boston Celtics put their Reebok Pump shoe on the map. He won the slam dunk contest by covering his eyes with his arm, and this helped the already growing brand to increase in popularity even further (Weinfuss, 2019).

This event's effects can be seen in the Google Ngrams graph where Reebok drastically increased in frequency between 1991 and 1996 (Figure 1). Eventually, however, Reebok started to lose popularity and has not regained it since. There is a big "what if" question here though. Many wonder what would have happened if Lebron James did not turn down a 10-million-dollar Reebok deal in the early 2000s (Davis, 2017). After failing to secure Lebron James, Reebok has not been able to bounce back. This deal would have been a boost to their financial success, and it ultimately fell through with Lebron James choosing Nike instead.

Adidas

The final brand included in this study is Adidas. Adidas entered the basketball picture in the late 1990s and has been steadily picking up players since. They had Kobe Bryant for a few years, and later signed Tracy McGrady, Kevin Garnett, Derrick Rose, and James Harden to name a few players (ceo4ceo, 2018). This goes hand in hand with a great increase in the frequency of the word Adidas since the late 1990s, and it has not declined since. Adidas signed many of these players early in their respective careers, and a similar trend could potentially happen with Puma, who seem to be taking a very similar approach to that of Adidas in the 1990s.

Another interesting insight that can be seen in the Ngrams graph is the correlation between each of the sports brands and the word basketball (Figure 1). It seems that Reebok followed a similar path to that of the word basketball for almost the entire graph. Rebook's frequency rose with that of the word "Basketball" and fell with it too. Adidas and Puma have very similar trends in frequency as well, but Adidas passed Puma in 2008 and the gap has only been getting larger since. Reebok also started to fall in popularity when the other two brands started to rise which is another interesting aspect in Figure 1.

Basketball

The word Basketball rose in frequency between the late 1980s and the late 1990s. It peaked from 1998 to 2002 (Figure 1). This coincides heavily with the career of Michael Jordan, who many believe to be the best basketball player of all time. He was drafted in 1984 and retired for a third and final time in 2003. It seems that the frequency of the word basketball peaked towards the end of his career and fell soon after he retired (Michael Jordan, n.d.).

NBA Finals Data

Ratings and viewers peaked in the NBA in the late 1990s largely due to the presence of Michael Jordan at the time too. He won multiple championships, and his high level of play had fans captivated everywhere. Since then, viewers and ratings have not been as high, and were especially low for the NBA Bubble in the 2019-2020 season. This bubble season is an abnormality, however, as it happened due to COVID-19 which is not a relationship that is explored in this chapter.

Table 2. History of Major Sports Brands Summary Table

Brand	Key Historical Points
Nike	Nike's basketball presence took off in the 1970s-1980s due to new, highly successful lines of basketball sneakers. The pinnacle of this success was the Air Jordan brand that is centered around star player Michael Jordan (Nike Basketball History, n.d.). An increase in frequency during the early 1990s in Figure 1 for both Michael Jordan and Nike can be seen.
Adidas	Adidas has been steadily adding to an impressive roster of endorsed NBA players since the 1990s. Some notable names include Kobe Bryant, Kevin Garnett, and James Harden (ceo4ceo, 2018). These players have had some positive impact on the frequency of Adidas. This is evidenced by the Adidas line in Figure 1 slowly creeping upwards in recent years.
Puma	Puma has been endorsing players for many years, but it has not been until recently that they have signed a plethora of them (Dodson, 2019). While these players have not necessarily generated a buzz about the brand yet (see Figure 1), the Ngrams frequency value is not decreasing by any means. Only time will tell if these players can have an impact on the brand value of Puma.
Reebok	Reebok seemed to be on their way up popularity-wise in the 1990s with their star player Dee Brown of the Boston Celtics winning the 1991 NBA Slam Dunk Contest. He won this contest in Reebok Pumps, and the frequency of Reebok in Figure 1 did go up for a few years (Weinfuss, 2019). Ever since the late 1990s, however, the frequency of Reebok has been going down and they are virtually irrelevant in professional basketball today.

Figure 1. Google Ngrams Frequency Graph

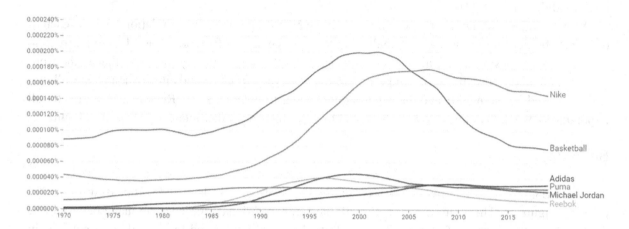

Financial Data

Below, Figure 2 displays the stock price by year for the major three brands of Nike, Adidas, and Puma. All three have increased especially since 2010. Nike used to be the least by value, but both this brand and Adidas have surpassed Puma in recent years in terms of the value per share. Nike also has a relatively smooth incline. This is significant, as this brand has been on the stock market the longest out of the major three. Adidas has a similar pattern, although it has only been public since 2006. Puma is shakier in terms of having a smooth line on this graph, but it does increase over time just as the other two brands do.

Figure 3 is a pie chart of the average stock price for Nike, Adidas, and Puma. The highest average price belongs to Adidas, which is then followed by Puma and Nike. Nike has been rising in recent years at an almost exponential rate however, and this low average can be attributed to the numerous years that Nike maintained a low price. It has only been recently that Nike stock has broken out (see Figure 2). Adidas having the highest average price here can be attributed to the few years that they have been on the stock market with a relatively high price. Adidas closed their first month on the stock market at a price of over 24$ which supports this. Puma's average stock price is the same story as Nike where they have only broken out in the last few years and had a very low price also.

Table 3 displays a correlational matrix for all the fields in the data set. There are some interesting insights that can be pulled from here, especially when it comes to stock price. As expected, the term Michael Jordan is heavily correlated to the term basketball (.78), and the term Nike (.88). As a player, Michael Jordan had a very heavy influence on the popularity of the game. He also signed with Nike early on in his career, and the Air Jordan brand was a major success (Nike Basketball History, n.d.). This is also inversely correlated to Adidas stock price, but this is due to a large increase since Adidas went public in 2006. Michael Jordan's term frequency has been going down since that point, as he is no longer an NBA player. Nike stock price is heavily correlated to both Adidas and Puma stock price, and also NBA revenue. If NBA revenue goes up, then it should be expected that the sports brands' shares value should go up too being highly correlated. If revenue decreases, then it should be expected that the stock prices decrease. With many high correlational relationships that can be seen among the fields, machine learning models should perform very well.

Figure 2. Average Sports Brand Stock Price by Year

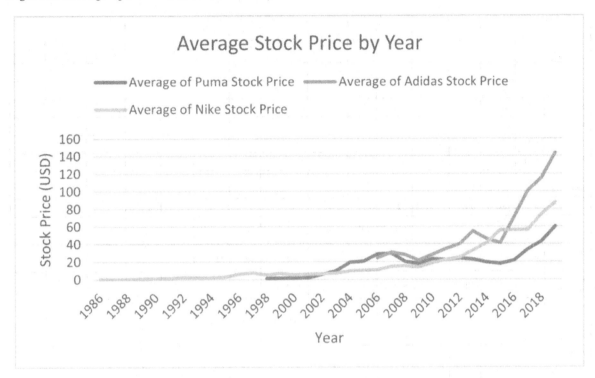

Figure 3. Average Sports Brand Stock Price Pie Chart

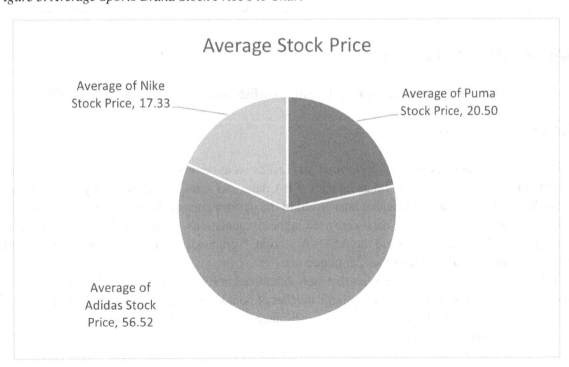

Table 3. Correlational Matrix of All Data Fields

	Year	Month	Puma	Reebok	Adidas	Nike	Michael Jordan	Basketball	Nike Stock Price	Adidas Stock Price	Puma Stock Price	NBA Finals AVG Rating	NBA Finals AVG Viewers	NBA Revenue	Brand Shares Value
Year	1.00														
Month	0.00	1.00													
Puma	0.81	0.00	1.00												
Reebok	0.49	0.00	0.68	1.00											
Adidas	0.97	0.00	0.77	0.41	1.00										
Nike	0.90	0.00	0.73	0.61	0.93	1.00									
Michael Jordan	0.75	0.00	0.72	0.89	0.71	0.88	1.00								
Basketball	0.24	0.00	0.48	0.88	0.22	0.51	0.78	1.00							
Nike Stock Price	0.83	0.03	-0.11	-0.54	0.66	0.40	-0.03	-0.61	1.00						
Adidas Stock Price	0.85	0.05	-0.79	-0.70	-0.34	-0.81	-0.83	-0.68	0.90	1.00					
Puma Stock Price	0.79	0.04	0.01	-0.73	0.71	-0.15	-0.80	-0.68	0.76	0.85	1.00				
NBA Finals AVG Rating	-0.64	0.00	-0.47	0.42	-0.75	-0.71	-0.09	0.13	-0.36	0.19	-0.37	1.00			
NBA Finals AVG Viewers	-0.15	0.00	-0.45	0.14	-0.43	-0.77	0.17	-0.06	0.07	0.29	-0.18	0.97	1.00		
NBA Revenue	0.90	0.00	-0.62	-0.81	0.41	-0.90	-0.81	-0.80	0.96	0.96	0.79	0.28	0.45	1.00	
Brand Shares Value	0.87	0.04	0.08	-0.51	0.77	0.52	0.04	-0.54	0.92	0.76	0.74	-0.45	0.01	0.87	1.00

MAIN FOCUS OF THE CHAPTER

Statistical Analysis of Frequency Data: Confidence Intervals and ANOVA

Confidence Intervals

For this section, calculations were performed and results were recorded prior to the expansion of the dataset. That is why none of the financial data, NBA data, and some of the frequency data fields are not included. Those fields were added later to aid in the performance of the machine learning models. This also means that less rows of data were used in these calculations, as the month index had not been added yet. For both this section and the ANOVA section, Ngrams data was used in two-year intervals from 1970 through 2018 for a total of 25 unique rows

Table 4 displays confidence intervals that were calculated in Excel, and there are four in total. Since Google Ngrams is based on an extremely large number of books, the frequency that each term shows up is a very low percentage. This translates to a small range for each confidence interval, and that is why each bound is to 10 decimal points.

For Puma, the level of confidence that μ falls within 0.0000240526 and 0.0000249366 is 95%. For Reebok, the level of confidence that μ falls within 0.0000153091 and 0.0000174369 is 95%. For Adidas, the level of confidence that μ falls within 0.0000148834 and 0.0000165997 is 95%. For Basketball, the level of confidence that μ falls within 0.0001234087 and 0.000129812 is 95%.

Table 4. Confidence Intervals for Original Frequency Data

Field	Bounds (Lower, Upper)	Conclusion
Puma	0.0000240526, 0.0000249366	95% confident that μ falls between these two bounds
Reebok	0.0000153091, 0.0000174369	95% confident that μ falls between these two bounds
Adidas	0.0000148834, 0.0000165997	95% confident that μ falls between these two bounds
Basketball	0.0001234087, 0.000129812	95% confident that μ falls between these two bounds

ANOVA

Below, six ANOVA calculations can be seen in Table 5. These cover brands vs brands and brands vs Basketball. Google Ngrams data was used in these calculations, and the critical value for all was 4.04. This value was obtained from the F distribution table at an alpha level of .05 where $v_2=48$ and $v_1=1$.

There was only one of these ANOVA calculations where the null hypothesis could not be rejected. This was for Reebok vs. Adidas, and the F value was 0.03 while the critical value was 4.04. There was not enough evidence here to reject that these two frequency data fields are the same. For the combinations of Puma vs Reebok, Puma vs Adidas, Puma vs Basketball, Reebok vs Basketball, and Adidas vs Basketball, the F value was greater than the critical value. This means that the null hypothesis should be rejected and that these frequency combinations are not the same.

Table 5. ANOVA For Original Frequency Data

Combination	F Value	Critical Value	Conclusion
Reebok vs Adidas	0.03	4.04	F<CV, null hypothesis cannot be rejected. Not enough evidence to reject that the frequencies of Reebok and Adidas are the same
Puma vs Reebok	7.33	4.04	F>CV, null hypothesis should be rejected. Frequencies of Puma and Reebok are not the same.
Puma vs Adidas	12.13	4.04	F>CV, null hypothesis should be rejected. Frequencies of Puma and Adidas are not the same.
Puma vs Basketball	445.71	4.04	F>CV, null hypothesis should be rejected. Frequencies of Puma and Basketball are not the same.
Reebok vs Basketball	157.49	4.04	F>CV, null hypothesis should be rejected. Frequencies of Reebok and Basketball are not the same.
Adidas vs Basketball	165.04	4.04	F>CV, null hypothesis should be rejected. Frequencies of Adidas and Basketball are not the same.

Machine Learning Models

Simple Models: Linear Regression, Lasso, and Ridge Regression

Before any machine learning models could be run, correlated fields had to be identified. These fields are crucial in any model at predicting the value of the target variable. Highly correlated fields were kept for the models ran, and the leftover fields were dropped. For the Nike stock price models, the fields used were: 'Year', 'Reebok', 'Adidas', 'Nike', 'Basketball', 'Adidas Stock Price', 'Puma Stock Price', 'NBA Finals AVG Rating', 'NBA Revenue', and 'Brand Shares Value'. For the Adidas stock price model, the fields are 'Year', 'Puma', 'Reebok', 'Basketball', 'Nike Stock Price', 'Puma Stock Price', 'NBA Finals AVG Viewers', 'NBA Revenue', and 'Brand Shares Value'. Finally, for the Puma stock price model, the fields are 'Year', 'Reebok', 'Adidas', 'Michael Jordan', 'Basketball', 'Nike Stock Price', 'Adidas Stock Price', 'NBA Finals AVG Rating', 'NBA Finals AVG Viewers', 'NBA Revenue', and 'Brand Shares Value'. These field lists are the same for both the simple machine learning models and the complex machine learning models. There are null values in many of these fields, and these were filled in using the overall means of each column.

To see if the value of a brand could be predicted, different machine learning models were run. With the smaller nature of this dataset, the most likely outcome is that the simple machine learning models will outperform the complex models. A more complex model may not be the best with the final dataset coming in at around 600 rows. Another note before the models are covered is that all had a 75/25 train/test split.

The major simple machine learning model that was performed was a linear regression. It was imported from the Scikit Learn library, and default parameters were used (Linear Models, n.d.). This is because there were no additional attributes that made a significant impact to the model's accuracy. A multiple linear regression "models the linear relationship between a single dependent continuous variable and more than one independent variable" (Multiple Linear Regression, n.d.). Building off this definition, a linear regression is machine learning because the dependent variable can be predicted through this method. In the case of this chapter, the dependent variable is the stock price of the target brand, and all of the other fields used to train the model are independent variables.

There were initially three regressions run in total. One was run for Nike stock price, one for Adidas stock price, and one for Puma stock price. The accuracy of each model was determined by the ".score" metric in Scikit Learn. Figure 4, Figure 5, and Figure 6 display single linear regressions of the stock price for each brand vs the other fields that were in each model. Since the formula for a multiple regression is universal and no parameters were changed in Python, Excel's generated multiple regression line fit plots were utilized to visually display the models.

Nike

The Nike Linear Regression was the most accurate model overall. It had an accuracy score of 95% for both the training dataset and the testing dataset. This closeness in accuracy between the two is a positive, as it implies that the training dataset is not overfit. In terms of predicting the value of Nike stock price in relation to the sport of basketball and other brands, this would be the best model to use out of this chapter. No additional varieties of regression were run on this field, as the results were satisfactory from the simple linear regression and a constraint was not seen as needed on the model.

Figure 4. Linear Regressions of Nike Stock Price

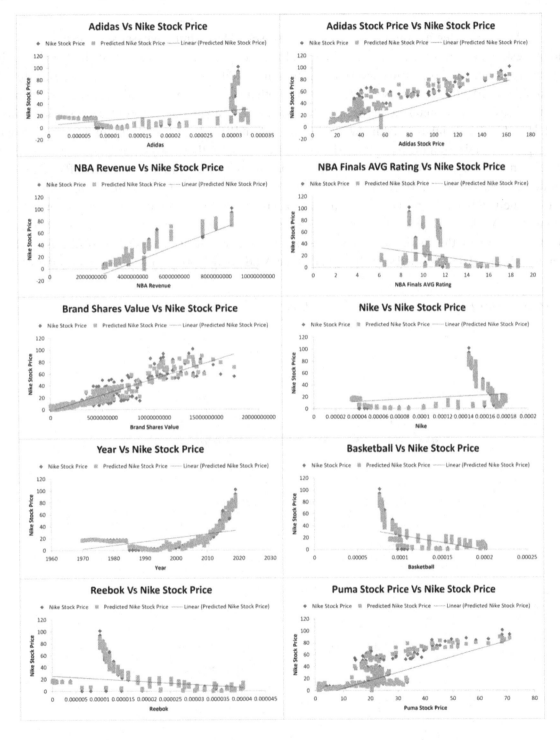

Adidas

The Adidas Linear Regression had decent results as well. The training dataset score came in at 79%, and the testing dataset score came in at 81% initially. Testing accuracy should not be higher than training accuracy, although the difference here was minimal. Additional varieties of regressions were also run in order to try and fix this issue. After running both a Ridge regression and a Lasso regression, the linear regression still maintained the best simple machine learning model for Adidas stock price (Linear Models, n.d.). The accuracy of both new models was around 10% lower for the training and testing data. The gap between the training and testing data was also worse for these two regressions, with the testing set being no less than 4% higher than the training dataset regardless of the alpha value. By adding this additional alpha constraint to the model different results were seen, but they were not favorable.

Ultimately, a linear regression with a training accuracy of 80% and a testing accuracy of 80% was obtained for Adidas stock price. This result was achieved by slightly increasing the test dataset size from 25% to 30%. Again, this model was not as accurate as the Nike linear regression. It is surprising, however, that this model performed so well given that the Adidas stock price only has fourteen years of data.

Figure 5. Linear Regressions of Adidas Stock Price

Puma

The final linear regression that was run was for Puma stock price. Similar to the Adidas stock price regressions, there was an issue here where the testing dataset's score was higher than the training dataset's score. The initial linear regression that was run had a training accuracy of 82% and a testing accuracy of 86%. Again, some additional regressions needed to be run to try and fix this issue.

Ridge and Lasso regressions were run but ultimately did not fix this issue of the training score being higher than the testing score. For Ridge, the best alpha constraint value was .0000000001. The accuracy achieved for this model was 84% for the training dataset and 87% for the testing dataset. The best Lasso model had an alpha value of .0000001. This model also had a training set accuracy of 84% and a testing accuracy of 87%. While the two new models closed the gap by 1% in accuracy, the issue of the testing accuracy being higher could not be resolved in terms of simple machine learning models. That being said, a decent accuracy was achieved with the Ridge regression and Lasso models in terms of predicting the value of Puma's stock price. It is no surprise that the Puma model fell just short in terms of accuracy to the Nike model. This is because Puma entered the stock market before Adidas and a few years after Nike, so it had the second least filled in null values.

Figure 6. Linear Regressions of Puma Stock Price

Complex Model: Neural Network

On top of simple regressions, some more complex machine learning models were also run. A neural network was run for Nike stock price, Adidas stock price, and Puma stock price. The specific neural network that was run in Python was the MLPClassifier out of Scikit Learn. (sklearn.neural_network. MLPClassifier, n.d.). MLP stands for Multi-Layer Perceptron, and it is a supervised machine learning model. This model can be compared to a logistic regression, and the difference is that the MLPClassifier has a non-linear hidden layer between the input and output layers. These attributes make the MLPClassifier able to solve both classification and regression problems (Neural network models (supervised), n.d.). Figure 7 below displays a conceptual multi-layer perceptron neural network model. This figure can be viewed as similar to the neural networks run in this chapter, as the default number of hidden layers (1 input, 1 output) are the same. These models were generally not as accurate as the regressions, but this falls in line with the simplicity of the dataset. Model results for this section can be found in Table 6.

Figure 7. MLPClassifier Conceptual Model with One Hidden Layer
(Created by author; adapted from Neural network models (supervised), n.d.)

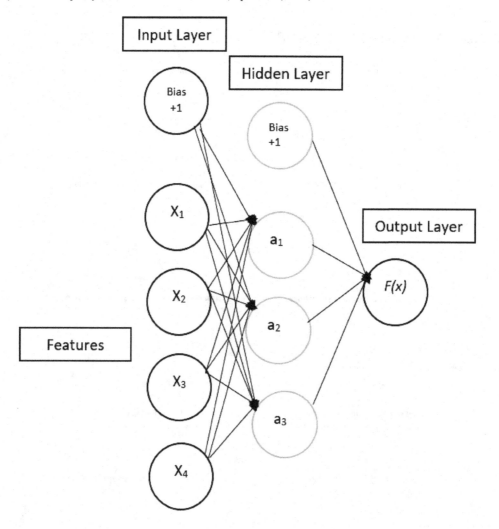

Complex models often take more time to run, and with that in mind a grid search was utilized for each model. A grid search essentially loops through a predefined list of parameters and goes through all possible combinations. It may take a while to run, but it is ultimately faster than manually adjusting parameters and is especially useful in more complex models such as neural networks that take longer on average to run. Parameters are simply stored in dictionary format, and the grid search returns the best scoring parameters which can then be passed into a machine learning model (Sharma, 2020).

The same list of parameters was passed through each model, and it covered a very large range of possibilities. The first parameter in the grid search was "random_state". This parameter "Determines random number generation for weights and bias initialization" (sklearn.neural_network.MLPClassifier, n.d.). A range from zero through nine was used for this. The next parameter in the grid search was "solver". The two values in this list were "adam" and "lbfgs". "Adam" typically works better for large datasets and "lbfgs" typically works better for smaller datasets (sklearn.neural_network.MLPClassifier, n.d.). The final parameter in the grid search is "max_iter". This is the maximum number of iterations that the model goes through until the solver converges (sklearn.neural_network.MLPClassifier, n.d.). Many values were in this list, as a small difference in the number of iterations may lead to a significant difference in model accuracy. The list was "2000, 2500, 3000, 3500, 4000, 4500, 5000, 7500, 10000". These parameters all together allow for a very complex model to be built and offer an intriguing comparison point between the simple and complex machine learning models that were run with this dataset.

Nike

The first neural network that was run was with Nike stock price as the target variable. The optimal parameters that were returned were the solver as "adam", the random state as 5, and the maximum number of iterations as 2000. The data was also scaled before it was passed through the model using MinMaxScaler. This scaler adjusts the values in the dataset to be between zero and one, and scaling is an important step when running a neural network (sklearn.preprocessing.MinMaxScaler, n.d.). The training dataset accuracy was 58% and the testing dataset accuracy was 27%. It was surprising that the ideal solver here was "Adam", as the dataset is not very large in size coming in at just over 600 rows. Even when passing the dataset through a grid search to obtain the best model, the neural network did not predict Nike's stock price very well at all with a low accuracy score and a large difference between the training and testing dataset accuracy scores.

Adidas

The next neural network that was run was with Adidas stock price as the target variable. The same list of parameters was also passed through the grid search for this model as the Nike stock price model. The data was also scaled with MinMaxScaler again. The optimal parameters obtained from this grid search was the solver as "adam", the random state as 1 and the maximum number of iterations as 100. The training set accuracy with these parameters was 73%, and the testing set accuracy was 71%. This is a lot better performing of a model than the Nike stock price neural network. The training set accuracy was slightly higher than the testing set, and it is also fairly accurate.

Puma

The final neural network that was run was for Puma stock price. The optimal parameters returned by the grid search for this model was "adam" as the solver, a random state of 2, and a maximum number of iterations as 100. The training set accuracy was 58%, and the testing set accuracy was 52%. Again, it was a low accuracy overall, but the difference between the training dataset score and the testing dataset score is not bad.

One final thing to note before the models can be compared is that the stock price is not available for every year as previously mentioned. This may have been a factor in some models not performing as well as others. These null values were simply just filled in with the mean of the respective field in order to run the models. Due to this, it was no surprise that Nike had the most accurate model overall while also having the most historical stock price data.

Table 6. Most Accurate Neural Network Model for Each Brand

Brand Name	Parameters	Accuracy
Nike	Solver: "Adam" Random State: 5 Maximum Iterations: 2000	Training: 58% Testing: 27%
Adidas	Solver: "Adam" Random State: 1 Maximum Iterations: 100	Training: 73% Testing: 71%
Puma	Solver: "Adam" Random State: 2 Maximum Iterations: 100	Training: 58% Testing: 52%

CONCLUSION

Nike Conclusion

To conclude, major takeaways and the best performing models will be covered. For Nike stock price, the best model was a simple linear regression. This had an accuracy of 95% for both the training dataset and testing dataset, and it would be a great model for predicting the stock price in the future. Referring to Figure 2 and the amount of historical data on Nike, it is no surprise that it is the best performing machine learning model. In Figure 2, Nike has the smoothest increase in stock price out of all the sports brands. It essentially has been increasing since the company went public, and it makes sense that a simple linear regression is great at predicting the value for this reason with time being a key factor. The neural network not performing well for Nike also makes sense when this is taken into consideration. Having a mean put in place for all the years that the stock price was unavailable may have been what lead to a poorly performing neural network model. Another factor which may have led to this is that it is simply a complex model. Complex machine learning models typically work better with datasets that contain a high amount of variety in the data. With the mean filled in for many rows, that was not the case here.

Adidas Conclusion

The best performing machine learning model for predicting Adidas' stock price was the simple linear regression, although the neural network was not far behind. The best accuracy score was 80% for both the training dataset and testing dataset for the regression models. The neural network was slightly behind the regression's accuracy with a score of 73% for the training dataset and 71% for the testing dataset. The neural network again fell short to the regressions for Adidas similar to what happened with the Nike machine learning models. It is suspected that the size of this dataset and the number of null values that had to be filled in are the leading factors in these models' shortcomings. With time, this model may increase in accuracy as more data is available to use in training. With Adidas stock price data only being available from 2006 and onward, it was expected that this predictive model would perform worse than the Nike regression. Referring to Figure 2, Adidas has increased over time almost steadily with a few dips in value, so this could be one of the key factors in the success of this model. Also, in Table 3 Adidas stock price has a heavy correlation to both NBA revenue and Year. Including both of these two fields in the model most likely played a factor in obtaining a max accuracy of 80% too.

Puma Conclusion

For Puma, the best performing machine learning models were the Ridge and Lasso regressions. The gap between the training dataset accuracy score and the testing dataset score was 1% less, and that is why these were selected as the best two models. The accuracy score was the same for both of these regressions, which is why it was not just one that was selected as the best model. The maximum accuracy score achieved was 84% for training and 87% for testing. It is slightly concerning that the accuracy score is higher for the testing dataset than the training dataset, but it is a relatively small difference. Referring to Table 3, it is not surprising that the model performed so well, as Puma stock price is moderately correlated to many different fields. In Figure 2 though, Puma has a relatively up and down pattern as it has increased in value over time. With this trend in mind, it is surprising that the regression performed so well. Another note on this same topic is the amount of data that had to be filled in before running the models. Puma has a limited stock price history similar to that of the other two brands, so it is surprising that the models performed so well with a decent sized chunk of the data being filled in with the column means.

Final Comparison Points

It can be seen through the various machine learning models conducted in this chapter that the stock price value of a sports brand can be predicted successfully. The Nike linear regression was especially successful at predicting a value for stock price. Data that is crucial to this involves NBA data, and even stock price data on other brands. This data can be seen to have a heavy influence on the stock price of a brand through both the high accuracy of the models, and the high correlation with brand shares value (Table 3). Fields such as these can be used in future models to predict the level of success of a sports brand on the stock market.

For all three brands, the simple machine learning models performed better than the complex models. The best simple machine learning model for Nike was over 30% more accurate for the training data and over 50% more accurate for the testing data than the best complex model. For Adidas, the difference was around 10% for both the training and testing data between the simple and complex models. For Puma, the difference was between 20% and 30% between the simple and complex models too. These differences are significant and could be caused by a variety of issues. The first one would be that complex machine learning models typically do not work very well for datasets that are smaller in nature. The second potential cause is that there simply was not enough real data, as a large number of nulls had to be filled in for the stock price fields. With these issues in mind, the various regressions ran were successful and did complete the task of predicting the stock price of all three of the target sports brands accurately.

REFERENCES

Ali Mahdi, H. A., Abbas, M., Mazar, T., & George, S. (2015). A Comparative Analysis of Strategies and Business Models of Nike, Inc. and Adidas Group with special reference to Competitive Advantage in the context of a Dynamic and Competitive Environment. *International Journal of Business Management and Economic Research.*

Beers, B. (2021, August 27). *Regression Definition.* Retrieved from Investopedia: https://www.investopedia.com/terms/r/regression.asp

Carew, J. M. (n.d.). *Predictive modeling.* Retrieved from TechTarget: https://searchenterpriseai.techtarget.com/definition/predictive-modeling

ceo4ceo. (2018, September 29). *Review of Adidas Basketball Brand History.* Retrieved from Adidas Live Wordpress: adidaslive.wordpress.com/2018/09/29/review-of-adidas-basketball-brand-history/

Davis, S. (2017, April 27). *LeBron James turned down $10 million from Reebok when he was an 18-year-old high school student, and it turned out to be a brilliant business decision.* Retrieved from Business Insider: https://www.businessinsider.com/lebron-james-turned-down-reebok-offer-nike-brilliant-2017-4

de Silva, K. C., Madhushani, A. L., & Jayalath, S. S. (2020, December). *The Impact of Brand Loyalty on Customer Purchase Intention: An Empirical Study on Basketball Shoe Brands of Adidas, Nike and Puma.* Retrieved from Research Gate: https://www.researchgate.net/profile/A-A-L-Madhushani-2/publication/345983988_The_Impact_of_Brand_Loyalty_on_Customer_Purchase_Intention_An_Empirical_Study_on_Basketball_Shoe_Brands_of_Adidas_Nike_and_Puma_in_Asia/links/5fb40b0045851518fdaffcda/The-Impact

Dodson, A. (2019, February 12). *The Forgotten History of Puma Basketball.* Retrieved from The Undefeated: theundefeated.com/features/the-forgotten-history-of-puma-basketball/

Google Books Ngram Viewer. (n.d.). Retrieved from Google Ngrams: https://books.google.com/ngrams

Humphreys, B. R. (2019). *The Effect of Superstars on Game Attendance: Evidence From the NBA.* Sage Journals.

Johnson, R. S. (1998, June 22). *The Jordan Effect The world's greatest basketball player is also one of its great brands. What is his impact on the economy?* Retrieved from IESE Business School: https://web.iese.edu/jestrada/PDF/Courses/ECOWAY/ECOWAY_Fortune-Jordan.pdf

Keefe, M. K. (2011, May). *The impact of athletic apparel company funding on grass roots basketball (2003–2008)*. Retrieved from Proquest: https://www.proquest.com/openview/5072ad398ba88df86cbcf c751e9608ba/1?pq-origsite=gscholar&cbl=18750&diss=y

Linear Models. (n.d.). Retrieved from Scikit Learn: https://scikit-learn.org/stable/modules/linear_model.html

Lynette Knowles Mathur, I. M. (1997). *The wealth effects associated with a celebrity endorser: The Michael Jordan phenomenon*. Gale Academic Onefile.

Maddock, I. I. P. (2018, April 23). *The Economic Implications of NBA Player*. Retrieved from The Claremont Colleges: https://scholarship.claremont.edu/cgi/viewcontent.cgi?article=2992&context=cmc_theses

Michael Jordan. (n.d.). Retrieved from Biography.com: www.biography.com/athlete/michael-jordan

Multiple Linear Regression. (n.d.). Retrieved from JavaTpoint: https://www.javatpoint.com/multiple-linear-regression-in-machine-learning

National Basketball Association total league revenue from 2001/02 to 2019/20(in billion U.S. dollars). (n.d.). Retrieved from Statista: https://www.statista.com/statistics/193467/total-league-revenue-of-the-nba-since-2005/

NBA Finals Ratings History (1988-Present). (n.d.). Retrieved from Sports Media Watch: https://www.sportsmediawatch.com/nba-finals-ratings-viewership-history/

Neural network models (supervised). (n.d.). Retrieved from Scikit Learn: https://scikit-learn.org/stable/modules/neural_networks_supervised.html

Nike Basketball History. (n.d.). Retrieved from Sneaker Files: https://www.sneakerfiles.com/nike/nike-basketball/

Sato, S., Ko, Y. J., Chang, Y., & Kay, M. J. (2018). How Does the Negative Impact of an Athlete's Reputational Crisis Spill Over to Endorsed and Competing Brands? *The Moderating Effects of Consumer Knowledge, 7*, 385–409.

Sharma, M. (2020, March 19). *Grid Search for Hyperparameter Tuning*. Retrieved from Towards Data Science: https://towardsdatascience.com/grid-search-for-hyperparameter-tuning-9f63945e8fec

sklearn.neural_network.MLPClassifier. (n.d.). Retrieved from Scikit Learn: https://scikit-learn.org/stable/modules/generated/sklearn.neural_network.MLPClassifier.html

sklearn.preprocessing.MinMaxScaler. (n.d.). Retrieved from Scikit Learn: https://scikit-learn.org/stable/modules/generated/sklearn.preprocessing.MinMaxScaler.html

Weinfuss, J. (2019, November 24). *Inside The Rise and Fall of the Iconic Reebok Pump on Its 30th Birthday*. Retrieved from ESPN: www.espn.com/nba/story/_/id/28149048/inside-rise-fall-iconic-reebok-pump-30th-birthday

Yahoo Finance Historical Data. (n.d.). Retrieved from Yahoo Finance: https://finance.yahoo.com/

Yang, Y., & Shi, M. (2011). Rise and fall of stars: Investigating the evolution of star status in professional team sports. [Elsevier.]. *International Journal of Research in Marketing*, 28(4), 352–366.

ADDITIONAL READING

Garcia-Lopez, F., Batyrshin, I., & Gelbukh, A. (2018). Analysis of relationships between tweets and stock market trends. *Journal of Intelligent & Fuzzy Systems*, 34(5), 3337–3347. doi:10.3233/JIFS-169515

Kamalov, F. (2020, May 4). Forecasting significant stock price changes using neural networks. Retrieved from EBSCOhost: http://bryant.idm.oclc.org/login?url=https://search.ebscohost.com/login.aspx?direct=true&db=aph&AN=146996807&site=ehost-live

Lv, D., Huang, Z., Li, M., & Xiang, Y. (2019). Selection of the optimal trading model for stock investment in different industries. *Public Library of Science* (PLOS). Retrieved from http://bryant.idm.oclc.org/login?url=https://search.ebscohost.com/login.aspx?direct=true&db=aph&AN=134679643&site=ehost-live

Mundra, A., Mundra, S., Verma, V., Srivastava, J., Balas, V., & Jain, L. C. (2020). A deep learning based hybrid framework for stock price prediction. *Journal of Intelligent & Fuzzy Systems*, 38(5), 5921–5931. doi:10.3233/JIFS-179679

Ntakaris, I. A., Kanniainen, J., Gabbouj, M., & Iosifidis, A. (2020). *Mid-price prediction based on machine learning methods with technical and quantitative indicators*. Public Library of Science. doi:10.1371/journal.pone.0234107

Shi, C., & Zhuang, X. (2019). A Study Concerning Soft Computing Approaches for Stock Price Forecasting. *Axioms*, 8(4), 116. doi:10.3390/axioms8040116

Sun, X.-Q., Shen, H.-W., Cheng, X.-Q., & Zhang, Y. (2016). Market Confidence Predicts Stock Price: Beyond Supply and Demand. *Public Library of Science*. Retrieved from http://bryant.idm.oclc.org/login?url=https://search.ebscohost.com/login.aspx?direct=true&db=aph&AN=116697775&site=ehost-live

Yu, P., & Yan, X. (2019, April 17). Stock price prediction based on deep neural networks. Retrieved from EBSCOhost: http://bryant.idm.oclc.org/login?url=https://search.ebscohost.com/login.aspx?direct=true&db=aph&AN=141999667&site=ehost-live

KEY TERMS AND DEFINITIONS

Correlation: A connection or relationship that is seen between two numbers.
Google Ngrams: Tool offered by Google that contains frequency data of a term in literature.
Michael Jordan: Michael Jordan is argued by many to be the greatest basketball player of all time and he carries a heavy influence on anything that he is involved in.

Multi-Layer Perception (MLP): MLP is a supervised machine learning model that can be compared to a logistic regression. One of the main differences is that the MLPClassifier has a non-linear hidden layer between the input and output layers. The attributes of this model make it good for both classification and regression problems. (Neural network models (supervised), n.d.). See Figure 7 for a conceptual example.

National Basketball Association (NBA): The premier professional basketball league in not only the United States, but also in the world.

Predictive Modeling: A mathematical process that seeks to predict future events or outcomes by analyzing patterns that are likely to forecast future results (Carew, n.d.).

Regression: A statistical method used in finance, investing, and other disciplines that attempts to determine the strength and character of the relationship between one dependent variable (usually denoted by Y) and a series of other variables (known as independent variables) (Beers, 2021).

Scikit Learn: Open-source Python library that offers predictive models and analysis metrics.

Stock Price: The value of a company on the stock market at a specific point in time.

Total Brand Value: Total brand value references a calculation that is as follows: å (Closing Stock Price * Volume of shares). All individual brand values are summed to reach this number.

Compilation of References

Abadi, M., Barham, P., Chen, J., Chen, Z., Davis, A., Dean, J., Devin, M., Ghemawat, S., Irving, G., Isard, M., Kudlur, M., Levenberg, J., Monga, R., Moore, S., Murray, D. G., Steiner, B., Tucker, P., Vasudevan, V., Warden, P., . . . Zheng, X. (2016, May 31). *TensorFlow: A system for large-scale machine learning.* https://arxiv.org/abs/1605.08695

Abdelrahman, A.A. (2020). *Artificial Intelligence and COVID-19: Identify COVID-19 from chest X ray Images by Artificial Intelligence.* LAP LAMBERT Academic Publishing.

Abdulaal, A., Patel, A., Charani, E., Denny, S., Mughal, N., & Moore, L. (2020, August 25). Prognostic Modeling of COVID-19 Using Artificial Intelligence in the United Kingdom: Model Development and Validation. *Journal of Medical Internet Research*, 22(8), e20259. doi:10.2196/20259 PMID:32735549

Abdulrahman, B. M. A., Ahmed, A. Y. A., & Abdellah, A. E. Y. (2018). Forecasting of Sudan Inflation Rates using ARIMA Model. *International Journal of Economics Financial Issues*, 8(3), 17.

Abu Mouch, S., Roguin, A., Hellou, E., Ishai, A., Shoshan, U., Mahamid, L., Zoabi, M., Aisman, M., Goldschmid, N., & Berar Yanay, N. (2021). Myocarditis following COVID-19 mRNA vaccination. *Vaccine*, 39(29), 3790–3793. doi:10.1016/j.vaccine.2021.05.087 PMID:34092429

Ackerman, D. (2021). *A machine-learning approach to finding treatment options for Covid-19.* MIT News Release. Retrieved February 16, 2021 from https://www.eurekalert.org/pub_releases/2021-02/miot-ama021221.php

Admin. (2021, January 1). *Perceptron - Deep Learning Basics.* Start-Tech Academy. https://starttechacademy.com/perceptron-deep-learning-basics/#:~:text=In%201958%20Frank%20Rosenblatt%20proposed%20the%20perceptron%2C%20a,was%20refined%20and%20perfected%20by%20Minsky%20and%20Papert

Agarwal, M., Saba, L., Gupta, S. K., Carriero, A., Falaschi, Z., Paschè, A., Danna, P., El-Baz, A., Naidu, S., & Suri, J. S. (2021, January 26). A Novel Block Imaging Technique Using Nine Artificial Intelligence Models for COVID-19 Disease Classification, Characterization and Severity Measurement in Lung Computed Tomography Scans on an Italian Cohort. *Journal of Medical Systems*, 45(3), 28. doi:10.100710916-021-01707-w PMID:33496876

Agbehadji, I. E., Awuzie, B. O., Ngowi, A. B., & Millham, R. C. (2020, August). Review of Big Data Analytics, Artificial Intelligence and Nature-Inspired Computing Models towards Accurate Detection of COVID-19 Pandemic Cases and Contact Tracing. *International Journal of Environmental Research and Public Health*, 17(15), 5330. doi:10.3390/ijerph17155330 PMID:32722154

Agency for Healthcare Research and Quality. (2019, June 25). Retrieved from https://meps.ahrq.gov/mepsweb/survey_comp/household.jsp

Agency for Healthcare Research and Quality. (n.d.). Retrieved from https://datatools.ahrq.gov/meps-hc

Agrebi, S., & Larbi, A. (2020). Use of artificial intelligence in infectious diseases. *Artificial Intelligence in Precision Health*, 415–438. doi:10.1016/B978-0-12-817133-2.00018-5

Ahmad, M. W., Mourshed, M., & Rezgui, Y. (2017). Trees vs Neurons: Comparison between random forest and ANN for high-resolution prediction of building energy consumption. *Energy and Bulidings*, *147*, 77–89. doi:10.1016/j.enbuild.2017.04.038

Ahmad, S. M., Busser, B. W., Huang, D., Cozart, E. J., Michaud, S., Zhu, X., Jeffries, N., Aboukhalil, A., Bulyk, M. L., Ovcharenko, I., & Michelson, A. M. (2014). Machine learning classification of cell-specific cardiac enhancers uncovers developmental subnetworks regulating progenitor cell division and cell fate specification. *Development*, *141*(4), 878–888. doi:10.1242/dev.101709 PMID:24496624

Ahmed, S., Hossain, T., Hoque, O. B., Sarker, S., Rahman, S., & Shah, F. M. (2021). Automated COVID-19 Detection from Chest X-Ray Images: A High-Resolution Network (HRNet) Approach. *Sn Comput. Sci*, *2*(4), 294. doi:10.100742979-021-00690-w PMID:34056622

AIC. (n.d.). Retrieved from https://stat.ethz.ch/R-manual/R-devel/library/stats/html/AIC.html

Akaike information criterion. (n.d.). In *Wikipedia*. https://en.wikipedia.org/wiki/Akaike_information_criterion

Alam, T. M., Shaukat, K., Hameed, I. A., Luo, S., Sarwar, M. U., Shabbir, S., Li, J., & Khushi, M. (2020). An Investigation of Credit Card Default Prediction in the Imbalanced Datasets. *IEEE Access: Practical Innovations, Open Solutions*, *8*, 201173–201198. doi:10.1109/ACCESS.2020.3033784

Algorithmia. (2019). *Six Open-Source Machine Learning Tools you should know*. Retrieved November 24, 2020 from https://algorithmia.com/blog/six-open-source-machine-learning-tools-you-should-know

Ali Mahdi, H. A., Abbas, M., Mazar, T., & George, S. (2015). A Comparative Analysis of Strategies and Business Models of Nike, Inc. and Adidas Group with special reference to Competitive Advantage in the context of a Dynamic and Competitive Environment. *International Journal of Business Management and Economic Research*.

Ali, Z., Hussain, I., Faisal, M., Nazir, H. M., Hussain, T., Shad, M. Y., . . . Hussain Gani, S. (2017). Forecasting drought using multilayer perceptron artificial neural network model. Advances in Meteorology.

Ali, S. R., Nguyen, D., Wang, B., Jiang, S., & Sadek, H. A. (2020). Deep learning identifies cardiomyocyte nuclei with high precision. *Circulation Research*, *127*(5), 696–698. doi:10.1161/CIRCRESAHA.120.316672 PMID:32486999

Allen Institute for AI. (2021, July 13). *COVID-19 open Research Dataset Challenge (CORD-19)*. Kaggle. https://www.kaggle.com/allen-institute-for-ai/CORD-19-research-challenge?select=metadata.csv

Allen, R. (2017). *Cheat Sheet of Machine Learning and Python (and Math) Cheat Sheets*. Retrieved December 30, 2020 from https://medium.com/machine-learning-in-practice/cheat-sheet-of-machine-learning-and-python-and-math-cheat-sheets-a4afe4e791b6

Alnaa, S. E., & Ahiakpor, F. (2011). ARIMA (autoregressive integrated moving average) approach to predicting inflation in Ghana. *Journal of Economics International Finance*, *3*(5), 328.

Alsaade & Al-Adhaileh. (2021). Developing a recognition system for classifying covid-19 using a convolutional neural network algorithm. *Computers, Materials & Continua*, *68*(1), 805–819. doi:10.32604/cmc.2021.016264

Altman, N. (1992). An introduction to kernel and nearest-neighbor nonparametric regression. *The American Statistician*, *46*, 175–185.

Al-Turjman, F. (2021). *Artificial Intelligence and Machine Learning for COVID-19*. Springer. doi:10.1007/978-3-030-60188-1

Álvarez-Díaz, M., González-Gómez, M., & Otero-Giráldez, M. S. (2019). Forecasting international tourism demand using a non-linear autoregressive neural network and genetic programming. *Forecasting*, *1*(1), 90–106. doi:10.3390/forecast1010007

Alzahrani, S. I., Aljamaan, I. A., & Al-Fakih, E. A. (2020). Forecasting the spread of the COVID-19 pandemic in Saudi Arabia using ARIMA prediction model under current public health interventions. *Journal of Infection and Public Health*, *13*(7), 914–919. doi:10.1016/j.jiph.2020.06.001 PMID:32546438

American Psychological Association. (2017). *Addressing the Mental and Behavioral Health Needs of Underserved Populations*. American Psychological Association. https://www.apa.org/advocacy/workforce-development/gpe/populations

Anand, A., Lamba, Y., & Roy, A. (2020). Forecasting COVID-19 Transmission in India Using Deep Learning Models. *Letters in Applied NanoBioScience*, *10*(2), 2044–2055. doi:10.33263/LIANBS102.20442055

Antoniades, C., Asselbergs, F. W., & Vardas, P. (2021). The year in cardiovascular medicine 2020: Digital health and innovation. *European Heart Journal*, *42*(7), 732–739. doi:10.1093/eurheartj/ehaa1065 PMID:33388767

Areekul, P., Senjyu, T., Toyama, H., & Yona, A. (2010). A Hybrid ARIMA and Neural Network Model for Short-Term Price Forecasting in Deregulated Market. *IEEE Transactions on Power Systems*, *25*(1), 524–530. doi:10.1109/TPWRS.2009.2036488

Arestis, P., Baddeley, M., & Sawyer, M. (2007, April). The Relationship Between Capital Stock, Unemployment and Wages in Nine EMU Countries. *Bulletin of Economic Research*, *59*(2), 13–15. doi:10.1111/j.0307-3378.2007.00254.x

Arestis, P., & Mariscal, B.-F. (2000). Capital shortages, unemployment and wages in the UK and Germany. *Scottish Journal of Political Economy*, *47*(5), 487–503. doi:10.1111/1467-9485.00175

Arga, K.Y. (2020). COVID-19 and the future of machine learning. *OMICS: A Journal of Integrative Biology*, 512-514. doi:10.1089/omi.2020.0093

Argyris, Y., Monu, K., Tan, P., Aarts, C., Jiang, F., & Wiseley, K. (2021). Using machine learning to compare provaccine and antivaccine discourse among the public on social media: Algorithm Development Study. *JMIR Public Health and Surveillance*, *7*(6), e23105. doi:10.2196/23105 PMID:34185004

Arias Velásquez, R. M., & Mejía Lara, J. V. (2020). Forecast and evaluation of COVID-19 spreading in USA with reduced-space Gaussian process regression. *Chaos, Solitons, and Fractals*, *136*, 109924. doi:10.1016/j.chaos.2020.109924 PMID:32501372

Arora, T., & Soni, R. (2021). A pre-screening approach for COVID-19 testing based on Belief Rule-Based Expert System. In COVID-19: Prediction, Decision-Making, and its Impacts. Springer Singapore. doi:10.1007/978-981-15-9682-7_3

Arora, P., Kumar, H., & Panigrahi, B. K. (2020). Prediction and analysis of COVID-19 positive cases using Deep Learning Models: A descriptive case study of India. *Chaos, Solitons, and Fractals*, *139*, 110017. doi:10.1016/j.chaos.2020.110017 PMID:32572310

Arunraj, N. S., & Ahrens, D. (2015). A hybrid seasonal autoregressive integrated moving average and quantile regression for daily food sales forecasting. *International Journal of Production Economics*, *170*, 321–335. doi:10.1016/j.ijpe.2015.09.039

Arya, S., & Devi, S. P. (2021). Prediction to Service Delivery: AI in Action. In COVID-19: Prediction, Decision-Making, and its Impacts. Springer Singapore. doi:10.1007/978-981-15-9682-7_12

Asnaoui, K. E., Chawki, Y., & Idri, A. (2020). *Automated methods for detection and classification pneumonia based on x-ray images using deep learning.* arXiv preprint arXiv:2003.14363.

Athey, S., Tibshirani, J., & Wager, S. (2019). Generalized random forests. *Annals of Statistics, 47*(2), 1148–1178. doi:10.1214/18-AOS1709

Atkeson, A. (2020). *What Will Be the Economic Impact of COVID-19 in the U.S.?* Rough Estimates of Disease Scenarios. doi:10.3386/w26867

Attia, Z. I., Kapa, S., Yao, X., Lopez-Jimenez, F., Mohan, T. L., Pellikka, P. A., Carter, R. E., Shah, N. D., Friedman, P. A., & Noseworthy, P. A. (2019). Prospective validation of a deep learning electrocardiogram algorithm for the detection of left ventricular systolic dysfunction. *Journal of Cardiovascular Electrophysiology, 30*(5), 668–674. doi:10.1111/jce.13889 PMID:30821035

Attia, Z. I., Noseworthy, P. A., Lopez-Jimenez, F., Asirvatham, S. J., Deshmukh, A. J., Gersh, B. J., Carter, R. E., Yao, X., Rabinstein, A. A., Erickson, B. J., Kapa, S., & Friedman, P. A. (2019). An artificial intelligence-enabled ECG algorithm for the identification of patients with atrial fibrillation during sinus rhythm: A retrospective analysis of outcome prediction. *Lancet, 394*(10201), 861–867. doi:10.1016/S0140-6736(19)31721-0 PMID:31378392

Ayan, E., & Ünver, H. M. (2019, April). Diagnosis of pneumonia from chest x-ray images using deep learning. In *2019 Scientific Meeting on Electrical-Electronics & Biomedical Engineering and Computer Science (EBBT)* (pp. 1-5). IEEE.

Bahl, A. (2019, November 22). *MAPE v/s MAE% v/s RMSE.* Retrieved from https://agrimabahl.medium.com/mape-v-s-mae-v-s-rmse-3e358fd58f65

Bahrami, M., & Sadeddin, S. (2021). *Classifying Cough Sounds to Predict COVID-19 Diagnosis.* Retrieved February 15, 2021 from https://blog.wolfram.com/2021/02/10/classifying-cough-sounds-to-predict-covid-19-diagnosis/

Baker, R. S., Bloom, N., & Davis, J. S. (2015). *Measuring Economic Policy Uncertainty.* National Bureau of Economic Research. doi:10.3386/w21633

Barrett, L., Payrovnaziri, S. N., Bian, J., & He, Z. (2019). Building computational models to predict one-year mortality in ICU patients with acute myocardial infarction and post myocardial infarction syndrome. *AMIA Joint Summits on Translational Science Proceedings. AMIA Joint Summits on Translational Science, 2019*, 407–416. PMID:31258994

Baruah, L. (2017). Performance Comparison of Binarized Neural Network with Convolutional Neural Network. *Digital Commons @ Michigan Tech.* doi:10.37099/mtu.dc.etdr/487

Bassi, P. R. A. S., & Attux, R. (2020). *A Deep Convolutional Neural Network Model for COVID-19 Detection using Chest X-rays.* Retrieved January 17, 2020 from https://arxiv.org/abs/2005.01578

Becker, G., & Newsom, E. (2003, May). Socioeconomic status and dissatisfaction with health care among chronically ill African Americans. *American Journal of Public Health.* https://www.ncbi.nlm.nih.gov/pmc/articles/PMC1447830/

Becker, A. S., Blüthgen, C., Sekaggya-Wiltshire, C., Castelnuovo, B., Kambugu, A., Fehr, J., & Frauenfelder, T. (2018). Detection of tuberculosis patterns in digital photographs of chest X-ray images using Deep Learning: Feasibility study. *The International Journal of Tuberculosis and Lung Disease, 22*(3), 328–335.

Beers, B. (2021, August 27). *Regression Definition.* Retrieved from Investopedia: https://www.investopedia.com/terms/r/regression.asp

Bellot, A., & Schaar, M. (2019). A hierarchical Bayesian model for personalized survival predictions. *IEEE Journal of Biomedical and Health Informatics, 23*(1), 72–80. doi:10.1109/JBHI.2018.2832599 PMID:29994056

Bellotti, T., & Crook, J. (2013). Forecasting and Stress Testing Credit Card Default using Dynamic Models. *International Journal of Forecasting*, 29(4), 563–574. doi:10.1016/j.ijforecast.2013.04.003

Bengio, Y., Courville, A. C., & Vincent, P. (2013). Representation learning: A review and new perspectives. *IEEE Transactions on Pattern Analysis and Machine Intelligence*, 35(8), 1798–1828. doi:10.1109/TPAMI.2013.50 PMID:23787338

Bengio, Y., Simard, P., & Frasconi, P. (1994). Learning long-term dependencies with gradient descent is difficult. *IEEE Transactions on Neural Networks*, 5(2), 157–166. doi:10.1109/72.279181 PMID:18267787

Benjamins, J. W., Hendriks, T., Knuuti, J., Juarez-Orozco, L. E., & van der Harst, P. (2019). A primer in artificial intelligence in cardiovascular medicine. *Netherlands Heart Journal; Monthly Journal of the Netherlands Society of Cardiology and the Netherlands Heart Foundation*, 27(9), 392–402. doi:10.100712471-019-1286-6 PMID:31111458

Benvenuto, D., Giovanetti, M., Vassallo, L., Angeletti, S., & Ciccozzi, M. (2020). Application of the ARIMA model on the COVID-2019 epidemic dataset. *Data in Brief*, 29, 105340. doi:10.1016/j.dib.2020.105340 PMID:32181302

Berk, M. L., & Monheit, A. C. (2001, March 01). The concentration of health care expenditures, revisited. *Health Affairs*, 20(2), 9–18. doi:10.1377/hlthaff.20.2.9 PMID:11260963

Bhapkar, H. R., Mahalle, P. N., Shinde, G. R., & Mahmud, M. (2021). Rough Sets in COVID-19 to Predict Symptomatic Cases. In COVID-19: Prediction, Decision-Making, and its Impacts. doi:10.1007/978-981-15-9682-7_7

Bhattacharyya, N. (2011). Incremental Healthcare Utilization and Expenditures for Allergic Rhinitis in the United States. *The Laryngoscope*, 121(9), 1830-1833.

Biau, G. (2012). Analysis of a Random Forests Model. *Journal of Machine Learning Research*, 3, 1063-1095.

Biedenbender, C., Berleant, D., Eversole, K., E. Hood, E., Leach, L., Mustell, R., R. Segall, R., & Vicuna, D. (2011). Text Mining: Using Rule Based and Neural Network Based Approaches. *2011 University of Arkansas at Little Rock (UALR) Student Research Expo.*

Bivens, J. (2019, January 30). *The economic costs and benefits of Airbnb.* Retrieved from Economic Policy Institute: https://www.epi.org/publication/the-economic-costs-and-benefits-of-airbnb-no-reason-for-local-policymakers-to-let-airbnb-bypass-tax-or-regulatory-obligations/

BMC. (2021). *BMC Helix Capacity Optimization.* BMC Datasheet. Retrieved February 18, 2021 from https://www.bmc.com/it-solutions/bmc-helix-capacity-optimization.html

Bock, J. (2018). *Quantifying macroeconomic expectations in stock markets using Google Trends.* Department of Finance, Warwick Business School, University of Warwick. doi:10.2139srn.3218912

Bodapati, S., Bandarupally, H., & Trupthi, M. (2020). COVID-19 Time Series Forecasting of Daily Cases, Deaths Caused and Recovered Cases using Long Short Term Memory Networks. *2020 IEEE 5th International Conference on Computing Communication and Automation (ICCCA).* 10.1109/ICCCA49541.2020.9250863

Bogacz, M. (2021, January 30). *Restaurant business RANKINGS 2020.* Kaggle. https://www.kaggle.com/michau96/restaurant-business-rankings-2020

Bonas, M., Nguyen, S., Olinsky, A., Quinn, J., & Schumacher, P. (2020). A Method to Determine the Size of the Resampled Data in Imbalanced Classification. *Contemporary Perspectives in Data Mining*, 4, 119.

Bootstrapping (statistics). (2021, July 15). Retrieved from https://en.wikipedia.org/wiki/Bootstrapping_(statistics)#Advantages

Boser, B. E., Guyon, I. M., & Vapnik, V. N. (1992). A training algorithm for optimal margin classifiers. *Proceedings of the Fifth Annual ACM Workshop on Computational Learning Theory*, 144-152. 10.1145/130385.130401

Box, G. E., Jenkins, G. M., Reinsel, G. C., & Ljung, G. M. (2015). *Time series analysis: forecasting and control* (5th ed.). Forecasting and Control.

Boyd, J. H., Hu, J., & Jagannathan, R. (2005). The Stock Market's Reaction to Unemployment News: Why Bad News Is Usually Good for Stocks. *The Journal of Finance*, *60*(2), 649–672. doi:10.1111/j.1540-6261.2005.00742.x

Branca, L., Sbolli, M., Metra, M., & Fudim, M. (2020). Heart failure with mid-range ejection fraction: Pro and cons of the new classification of heart failure by European Society of Cardiology guidelines. *ESC Heart Failure*, *7*(2), 381–399. doi:10.1002/ehf2.12586 PMID:32239646

Braunwald, E. (2013). Heart failure. *JACC. Heart Failure*, *1*(1), 1–20. doi:10.1016/j.jchf.2012.10.002 PMID:24621794

Breiman, L. (1994). *Bagging Predictors*. Technical Report.

Breiman, L., Friedman, J. H., Olshen, R. A., & Stone, C. J. (1984). Classification and regression trees. Wadsworth & Brooks/Cole Advanced Books & Software.

Breiman, L. (2001). Random Forests. *Machine Learning*, *45*(1), 5–32. doi:10.1023/A:1010933404324

Broman, C. L. (2012). Race differences in the receipt of mental health services among young adults. *Psychological Services*, *9*(1), 38–48. doi:10.1037/a0027089 PMID:22449086

Brownlee, J. (2017). *A Gentle Introduction to Long Short-Term Memory Networks by the Experts*. Retrieved December 26, 2020 from https://machinelearningmastery.com/gentle-introduction-long-short-term-memory-networks-experts/

Brush, K. (2019). *Chatbot*. Retrieved May 9, 2021 from https://searchcustomerexperience.techtarget.com/definition/chatbot?vgnextfmt=print

Bullock, J., Luccioni, A., Pham, K. H., & Luengo-Oroz, M. (2020). Mapping the Landscape of Artificial Intelligence Applications against COVID-19. *Journal of Artificial Intelligence Research*, *69*, 807–845. doi:10.1613/jair.1.12162

Bursi, F., Weston, S. A., Redfield, M. M., Jacobsen, S. J., Pakhomov, S., Nkomo, V. T., Meverden, R. A., & Roger, V. L. (2006). Systolic and diastolic heart failure in the community. *Journal of the American Medical Association*, *296*(18), 2209–2216. doi:10.1001/jama.296.18.2209 PMID:17090767

Caballé, N., Castillo-Sequera, J., Gomez-Pulido, J. A., Gómez, J., & Polo-Luque, M. (2020). Machine learning applied to diagnosis of human diseases: A systematic review. *Applied Sciences (Basel, Switzerland)*, *10*(15), 5135. Advance online publication. doi:10.3390/app10155135

Cai, F. (2020). DarwinAI open-source COVID-Net as medical image in COVID-19 diagnosis debate continues. *Synced: AI Technology & Industry Review*. Retrieved May 17, 2020 from https://syncedreview.com/2020/04/02/darwinai-open-sources-covid-net-as-medical-imaging-in-covid-19-diagnosis-debate-continues/

Callaway, E. (2020). 'It will change everything': DeepMind's AI makes gigantic leap in solving protein structures. *Nature*, *588*(7837), 203–204. doi:10.1038/d41586-020-03348-4 PMID:33257889

Campesato, O. (2020). *Artificial Intelligence, Machine Learning, and Deep Learning*. Mercury Learning & Information.

Cang, S. (2011). A non-linear tourism demand forecast combination model. *Tourism Economics*, *17*(1), 5–20. doi:10.5367/te.2011.0031

Carew, J. M. (n.d.). *Predictive modeling*. Retrieved from TechTarget: https://searchenterpriseai.techtarget.com/definition/predictive-modeling

Castle, N. (2017). *6 Common Machine Learning Applications for Business*. Retrieved May 9, 2021 from https://blogs.oracle.com/ai-and-datascience/post/6-common-machine-learning-applications-for-business

Centers for Disease Control and Prevention. (2020, March 9). *Pneumonia*. Centers for Disease Control and Prevention. https://www.cdc.gov/pneumonia/index.html

Centers for Disease Control and Prevention. (2021). *Vaccines for COVID-19*. Centers for Disease Control and Prevention. https://www.cdc.gov/coronavirus/2019-ncov/vaccines/index.html

ceo4ceo. (2018, September 29). *Review of Adidas Basketball Brand History*. Retrieved from Adidas Live Wordpress: adidaslive.wordpress.com/2018/09/29/review-of-adidas-basketball-brand-history/

Céspedes, N., Irfan, B., Senft, E., Cifuentes, C. A., Gutierrez, L. F., Rincon-Roncancio, M., Belpaeme, T., & Múnera, M. (2021). A socially assistive robot for long-term cardiac rehabilitation in the real world. *Frontiers in Neurobototics*, *15*, 1–19. doi:10.3389/fnbot.2021.633248 PMID:33828473

Chakraborty, T., & Ghosh, I. (2020). Real-time forecasts and risk assessment of novel coronavirus (COVID-19) cases: A data-driven analysis. doi:10.1101/2020.04.09.20059311

Chandra, R., Jain, A., & Chauhan, D. S. (2021, January 28). *Deep learning via LSTM models for COVID-19 infection forecasting in India*. Retrieved September 30, 2021, from https://arxiv.org/abs/2101.11881

Chang, H.-Y., Boyd, C. M., Leff, B., Lemke, K. W., Bodycombe, D. P., & Weiner, J. P. (2016, September). (2016-09). Identifying Consistent High-cost Users in a Health Plan: Comparison of Alternative Prediction Models. *Medical Care*, *54*(9), 852–859. doi:10.1097/MLR.0000000000000566 PMID:27326548

Chang, S., Kim, H., Suh, Y. J., Choi, D. M., Kim, H., Kim, D. K., Kim, J. Y., Yoo, J. Y., & Choi, B. W. (2021). Development of a deep learning-based algorithm for the automatic detection and quantification of aortic valve calcium. *European Journal of Radiology*, *137*, 109582. Advance online publication. doi:10.1016/j.ejrad.2021.109582 PMID:33578089

Charleonnan, A. (2016). Credit Card Fraud Detection using RUS and MRN Algorithms. *2016 Management and Innovation Technology International Conference (MITicon)*, MIT-73-MIT-76. 10.1109/MITICON.2016.8025244

Chatfield, C. (2001). *Time-series forecasting*. Chapman & Hall/CRC Press.

Chawki, M. (2021). Artificial Intelligence (AI) joins the Fight against COVID-19. In COVID-19: Prediction, Decision-Making, and its Impacts. Springer Singapore. doi:10.1007/978-981-15-9682-7_1

Chawla, N. V., Bowyer, K. W., Hall, L. O., & Kegelmeyer, W. P. (2002). SMOTE: Synthetic minority over-sampling technique. *Journal of Artificial Intelligence Research*, *16*, 321–357.

Chen, Y., Jiang, G., Li, Y., Tang, Y., Xu, Y., Ding, S., Xin, Y., & Lu, Y. (2020). A Survey on Artificial Intelligence in Chest Imaging of COVID-19. *BIO Integration*, *1*(3), 137–146. doi:10.15212/bioi-2020-0015

Chen, J., Li, W., & Xiang, M. (2020). Burden of valvular heart disease, 1990-2017: Results from the Global Burden of Disease Study 2017. *Journal of Global Health*, *10*(2), 020404. Advance online publication. doi:10.7189/jogh.10.020404 PMID:33110570

Chen, M., Ju, C. J. T., Zhou, G., Chen, X., Zhang, T., Chang, K. W., Zaniolo, C., & Wang, W. (2019). Multifaceted protein–protein interaction prediction based on Siamese residual RCNN. *Bioinformatics (Oxford, England)*, *35*(14), i305–i314. doi:10.1093/bioinformatics/btz328 PMID:31510705

Chen, X., Diaz-Pinto, A., Ravikumar, N., & Frangi, A. F. (2020). Deep learning in medical image registration. *Progress in Biomedical Engineering, 3*(1). Advance online publication. doi:10.1088/2516-1091/abd37c

Chen, X., & Ishwaran, H. (2012). Random forests for genomic data analysis. *Genomics, 99*(6), 323–329. doi:10.1016/j.ygeno.2012.04.003 PMID:22546560

Chimmula, V. K., & Zhang, L. (2020). Time series forecasting of COVID-19 transmission in Canada using LSTM networks. *Chaos, Solitons, and Fractals, 135*, 109864. doi:10.1016/j.chaos.2020.109864 PMID:32390691

Chinonso, U. E., & Justice, O. I. (2016). Modelling Nigeria's urban and rural inflation using Box-Jenkins model. *Scientific Papers. Series Management, Economic Engineering in Agriculture and Rural Development, 16*(4), 61-68.

Chishti, W. A., & Awan, S. M. (2019). Deep Neural Network a Step-by-Step Approach to Classify Credit Card Default Customer. *2019 International Conference on Innovative Computing (ICIC)*, 1–8. 10.1109/ICIC48496.2019.8966723

Cho, K., van Merrienboer, B., Gulcehre, C., Bahdanau, D., Bougares, F., Schwenk, H., & Bengio, Y. (2014). *Learning Phrase Representations using RNN Encoder-Decoder for Statistical Machine Translation*. doi:10.3115/v1/D14-1179

Cho, K., van Merrienboer, B., Gulcehre, C., Bahdanau, D., Bougares, F., Schwenk, H., & Bengio, Y. (2014). Learning phrase representations using RNN Encoder-Decoder for statistical machine translation. *arXivLabs*. https://arxiv.org/abs/1406.1078v3

Choi, E., Schuetz, A., Stewart, W., & Sun, J. (2016). Using recurrent neural network models for early detection of heart failure onset. *Journal of the American Medical Informatics Association: JAMIA, 24*(2), 361–370. doi:10.1093/jamia/ocw112 PMID:27521897

Chollet, F. (2020). *The Keras Blog*. The Keras Blog ATOM. https://blog.keras.io/author/francois-chollet.html

Chollet, F. (2017). *Deep Learning with Python*. Manning Publications.

Chollet, F. (2017). Xception: Deep learning with depthwise separable convolutions. In *Proceedings of The IEEE Conference on Computer Vision And Pattern Recognition* (pp. 1251-1258). IEEE.

Choubey, A. M. (2018). *Predicting Credit Default Risk via Statistical Model and Machine Learning Algorithms* (Masters Thesis in Economics). The University of North Carolina at Charlotte (UNCC).

Chouldechova, A., & Roth, A. (2020, May). A snapshot of the frontiers of fairness in machine learning. *Communications of the ACM, 63*(5), 82–89. doi:10.1145/3376898

Chow, J. C.-C., Jaffee, K., & Snowden, L. (2003). Racial/Ethnic Disparities in the Use of Mental Health Services in Poverty Areas. *American Journal of Public Health, 93*(5), 792–797. doi:10.2105/AJPH.93.5.792 PMID:12721146

Chung, M. K., Zidar, D. A., Bristow, M. R., Cameron, S. J., Chan, T., Harding, C. V. III, Kwon, D. H., Singh, T., Tilton, J. C., Tsai, E. J., Tucker, N. R., Bernard, J., & Loscalzo, J. (2021). COVID-19 and cardiovascular disease: From bench to bedside. *Circulation Research, 128*(8), 1214–1236. doi:10.1161/CIRCRESAHA.121.317997 PMID:33856918

Colak, A. B. (2021). COVID-19 Projections Using Machine Learning. *Coronaviruses: The World's First International Journal Dedicated to Coronaviruses*. Retrieved August 9, 2020 from https://www.eurekaselect.com/node/185917/article/prediction-of-infection-and-death-ratio-of-covid-19-virus-in-turkey-by-using-artificial-neural-network-ann

Cole, G. D., Dhutia, N. M., Shun-Shin, M. J., Willson, K., Harrison, J., Raphael, C. E., Zolgharni, M., Mayet, J., & Francis, D. P. (2015). Defining the real-world reproducibility of visual grading of left ventricular function and visual estimation of left ventricular ejection fraction: Impact of image quality, experience and accreditation. *The International Journal of Cardiovascular Imaging, 31*(7), 1303–1314. doi:10.100710554-015-0659-1 PMID:26141526

Connor, J. T., Martin, R. D., & Atlas, L. E. (1994). Recurrent Neural Networks and robust time series prediction. *IEEE Transactions on Neural Networks*, 5(2), 240–254. doi:10.1109/72.279188 PMID:18267794

Cook, A. (2019, March 18). *Interesting data to visualize*. Kaggle. https://www.kaggle.com/alexisbcook/data-for-datavis

Counts, P. G. T. N. N. (2016, January 25). Reducing Health Care Costs Through Early Intervention On Mental Illnesses: Health Affairs Blog. *Health Affairs*.

Cruz Rivera, S., Liu, X., Chan, A.-W., Denniston, A. K., Calvert, M. J., Darzi, A., Holmes, C., Yau, C., Moher, D., Ashrafian, H., Deeks, J. J., Ferrante di Ruffano, L., Faes, L., Keane, P. A., Vollmer, S. J., Lee, A. Y., Jonas, A., Esteva, A., Beam, A. L., ... Rowley, S. (2020). Guidelines for clinical trial protocols for interventions involving artificial intelligence: The SPIRIT-AI extension. *Nature Medicine*, 26(9), 1351–1363. doi:10.103841591-020-1037-7 PMID:32908284

Cruz-Mendoza, I., Quevedo-Pulido, J., & Adanaque-Infante, L. (2020). LSTM perfomance analysis for predictive models based on Covid-19 dataset. *2020 IEEE XXVII International Conference on Electronics, Electrical Engineering and Computing (INTERCON)*. 10.1109/INTERCON50315.2020.9220248

Cui, Z., Ke, R., Pu, Z., & Wang, Y. (2020). Stacked bidirectional and unidirectional LSTM recurrent neural network for forecasting network-wide traffic state with missing values. *Transportation Research Part C, Emerging Technologies*, 118, 102674. doi:10.1016/j.trc.2020.102674

Cutler, A., Cutler, D. R., & Stevens, J. R. (2012) Random forests. In C. Zhang & Y. Ma (Eds.), Ensemble Machine Learning (pp. 157-175). Springer. doi:10.1007/978-1-4419-9326-7_5

Cutler, D. R. (2007, November 1). Random Forests for Classification in Ecology. *Journal of Ecological Society of America*, 88(11), 2783–2792. PMID:18051647

Da Silva, R. G., Ribeiro, M. H., Mariani, V. C., & dos Coelho, L. (2020). Forecasting Brazilian and American COVID-19 cases based on artificial intelligence coupled with climatic exogenous variables. *Chaos, Solitons, and Fractals*, 139, 110027. doi:10.1016/j.chaos.2020.110027 PMID:32834591

Dabbura, I. (2018, September 17). *K-means Clustering: Algorithm, Applications, Evaluation Methods, and Drawbacks*. Retrieved from towards (data science): https://towardsdatascience.com/K-means-clustering-algorithm-applications-evaluation-methods-and-drawbacks-aa03e644b48a

Daley, S. (2021). *23 Examples of Artificial Intelligence Shaking up Business as Usual*. Retrieved May 9, 2021 from https://builtin.com/artificial-intelligence/examples-ai-in-industry

Dalip, D. (2020). AI-Enabled Framework to Prevent COVID-19 from Further Spreading. In *Intelligence Systems and Methods to Combat Covid-19* (pp. 29–33). Springer Press. doi:10.1007/978-981-15-6572-4_4

Daniel, G. G. (2013). Artificial Neural Network. In A. L. C. Runehov & L. Oviedo (Eds.), *Encyclopedia of Sciences and Religions*. Springer. doi:10.1007/978-1-4020-8265-8_200980

Darling, K. (2021). *The new breed: What our history with animals reveals about our future with robots*. Henry Holt and Company.

Das, V. K. (2020, October 11). *K-means clustering vs hierarchical clustering*. Retrieved from Global Tech Council: https://www.globaltechcouncil.org/clustering/K-means-clustering-vs-hierarchical-clustering/

Datkhile, A., Chandak, K., Bhandari, S., Gajare, H., & Karyakarte, M. (2020). Statistical Modelling on Loan Default Prediction Using Different Models. *IJRESM*, 3(3), 3–5.

Datta, K. (2011). ARIMA forecasting of inflation in the Bangladesh economy. *The IUP Journal of Bank Management*, *10*(4), 7–15.

David, D. (2020). *15 Undiscovered & Open Source Machine Learning Frameworks You Need to Know in 2020*. #Machine Learning. Retrieved November 24, 2020 from https://www.freecodecamp.org/news/15-undiscovered-open-source-machine-learning-frameworks-you-need-to-know-in-2020/

Davis, S. (2017, April 27). *LeBron James turned down $10 million from Reebok when he was an 18-year-old high school student, and it turned out to be a brilliant business decision.* Retrieved from Business Insider: https://www.businessinsider.com/lebron-james-turned-down-reebok-offer-nike-brilliant-2017-4

de Castro Vieira, J. R., Barboza, F., Sobreiro, V. A., & Kimura, H. (2019). Machine Learning Models for Credit Analysis Improvements: Predicting low-income families' default. *Applied Soft Computing*, *83*, 105640. doi:10.1016/j.asoc.2019.105640

de Silva, K. C., Madhushani, A. L., & Jayalath, S. S. (2020, December). *The Impact of Brand Loyalty on Customer Purchase Intention: An Empirical Study on Basketball Shoe Brands of Adidas, Nike and Puma.* Retrieved from Research Gate: https://www.researchgate.net/profile/A-A-L-Madhushani-2/publication/345983988_The_Impact_of_Brand_Loyalty_on_Customer_Purchase_Intention_An_Empirical_Study_on_Basketball_Shoe_Brands_of_Adidas_Nike_and_Puma_in_Asia/links/5fb40b0045851518fdaffcda/The-Impact

Deane, S. (2021, January 26). *2021 Airbnb Statistics: Usage, demographics, and revenue growth.* Retrieved from STRATOS (Jet Charters, Inc.): https://www.stratosjets.com/blog/airbnb-statistics/

DeGrave, A. J., Janizek, J. D., & Lee, S. I. (2021). AI for radiographic COVID-19 detection selects shortcuts over signal. *Nature Machine Intelligence*, *3*(7), 610–619. Advance online publication. doi:10.103842256-021-00338-7

Deng, J., Dong, W., Socher, R., Li, L.-J., Li, K., & Fei-Fei, L. (2009). Imagenet: A large-scale hierarchical image database. In *2009 IEEE Conference on Computer Vision and Pattern Recognition* (pp. 248–255). IEEE.

Deng, L. (2014). A tutorial survey of architectures, algorithms, and applications for deep learning. *APSIPA Transactions on Signal and Information Processing*, *3*(E2), e2. Advance online publication. doi:10.1017/atsip.2013.9

Dhillon, J., Eluri, N. P., Kaur, D., Chhipa, A., Gadupudi, A., Eravi, R. C., & Pirouz, M. (2021). Analysis of Airbnb Prices using Machine Learning Techniques. In *2021 IEEE 11th Annual Computing and Communication Workshop and Conference (CCWC)* (pp. 297-303). IEEE.

Dias, R. D., Shah, J., & Zenati, M. A. (2020). Artificial intelligence in cardiothoracic surgery. *Minerva Cardioangiologica*, *68*(5), 532–538. doi:10.23736/S0026-4725.20.05235-4 PMID:32989966

Diller, G.-P., Kempny, A., Babu-Narayan, S. V., Henrichs, M., Brida, M., Uebing, A., Lammers, A. E., Baumgartner, H., Li, W., Wort, S. J., Dimopoulos, K., & Gatzoulis, M. A. (2019). Machine learning algorithms estimating prognosis and guiding therapy in adult congenital heart disease: Data from a single tertiary centre including 10 019 patients. *European Heart Journal*, *40*(13), 1069–1077. doi:10.1093/eurheartj/ehy915 PMID:30689812

Dodson, A. (2019, February 12). *The Forgotten History of Puma Basketball.* Retrieved from The Undefeated: theundefeated.com/features/the-forgotten-history-of-puma-basketball/

Donges, N. (2019, June 16). *A complete guide to the random forest algorithm.* Retrieved from Built In: https://builtin.com/data-science/random-forest-algorithm

Dorogush, A. V., Ershov, V., & Gulin, A. (2018). *CatBoost: gradient boosting with categorical features support.* arXiv preprint arXiv:1810.11363.

Dozat, T. (2016). Incorporating Nesterov momentum into Adam. *Workshop Track of ICLR 2016*. Retrieved July 10, 2021 from https://openreview.net/pdf/OM0jvwB8jIp57ZJjtNEZ.pdf

Dubchak, I., Muchnik, I., Holbrook, S. R., & Kim, S. H. (1995). Prediction of Protein Folding Class using Global Description of Amino Acid Sequence. *Proceedings of the National Academy of Sciences of the United States of America, 92*(19), 8700–8704. doi:10.1073/pnas.92.19.8700 PMID:7568000

Dubchak, I., Muchnik, I., Mayor, C., Dralyuk, I., & Kim, S. H. (1999). Recognition of a Protein Fold in the Context of the SCOP Classification. *Proteins, 35*(4), 401–407. doi:10.1002/(SICI)1097-0134(19990601)35:4<401::AID-PROT3>3.0.CO;2-K PMID:10382667

Duchi, J., Hazan, E., & Singer, Y. (2011). Adaptive subgradient methods for online learning and stochastic optimization. *Journal of Machine Learning Research, 12*(7).

Duflos, C., Troude, P., Strainchamps, D., Segouin, C., Logeart, D., & Mercier, G. (2020). Hospitalization for acute heart failure: The in-hospital care pathway predicts one-year readmission. *Scientific Reports, 10*(1), 10644. Advance online publication. doi:10.103841598-020-66788-y PMID:32606326

Du, X., Zhang, W., Zhang, H., Chen, J., Zhang, Y., Warrington, J. C., Brahm, G., & Li, S. (2018). Deep regression segmentation for cardiac bi-ventricle MR images. *IEEE Access: Practical Innovations, Open Solutions, 6*, 3828–3838. doi:10.1109/ACCESS.2017.2789179

Du, X., Zhang, Y., Yao, Y., Hu, C., & Sun, S. (2017). DeepPPI: Boosting Prediction of protein-protein Interactions with Deep Neural Networks. *Journal of Chemical Information and Modeling, 57*(6), 1499–1510. doi:10.1021/acs.jcim.7b00028 PMID:28514151

Ebiaredoh-Mienye, S. A., Esenogho, E., & Swart, T. (2020). *Effective Feature Learning using Stacked Sparse Autoencoder for Improved prediction of Credit Card Default*. Project. https://www.researchgate.net/profile/Ebenezer-Esenogho/publication/341510387_Effective_Feature_Learning_using_Stacked_Sparse_Autoencoder_for_Improved_prediction_of_Credit_Card_Default/links/5ec515a6458515626cb85ac0/Effective-Feature-Learning-using-Stacked-Sparse-Autoencoder-for-Improved-prediction-of-Credit-Card-Default.pdf

Elghamrawy, S. (2020) An H2O's Deep Learning-Inspired Model Based on Big Data Analytics for Coronavirus Disease (COVID-19) Diagnosis. In Big Data Analytics and Artificial Intelligence Against COVID-19: Innovation Vision and Approach. Springer. doi:10.1007/978-3-030-55258-9_16

Enriko, I. K. A., Suryanegara, M., & Gunawan, D. (2016). Heart disease prediction system using k-nearest neighbor algorithm with simplified patient's health parameters. *Journal of Telecommunication. Electronic and Computer Engineering, 8*(12), 59–65.

Eom, J.-H., Kim, S.-C., & Zhang, B.-T. (2008). AptaCDSS-E: A classifier ensemble-based clinical decision support system for cardiovascular disease level prediction. *Expert Systems with Applications, 34*(4), 2465–2479. doi:10.1016/j.eswa.2007.04.015

Erion, G., Janizek, J. D., Sturmfels, P., Lundberg, S. M., & Lee, S.-I. (2021). Improving performance of deep learning models with axiomatic attribution priors and expected gradients. *Nature Machine Intelligence, 3*(7), 620–631. Advance online publication. doi:10.103842256-021-00343-w

European Centre for Disease Prevention and Control (ECDC). (2021). *Download COVID-19 datasets*. Retrieved January 17, 2021 from https://www.ecdc.europa.eu/en/covid-19/data

Everitt, B., Landau, S., & Leese, M. (2011). *Cluster analysis* (5th ed.). Wiley Series in Probability and Statistics. doi:10.1002/9780470977811

Expert.ai Team. (2020, May 06). *What is Machine Learning? A Definition*. Retrieved from expert.ai: https://www.expert.ai/blog/machine-learning-definition/

Faggella, D. (2020). *7 Applications of Machine Learning in Pharma and Medicine*. Emerj AI Research and Advisory Company. Retrieved May 9, 2021 from https://emerj.com/ai-sector-overviews/machine-learning-in-pharma-medicine/

Fahlman, S. E., & Lebiere, C. (1990). The Cascade-Correlation Learning Architecture. In D. S. Touretzky (Ed.), *Advances in Neural Networks in Information Processing Systems 2* (pp. 524–532). Morgan Kaufmann Publishers Inc.

Fan, J., Cao, X., Xue, Z., Yap, P. T., & Shen, D. (2018). Adversarial similarity network for evaluating image alignment in deep learning based registration. In A. Frangi, J. Schnabel, C. Davatzikos, C. Alberola-López, & G. Fichtinger (Eds.), *MICCAI 2018. Lecture notes in computer science, 11070*. Medical image computing and computer assisted intervention. Springer. doi:10.1007/978-3-030-00928-1_83

Farshidfar, F., Koleini, N., & Ardehali, H. (2021). Cardiovascular complications of COVID-19. *JCI Insight*, *6*(13), e148980. Advance online publication. doi:10.1172/jci.insight.148980 PMID:34061779

Faruk, D. Ö. (2010). A hybrid neural network and ARIMA model for water quality time series prediction. *Engineering Applications of Artificial Intelligence*, *23*(4), 586–594. doi:10.1016/j.engappai.2009.09.015

Fatima, H., Mahmood, F., Sehgal, S., Belani, K., Sharkey, A., Chaudhary, O., Baribeau, Y., Matyal, R., & Khabbaz, K. R. (2020). Artificial intelligence for dynamic echocardiographic tricuspid valve analysis: A new tool in echocardiography. *Journal of Cardiothoracic and Vascular Anesthesia*, *34*(10), 2703–2706. doi:10.1053/j.jvca.2020.04.056 PMID:32540242

Fattah, J., Ezzine, L., Aman, Z., El Moussami, H., & Lachhab, A. (2018). Forecasting of demand using ARIMA model. *International Journal of Engineering Business Management*, *10*, 184797901880867. doi:10.1177/1847979018808673

Federal Reserve Bank of St. Louis. (2020). *FRED Economic Data*. Retrieved from *Economic Research*: https://fred.stlouisfed.org/

Feizi, N., Tavakoli, M., Patel, R., & Atashzar, S. (2021). Robotics and AI for teleoperation, tele-assessment, and tele-training for surgery in the era of COVID-19: Existing challenges and future vision. *Frontiers in Robotics and AI*, *8*, 610677. Advance online publication. doi:10.3389/frobt.2021.610677 PMID:33937347

Fernandes, N. (2020). Economic Effects of Coronavirus Outbreak (COVID-19) on the World Economy. SSRN *Electronic Journal*. doi:10.2139/ssrn.3557504

Fernandes, F. T., de Oliveira, T. A., Teixeira, C. E., Batista, A. F. M., Dalla Costa, G., & Chiavegatto Filho, A. D. P. (2021). A multipurpose machine learning approach to predict COVID-19 negative prognosis in São Paulo, Brazil. *Scientific Reports*, *11*(1), 3343. doi:10.103841598-021-82885-y PMID:33558602

Feroze, N. (2020). Forecasting the patterns of COVID-19 and causal impacts of lock-down in top five affected countries using Bayesian Structural Time Series Models. *Chaos, Solitons, and Fractals*, *140*, 110196. doi:10.1016/j.chaos.2020.110196 PMID:32834662

Fischer, S. H. (2021, January 8). *Use of Telehealth Jumped as Pandemic Shutdown Began; Use Is Highest for Mental Health Services*. RAND Corporation. https://www.rand.org/news/press/2021/01/11/index1.html

Fischer, S. H., Uscher-Pines, L., Roth, E., & Breslau, J. (2021). The Transition to Telehealth during the First Months of the COVID-19 Pandemic: Evidence from a National Sample of Patients. *Journal of General Internal Medicine*, *36*(3), 849–851. doi:10.100711606-020-06358-0 PMID:33409884

Fish, K. E., & Segall, R. S. (2002). *A Visual Analysis of Learning Rule Effects and Variable Importance for Neural Networks Employed in Data Mining Operations.* Acxiom Data Engineering Laboratory Working Paper Series, ADEL-WP-02-03, Publication in Collaboration with University of Arkansas at Little Rock (UALR) Donaghey Cyber College.

Fouladi, S., Ebadi, M. J., Safaei, A. A., Bajuri, M. Y., & Ahmadian, A. (2021). Efficient deep neural networks for classification of COVID-19 based on CT images: Virtualization via software defined radio. *Computer Communications*, *176*, 234–248. doi:10.1016/j.comcom.2021.06.011 PMID:34149118

Freund, Y., Iyer, R., Schapire, R. E., & Singer, Y. (2003). An efficient boosting algorithm for combining preferences. *Journal of Machine Learning Research, 4*, 933–969.

Friedman, J., Hastie, T., & Tibshirani, R. (2009). The Elements of Statistical Learning: Data Mining, Inference, and Prediction. New York: Springer. https://doi.org/ doi:10.1007/978-0-387-84858-7

Fries, J. A., Varma, P., Chen, V. S., Xiao, K., Tejeda, H., Saha, P., Dunnmon, J., Chubb, H., Maskatia, S., Fiterau, M., Delp, S., Ashley, E., Ré, C., & Priest, J. R. (2019). Weakly supervised classification of aortic valve malformations using unlabeled cardiac MRI sequences. *Nature Communications*, *10*(1), 3111. Advance online publication. doi:10.103841467-019-11012-3 PMID:31308376

G2. (2020). *Best machine learning software.* Retrieved May 31, 2020 from https://www.g2.com/categories/machine-learning#grid

Gallagher, M. B. (2020). Model quantifies the impact of quarantine measures of COVID-19's spread. *MIT News.* Retrieved May 17, 2020 from https://news.mit.edu/2020/new-model-quantifies-impact-quarantine-measures-covid-19-spread-0416

Gallagher, W. (2020, July 1). *For People in Underserved Communities, Getting Mental Health Care Is a Struggle.* Black Bear Lodge. https://blackbearrehab.com/blog/for-people-in-underserved-communities-getting-mental-health-care-is-a-struggle/

Gao, J., Zheng, P., Jia, Y., Chen, H., Mao, Y., Chen, S., Wang, Y., Fu, H., & Dai, J. (2020). Mental Health Problems and Social Media Exposure During COVID-19 Outbreak. SSRN *Electronic Journal.* doi:10.2139/ssrn.3541120

Garima, S., Navita, S., & Gulshan, W. (2012). Neural Network Model for Prediction of PPI using Domain Frequency & Association Score Base Classification of Protein Pairs. *International Journal of Advanced Research in Computer Science, 3*(3), 234–238.

Gedefaw, L., Ullah, S., Leung, P. H. M., Cai, Y., Yip, S. P., & Huang, C. L. (2021). Inflammasome activation-induced hypercoagulopathy: Impact on cardiovascular dysfunction triggered in COVID-19 patients. *Cells*, *10*(4), 916. doi:10.3390/cells10040916 PMID:33923537

Genuer, R., Poggi, J.-M., Tuleau-Malot, C., & Vialaneix, N. (2017). Random Forests for Big Data. Big Data Research, 9, 28-46. doi:10.1016/j.bdr.2017.07.003

Genuer, R., Poggi, J.-M., & Tuleau-Malot, C. (2010). Variable selection using random forests. *Pattern Recognition Letters, 31*(14), 2225–2236. doi:10.1016/j.patrec.2010.03.014

Geron, A. (2020). *Hands-On Machine Learning with Scikit-Learn, Keras, and TensorFlow: Concepts, Tools, and Techniques to Build Intelligent Systems* (2nd ed.). O'Reilly Media.

Ghahnavieh, A. E. (2019). Time series forecasting of styrene price using a hybrid ARIMA and neural network model. *Independent Journal of Management & Production, 10*(3), 915–933. doi:10.14807/ijmp.v10i3.877

Ghany, K. K., Zawbaa, H. M., & Sabri, H. M. (2021). COVID-19 prediction using LSTM algorithm: GCC case study. *Informatics in Medicine Unlocked, 23*, 100566. doi:10.1016/j.imu.2021.100566 PMID:33842686

Gislason, P.O., Benediktsson, J.A. & Sveinsson, J.R. (2006, March). Random Forests for land cover classification. *Pattern Recognition Letters, 27*(4), 294-300. doi:10.1016/j.patrec.2005.08.011

Godarzi, A. A., Amiri, R. M., Talaei, A., & Jamasb, T. (2014). Predicting oil price movements: A dynamic Artificial Neural Network approach. *Energy Policy, 68*, 371–382. doi:10.1016/j.enpol.2013.12.049

Gonzalo, J., & Taamouti, A. (2017, June 23). The reaction of stock market returns to unemployment. *Studies in Nonlinear Dynamics and Econometrics, 21*(4), 78–80.

Goodfellow, I., Bengio, Y., & Courville, A. (2016). *Deep learning*. MIT Press.

Google Books Ngram Viewer. (n.d.). Retrieved from Google Ngrams: https://books.google.com/ngrams

Gorbalenya, A. E., Baker, S. C., Baric, R. S., Groot, R. J., Haagmans, B. L., Gulyaeva, A. A., Drosten, C., Ziebuhr, J., Sola, I., Sidorov, I. A., Samborskiy, D. V., Leo, L. M., Poon, L. L. M., Perlman, S., Penzar, D., Neuman, B. W., Leontovich, A. M., & Lauber, C. (2020). The species Severe acute respiratory syndrome-related coronavirus: Classifying 2019-nCoV and naming it SARS-CoV-2. *Nature Microbiology, 5*(4), 536–544. doi:10.103841564-020-0695-z PMID:32123347

Gordon, R. (1997). Is there a trade-off between unemployment and productivity growth? In D. Snower & G. de la Dehesa (Eds.), *Unemployment Policy: Government Options for the Labour Market* (pp. 433–463). Cambridge University Press. doi:10.1017/CBO9780511752025.033

Gortmaker, S. L., Hosmer, D. W., & Lemeshow, S. (2013). Applied Logistic Regression. *Contemporary Sociology, 23*, 89–151. Advance online publication. doi:10.1002/9781118548387.ch4

Goswami, P. N. (2021). MCNNet: Generalizing Fake News Detection with a Multichannel Convolutional Neural Network using a Novel COVID-19 Dataset. *CODS COMAD 2021: 8th ACM IKDD CODS and 26th COMAD.* Retrieved February 15, 2021 from https://dl.acm.org/doi/10.1145/3430984.3431064

Gower, J. C., & Ross, G. J. (1969). Minimum Spanning Trees and Single Linkage Cluster Analysis. *Applied Statistics, 18*(1), 54. doi:10.2307/2346439

Graff, C. G., & Sidky, E. Y. (2015). Compressive sensing in medical imaging. *Applied Optics, 54*(8), C23–C44. doi:10.1364/AO.54.000C23 PMID:25968400

Graves, A., & Jaitly, N., & Mohamed, A-R. (2013). Hybrid speech recognition with Deep Bidirectional LSTM. *2013 IEEE Workshop on Automatic Speech Recognition and Understanding.* 10.1109/ASRU.2013.6707742

Grawitch, M. (2009). Faulty Assumptions in Creating a Psychologically Healthy Workplace. *PsycEXTRA Dataset.* doi:10.1037/e686382011-001

Guo, Q., Lu, X., Gao, Y., Zhang, J., Yan, B., Su, D., Song, A., Zhao, X., & Wang, G. (2017). Cluster analysis: A new approach for identification of underlying risk factors for coronary artery disease in essential hypertensive patients. *Scientific Reports, 7*(1), 43965. Advance online publication. doi:10.1038rep43965 PMID:28266630

Guo, Y., Yu, L., Wen, Z., & Li, M. (2008). Using support vector machine combined with auto covariance to predict protein–protein interactions from protein sequences. *Nucleic Acids Research, 36*(9), 3025–3030. doi:10.1093/nar/gkn159 PMID:18390576

Gupta, D. K., & Goyal, S. (2018). Credit Risk Prediction Using Artificial Neural Network Algorithm. *International Journal of Modern Education and Computer Science, 10*(5), 9–16. doi:10.5815/ijmecs.2018.05.02

Gupta, D., Mahajan, A., & Gupta, S. (2020). Social Distancing and Artificial Intelligence-Understanding the Duality in the Times of COVID-19. In *Intelligence Systems and Methods to Combat Covid-19* (pp. 75–81). Springer Press. doi:10.1007/978-981-15-6572-4_9

Guresen, E., Kayakutlu, G., & Daim, T. U. (2011). Using artificial neural network models in stock market index prediction. *Expert Systems with Applications*, *38*(8), 10389–10397. doi:10.1016/j.eswa.2011.02.068

Halasz, G., Sperti, M., Villani, M., Michelucci, U., Agostoni, P., Biagi, A., Rossi, L., Botti, A., Mari, C., Maccarini, M., Pura, F., Roveda, L., Nardecchia, A., Mottola, E., Nolli, M., Salvioni, E., Mapelli, M., Deriu, M., Piga, D., & Piepoli, M. (2021). A Machine Learning Approach for Mortality Prediction in COVID-19 Pneumonia: Development and Evaluation of the Piacenza Score. *Journal of Medical Internet Research*, *23*(5), e29058. doi:10.2196/29058 PMID:33999838

Hamadneh, N. N., Khan, W. A., Ashraf, W., Atawneh, S. H., Khan, I., & Hamadneh, B. N. (2021). *Artificial Neural Networks for Prediction of COVID-19 in Saudi Arabia*. Computers, Materials & Continua. doi:10.32604/cmc.2021.013228

Hammoudi, K., Benhabiles, H., Melkemi, M., Dornaika, F., Arganda-Carreras, I., Collard, D., & Scherpereel, A. (2021). Deep learning on chest x-ray images to detect and evaluate pneumonia cases at the era of covid-19. *Journal of Medical Systems*, *45*(7), 1–10.

Hanfi, S. A. (2020). *A Neural Networks based approach to detect Covid-19 through Chest X-Ray*. Retrieved December 24, 2020 from https://sohailahmedhanfi.medium.com/a-neural-networks-based-approach-to-detect-covid-19-through-chest-x-ray-c11c2b44824d

Hasan, M. (2020). *Top 20 best AI and machine learning software and framework in 2020*. Retrieved May 31, 2020 from https://www.ubuntupit.com/best-ai-and-machine-learning-software-and-frameworks/

Haskins, G., Kruecker, J., Kruger, U., Xu, S., Pinto, P. A., Wood, B. J., & Yan, P. (2018). Learning deep similarity metric for 3D MR–TRUS image registration. *International Journal of Computer Assisted Radiology and Surgery*, *14*(3), 417–425. doi:10.100711548-018-1875-7 PMID:30382457

Haykin, S. (2020). Neural Networks and Learning Machines (3rd ed.). Pearson India Education Services.

He, K., Zhang, X., Ren, S., & Sun, J. (2016). Deep residual learning for image recognition. In *Proceedings of The IEEE Conference on Computer Vision and Pattern Recognition* (pp. 770-778). IEEE.

Henderson, M. (2019). Machine learning for beginners 2019. Independently Published.

Henderson, C., Evans-Lacko, S., & Thornicroft, G. (2013). Mental Illness Stigma, Help Seeking, and Public Health Programs. *American Journal of Public Health*, *103*(5), 777–780. doi:10.2105/AJPH.2012.301056 PMID:23488489

Hendrickson, H. (1994). Fluorescence-Based Assays of Lipases, Phospholipases, and Other Lipolytic Enzymes. *Analytical Biochemistry*, *219*(1), 1–8. doi:10.1006/abio.1994.1223 PMID:8059934

Hernandez-Suarez, D. F., Ranka, S., Kim, Y., Latib, A., Wiley, J., Lopez-Candales, A., Pinto, D. S., Gonzalez, M. D., Ramakrishna, H., Sanina, C., Nieves-Rodriguez, B. G., Rodriguez-Maldonado, J., Maldonado, R. F., Rodriguez-Ruiz, I. J., da Luz Sant'Ana, I., Wiley, K. A., Cox-Alomar, P., Villablanca, P. A., & Roche-Lima, A. (2021). Machine-learning-based in-hospital mortality prediction for transcatheter mitral valve repair in the United States. *Cardiovascular Revascularization Medicine*, *22*, 22–28. doi:10.1016/j.carrev.2020.06.017 PMID:32591310

Hinton, G.E., Vinyals, O. & Dean, J. (2015). *Distilling the knowledge in a neural network*. ArXiv, abs/1503.02531.

Hinton, G., & Sejnowski, T. J. (1999). *Unsupervised learning: Foundations of neural computation*. Bradford Books. doi:10.7551/mitpress/7011.001.0001

Ho Ha, S., & Krishnan, R. (2012). Predicting Repayment of the Credit Card Debt. *Computers & Operations Research*, *39*(4), 765–773. doi:10.1016/j.cor.2010.10.032

Hochreiter, S., & Schmidhuber, J. (1997, November 15). *Long Short-Term Memory*. Neural Computation. https://direct.mit.edu/neco/article/9/8/1735/6109/Long-Short-Term-Memory

Hochreiter, S., & Schmidhuber, J. (1997). Long short-term memory. *Neural Computation*, *9*(8), 1735–1780. doi:10.1162/neco.1997.9.8.1735 PMID:9377276

Ho, D., Quake, S. R., McCabe, E. R. B., Chng, W. J., Chow, E. K., Ding, X., Gelb, B. D., Ginsburg, G. S., Hassenstab, J., Ho, C.-M., Mobley, W. C., Nolan, G. P., Rosen, S. T., Tan, P., Yen, Y., & Zarrinpar, A. (2020). Enabling technologies for personalized and precision medicine. *Trends in Biotechnology*, *38*(5), 497–518. doi:10.1016/j.tibtech.2019.12.021 PMID:31980301

Hossin, M., & Sulaiman, M.N. (2015). A Review on Evaluation Metrics for Data Classification Evaluations. *International Journal of Data Mining & Knowledge Management Process*, *52*, 1–11.

Howard, A. G., Zhu, M., Chen, B., Kalenichenko, D., Wang, W., Weyand, T., . . . Adam, H. (2017). *Mobilenets: Efficient convolutional neural networks for mobile vision applications.* arXiv preprint arXiv:1704.04861.

Hsu, T. C., Liou, S. T., Wang, Y. P., Huang, Y. S., & Che-Lin. (2019). Enhanced Recurrent Neural Network for Combining Static and Dynamic Features for Credit Card Default Prediction. *ICASSP, IEEE International Conference on Acoustics, Speech and Signal Processing - Proceedings*, 1572–1576. doi:10.1109/ICASSP.2019.8682212

Huang, J., Lu, J., & Ling, C. X. (2003). Comparing naive Bayes, decision trees, and SVM with AUC and accuracy. *Third IEEE International Conference on Data Mining*, 553-556. 10.1109/ICDM.2003.1250975

Huang, S., Yang, J., Fong, S., & Zhao, Q. (2021). Artificial intelligence in the diagnosis of COVID-19: Challenges and perspectives. *International Journal of Biological Sciences*, *17*(6), 1581–1587. doi:10.7150/ijbs.58855 PMID:33907522

Hubel, D. H., & Wiesel, T. N. (1962). Receptive fields, binocular interaction and functional architecture in the cat's visual cortex. *The Journal of Physiology*, *160*(1), 106–154. doi:10.1113/jphysiol.1962.sp006837 PMID:14449617

Hudson, C. G. (2005). Socioeconomic Status and Mental Illness: Tests of the Social Causation and Selection Hypotheses. *The American Journal of Orthopsychiatry*, *75*(1), 3–18. doi:10.1037/0002-9432.75.1.3 PMID:15709846

Humphreys, B. R. (2019). *The Effect of Superstars on Game Attendance: Evidence From the NBA.* Sage Journals.

Hurt, B., Kligerman, S., & Hsiao, A. (2020). Deep learning localization of pneumonia: 2019 coronavirus (COVID-19) outbreak. *Journal of Thoracic Imaging*, *35*(3), W87-W89. doi:10.1097/RTI.0000000000000512

Hyndman, R.J., & Athanasopoulos, G. (2018). *Forecasting: principles and practice* (2ⁿᵈ ed.). OTexts. OTexts.com/fpp2

Inside Big Data Editorial Team. (2021, February 5). *AI Solving Real-world Problems and AI Ethics Among Top Trends for 2021, According to Oxylabs' AI and ML Advisory Board.* Retrieved February 15, 2021 from https://insidebigdata.com/2021/02/05/ai-solving-real-world-problems-and-ai-ethics-among-top-trends-for-2021-according-to-oxylabs-ai-and-ml-advisory-board/

Irmak, E. (2020). Implementation of convolutional neural network approach for COVID019 disease detection. *Physiological Genomics*, *52*(12), 590–601. doi:10.1152/physiolgenomics.00084.2020 PMID:33094700

Islam, S. R., Eberle, W., & Ghafoor, S. K. (2018). *Credit Default Mining using Combined Machine Learning and Heuristic Approach.* ArXiv.

Ismail, B., & Anil, M. (2014). Regression methods for analyzing the risk factors for a life style disease among the young population of India. *Indian Heart Journal*, *66*(6), 587–592. doi:10.1016/j.ihj.2014.05.027 PMID:25634389

Jaadi, Z. (2021, April 7). *A step-by-step explanation of Principal Component Analysis (PCA)*. Retrieved from Built In: https://builtin.com/data-science/step-step-explanation-principal-component-analysis

Jaiswal, A. K., Tiwari, P., Kumar, S., Gupta, D., Khanna, A., & Rodrigues, J. J. (2019). Identifying pneumonia in chest X-rays: A deep learning approach. *Measurement*, *145*, 511–518.

Jansen, S. (2018). *Hands-On Machine Learning for Algorithmic Trading*. Packt Publishing, Ltd.

Jansson, B. S. (2020). Practicing Policy Advocacy in the Mental Health and Substance Abuse Sector. In Social welfare policy and advocacy: advancing social justice through eight policy sectors (pp. 289–332). Sage.

Jat, D. S., & Singh, C. (2020). Artificial Intelligence-Enabled Robotic Drones for COVID-19 Outbreak. In *Intelligence Systems and Methods to Combat Covid-19* (pp. 37–46). Springer Press. doi:10.1007/978-981-15-6572-4_5

Jennings, C. W., & Glass, S. (2020). *COVID-19 public dataset program: Making data freely accessible for better public outcomes*. Retrieved December 25, 2020 from https://cloud.google.com/blog/products/data-analytics/free-public-datasets-for-covid19

Jing, Y., Bian, Y., Hu, Z., Wang, L., & Xie, X.-Q. (2018). Deep learning for drug design: An artificial intelligence paradigm for drug discovery in the big data era. *The AAPS Journal*, *20*(3), 58–58. doi:10.120812248-018-0210-0 PMID:29603063

John Hopkins University (JHU). (2021). *COVID-19 Dashboard by the Center for Systems Science and Engineering (CSSE)*. https://publichealthupdate.com/jhu/

Johnson, R. S. (1998, June 22). *The Jordan Effect The world's greatest basketball player is also one of its great brands. What is his impact on the economy?* Retrieved from IESE Business School: https://web.iese.edu/jestrada/PDF/Courses/ECOWAY/ECOWAY_Fortune-Jordan.pdf

Jones, B., Reed, B., & Hayanga, J. W. A. (2020). Autonomously driven: Artificial intelligence in cardiothoracic surgery. *The Annals of Thoracic Surgery*, *110*(2), 373. doi:10.1016/j.athoracsur.2020.02.074 PMID:32277880

Jones, H. (2018). *Machine Learning: The Ultimate Guide to machine learning, neural networks and deep learning for beginners who want to understand applications, artificial intelligence, data mining, big data and more*. CreateSpace Independent Publishing Platform.

Jong, P. d., & Heller, G. Z. (2008). *Generalized Linear Models for Insurance Data*. Cambridge University Press. doi:10.1017/CBO9780511755408

Joshi, A., Dey, N., & Santosh, K. C. (2020). *Intelligence Systems and Methods to Combat Covid-19*. Springer Press. doi:10.1007/978-981-15-6572-4

Juhola, M., Joutsijoki, H., Penttinen, K., & Aalto-Setälä, K. (2018). Detection of genetic cardiac diseases by Ca^{2+} transient profiles using machine learning methods. *Scientific Reports*, *8*(1), 9355. Advance online publication. doi:10.103841598-018-27695-5 PMID:29921843

Jumper, J., Evans, R., Pritzel, A., Green, T., Figurnov, M., Ronneberger, O., Tunyasuvunakool, K., Bates, R., Žídek, A., Potapenko, A., Bridgland, A., Meyer, C., Kohl, S. A. A., Ballard, A. J., Cowie, A., Romera-Paredes, B., Nikolov, S., Jain, R., Adler, J., ... Hassabis, D. (2021). Highly accurate protein structure prediction with AlphaFold. *Nature*, *596*(7873), 583–589. doi:10.103841586-021-03819-2 PMID:34265844

Kadurin, A., Nikolenko, S., Khrabrov, K., Aliper, A., & Zhavoronkov, A. (2017). druGAN: An advanced generative adversarial autoencoder model for de novo generation of new molecules with desired molecular properties in Silico. *Molecular Pharmaceutics*, *14*(9), 3098–3104. doi:10.1021/acs.molpharmaceut.7b00346 PMID:28703000

Kahn, A. I., Shah, A. I., & Bhat, M. (2020). *CoroNet: A Deep Neural Network for Detection and Diagnosis of COVID-19 from Chest X-ray Images*. Retrieved May 16, 2020 from https://www.researchgate.net/publication/340598559_CoroNet_A_Deep_Neural_Network_for_Detection_and_Diagnosis_of_Covid-19_from_Chest_X-ray_Images

Kaiser, M. S., AlMamun, A., Mahmud, M., & Tania, M. H. (2021). COVID-19: Prediction, Decision-Making, and its Impacts. Springer Singapore. doi:10.1007/978-981-15-9682-7_10

Kalehbasti, P. R., Nikolenko, L., & Rezaei, H. (2021). *Airbnb Price Prediction Using Machine Learning and Sentiment Analysis*. Machine Learning and Knowledge Extraction. doi:10.1007/978-3-030-84060-0_11

Kaliyar, R. K., Goswami, A., & Narang, P. (2021). *MCNNet: Generalizing Fake News Detection with a Multichannel Convolutional Neural Network using a Novel COVID-19 Dataset*. Retrieved February 15, 2021 from https://dl.acm.org/doi/10.1145/3430984.3431064

Kambezidis, H. (2012). *Comprehensive Renewable Energy*. Elsevier.

Karimi-Bidhendi, S., Arafati, A., Cheng, A. L., Wu, Y., Kheradvar, A., & Jafarkhani, H. (2020). Fully-automated deep-learning segmentation of pediatric cardiovascular magnetic resonance of patients with complex congenital heart diseases. *Journal of Cardiovascular Magnetic Resonance*, *22*(1), 80. Advance online publication. doi:10.118612968-020-00678-0 PMID:33256762

Karra, S. (2020, October 6). *LSTM for Time Series predictions*. Medium. https://sailajakarra.medium.com/lstm-for-time-series-predictions-cc68cc11ce4f

Kaxiras, E., Neofotistos, G., & Angelaki, E. (2020). The first 100 days: Modeling the evolution of the COVID-19 pandemic. *Chaos, Solitons, and Fractals*, *138*, 110114. doi:10.1016/j.chaos.2020.110114 PMID:32834582

Keefe, M. K. (2011, May). *The impact of athletic apparel company funding on grass roots basketball (2003–2008)*. Retrieved from Proquest: https://www.proquest.com/openview/5072ad398ba88df86cbcfc751e9608ba/1?pq-origsite=gscholar&cbl=18750&diss=y

Kelleher, J. D., Mac Namee, B., & D'Arcy, A. (2015). *Fundamentals of Machine Learning for Predictive Data Analytics: Algorithms, Worked Examples, and Case Studies*. The MIT Press.

Kent, J. (2020a). *Machine Learning Models Forecast Likelihood of COVID-19 Mortality*. Retrieved November 26, 2020 from https://healthitanalytics.com/news/machine-learning-models-forecast-likelihood-of-covid-19-mortality

Kent, J. (2020b). Google Makes COVID-19 Datasets Freely Available to Researchers. *Health IT Analytics*. Retrieved December 24, 2020 from https://healthitanalytics.com/news/google-makes-covid-19-datasets-freely-available-to-researchers

Kent, J. (2020c). Big Data Analytics Show COVID-19 Spread, Outcomes by Region. *HealthITAnalytics*. Retrieved February 15, 2021 from https://healthitanalytics.com/news/big-data-analytics-show-covid-19-spread-outcomes-by-region

Kent, J. (2020d). Intersection of Big Data Analytics, COVID-19 Top Focus of 2020. *HealthITAnalytics*. Retrieved February 15, 2021 https://healthitanalytics.com/news/intersection-of-big-data-analytics-covid-19-top-focus-of-2020

Kermany, D., Zhang, K., & Goldbaum, M. (2018). Labeled optical coherence tomography (OCT) and Chest X-Ray images for classification. *Mendeley Data*, *2*. Advance online publication. doi:10.17632/rscbjbr9sj.2

Khandelwal, I., Adhikari, R., & Verma, G. J. P. C. S. (2015). Time series forecasting using hybrid ARIMA and ANN models based on DWT decomposition. *Procedia Computer Science, 48*, 173–179. doi:10.1016/j.procs.2015.04.167

Khazan, O. (2016, June 1). It's Hard to Get Therapy Unless You're White. *The Atlantic.* https://www.theatlantic.com/health/archive/2016/06/the-struggle-of-seeking-therapy-while-poor/484970/

Khera, A. V., Chaffin, M., Zekavat, S. M., Collins, R. L., Roselli, C., Natarajan, P., Lichtman, J. H., D'Onofrio, G., Mattera, J., Dreyer, R., Spertus, J. A., Taylor, K. D., Psaty, B. M., Rich, S. S., Post, W., Gupta, N., Gabriel, S., Lander, E., Chen, Y.-D. I., ... Kathiresan, S. (2018). Whole-genome sequencing to characterize monogenic and polygenic contributions in patients hospitalized with early-onset myocardial infarction. *Circulation, 139*(13), 1593–1602. doi:10.1161/CIRCULATIONAHA.118.035658 PMID:30586733

Khosla, P. H., Mittal, M., Sharma, D. & Goyal, L. M. (2021). *Predictive and Preventive Measures for Covid-19 Pandemic.* Springer.

Kido, T., Kido, T., Nakamura, M., Kouki, W., Schmidt, M., Forman, C., & Mochizuki, T. (2016). Compressed sensing real-time cine cardiovascular magnetic resonance: Accurate assessment of left ventricular function in a single-breath-hold. *Journal of Cardiovascular Magnetic Resonance, 18*(1), 50. Advance online publication. doi:10.118612968-016-0271-0 PMID:27553656

Kilbourne, A. M., Beck, K., Spaeth-Rublee, B., Ramanuj, P., O'Brien, R. W., Tomoyasu, N., & Pincus, H. A. (2018). Measuring and improving the quality of mental health care: A global perspective. *World Psychiatry; Official Journal of the World Psychiatric Association (WPA), 17*(1), 30–38. doi:10.1002/wps.20482 PMID:29352529

Kilic, M., & Wachter, J. (2018, December). Risk, Unemployment, and the Stock Market: A Rare-Event-Based Explanation of Labor Market Volatility. *Review of Financial Studies, 31*(12), 4762–4814. doi:10.1093/rfs/hhy008

Kim, K.-P., & Song, S.-W. (2018). A Study on Prediction of Business Status. *Korea Journal of Artificial Intelligence*, 23–27.

Kim, S., & Kim, H. (2016). A new metric of absolute percentage error for intermittent demand forecasts. *International Journal of Forecasting, 32*(3), 669–679. doi:10.1016/j.ijforecast.2015.12.003

Kingma, D. P., & Ba, J. (2014). *Adam: A method for stochastic optimization.* arXiv preprint arXiv:1412.6980.

Kitzman, D. W., Hundley, W. G., Brubaker, P. H., Morgan, T. M., Moore, J. B., Stewart, K. P., & Little, W. C. (2010). A randomized double-blind trial of enalapril in older patients with heart failure and preserved ejection fraction: Effects on exercise tolerance and arterial distensibility. *Circulation: Heart Failure, 3*(4), 477–485. doi:10.1161/CIRCHEARTFAILURE.109.898916 PMID:20516425

Knott, K., Seraphim, A., Augusto, J., Xue, H., Chacko, L., Aung, N., Petersen, S. E., Cooper, J. A., Manisty, C., Bhuva, A. N., Kotecha, T., Bourantas, C. V., Davies, R. H., Brown, L. A. E., Plein, S., Fontana, M., Kellman, P., & Moon, J. (2020). The prognostic significance of quantitative myocardial perfusion: An artificial intelligence-based approach using perfusion mapping. *Circulation, 141*(16), 1282–1291. doi:10.1161/CIRCULATIONAHA.119.044666 PMID:32078380

Kösesoy, R., Gök, M., & Öz, C. (2019). A New Sequence Based Encoding for Prediction of Host–Pathogen Protein Interactions. *Computational Biology and Chemistry, 78*, 170–177. doi:10.1016/j.compbiolchem.2018.12.001 PMID:30553999

Krittanawong, C., Johnson, K. W., Hershman, S. G., & Tang, W. H. W. (2018). Big data, artificial intelligence and cardiovascular precision medicine. *Expert Review of Precision Medicine and Drug Development, 3*(5), 305–317. doi:10.1080/23808993.2018.1528871

Krittanawong, C., Johnson, K. W., Rosenson, R. S., Wang, Z., Aydar, M., Baber, U., Min, J. K., Tang, W. H. W., Halperin, J. L., & Narayan, S. M. (2019). Deep learning for cardiovascular medicine: A practical primer. *European Heart Journal*, *40*(25), 2058–2073. doi:10.1093/eurheartj/ehz056 PMID:30815669

Krittanawong, C., Zhang, H., Wang, Z., Aydar, M., & Kitai, T. (2017). Artificial intelligence in precision cardiovascular medicine. *Journal of the American College of Cardiology*, *69*(21), 2657–2664. doi:10.1016/j.jacc.2017.03.571 PMID:28545640

Krizhevsky, A. (2009). *Learning Multiple Layers of Features from Tiny Images*. Technical Report TR-2009, University of Toronto.

Krizhevsky, A., Sutskever, I., & Hinton, G. E. (2012). Imagenet classification with deep convolutional neural networks. *Advances in Neural Information Processing Systems*, *25*, 1097–1105.

Kruppa, J., Schwarz, A., Arminger, G., & Ziegler, A. (2013). Consumer Credit Risk: Individual Probability Estimates using Machine Learning. *Expert Systems with Applications*, *40*(13), 5125–5131. doi:10.1016/j.eswa.2013.03.019

Kuncheva, L. I., & Whitaker, C. J. (2003). Measures of diversity in classifier ensembles and their relationship with the ensemble accuracy. *Machine Learning*, *51*(2), 181–207. doi:10.1023/A:1022859003006

Küstner, T., Fuin, N., Hammernik, K., Bustin, A., Qi, H., Hajhosseiny, R., Masci, P. G., Neji, R., Rueckert, D., Botnar, R. M., & Prieto, C. (2020). CINENet: Deep learning-based 3D cardiac CINE MRI reconstruction with multi-coil complex-valued 4D spatio-temporal convolutions. *Scientific Reports*, *10*(1), 13710. Advance online publication. doi:10.103841598-020-70551-8 PMID:32792507

Lai, L. (2020). Loan Default Prediction with Machine Learning Techniques. *2020 International Conference on Computer Communication and Network Security (CCNS)*, 5–9. 10.1109/CCNS50731.2020.00009

Lalmuanawma, S., Hussain, J., & Chhakchhuak, L. (2020, October). Applications of machine learning and artificial intelligence for Covid-19 (SARS-CoV-2) pandemic: A review. *Chaos, Solitons, and Fractals*, *139*, 110059. doi:10.1016/j.chaos.2020.110059 PMID:32834612

Larroza, A., López-Lereu, M. P., Monmeneu, J. G., Gavara, J., Chorro, F. J., Bodí, V., & Moratal, D. (2018). Texture analysis of cardiac cine magnetic resonance imaging to detect non-viable segments in patients with chronic myocardial infarction. *Medical Physics*, *45*(4), 1471–1480. doi:10.1002/mp.12783 PMID:29389013

Lavecchia, A. (2019). Deep learning in drug discovery: Opportunities, challenges and future prospects. *Drug Discovery Today*, *24*(10), 2017–2032. doi:10.1016/j.drudis.2019.07.006 PMID:31377227

Learning, U. C. I. M. (2017, September 27). *Restaurant data with consumer ratings*. Kaggle. https://www.kaggle.com/uciml/restaurant-data-with-consumer-ratings

LeCun, Y., Bengio, Y., & Hinton, G. (2015). Deep learning. *Nature*, *521*(7553), 436–444. doi:10.1038/nature14539 PMID:26017442

Lee, E. K., Tran, D. D., Keung, W., Chan, P., Wong, G., Chan, C. W., Costa, K. D., Li, R. A., & Khine, M. (2017). Machine learning of human pluripotent stem cell-derived engineered cardiac tissue contractility for automated drug classification. *Stem Cell Reports*, *9*(5), 1560–1572. doi:10.1016/j.stemcr.2017.09.008 PMID:29033305

Lee, J. H., Ó Hartaigh, B., Han, D., Rizvi, A., Lin, F. Y., & Min, J. K. (2016). Fractional flow reserve measurement by computed tomography: An alternative to the stress test. *Interventional Cardiology (London, England)*, *11*(2), 105–109. doi:10.15420/icr.2016:1:2 PMID:29588715

Leiner, T., Rueckert, D., Suinesiaputra, A., Baeßler, B., Nezafat, R., Išgum, I., & Young, A. A. (2019). Machine learning in cardiovascular magnetic resonance: Basic concepts and applications. *Journal of Cardiovascular Magnetic Resonance*, *21*(1), 61. Advance online publication. doi:10.118612968-019-0575-y PMID:31590664

LeMaire, S. A., McDonald, M.-L. N., Guo, D. C., Russell, L., Miller, C. C. III, Johnson, R. J., Bekheirnia, M. R., Franco, L. M., Nguyen, M., Pyeritz, R. E., Baravia, J. E., Devereux, R., & Maslen, C. (2011). Genome-wide association study identifies a susceptibility locus for thoracic aortic aneurysms and aortic dissections spanning FBN1 at 15q21.1. *Nature Genetics*, *43*(10), 996–1000. doi:10.1038/ng.934 PMID:21909107

Leong, B., & Jordon, S. (2020). *Artificial Intelligence and the COVID-19 Pandemic*. Retrieved May 16, 2020 from https://fpf.org/2020/05/07/artificial-intelligence-and-the-covid-19-pandemic/

Leong, O. J., & Jayabalan, M. (2019). A Comparative Study on Credit Card Default Risk Predictive Model. *Journal of Computational and Theoretical Nanoscience*, *16*(8), 3591–3595. doi:10.1166/jctn.2019.8330

Leow, M., & Crook, J. (2014). Intensity Models and Transition Probabilities for Credit Card Loan Delinquencies. *European Journal of Operational Research*, *236*(2), 685–694. doi:10.1016/j.ejor.2013.12.026

Liaw, A., & Wiener, M. (2002). Classification and Regression by Random Forest. *R News*, *2/3*. doi:10.1057/9780230509993

Lindman, B. R., Clavel, M.-A., Mathieu, P., Iung, B., Lancellotti, P., Otto, C. M., & Pibarot, P. (2016). Calcific aortic stenosis. *Nature Reviews Disease Primers, 2. Artricle*, *16006*(1). Advance online publication. doi:10.1038/nrdp.2016.6 PMID:27188578

Linear Models. (n.d.). Retrieved from Scikit Learn: https://scikit-learn.org/stable/modules/linear_model.html

Lin, S., Li, Z., Fu, B., Chen, S., Li, X., Wang, Y., Wang, X., Lv, B., Xu, B., Song, X., Zhang, Y.-J., Cheng, X., Huang, W., Pu, J., Zhang, Q., Xia, Y., Du, B., Ji, X., & Zheng, Z. (2020). Feasibility of using deep learning to detect coronary artery disease based on facial photo. *European Heart Journal*, *41*(46), 4400–4411. doi:10.1093/eurheartj/ehaa640 PMID:32818267

Lin, Y., & Jeon, Y. (2006). Random Forests and Adaptive Nearest Neighbors. *Journal of the American Statistical Association*, *101*(474), 578–590. doi:10.1198/016214505000001230

Li, Q., Wang, J., Tao, H., Zhou, Q., Chen, J., Fu, B., Qin, W. Z., Li, D., Hou, J. L., & Zhang, W. H. (2020). The prediction model of warfarin individual maintenance dose for patients undergoing heart valve replacement, based on the Back Propagation Neural Network. *Clinical Drug Investigation*, *40*(1), 41–53. doi:10.100740261-019-00850-0 PMID:31586305

Lisboa, P. J. G., Vellido, A., & Edisbury, B. (2000). *Business Applications of Neural Networks: The state-of-the-art of real-world applications*. World Scientific Press. doi:10.1142/4238

Litjens, G., Kooi, T., Bejnordi, B. E., Setio, A. A. A., Ciompi, F., Ghafoorian, M., ... Sánchez, C. I. (2017). A survey on deep learning in medical image analysis. *Medical Image Analysis*, *42*, 60–88.

Liu, X., Cruz Rivera, S., Moher, D., Calvert, M. J., Denniston, A. K., Ashrafian, H., Beam, A. L., Chan, A.-W., Collins, G. S., Deeks, A. D. J. J., ElZarrad, M. K., Espinoza, C., Esteva, A., Faes, L., Ferrante di Ruffano, L., Fletcher, J., Golub, R., Harvey, H., Haug, C., ... Yau, C. (2020). Reporting guidelines for clinical trial reports for interventions involving artificial intelligence: The CONSORT-AI extension. *The Lancet. Digital Health*, *2*(10), e537–e548. doi:10.1016/S2589-7500(20)30218-1 PMID:33328048

Li, W., Ma, J., Shende, N., Castaneda, G., Chakladar, J., Tsai, J. C., Apostol, L., Honda, C. O., Xu, J., Wong, L. M., Zhang, T., Lee, A., Gnanasekar, A., Honda, T. K., Kuo, S. Z., Yu, M. A., Chang, E. Y., Rajasekaran, M. R., & Ongkeko, W. M. (2020). Using machine learning of clinical data to diagnose COVID-19: A systematic review and meta-analysis. *BMC Medical Informatics and Decision Making*, *20*(1), 247. Retrieved December 24, 2020, from. doi:10.118612911-020-01266-z PMID:32993652

Li, X., & Wu, X. (2015). Constructing Long Short-Term Memory based deep Recurrent Neural Networks for large vocabulary speech recognition. *2015 IEEE International Conference on Acoustics, Speech and Signal Processing (ICASSP)*. 10.1109/ICASSP.2015.7178826

Li, Y., Li, Y., & Li, Y. (2019). What factors are Influencing Credit Card Customer's Default Behavior in China? A study based on survival analysis. *Physica A*, *526*, 120861. doi:10.1016/j.physa.2019.04.097

Loungani, P., Rush, M., & Tave, W. (1990). Stock market dispersion and unemployment. *Journal of Monetary Economics*, *25*(3), 367–388. doi:10.1016/0304-3932(90)90059-D

Louppe, G. (2014). *Understanding Random Forests: From Theory to Practice* (Ph.D. Dissertation). University of Liège, Faculty of Applied Sciences, Department of Electrical Engineering & Computer Science. Retrieved August 14, 2021 from https://arxiv.org/pdf/1407.7502.pdf

Luo, Y., Ahmad, F. S., & Shah, S. J. (2017). Tensor factorization for precision medicine in heart failure with preserved ejection fraction. *Journal of Cardiovascular Translational Research*, *10*(3), 305–312. doi:10.100712265-016-9727-8 PMID:28116551

Lu, S., Sears, A., Radish, J., Segall, R. S., & Hahn, T. F. (2014). Discovery of Strong Association Rules for Attributes from Data for Program of All-Inclusive Care for the Elderly. *Journal of Systemics, Cybernetics and Informatics*, *12*(1), 21–26.

Lu, S., & Segall, R. S. (2013). Linkage in Medical Records and Bioinformatics Data. *International Journal of Information and Decision Sciences*, *5*(2), 169–187. doi:10.1504/IJIDS.2013.053803

Luthra, R., Nath, G., & Chellani, R. (2019). *A Review on Class Imbalanced Correction Techniques: A Case of Credit Card Default Prediction on A Highly Imbalanced Dataset*. Praxis Business School.

Lv, D., Wang, Y., Wang, S., Zhang, Q., Qi, W., Li, Y., & Sun, L. (2021, May). A Cascade-SEME network for COVID-19 detection in chest x-ray images. *Medical Physics*, *48*(5), 2337–2353. doi:10.1002/mp.14711 PMID:33778966

Lynette Knowles Mathur, I. M. (1997). *The wealth effects associated with a celebrity endorser: The Michael Jordan phenomenon*. Gale Academic Onefile.

Machine learning in translation [Editorial]. (2021). *Nature Biomedical Engineering, 5*, 485–486. doi:10.1038/s41551-021-00758-1

Maddock, I. I. P. (2018, April 23). *The Economic Implications of NBA Player*. Retrieved from The Claremont Colleges: https://scholarship.claremont.edu/cgi/viewcontent.cgi?article=2992&context=cmc_theses

Mahapatra, D., Ge, Z., Sedai, S., & Chakravorty, R. (2018, September). Joint registration and segmentation of xray images using generative adversarial networks. In *International Workshop on Machine Learning in Medical Imaging* (pp. 73-80). Springer.

Mahapatra, S., Gupta, V. R., Sahu, S. S., & Panda, G. (2021). Deep Neural Network and Extreme Gradient Boosting Based Hybrid Classifier for Improved Prediction of Protein-Protein Interaction. *IEEE/ACM Transactions on Computational Biology and Bioinformatics*, 1–1. doi:10.1109/TCBB.2021.3061300 PMID:33621179

Majhi, R., Thangeda, R., Sugasi, R. P., & Kumar, N. (2020). Analysis and prediction of COVID-19 trajectory: A machine learning approach. *Journal of Public Affairs, e2537.* doi:10.1002/pa.2537 PMID:33349741

Mak, K.-K., & Pichika, M. R. (2018). Artificial intelligence in drug development: Present status and future prospects. *Drug Discovery Today, 24*(3), 773–780. doi:10.1016/j.drudis.2018.11.014 PMID:30472429

Makridakis, S. (1989). Why combining works? *International Journal of Forecasting, 5*(4), 601–603. doi:10.1016/0169-2070(89)90017-4

Makridakis, S. (1993). Accuracy measures: Theoretical and practical concerns. *International Journal of Forecasting, 9*(4), 527–529. doi:10.1016/0169-2070(93)90079-3

Maleki, M., Mahmoudi, M. R., Wraith, D., & Pho, K.-H. (2020). Time series modelling to forecast the confirmed and recovered cases of COVID-19. *Travel Medicine and Infectious Disease, 37,* 101742. doi:10.1016/j.tmaid.2020.101742

Maliszewska, M., Mattoo, A., & van der Mensbrugghe, D. (2020). *The Potential Impact of COVID-19 on GDP and Trade: A Preliminary Assessment.* doi:10.1596/1813-9450-9211

Mandair, D., Tiwari, P., Simon, S., Colborn, K. L., & Rosenberg, M. A. (2020). Prediction of incident myocardial infarction using machine learning applied to harmonized electronic health record data. *BMC Medical Informatics and Decision Making, 20*(1), 252. Advance online publication. doi:10.118612911-020-01268-x PMID:33008368

Marcus, G. (2018). *Deep learning: A critical appraisal.* arXiv preprint arXiv:1801.00631.

Marques, J. A. L., Gois, F. N. B., Xavier-Neto, J., & Fong, S. J. (2021). *Predictive Models for Decision Support in the COVID-19 Crisis.* Springer. doi:10.1007/978-3-030-61913-8

Martin-Isla, C., Campello, V. M., Izquierdo, C., Raisi-Estabragh, Z., Baeßler, B., Petersen, S. E., & Lekadir, K. (2020). Image-based cardiac diagnosis with machine learning: A review. *Frontiers in Cardiovascular Medicine, 7*(1), 1. Advance online publication. doi:10.3389/fcvm.2020.00001 PMID:32039241

Mathur, P., Srivastava, S., Xu, X., & Mehta, J. L. (2020). Artificial intelligence, machine learning, and cardiovascular disease. *Clinical Medicine Insights. Cardiology, 14.* Advance online publication. doi:10.1177/1179546820927404 PMID:32952403

Mazumder, S. (2020). *Comparative Study of Five Supervised Machine Learning Methods.* doi:10.13140/RG.2.2.16997.14568

Mbuvha, R., Boulkaibet, I., & Marwala, T. (2019). *Automatic Relevance Determination Bayesian Neural Networks for Credit Card Default Modelling.* ArXiv.

McFrockman, J. (2020). Artificial Intelligence Mastery: 4 Books in 1: Machine Learning and Artificial Intelligence for beginners+AI for Business+AI Superpowers and Data Analytics+IOT, Data Science and DL, Updated Edition. Independently Published.

McKinney, W. (2010, January 1). *Pandas: A Foundational Python Library for Data Analysis and Statistics: Semantic Scholar.* Academic Press.

Meehan, J., Chou, C.-A., & Khasawneh, M. T. (2015). Predictive modeling and analysis of high-cost patients. *IIE Annual Conference. Proceedings,* 2566-2575.

Méndez-Lucio, O., Baillif, B., Clevert, D.-A., Rouquie, D., & Wichard, J. (2020). De novo generation of hit-like molecules from gene expression signatures using artificial intelligence. *Nature Communications, 11*(1), 10. Advance online publication. doi:10.103841467-019-13807-w PMID:31900408

Meng, X., Bradley, J., Yavuz, B., Sparks, E., Venkataraman, S., Liu, D., Freeman, J., Tsai, D. B., & Zadeh, R. (2015). *MLlib: Machine Learning in Apache Spark.* arXiv:1505.06807.

Mental Health Foundation. (2016, July 9). *Physical health and mental health.* https://www.mentalhealth.org.uk/a-to-z/p/physical-health-and-mental-health

MEPS. (2020). *HC-207 2018 Medical Conditions.* Retrieved from https://meps.ahrq.gov/data_stats/download_data/pufs/h207/h207doc.pdf

Mercier, G., Georgescu, V., & Bousquet, J. (2015). Geographic variation in potentially avoidable hospitalizations in France. *Health Affairs, 34*(5), 836–843. doi:10.1377/hlthaff.2014.1065 PMID:25941286

Merh, N., Saxena, V. P., & Pardasani, K. R. (2010). A comparison between hybrid approaches of ANN and ARIMA for Indian stock trend forecasting. *Business Intelligence Journal, 3*(2), 23–43.

Michael Jordan. (n.d.). Retrieved from Biography.com: www.biography.com/athlete/michael-jordan

Miliard, M. (2021). Northwell machine learning model can predict COVID-19 respiratory failure. *Heath Care IT News.* Retrieved February 16, 2021 from https://www.healthcareitnews.com/news/northwell-machine-learning-model-can-predict-covid-19-respiratory-failure

Miranda, E., Irwansyah, E., Amelga, A. Y., Maribondang, M. M., & Salim, M. (2016). Detection of cardiovascular disease risk's level for adults using naive Bayes classifier. *Healthcare Informatics Research, 22*(3), 196–205. doi:10.4258/hir.2016.22.3.196 PMID:27525161

Mitchell, T. M. (1997). *Machine learning.* McGraw-Hill.

Mohanty, S. N., Saxena, S. K., Chatterjee, J. M., & Satpathy, S. (2021). *Application of Artificial Intelligence in COVID-19.* Springer.

Mollalo, A., Rivera, K. M., & Vahedi, B. (2020). Artificial Neural Network Modeling of Novel Coronavirus (COVID-19) Incidence Rates across the Continental United States. *International Journal of Environmental Research and Public Health, 17*(12), 4204. doi:10.3390/ijerph17124204 PMID:32545581

Mongan, J., Moy, L., & Kahn, C. E. Jr. (2020). Checklist for Artificial Intelligence in Medical Imaging (CLAIM): A guide for authors and reviewers. *Radiology. Artificial Intelligence, 2*(2), e200029. doi:10.1148/ryai.2020200029 PMID:33937821

Moustris, G. P., Hirides, S. C., Deliparaschos, K. M., & Konstantinidis, K. M. (2011). Evolution of autonomous and semi-autonomous robotic surgical systems: A review of the literature. *International Journal of Medical Robotics and Computer Assisted Surgery, 7*(4), 375–392. doi:10.1002/rcs.408 PMID:21815238

Mukherjee, H., Ghosh, S., Dhar, A., Obaidullah, S. M., Santosh, K. C., & Roy, K. (2021). Shallow Convolutional Neural Network for COVID-19 Outbreak Screening Using Chest X-rays. *Cognitive Computation.* Advance online publication. doi:10.100712559-020-09775-9 PMID:33564340

Multiple Linear Regression. (n.d.). Retrieved from JavaTpoint: https://www.javatpoint.com/multiple-linear-regression-in-machine-learning

Nahar, J., Imam, T., Tickle, K. S., & Chen, Y.-P. P. (2013). Association rule mining to detect factors which contribute to heart disease in males and females. *Expert Systems with Applications, 40*(4), 1086–1093. doi:10.1016/j.eswa.2012.08.028

Nair, V., & Hinton, G. E. (2010). Rectified linear units improve restricted boltzmann machines. *Proceedings of the 27th International Conference on Machine Learning (ICML-10),* 807-814.

Narin, A., Kaya, C., & Pamuk, Z. (2021). *Automatic detection of coronavirus disease (COVID-19) using X-ray images and deep convolutional neural networks.* Pattern Anal Applic. doi:10.100710044-021-00984-y

National Basketball Association total league revenue from 2001/02 to 2019/20(in billion U.S. dollars). (n.d.). Retrieved from Statista: https://www.statista.com/statistics/193467/total-league-revenue-of-the-nba-since-2005/

National Institutes of Health. (2020). *Open-Access Data and Computational Resources to Address COVID-19.* Office of Data Science Strategy. Retrieved December 24, 2020 from https://datascience.nih.gov/covid-19-open-access-resources

Nawaz, M. S., Fournier-Viger, P., Shojaee, A., & Fujita, H. (2021). Using artificial intelligence techniques for COVID-19 genome analysis. *Applied Intelligence, 51*(5), 3086–3103. doi:10.100710489-021-02193-w PMID:34764587

NBA Finals Ratings History (1988-Present). (n.d.). Retrieved from Sports Media Watch: https://www.sportsmediawatch.com/nba-finals-ratings-viewership-history/

Neema, S., & Soibam, B. (2017). The Comparison of Machine Learning Methods to achieve Most Cost-Effective Prediction for Credit Card Default. *Journal of Management Science and Business Intelligence, 9264,* 36–41. doi:10.5281/zenodo.851527

Neural network models (supervised). (n.d.). Retrieved from Scikit Learn: https://scikit-learn.org/stable/modules/neural_networks_supervised.html

Niazkar, H. R., & Niazkar, M. (2020). Application of artificial neural networks to predict the COVID-19 outbreak. *Global Health Research and Policy, 5*(1), 50. doi:10.118641256-020-00175-y PMID:33292780

Nicholson, C. (2020). *A Beginner's Guide to LSTMs and Recurrent Neural Networks.* Retrieved December 26, 2020 from https://wiki.pathmind.com/lstm

Nielsen, M. (2016). A visual proof that neural nets can compute any function. In *Artificial Neural Networks and Deep Learning.* Determination Press. http://neuralnetworksanddeeplearning.com/chap4.html

Nike Basketball History. (n.d.). Retrieved from Sneaker Files: https://www.sneakerfiles.com/nike/nike-basketball/

Ni, Q., Sun, Z. Y., Qi, L., Chen, W., Yang, Y., Wang, L., ... Zhang, L. J. (2020). A deep learning approach to characterize 2019 coronavirus disease (COVID-19) pneumonia in chest CT images. *European Radiology, 30*(12), 6517–6527.

Niraula, P., Mateu, J., & Chaudhuri, S. (2021). A Bayesian machine learning approach for spatio-temporal prediction of COVID-19 cases. doi:10.21203/rs.3.rs-636809/v1

Nirschl, J. J., Janowczyk, A., Peyster, E. G., Frank, R., Margulies, K. B., Feldman, M. D., & Madabhushi, A. (2018). A deep-learning classifier identifies patients with clinical heart failure using whole-slide images of H&E tissue. *PLoS One, 13*(4), e0192726. doi:10.1371/journal.pone.0192726 PMID:29614076

Nishiga, M., Wang, D. W., Han, Y., Lewis, D. B., & Wu, J. C. (2020). COVID-19 and cardiovascular disease: From basic mechanisms to clinical perspectives. *Nature Reviews. Cardiology, 17*(9), 543–558. doi:10.103841569-020-0413-9 PMID:32690910

Niu, G., & Olinsky, A. (2020). Generalized Linear Model for Automobile Fatality Rate Prediction in R. In R. S. Segall & G. Niu (Eds.), *Open Source Software for Statistical Analysis of Big Data: Emerging Research and Opportunities* (pp. 137–161). IGI Global. doi:10.4018/978-1-7998-2768-9.ch005

Niu, G., Segall, R. S., Zhao, Z., & Wu, Z. (2021). A Survey of Open Source Statistical Software (OSSS) and Their Data Processing Functionalities. *International Journal of Open Source Software and Processes, 12*(1), 1–20. doi:10.4018/IJOSSP.2021010101

Norgeot, B., Quer, G., Beaulieu-Jones, B. K., Torkamani, A., Dias, R., Gianfrancesco, M., Arnaout, R., Kohane, I. S., Saria, S., Topol, E., Obermeyer, Z., Yu, B., & Butte, A. J. (2020). Minimum information about clinical artificial intelligence modeling: The MI-CLAIM checklist. *Nature Medicine*, 26(9), 1320–1324. doi:10.103841591-020-1041-y PMID:32908275

Nyoni, T., & Nathaniel, S. P. (2018). *Modeling rates of inflation in Nigeria: an application of ARMA, ARIMA and GARCH models*. https://mpra.ub.uni-muenchen.de/91351/MPRAPaperNo.91351

Nyoni, T. (2018). Modeling and Forecasting Inflation in Kenya: Recent Insights from ARIMA and GARCH analysis. *Dimorian Review*, 5(6), 16–40.

NYTimes. (n.d.). *Nytimes/Covid-19-Data*. GitHub. https://github.com/nytimes/covid-19-data/tree/30cc9e39b9695393 f91c0a61a50c659195cbfb49

Oikonomou, E. K., Mohamed, M. M., Desai, M. Y., Mancio, J., Alashi, A., Hutt, E., Centeno, E. H., Thomas, S., Herdman, L., Kotanidis, C. P., Thomas, K. E., Griffin, B. P., Flamm, S. D., Antonopoulos, A. S., Shirodaria, C., Sabharwal, N., Deanfield, J., Neubauer, S., Hopewell, J. C., ... Antoniades, C. (2018). Non-invasive detection of coronary inflammation using computed tomography and prediction of residual cardiovascular risk (the CRISP CT study): A post-hoc analysis of prospective outcome data. *Lancet*, 392(10151), 929–939. doi:10.1016/S0140-6736(18)31114-0 PMID:30170852

Oja, E. (1994). Neural Networks – Advantages and Applications. Machine Intelligence and Pattern Recognition. In E. S. Gelsema & L. S. Kanal (Eds.), *Pattern Recognition in Practice IV: Multiple Paradigms, Comparative Studies and Hybrid Systems* (Vol. 16, pp. 359–365). Elsevier.

Olah, C. (2015). *Understanding LSTM Networks*. Understanding LSTM Networks -- colah's blog. https://colah.github. io/posts/2015-08-Understanding-LSTMs/

Oliphant, T. E. (2015). *Guide to NumPy* (2nd ed.). CreateSpace Independent Publishing Platform.

Olurotimi, O. (1994). Recurrent neural network training with feedforward complexity. *IEEE Transactions on Neural Networks*, 5(2), 185–197. doi:10.1109/72.279184 PMID:18267790

Orita, K., Sawada, K., Matsumoto, N., & Ikegaya, Y. (2020). Machine-learning-based quality control of contractility of cultured human-induced pluripotent stem-cell-derived cardiomyocytes. *Biochemical and Biophysical Research Communications*, 526(3), 751–755. doi:10.1016/j.bbrc.2020.03.141 PMID:32265031

Orr, M. J. (1996). *Introduction to radial basis function networks*. Centre for Cognitive Science, University of Edinburgh.

Orwat, S., Arvanitaki, A., & Diller, G. P. (2021). A new approach to modelling in adult congenital heart disease: Artificial intelligence. *Revista Espanola de Cardiologia*, 74(7), 573–575. doi:10.1016/j.recesp.2020.12.009 PMID:33478913

Owusu-Fordjour, C., Koomson, C. K., & Hanson, D. (2020, January 1). The Impact Of Covid-19 On Learning - The Perspective of the Ghanaian Student. *Semantic Scholar. European Journal of Education Studies*. Doi:10.46827/EJES. V0I0.3000

Ozlurk, T., Talo, M., Yildirim, E. A., Baloglu, U. B. Y., & Rajendra-Acharya, U. (2020). Automated detection of COVID-19 cases using deep neural networks with X-ray images. *Computers in Biology and Medicine*. Retrieved May 16, 2020 from https://www.ncbi.nlm.nih.gov/pmc/articles/PMC7187882/ doi:10.1016/j.compbiomed.2020.103792

Pakulis, A. (2020, February 25). *Fact Sheet: Impact of the President's 2021 Budget on Health*. First Focus on Children. https://firstfocus.org/resources/fact-sheet/fact-sheet-impact-of-the-presidents-2021-budget-on-health

Pal, R., Sekh, A. A., Kar, S., & Prasad, D. K. (2020). *Neural Network Based Country Wise Risk Prediction of COVID-19*. doi:10.20944/preprints202004.0421.v1

Palm, F. C., & Zellner, A. (1992). To combine or not to combine? Issues of combining forecasts. *Journal of Forecasting*, *11*(8), 687–701. doi:10.1002/for.3980110806

Palm, G. (1986). Warren McCulloch and Walter Pitts: A Logical Calculus of the Ideas Immanent in Nervous Activity. *Brain Theory*, 229–230. Advance online publication. doi:10.1007/978-3-642-70911-1_14

Pan, S. J., & Yang, Q. (2009). A survey on transfer learning. *IEEE Transactions on Knowledge and Data Engineering*, *22*(10), 1345–1359.

Pan, W.-F. (2018). Does the stock market really cause unemployment? A cross-country analysis. *The North American Journal of Economics and Finance*, *44*(C), 34–43. doi:10.1016/j.najef.2017.11.002

Patel, L., Shukla, T., Huang, X., Ussery, D. W., & Wang, S. (2020). Machine learning methods in drug discovery. *Molecules (Basel, Switzerland)*, *25*(22), 5277. doi:10.3390/molecules25225277 PMID:33198233

Pathan, R. K., Biswas, M., & Khandaker, M. U. (2020). Time series prediction of COVID-19 by mutation rate analysis using recurrent neural network-based LSTM model. *Chaos, Solitons, and Fractals*, *138*, 110018. doi:10.1016/j.chaos.2020.110018 PMID:32565626

Patil, M., Singh, S., Henderson, J., & Krishnamurthy, P. (2021). Mechanisms of COVID-19-induced cardiovascular disease: Is sepsis or exosome the missing link? *Journal of Cellular Physiology*, *236*(5), 3366–3382. doi:10.1002/jcp.30109 PMID:33078408

Patlolla, C. R. (2018, December 10). *Understanding the concept of hierarchical clustering technique.* Retrieved from Towards Data Science: https://towardsdatascience.com/understanding-the-concept-of-hierarchical-clustering-technique-c6e8243758ec

Paul, D., Sanap, G., Shenoy, S., Kalyane, D., Kalia, K., & Tekade, R. K. (2020). Artificial intelligence in drug discovery and development. *Drug Discovery Today*, *26*(1), 80–93. doi:10.1016/j.drudis.2020.10.010 PMID:33099022

Pawade, T. A., Newby, D. E., & Dweck, M. R. (2015). Calcification in aortic stenosis: The skeleton key. *Journal of the American College of Cardiology*, *66*(5), 561–577. doi:10.1016/j.jacc.2015.05.066 PMID:26227196

Pearson, G. S., Hines-Martin, V. P., Evans, L. K., York, J. A., Kane, C. F., & Yearwood, E. L. (2015). Addressing Gaps in Mental Health Needs of Diverse, At-Risk, Underserved, and Disenfranchised Populations: A Call for Nursing Action. *Archives of Psychiatric Nursing*, *29*(1), 14–18. doi:10.1016/j.apnu.2014.09.004 PMID:25634869

Peng, P., Lekadir, K., Gooya, A., Shao, L., Petersen, S. E., & Frangi, A. F. (2016). A review of heart chamber segmentation for structural and functional analysis using cardiac magnetic resonance imaging. *Magnetic Resonance Materials in Physics. Biology and Medicine (Aligarh)*, *29*(2), 155–195. doi:10.100710334-015-0521-4 PMID:26811173

Peng, Y., Chen, X., Rong, Y., Pang, C., Chen, X., & Chen, H. (2021). Real-time prediction of the daily incidence of COVID-19 in 215 countries and territories using machine learning: Model Development and Validation. *J Med Internet*, *23*(6), e24285. doi:10.2196/24285 PMID:34081607

Perez, M. V., Mahaffey, K. W., Hedlin, H., Rumsfeld, J. S., Garcia, A., Ferris, T., Balasubramanian, V., Russo, A. M., Rajmane, A., Cheung, L., Hung, G., Lee, J., Kowey, P., Talati, N., Nag, D., Gummidipundi, S. E., Beatty, A., Hills, M. T., Desai, S., ... Turakhia, M. P. (2019). Large-scale assessment of a smartwatch to identify atrial fibrillation. *The New England Journal of Medicine*, *381*(20), 1909–1917. doi:10.1056/NEJMoa1901183 PMID:31722151

Petitjean, C., & Dacher, J.-N. (2010). A review of segmentation methods in short axis cardiac MR images. *Medical Image Analysis*, *15*(2), 169–184. doi:10.1016/j.media.2010.12.004 PMID:21216179

Pham, T. D. (2020). A comprehensive study on classification of COVID-19 on computed tomography with pretrained convolutional neural networks. *Scientific Reports*, *10*(1), 16942. doi:10.103841598-020-74164-z PMID:33037291

Piccini, N. (2019). *101 Machine Learning Algorithms for Data Science with Cheat Sheets*. R-bloggers. Retrieved January 17, 2021 from https://blog.datasciencedojo.com/machine-learning-algorithms/

Piehler, J. (2005). New Methodologies for Measuring Protein Interactions in Vivo and in Vitro. *Current Opinion in Structural Biology*, *15*(1), 4–14. doi:10.1016/j.sbi.2005.01.008 PMID:15718127

Pierpont, M. E., Brueckner, M., Chung, W. K., Garg, V., Lacro, R. V., McGuire, A. L., Mital, S., Priest, J. R., Pu, W. T., Roberts, A., Ware, S. M., Gelb, B. D., & Russell, M. W. (2018). Genetic basis for congenital heart disease: Revisited: A scientific statement from the American Heart Association. *Circulation*, *138*(21), e653–e711. doi:10.1161/CIR.0000000000000606 PMID:30571578

Pitt, B., Pfeffer, M. A., Assmann, S. F., Boineau, R., Anand, I. S., Claggett, B., Clausell, N., Desai, A. S., Diaz, R., Fleg, J. L., Gordeev, I., Harty, B., Heitner, J. F., Kenwood, C. T., Lewis, E. F., O'Meara, E., Probstfield, J. L., Shaburishvili, T., Shah, S. J., ... McKinlay, S. M. (2014). Spironolactone for heart failure with preserved ejection fraction. *The New England Journal of Medicine*, *370*(15), 1383–1392. doi:10.1056/NEJMoa1313731 PMID:24716680

Poplin, R., Varadarajan, A. V., Blumer, K., Liu, Y., McConnell, M. V., Corrado, G. S., Peng, L., & Webster, D. R. (2018). Predicting cardiovascular risk factors from retinal fundus photographs using deep learning. *Nature Biomedical Engineering*, *2*(3), 158–164. doi:10.103841551-018-0195-0 PMID:31015713

Porumb, M., Iadanza, E., Massaro, S., & Pecchia, L. (2020). A convolutional neural network approach to detect congestive heart failure. *Biomedical Signal Processing and Control*, *55*, 101597. Advance online publication. doi:10.1016/j.bspc.2019.101597

Poulopoulos, D. (2020). 5 Datasets About COVID-19 you can Use Right Now. *Towards Data Science*. Retrieved December 25, 2020 from https://towardsdatascience.com/5-datasets-about-covid-19-you-can-use-right-now-46307b1406a

Pratt, M. K. (2020). 10 Common Uses for Machine Learning Applications in Business. *Tech Target*. Retrieved May 9, 2021 from https://searchenterpriseai.techtarget.com/feature/10-common-uses-for-machine-learning-applications-in-business.

Prayoga, Suhartono, & Rahayu. (2017). Forecasting currency circulation data of Bank Indonesia by using hybrid ARIMAX-ANN model. AIP Conference Proceedings, 1842. doi:10.1063/1.4982867

Prokhorenkova, L., Gusev, G., Vorobev, A., Dorogush, A. V., & Gulin, A. (2017). *CatBoost: unbiased boosting with categorical features*. arXiv preprint arXiv:1706.09516.

Puig, O., Caspary, F., Rigaut, G., Rutz, B., Bouveret, E., Bragado-Nilsson, E., Wilm, M., & Séraphin, B. (2001). The Tandem Affinity Purification (TAP) Method: A General Procedure of Protein Complex Purification. *Methods (San Diego, Calif.)*, *24*(3), 218–229. doi:10.1006/meth.2001.1183 PMID:11403571

Qian, N. (1999). On the momentum term in gradient descent learning algorithms. *Neural Networks*, *12*(1), 145–151.

Qin, C., Schlemper, J., Caballero, J., Price, A. N., Hajnal, J. V., & Rueckert, D. (2019). Convolutional recurrent neural networks for dynamic MR image reconstruction. *IEEE Transactions on Medical Imaging*, *38*(1), 280–290. doi:10.1109/TMI.2018.2863670 PMID:30080145

Quer, G., Arnaout, R., Henne, M., & Arnaout, R. (2021). Machine learning and the future of cardiovascular care: *JACC* state-of-the-art review. *Journal of the American College of Cardiology*, *77*(3), 300–313. doi:10.1016/j.jacc.2020.11.030 PMID:33478654

Quinlan, J. R. (1986). Induction of decision trees. *Machine Learning*, *1*(1), 81–106. doi:10.1007/BF00116251

Rahimzadeh, M., & Attar, A. (2020). A modified deep convolutional neural network for detecting COVID-19 and pneumonia from chest X-ray images based on the concatenation of Xception and ResNet50V2. *Informatics in Medicine Unlocked, 19*, 100360.

Rahimzadeh, M., Attar, A., & Sakhaei, S. M. (2021). A fully automated deep learning-based network for detecting COVID-19 from a new and large lung CT scan dataset. *Biomedical Signal Processing and Control, 68*(July), 102588. Advance online publication. doi:10.1016/j.bspc.2021.102588 PMID:33821166

Rahman, T., Chowdhury, M. E., Khandakar, A., Islam, K. R., Islam, K. F., Mahbub, Z. B., ... Kashem, S. (2020). Transfer learning with deep convolutional neural network (CNN) for pneumonia detection using chest X-ray. *Applied Sciences (Basel, Switzerland), 10*(9), 3233.

Rajpurkar, P., Irvin, J., Zhu, K., Yang, B., Mehta, H., Duan, T., . . . Ng, A. Y. (2017). *Chexnet: Radiologist-level pneumonia detection on chest x-rays with deep learning.* arXiv preprint arXiv:1711.05225.

Ramchandani, A., Fan, C., & Mostafavi, A. (2020). DeepCOVIDNet: An Interpretable Deep Learning Model for Predictive Surveillance of COVID-19 Using Heterogeneous Features and Their Interactions. *IEEE Access: Practical Innovations, Open Solutions, 8*, 159915–159930. doi:10.1109/ACCESS.2020.3019989 PMID:34786287

Ramezani, N. (2020). Modern Statistical Modeling in Machine Learning and Big Data Analytics: Statistical models for continuous and categorical variables. Handbook of Research on Big Data Clustering and Machine Learning, 135-151.

Rao, A. S. R. S., & Vazquez, J. A. (2020, July). Identification of COVID-19 can be quicker through artificial intelligence framework using a mobile phone-based survey when cities and towns are under quarantine. *Infection Control and Hospital Epidemiology, 41*(7), 826–830. doi:10.1017/ice.2020.61 PMID:32122430

Reactome. (2020). *COVID-19: SARS-CoV-2 infection pathway released.* Retrieved February 16, 2021 from https://reactome.org/about/news/161-version-74-released

Reddi, S. J., Kale, S., & Kumar, S. (2019). *On the convergence of adam and beyond.* arXiv preprint arXiv:1904.09237.

Ren, H., Zhao, L., Zhang, A., Song, L., Liao, Y., Lu, W., & Cui, C. (2020). Early forecasting of the potential risk zones of COVID-19 in China's megacities. *The Science of the Total Environment, 729*, 138995. doi:10.1016/j.scitotenv.2020.138995 PMID:32353723

Rezaeian-Zadeh, M., & Tabari, H. (2012). MLP-based drought forecasting in different climatic regions. *Theoretical and Applied Climatology, 109*(3-4), 407–414. doi:10.100700704-012-0592-3

Rhys, H. I. (2020). *Machine Learning with R, the Tidyverse, and Mlr* (1st ed.). Manning Publications.

Rigaut, G., Shevchenko, A., Rutz, B., Wilm, M., Mann, M., & Séraphin, B. (1999). A Generic Protein Purification Method for Protein Complex Characterization and Proteome Exploration. *Nature Biotechnology, 17*(10), 1030–1032. doi:10.1038/13732 PMID:10504710

Riley, G. (2007). Long-Term Trends in the Concentration of Medicare Spending. *Health Affairs, 26*(3), 808-816.

Roberts, M., Driggs, D., Thorpe, M., Gilbey, J., Yeung, M., Ursprung, S., Aviles-Rivero, A. I., Etmann, C., McCague, C., Beer, L., Weir-McCall, J. R., Teng, Z., Gkrania-Klotsas, E., Rudd, J. H. F., Sala, E., & Schönlieb, C.-B. (2021). Common pitfalls and recommendations for using machine learning to detect and prognosticate for COVID-19 using chest radiographs and CT scans. *Nature Machine Intelligence, 3*(3), 199–217. doi:10.103842256-021-00307-0

Robinson, A. J., Cook, G. D., Ellis, D. P. W., Fosler-Lussier, E., Renals, S. J., & Williams, D. A. G. (2002). Connectionist speech recognition of Broadcast News. *Speech Communication, 37*(1-2), 27–45. doi:10.1016/S0167-6393(01)00058-9

Robnik-Šikonja, M. (2004). Improving Random Forests. *Proceedings of 15th European Conference on Machine Learning (ECML)*, 359-370.

Rodbard, H. W., Green, A. J., Fox, K. M., & Grandy, S. (2009). Impact of type 2 diabetes mellitus on prescription medication burden and out-of-pocket healthcare expenses. *Diabetes Research and Clinical Practice*, *87*(3), 360–365. doi:10.1016/j.diabres.2009.11.021 PMID:20047768

Rogers, A. J., Selvalingam, A., Alhusseini, M. I., Krummen, D. E., Corrado, C., Abuzaid, F., Baykaner, T., Meyer, C., Clopton, P., Giles, W., Bailis, P., Niederer, S., Wang, P. J., Rappel, W.-J., Zaharia, M., & Narayan, S. M. (2021). Machine learned cellular phenotypes in cardiomyopathy predict sudden death. *Circulation Research*, *128*(2), 172–184. doi:10.1161/CIRCRESAHA.120.317345 PMID:33167779

Rohé, M.-M., Datar, M., Heimann, T., Sermesant, M., & Pennec, X. (2017). SVF-Net: Learning deformable image registration using shape matching. In M. Descoteaux, L. Maier-Hein, A. Franz, P. Jannin, D. Collins, & S. Duchesne (Eds.), Medical image computing and computer assisted intervention: Vol. 10433. *MICCAI 2017. Lecture notes in computer science*. Springer. doi:10.1007/978-3-319-66182-7_31

Rokach, L. (2010). Ensemble-based classifiers. *Artificial Intelligence Review*, *33*(1-2), 1–39. doi:10.100710462-009-9124-7

Romaguera, L. V., Romero, F. P., Filho, C. F. F. C., & Costa, M. G. F. (2017). Myocardial segmentation in cardiac magnetic resonance images using fully convolutional neural networks. *Biomedical Signal Processing and Control*, *44*, 48–57. doi:10.1016/j.bspc.2018.04.008

Ronneberger, O., Fischer, P., & Brox, T. (2015). U-Net: convolutional networks for biomedical image segmentation. In N. Navab, J. Hornegger, W. Wells, & A. Frangi (Eds.), Medical image computing and computer-Assisted intervention: Vol. 9351. *MICCAI 2015. Lecture notes in computer science*. Springer. doi:10.1007/978-3-319-24574-4_28

Rosebrock, A. (2020). *Detecting COVID-19 in x-ray images with Keras, TensorFlow, and Deep Learning*. Retrieved May 17, 2020 from https://www.pyimagesearch.com/2020/03/16/detecting-covid-19-in-x-ray-images-with-keras-tensorflow-and-deep-learning/

Rosner, C. M., Genovese, L., Tehrani, B. N., Atkins, M., Bakhshi, H., Chaudhri, S., Damluji, A. A., de Lemos, J. A., Desai, S. S., Emaminia, A., Flanagan, M. C., Khera, A., Maghsoudi, A., Mekonnen, G., Muthukumar, A., Saeed, I. M., Sherwood, M. W., Sinha, S. S., O'Connor, C. M., & deFilippi, C. R. (2021). Myocarditis temporally associated with COVID-19 vaccination. *Circulation*, *144*(6), 502–505. doi:10.1161/CIRCULATIONAHA.121.055891 PMID:34133885

Ruano, M. G., & Ruano, A. E. (2013). On the Use of Artificial Neural Networks for Biomedical Applications. In Soft Computing, AISC 195, 433-451. doi:10.1007/978-3-642-33941-7_40

Ruder, S. (2016). *An overview of gradient descent optimization algorithms*. arXiv preprint arXiv:1609.04747.

Russo, R. R. (2019). Neural Networks for Beginners: An Easy Textbook for Machine Learning Fundamentals to Guide You Implementing Neural Networks with Python and Deep Learning. Independently Published.

Ruuskanen, O., Lahti, E., Jennings, L. C., & Murdoch, D. R. (2011). Viral pneumonia. *Lancet*, *377*(9773), 1264–1275.

Safri, Y. F., Arifudin, R., & Muslim, M. A. (2018). K-Nearest Neighbor and Naive Bayes Classifier Algorithm in Determining the Classification of Healthy Card Indonesia Giving to The Poor. *Scientific Journal of Informatics*, *5*(1), 18. doi:10.15294ji.v5i1.12057

Sak, H., Senior, A., & Beaufays, F. (n.d.). *Long Short-Term Memory Based Recurrent Neural Network Architectures for Large Vocabulary Speech Recognition*. https://www.arxiv-vanity.com/papers/1402.1128/

Sandfort, V., Yan, K., Pickhardt, P. J., & Summers, R. M. (2019). Data augmentation using generative adversarial networks (CycleGAN) to improve generalizability in CT segmentation tasks. *Scientific Reports*, *9*(1), 1–9.

Sandulescu, V., & Chiru, M. (2016). *Predicting the future relevance of research institutions-The winning solution of the KDD Cup 2016*. arXiv preprint arXiv:1609.02728.

Sang, Y., & Ruan, D. (2020). Enhanced image registration with a network paradigm and incorporation of a deformation representation model. *2020 IEEE 17th International Symposium on Biomedical Imaging (ISBI)*, 91-92. 10.1109/ISBI45749.2020.9098395

Santos, C. A. G., & Silva, G. B. L. (2013). Daily streamflow forecasting using a wavelet transform and artificial neural networkhybrid models. *Hydrological Sciences Journal*, *59*(2), 312–324. doi:10.1080/02626667.2013.800944

Santosh, K. C., & Joshi, A. (2021). COVID-19: Prediction, Decision-Making, and its Impacts. Springer Nature Singapore Pte Ltd.

Sariannidis, N., Papadakis, S., Garefalakis, A., Lemonakis, C., & Kyriaki-Argyro, T. (2020). Default Avoidance on Credit Card Portfolios using Accounting, Demographical and Exploratory Factors: Decision Making based on Machine Learning (ML) Techniques. *Annals of Operations Research*, *294*(1–2), 715–739. doi:10.100710479-019-03188-0

Sarki, R., Ahmed, K., Wang, H., Zhang, Y., & Wang, K. (2021). *Automated Detection of COVID-19 through Convolutional Neural Network using Chest x-ray images*. Retrieved February 15, 2021 from https://www.medrxiv.org/content/10.1101/2021.02.06.21251271v1

SAS. (2020a). *Artificial intelligence: What is it and why it matters*. Retrieved May 31, 2020 from https://www.sas.com/en_us/insights/analytics/what-is-artificial-intelligence.html

SAS. (2020b). *Neural Networks: What they are and why they matter*. Retrieved May 31, 2020 from https://www.sas.com/en_us/insights/analytics/neural-networks.html

SAS. (2020c). *SAS Visual Data Mining and Machine Learning*. Retrieved May 31, 2020 from https://www.sas.com/en_us/software/visual-data-mining-machine-learning.htm

Sato, S., Ko, Y. J., Chang, Y., & Kay, M. J. (2018). How Does the Negative Impact of an Athlete's Reputational Crisis Spill Over to Endorsed and Competing Brands? *The Moderating Effects of Consumer Knowledge*, *7*, 385–409.

Sayjadah, Y., Hashem, I. A. T., Alotaibi, F., & Kasmiran, K. A. (2018). Credit Card Default Prediction using Machine Learning Techniques. *2018 Fourth International Conference on Advances in Computing, Communication & Automation (ICACCA)*, 1–4. 10.1109/ICACCAF.2018.8776802

Schifferer, B. (2020, September 23). *Winning Solution of RecSys2020 Challenge*. Medium. https://medium.com/rapids-ai/winning-solution-of-recsys2020-challenge-gpu-accelerated-feature-engineering-and-training-for-cd67c5a87b1f

Schmidhuber, J. (2015). Deep learning in neural networks: An overview. *Neural Networks*, *61*, 85–117.

Scornet, E., Biau, G., & Vert, J.-P. (2015, August). Consistency of random forests. *Annals of Statistics*, *43*(4), 1716–1741. doi:10.1214/15-AOS1321

Seber, G. A. F., & Lee, A. J. (2012). *Linear regression analysis* (2nd ed.). John Wiley & Sons.

Segall, R. S. (2001). Final Report for U. S. Air Force Summer Faculty Fellowship (AF/SFFP): Applications of Neural Networks, Data Mining and Warehousing to Artificial Intelligence and Sensor Array Pattern Recognition. National Research Council (NRC).

Segall, R. S. (2003). *Incorporating Data Mining and Computer Graphics for Modeling of Neural Networks.* Acxiom Data Engineering Laboratory Working Paper Series, ADEL-WP-03-02, Publication in Collaboration with University of Arkansas at Little Rock (UALR) Donaghey Cyber College.

Segall, R. S. (2020). *Applications of Artificial Intelligence to COVID-19.* Invited Virtual Plenary Address at 24th Multi-conference on Systemics, Cybernetics, and Informatics (WMSCI 2020), September 13-16, 2020.

Segall, R. S. (2021). *Applications of Machine Learning and Neural Networks for COVID-19.* 2021 Virtual Conference of MidSouth Computational and Bioinformatics Society (MCBIOS 2021), April 26-30, 2021.

Segall, R. S., & Lu, S. (2015). Information Retrieval by Linkage Discovery. In Encyclopedia of Information Science & Technology (pp. 3932–3939). IGI Global.

Segall, R. S., & Lu, S. (2018). Data Linkage Discovery Applications. In Encyclopedia of Information Science and Technology (IST), 4th edition. IGI Global.

Segall, R. S., & Zhang, Q. (2009). Comparing Four Data Mining Software. In Encyclopedia of Data Warehousing and Mining (2nd ed., pp. 269-277). IGI Global Publishing Inc.

Segall, R. S. (1995, July). Some Mathematical and Computer Modelling of Neural Networks. *Applied Mathematical Modelling*, *19*(7), 386–399. doi:10.1016/0307-904X(95)00021-B

Segall, R. S. (1996). Comparing Learning Rules of Neural Networks Using Computer Graphics; *Proceedings of the Twenty-seventh Annual Conference of the Southwest Decision Sciences Institute.*

Segall, R. S. (2004). Incorporating Data Mining and Computer Graphics for Modeling of Neural Networks. *Kybernetes: The International Journal of Systems & Cybernetics*, *33*(8), 1258–1276. doi:10.1108/03684920410545252

Segall, R. S., & Lu, S. (2014). *Linkage Discovery with Glossaries. In Encyclopedia of Business Analytics & Optimization* (pp. 1411–1421). IGI Global. doi:10.4018/978-1-4666-5202-6.ch128

Segall, R. S., & Zhang, Q. (2006). Applications of Neural Network and Genetic Algorithm Data Mining Techniques in Bioinformatics Knowledge Discovery – A Preliminary Study. *Proceedings of the Thirty-seventh Annual Conference of the Southwest Decision Sciences Institute*, *37*(1).

Segal, M., & Xiao, Y. (2011). Multivariate random forests. *WIRES Data Mining and Knowledge Discovery*, *1*(1), 80–87. doi:10.1002/widm.12

Sekelj, S., Sandler, B., Johnston, E., Pollock, K. G., Hill, N. R., Gordon, J., Tsang, C., Khan, S., Ng, F. S., & Farooqui, U. (2021). Detecting undiagnosed atrial fibrillation in UK primary care: Validation of a machine learning prediction algorithm in a retrospective cohort study. *European Journal of Preventive Cardiology*, *28*(6), 598–605. doi:10.1177/2047487320942338 PMID:34021576

Sengupta, P. P., Huang, Y.-M., Bansal, M., Ashrafi, A., Fisher, M., Shameer, K., Gall, W., & Dudley, J. T. (2016). Cognitive machine-learning algorithm for cardiac imaging: A pilot study for differentiating constrictive pericarditis from restrictive cardiomyopathy. *Circulation: Cardiovascular Imaging*, *9*(6), e004330. doi:10.1161/CIRCIMAGING.115.004330 PMID:27266599

Sengupta, P. P., Shrestha, S., Berthon, B., Messas, E., Donal, E., Tison, G. H., Min, J. K., D'hooge, J., Voigt, J.-U., Dudley, J., Verjans, J. W., Shameer, K., Johnson, K., Lovstakken, L., Tabassian, M., Piccirilli, M., Pernot, M., Yanamala, N., Duchateau, N., ... Arnaout, R. (2020). Proposed requirements for cardiovascular imaging-related machine learning evaluation (PRIME): A checklist: Reviewed by the American College of Cardiology Healthcare Innovation Council. *JACC: Cardiovascular Imaging*, *13*(9), 2017–2035. doi:10.1016/j.jcmg.2020.07.015 PMID:32912474

Shademan, A., Decker, R. S., Opfermann, J. D., Leonard, S., Krieger, A., & Kim, P. C. W. (2016). Supervised autonomous robotic soft tissue surgery. *Science Translational Medicine*, *8*(337), 337ra64. Advance online publication. doi:10.1126citranslmed.aad9398 PMID:27147588

Shahid, F., Zameer, A., & Muneeb, M. (2020). Predictions for COVID-19 with deep learning models of LSTM, GRU and Bi-LSTM. *Chaos, Solitons, and Fractals*, *140*, 110212. doi:10.1016/j.chaos.2020.110212 PMID:32839642

Sharma, M. (2020, March 19). *Grid Search for Hyperparameter Tuning*. Retrieved from Towards Data Science: https://towardsdatascience.com/grid-search-for-hyperparameter-tuning-9f63945e8fec

Sharma, P. (2019, August 19). *The most comprehensive guide to K-means clustering you'll ever need*. Retrieved from Analytics Vidhya: https://www.analyticsvidhya.com/blog/2019/08/comprehensive-guide-K-means-clustering/

Shastri, S., Singh, K., Kumar, S., Kour, P., & Mansotra, V. (2020). Time series forecasting of Covid-19 using deep learning models: India-USA comparative case study. *Chaos, Solitons, and Fractals*, *140*, 110227. doi:10.1016/j.chaos.2020.110227 PMID:32843824

Shelke, M. M. S., Deshmukh, P. R., & Shandilya, V. K. (2017, April). A Review on imbalanced data handling using undersampling and oversampling technique. *International Journal of Recent Trends in Engineering & Research*, *3*(4). Advance online publication. l doi:0.23883/lJRTER.2017. 3168.0UWXM

Shen, J. (2007). Predicting Protein-Protein Interactions based only on Sequences Information. *Proceedings of the National Academy of Sciences*, *104*(11), 4337–4341. 10.1073/pnas.0607879104

Sherazi, S. W. A., Jeong, Y. J., Jae, M. H., Bae, J.-W., & Lee, J. Y. (2019). A machine learning-based 1-year mortality prediction model after hospital discharge for clinical patients with acute coronary syndrome. *Health Informatics Journal*, *26*(2), 1289–1304. doi:10.1177/1460458219871780 PMID:31566458

Shi, X., Chen, Z., Wang, H., & Yeung, D.-Y. (1970, January 1). *Convolutional LSTM Network: A Machine Learning Approach for Precipitation Nowcasting*. Advances in Neural Information Processing Systems. https://proceedings.neurips.cc/paper/5955-convolutional-lstm-network-a-machine-learning-approach-for-precipitation-nowcasting

Shi, F., Wang, J., Shi, J., Wu, Z., Wang, Q., Tang, Z., He, K., Shi, Y., & Shen, D. (2020). *Review of Artificial Intelligence Techniques in Imaging Data Acquisition, Segmentation and Diagnosis for COVID-19*. IEEE Rev Biomed Eng.

Shim, R., Koplan, C., Langheim, F. J. P., Manseau, M. W., Powers, R. A., & Compton, M. T. (2014). The Social Determinants of Mental Health: An Overview and Call to Action. *Psychiatric Annals*, *44*(1), 22–26. doi:10.3928/00485713-20140108-04

Shirmohammadi-Khorram, N., Tapak, L., Hamidi, O., & Maryanaji, Z. (2019). A comparison of three data mining time series models in prediction of monthly brucellosis surveillance data. *Zoonoses and Public Health*, *66*(7), 759–772. doi:10.1111/zph.12622 PMID:31305019

Shorten, C., & Khoshgoftaar, T. M. (2019). A survey on image data augmentation for deep learning. *Journal of Big Data*, *6*(1), 1–48.

Shortliffe, E. H. (1976). Copyright. *Computer-Based Medical Consultations: Mycin*. Advance online publication. doi:10.1016/B978-0-444-00179-5.50003-2

Shuja, J., Alanazi, E., Alasmary, W., & Alashaikh, A. (2020). COVID-19 open source data sets: A comprehensive survey. *Applied Intelligence*, 1–30. Advance online publication. doi:10.100710489-020-01862-6 PMID:34764552

Sibande, X., Gupta, R., & Wohar, M. (2019). Time-varying causal relationship between stock market and unemployment in the United Kingdom: Historical evidence from 1855 to 2017. *Journal of Multinational Financial Management, 49,* 81–88. doi:10.1016/j.mulfin.2019.02.003

Sifrim, A., Hitz, M. P., Wilsdon, A., Breckpot, J., Turki, S. H., Thienpont, B., McRae, J., Fitzgerald, T. W., Singh, T., Swaminathan, G. J., Prigmore, E., Rajan, D., Abdul-Khaliq, H., Banka, S., Bauer, U. M. M., Bentham, J., Berger, F., Bhattacharya, S., Bu'Lock, F., ... Hurles, M. E. (2016). Distinct genetic architectures for syndromic and nonsyndromic congenital heart defects identified by exome sequencing. *Nature Genetics, 48*(9), 1060–1065. doi:10.1038/ng.3627 PMID:27479907

Silvestrini, R. T., & Burke, S. E. (2018). *Linear Regression Analysis with JMP and R.* ASQ Quality Press.

Singh, D., Kumar, V., & Kaur, M. (2020). Classification of COVID-19 patients from chest CT images using multi-objective differential evolution-based convolutional neural networks. *European Journal of Clinical Microbiology & Infectious Diseases.* Retrieved May 16, 2020 from https://link.springer.com/content/pdf/10.1007/s10096-020-03901-z.pdf

Singh, S., Parmar, K. S., Kumar, J., & Makkhan, S. J. (2020). Development of new hybrid model of discrete wavelet decomposition and autoregressive integrated moving average (ARIMA) models in application to one month forecast the casualties cases of COVID-19. *Chaos, Solitons, and Fractals, 135,* 109866. doi:10.1016/j.chaos.2020.109866 PMID:32395038

sklearn.neural_network.MLPClassifier. (n.d.). Retrieved from Scikit Learn: https://scikit-learn.org/stable/modules/generated/sklearn.neural_network.MLPClassifier.html

sklearn.preprocessing.MinMaxScaler. (n.d.). Retrieved from Scikit Learn: https://scikit-learn.org/stable/modules/generated/sklearn.preprocessing.MinMaxScaler.html

Snaauw, G., Gong, D., Maicas, G., van den Hengel, A., Niessen, W. J., Verjans, J., & Carneiro, G. (2019, 04). End-to-end diagnosis and segmentation learning from cardiac magnetic resonancei Imaging. *2019 IEEE 16th International Symposium on Biomedical Imaging (ISBI 2019),* 802-805. 10.1109/ISBI.2019.8759276

So, D. (2020). *Alibaba News Roundup: Tech Takes on the Outbreak.* Retrieved May 17, 2020 from https://www.alizila.com/alibaba-news-roundup-tech-takes-on-the-outbreak/

Solomon, S. D., McMurray, J. J. V., Anand, I. S., Ge, J., Lam, C. S. P., Maggioni, A. P., Martinez, F., Packer, M., Pfeffer, M. A., Pieske, B., Redfield, M. M., Rouleau, J. L., van Veldhuisen, D. J., Zannad, F., Zile, M. R., Desai, A. S., Claggett, B., Jhund, P. S., Boytsov, S. A., ... Lefkowitz, M. P. (2019). Angiotensin-neprilysin inhibition in heart failure with preserved ejection fraction. *The New England Journal of Medicine, 381*(17), 1609–1620. doi:10.1056/NEJMoa1908655 PMID:31475794

Sounderajah, V., Ashrafian, H., Aggarwal, R., De Fauw, J., Denniston, A. K., Greaves, F., Karthikesalingam, A., King, D., Liu, X., Markar, S. R., McInnes, M. D. F., Panch, T., Pearson-Stuttard, J., Ting, D. S. W., Golub, R. M., Moher, D., Bossuyt, P. M., & Darzi, A. (2020). Developing specific reporting guidelines for diagnostic accuracy studies assessing AI interventions: The STARD-AI Steering Group. *Nature Medicine, 26*(6), 807–808. doi:10.103841591-020-0941-1 PMID:32514173

Sousa, P. L., Sculco, P. K., Mayman, D. J., Jerabek, S. A., Ast, M. P., & Chalmers, B. P. (2020). Robots in the operating room during hip and knee arthroplasty. *Current Reviews in Musculoskeletal Medicine, 13*(3), 309–317. doi:10.100712178-020-09625-z PMID:32367430

Spaccarotella, C. A. M., Polimeni, A., Migliarino, S., Principe, E., Curcio, A., Mongiardo, A., Sorrentino, S., De Rosa, S., & Indolfi, C. (2020). Multichannel electrocardiograms obtained by a smartwatch for the diagnosis of ST-segment changes. *JAMA Cardiology*, 5(10), 1176–1180. doi:10.1001/jamacardio.2020.3994 PMID:32865545

Spaccarotella, C., Santarpia, G., Curcio, A., & Indolfi, C. (2021). The smartwatch detects ECG abnormalities typical of Brugada syndrome. *The Journal of Cardiovascular Medicine*. Advance online publication. doi:10.2459/JCM.0000000000001216 PMID:34054105

Srikusan, R., & Karunamoorthy, M. (2021). Implementing Early Detection System for COVID-19 using Anomaly Detection. In COVID-19: Prediction, Decision-Making, and its Impacts. Springer Singapore. doi:10.1007/978-981-15-9682-7_5

Srivastava, N., Hinton, G., Krizhevsky, A., Sutskever, I., & Salakhutdinov, R. (1970, January 1). Dropout: A Simple Way to Prevent Neural Networks from Overfitting. *Journal of Machine Learning Research*. https://jmlr.org/papers/v15/srivastava14a.html

Srivastava, S. (2019, February 27). *Uber traffic data visualization*. Kaggle. https://www.kaggle.com/shobhit18th/uber-traffic-data-visualization

Stephen, O., Sain, M., Maduh, U. J., & Jeong, D. U. (2019). An efficient deep learning approach to pneumonia classification in healthcare. *Journal of Healthcare Engineering*.

Stirenko, S., Kochura, Y., Alienin, O., Rokovyi, O., Gordienko, Y., Gang, P., & Zeng, W. (2018, April). Chest X-ray analysis of tuberculosis by deep learning with segmentation and augmentation. In *2018 IEEE 38th International Conference on Electronics and Nanotechnology (ELNANO)* (pp. 422-428). IEEE.

Stone, J. V. (2019). *Artificial Intelligence engines: A tutorial introduction to the mathematics of deep learning*. Sebtel Press.

Strobl, C., Boulesteix, A.-L., Kneib, T., Augustin, T., & Zeileis, A. (2008). Conditional variable importance for random forests. *BMC Bioinformatics*, 9(1), 307. Advance online publication. doi:10.1186/1471-2105-9-307 PMID:18620558

Subramanian, B. (2021, January 31). *Deep Learning: Fighting Covid-19 with Neural Networks*. Data Science Foundation, U.K. Retrieved February 15, 2021 from https://datascience.foundation/sciencewhitepaper/deep-learning-fighting-covid-19-with-neural-networks

Subramanian, M., Wojtusciszyn, A., Favre, L., Boughorbel, S., Shan, J., Letaief, K. B., Pitteloud, N., & Chouchane, L. (2020). Precision medicine in the era of artificial intelligence: Implications in chronic disease management. *Journal of Translational Medicine*, 18(1), 472. Advance online publication. doi:10.118612967-020-02658-5 PMID:33298113

Sun, L. (2021, May 7). *LSTM for Stock Price Prediction*. Medium. https://towardsdatascience.com/lstm-for-google-stock-price-prediction-e35f5cc84165

Sun, T., & Vasarhelyi, M. A. (2018). Predicting Credit Card Delinquencies: An Application of Deep Neural Networks. *Intelligent Systems in Accounting, Finance & Management*, 25(4), 174–189. doi:10.1002/isaf.1437

Szegedy, C., Liu, W., Jia, Y., Sermanet, P., Reed, S., Anguelov, D., . . . Rabinovich, A. (2015). Going deeper with convolutions. In *Proceedings of The IEEE Conference On Computer Vision and Pattern Recognition* (pp. 1-9). IEEE.

Tali, S. H. S., LeBlanc, J. J., Sadiq, Z., Oyewunmi, O. D., Camargo, C., Nikpour, B., Armanfard, N., Sagan, S. M., & Jahanshahi-Anbuhi, S. (2021, May 12). Tools and Techniques for Severe Acute Respiratory Syndrome Coronavirus 2 (SARS-CoV-2)/COVID-19 Detection. *Clinical Microbiology Reviews*, 34(3), e00228–e20. doi:10.1128/CMR.00228-20 PMID:33980687

Talylor, M. (2017). *Neural Networks: A visual introduction for beginners*. Blue Windmill Media.

Tan, M., & Le, Q. (2019, May). Efficientnet: Rethinking model scaling for convolutional neural networks. In *International Conference on Machine Learning* (pp. 6105-6114). PMLR.

Tan, P.-N., Steinbach, M., Karpatne, A., & Kumar, V. (2020). *Introduction to Data Mining*. Pearson.

Taresh, M.M., Zhu, N., Ali, T.A.A., Hameed, A.S., & Mutar, M.L. (2021). Transfer Learning to Detect COVID-19 Automatically from X-Ray Images Using Convolutional Neural Networks. *International Journal of Biomedical Imaging*. doi:10.1155/2021/8828404

The New York Times. (2021). *Coronavirus (Covid-19) Data in the United States*. GitHub. https://github.com/nytimes/covid-19-data

Theobald, O. (2017). Machine Learning for Absolute Beginners (2nd ed.). Independently Published.

Theodoris, C. V., Zhou, P., Liu, L., Zhang, Y., Nishino, T., Huang, Y., Kostina, A., Ranade, S. S., Gifford, C. A., Uspenskiy, V., Malashicheva, A., Ding, S., & Srivastava, D. (2021). Network-based screen in iPSC-derived cells reveals therapeutic candidate for heart valve disease. *Science, 371*(6530), eabd0724. Advance online publication. doi:10.1126cience.abd0724 PMID:33303684

Thoenes, M., Agarwal, A., Grundmann, D., Ferrero, C., McDonald, A., Bramlage, P., & Steeds, R. P. (2021). Narrative review of the role of artificial intelligence to improve aortic valve disease management. *Journal of Thoracic Disease, 13*(1), 396–404. doi:10.21037/jtd-20-1837 PMID:33569220

Thomas, M. (2020). *15 Examples of Machine Learning in Healthcare that are Revolutionizing Medicine*. Built in. Retrieved May 9, 2021 from https://builtin.com/artificial-intelligence/machine-learning-healthcare

Thomas, S., Jenkins, R., & Wright, F. (2016). Promoting Mental Health and Preventing Mental Illness in General Practice. *London Journal of Primary Care*. https://pubmed.ncbi.nlm.nih.gov/28250821/

Ting, D. S. W., Carin, L., Dzau, V., & Wong, T. Y. (2020, March 27). Digital technology and COVID-19. *Nature News*. https://www.nature.com/articles/s41591-020-0824-5

Toba, S., Mitani, Y., Yodoya, N., Ohashi, H., Sawada, H., Hayakawa, H., Mirayama, M., Futsuki, A., Yamamoto, N., Ito, H., Konuma, T., Shimpo, H., & Takao, M. (2020). Prediction of pulmonary to systemic flow ratio in patients with congenital heart disease using deep learning-based analysis of chest radiographs. *JAMA Cardiology, 5*(4), 449–457. doi:10.1001/jamacardio.2019.5620 PMID:31968049

Topol, E. J. (2020). Welcoming new guidelines for AI clinical research. *Nature Medicine, 26*(9), 1318–1320. doi:10.103841591-020-1042-x PMID:32908274

Trehan, D. (2020, July 2). *Why choose random forest and not decision trees*. Retrieved from *Towards AI*: https://towardsai.net/p/machine-learning/why-choose-random-forest-and-not-decision-trees

TrustRadius. (2020). *Machine Learning Tools*. Retrieved May 31, 2020 from https://www.trustradius.com/machine-learning

Tsymbal, A., Pechenizkiy, M., & Cunningham, P. (2006). Dynamic Integration with Random Forests. *European Conference on Machine Learning*, 801-808. Retrieved August 15,2021 from http://citeseerx.ist.psu.edu/viewdoc/download?doi=10.1.1.391.1720&rep=rep1&type=pdf

Tunyasuvunakool, K., Adler, J., Wu, Z., Green, T., Zielinski, M., Žídek, A., Bridgland, A., Cowie, A., Meyer, C., Laydon, A., Velankar, S., Kleywegt, G. J., Bateman, A., Evans, R., Pritzel, A., Figurnov, M., Ronneberger, O., Bates, R., Kohl, S. A. A., ... Hassabis, D. (2021). Highly accurate protein structure prediction for the human proteome. *Nature, 596*(7873), 590–596. doi:10.103841586-021-03828-1 PMID:34293799

Tuppin, P., Cuerq, A., de Peretti, C., Fagot-Campagna, A., Danchin, N., Juillière, Y., Alta, F., Allemand, H., Bauters, C., Drici, M.-D., Hagège, A., Jondeau, G., Jourdain, P., Leizorovica, A., & Paccaud, F. (2014). Two-year outcome of patients after a first hospitalization for heart failure: A national observational study. *Archives of Cardiovascular Diseases*, *107*(3), 158–168. doi:10.1016/j.acvd.2014.01.012 PMID:24662470

U.S. Department of Health and Human Services. (2020). *Mental Illness*. National Institute of Mental Health. https://www.nimh.nih.gov/health/statistics/mental-illness.shtml

Ullah, M. A., Alam, M. M., Sultana, S., & Toma, R. S. (2018). Predicting Default Payment of Credit Card Users: Applying Data Mining Techniques. *2018 International Conference on Innovations in Science, Engineering and Technology (ICISET), October*, 355–360. 10.1109/ICISET.2018.8745571

Ulloa Cerna, A. E., Jing, L., Good, C. W., vanMaanen, D. P., Raghunath, S., Suever, J. D., Nevius, C. D., Wehner, G. J., Hartzel, D. N., Leader, J. B., Alsaid, A., Patel, A. A., Kirchner, H. L., Pfeifer, J. M., Carry, B. J., Pattichis, M. S., Haggerty, C. M., & Fornwalt, B. K. (2021). Deep-learning-assisted analysis of echocardiographic videos improves predictions of all-cause mortality. *Nature Biomedical Engineering*, *5*(6), 546–554. doi:10.103841551-020-00667-9 PMID:33558735

Umer, M., Ashraf, I., & Ullah, S. (2021). *COVINet: A convolutional neural network approach for predicting COVID-19 from chest X-ray images. J Ambient Intell Human Comput*. doi:10.100712652-021-02917-3

Unnithan, C., Hardy, J., & Lilley, N. (2021). AI for Covid-19: Conduits for Public Heath Surveillance. In COVID-19: Prediction, Decision-Making, and its Impacts. Springer Singapore. doi:10.1007/978-981-15-9682-7_2

Vaid, A., Somani, S., Russak, A. J., De Freitas, J. K., Chaudhry, F. F., Paranjpe, I., Johnson, K. W., Lee, S. J., Miotto, R., Richter, F., Zhao, S., Beckmann, N. D., Naik, N., Kia, A., Timsina, P., Lala, A., Paranjpe, M., Golden, E., Danieletto, M., ... Glicksberg, B. S. (2020). Machine Learning to Predict Mortality and Critical Events in a Cohort of Patients With COVID-19 in New York City: Model Development and Validation. *Journal of Medical Internet Research*, *22*(11), e24018. doi:10.2196/24018 PMID:33027032

Vamathevan, J., Clark, D., Czodrowski, P., Dunham, I., Ferran, E., Lee, G., Li, B., Madabhushi, A., Shah, P., Spitzer, M., & Zhao, S. (2019). Applications of machine learning in drug discovery and development. *Nature Reviews. Drug Discovery*, *18*(6), 463–477. doi:10.103841573-019-0024-5 PMID:30976107

Van den Eynde, J., Vaesen Bentein, H., Decaluwé, T., De Praetere, H., Wertan, M. C., Sutter, F. P., Balkhy, H. H., & Oosterlinck, W. (2021). Safe implementation of robotic-assisted minimally invasive direct coronary artery bypass: Application of learning curves and cumulative sum analysis. *Journal of Thoracic Disease*, *13*(7), 4260–4270. doi:10.21037/jtd-21-775 PMID:34422354

Van der Maaten, L., Postma, E., & van den Herik, J. (2009). *Dimensionality reduction: A comparative review*. https://members.loria.fr/moberger/Enseignement/AVR/Exposes/TR_Dimensiereductie.pdf

Van Veen, F., & Leijnen, S. (2019). *A mostly complete chart of Neural Networks*. The Neural Network Zoo. Retrieved December 28, 2020 from https://www.asimovinstitute.org/neural-network-zoo

Vanhoucke, V., Senior, A., & Mao, M. Z. (2011). Improving the speed of neural networks on CPUs. In *Deep Learning and Unsupervised Feature Learning Workshop*. NIPS.

Varughese, J., & Allen, R. P. (2001). Fatal Accidents Following Changes in Daylight Savings Time: The American Experience. *Sleep Medicine*, *2*(1), 31–36. doi:10.1016/S1389-9457(00)00032-0 PMID:11152980

Vasanawala, S. S., Alley, M. T., Hargreaves, B. A., Barth, R. A., Pauly, J. M., & Lustig, M. (2010). Improved pediatric MR imaging with compressed sensing. *Radiology*, *256*(2), 607–616. doi:10.1148/radiol.10091218 PMID:20529991

Vaswani, A., Shazeer, N., Parmar, N., Uszkoreit, J., Jones, L., Gomez, A. N., Kaiser, L., & Polosukhin, I. (2017, December 6). *Attention is all you need*. Retrieved September 30, 2021, from https://arxiv.org/abs/1706.03762

Velagaleti, R. S., Pencina, M. J., Murabito, J. M., Wang, T. J., Parikh, N. I., D'Agostino, R. B., Levy, D., Kannel, W. B., & Vasan, R. S. (2008). Long-term trends in the incidence of heart failure after myocardial infarction. *Circulation*, *118*(20), 2057–2062. doi:10.1161/CIRCULATIONAHA.108.784215 PMID:18955667

Velasco, L. C. P., Serquiña, R. P., Zamad, M. S. A. A., & Juanico, B. F. (2019). Performance Analysis of Multilayer Perceptron Neural Network Models in Week-Ahead Rainfall Forecasting. *International Journal of Advanced Computer Science and Applications*, *10*(3). Advance online publication. doi:10.14569/IJACSA.2019.0100374

Verde, L., De Pietro, G., Ghoneim, A., Alrashoud, M., Al-Mutib, K. N., & Sannino, G. (2021). Exploring the Use of Artificial Intelligence Techniques to Detect the Presence of Coronavirus Covid-19 Through Speech and Voice Analysis. *IEEE Access: Practical Innovations, Open Solutions*, *9*, 65750–65757. doi:10.1109/ACCESS.2021.3075571

Verikas, A., Gelzinis, A., & Bacauskiene, M. (2011, February). Mining data with random forests: A survey and results of new tests. *Pattern Recognition*, *44*(2), 330–349. doi:10.1016/j.patcog.2010.08.011

Vieira, A., & Ribeiro, B. (2018). Introduction to Deep Learning Business Applications for Developers: From Conversational Bots in Customer Service to Medical Image Processing. Apress.

Virani, S. S., Alonso, A., Aparicio, H. J., Benjamin, E. J., Bittencourt, M. S., Callaway, C. W., Carson, A. P., Chamberlain, A. M., Cheng, S., Delling, F. N., Elkind, M. S. V., Evenson, K. R., Ferguson, J. F., Gupta, D. K., Khan, S. S., Kissela, B. M., Knutson, K. L., Lee, C. D., Lewis, T. T., ... Tsao, C. W. (2021). Heart disease and stroke statistics—2021 update: A report from the American Heart Association. *Circulation*, *143*(8), e254–e743. doi:10.1161/CIR.0000000000000950 PMID:33501848

Volkovs, M., Yu, G. W., & Poutanen, T. (2017). Content-based neighbor models for cold start in recommender systems. In *Proceedings of the Recommender Systems Challenge 2017* (pp. 1-6). Academic Press.

Wang, D., Mo, J., Zhou, G., Xu, L., & Liu, Y. (2020) An efficient mixture of deep and machine learning models for COVID-19 diagnosis in chest X-ray images. *PLoS ONE, 15*(11). Retrieved December 25, 2020 from https://journals.plos.org/plosone/article?id=10.1371/journal.pone.0242535 doi:10.1371/journal.pone.0242535

Wang, H., Li, G., Wang, G., Peng, J., Jiang, H., & Liu, Y. (2016, December 8). Deep learning based ensemble approach for probabilistic wind power forecasting. *Applied Energy*. https://www.sciencedirect.com/science/article/pii/S0306261916317421

Wang, L. (2020). Convolutional neural network detects COVID-19 from chest radiography images. *Vision Systems Design*. Retrieved May 16, 2020 from https://www.vision-systems.com/non-factory/life-sciences/article/14173262/covid-19-chest-radiography-deep-learning-virus-detection

Wang, L. (2020). Convolutional Neural Network detects COVID-19 from Chest Radiography Images. *Vision Systems Design*. Retrieved May 16, 2020 from https://www.vision-systems.com/non-factory/life-sciences/article/14173262/covid-19-chest-radiography-deep-learning-virus-detection

Wang, L., & Wong, A. (2020). *COVID-Net: A Tailored Deep Convolutional Neural Network Design for Detection of COVID-19 Cases from Chest X-Ray Images*. Retrieved May 16, 2020 from https://arxiv.org/abs/2003.09871

Wang, J.-J., Wang, J.-Z., Zhang, Z.-G., & Guo, S.-P. (2012). Stock index forecasting based on a hybrid model. *Omega*, *40*(6), 758–766. doi:10.1016/j.omega.2011.07.008

Wang, L., & Shen, L. (2020). A CONVLSTM-combined hierarchical attention network for saliency detection. *2020 IEEE International Conference on Image Processing (ICIP)*. 10.1109/ICIP40778.2020.9190788

Wang, L., You, Z. H., Xia, S. X., Chen, X., Yan, X., Zhou, Y., & Liu, F. (2017). An Improved Efficient Rotation Forest Algorithm to predict the Interactions among Proteins. *Soft Computing*, *22*(10), 3373–3381. doi:10.100700500-017-2582-y

Wang, P., Zheng, X., Li, J., & Zhu, B. (2020). Prediction of epidemic trends in COVID-19 with logistic model and machine learning technics. *Chaos, Solitons, and Fractals*, *139*, 110058. doi:10.1016/j.chaos.2020.110058 PMID:32834611

Weinfuss, J. (2019, November 24). *Inside The Rise and Fall of the Iconic Reebok Pump on Its 30th Birthday*. Retrieved from ESPN: www.espn.com/nba/story/_/id/28149048/inside-rise-fall-iconic-reebok-pump-30th-birthday

Wenger, N. K., & Lewis, S. J. (2021). Incremental change versus disruptive transformation: COVID-19 and the cardiovascular community. *Circulation*, *143*(19), 1835–1837. doi:10.1161/CIRCULATIONAHA.121.053860 PMID:33820438

West, J., Ventura, D., & Warnick, S. (2007). *Spring research presentation: A theoretical foundation for inductive transfer*. Brigham Young University, College of Physical and Mathematical Sciences. https://web.archive.org/web/20070801120743/http://cpms.byu.edu/springresearch/abstract-entry?id=861

Whitney, D. G., Kamdar, N. S., Ng, S., Hurvitz, E. A., & Peterson, M. D. (2019). Prevalence of high-burden medical conditions and health care resource utilization and costs among adults with cerebral palsy. *Clinical Epidemiology*, *11*, 469–481. doi:10.2147/CLEP.S205839 PMID:31417318

Wieczorek, M., Siłka, J., & Woźniak, M. (2020). Neural network powered COVID-19 spread forecasting model. *Chaos, Solitons, and Fractals*, *140*, 110203. doi:10.1016/j.chaos.2020.110203 PMID:32834663

Wikipedia. (2020). *Comparison of Deep Learning Software*. https://en.wikipedia.org/wiki/Comparison_of_deep-learning_software

Wikipedia. (2021a). *Gated Recurrent Unit (GRU)*. Author.

Wikipedia. (2021a). *Neural Networks*. Retrieved January 2, 2021 from https://en.wikipedia.org/wiki/Neural_network

Wikipedia. (2021b). *Long Short-Term Memory*. Retrieved January 24, 2021 from https://en.wikipedia.org/wiki/Long_short-term_memory

Wikipedia. (2021b). *Machine Learning*. Retrieved January 2, 2021 from https://en.wikipedia.org/wiki/Machine_learning

Wikipedia. (2021c). *Artificial Intelligence*. Retrieved January 2, 2021 from https://en.wikipedia.org/wiki/Artificial_intelligence

Wikipedia. (2021c). *Tensor Flow*. Retrieved February 16, 2021 from https://en.wikipedia.org/wiki/TensorFlow

Wikipedia. (2021d). *Open Source Software*. Retrieved February 18, 2021 from https://en.wikipedia.org/wiki/Open-source_software

Wikipedia. (2021e). *Multifactor Dimensionality Reduction (MDR)*. Retrieved February 18, 2021 from https://en.wikipedia.org/wiki/Multifactor_dimensionality_reduction

Williams, D., & Williams-Morris, R. (2000). Racism and Mental Health: The African American experience. *Ethnicity & Health*, *5*(3-4), 243–268. doi:10.1080/713667453 PMID:11105267

Wolterink, J., Leiner, T., Viergever, M. A., & Išgum, I. (2018). Automatic segmentation and disease classification using cardiac cine MR images. In M. Pop, M. Sermesant, J. Zhao, S. Li, K. McLeod, A. Young, K. Rhode, & T. Mansi (Eds.), Statistical atlases and computational models of the heart. Atrial segmentation and LV quantification challenges (pp. 101-110). Springer. doi:10.1007/978-3-319-75541-0_11

World Health Organization (WHO). (2020). *Coronavirus disease 2019 (COVID-19), Situation Report 162*. WHO.

World Health Organization. (2019). *Special initiative for mental health (2019-2023)*. World Health Organization. https://www.who.int/mental_health/evidence/special_initiative_2019_2023/en/

World Health Organization. (2020). *Coronavirus Disease (COVID-19) Situation Reports*. World Health Organization. https://www.who.int/emergencies/diseases/novel-coronavirus-2019/situation-reports

Wu, Z., Zhao, Z., & Niu, G. (2020). Introduction to the Popular Open Source Statistical Software (OSSS). In R. S. Segall & G. Niu (Eds.), *Open Source Software for Statistical Analysis of Big Data: Emerging Research and Opportunities* (pp. 73–110). IGI Global. doi:10.4018/978-1-7998-2768-9.ch003

Xu, P., Ding, Z., & Pan, M. (2017). An Improved Credit Card Users Default Prediction Model based on RIPPER. *2017 13th International Conference on Natural Computation, Fuzzy Systems and Knowledge Discovery (ICNC-FSKD)*, 1785–1789. 10.1109/FSKD.2017.8393037

Xu, S., Zhang, Z., Wang, D., Hu, J., Duan, X., & Zhu, T. (2017, March 10–12). *Cardiovascular risk prediction method based on CFS subset evaluation and random forest classification framework* [Paper presentation]. 2017 IEEE 2nd International Conference on Big Data Analysis (ICBDA), Beijing, China. 10.1109/ICBDA.2017.8078813

Xu, P., Ding, Z., & Pan, M. Q. (2018). A Hybrid Interpretable Credit Card Users Default Prediction Model based on RIPPER. *Concurrency and Computation*, *30*(23), 1–12. doi:10.1002/cpe.4445

Yadav, P. (2018, November 13). *Decision tree in machine learning*. Retrieved from *Towards Data Science*: https://towardsdatascience.com/decision-tree-in-machine-learning-e380942a4c96

Yadav, M., Perumal, M., & Srinivas, M. (2020). Analysis on novel coronavirus (COVID-19) using machine learning methods. *Chaos, Solitons, and Fractals*, *139*, 110050. doi:10.1016/j.chaos.2020.110050 PMID:32834604

Yahoo Finance Historical Data. (n.d.). Retrieved from Yahoo Finance: https://finance.yahoo.com/

Yang, J.-H., Cheng, C.-H., & Chan, C.-P. (2017). A Time-Series Water Level Forecasting Model Based on Imputation and Variable Selection Method. *Computational Intelligence and Neuroscience*, *2017*, 1–11. doi:10.1155/2017/9478952 PMID:29250110

Yang, S., & Zhang, H. (2018). Comparison of Several Data Mining Methods in Credit Card Default Prediction. *Intelligent Information Management*, *10*(05), 115–122. doi:10.4236/iim.2018.105010

Yang, Y., & Shi, M. (2011). Rise and fall of stars: Investigating the evolution of star status in professional team sports. [Elsevier.]. *International Journal of Research in Marketing*, *28*(4), 352–366.

Yang, Y., Sun, J., Li, H., & Xu, Z. (2016, December 5-12). *Deep ADMM-Net for compressive sensing MRI* [Paper presentation]. Annual Conference on Neural Information Processing Systems, Barcelona, Spain.

Yates, E. J., Yates, L. C., & Harvey, H. (2018, September). Machine learning "red dot": Open-source, cloud, deep convolutional neural networks in chest radiograph binary normality classification. *Clinical Radiology*, *73*(9), 827–831. doi:10.1016/j.crad.2018.05.015 PMID:29898829

Yeh, I.-C., & Lien, C. (2009). The Comparisons of Data Mining Techniques for the Predictive Accuracy of Probability of Default of Credit Card Clients. *Expert Systems with Applications*, *36*(2), 2473–2480. doi:10.1016/j.eswa.2007.12.020

Yeşilkanat, C. M. (2020). Spatio-temporal estimation of the daily cases of COVID-19 in worldwide using random forest machine learning algorithm. *Chaos, Solitons, and Fractals*, *140*, 110210. doi:10.1016/j.chaos.2020.110210 PMID:32843823

Yeung, M. W., Benjamins, J. W., van der Harst, P., & Juárez-Orozco, L. (2021). Machine learning in cardiovascular genomics, proteomics, and drug discovery. In S. J. Al'Aref, G. Singh, L. Baskaran, & D. Metaxas (Eds.), *Machine learning in cardiovascular medicine* (pp. 325–352). Academic Press. doi:10.1016/B978-0-12-820273-9.00014-2

Yiangou, L., Davis, R. P., & Mummery, C. L. (2021). Using cardiovascular cells from human pluripotent stem cells for COVID-19 research: Why the heart fails. *Stem Cell Reports*, *16*(3), 385–397. doi:10.1016/j.stemcr.2020.11.003 PMID:33306986

Yontar, M., Namli, Ö. H., & Yanik, S. (2020). Using Machine Learning Techniques to develop Prediction Models for Detecting Unpaid Credit Card Customers. *Journal of Intelligent & Fuzzy Systems*, *39*(5), 6073–6087. doi:10.3233/JIFS-189080

You, Z. H., Huang, W. Z., Zhang, S., Huang, Y. A., Yu, C. Q., & Li, L. P. (2019). An Efficient Ensemble Learning Approach for Predicting Protein-Protein Interactions by Integrating Protein Primary Sequence and Evolutionary Information. *IEEE/ACM Transactions on Computational Biology and Bioinformatics*, *16*(3), 809–817. doi:10.1109/TCBB.2018.2882423 PMID:30475726

You, Z. H., Lei, Y. K., Zhu, L., Xia, J., & Wang, B. (2013). Prediction of Protein-Protein Interactions from Amino Acid Sequences with Ensemble Extreme Learning Machines and Principal Component Analysis. *BMC Bioinformatics*, *14*(S8), S10. Advance online publication. doi:10.1186/1471-2105-14-S8-S10 PMID:23815620

Yutzey, K. E., Demer, L. L., Body, S. C., Huggins, G. S., Towler, D. A., Giachelli, C. M., Hofmann-Bowman, M. A., Mortlock, D. P., Rogers, M. B., Sadeghi, M. M., & Aikawa, E. (2014). Calcific aortic valve disease: A consensus summary from the Alliance of Investigators on Calcific Aortic Valve Disease. *Arteriosclerosis, Thrombosis, and Vascular Biology*, *34*(11), 2387–2393. doi:10.1161/ATVBAHA.114.302523 PMID:25189570

Yu, Y. (2020). The Application of Machine Learning Algorithms in Credit Card Default Prediction. *2020 International Conference on Computing and Data Science (CDS)*, 212–218. 10.1109/CDS49703.2020.00050

Zaremba, W., Sutskever, I., & Vinyals, O. (2014, September 11). *Recurrent Neural Network Regularization*. https://arxiv.org/abs/1409.2329v2

Zech, J. R., Badgeley, M. A., Liu, M., Costa, A. B., Titano, J. J., & Oermann, E. K. (2018). Variable generalization performance of a deep learning model to detect pneumonia in chest radiographs: A cross-sectional study. *PLoS Medicine*, *15*(11), e1002683.

Zeiler, M. D. (2012). *Adadelta: An adaptive learning rate method.* arXiv preprint arXiv:1212.5701.

Zhang, C. (2020). A Survey of China's Artificial Intelligence Solutions in Response to the COVID-19 Pandemic: 87 Case Studies from 700+ AI Vendors in China. *Synced Review*.

Zhang, H. (2004). The optimality of naive Bayes. *Proceedings of Florida Artificial Intelligence Research Society (FLAIRS)*. https://www.aaai.org/Papers/FLAIRS/2004/Flairs04-097.pdf

Zhang, J., Xie, Y., Li, Y., Shen, C., & Xia, Y. (2020). *Covid-19 screening on chest x-ray images using deep learning based anomaly detection.* arXiv preprint arXiv:2003.12338

Zhang, G., Patuwo, B. E., & Hu, M. Y. (1998). Forecasting with artificial neural networks: The state of the art. *International Journal of Forecasting, 14*(1), 35–62. doi:10.1016/S0169-2070(97)00044-7

Zhang, J., Zulkernine, M., & Haque, A. (2008, August 19). Random-Forests-Based Network Intrusion Detection Systems. *IEEE Xplore, 38*(5), 649–659.

Zhang, Z. (2016). Introduction to Machine Learning: K-nearest Neighbors. *Annals of Translational Medicine, 4*(11), 218. doi:10.21037/atm.2016.03.37 PMID:27386492

Zhao, H. (2020). AI CT scan analysis for CONVID-19 detection and patient monitoring. *Synced: AI Technology & Industry Review*. Retrieved May 17, 2020 from https://syncedreview.com/2020/03/18/ai-ct-scan-analysis-for-covid-19-detection-and-patient-monitoring/

Zhao, H. (2020). AI CT Scan Analysis for CONVID-19 Detection and Patient Monitoring. *Synced: AI Technology & Industry Review*. Retrieved May 17, 2020 from https://syncedreview.com/2020/03/18/ai-ct-scan-analysis-for-covid-19-detection-and-patient-monitoring/

Zhao, J., Zhang, Y., He, X., & Xie, P. (2020). *COVID-CT-Dataset: A CT scan dataset about COVID-19*. Retrieved May 17, 2020 from https://arxiv.org/pdf/2003.13865.pdf

Zhao, J., Feng, Q., Wu, P., Lupu, R. A., Wilke, R. A., Wells, Q. S., Denny, J. C., & Wei, W.-Q. (2019). Learning from longitudinal data in electronic health record and genetic data to improve cardiovascular event prediction. *Scientific Reports, 9*(1), 717. doi:10.103841598-018-36745-x PMID:30679510

Zhavoronkov, A., Ivanenkov, Y. A., Aliper, A., Veselov, M. S., Aladinskiy, V. A., Aladinskaya, A. V., Terentiev, V. A., Polykovskiy, D. A., Kuznetsov, M. D., Asadulaev, A., Volkov, Y., Zholus, A., Shayakhmetov, R. R., Zhebrak, A., Minaeva, L. I., Zagribenlnyy, B. A., Lee, L. H., Soll, R., Madge, D., ... Aspuru-Guzik, A. (2019). Deep learning enables rapid identification of potent DDR1 kinase inhibitors. *Nature Biotechnology, 37*(9), 1038–1040. doi:10.103841587-019-0224-x PMID:31477924

Zhou, X., Park, B., Choi, D., & Han, K. (2018). A Generalized Approach to Predicting Protein-Protein Interactions between Virus and Host. *BMC Genomics, 19*(S6), 568. Advance online publication. doi:10.118612864-018-4924-2 PMID:30367586

Zoabi, Y., Deri-Rozov, S., & Shomron, N. (2021, January 4). Machine learning-based prediction of COVID-19 diagnosis based on symptoms. *NPJ Digital Medicine, 4*(1), 3. doi:10.103841746-020-00372-6 PMID:33398013

Zunicd. (n.d.). *Zunicd/Bank-Churn-Prediction: Bank customers churn dashboard with predictions from several machine learning models*. GitHub. https://github.com/zunicd/Bank-Churn-Prediction

About the Contributors

Richard S. Segall is Professor of Information Systems & Business Analytics (ISBA) at Arkansas State University where he is also on the faculty of the Environmental Sciences program and has taught for ten years in the Master of Engineering Management (MEM) Program in the College of Engineering & Computer Science. He is also Affiliate Faculty at University of Arkansas at Little Rock (UALR) where he serves on thesis committees. He holds BS/MS in mathematics, MS in operations research and statistics from Rensselaer Polytechnic Institute in Troy, New York, and PhD in operations research form University of Massachusetts at Amherst. He has served on faculty of Texas Tech University, University of Louisville, University of New Hampshire, University of Massachusetts-Lowell, and West Virginia University. His research interests include data mining, Big Data, text mining, web mining, database management, and mathematical modeling. His funded research includes that by U.S. Air Force (USAF), National Aeronautical and Space Administration (NASA), Arkansas Biosciences Institute (ABI), and Arkansas Science & Technology Authority (ASTA). He is on the Editorial Boards of International Journal of Data Mining, Modelling and Management (IJDMMM), and International Journal of Data Science (IJDS). Dr. Segall is author or co-author of 44 Journal Articles, 21 Book Chapters, and 68 Conference Proceedings. Dr. Segall is Lead editor of Open Source Software for Statistical Analysis of Big Data; Handbook of Big Data Storage and Visualization Techniques (2 volumes); and Research and Applications in Global Supercomputing; and co-Editor of Visual Analytics of Interactive Technologies: Applications to Data, Text & Web Mining; all published by IGI Global. Dr. Segall is a member of the Center for No-Boundary Thinking (CNBT) and was a member of the former Center for Plant-Powered Production (P3) from 2008 to 2016, and served as Local Arrangements Chair of the MidSouth Computational Biology and Bioinformatics Society (MCBIOS) conference held at Arkansas State University. Dr. Segall is the recipient of the 2015 and 2019 Awards for Excellence in Research by the Neil Griffin College of Business and the 2020 University Award for Excellence in Scholarship (Research) of Arkansas State University.

Gao Niu is an Assistant Professor in Actuarial Science and Program Coordinator of Actuarial Math Program at Bryant University. He also serves as a Faculty Consultant of the Janet & Mark L Goldenson Center for Actuarial Research at the University of Connecticut. He has a doctorate in actuarial science from the University of Connecticut, is an Associate of the Casualty Actuarial Society and a Member of the American Academy of Actuaries. Dr. Niu has years of experience in academic actuarial research and consulting practice. His research area includes but not limited to the following: big data analytics application in insurance industry, property and casualty insurance practice, predictive modeling, agent-based modeling, financial planning, life insurance and health insurance pricing, reserving and data mining.

* * *

Houwei Cao is an Assistant Professor in the Department of Computer Science at New York Institute of Technology (NYIT). She was an adjunct professor at the Computer Science and Engineering Department of the Tandon School of Engineering of New York University before joining NYIT. She obtained her PhD degree in Electronic Engineering from the Chinese University of Hong Kong in 2011, and was a postdoctoral fellow at University of Pennsylvania from 2011 to 2014. Her main areas of research are signal processing, machine learning, data mining and their applications in human-centric data analytics, with emphasis on developing computational methods, algorithms, and models for speech recognition, natural language processing, multimodal affective computing, social network analysis, and healthcare information systems. She won the audio-visual emotion recognition challenge (AVEC) in 2012. Her research has been supported by the NSF, Northrop Grumman, and NYIT. Dr. Cao is a member of International Speech Communication Association (ISCA), the Association for the Advancement of Affective Computing (AAAC), and IEEE. She has served as program committee members and/or reviewers for more than ten journals and conferences in speech and language processing, affective computing, and computer vision.

Martin Chanza is a Doctor in Statistics and he is a senior lecturer in the Department of Statistics and Operations Research, North-West University, South Africa. He is specializing in time series analysis, forecasting models, panel data models, econometrics models, operational risk models, data mining, and machine learning models.

Tianchuan Gao is a first-year master's student at Columbia University Mailman School of Public Health studying Biostatistics. He is interested in statistical learning methods for analyzing high-dimensional data. His research interest also includes Data Science, Predictive Modeling/Machine Learning and Survival Analysis.

Guanzhou Hou is a graduate student of Financial Econometrics major at Johns Hopkins University. He has a Bachelor's degree in Economics from the University of Connecticut. He worked at Yuanrui Electric Power Technology from 2016 - 2018. His current research includes but not limited to asset pricing finance, machine learning, big data analyitcs, statistical modeling.

Siddharth Jain has completed his Masters in Data Science from Liverpool John Moores University, UK. He also holds a Post Graduate degree in Data Science from International Institute of Technology, Bengaluru, India. He has done his Bachelor of Engineering in Computer Science from Pune University, India. He has keen interest in Data analytics and is enthusiastic about contributing to the Banking, Financial Services and Insurance industry given an experience of over 20 years in the same domain.

Manoj Jayabalan is a post doctorate fellow in the Faculty of Engineering & Technology, Liverpool John Moores University, UK. Manoj obtained his Ph.D. in Computing from Asia Pacific University of Technology & Innovation, Malaysia with research area focusing on health informatics and data science. He has completed his MSc. in Software Engineering from Staffordshire University, UK. He also holds a B.Eng. in Computer Science from Anna University, India. He was previously head of the Asia Pacific Center for Analytics (APCA), Malaysia. Moreover, he has received numerous excellence award for teaching and research in Asia Pacific University of Technology & Innovation, Malaysia. Mining, Machine Learning, Health Informatics, and Software Engineering. His area of expertise in the data analytics in performing data wrangling, and implementing models. He has supervised many industrial projects, master dissertations and mentored students for National level competitions. He has been invited guest speakers for several talks on Big Data and conducted many workshops.

Fangjun Li is a Research Scholar of the Janet & Mark L Goldenson Center for Actuarial Research at the University of Connecticut. She earned Master of Science degree in Mathematics with concentration in Actuarial Science from the University of Connecticut. Her research concentrate on life insurance pricing, reserving and mortality risk modeling.

Xiang Li is a master's student at Weill Cornell Medicine of Cornell University, his major is biostatistics & data science.

Jingxi Liao is a PhD student at University of Central Florida. His major is mathematics with financial math track. His research interest is in optimal control that concentrate on different kinds of financial products, such as optimization of pricing option.

Xiangming Liu, who graduated from the University of Connecticut with Master's degree of Applied Financial Mathematics in 2014, is interested in using Python for modeling and predicting. She loves learning new things both in technology and personal development. She recently is seeking approaches to apply machine learning methods to analyze data and present results in visualizations in the area of insurance and other financial industry.

Jason Michaud is currently a student at Bryant University with an anticipated graduation date of May 2023. The degree that he is pursuing is a Bachelor of Science in Data Science with a minor in Business Administration. Through his education to date, he has gained experience in Python, data visualization, machine learning, and statistics. Through his experience in machine learning and statistics, he has gained a research interest in both of these areas. He also has developed a research interest in COVID-19 Tweets and is currently analyzing the psychological impact of this pandemic through topic modeling and retweet network analysis as of Summer 2021.

Gomolemo Motlhwe is a Master's student in the department of Business Statistics and Operations Research, North West University, South Africa. He is focusing his research on the application of machine learning models to time series data.

Son Nguyen earned his master's degree in applied mathematics and doctoral degree in mathematics, statistics emphasis, both at Ohio University. He is currently an assistant professor at the department of mathematics at Bryant University. His primary research interests lie in dimensionality reduction, imbalanced learning, and machine learning classification. In addition to the theoretical aspects, he is also interested in applying statistics to other areas such as finance and healthcare.

Alan Olinsky is a professor of mathematics and information systems analytics at Bryant University. He earned his PhD in Management Science from the University of Rhode Island and his research interests include multivariate statistics, management science, business analytics, and data mining. He is past president of the Rhode Island Chapter of the American Statistical Association and has appeared several times as an expert witness in statistical matters at hearings and trials.

John Quinn is a Professor of Mathematics at Bryant University and has been teaching there since 1991. Prior to teaching, Professor Quinn was a mechanical engineer at the Naval Underwater Systems Center (now the Naval Undersea Warfare Center) in Newport, R.I. He received his Sc.B. degree from Brown University in 1978, and his M.S. and Ph.D. degrees from Harvard University in 1987 and 1991, respectively. Professor Quinn has had articles published in multiple areas. He has done previous research in mathematical programming methods and computable general equilibrium models in economics. He currently does research in data mining applications, predictive modeling of rare events and simulation models.

Matthew Quinn is a PhD student in Biostatistics at Harvard University's T.H. Chan School of Public Health. His primary interests include researching methods and applications in computational statistics. His projects currently include developing methods for analyzing changepoints in mobile health data and for identifying differential protein binding sites on the human genome. He has previously worked at Worcester Polytechnic Institute to investigate machine learning methods for categorizing scanning electron microscope images of carbon nanotubes. Additionally, he has worked on research at Harvard to develop statistical tools that help link resources between brick-and-mortar classes and Massive Open Online Courses (MOOCs).

Mogari Ishmael Rapoo holds MSc. in Statistics and he is a Lecturer in the Department of Statistics and Operations Research, North West University, Mafikeng, South Africa. He is currently about to register for his PhD and his area of specialization are Machine learning, Econometrics and Time series.

Juan Shu is a third-year Ph.D. student at the Department of Statistics, Purdue University.

Fan Wu is a fourth-year Ph.D. student at the Department of Statistics, Purdue University.

Zichen Zhao is a graduate student of biostatistics major at Yale University. He has a Bachelor's degree in Actuarial Science from the University of Connecticut. He Worked at multiple investment and insurance companies such as Goldman Sachs, Sunshine Insurance Group. His current research includes but not limited to actuarial science, big data analytics, predictive modeling, machine learning, statistical modeling.

Index

P

R

S

T

U

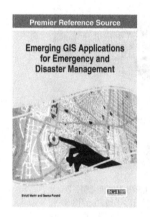
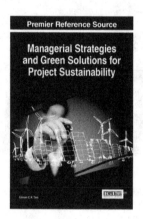

IGI Global
PUBLISHER of TIMELY KNOWLEDGE
www.igi-global.com

Publisher of Peer-Reviewed, Timely, and
Innovative Academic Research Since 1988

IGI Global's Transformative Open Access (OA) Model:
How to Turn Your University Library's Database Acquisitions Into a Source of OA Funding

Well in advance of Plan S, IGI Global unveiled their OA Fee Waiver (Read & Publish) Initiative. Under this initiative, librarians who invest in IGI Global's InfoSci-Books and/or InfoSci-Journals databases will be able to subsidize their patrons' OA article processing charges (APCs) when their work is submitted and accepted (after the peer review process) into an IGI Global journal.

How Does it Work?

Step 1: **Library Invests in the InfoSci-Databases:** A library perpetually purchases or subscribes to the InfoSci-Books, InfoSci-Journals, or discipline/subject databases.

Step 2: **IGI Global Matches the Library Investment with OA Subsidies Fund:** IGI Global provides a fund to go towards subsidizing the OA APCs for the library's patrons.

Step 3: **Patron of the Library is Accepted into IGI Global Journal (After Peer Review):** When a patron's paper is accepted into an IGI Global journal, they option to have their paper published under a traditional publishing model or as OA.

Step 4: **IGI Global Will Deduct APC Cost from OA Subsidies Fund:** If the author decides to publish under OA, the OA APC fee will be deducted from the OA subsidies fund.

Step 5: **Author's Work Becomes Freely Available:** The patron's work will be freely available under CC BY copyright license, enabling them to share it freely with the academic community.

Note: This fund will be offered on an annual basis and will renew as the subscription is renewed for each year thereafter. IGI Global will manage the fund and award the APC waivers unless the librarian has a preference as to how the funds should be managed.

Hear From the Experts on This Initiative:

"I'm very happy to have been able to make one of my recent research contributions *freely available* along with having access to the *valuable resources* found within IGI Global's InfoSci-Journals database."

— **Prof. Stuart Palmer,**
Deakin University, Australia

"Receiving the support from IGI Global's OA Fee Waiver Initiative *encourages me to continue my research work without any hesitation.*"

— **Prof. Wenlong Liu**, College of Economics and Management at Nanjing University of Aeronautics & Astronautics, China

For More Information, Scan the QR Code or Contact:
IGI Global's Digital Resources Team at eresources@igi-global.com.

Printed in the United States
by Baker & Taylor Publisher Services